I0038771

Regenerating Urban Land

**URBAN
DEVELOPMENT
SERIES**

The Urban Development Series discusses the challenge of urbanization
and what it will mean for developing countries in the decades ahead.
The Series aims to delve substantively into the core issues framed by
the World Bank's 2009 Urban Strategy, *Systems of Cities: Harnessing
Urbanization for Growth and Poverty Alleviation.* Across the five
domains of the Urban Strategy, the Series provides a focal point for
publications that seek to foster a better understanding of: the core
elements of the city system; pro-poor policies; city economies; urban
land and housing markets; sustainable urban environment; and other
issues germane to the urban development agenda.

Cities and Climate Change: Responding to an Urgent Agenda
*Climate Change, Disaster Risk, and the Urban Poor: Cities Building
    Resilience for a Changing World*
*East Asia's Changing Urban Landscape: Measuring a Decade of Spatial
    Growth, 2000-2010*
*The Economics of Uniqueness: Investing in Historic City Cores and
    Cultural Heritage Assets for Sustainable Development*
*Financing Transit-Oriented Development with Land Values: Adapting
    Land Value Capture in Developing Countries*
*Regenerating Urban Land: A Practitioner's Guide to Leveraging Private
    Investment*
*Transforming Cities with Transit: Transit and Land-Use Integration for
    Sustainable Urban Development*
*Urban Risk Assessments: An Approach for Understanding Disaster and
    Climate Risk in Cities*

All books in the Urban Development Series are available for free at
https://openknowledge.worldbank.org/handle/10986/2174

Regenerating Urban Land

A Practitioner's Guide to Leveraging Private Investment

Rana Amirtahmasebi
Mariana Orloff
Sameh Wahba
Andrew Altman

WORLD BANK GROUP

© 2016 International Bank for Reconstruction and Development / The World Bank
1818 H Street NW, Washington, DC 20433
Telephone: 202-473-1000; Internet: www.worldbank.org

Some rights reserved
1 2 3 4 19 18 17 16

This work is a product of the staff of The World Bank with external contributions. The findings, interpretations, and conclusions expressed in this work do not necessarily reflect the views of The World Bank, its Board of Executive Directors, or the governments they represent. The World Bank does not guarantee the accuracy of the data included in this work. The boundaries, colors, denominations, and other information shown on any map in this work do not imply any judgment on the part of The World Bank concerning the legal status of any territory or the endorsement or acceptance of such boundaries.

Nothing herein shall constitute or be considered to be a limitation upon or waiver of the privileges and immunities of The World Bank, all of which are specifically reserved.

Rights and Permissions

This work is available under the Creative Commons Attribution 3.0 IGO license (CC BY 3.0 IGO) http://creativecommons.org/licenses/by/3.0/igo. Under the Creative Commons Attribution license, you are free to copy, distribute, transmit, and adapt this work, including for commercial purposes, under the following conditions:

Attribution—Please cite the work as follows: Amirtahmasebi, Rana, Mariana Orloff, Sameh Wahba, and Andrew Altman. *Regenerating Urban Land: A Practitioner's Guide to Leveraging Private Investment.* 2016. Urban Development Series. Washington, DC: World Bank. doi: 10.1596/978-1-4648-0473-1. License: Creative Commons Attribution CC BY 3.0 IGO

Translations—If you create a translation of this work, please add the following disclaimer along with the attribution: *This translation was not created by The World Bank and should not be considered an official World Bank translation. The World Bank shall not be liable for any content or error in this translation.*

Adaptations—If you create an adaptation of this work, please add the following disclaimer along with the attribution: *This is an adaptation of an original work by The World Bank. Views and opinions expressed in the adaptation are the sole responsibility of the author or authors of the adaptation and are not endorsed by The World Bank.*

Third-party content—The World Bank does not necessarily own each component of the content contained within the work. The World Bank therefore does not warrant that the use of any third-party-owned individual component or part contained in the work will not infringe on the rights of those third parties. The risk of claims resulting from such infringement rests solely with you. If you wish to re-use a component of the work, it is your responsibility to determine whether permission is needed for that re-use and to obtain permission from the copyright owner. Examples of components can include, but are not limited to, tables, figures, or images.

All queries on rights and licenses should be addressed to the Publishing and Knowledge Division, The World Bank, 1818 H Street NW, Washington, DC 20433, USA; fax: 202-522-2625; e-mail: pubrights@worldbank.org.

ISBN (paper): 978-1-4648-0473-1
ISBN (electronic): 978-1-4648-0474-8
DOI: 10.1596/978-1-4648-0473-1

Cover photo: HCP Design Planning and Management Ltd. Ahmedabad, India

Cover design: Bill Pragluski of Critical Stages

Library of Congress Cataloging-in-Publication Data has been requested.

Contents

Figures

Photographs

Tables

Foreword

Today, cities face an ever-increasing demand for land. Urbanization is the defining phenomenon of our time. For the first time in history, more than half the world's population lives in cities, with 90 percent of urban growth taking place in the developing world. This high rate of urban growth has put pressure on cities in various ways. Due to lack of access to urban land within city boundaries, one billion urban residents already live in overpopulated slums to be close to economic activity and jobs.

How do cities respond to the rising demand for land? In many cases, citizens are forced to respond by moving to marginal areas in new low-density developments on the urban periphery, resulting in a sprawling urban footprint. But sustainable cities with a strong vision for the future respond to demand for land by densifying existing urban cores, where pockets of underused land or dilapidated inner cities exist. Higher density is associated with economic growth and social integration. Building denser cities also means lower carbon emissions and less pollution, which is why regeneration of underused urban land and infill development contribute to sustainable development of cities.

Developing underused urban land requires reversing the process of economic, social, and physical decay in urban areas. These projects aim at environmental remediation of brownfields, creating vibrant waterfronts and addressing social and economic decline in inner cities. But in most cases, deterioration of urban areas or contamination of brownfield sites has reached the stage at which regeneration does not necessarily occur naturally through market forces. In most cases, key catalytic public sector investments trigger the recovery. Urban regeneration projects encompass a variety of interventions that local governments (with participation of the private sector and the community) take to improve the conditions and intensify the use of an existing urban area to accommodate population and economic activities, as opposed to developing new urban areas in peripheral land.

Regeneration of underutilized urban land also contributes to creation of sustainable communities in cities. Such communities are successful for the following four reasons: environmental sustainability, resilience to natural disasters, inclusiveness, and competitiveness. Environmentally, urban regeneration processes can accelerate cleanup and remediation of existing polluted sites and waters and help achieve higher environmental standards by financing cleanup activities of brownfield sites. Similarly, these projects could have built-in elements of resiliency through sound treatment of water catchment areas and potential resettlement of informal settlements in disaster-prone regions. Revitalizing urban areas can increase inclusiveness by providing opportunities for a new supply of affordable housing and by building new public infrastructure and open spaces for the enjoyment of a larger urban community. Finally, urban regeneration initiatives can infuse new revenue- and tax-generating activities on previously unproductive land, while creating new opportunities for businesses and for local economic development in the community.

Urban regeneration projects are by nature complex and hard to finance. They require a capable local government that can put together all the pieces that such a multisectoral and multistakeholder project requires. These projects also demand an institutional structure conducive to long-term processes that can sustain initiatives for long periods of time regardless of political swings or bureaucratic reassignments. Financing urban regeneration projects is an additional challenge, as the private sector often deems investment in regeneration projects to be risky compared with new development. In many cities, the land tagged for regeneration is under fragmented ownership and requires assembly and readjustment. The existence of informal settlements and renters adds to the complexity by requiring measurements for equitable development and adding cost and time for potential compensation and resettlement. Despite all of these difficulties, there are many successful examples of equitable regeneration in the cities of the global north and south. These cities have capitalized on their active private sector (when one existed) or have designed an attractive regulatory environment to incentivize participation when the private sector was not stimulated enough to invest.

While private sector participation has been mainstreamed in infrastructure and service-delivery projects, its presence in larger, integrated urban regeneration projects has been limited. This is mainly because of the assumed investment risk and potential low rate of return due to delays or pauses in the process. Many aspects of project design, such as cohesion and clarity in public sector processes and procedures, remediation of contaminated land, and community participation, slow down progress and discourage private sector participation. But in recent decades, many cities have undertaken successful urban regeneration projects with significant participation of the private sector. From Johannesburg to Ahmedabad, from Seoul to Santiago, cities are designing effective multistakeholder processes that leverage private sector investment for urban development.

This guidebook provides a menu of options for leveraging private sector investment in urban regeneration initiatives. The goal is to make available to subnational governments and local planners a variety of tools to systematically identify the sequence of actions for leveraging public assets and attracting private sector investment in regeneration projects. The choice and use of these tools depends on each city's institutional and technical capacity, level of autonomy, and ability to manage its municipal finances. The case studies in this book highlight how a city that possesses considerable land assets can use the appropriate tools to achieve regeneration goals. In cities with limited public assets, the guidebook presents methods for leveraging local governments' regulatory powers to incentivize private investment in regeneration initiatives. The hope is that local governments can use the information curated in this volume to move toward infill development and densification of their urban cores, building more desirable urban environments in which their citizens can live, work, and thrive.

Ede Jorge Ijjasz-Vasquez
Senior Director
Social, Urban, Rural and Resilience Global Practice
The World Bank Group

Acknowledgments

This book was written and edited by Rana Amirtahmasebi, Mariana Orloff, Sameh Wahba, and Andrew Altman. Core contributors are Chirayu Bhatt, Isabel Brain, Jean Chia, Diana Giambiagi, Remy Guo, Sanghoon Jung, Myounggu Kang, In-Keun Lee, Valerie Santos, Jong-ho Shin, and Lan Wang.

The book draws on case studies from eight cities: Buenos Aires, Argentina; Santiago, Chile; Shanghai, China; Ahmedabad, India; Seoul, Republic of Korea; Singapore; Washington, DC, United States; and Johannesburg, South Africa. Each case study was developed by a consultant or a group of consultants, with assistance and oversight from various local entities or individuals.

Buenos Aires: The lead author was Diana Giambiagi. The team would like to thank Alfredo Garay (CAPMSA president), Marcela Suárez (CAPMSA urban planning and project manager), and Rodrigo Martinez Daveño (CAPMSA president of fiscal commission) for their insights and the information provided.

Santiago: The lead author was Isabel Brain. The team would like to thank Pablo Trivelli and Pablo Contrucci (who started the Santiago Repopulation Plan) and Bernabe Aravena and Claudio Maggi from the Santiago Development Corporation for providing information and insights on the project.

Shanghai: The lead author was Lan Wang. Jie Su, Gang Liu, Hao Gu, and Yahui Zhong provided research assistance. The team is grateful to Albert Kain Bon Chan and Vincent Hong Sui Lo of Shui On Land Limited; Yaliang Chen (formerly of urban Planning Administration Bureau of Luwan District); Lin Wang and Meitang Ye of Shanghai Urban Planning Administration Bureau; Henry Cheng; and Benjamin Wood for agreeing to be interviewed and for providing information.

Ahmedabad: The lead author was Chirayu Bhatt. The team expresses its thanks to Dr. Bimal Patel and the staff of the Sabarmati Riverfront Development Corporation, the Ahmedabad Municipal Corporation, and HCP Design, Planning, and Management Pvt, Ltd. for their support.

Seoul: The lead author was Myounggu Kang. In-Keun Lee, Jong-ho Shin, and Sanghoon Jung co-developed this case study. The team is grateful to the metropolitan government of Seoul and the Seoul Institute for providing assistance and insights.

Singapore: The lead authors were Remy Guo and Jean Chia. The team would like to thank the Urban Redevelopment Authority and the Centre for Livable Cities of Singapore for providing material and support in developing this case study.

Washington, DC: The lead authors were Mariana Orloff and Andrew Altman. The team benefited from advice and insights of former Washington, DC, mayor Anthony Williams; Uwe Brandes of Georgetown University; Stephen Green of the NHP Foundation; Alex Nyhan of Forest City; Michael Stevens and Tammy Shoham of the Capitol Riverfront BID; Brett Banks of the General Services Administration; and Barbara Smith of the U.S. Environmental Protection Agency.

Johannesburg: The lead author was Rana Amirtahmasebi. The peer reviewers were Tanya Zack and Mark Napier. The case was prepared with the help and insights of Sharon Lewis (formerly of JDA), Graeme Gotz of Gauteng City Region Observatory, Renney Plit of Afhco, and Anne Steffny of the Johannesburg CID Forum.

Stephen Karam (program leader, World Bank), Olga Kaganova (consultant), and Jordan Schwartz (head, Global Infrastructure Facility, World Bank) peer-reviewed the concept note and provided direction for the publication from the onset. Peer reviewers of the final document included Olga Kaganova, Stephen Karam, Barjor Mehta (lead urban specialist, World Bank), and Wael Zakout (lead land administration specialist, World Bank).

The publication of the book was supported by the following World Bank operational staff: Barjor Mehta, Stephen Karam, Joanna McLean Masic, and Angelica Nunez.

Adelaide Barra, Vivian Cherian, Ruth Maturan Cruz, and Brett Beasley provided logistical and administrative assistance. Lauren Bradford and Max Budovitch provided research assistance to the team. Laura De Brular assisted in production. The work was supported by the World Bank Social, Urban, Rural, and Resilience Global Practice under the overall guidance of Sameh Wahba and Ellen Hamilton.

Preparation of this book was facilitated by the Public-Private Infrastructure Advisory Facility (PPIAF) and the Culture and Sustainable Development Global Partnership Facility. PPIAF is a multidonor technical assistance facility aimed at helping developing countries improve the quality of their infrastructure through private sector involvement. For more information on the facility, visit http://www.ppiaf.org. The Culture and

Sustainable Development Global Partnership Facility is funded by the governments of Italy and India and is managed by the World Bank.

The publication of the book was managed by the World Bank's Publishing and Knowledge Division under the supervision of Susan Graham, Patricia Katayama, and Stephen Pazdan. Graphics were prepared by Allied Design and Urbanism. The book was edited by Barbara Balaj and Dana Lane. The corresponding website was developed by Daniel Cramer of Blue Tundra.

About the Authors

Principal Authors

Rana Amirtahmasebi is an urban planner and architect with a passion for designing systems, policies, and products to improve and adjust the conditions of human settlements. Rana is experienced in policy analysis and design and program implementation in community and local economic development, conservation of historic cities, settlement design and upgrading, and land governance frameworks. Her professional affiliations, in addition to the World Bank, include Pelli-Clarke-Pelli; New York City government; Bavand Consultants, Tehran, Iran; and the Aga Khan Foundation. Rana holds master's degrees in advanced urbanism studies and city planning from the Massachusetts Institute of Technology and also graduated with a master's degree in architectural engineering from Azad University in her hometown of Tehran, Iran. Follow her on twitter @amirtahmasebi.

Mariana Orloff is an associate at the Ross Center for Sustainable Cities at the World Resources Institute (WRI). She is part of the urban development team and coordinates among urban planning, land use, and transit-oriented development programs. Prior to joining WRI, Mariana worked as a consultant in the Urban Sector at the World Bank on both lending and knowledge projects (Latin America and Caribbean Region), and in the Global Urban and Resilience Unit on local economic development, slum upgrading, housing, and land use. Mariana holds a BA in political science and international relations from the Catholic University of La Plata, Argentina, and master's degrees in public policy and urban planning from the University of Michigan.

Sameh Wahba is practice manager for urban and disaster risk management in the Africa Region at the World Bank. Prior to this position, he managed the Global Urban and Resilience Unit, where he was responsible for the World Bank's urban policy, strategy, analytics, and partnerships at the global level. He also worked as Sustainable Development Sector leader for Brazil and as an urban specialist focused on housing, land, and local economic development in both the Latin America and the Caribbean and the Middle East and North Africa regions. Before joining the World Bank, he worked at the Institute of Housing and Urban Development Studies in Rotterdam and at the Harvard Center for Urban Development Studies. He holds a PhD in urban planning from Harvard University.

Andrew Altman is a leading practitioner in transforming cities and implementing public-private partnerships. He was the founding chief executive officer of the London Olympic Park Legacy Company in London, where he led the master planning and the development of the 600-acre 2012 Olympic Park into a new international growth center. He was the deputy mayor for economic development and planning and chair of the City Planning Commission for the city of Philadelphia. Andrew first established himself as an internationally recognized urban planner in Washington, DC, when he was the city's planning director and transformed a neglected planning department into a leader in the planning profession. Andrew has also worked in the private sector and is currently the managing principal of Fivesquares Development, a newly formed real estate development and consulting company based in Washington, DC, which focuses on innovative urban and transit-oriented projects. Andrew has numerous affiliations and fellowships, including the Brookings Institution, Loeb Fellowship from Harvard University, the German Marshall Fund, and the Technion-Israel Institute of Technology. He holds a master's degree in city planning from the Massachusetts Institute of Technology.

Contributing Authors

Chirayu Bhatt is an architect and urban planner with over 12 years of experience working on urban projects in the United States, the Middle East, Southeast Asia, and India. He works with CEPT University in Ahmedabad, where he manages the president's office and teaches in the graduate program in planning. His interests are policy, development regulations, public participation, and consensus building.

Isabel Brain is an independent consultant, researcher, and sociologist. She holds a master's degree in public administration from Harvard University. She cofounded and directed the urban program (Pro Urbana) at the Universidad Católica de Chile and the Social Research Center of the TECHO Foundation. Her experience focuses primarily on land markets, housing policy, urban segregation, citizen participation, and land readjustment.

Jean Chia holds a bachelor's degree in economics and a master's degree in environmental management from the National University of Singapore. She has worked in the international natural resources and commodities sector at the government of Singapore's economic agency, International Enterprise Singapore, as well as at the International Trading Institute at Singapore Management University. At the Centre for Liveable Cities (CLC), set up under the Ministry of National Development and Ministry of Environment and Water Resources in Singapore, she was involved in research and capability development and was part of the organizing team for the biennial World Cities Summit. She is currently an adjunct researcher with CLC.

Diana Giambiagi is an urban planner with a strong background in regeneration and land-use planning. She holds a master's degree in urban development planning from University College, London. Diana received the Japan Inter-American Development Bank Scholarship Award. Today she leads CH2M HILL's Urban programs Business Group in Latin America, coordinating inputs from the planning, land development, transportation, maritime, water, and infrastructure teams. Since 2010, she has been a visiting professor at the Universidad Torcuato Di Tella in the urban economics master's degree program.

Remy Guo is senior assistant director at the Centre for Liveable Cities, where he is involved in planning- and development-related research. Prior to joining CLC in 2013, Remy was a practicing urban designer and architect in the private sector; he completed various local and international projects, ranging from district-level master plans and urban design proposals to architectural construction projects.

Sanghoon Jung is an assistant professor in the Department of Urban Planning at Gachon University, Republic of Korea. He holds a PhD in Design from Harvard University's Graduate School of Design and Bachelor and Masters degrees from Seoul National University, Republic of Korea. His research focuses on the international transfer and localization of urban planning and design.

Myounggu Kang is professor of urban and regional planning at the University of Seoul and the former director-general of the International Urban Development Collaboration in the Seoul metropolitan government. He earned his bachelor's and master's degrees from Seoul National University and his master's of city planning and PhD from the Massachusetts Institute of Technology.

In-Keun Lee is the head of Land and Housing Institute (LHI), the research arm of the LHI Corporation. Before joining LHI, he served in the metropolitan government of Seoul for 32 years, including as director-general of the Cheonggyecheon Restoration Project, as director-general for urban planning, and as assistant mayor for infrastructure. He studied engineering at Seoul National University and holds a PhD in civil engineering from City University, London.

Valerie Santos is a senor urban specialist at the World Bank Group. She works with national and local governments around the globe on urban economic development strategies, financing local infrastructure, regeneration of center cities and waterfronts, metropolitan management, and housing and has advised on urban projects in Brazil, Colombia, Georgia, Guatemala, Jamaica, Panama, Peru, the Philippines, and South Africa. Valerie brings more than 15 years of experience in real estate and urban development and in structuring public-private agreements. Before joining the World Bank Group, she served as deputy mayor for planning and economic development in Washington, DC. During her tenure, the city invested in transforming hundreds of acres of underutilized land into parks and mixed-use and commercial developments, implemented ambitious neighborhood revitalization initiatives in underserved communities, and Valerie was responsible for a portfolio of projects valued at more than $13 billion. Valerie holds master's degrees in business administration and public policy from Harvard University and a bachelor's degree from Santa Clara University.

Jong-ho Shin currently holds a professorship at Konkuk University, Seoul, Republic of Korea. He studied at the Imperial College, London; the Korea Advanced Institute of Science and Technology; and Korea University. He worked for the metropolitan government of Seoul for 17 years and was responsible for the design and planning of the Cheonggyecheon Restoration Project.

Lan Wang is associate professor of urban planning at the University of Tongji, Shanghai, China. Her research interests include urban planning in globalizing cities with a focus on urban regeneration and new town development. She has been assistant dean of the College of Architecture and Urban Planning at Tongji University since 2014 and the secretary-general of the National Steering Committee of China Urban and Rural Planning Education since 2010. Lan holds a PhD from the University of Illinois, Chicago.

Executive Summary

What Triggers an Urban Regeneration Process?

Every city has pockets of underused and underutilized land or distressed and decaying urban areas. These pockets of underused land weaken the city's image, livability, and productivity. They are usually the result of changes in the urban growth and productivity patterns. Urban regeneration policies either target inner city declining neighborhoods or vacant land parcels. We have documented eight cities in this volume that have faced major challenges of this kind.

Consider the city of Santiago, which had been facing high urban deterioration for several decades. It lost almost 50 percent of its population and 33 percent of the housing stock between 1950 and 1990. This was mainly because of the ongoing trend that favored low-density suburban housing developments and the relocation of informal settlements in other municipalities within the metropolitan region. The loss of population was coupled with the deterioration of the built environment, the 1985 earthquake, a sharp decrease in real estate investment, high crime, pollution, and the lack of investment in public spaces. Similarly, Buenos Aires found itself unsustainably sprawling to the north and northwest and away from downtown, while its 170-hectar prime waterfront land, with some significant architectural and industrial heritage, was left vacant and underused. The initiative to rehabilitate the port area, called Puerto Madero, played a key role in the regeneration of Buenos Aires' traditional administrative and central business district and came to rescue the downtown.

The decaying inner city areas do not affect only the impoverished; these areas marginalize and exclude the residents, and they can have a long-term negative effect on their upward mobility. For example, the inner city of Johannesburg, suffering from spatial segregation policies of the

apartheid era, experienced a slow decline in the 1950s, which was accelerated in the 1980s and 1990s by out-migration of the white population
and businesses to new suburban centers on its north side. In the 1990s,
the inner city found itself struggling with excessive crime, physical decline,
uncontrollable informal retail activity, lack of public transportation, and
bankruptcy of service delivery institutions. These problems resulted in
major disinvestment in the inner city, leaving it with many vacant buildings, overdue taxes, and a large squatter population.

In Ahmedabad, the Sabarmati Riverfront Development project was a
response to the deteriorating ecological health of the riverfront and the
reduced public access to this natural asset. Deterioration of the riverfront in
Ahmedabad started because of a change in economic productivity resulting
from the closure of mills along the river. The unemployed laborers of the
abandoned mills started to live on the riverbed, forming large informal settlements in water catchment areas, which in turn reduced the flood management capacity of the river. This transformed the riverfront to an unsafe and
unclean area for the informal settlements, and it denied the city from enjoy-
ing its natural endowment. Washington, DC had a similar challenge. The
capital city of one of the wealthiest nations on the planet struggled with a
polluted Anacostia River, which runs seven miles along its eastern border.
Initially the commercial lifeline of the city, the Anacostia River had one of
the worst water quality ratings in the nation. Decades of unsound urban
policies and the exit of manufacturing firms resulted in the decay of this
postindustrial riverfront area. The river has long represented a dividing line
in the city, symbolizing the stark segregation by race and class. This area,
targeted for regeneration, had a high concentration of poverty, deteriorating
public housing, and a racially segregated African American population.

Taipingqiao, a historically significant neighborhood in Shanghai, had
become a public housing shantytown. The housing policies of 1950–80
rendered many of Shanghai's historic areas prime targets for developers to
build to the maximum floor area ratio. Taipingqiao, however, followed a
different development model than many of its neighbors; it embraced its
historic fabric and leveraged it to create value. Taipingqiao developers valued historic preservation and mixed land uses, making this development a
model that was followed by many other Chinese cities. Another Asian city,
Seoul, saw a major decrease in residential and commercial activity in its
downtown, which comprised small plots, narrow roads, and very high land
prices, rendering development too costly. Add to this a debate over renovating a major elevated highway that would cover a historic stream in the
downtown area. This debate triggered discussions on improving the environmental conditions and public spaces of downtown Seoul.

To tackle the issues of decline and urban decay, these cities and others
have designed complex processes of urban regeneration. Rarely are urban
regeneration projects implemented solely by the public sector. The need for
massive financial resources is one factor. However, even if the government
could provide the necessary resources for regenerating urban land,

the buy-in from the community and business sector is needed to ensure the sustainability of regeneration efforts. Consequently, the participation of the private sector is a determining factor in whether the regeneration of underutilized urban land is successful.

To this end, this volume builds on the experience of these eight cities from around the globe that successfully used their land assets and regulatory powers to leverage and incentivize private participation in urban regeneration. The cases vary in the institutional and political context, policy and regulatory tools used, and the extent of community participation and governance structure. What they have in common is significant private sector participation in the regeneration and rehabilitation of decaying urban areas.

To help identify the sequence of actions needed for a regeneration process, this book identifies four distinct phases: scoping, planning, financing, and implementation. Each phase includes a set of unique tools that local governments can use to systematically design a regeneration process. In addition to the four phases, the book also defines three major assets that the city must manage for urban regeneration; these are land, community, and the environment. The phases, tools, and assets are presented in figure ES.1.

Envisioning Change: The Scoping Phase

A transformational urban regeneration process—either for the city as a whole or for a specific land parcel—starts with a scoping exercise. Scoping is a process that provides decision makers with a strategic assessment to identify and promote regeneration. Scoping provides an analytical foundation and engagement process that the city leaders can use to generate choices and to debate and decide on the best course of action. A sound scoping process supplies city leaders with analytical tools to confront issues facing the city that are vital to its future and to make strategic decisions on the direction they want their city to pursue. Scoping is both forward looking and backward looking. It is forward looking, in that it analyzes what is required for the city and regeneration area to be successful in the future, and backward looking, in that it takes into account the city's history and the unique "DNA," which are precedents for prudent action that can be capitalized on.

The scoping phase could span several decades. For example, in Ahmedabad, the vision of a vibrant riverfront for the city started in the 1960s by a French architect, and it was followed up in the 1970s by the Riverfront Development Group who proposed an incremental approach to creating a public riverfront along the banks of the river. However, the city was financially struggling at the time, and without a clear approach to financing and implementing the proposals, this plan was going to remain on paper. In this case, the key to jump-starting the scoping process of the Sabarmati riverfront regeneration was envisioning a mechanism for financing the project.

Figure ES.1   Tools for urban regeneration

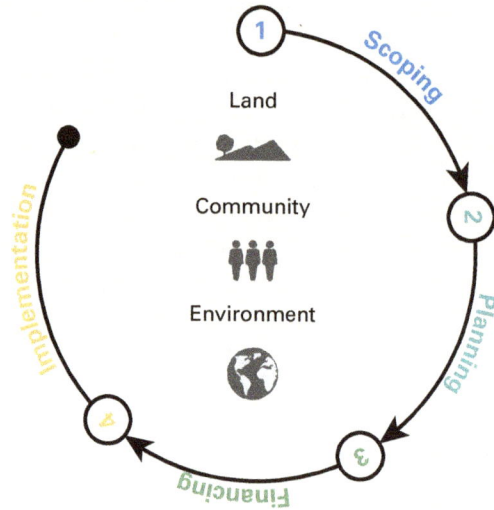

In Johannesburg, similar to Ahmedabad, the scoping process was started by the private sector, and it was continued by the government. Various scoping exercises were done through collaborative processes and over the course of 20 years. The scoping process in Johannesburg is also unique in that it acted as a convener of ideas presented by various groups of stakeholders. The vision for the inner city evolved from a "dynamic city that works" and is "livable, safe, well managed, and welcoming" in 1996, to financial viability, budget reform, and privatization of services in 2002, to municipal strategy and economic growth in 2030. The drivers behind these visions also changed from communities and private sector in 1996 to the city council and local and provincial governments. The private sector remained very active throughout.

The scoping process can also act as an organizing framework as it did in Washington, DC. The planning team used the scoping phase as a means to heal the city with new leadership and new control of its destiny. Washington's downtown area was nearly built out, and the city's pattern of growth was moving steadily eastward toward and across the Anacostia River. The team behind the vision understood that the capacity of the capital city to grow was inextricably linked to recentering its growth in the coming decades on the Anacostia River.

The scoping phase needs to consider the overall growth of the city and not just the targeted regeneration area. In fact, scoping can be a tool to determine the future growth direction of the city. For example, in Buenos Aires, the scoping phase not only focused on regenerating the port area into higher-value land uses, it also envisioned the revitalization of the central business district, overcoming years of disinvestment and changing the public's perception of the downtown area. Similar to Ahmedabad and Johannesburg, all of the planning efforts for the city since the 1960s had included ideas about new uses for this centrally located land; yet none of these plans was ever executed because of the administrative and financial challenges.

Similarly, the goal of the Santiago repopulation program was rebuilding the residential role of the city. Based on detailed and sound analytical work, Santiago's Repopulation Program (SRP) was designed to attract 100,000 new residents to the district in the course of 15 years. The SRP was created based on a series of studies and scoping exercises. One major study compared the costs of developing housing solutions in consolidated areas of the city with the costs of urban expansion, and it showed that building in peripheral areas was almost 18 times more expensive for the city than in consolidated areas. The visioning phase clearly showed that the city would benefit from infill development, and the goals were arranged accordingly.

In Shanghai, the site was tagged for regeneration at a time of large-scale demolition and construction. In the 1990s, establishment of land markets provided a legal framework for private developers to rent land for real estate development. Based on a preexisting relationship with Shui On Land Limited, a developer from Hong Kong SAR, China, the district government asked the company to create a vision of redevelopment. The company hired a multinational planning firm to develop a master plan for the entire Taipingqiao neighborhood. A significant part of this process was the company's emphasis on preserving the traditional architecture of two blocks within Taipingqiao, against the market behavior of the time and the objection of the local government.

Designing a Web of Actions and Institutions: The Planning Phase

While the scoping phase provides an analytical foundation and an overarching rationale and narrative for the regeneration project, the planning framework establishes the long-term vision and context. This step is vital to sustaining the regeneration vision through the inevitable changes and unforeseen challenges of the market and political cycles. However, it is important that the plan not be overly rigid, because it will discourage private investment. An effective planning framework will balance vision and planning principles, and it will facilitate negotiation among the public, private, and community sectors.

A sound planning framework brings together an inspiring vision with a clear regulatory process. This will provide the private sector with the assurance to invest and take risks, and it assures communities that public goals will be achieved and not subordinated purely to the dictates of the market. Using the findings of the scoping exercise, the planning phase of a regeneration process must detail all the vital elements and assets, including land, community, and the environmental issues.

There are various ways to start the planning phase. In some cases, planning starts with defining the organizational framework for taking on the regeneration project while in other cases, a master plan is developed to spatially define the process. In Buenos Aires, the planning phase started with the creation of a new corporation, which through a national competition developed a master plan to guide the development of its port area. This plan was broad and simple; it consisted of a basic subdivision and massing design and mechanisms to allocate land parcels to different private partners to be developed for different uses. In Ahmedabad, once a special purpose vehicle was established, the planning phase began. The plan was centered on reclaiming about 200 hectares of land on both sides of the river and building a continuous promenade along the east and west banks, while reducing the risk of erosion and flooding in the vicinity. The plan also envisioned implementation mechanisms and financing strategies, and it created a new identity for Ahmedabad by providing the city with new cultural, trade, and social amenities.

Singapore's regeneration started in a context different from the other cities featured in this volume. Because Singapore was a new city-state, the idea was to develop a comprehensive planning framework. The planning system in Singapore brings together the policies and programs of various government agencies and incorporates them into a national urban policy document, known as the concept plan, which is valid for 40–50 years. This concept plan is then followed by a master plan, which translates the broad and long-term strategies of the concept plan into detailed plans for implementation of 10–15 years and guides the exercise of development controls. The planning system in Singapore requires a high degree of coordination among various entities of the local government. It allows for conflicts among different agencies to be resolved early and for trade-offs to be dealt with in constructive and innovative ways.

Some of the cases in this volume outline a participatory process in their planning efforts. Washington, DC's planning phase for the regeneration of the Anacostia River is one of the most successful examples of participatory planning. Under the direction of the Office of Planning, a 150-member steering committee was formed to support the planning process and to provide a forum for handling the major public policy disputes related to the river. Likewise, Johannesburg's local government arranged to involve various stakeholder groups in the planning process. The regeneration summit and resulting charter of 2007 created a consultative process that involved inner city stakeholders in six working groups on various topics of concern. The charter also developed a plan for the future regeneration of Johannesburg, which focused on the findings of these six working groups and their focus areas. In addition, the charter recommended a spatial development plan be designed for the inner city and Johannesburg as a whole, which would act as a new framework.

The planning phase in Santiago concerned infill development and attracting new residents to the entire municipal territory. The scope was so ambitious that there was no hope for success without the participation of the private sector. The planning phase focused on convincing the private developers to invest in the inner city, stimulating demand for housing and changing the image of the city. The plan focused on using the existing national housing subsidy, demonstrating the considerable demand for housing, and collaborating with private developers. The diagnostic studies that assessed the city's urban and socioeconomic structure were shared with the community.

In Shanghai, the regeneration of the Taipingqiao neighborhood was planned by the government in consultation with a development company. The Master Plan of Taipingqiao allowed for a 10–15 year development process, leveraging the investment return from housing development to support the construction of a lake and a park. However, this process did not engage with the extensive informal settlement population that inhabits the rundown neighborhoods for which the regeneration project was planned.

In Seoul, restoration of the Cheonggyecheon stream was at the heart of mayoral election debates, because the two strong mayoral candidates had very different views on it. Opening up this topic in the mayoral debates enabled active communication and social consensus formation between the government and among its citizens. Three different bodies were established to manage the restoration: the Cheonggyecheon Restoration Headquarters, a Research Group, and a Citizens' Committee. They handled research activities related to the restoration and developed basic plans and the organizational structure to jump-start the process. The resulting Downtown Development Plan was a systematic reorganization of the Cheonggyecheon neighborhood and a long-term development of downtown area, which leveraged the public investment in the Cheonggyecheon restoration to create a new downtown Seoul.

Incentivizing Private Funding: The Financing Phase

Whether an urban regeneration initiative is led by the public sector or the private sector can affect the financing tools available to its lead sponsor. Large-scale urban regeneration projects are complex and require immense resources to be planned and implemented properly. Few cities have the resources to finance the costs of such large initiatives outright. Partnerships with the private sector are necessary not only to share the costs but also the risks and technical capacities. Typically, cities deploy a combination of internal and external funding sources, policy and regulatory tools, and strategic partnerships with the private sector to finance their urban regeneration vision.

Many factors affect the methods used for financing urban regeneration initiatives. The most important factor is the national, legal, and institutional context for the project and the amount of control a city has over its fiscal management—specifically its ability to raise and allocate revenue (for example, a city's ability to access municipal bond markets). Another important factor is the city's capacity to use innovative financing techniques, such as tax increment financing or development rights transfers to support specific real estate and economic development strategies. Based on the case studies in this volume, there are two distinct groups of instruments used for financing urban regeneration: financial tools and regulatory tools. Financial tools involve direct financing assistance, such as various value capture methods (impact fees, special assessments, exactions). Regulatory instruments are essential for leveraging a city's regulatory powers to incentivize private sector participation (tax-based and non-tax-based incentives, zoning, land-use regulations, and development rights transfers).

Among the case studies, Ahmedabad, Santiago, and Washington, DC employed innovative financing schemes. In Ahmedabad, 14 percent of the reclaimed land was used to finance the entire regeneration of the Sabarmati riverfront, including capital improvements, public spaces, and interest on loans. The city used its existing serviced public land as collateral for a loan through a central government financial institution, called Housing and Urban Development Corporation. This pragmatic approach lowered the perceived risk of borrowing. Had the collateral been the actual riverfront land, whose existence and value depended on the timeliness and success of the project, there might have been a greater collective push to complete the various stages of the project more expeditiously.

In some cases, where public land is owned by the central government, special legislation may be required to transfer the land to the local government. This was the case in Washington, DC, where the local government worked with the national government to take control of 200 acres of federal waterfront land, which was key to the city's plans to transform areas bordering both sides of the Anacostia River. This was a great achievement for the city, since the land transfer placed the land on tax rolls, which would produce significant revenue contingent upon redevelopment. In addition, the city used a US\$230 million payment-in-lieu-of-taxes bond to pay for the infrastructure investments and green spaces. To build a baseball stadium, the city sold US\$535 million in municipal bonds to be repaid by stadium-generated revenues and by a special tax on businesses within the area. The city also established a business improvement district, which imposed a fee, paid by local businesses, to maintain green public spaces in the area.

While urban regeneration is usually the responsibility of the local government, national regulations and incentives can also be used to facilitate the process. In Santiago, the local government used an existing national subsidy to encourage private developers to invest in the municipal district. The existing policy provided tax benefits to properties constructed or renovated in areas designated for urban renovation, freezing their valuation for tax purposes for 20 years (starting in 1987). This subsidy program was especially innovative in its allocation criteria, which included geographical boundaries of the targeted zone. Likewise, policy makers in Johannesburg used a national tax incentive to leverage private sector investment in regenerating the blighted inner city neighborhoods. This law, described as a driving force behind the surge in inner city real estate investments, allowed the municipalities to designate priority areas for regeneration efforts listed in their integrated plans as urban development zones. The incentive works in the form of an accelerated depreciation from eligible taxpayers' taxable income, if the income comes from the construction or renovation of all or part of a building in the inner city. Johannesburg also legislated city improvement districts to absorb more private funding for security, closed circuit TV cameras, public space upgrades, and social and educational programs. Finally, area-based initiatives by the Johannesburg Development Agency achieved substantial leverage ratios of public to private sector investments.

Some cities have an investment climate that is already attractive to the private sector. In such cases, the local government uses its regulatory power to ease some of the procedures and rules required for development. For example, in Shanghai, the local government piggybacked on the wave of increased private sector investment in urban development and used its valuable asset—public land—to encourage the regeneration of rundown areas. By building infrastructure and providing a friendly regulatory environment, the government created incentives for private sector investment. In contrast to Shanghai, which outsourced the regeneration process to a private sector developer, the city of Seoul took on the regeneration of the Cheonggyecheon stream with a large upfront investment. The city was confident that once completed, the stream would act as a catalyst to accelerate private sector funding and regenerating the decaying downtown area. The transformation of the Cheonggyecheon stream area increased land prices and rents and boosted the economic activity and population in downtown Seoul.

In many cases, cities use autonomous corporations to finance and implement regeneration initiatives. For example, financing the regeneration of Puerto Madero in Buenos Aires was implemented through a public limited corporation, which was regulated by the commercial code. The federal government and the city government contributed to the capital stock in equal parts. The company had the ability to issue shares in order to attract private, national, and foreign funds. The decree also transferred the property of the 170 hectares of public land to the corporation. The statute of the corporation set the capital stock in Arg$40 million represented by 40,000 common shares. Each share was entitled to one vote. By a resolution at the ordinary shareholders' meeting, the capital stock could be raised to five times the amount previously set.

The case studies in this volume exhibit innovation and creativity in the ways cities can use their unique regulatory powers and public resources to finance large-scale interventions. However, financing is only one phase of the process. Urban regeneration projects are by definition lengthy and complex, and they engage the public and private sectors in a diverse set of interrelationships. After the scoping and planning phases are completed and the financing scheme is decided, the project enters the implementation phase.

Evolution from Ideas to Action: The Implementation Phase

The implementation phase translates the vision for long-term change into the financial, contractual, and institutional relationships between the public and private sectors. This phase includes structuring sound institutions and an organizational structure that is viable and sustainable and can exist through multiple political administrations. It also involves developing sound contracts that translate the vision into a tangible partnership between public and private sectors.

Political leadership may be the most important factor throughout the process, especially in the implementation phase. Because regeneration is a long-term, transformative process, there is disruption and risk, and political leadership is essential to managing the change process so that all stakeholders feel engaged in the process, understand its importance to the future of the city, and have genuine outlets to participate. The longitudinal test of political leadership is whether the vision is sustained through changes in political and economic cycles and results not in community division but greater cohesion.

Another major indicator of success in the implementation phase is to clearly map out the life of the project and the expected project cycle and phases, accounting for uncertainties. Up next is the phasing and breakdown of a large project into manageable components. The handover process must account for the complex set of interdependencies between the large scale investments and construction projects, such as major infrastructure (utilities, transport, park systems, brownfield cleanup), and the microdelivery of commercial and residential projects that need to establish a "sense of place" and feel complete even though the ultimate build-out of the regeneration project will progress over a longer period. One last important component of implementation is determining the optimal institutional structure for project delivery and assigning the powers and tools to various entities. This affects the structure of contracts, handover, and sustainability of the project.

Outlined in the eight case studies in this volume are various implementation mechanisms. Each city has used its organizational structure and legal and regulatory framework to design a sound implementation process. In four of the case studies (Buenos Aires, Washington DC, Santiago, and Ahmedabad), the local government implemented the regeneration project through some kind of a standalone corporation. In Buenos Aires, the Corporacion Antiguo Puerto Madero Sociedad Anonima (CAMPSA) was established, with representation from the federal government (through Ministry of Finance, the Ministry of Public Works, and the Interior

Ministry) and the city government. CAMPSA's board was initially composed of six directors: four on behalf of the federal government and two for the city of Buenos Aires. Each member had one vote, and only in the event of a draw would the president's vote count double.

Another example of an autonomous corporation set up for executing an urban regeneration project was in Ahmedabad. The corporation was a Special Purpose Vehicle (SPV) within the Ahmedabad Municipal Corporation. With a diverse Board of Directors comprising various private sector members and political and bureaucratic interests from both the ruling and the opposition parties, the regeneration of the Sabarmati Riverfront was viewed as a civic project rather than a project aligned with a certain party's agenda. This arrangement also ensured the sustainability of the project when it transitioned from one administration to another.

The implementation of the SRP was delegated to Santiago's Development Corporation (SDC), which developed partnerships with the private sector. Like other municipal corporations in Chile, SDC is ruled by private law, and it was therefore authorized to enter into contracts with public or private institutions, receive contributions, and borrow from private banks or financial entities. By employing such a flexible institutional structure, SDC's executive directors played the role of public entrepreneurs, working on behalf of the community while using the financial instruments available to the private sector. The public-private partnership agreements between SDC and other actors were regulated in the same manner as contracts between two private sector entities. In addition, the SDC worked closely with the municipality, as the mayor was the president of the corporation.

In Washington, DC, the District of Columbia Office of Planning was designated as the lead agency in the urban regeneration process. It was believed that creating a single development corporation would ensure that the various components of the Anacostia Waterfront Initiative were coordinated to maximize the benefits of this natural asset to the District of Columbia. To that end, the District government-chartered Anacostia Waterfront Corporation was established. With a board that included both mayoral appointees as well as ex-officio members from both the District and federal agencies, the corporation was an entity poised to become a development partner for both municipal and federal agencies.

Two of the case studies—Johannesburg and Singapore—have used a stand-alone agency within the local government to undertake urban regeneration of decaying areas within their inner cities. The Urban Redevelopment Authority in Singapore was established in the 1970s as an autonomous statutory board under the Ministry of National Development, which focused on the comprehensive redevelopment of the central area. This hugely successful initiative transformed the central area into a modern financial and business hub by executing 155 development projects between 1967 and 1989. Similarly, the Johannesburg Development Agency (JDA) was mandated to regenerate the inner city and to develop transit areas and economic development strategies across the metropolitan area. Its role as an economic development agency was to support the city's growth and development strategy and to act as the management body to initiate development within the central business district. The JDA has successfully undertaken a range of capital-based projects throughout the city since its inception, creating a favorable environment to attract new investment and increase occupancy levels in the inner city.

In some cases, public and private sectors collaborate within a flexible framework. This was the case in Shanghai, where the district government collaborated with the municipal government to facilitate the implementation process. The review and approval procedure had to be revised to make the preservation of the historic buildings feasible. For instance, the Shanghai Urban Planning Administrative Bureau transferred the authority to review the transportation and construction permits from the municipal level to the committee at the district level to facilitate the approval process.

In Seoul, the institutional arrangements for the Cheonggyecheon restoration project used a triangular implementation system of the citizens' committee, the project headquarters, and a research group. Each of these entities was comprised of government officials, experts, and citizens. This system was designed to simultaneously promote efficient project implementation, collect public opinion, and build public relations. The project headquarters office was launched within city hall to act as the main implementation arm of the project. Focusing solely on the site works, the mayor hosted weekly meetings to maximize efficiency and collaboration. The Cheonggyecheon Research Group was established under the Seoul Development Institute and it was tasked with conducting research on the basic data and blueprint for the Cheonggyecheon restoration, including on transportation, land use, urban planning, environment, and culture. It also organized a variety of seminars and meetings with experts, and it promoted the restoration project through academic events, public relations, and media outlets. Finally, the Citizens' Committee was established to serve as an official channel to collect the citizens' opinions and concerns regarding the project.

The process of urban regeneration is broken down into phases for the sake of simplification and comparison. These phases can vary in length and depth, depending on a given city's legal and institutional context. Table ES.1 summarizes these phases in the case studies examined in this volume. It attempts to provide a glance at the process, financing scheme, and timeline of each case.

Leveraging Urban Assets for Regeneration

The processes and phases summarized in this volume revolve around the three main assets cities possess to leverage for urban redevelopment: land, community, and the environment. Large-scale urban regeneration

Table ES.1   The process of urban regeneration for eight case studies in this volume

Case study characteristics	Scoping	Planning	Financing	Implementation
Puerto Madero, Buenos Aires, Argentina				
Type: Port rehabilitation *Parcel size:* 170 hectares (40 ha are water bodies) *Institution in charge:* CAPMSA, a public limited corporation *Timeline:* 1989–2012 *Investments:* Total land sold was around US$300 million. CAPMSA invested US$113 million in infrastructure, with a total operational cost of US$92 million. Total investment in 2009 reached US$1.7 billion.	• Economic growth context and regulatory environment that allowed for privatization of public land; • 1986 feasibility study synthesized successive plans, mapped the tenancy, mapped heritage buildings, and outlined alternative access routes.	• Master plan through a call for proposals (1992); • CAPMSA conceived of the master plan as an instrument of negotiation with the developers; • Puerto Madero would accommodate the expansion of the central business area and develop cultural and recreational areas.	• Self-financing scheme through the sale of public land; • Early financial resources of consisted of rents and the sale of demolition material. The revenues were used to pay for office rental, the master plan, and a marketing strategy. • Buenos Aires City maintains roads and parks in the area.	• Preparation of land (regularization of ownership, survey, new zoning for the area); • Transfer of national land to the development corporation "CAPMSA"; • Land sold in three stages and destined for mixed use • During the third stage, Puerto Madero was officially incorporated into the city with the status of a "district".
Santiago Repopulation Program (SRP), Chile				
Type: Downtown revitalization and repopulation *Parcel size:* 23 sq km *Institution in charge:* Santiago Development Corporation (SDC) *Timeline:* 1990–present *Investments:* The total subsidies from 1992 to 2002 were US$138.8 million. Private investment has reached US$3 billion. The municipal revenues from property taxes increased 85.1 percent from 2001 to 2013.	• *Vision exercise:* plan for the Renovation of Santiago, with public participation; • *Scoping study* found out that the cost of urban expansion (to the government) in the urban core is much lower than the suburbs.	• Identification of available land for redevelopment (land bank); • Redefinition of the national housing subsidy to fit Santiago's needs; • Compilation of housing demand • Marketing and advertisement.	• Private sector financing of construction through the National Housing Subsidy Program; • For the first time in Chile, subsidies were targeted based on a geographical or urban definition of the area—instead of income criteria.	• As the SRP became more consolidated, the private sector became the main driver of housing production, and the role of the SDC diminished; • Collaborating with private developers through the repopulation agreements; • The SRP was implemented by the Santiago Development Corporation, in collaboration with the private sector.

(Table continues on next page)

Table ES.1   The process of urban regeneration for eight case studies in this volume *(continued)*

Case study characteristics	Scoping	Planning	Financing	Implementation
Xintiandi, Shanghai, China				
Type: Historic downtown redevelopment *Parcel size:* 3 ha (two-block development) *Institution in charge:* Shui On Land Limited (SOL). *Investments:* The total cost of the Xintiandi project was about US$175 million. Government spending or revenues are unknown.	• SOL signed an agreement with the Luwan District government, by which SOL would pay for the relocation, land, and a portion of infrastructure and redevelopment of the site. In return, local government provided SOL with development rights for the entire Taipingqiao neighborhood.	• Master plan for the entire Taipingqiao neighborhood (1997) • Shanghai Planning Department offered simplified approval procedures to expedite implementation. • Construction regulations were also softened.	• The investment return from housing and office space supported the construction of the Taipingqiao lake and park. • SOL used cross-subsidization to afford the conservation of Xintiandi by redeveloping the entire 52 hectares of Taipingqiao. • SOL paid for relocation compensation.	• Implementation and project phasing were adjusted based on macroeconomic conditions and their impact on housing demand. Early investment concentrated on the redevelopment of the historic area and urban public space, instead of housing and office space. • A subordinate real estate development company of Luwan District established a joint venture with SOL to assist with bureaucratic procedures and approvals.
Sabarmati Riverfront Development Ahmedabad, India				
Type: Waterfront redevelopment *Parcel size:* 12 km long, 200 hectares of gained land *Institution in charge:* Sabarmati Riverfront Development Corporation Limited *Timeline:* 1997–present *Investments:* Project expenses amount to Rs 1100 Crores (about US$180 million). Revenues will be provided through the sale of 29 ha (14.5 percent) of the reclaimed land area.	• Feasibility study suggested to train the width of the river to 275 meters and gain land • Political consensus was built through - creation of a special-purpose vehicle headed by a board of directors with representation of two main political parties.	• Make the riverfront accessible to the public, stop the flow of sewage, and keep the river clean and reduce the risk of erosion; • Manage the informal settlements; • Enhance connections between the east and west sides of Ahmedabad; • Create a stronger identity for Ahmedabad and provide the city with new cultural and social amenities.	• Loans from HUDCO (a large national infrastructure funding agency) and the Ahmedabad Municipal Corporation, using land as collateral; • Twenty percent of the reclaimed land was to be sold to finance the entire cost of the project.	• Implementation outsourced by hiring private sector consultants to oversee development management services; • Land transfer from state government • Relocation of informal settlements; • Reconciliation of municipal land records through *melavni*.[a]

Table ES.1 The process of urban regeneration for eight case studies in this volume *(continued)*

Case study characteristics	Scoping	Planning	Financing	Implementation
Restoration of Cheonggyecheon Stream, Seoul, Korea, Rep.				
Type: Downtown redevelopment *Parcel size:* 5.8 km *Institution in charge:* Tripartite implementation structure, representing citizens, research, and implementation: Restoration Headquarters, Research Group, and a Citizens' Committee *Timeline:* 2002–05 *Investments:* Total project costs were US$ 323 million, paid fully by the city. After restoration, land prices increased by 30 percent.	• Vision came from a mayoral candidate that won the 2002 election; before, restoring the river was considered too expensive and complicated; • The city decided to demolish the elevated highway and create an eco-friendly waterfront, and restore the historical value of the stream through public investment.	• Downtown Development Plan (2003); Master Plan for the Cheonggyecheon Restoration (2004); • Public discussion topics included development direction, economic effect, traffic congestion, environment and ecology, water supply, neighborhood development, historic preservation and implementation system; • Transportation planning was among the toughest issues that the government had to address, given the removal of busy roads in the downtown.	• The project was 100 percent financed by the Seoul metropolitan government; • The budget came from city's capital budget, downsizing less urgent projects, and introducing creative work procedures to enhance the efficiency of the city administration; • Public investment was viewed as a catalyst for leveraging private investment in downtown and its economy.	• The project was phased with initial public investment in the restoration of the river, public amenities, and environmental cleanup, followed by private investment in the surrounding land; • The project team employed a triangular implementation system. This framework was designed to simultaneously promote efficient project implementation, collect public opinion, and build public relations; • A fast-track, design-build system was adopted so that the construction could be completed before the seasonal floods in the summer.
Anacostia Waterfront Initiative, Washington, DC, United States				
Type: Waterfront redevelopment *Parcel size:* 36 miles of riverfront *Institution in Charge:* Anacostia Waterfront Corporation (AWC) and DC government	Previous events for momentum gathering: • Decision of the United States Navy to move NAVSEA to the southeast Washington; • Election of Mayor Williams	• Memorandum of understanding with federal government • Creation of AWI • Creation of the corporation AWC	• PILOT Bonds • Business Improvement District • HOPE VI (affordable housing grant) • Municipal bonds for stadium construction	Some implementation milestones: • National Congress passed the Southeast Federal Center Public Private Redevelopment Act, allowing for PPP to redevelop the land • Relocation of the U.S. Department of Transportation to the area

(Table continues on next page)

Table ES.1 The process of urban regeneration for eight case studies in this volume *(continued)*

Case study characteristics	Scoping	Planning	Financing	Implementation
Timeline: 2000–2030 *Investments:* US$25 billion was invested (private and public) in the project, which is projected to yield US$1.5 billion in additional tax revenues for the district per year.	• Planning a ballpark and other attractions to extract additional revenue from the area.	• Some important planning documents: • National Capital Planning Commission Legacy Plan • Extensive consultations • AWI framework • Neighborhood plans	• Additional sale taxes for big businesses (ballpark)	• Navy Yards and Yards Park • Redevelopment of Public Housing • Federal transfer of lands to local government

Redevelopment of the Golden Shoe District, Singapore River, and Marina Bay, Singapore

Case study characteristics	Scoping	Planning	Financing	Implementation
Type: Waterfront redevelopment (Golden Shoe District, Singapore River, and Marina Bay) *Institution in charge:* Urban Redevelopment Authority, Housing Development Board, and other national agencies. *Timeline:* 1960–present *Investment:* This was a national level program and estimating the exact investment amount is not possible.	• UN technical assistance for planning, 1962 and 1963; • The government decided that the area should be redeveloped into a financial center.	• Singapore's First Concept Plan (1971) • Plot ratios were established in view of the road capacity and traffic in the area; • Site coverage was maximized at 100 percent; urban design guidelines were developed, specifying a podium and tower configuration to maintain visual uniformity and human scale; the views of the harbor were preserved.	• Public land acquisition for a broad variety of purposes and low compensation • Development charge system • Government land sales • Construction of public housing • Removal of rent controls • A minimum of 2 percent of the total development costs was to be spent on landscaping as stipulated in the land sale condition	• Resettlement measures, including a meticulous compensation formula established by the government; • Environmental cleanup of the river • Urban conservation of shophouses • Public investment in infrastructure and public spaces.

Table ES.1 The process of urban regeneration for eight case studies in this volume *(continued)*

Case study characteristics	Scoping	Planning	Financing	Implementation
Inner City, Johannesburg, South Africa				
Type: Inner city *Parcel size:* 18 sq km *Institution in charge:* Johannesburg Development Agency *Timeline:* 1991–present *Investment:* The JDA invested about R 3.6 billion (US$ 225 million) on Area Based Initiatives. When combined with new property development, the private sector has invested a total of R11 billion in Inner City properties since 2000.	Many visions and plans were developed including: • Strategic Initiative for Central Johannesburg • The Golden Heartbeat of Africa • Provincial four-point plan • Spatial and Economic Framework for the Inner City • iGoli 2002 • iGoli 2010 • iGoli 2030 Most of these plans stay as visioning exercises and lack the level of granularity needed for an implementable plan.	There were many plans over the years. The notable ones are: • The 2004 Inner City Regeneration Business Plan • Inner City Summit and charter in 2007 addressed the issue of derelict buildings in the Inner City, inner city housing Action Plan, PPP development, and economic and spatial development. • In 2013, the City of Johannesburg released its Inner City Transformation Roadmap.	• City improvement districts • National level UDZ tax incentives • Trust for the Urban Housing Foundation loans • JDA's capital budget is supplied by the local government, grants from other government departments, the National Treasury, the Department of Public Works, and so on; • The JDA's operating budget comes from a 5 percent fee on all projects and a transfer received from the City.	• Provincial governments move to CBD (1994) • Projects that aimed at boosting private sector investment in the inner city • Area-based initiatives by JDA had a large leverage ratio • Crime prevention measures • Public arts and public space upgrades • Better Buildings Program (to deal with dilapidated housing)

Note: AWC = Anacostia Waterfront Corporation; AWI = Anacostia Waterfront Initiative; CAPMSA = Corporacion Antiguo Puerto Madero Sociedad Anonima; CBD = central business district; HUDCO = Housing and Urban Development Corporation; iGoli = is *Johannesburg* in local language; km = kilometer; PPP = public-private partnership; SDC = Santiago Development Corporation; SOL = Shui On Land Limited; sq = square; SRFDCL = Sabarmati Riverfront Development Corporation Limited; SRP = Santiago Repopulation Program; UDZ = urban development zone; UN = United Nations.

a. *Melavni*—which means *to match* in the local language—reconciles the paper records of land ownership with the actual on-the-ground ownership of land (Ballaney 2008).

projects usually involve all three assets. First, land is the most valuable asset for municipal governments. There are many ways that governments can leverage land for urban regeneration, including using land as collateral for borrowing in capital markets, or from local and national banks, or auctions and leaseholds. Yet regardless of how land is used for revenue generation, a strong regulatory framework is usually necessary to maximize these benefits. Second, the community that lives in or around the regeneration area (or the urban citizens as a whole) needs to be considered and involved in the regeneration process to ensure equitable development and to avoid displacement and gentrification. The process should enable the local community to have a voice in how their local area will be redeveloped and reused. Third, almost all urban regeneration projects have to face environmental challenges, because they mostly take place in brownfields, waterfronts, or old deprived urban areas around the city center. Therefore, the environmental aspects of the project must be considered an integral part of designing a sustainable process. These three assets are briefly presented here.

Land

Planning for regeneration of underused urban land starts with developing a clear understanding of the land ownership regime in the city. There are various regimes of land ownership/control such as public, private, communal, and endowment/trust. In many cases, the existence of informal settlements and informal tenure can be a challenge in executing an equitable regeneration project. Informal development is associated with a range of legal degrees depending on the country's political and legal context, the length and nature of informal land occupancy, and the presence of adverse possession regulations and property disputes.

Local governments have many policy and regulatory tools at their disposal to determine and control the use of land and the physical shape of the urban environment, and to encourage the private sector to invest in the city. At a larger scale, these tools include land-use planning and zoning regulations. Zoning is a planning control tool for regulating the built environment and creating functional real estate markets. Another issue in managing land is readjustment and assembly, and this is where fragmented land ownership presents a challenge to regeneration. Governments use a variety of voluntary and involuntary methods to acquire and assemble land from private interests in order to implement urban development and transformation projects. The general policy recommendation encourages land assembly through achieving consensus or negotiation. Many countries have shifted their policies toward assembling land through voluntary purchases, which have proven to be cheaper, faster, and more popular. One of the other tools that can be used to manage land assets, discourage speculation, and encourage development is to tax vacant land parcels. Many governments around the world have used this tool to motivate the private sector to develop vacant land. However, governments should not use this tool solely to address budget issues. Rather, they should use this tool to change the behavior of the private sector and block speculation.

The case studies present a variety of options in leveraging land assets for regeneration. In Shanghai, land was leased to the private sector developer through negotiations. Buenos Aires used its wealth of public land as an equity contribution to the Puerto Madero Development Corporation. Singapore used a mandatory land assembly regulation to assemble smaller land parcels and to make them ready for large-scale development. In Washington, DC, riverfront lands fell under the jurisdiction of multiple federal and local authorities and agencies, not one of which had a clear mandate for revitalizing the waterfront. Transfering all of these land assets to the city and creating one entity for managing them was the key to the project's success. In Santiago, the SDC began its regeneration efforts by conducting a land market assessment with the update of a 1987 cadastre of vacant or highly deteriorated/underutilized properties. The process of updating the cadastre included identifying 90 hectares of land owned by private and public entities that qualified for redevelopment.

Community

Community participation and public involvement in the planning of development projects are fundamental for project success and sustainability. First, participation is necessary because the public expresses its democratic right to be involved in the public policy process. Second, it allows the communities to express their needs and aspirations, which subsequently feed into the policy-making, delivery, and monitoring process. Third, participation allows for greater efficiencies throughout the project delivery process.

There are also very practical implications for community participation during an urban regeneration project. First, end users add valuable content and information based on local knowledge and personal experience. Public involvement, if done effectively, can improve the outcome of the project. Second, participation is a positive way to channel public interest that can otherwise manifest itself as uninformed opposition and protest. Participation in the planning and design of a project, in particular, gives people the opportunity to influence decisions that will affect their daily lives. Third, when people are involved early on in the design and creation of the plan, they are more likely to support the results. Thus a well-run, inclusive process can improve outcomes.

Among the case studies documented in this volume, some have employed community participation methods successfully. In Washington DC, the Office of Planning sponsored more than 30 community workshops and focus group sessions in six neighborhood target areas, attended by more than 5,000 individuals. In Seoul, the strongest opponents to the restoration of Cheonggyecheon Stream were the local merchants who worried about traffic, congestion, and potential negative impacts on their businesses. Some 4,200 meetings were held for negotiations between the city officials and the local merchants. In Santiago, the city administration shared reports and assessments with the community through a participatory strategy. More than 16,000 residents and 1,200 community leaders and organizations took part in council meetings under the slogan: "Santiago, a Task of All." The outcome of this dialogue with the community was the clear demand from the residents to stop the exodus of inhabitants and to restore the quality of life in Santiago. Community participation was especially important in Johannesburg, because the city was recovering from segregation policies of the apartheid era. The planning process became a forum for aligning different interests and distant members of the community for a shared decision regarding the regeneration of the inner city.

Environment

Environmental endowments or liabilities are major determinants of how urban regeneration initiatives are financed, planned, and implemented. This is because many of the underused urban land parcels are located along water bodies and in former industrial corridors (brownfields), central urban areas, postwar areas, large high-rise public housing blocks, military sites, or railway corridors. As a consequence, past land uses and potential contamination need to be investigated and, when necessary, the project team needs to create an environmental cleanup plan that includes a financing scheme. There is a remarkable variation in the definition and severity of industrial contamination across countries. Industrialized countries with a history of industrialization and the largest number of contaminated sites tend to have the most well-defined policies and regulations for contaminated sites. However, many other countries—especially those in the developing world—lack the definitions and/or regulations related to site contamination. Many regeneration sites may have real or perceived contamination problems. If contamination is suspected, it is essential to conduct an environmental assessment very early in the process, during the scoping period, to get a first notion of the potential cleanup costs. This is extremely important because contamination cleanup might be so expensive that the project would not be financially viable.

In Washington DC, the regeneration program needed considerable public investment to clean up the river before they could trigger private investment. The cost of environmental remediation for the land, which had been used as an industrial site for 200 years, was covered by the federal government. Another case study with significant environmental benefits was the restoration of Cheonggyecheon Stream, which resulted in lowering the downtown temperatures. Because the project involved removing an air-blocking elevated highway, a wind corridor was established and air pollution decreased. The water ecosystem was also restored so that the number of wildlife fish species, birds, insects, and plants increased in the area. In Ahmedabad, the environmental underpinning of the regeneration was to reduce the risk of erosion and overflow to flood-prone neighborhoods that were the victims of unplanned development. The project also stopped the flow of untreated sewage to keep the river clean and pollution free from the informal settlements and nearby developments. In Singapore, a national campaign was launched in 1977 to clean up the Singapore River. The government recognized the negative impact of poor environmental conditions on the city-state's image at the same time it embraced the Singapore River's historical importance and potential for redevelopment. Most important, the government recognized the need to conserve and protect water resources in the city-state and to work toward water security.

A Note on the Tools and Case Studies

The tools presented in this book have yielded successful results in many cities around the world; but the authors would like to stress that no one tool is universally applicable to all cities and all regulatory environments. The success of any urban regeneration project is first and foremost dependent on the political leadership behind it. Beyond that, this book hopes to present a well-curated collection of tools, which we believe could be instrumental in incentivizing the private sector to take on a role in regenerating underused urban areas.

The case studies presented in this volume are not free of criticism and problems. The goal has been to single out successful policy and finance tools in each case study, while pointing out the issues and challenges the city faced during the process. The intention was to select a variety of cities from different regions and address different typologies of underused urban land. The cases address inner cities, brownfields, port areas, waterfronts, and historic neighborhoods. The degree of private participation varies among cases, but our study shows that each of the case study cities has leveraged private sector financing in some way and to some degree.

Last, while the book offers various project planning, financing, and implementation tools to be used in any city, no single tool is universally applicable to all cities and all situations. While we believe that with strong political leadership, any city can start an urban regeneration process, the successful use of many advanced finance and land-planning tools are dependent on a sound and well-enforced zoning regulation regime and property tax system. Without such arrangements in place, incentive-based tools and other fiscal and regulatory tools discussed are hard to use. Similarly, several tools mentioned in the financing section require creditworthiness and access to capital markets, which may not be the case for many cities. To this end, this book is also accompanied by an online decision tool, which presents the tools based on a short survey of specific issues the city faces and its regulatory and financial environment. The website can be accessed at http://urban-regeneration.worldbank.org.

How to Use This Book

This book is a practical tool for city managers and planning officials; it provides them with a wide variety of options for conceiving and implementing an urban regeneration project. The toolbox is not exhaustive, but it offers many possible models for cities to implement projects according to the unique circumstances (the financial situation, technical capacity, timeline, and priorities) of each city.

Organization of the Book

This book works as an introductory primer for a technical team looking to learn about regeneration from start to finish and the broad array of options available for implementing a regeneration project. But the guidebook has been developed with independent modules that are self-contained and self-explanatory. For example, if a city official is interested in learning about different ways to leverage land for urban regeneration, the guidebook is a good starting point.

The book is divided into two parts: Part I is titled "Guidebook" and Part II is titled "Case Studies." Part I, the guidebook, has three distinct sections that follow a process-plus-assets logic. The first section is the toolbox, which describes the process of an urban regeneration project, following a typical project cycle: scoping, planning, financing, and implementation. Each of the four phases includes specific tools for implementation, illustrated with relevant examples from the case studies. Some tools included in the book are the macrolevel and microlevel analysis (in scoping); different planning instruments, such as master plans, and a variety of institutional arrangements for regeneration projects (in planning); a variety of financial tools (tax-increment financing, business improvement districts) and regulatory tools (transferable development rights, density bonus) in phase 3; and a series of considerations regarding leadership and risk analysis (in phase 4, implementation). After reading the toolbox section, the reader should have a clear sense of the many different paths that can be followed for a regeneration project, the many tools available, the complexity of the task, and the main milestones in the process.

The second section is structured around the assets that cities can count on to implement an urban regeneration project. The assets directly affected by the urban regeneration projects are land, community, and the environment. However, land and environment can also be liabilities, because sometimes the cost of cleanup and decontamination of these assets surpasses their value. This section addresses various tools for managing, protecting, and leveraging these assets for a more successful regeneration project. After reviewing this section, the reader should understand how the three main assets will contribute (or hinder) project implementation.

The third section looks at the social impacts of urban regeneration projects, both positive and negative, and at tools that can be used to avoid unwanted impacts, such as gentrification or population displacement. This section also covers a variety of social components for regeneration projects with a broader social agenda. The list is not exhaustive, but after reviewing the section, the reader should be able to look at the different social components of a regeneration project and begin the process of determining which, if any, should be included in the project.

The guidebook portion of the book ends by briefly summarizing lessons learned in urban regeneration projects and extracts the main experiences from the case studies developed for the book. Part II of the book includes the eight case studies, each broken down in phases (scoping, planning, financing, and implementation) for further research and review. The cases include examples of urban regeneration projects in Buenos Aires, Santiago, Shanghai, Ahmedabad, Seoul, Washington, DC, Singapore, and Johannesburg. Examples of the different instruments used in these case studies are detailed (when applicable) throughout the book.

The tools presented in the book are also available through an online decision tool, which presents the relevant content in a dynamic way, after the user takes a short survey. Visit *http://urban-regeneration.worldbank.org*.

Abbreviations

ABI	area-based initiative
AFHCO	Affordable Housing Company
AGP	General Administration of Ports
AMC	Ahmedabad Municipal Corporation
APEC	Asia-Pacific Economic Cooperation
ASP	average selling price
AUDA	Ahmedabad Urban Development Authority
AUSA	Urban Highways SA
AWC	Anacostia Waterfront Corporation
AWI	Anacostia Waterfront Initiative
BACSA	Business against Crime South Africa
BBP	Better Buildings Program
BID	business improvement district
BPMC	Bombay Provincal Municipal Corporation
BPMCA	Bombay Provincal Municipal Corporation ACT
CABA	Autonomous City of Buenos Aires
CABE	Commission for Architects and the Built Environment
CAPMSA	Corporación Antiguo Puerto Madero Sociedad Anónima
CBD	central business district
CCHC	Chilean Chamber of Construction
CE	Common Era
CEPAC	certificates of additional construction potential bonds
CGP	Participation and Management Centers
CID	city improvement district
CJP	Central Johannesburg Partnership
CMF	Common Municipal Fund
CMO	Construction Management Office
COO	chief operations officer

CST	Common Services Tunnel
DCHA	District of Columbia Housing Authority
DCP	detailed control plan
DGP	Development Guide Plan
DIF	district improvement fund
DOT	Department of Transportation
DP	displaced person
EIA	environmental impact assessment
EPA	Environmental Protection Agency
EPC	Environmental Planning Collaborative
FAR	floor area ratio
FIFA	International Federation of Association Football
FSI	floor space index
GBA	Buenos Aires Greater Metropolitan Area
GDP	gross domestic product
GFA	gross floor area
GIS	geographic information systems
GRA	gross floor area
GSA	General Services Administration
GTPUDA	Gujarat Town Planning and Urban Development Act
ha	hectare
HDB	Housing and Development Board
HUD	Housing and Urban Development
HUDCO	Housing and Urban Development Corporation
IAS	Indian Administrative Service
ICO	Inner City Office
ICT	information and communications technologies
iGoli	Johannesburg in local language
JDA	Johannesburg Development Agency
JICBC	Johannesburg Inner City Business Coalition
JICDF	Johannesburg Inner City Development Forum
IHP	inclusionary housing program
INE	National Statistics Institute (Chile)
IRS	Internal Revenue Service
IZ	inclusionary zoning
km	kilometer, kilometers
LEED	Leadership in Energy and Environmental Design
LVC	land value capture
m	meter, meters
MHUD	Ministry of Housing and Urban Development
MINVU	Ministerio de Vivienda y Urbanismo
MND	Ministry of National Development
MOU	memorandum of understanding
NCPC	National Capital Planning Commission
NGO	nongovernmental organization
OECD	Organisation for Economic Co-operation and Development

OP	Office of Planning
PILOT	payment-in-lieu-of-taxes
PPP	public-private partnership
REHA	Housing Rehabilitation Program
RLF	revolving loan fund
SCA	Central Society of Architects
SDC	Santiago Development Corporation
SEFC	Southeast Federal Center
SMD	Santiago's Municipal District
SME	small and medium enterprise
SMR	Santiago metropolitan region
SMS	short message service
SOL	Shui On Land Limited
SOM	Skidmore, Owings and Merrill
SPE	special purpose entity
SPV	special purpose vehicle
sq m	square meters
SRFDCL	Sabarmati River Front Development Corporation
SRP	Santiago Repopulation Program
STA	state tax administration
STCM	Standing Conference of Towns and Municipalities
SUR	subsidy for urban renovation
TA	technical assistance
TDR	transferable development rights
TIF	tax increment financing
TPS	town planning scheme
TUHF	Trust for the Urban Housing Foundation
UBA	University of Buenos Aires
UDA	urban development area
UDZ	urban development zone
UF	unidades de foment
UNDP	United Nations Development Programme
URA	Urban Redevelopment Authority
URD	Urban Renewal Department
UTM	unidad tributaria mensual

Part I
Guidebook

Process

Chapter 1 of the guidebook explains the urban regeneration process through the phases of scoping, planning, financing, and implementation. Figure 1.1 provides an overview of these phases.

Phase 1: Scoping

Scoping is a process during which decision makers conduct a strategic assessment to identify and promote regeneration either for the city as a whole or for a specific land parcel, such as a port, downtown, or neighborhood area. It involves a process of long-term, transformational change as city leaders develop a "road map" to make difficult choices about the future of their city or for particular areas of the city. Through the scoping process, city leaders also develop and utilize analytical tools to confront issues facing the city that are vital to its future. The process helps city leaders make strategic decisions about the direction they want their city to pursue.

The scoping process involves the following key components:

- Generating a vision
- Analyzing the economic, social, and physical characteristics of the city or area
- Analyzing the regional and global position of the city or area
- Identifying the opportunities for change and interventions to promote regeneration
- Identifying the barriers to regeneration
- Analyzing the capacity for change in the public, private, civic, and community sectors
- Identifying key actions to initiate change

Figure 1.1   Defining the process of urban regeneration projects

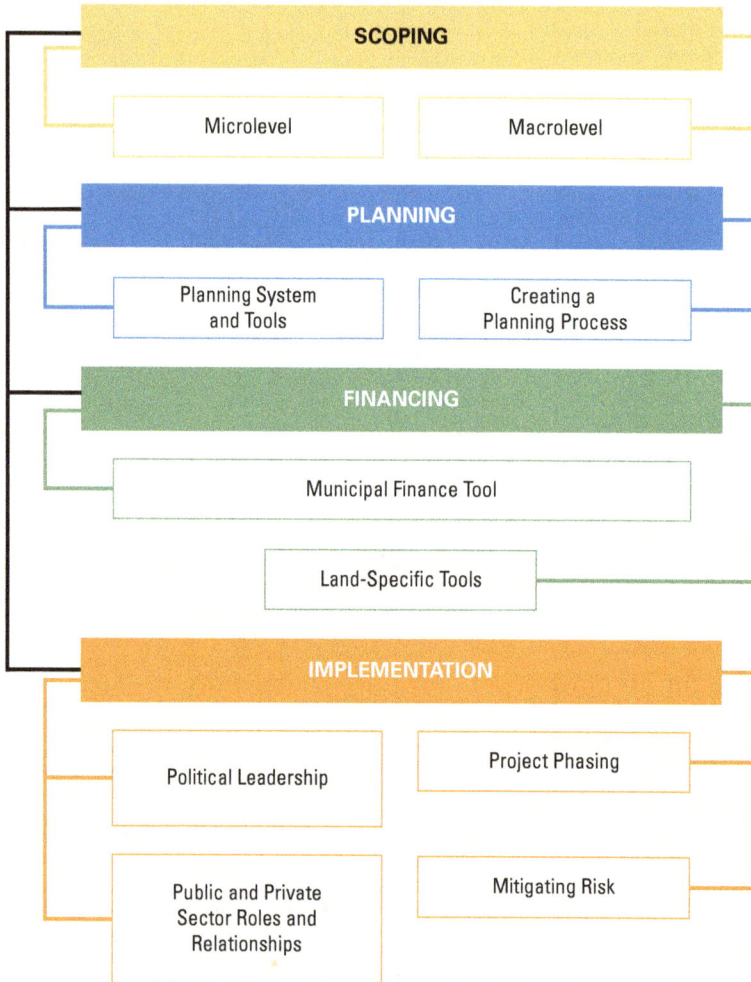

The scoping process can be applied to a range of situations and interventions, such as revamping the system for the provision of affordable housing, rethinking transportation expenditures, or completely redeveloping a neighborhood in urgent need of rehabilitation.

Ideally, the scoping process is an empirically grounded and inclusive process that integrates quantitative and qualitative data with a participatory planning process tailored to the unique dynamics of the city. The process provides a clear set of choices for policy and action. City planners can use the quantitative and qualitative data generated through the scoping analysis as a "tool" and as a foundation for a strategic planning process that engages public, private, civic, and community leadership in developing a vision for the city. Data can then be used to create an action plan to initiate major policy changes and options for regeneration. Crucially, the scoping process allows for broad community dialogue and the careful weighing of the economic, financial, political, and social consequences of different paths of action.

The scoping process is both forward and backward looking. It is forward looking because it involves analyzing what is required for the city and regeneration area to be successful in the future. It is backward looking because it involves an understanding of the city's history and its unique composition.

The Two Levels of Scoping

Scoping activities can be developed on the macrolevel and the microlevel. The macrolevel scoping exercise seeks to shed light on the key forces shaping the city from a diversity of perspectives—economic, physical, institutional, political, social, and historical—to develop a set of regeneration options for city leaders to consider. The macrolevel scoping provides the "big picture frame" that supplies the context for identifying options, making decisions, and executing a targeted regeneration program—whether it be an area for a policy or for a geographic intervention. In this regard, scoping is intended to be strategic and action oriented rather than comprehensive or exhaustive.

Conversely, the "microlevel" scoping takes into account the city's key challenges, vision, and goals. It translates them into a set of policy and project choices. The microlevel scoping analysis generates a more fine-tuned and focused context for developing specific regeneration interventions. The identification of these interventions is intended to assist the city leaders in understanding how and where to make strategic investments that will be transformational in achieving larger economic growth and equity goals. It also helps show why these interventions are important relative to other possible courses of action. If a regeneration area has already been identified, the analysis will provide important contextual information as to why this area is important to achieving the city's larger goals, as well as how it can fit into the larger citywide agenda for change. The microanalysis could also include more targeted analyses of the city's economic sectors that may need to be strengthened. So too could it provide an analysis of the conditions for specific areas of the city that are candidates for major regeneration programs, including public-private partnerships (PPPs) to rebuild distressed or obsolete areas of the city.

Why Scoping Is a Fundamental First Phase for Any Regeneration Project

Scoping helps city leaders develop a clear and powerful vision from the outset. The scoping process is intended to provide an analytical foundation and engagement process for a regeneration program that will arm city leaders with an empirical basis to generate choices. Large-scale urban interventions tend to be highly complex because they lay the foundation for systemic long-term change in city conditions. This entails substantial political risks and financial commitments that, by definition, engender controversy. Furthermore, to be effective in changing the city, these urban interventions require long-term commitments and changes in policy. Furthermore, changes may also be needed in institutional and delivery structures. So too, public and private commitments of funds must be secured.

Because powerful constituencies can exert significant political pressure to advance projects that are not in the best interests of the city, the scoping process is especially critical for mayors and other government leaders. Scoping serves as a counterbalance to these very real and powerful voices and pressures. The strategic analysis can be used to weigh competing political priorities and limited resources so that more informed strategic decisions can be made.

As city leaders embark on these regeneration initiatives, much is at stake. First, large amounts of investment funds must be raised for these high-profile, large-scale regeneration projects. Second, leaders must utilize their scarce political and reputational capital to see the project to fruition. Leaders must also be responsive to their constituencies and actively engage with and involve the private sector and civil society. Therefore, it is critical that the larger rationale is thoughtfully established as to why a specific project, policy, or geographic area has been selected and found worthy of support.

The scoping process should be seen as an opportunity to bring together a diverse group of stakeholders to generate a common vision for city regeneration initiatives. Members of the coalition in favor of the initiatives will also need to work together to build a constituency to counter the inevitable pressure to shift resources from more immediate needs. Thus, scoping is an essential part of the public-private development process. To take one case study, the city of Johannesburg went through an extensive visioning and scoping process over the course of decades. A summary of these efforts is outlined in box 1.1.

Scoping Out the Options

The analytical dimension of the scoping process can be divided into two interrelated components. These include the "macroanalysis" of the city (and region) at large and the "microanalysis." This section will outline the key factors that comprise both levels of analysis. It is intended as a guide, not an exhaustive inventory of all the factors that could be assessed. Moreover, the scoping factors need to be tailored to unique local characteristics and conditions. This section will therefore describe the types of strategic data and factors that should be considered in the scoping process.

Box 1.1   Decades of the "visioning" process in the regeneration of Johannesburg's inner city

Contrary to many other city visions in which the public sector takes the leading role, the "visioning" process for the regeneration of Johannesburg's inner city was started by the private sector. It was a long and collaborative process that played out over the course of 20 years. The Johannesburg process is particularly interesting for another important historical reason. It began immediately after the dismantling of the apartheid regime in South Africa. For the first time, it followed a participatory course in which various groups—including formerly segregated citizens—could partake. The process included many initiatives and plans. The major milestones are summarized below.

1991: Strategic Workshop Initiative

In 1991, the major business owners in the inner city organized the Strategic Workshop Initiative with 25 key participants. While this workshop was effective in identifying priority areas of concern in the inner city, its major achievement was the formation of a new private sector body to address these issues. This entity, called the Central Johannesburg Partnership, was committed to involving and working cooperatively with all stakeholders. This structure played a key role in the development of the inner city, and it was later transformed into a nonprofit organization.

1996: Johannesburg Inner City Development Forum

In 1996, inner city stakeholders joined together in a common platform called the Johannesburg Inner City Development Forum to develop a new vision for the inner city. Four separate groups of stakeholders submitted their visions for the city: the metropolitan government, the provincial government, the community, and the business sector. These four visions were then combined and consolidated into one vision during a workshop, which brought together all four groups. This vision was named "Johannesburg: The Golden Heartbeat of Africa" and called for the following:

- A dynamic city that works
- A livable, safe, well-managed, and welcoming city
- A people-centered, accessible city that celebrates cultural diversity
- A vibrant 24-hour city—a city for residents, workers, tourists, entrepreneurs, and learners
- A city focused on the twenty-first century
- A city that respects its heritage and capitalizes on its position in South Africa, Africa, and the world—a truly global city
- A city that is the trading hub of Africa, thriving through participation, partnerships, and the spirit of UBUNTU![a]

2002: iGoli 2030

This vision followed the previous two iGoli plans, iGoli 2002 and 2010, which had shorter horizons and were more inward focused.[b] The iGoli 2030 plan launched a crucial, comprehensive economic development strategy that was lacking in previous plans. It envisioned Johannesburg as a world-class city in 2030, "with service delivery efficiencies that meet world best practice." It also laid out a vision for a specialized service-oriented economy and labor force that would be strongly outwardly oriented such that the city economy world operate on a global scale. The vision aimed for strong economic growth that would raise the city's tax base and would have strong private sector investment returns as well as a population with disposable income that would drive up the living standard and the quality of life.

2007: City Summit and Charter

The mayor undertook this initiative. It was probably the most substantial effort to date in creating a real vision and direction for the regeneration of Johannesburg. The 2010 FIFA World Cup in South Africa

(Box continues on next page)

Box 1.1   Decades of the "visioning" process in the regeneration of Johannesburg's inner city *(continued)*

also served as an impetus and a goal to aim for, particularly with respect to achieving some stability in the inner city.

The goals of the 2007 summit were to "mobilize stakeholders towards a refocused agenda for regeneration, agree on the critical issues of concern and develop a programme of solutions." The summit was organized around six specific sectors and involved numerous working groups looking to define primary areas of concern. The consequent charter envisioned the inner city as a place

- That will be developed in a balanced way to accommodate all people and interests;
- That remains the vibrant business heart of Johannesburg as a whole but which balances future commercial, retail, and light manufacturing development with a large increase in residential density;
- That works as a key mixed-income, mixed-use residential node;
- That is the first entry into Johannesburg but also a place where people want to stay because it offers a high-quality urban environment with social and educational facilities, public open spaces, and entertainment opportunities;
- That serves as both the key transportation transit point for the entire region and a destination point in itself; and
- Where the prevailing urban management, safety, and security concerns are a thing of the past.

Source: City of Johannesburg, http://www.joburg.org.za/index.php?option=com_content&task=view&id=132 6&Itemid=58. Accessed December 2015.
a. See http://www.joburg.org.za/index2.php?option=com_content&task=view&id=4754&pop=1&page=0&Item id=266. Accessed December 2015.
b. iGoli is the name of Johannesburg in the local language.

Tool: Macrolevel Scoping

At this stage, the city leaders seek to understand the key forces shaping the city from a diversity of perspectives—economic, physical, institutional, political, social, and historical. City leaders can then develop a set of regeneration options for larger consideration.

Scoping provides the "big picture frame," that is, the context and basis for identifying, deciding on, and executing a targeted regeneration program. This can include areas for policy development or reform or for geographic intervention. At this stage of analysis, specific types of data are needed, including:

- *Economic data.* These data determine the position of the city relative to the region, country, and global environment. It can help decision makers answer such questions as, What are the strengths and weaknesses of the city? What are the drivers of the economy and its economic base?
- *Economic sectors.* Achieving a better understanding of the city's economic sectors will be critical to establishing the baseline from which

the focal points and direction for regeneration will be determined. This analysis explores the condition of the city's various sectors. It can help answer questions about which economic sectors are growing and should be supported, which have the greatest potential for growth and should be nurtured, and which are declining.

- *Growth dynamics*. This analysis will delve into the fundamentals of how the city is growing or contracting, as well as the underlying market and political forces shaping its growth or decline, as the case may be. In particular, the growth dynamic will need to be understood at multiple levels: the growth of the city within the state, region, and the city itself. For instance, what is the relationship between the growth of the city and the vitality of the regional, state, and national economy as a percentage of gross domestic product (GDP) and employment? Where are the market and population dynamics pushing growth or forcing contraction? To what extent is the growth dynamic a result of, or influenced by, market forces versus government intervention?

- *Socioeconomic and demographic analysis*. This analysis explores issues such as inequality, aging, special populations, and migration. Other areas of concern include areas of concentrated poverty, transitional neighborhoods, and the rate of change of areas that are vulnerable to decline or gentrification, as well as those that are stable.

- *Physical analysis*. This analysis takes note of the civic structure of the city, building forms, and urban patterns. For instance, it can help city planners answer questions such as, What are the basic form and block structures of the city? What parcels of land are available and in which areas? Based on the civic structure of the city, what areas have potential for growth and change? The analysis differentiates between areas for intensification, redevelopment, and new extensions.

- *Assets, networks, and social media mapping*. This analysis investigates the major defining assets of the city that should be increased and strengthened and includes the city's community organizations, institutions, business organizations, and social media that form the foundation for exchange and communication networks in the city.

- *Infrastructure*. This analysis examines the major infrastructure needed for the growth of the city and the regeneration site. It also considers related questions such as, what infrastructure is needed, or scheduled for delivery? What infrastructure is funded, underfunded, or completely unfunded? What financial and technical capacities exist to deliver major new infrastructure? For example, in the case of Santiago, a thorough analysis of the cost of providing infrastructure within the city versus the suburbs showed the need for infill development (see box 1.2 and table B1.2.1).

- *Housing*. This analysis takes note of the basic condition of the housing stock and performance of the housing market in serving a diverse

Box 1.2   The case of Santiago, Chile: Analysis of sprawl and the cost of providing infrastructure

Many of the elements of macroanalysis have been addressed in the case studies presented here. For instance, the "Plan for the Renovation of Santiago," initiated in 1990, was based on a series of studies. One of the major studies was "The Imperatives of the Urban Renovation of Santiago: The Costs of the Expansion," which was developed in 1987 by the Santiago Development Corporation. It compared the costs of developing housing solutions in consolidated areas of the city versus areas of urban expansion outside of or on the periphery of the city. The results led to a key discovery, that building in peripheral areas was almost 18 times more expensive than building in consolidated areas of the city (see table B1.2.1).

Table B1.2.1   Costs of incorporating a new residential unit in the city center versus the periphery in Santiago
US$

Item	City center	City periphery
Infrastructure	178	740
Water pipes	45	236
Sewage	12	98
Rainwater drainage	0	12
Electric power networks	112	161
Access and circulation roads	9	234
Urban equipment	185	5,747
Health	0	237
Education	0	4,100
Police surveillance	133	1,361
Sports and recreation	72	49
Total	**363**	**6,487**

Source: Verdugo 2003.

In 1990, the mayor of Santiago commissioned the Catholic University to undertake a complete economic and social assessment of the district in order to design a development plan. The report found that the intensive industrial activity in the district had caused a decrease in the quality of life and increased the expulsion of residents. The study's recommendation was to reactivate the housing market within the municipal district, regulate industrial activity, rehabilitate tenement halls, and invest in public spaces.

The mayor used these recommendations to start a community discussion about urban renewal. Subsequently, the Municipality of Santiago developed a strategic vision with the goal of recovering the residential community in the Santiago Municipal District. The Santiago Repopulation Program's objective was to attract 100,000 new residents to the district over the course of 15 years. The strategic analysis concluded that in order to stop the exodus of residents and attract new ones, the municipality needed to simultaneously work on three fronts by (a) attracting private sector investment in housing; (b) improving the deteriorated physical environment through public investments; and (c) changing people's perceptions of the Santiago Municipal District through public campaigns.

Source: Based on the case study of Santiago in chapter 5.

range of the population's housing needs. It also records the quality of housing stock, demand for new housing, and rehabilitation of older or substandard units.

- *Fiscal analysis.* This analysis incorporates the basic fiscal outlook for the city, including the status of the city budget and municipal finances. In addition, it examines the debt burden of the city, as well as current and future obligations that put pressure on the city's financial resources. It measures the capacity of the city to engage in creative financing and examines the tools available for off-budget financing for urban regeneration. It asks several important questions: Have public sector interventions been sound and generated a return on investment, or have they been largely politically determined and distributed based on political versus market or growth considerations?

- *Political analysis.* This analysis includes an assessment of the various interested constituencies and their key priorities, demands, and goals with regard to city regeneration. It also includes an assessment of the relationship of the city to the state and national governments in terms of potential support for large-scale interventions through legislation, financing, capital projects, and so on.

- *Market assessment and state of the private sector.* This analysis helps policy makers understand and interpret the overall market position of the city. It examines the impediments to determining and managing urban growth. Key findings about the state of the private sector and its strength, various industries, and concentration of various industries provide valuable input. In cases such as Johannesburg with a very active private sector, the analysis took note of this engagement in terms of the larger agenda of city development. In particular, it examined the emerging industries and the need to engage a new generation of private sector leaders.

- *Institutions.* Determining which major institutions are key to supporting a city's growth and development is crucial to the regeneration initiative. Such analysis helps focus on key institutional questions, such as, How strong and engaged are universities, hospitals, and research facilities? Can existing institutions take on the planning and implementation of the project or should a standalone entity be established? How can these institutions be better leveraged to support the city's goals and growth objectives? Is there a strong network of community-based organizations that can participate in regeneration or will this need to be created?

- *Historical analysis.* An appreciation of the city's past is critical in envisioning its future. The unique composition of the city—the basic elements of its form and function—would be analyzed to provide insight into building on the positive qualities of the city. At the same time, an analysis will shed light on problematic areas and reasons for their existence. The historical analysis would range from understanding the built and natural forms of the city, to the changing role of the city in the global economy, to the cultural aspects of the city that give it its unique character.

- *Best practices.* Given the potential interventions suggested by the analysis, best practices would be sought and analyzed for their potential relevance and lessons learned. The goal is not necessarily to import these practices as a whole. Rather, the goal would be to learn how the lessons can be best applied to the potential regeneration schemes.

Tool: Microlevel Scoping

At the microscoping level, city leaders try to understand key challenges and goals and translate them into a set of policy and project choices. The analysis generates a more fine-tuned and focused context for developing specific opportunities for city regeneration interventions. To draw contrast between microlevel and macrolevel analyses, macrolevel focuses on the whole city's direction of growth while microlevel analysis focuses on the site or the area targeted for regeneration.

The identification of specific interventions is intended to assist the city's leaders in understanding how and where to make strategic investments that will lead to transformational economic growth and greater equity for its population. Officials can also gain a greater understanding about these interventions and their comparative relevance to other possible courses of action. In addition, the microanalysis could include more targeted analyses of the economic sectors of the city that need to be strengthened. Alternatively, it could include an analysis of the conditions of specific areas of the city that will need to be targeted in any major regeneration program. It can also help city leaders in establishing the critical PPPs that will be needed to rebuild distressed or obsolete areas of the city.

The microanalysis involved in the scoping process is intended to narrow the scale of focus, either by geography or by policy topic. It aims to present stakeholders with clear options and the next logical steps in developing a regeneration program for supporting PPPs. The microanalysis also goes into greater depth for a discrete number of regeneration options. The example in box 1.3 illustrates both stages of the scoping exercise for a given city.

The microscoping analysis could include options for a number of different sites or policies, or it could focus on one option in greater depth. In either scenario, the microanalysis would include the following elements:

- *Setting a vision.* What is the vision for the project identified within the context of the larger vision for the city? The notion of a vision is often dismissed as too ethereal to be useful. However, it is actually core to articulating the direction of the project. For it to be effective, it should be clear and aspirational, and it should provide a benchmark against which to measure progress.

Box 1.3   **An example of macroanalysis and microanalysis**

To understand these types of analyses better, it is useful to imagine a city for which the macroanalysis has been concluded. Imagine the city's economy is declining due to the loss of its manufacturing base and competition from cities that have a lower cost basis. However, due to the city's extensive trans-port network, location along a potentially scenic waterfront, and the existence of strong local educa-tional institutions, the economy has the requisite ingredients to transition to a new, more globally competitive service-based economy.

The key is to unlock a sufficiently large tract of land to provide space for the new service economy to grow. Based on the macroassessment, the microanalysis of the scoping exercise would begin. Specifically, it would identify options for key sites that could provide the foundation for a new economic position for the city. Sites would be assessed in terms of the advantages/disadvantages of each to meet the macrogoals of a service-based economy. A number of factors would need to be considered, such as:

- The ability to assemble the sites into one cohesive area
- The cost of infrastructure
- The social impacts, such as displacement of population
- The readiness and capability of educational institutions to train the workforce and teach the skills required to succeed in the new economy
- The housing and amenities that workers will require
- The capacity of the public and private sectors to deliver the project
- The time horizon by which the project can be delivered—as well as consideration of the potential barriers and risks to successful implementation
- A stakeholder analysis of the different interests that should be engaged in the process

This could be summarized in a matrix of options that would weigh the evaluated sites against the larger macroanalysis and goals that were established in the first phase of the scoping exercise.

- *Geography.* Selecting the right target regeneration area is critical. In this context, the scale and extent of the area targeted for regen-eration should be carefully considered and defined. If it is too large, it could raise costs and expectations beyond what can be realistically delivered. It may also be too broad and generic to motivate capital deployment by the public and especially the private sector. If too small, it may not be ambitious enough to spur the transformational change required to realize the new vision for the city.
- *Growth dynamic of the targeted area.* The analysis would exam-ine the current growth dynamic of the area relative to the city. It would also seek to answer questions such as, What are the core economic drivers of the area? Are the core drivers commerce, inno-vation economy, services, or tourism? What can be supported or will need to be changed in order to make the target area serve as a greater contributor to the economy of the city, region, and nation?

- *Asset mapping.* Assets can include environmental or cultural endowments, a skilled labor force nearby, universities or research institutions, and so on. The main anchors and strengths of the area should be identified and assessed for their capacity and ability to participate in the regeneration program.
- *Market.* A basic assessment of the market dynamics of the target area should include the potential or real growth of key sectors, land values, and real estate values.
- *Physical survey.* A basic survey of the physical form and conditions of the built environment would need to be completed. This would include an analysis of the obsolescence of buildings, as well as the condition of streets and supporting infrastructure.
- *Obstacles to growth.* What are the current obstacles to growth that would need to be addressed? These might be infrastructure weaknesses and gaps, fragmentation of land ownership, lack of an accurate cadastre, insufficient market demand, community opposition, and potential relocation of the population. What is clear is that there must exist obstacles to regeneration of the area. These obstacles must have weakened and discouraged investment. The microlevel scoping exercise must identify these obstacles.
- *Potential range of project costs and funding sources.* Is the potential cost of the project something leaders are willing to consider even if there are no readily identifiable sources of public and/or private funding available? Is the lack of financing a "nonstarter" or are the parties willing to proceed and accept funding uncertainty? Are there new and unexplored options for creative financing? How have other cities dealt with financing issues?
- *Community mapping and local dynamics.* This addresses questions such as, What are the key community issues and dynamics that would need to be addressed? What are the important social networks that exist and need to be understood? What are the strengths of local community organizations? How well organized is the community, and is it fully representative of the area's population? Are there groups that do not traditionally participate that would need to be engaged through alternative means?
- *Socioeconomic considerations.* Again, a series of questions would need to be considered. For example, How would the proposed regeneration project benefit the current population and lower-income populations through targeting jobs, housing, and services? What are the base assumptions and conditions that would need to be in place to proceed with regeneration? These might include replacement of housing, relocation of displaced households, building of community facilities, and equity participation of small businesses.

The scoping process is further illustrated in figure 1.2.

Figure 1.2 **The scoping process**

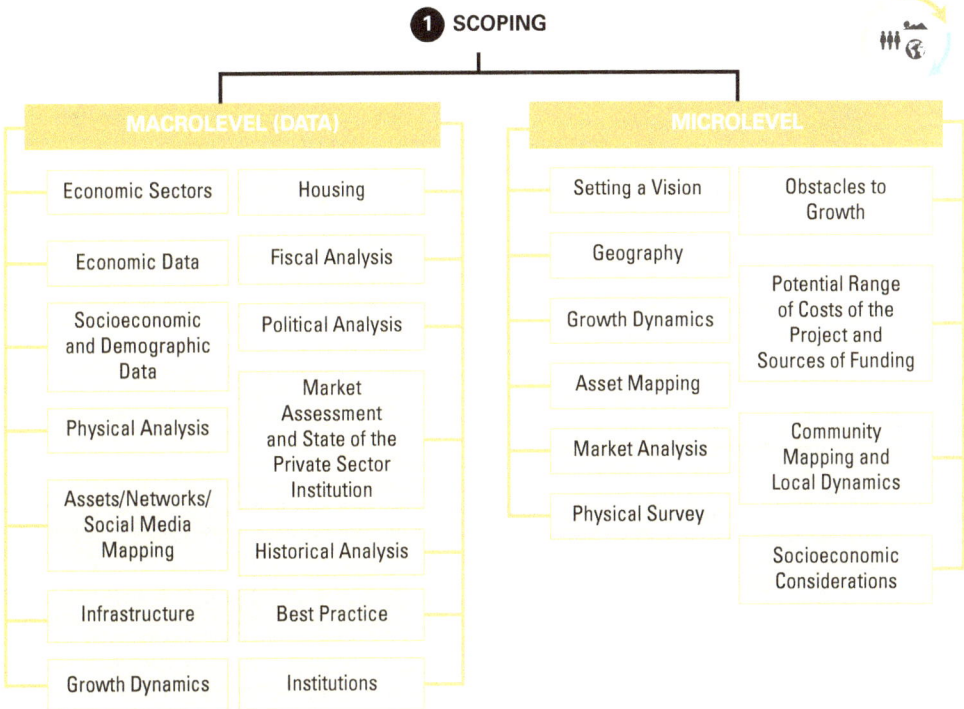

1 SCOPING

MACROLEVEL (DATA)		MICROLEVEL	
Economic Sectors	Housing	Setting a Vision	Obstacles to Growth
Economic Data	Fiscal Analysis	Geography	Potential Range of Costs of the Project and Sources of Funding
Socioeconomic and Demographic Data	Political Analysis	Growth Dynamics	
Physical Analysis	Market Assessment and State of the Private Sector Institution	Asset Mapping	Community Mapping and Local Dynamics
Assets/Networks/ Social Media Mapping		Market Analysis	
	Historical Analysis	Physical Survey	
Infrastructure	Best Practice		Socioeconomic Considerations
Growth Dynamics	Institutions		

Phase 2: Planning

The planning section of the guidebook has three distinctive parts. First, it starts by laying the foundation of various planning systems and frameworks that could be employed. It includes a thorough description of the master planning process. It concludes with a piece about the importance of defining the design standards early in the planning process so that the regeneration project can result in a better urban environment.

The second section describes developing planning processes for partnering with the private sector. These include parallel implementation methods through joint ventures or creating autonomous corporations to take on the regeneration project under the commercial code. The importance of defining the implementation processes from early on is also emphasized.

Third, a way to bridge the planning and implementation phases by preparing for changes to come is presented. Figure 1.3 provides an illustration of this aspect.

Planning Systems and Tools
Tool: Defining the Planning Framework

Each city government will adopt a different approach to planning their urban regeneration projects. In general, governments must first examine the

Figure 1.3   The planning process for urban regeneration projects

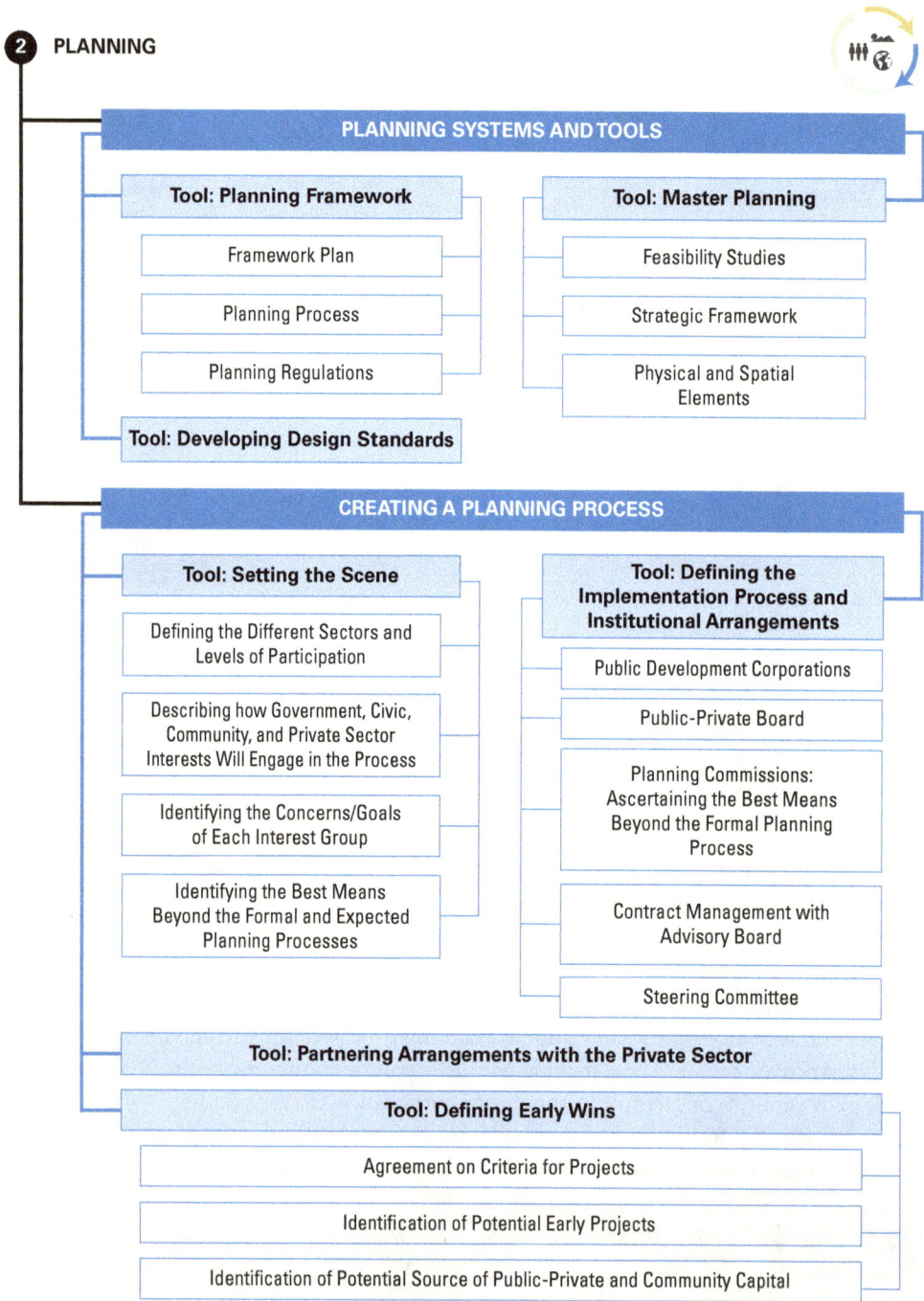

2   PLANNING

PLANNING SYSTEMS AND TOOLS

Tool: Planning Framework

Framework Plan

Planning Process

Planning Regulations

Tool: Developing Design Standards

Tool: Master Planning

Feasibility Studies

Strategic Framework

Physical and Spatial Elements

CREATING A PLANNING PROCESS

Tool: Setting the Scene

Defining the Different Sectors and Levels of Participation

Describing how Government, Civic, Community, and Private Sector Interests Will Engage in the Process

Identifying the Concerns/Goals of Each Interest Group

Identifying the Best Means Beyond the Formal and Expected Planning Processes

Tool: Defining the Implementation Process and Institutional Arrangements

Public Development Corporations

Public-Private Board

Planning Commissions: Ascertaining the Best Means Beyond the Formal Planning Process

Contract Management with Advisory Board

Steering Committee

Tool: Partnering Arrangements with the Private Sector

Tool: Defining Early Wins

Agreement on Criteria for Projects

Identification of Potential Early Projects

Identification of Potential Source of Public-Private and Community Capital planning frameworks that either exist or need to be created to guide and govern the regeneration initiative. There are three basic elements of the planning framework that need to be in place to guide and ensure successful urban regeneration:

- *Framework plan.* Often called a "strategic plan" or a "vision plan," this document articulates a clear vision for the regeneration project based on the findings of the scoping phase. It has a long-term horizon, explicates the context and rationale for why the regeneration project is important to the city and region, and provides comprehensive goals for the area. It also addresses the interrelationship between the economic, physical, social, and institutional dimensions of the regeneration program. It is necessarily general in nature as it is intended more to articulate the big picture ideas, goals, and principles that will guide the project. This type of plan is to be differentiated from a traditional "comprehensive plan" that attempts to address in depth and in detail all of the elements required to govern the long-range growth of the city. In essence, the planning framework is conceptual. While providing a powerful long-term vision, it does not attempt to define each and every policy and detail necessary to achieve that vision. The data included in these plans are usually only of sufficient detail to support the vision, promote consensus, and motivate action.
- *Planning process.* The planning process should be inclusive, clear and objective. Establishing a clear process and mechanisms by which the public, private, and community sectors will interact in the development and implementation of the regeneration project is critical to building confidence. Deciding on a process is important to setting the "terms of engagement" and the ways in which these sectors will formally and informally interact, such as through formal planning commissions (if any exist), advisory groups, local boards, and so on. The level of authority of the participation mechanisms must be carefully defined so there are not excessive layers of decision-making or entities with conflicting mandates and powers. Clear structures are necessary for project approvals. Care must be taken to ensure that land use processes—which are often subjected to political influence—are structured to promote professionalism and independent judgment whereby decisions are made on the basis of sound planning principles.
- *Planning regulations.* The legal regime establishes the rules of the game, specifically the regulations that will frame the planning process. The vision and goals of the planning framework are translated into land use and building regulations that will govern what is built in the regeneration area. Social goals for regeneration projects are also incorporated into the planning process and regulations and can include a mandatory minimum level of affordable housing, environmental and design requirements, the treatment of historic structures, and so on.[1] The planning regulations, which traditionally encompass zoning,

site planning and subdivision, building regulations, environmental regulations, and health and safety codes are fundamental to establishing the predictability and certainty that are a prerequisite to attracting private investment. The more discretionary and unclear the regulations are, the more uncertainty will be created for investors and developers. This in turn will deter investment and the willingness of the private sector to take risks. Likewise for the community, the lack of clear regulations will increase the level of concern and anxiety over how projects are approved and what will ultimately be built in their community. Often in regeneration areas where investment is being actively promoted, special regulations or "zones" are created. These involve the creation of streamlined approval processes and the adoption of new regulations specific to the goals of the regeneration area. These measures can be a powerful tool to overcome the higher barriers to entry often associated with particularly rundown areas slated for regeneration.

Local governments differ in the way they arrive at their planning framework. Some may not conduct the kind of granular-level planning that is typically needed for urban regeneration. Some may outsource the planning activities to other entities, including the private sector. However the planning process and regulations agreed to will be essential to establishing the long-term vision and context for the regeneration project. Indeed, the planning framework will be vital to sustaining the regeneration vision through the inevitable changes and unforeseen challenges of market and political cycles. On a cautionary note, governments should *not* create overly strict planning regimes that are inflexible and deter investment by trying to dictate and rigidly regulate outcomes.

The aim of an effective planning framework is to balance a clear vision with planning principles and a dynamic process, that allows for engagement and negotiation among the public, private and community sectors. To be successful, the planning framework must promulgate an inspiring vision matched with a predictable and clear regulatory process that instills in the private sector the confidence to invest and take risks. Likewise, it should also instill the necessary confidence in communities and governments that public goals will be achieved and will not be subordinated purely to the dictates of the market. Regardless of the planning framework of the city, in most cases a master plan will be necessary to guide urban regeneration.

Tool: Master Planning

A master plan is a dynamic long-term planning document that provides a conceptual layout to guide future growth and development. Master planning is about making the connection between buildings, social settings, and their surrounding environments. A master plan includes analysis, recommendations, and proposals for a site's population, economy, housing, transportation, community facilities, and land use. It is based on public input, surveys, planning initiatives, existing development, physical characteristics, and social and economic conditions.

Master planning can assume some or all of these roles:

- Develop a phasing and implementation schedule and identify priorities for action.
- Act as a framework for regeneration and attract private sector investment.
- Conceptualize and shape the three-dimensional urban environment.
- Define public, semiprivate, and private spaces and public amenities.
- Determine the mix of uses and their physical relationship.
- Engage the local community and act as a consensus builder.

As city regeneration initiatives are generally long-term propositions, it is important to consider the master plan as a dynamic document that can be altered based on changing project conditions over time. For example, in the case of the Santiago repopulation program detailed in this volume, the municipal master plan was modified 29 times during the implementation phase. These changes sought to either allow for more density and height in some areas, or to restrict and lower the height of the buildings—including the definition of areas under patrimonial protection (Arraigada, Moreno, and Rovirosa 2007). This flexibility has been beneficial to the real estate sector, enabling increases in the number of floors and housing units per building.

Master plans can have an important role in determining the shape of the urban environment. If not well conceived, they can lead to problems in the future. For instance, one of the criticisms of Santiago's master plan was that it was *too* flexible in setting standards for beautification and building volume design. Hence, the quality of these buildings in terms of architectural design and construction materials was considered one of the weaknesses of the repopulation program (see photograph 1.1). The residents also criticized the unpleasant contrast of the high tower buildings with the existing historic urban fabric, as well as the fact that the new towers are not well integrated within the traditional neighborhoods. All of these issues could have been addressed well in advance as part of the master plan.

The Process of Developing a Master Plan
Depending on the role of the master plan, it could have various sections and be developed in several ways. However, some common denominators for a good master plan are explained in this section (see figure 1.4).

Feasibility Study: The feasibility study is an objective review of available options for development. It includes findings, analysis, and conclusions from the visioning and scoping exercises for a given site or inner-city area. It indicates whether the chosen site is suitable for the intended function, taking into account the financial, social, and environmental aspects of each proposal. Many comprehensive master plans start with a feasibility study in order to understand the site's geographic, environmental, and historic context. This process builds on the information collected and analysis developed during the scoping phase. Any background reports that are deemed necessary (that is, hydrology, environment, cultural

Photograph 1.1   Lack of attention to urban design, building heights, and massing brought on criticism of the Santiago repopulation program

© Ana M. Valenzuela. Used with permission. Permission required for re-use.

heritage, transport, and so on) should also be commissioned at this stage to inform the master planning process (Blackmore 1990). For an example of a successful feasibility study see box 1.4.

Strategic Framework: The strategic framework accompanies the master plan and sets the scene in establishing baseline information related to the physical, social, and economic context of the site and surroundings. This background information should outline the site location and dimensions, topography, and existing uses. It should highlight the current zoning regulations and relevant/applicable planning policies, as well as any particularly important opportunities and constraints relevant to the site (CABE 2008; Growth Areas Authority 2009). In summary, the strategic framework includes:

- Physical aspects of the regeneration project
- Vision and scope prepared during the scoping phase
- Various elements or functions that could act as catalysts for change
- Business case for development
- Strategic delivery issues and options
- Guidelines about how the strategic framework will inform and impact design (CABE 2008)

Figure 1.4   **Process and elements of a master plan**

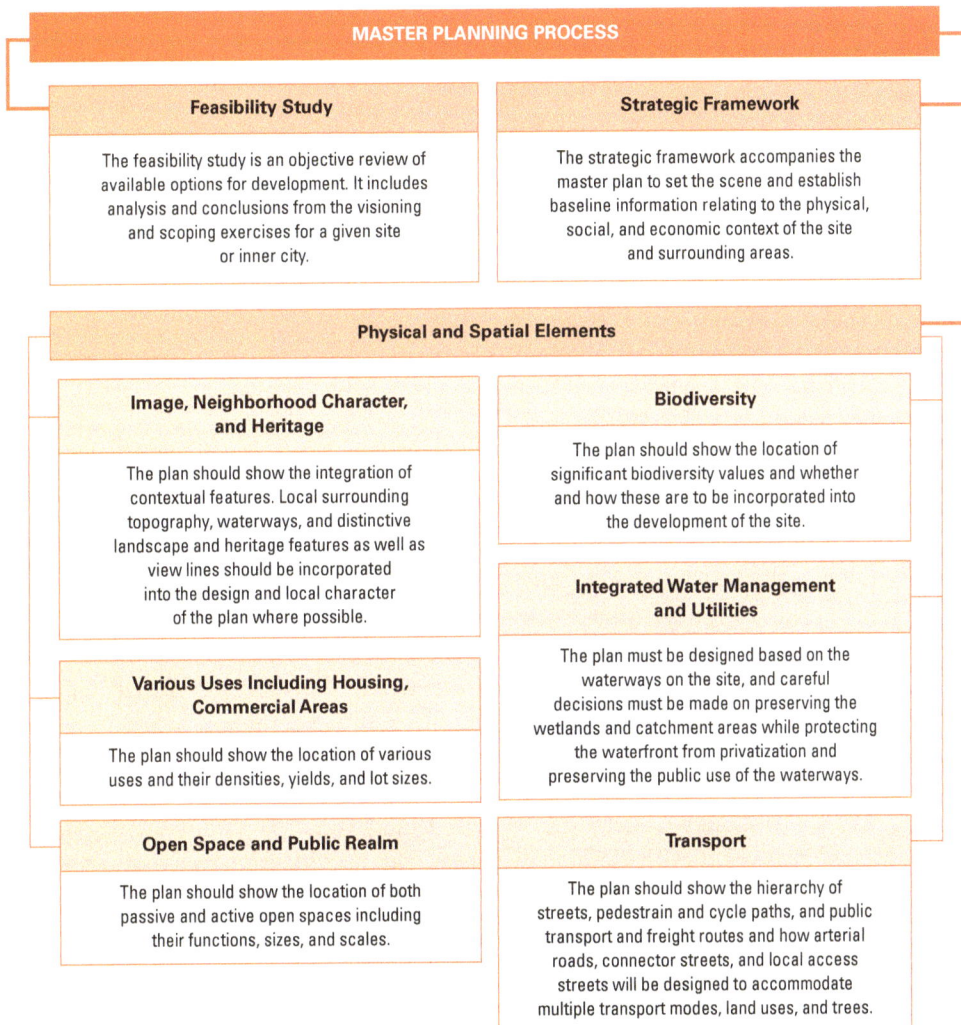

MASTER PLANNING PROCESS

Feasibility Study	Strategic Framework
The feasibility study is an objective review of available options for development. It includes analysis and conclusions from the visioning and scoping exercises for a given site or inner city.	The strategic framework accompanies the master plan to set the scene and establish baseline information relating to the physical, social, and economic context of the site and surrounding areas.

Physical and Spatial Elements	

Image, Neighborhood Character, and Heritage	Biodiversity
The plan should show the integration of contextual features. Local surrounding topography, waterways, and distinctive landscape and heritage features as well as view lines should be incorporated into the design and local character of the plan where possible.	The plan should show the location of significant biodiversity values and whether and how these are to be incorporated into the development of the site.

Various Uses Including Housing, Commercial Areas	Integrated Water Management and Utilities
The plan should show the location of various uses and their densities, yields, and lot sizes.	The plan must be designed based on the waterways on the site, and careful decisions must be made on preserving the wetlands and catchment areas while protecting the waterfront from privatization and preserving the public use of the waterways.

Open Space and Public Realm	Transport
The plan should show the location of both passive and active open spaces including their functions, sizes, and scales.	The plan should show the hierarchy of streets, pedestrain and cycle paths, and public transport and freight routes and how arterial roads, connector streets, and local access streets will be designed to accommodate multiple transport modes, land uses, and trees.

The strategic framework is critical for developing a sound spatial master plan in the next stage. It includes all of the studies and analysis that are needed before entering the design phase, especially urban design analysis, which provides options for various urban form scenarios.

In the strategic planning phase, the team also determines which core competencies are required to develop the master plan. These could include urban design and planning, landscape design, transportation planning, economic development, cost planning/surveying, cultural heritage, specific industry sector analysis, and urban sociology and crime statistics (CABE 2008).

Box 1.4   Feasibility study for Sabarmati Riverfront development project

In the case of the Sabarmati Riverfront Development Corporation in India, the board commissioned a feasibility study be conducted by a local nonprofit environmental planning group. This study was completed within a matter of months. The study assessed the feasibility of the new proposal for constraining the width of the existing river. The proposal, as outlined in the 1997 study, specifically called for constraining the width of the existing river to 275 meters. The river's unconstrained width varied from 340 meters to 600 meters throughout. The study found out that the land reclaimed through this river training would be about 162 hectares (which subsequently increased to 200 hectares) spread along 9 kilometers (km) (which subsequently expanded to 12 km) along the west and east banks of the river. According to the feasibility study, the sale of 20 percent of this land would finance the entire cost of the project, whereas the rest of the reclaimed land could be used for public benefits, such as new streets, parks, and other city amenities. A key feature of this proposal was a continuous promenade along the east and west banks of the river. The study also proposed implementation mechanisms and financing strategies.

Physical and Spatial Elements of a Master Plan: Once the feasibility study and strategic framework have been undertaken, the physical master planning process continues. Based on the first two phases, master plans establish and develop options for land use, which will later be translated into three-dimensional models to identify the resulting development needs, as well as costs and values. In summary, the spatial master plan should include elements such as massing, height, densities, orientation, grids and blocks (without architectural or style details) transportation systems, and open spaces (CABE 2008). The master plan should also cover some or all of the following elements to ensure an overall holistic and successful design and use outcome:

- *Image, neighborhood character, and heritage.* The plan should show the integration of contextual features. Local surrounding topography, water, and distinctive landscape and heritage features should be incorporated into the design of the plan where possible. These elements have an immense impact on the character of the urban area (see box 1.5). For instance, the master plan for the two blocks of Xintiandi within the Taipingqiao neighborhood of Shanghai preserved the original *shikumen* buildings—despite opposition from the government and the perceived lack of a business case. The project was successful in generating much economic value through preservation efforts, resulting in a rise in land prices of adjacent areas. These areas were later developed into high-density office and residential buildings. The important point in this case is that high-density allowance in adjacent areas was used as a cross-subsidization tool in preserving these two blocks. Indeed, the developer admits that without high returns

Box 1.5   **What determines the character of an urban area?**

Urban designers and architects have used the term "character" or "sense of place" since the early days of urban design. But what defines the character of a place and what impacts it? According to Kevin Lynch, neighborhood character is determined by its history, cultural identity, landscape, and architecture. Character also means that the urban area is remarkable and coherent in a way that serves as a basis for pride, affection, and a sense of community. The character of a place is influenced by many factors, including:

- The built environment, including building bulk and height
- The relationship of built form to topography, geography, and the natural features around which the settlement has grown
- The mix of uses
- The quality and pattern of open spaces and streets
- The hierarchy and relationship between the public and private realms
- The streetscape, landscape, building materials, and views
- The historic elements such as culturally significant buildings and historic fabric

Source: Lynch, Banerjee, and Southworth 1990.

from the adjacent developments, the preservation project would have been financially unfeasible. This is further detailed in chapter 6, which describes the preservation of the two blocks of Xintiandi in Shanghai.

- *Various uses including housing and commercial areas.* The plan should show the location of various types of uses, densities, yields, and lot sizes. When developing housing, a variety of housing types, sizes, and tenures must be considered. In this context, the plan should also ensure appropriate housing density and diversity. The master plan should also be flexible enough to allow for change over time in housing diversity as communities mature (Growth Areas Authority 2009). Similarly, commercial areas should be planned within other areas to promote mixed-use neighborhoods, which are vibrant at all hours of the day. Entertainment and retail land uses should also be integrated in the master plan. Finally, the master plan should contain a strategy for the layout of streets that will best fit the character of the site.
- *Open space and the public realm.* Jurisdictions around the world will require different open space prescriptions. Plans should show the location of open spaces including function, size, and scale. However, both qualitative and quantitative measures, as well as the ratio of active and passive uses, should be taken into account in the design and layout. The broader connection to the larger open space network as a whole should also be considered. For example, the New York City Planning Department works on the basis that "the open space

ratio is the amount of open space required in a residential zoning lot in noncontextual districts, expressed as a percentage of the total floor area on the zoning lot." For example, if a building with 20,000 square feet of floor space has an open space requirement of 20, this would mean that 4,000 square feet of open space would be required in the zoning lot (0.20 × 20,000 square feet) (City of New York 2014b). Another example is the case of Shanghai, where in 2003 the municipal government introduced the policy of "double increase and double decrease," which was applied to the central city. The "double increase" required an increase in green space and open space in new developments, whereas the "double decrease" required a decrease in the building floor area and the floor area ratio (FAR) of these developments to improve the living quality of the central city. This resulted in contract renegotiations between the private and public sectors and ensured a more balanced urban environment in the center of the city.

- *Biodiversity.* The plan should show the location of significant biodiversity values, as well as whether and how these are to be incorporated into the development of the site. Biodiversity and environmental factors should also be planned for at the beginning of regeneration projects in order to protect, enhance, manage, and strike a balance between development uses and flora and fauna sustainability. Doing so will help to avoid any policy issues at a later stage. For example, a site may be home to an endangered species, which may require the redesign of the site or relocation of the species. Therefore, it is particularly important to survey the land and assess biodiversity early in the process (Growth Areas Authority 2009).

- *Integrated water management and utilities.* The plan's design should be based on the site waterways, making careful decisions to preserve the wetlands and catchment areas. At the same time, there is a need to protect the waterfront from being fully privatized and to preserve the public use of the waterways. Consideration needs to be given to existing and new waterways and catchments, as well as to utility infrastructure in the design of the site. This will help to ensure the supply of water, electricity, gas, sewage, and telecommunications infrastructure to all site lots. The capacity of the waterways will also need to be taken into account. Allowances should be made for expansion where required to prevent flooding. Further allowances should also be made for the development of new retarding basins or preservation of existing wetlands—while ensuring efficiencies have been achieved by incorporating a water-sensitive urban design (Growth Areas Authority 2009). An example occurred in Ahmedabad, India, where a series of retaining walls were used along the waterfront redevelopment to prevent flooding and erosion. Underground sewer lines, which had been affecting local informal development along the river's edge were also integrated (see chapter 7). In this regard, the size of utility easements also needs to be considered to ensure minimal impact on development.

- *Transport.* The plan should show the hierarchy of streets, pedestrian and cycle paths, and public transport and freight routes. It should also outline how arterial roads, connector streets, and local access streets will be designed to cater to multiple transport modes, land uses, and trees. Priority should be given to public transport, and walking and cycling should be encouraged through the layout of paths (CABE 2008; Growth Areas Authority 2009). For example, in Washington, DC, the government was successful in integrating existing transport and land use planning into the Anacostia Master Plan. It then built a complete system, including a new waterfront metro station as a centerpiece. This in turn enabled the reopening of a number of streets and reestablishment of a grid network. It also allowed for a walking trail along the length of the waterfront (see chapter 9).

Tool: Developing Design Standards

The thoughtful design of high-quality buildings and public spaces is vital not only to the improvement of the standard of living and work environment of regeneration areas but also to the creation of economic value for the regeneration site. Indeed, the success of regeneration projects depends on the design quality of the built environment that is incorporated into the planning phase. For example, it is known that well-designed, open spaces generate significant value for residential properties. So too, the current economic trend favoring creative industries is demanding lively mixed-use districts to attract the creative class.[2] Good urban design can also add social and environmental value, turning the urban space into a place to "mix and mingle" while merging the city with its environment (for a list of potential value-added by good urban design projects, see table 1.1). Throughout the life of the regeneration project, the process of how design will be negotiated must be addressed and provided for in the attendant contract. However, it must also be recognized that this is a shared responsibility for both the public and private sectors.

How to Define the Private Sector Role in Development of Design Standards

There are many options along the continuum of public and private sector involvement in the design process. These range from the public sector having a more passive regulatory role through the planning and permitting process, to having its own design staff who review and negotiate the design of each project in the regeneration area. Although a master plan is an essential foundation for the regeneration project, it is not sufficient for monitoring various elements of urban design. There must be an ongoing process whereby the public and private sectors are actively involved in the design process. The private sector will often resist this and will be justifiably concerned that the public sector might create regulatory uncertainty and additional time and money constraints. However, this is exactly the balance that must be struck in developing a process that leads to the design of superior places and buildings.

Table 1.1   Benefits of a sound urban design strategy

Good design adds economic value by	Good design adds social and environmental value by
• Producing high returns on investments	• Creating well-connected, inclusive, and accessible new places
• Making new places more attractive at lower cost than projects proposed by local competition	• Delivering mixed-use environments with a broad range of facilities and amenities available to all
• Responding to occupier demand	• Delivering development that is sensitive to the local context
• Reducing management, maintenance, energy, and security costs	• Enhancing the sense of safety and security within and beyond the development
• Contributing to a more contented and productive workforce	• Returning inaccessible or run-down areas and amenities to beneficial public use
• Supporting the life-giving, mixed-use elements in the development	• Boosting civic pride and enhancing civic image
• Creating an urban regeneration and place-making market dividend	• Creating more energy-efficient and less polluting development
• Differentiating places and raising their prestige	• Conserving urban heritage
• Opening investment opportunities, raising confidence in development opportunities, and attracting grant funding	
• Providing opportunities for wealth generation by inhabitants	
• Reducing costs to the public of rectifying urban design mistakes	

Source: CABE 2008.

There are many ways to address private sector concerns regarding uncertainty and delays, including (a) developing and adopting design guidelines that provide direction, but still allow for creativity and flexibility; (b) setting timeframes for reviews—if the deadlines are not met, then projects would be "deemed approved"; and (c) establishing design panels of outside experts agreed to by both public and private sector parties.

Master plans usually define an urban design vision and attendant controls. However, they should not necessarily define specific architectural styles, which should be left to architects during the implementation and delivery of the site development. Design standards should establish the aim of design quality and create a framework within which good quality architecture and design can flourish (CABE 2008).

Design guidelines can either be incorporated into the land use regulations or adopted as stand-alone provisions. Such guidelines should translate the aspirations of the regeneration program into ideas for the evolution of the three-dimensional physical form of the area. The guidelines might include establishing more explicit building specifications (for instance, height, setbacks, ground floor dimensions, and so on) for private and public parcels so that an overall design for the area is achieved. Alternatively, they might include recommendations for the government about the design of the public realm and important "place-making" interventions. These can include the design of open public spaces, the dimensions and materials for sidewalks and streets, and street lighting, as well as other key public infrastructure investments that comprise the physical environment.

Creating a Planning Process and Defining the Roles of the Private and Public Sectors

The planning phase should assess the capacities of the public, private, and civic sectors to implement the plans. This process could also be used as an organizing construct for the public and private sectors to prepare for a city's regeneration, including identifying leadership and capital sources, and building broad-based and diverse coalitions.

The process should also include a preliminary identification of the leadership for the project. It is important to carefully map and define the leadership network that will be critical to the success of the regeneration project. Based on this leadership mapping, a process would be customized to motivate the participation and support of political, business, civic, and community leadership.

For example, in Seoul, the Republic of Korea, the project headquarters office for the restoration of Cheonggyecheon was launched within the city hall to ensure efficient communication and project implementation. Focusing strictly on the actual works at the site, the headquarters office conducted a weekly meeting hosted by the mayor to maximize efficiency and collaboration. The organization was modified continually to adapt to the evolving work stages.

In addition, the Cheonggyecheon Research Group was established under the Seoul Development Institute to support the restoration project. Its mandate was to conduct research projects, collect basic data, and devise a blueprint for the Cheonggyecheon restoration. The group contributed to the project by researching issues regarding transportation, land use, urban planning, environmental and cultural issues. It also organized a variety of seminars and meetings with experts and conducted a variety of activities to promote the restoration through academic events, public relations campaigns, and media outlets.

Finally, the Cheonggyecheon Citizens' Committee was established to serve as an official channel to solicit the opinions and concerns of the citizenry with regard to the project. Experts from the Cheonggyecheon Revival Research Group joined the committee, along with other experts and citizen representatives of various backgrounds. The committee's primary role was to set the directions for the restoration project. It was given rights to audit and monitor, as well as to simply advise on the project. The committee also had legally binding rights according to special enacting ordinances. In addition to deliberation and assessment, the committee conducted a series of hearings and briefings to garner public opinion, build public consensus, and encourage citizens to participate in the project (see chapter 8). Figure 1.5 illustrates these arrangements.

Figure 1.5   **Triangular implementation system for the Cheonggyecheon Restoration Project**

Citizens' Committee

- Develop restoration principles
- Collect public opinions
- Promote public relations

Project Office

- Plan project
- Execute project plans
- Establish cooperation with interest groups

Cheonggyecheon Restoraton Project

Research Center

- Establish policy
- Conduct survey
- Study feasibility

Tool: Setting the Scene

As noted, given the scale of change typically envisioned in urban regeneration initiatives, strong relationships between the public and private sectors will need to be forged early in the process so that there is a "buy-in" or ownership of the project. It is critical to think ahead early in the planning process and not wait until the end to identify and engage potential private, civic, and public partners. These groups will act as the main implementers, change agents, and advocates for regeneration. Indeed, the key to successful PPPs in urban regeneration is to "engage early and often." The planning process should be based on the following analyses:

- Defining the different sectors and levels of participation that will be required to ensure an inclusive process, especially with respect to potential private sector partners that might participate in future PPPs.
- Describing how government, civic, community, and private sector interests and leadership will engage in the process through a variety of forums, such as steering committees, open forums, private negotiations, and so on; defining both the formal and informal structures for participation.
- Identifying the concerns/goals of each interest group so that, to the fullest extent possible, all the issues, risks, and opportunities related to

each group and their "negotiating positions" are understood and factored into the design process.

- Ascertaining the best means beyond the formal planning process to ensure inclusiveness and engagement of the broadest diversity of sectors and populations (including those populations that may not traditionally participate) through communications vehicles, such as social media, direct surveys, smaller forums, street-level conversations, and design "charrettes."[3]

Tool: Defining the Implementation Process and Institutional Arrangements

Determining the optimum institutional structures will be key to the success of the project. Institutional arrangements may range from formal to informal, with varying degrees of authority, accountability, and responsibility for coordination, handover, and delivery. Depending on the project requirements and whether it is public or private sector-led, there are a number of options for the types of vehicles that might be created to guide, monitor, and maintain the regeneration project to ensure coordination and results. These entities might have a range of powers depending on the scale and complexity of what is required to catalyze and sustain the regeneration project.

Given the complicated nature of development, a useful and very broad delineation of public and private roles will be needed to distinguish between land development and development of the buildings. In this instance, it is the public sector that potentially assumes more of a role in the delivery of some services, such as parks and transportation improvements. For its part, the private sector delivers the buildings and public amenities that will attract people to the regenerated areas. Financing, governance, and operational responsibilities can then flow from this.

Although this is necessarily a general construct, it can be useful as a guide for land or vertical development. For example, it is often the case that the public sector will build and manage affordable housing. A key and commonly used method for the public sector to maintain control, ensure competition, and protect its interests is to release parcels for development only when necessary. Parcels are offered through a competitive process to ensure that the highest quality and best financial offer is achieved. The extent of public land ownership is a key determinant of the type of public-private institutional arrangement that will be possible. Further, it gives the public sector broad latitude in using land as an incentive and source of leverage in achieving a city's regeneration.

One example of institutional arrangements in this type of development is public development corporations established by the government to directly lead and manage regeneration projects, such as the Battery Park City Authority in New York City. It led the 40-year-old redevelopment of 80 acres of prime waterfront land in Lower Manhattan. Likewise, in the United Kingdom, the London Legacy Development Corporation was created to lead the development of the 600-acre Olympic Park following the 2012 London Olympics.

Other models involve public sector organizations, such as planning commissions or advisory entities that rely more on regulations and the enforcement of contracts than direct involvement in the delivery of development projects. Some examples are summarized below; however, more arrangements could be possible depending on each country's specific regulatory environment.

- *Public development corporations*. This is the most formal type of organization created to manage project development and handover. It can have a full range of powers, depending on project requirements and political will, including eminent domain,[4] land use, financing, development and construction expertise, marketing, master planning, design review, and facilitation. More information regarding these corporations is detailed in box 1.6.
- *Public-private board*. The term "board" is used here to include various public-private arrangements—from joint legal entities to contractual relations, such as concession leases.[5] Depending on whether and how public land is contributed to the regeneration venture, the board can be more or less formal. If the public sector is an equity partner, it would fully participate in all project decisions and would be responsible for project oversight, handover, and performance. However, even if public land is not contributed as equity, joint venture arrangements can be organized to allow for significant joint-decision making, project oversight, and assurance. Some potential examples of such boards or corporations are covered in box 1.7.
- *Planning commissions*. These entrust delivery to the private sector. Public sector involvement would be limited to regulatory oversight through a planning body that would ensure the master plan is being implemented pursuant to its approval.
- *Contract management with advisory board*. A project is managed largely through contract performance depending on the differing roles of the public and private sectors. There might be an advisory board to monitor progress and resolve conflicts. However, it is largely a contract-driven relationship that defines handover until and unless there are nonperformance issues.
- *Steering committee*. The least formal arrangement, the steering committee structure is a forum to bring together the diverse interests engaged in the regeneration project to monitor implementation, resolve problems, and provide advice on project-related issues. It is best used to either supplement other vehicles with a more formal structure, or when the project is private-sector-led and delivery is largely within its purview. The committee structure would be useful in galvanizing outside resources and maintaining and promoting the profile of the project. It can also work to resolve any major tensions that might surface.

Providing for ongoing operations and maintenance is critical to project sustainability and must be planned for in advance. This "aftercare" of

Box 1.6   **Urban development corporations**

In general, there are three main institutional models for handling urban landholdings by the government:

- *In house:* Implemented by governmental departments or public agencies themselves;
- *Corporate model:* Implemented by a government–established company, often called a "special purpose corporation," which is tasked with managing some specific asset management work;
- *Public-private partnerships (PPPs):* Implemented through engaging the private sector within this partnership framework (Kaganova 2011).

Countries embarking on city regeneration initiatives have established different practices within the corporate model. These corporations often act as private entities and are empowered under the commercial code. Importantly, they also have a degree of separation from the government. Their responsibilities include land acquisition, infrastructure provision, and releasing vacant land for market sale. They are also tasked with building housing for low-income families, managing properties used by governments, and so on (Kaganova 2011).

City regeneration carried out by a special purpose corporation often involves the use of special regulatory powers. These powers enhance the project's ability to create development value through project-specific density arrangements, a situation referred to as density financing (Sagalyn 2007). A review of these corporations has shown that in addition to land development, almost all of them are involved in economic development; in recent years, low-income housing has also been included in some of their mandates. Furthermore, to avoid conflict of interest, such corporations separate real estate and land development roles from the regulatory and planning roles of the government (Kaganova 2011).

In the United Kingdom, for example, urban development corporations were established as land development entities to bring derelict land back to the market. They were involved in planning, reclaiming, and reassembling land using eminent domain. They were also in charge of developing infrastructure and social services as necessary. In addition, they filled the gap between development costs and the value of developed land (Greenstein and Sungu-Eryilmaz 2004). Whereas some of these corporations are structured to deliver a regeneration plan as part of the national development plan, others are the product of local bottom-up efforts. As such, they are not subject to national coordination or planned programs of national resourcing (Clark, Huxley, and Mountford 2010). Cities in Europe are increasingly using publicly funded development corporations through which they grant operational concessions for major urban and transport projects.

projects during and after construction includes provisions for security, the upkeep and programming of the public realm, and providing for the needs of the local community. A well-established vehicle is a business improvement district (BID), which is covered in the financing section of this chapter.

The key point is that it is never too early to plan for the best range of organizational entities that the regeneration project might require. Indeed, there can be multiple entities, each with its own focus that can be created or supported to ensure long-term success. It is therefore not a simple matter of whether regeneration is public or private. Rather, it will usually be a complex mix that requires careful consideration of a range of options for how the public, private, community, and civic sectors can best interact, as well as the institutional arrangements that are best suited to the aspirations of the leadership and demands of the project.

One example involving thorough institutional arrangements in urban regeneration projects concerns the Santiago Repopulation Program (see chapter 5), delegated to the Santiago Development Corporation (SDC). The SDC was conceived as the executive arm for the implementation of the Santiago Regeneration Plan. Its flexible institutional structure facilitated the negotiations and partnerships developed with the private sector. Municipal corporations in Chile are ruled by the private law. Thus, they are authorized to enter into contract with public or private institutions, receive contributions, and borrow from private banks or financial entities, and so on. This institutional feature allowed SDC's executive directors to play the role of public entrepreneurs, working on behalf of the community—and using the financial instruments available to the private sector. The PPP agreements between the SDC and other actors were regulated in the same manner as contracts between two private actors. However, beyond its managerial attributes, the SDC worked closely with the municipality, as the mayor was the president of the corporation. For more details, see table 1.2 for the organizational chart of the corporation.

Box 1.7   Types of public-private cooperation

A variety of questions should be posed in determining the type of public-private cooperation for urban regeneration. For example, is the public sector interested in playing a more active and involved role in the process? To what extent do city leaders want the private sector to deliver and the public sector to act as guardian of the public interest and beneficiary of regeneration? The answer to these questions of course depends on how much is required of the public sector for the regeneration program, especially if it entails direct funding.

The organizational structure of public-private cooperation is an important element in the success of such partnerships. There are many variations of such cooperation, from creating wholly or partially owned public companies, to fifty-fifty partnerships, to more passive ones in which the public sector participates through contractual land and profit-sharing arrangements. In considering different cooperation models, it is critical to be clear about the roles, authority, level of responsibility, decision making, and risk the public sector is seeking and willing to assume relative to the private sector. A lack of clarity on any of these issues will create barriers to effective project implementation. These roles must be defined from the very conception of the project. The three examples below are illustrations of the possibilities for passive, active, and hybrid models.

Passive Model. Assume for illustrative purposes that the public sector is the majority land owner and wishes to retain long-term land ownership. However, the public sector is not interested in having any direct involvement in implementing or delivering the project. Rather, it prefers that the private sector assume full responsibility for all aspects of the project, including infrastructure, site preparation, and vertical construction. A cooperation arrangement to achieve these objectives would be structured whereby the public sector enters into a long-term ground lease (from between 99–199 years) with a private developer. The arrangement would establish some of the following parameters: project objectives (specifying the type of development the public desires, the quantum of the development, and social targets, such as levels of affordability); phasing requirements; schedule for land payments, ground leases, and the formula for

(Box continues on next page)

Box 1.7 **Types of public-private cooperation** *(continued)*

profit sharing; remedies for nonperformance and default; and key decisions requiring the approval of both parties and/or those that are held as reserve matters for the public sector.

Once the cooperation is established, the public sector role is largely limited to monitoring performance, participating in major decisions, and ensuring that its social and investment goals are being achieved. The governance structure might consist of a board of directors with equal representation of both parties that meets on a regular basis. The private sector is clearly empowered to deliver the project pursuant to the agreement.

Active Model. In this model, the public sector is the primary entity responsible for actual delivery of the project. It assumes all execution risk and responsibility and acts as a developer would in managing the land and vertical development process. This is rarely used in its pure form due to the lack of expertise in the public sector and the high level of execution risk this entails. However, there are instances, often in the case of the development of large-scale public housing, that the public sector has assumed such a prominent role. The cooperation model here might have the private sector assuming some of the risk and delivery responsibilities, such as developing some of the parcels or infrastructure financing. In this model, the venture is controlled largely by the public sector, with the private sector playing a more narrowly defined role.

Hybrid Model. This model is more typical of city regeneration projects. As an example, assume the majority of the land is owned by the public sector and requires significant infrastructure development, especially in the early stages. The public sector is concerned with the quality of the urban environment and wants to maintain a long-term active role in its development. However, it does not want to deliver the vertical construction or assume such a high risk. In this model, the cooperation would be structured in such a way that the public sector acts as the land developer responsible for the funding and delivery of area-wide infrastructure (not parcel specific). For its part, the private sector would be responsible for building and financing the vertical construction.

The venture would clearly delineate the respective roles, investment requirements, and profit-sharing and decision-making arrangements. In this way, all parties would understand and agree on the clear division of financing and execution responsibilities. Given the interdependence between the public and private sectors in delivering the regeneration project, issues such as the phasing of development, timing and obligations for capital investment and capital calls, and the level of decision making on key aspects of project conception and execution will need to be well articulated and fully documented.

These examples highlight the complexity of public-private arrangements. In deciding on the appropriate arrangement, the public sector should generally be very clear about the extent of its own capacity and expertise.

Tool: Partnering Arrangements with the Private Sector

Whether an urban regeneration initiative is led by the public or private sector, there are various types of structures that can be adopted for creating a mutually beneficial partnership between them. The most appropriate approach will depend on the specific institutional, market, and political context. Whereas some municipalities may be open to sharing risks with private parties through joint-venture forms of PPPs, other cities may be legally constrained from or have limited human resource capacity to prepare, procure, and manage high-quality agreements with the private sector. Many countries have regulatory limitations on

Table 1.2 Organization of the Santiago Development Corporation

Presidency	President (mayor) Vice president (municipal secretary of planning)
Executive director	Director Vice director Manager of administration and finance
Directors (5 elected members)	Representative of universities President of the Architects Association Representative of the Chamber of Commerce of Santiago Representative of NGOs Representative of firms of Santiago
Assembly of associates (35 members with urban interests)	Guilds (Architects Association, Engineers Association, Chamber of Commerce of Santiago, Developers Association, SMEs Association) Representatives of banks Representatives of universities Representative of Ministry of Housing and Urban Development Housing Cooperatives Representatives of real estate developers Representatives of neighborhood development committees Representative of the Neighbors Association

Source: Authors' elaboration based on Parra and Dooner (2001); Contrucci (2013).
Note: NGOs = nongovernmental organizations; SMEs = small and medium enterprises.

municipal public-private agreements and may require that a city use a concessional approach for any agreement with a potential developer or investor.

Regardless of structure, attracting private capital and high-quality development partners to invest in a proposed urban regeneration plan will require that certain core conditions are met. Predictability of up-front and ongoing project costs and anticipated future revenues are investor prerequisites in determining a project's feasibility. Risk identification and mitigation are critical for any investor—and can be as important as a project's expected rates of return. Thus, for a city to attract private investors and developers to buy into a municipal vision for urban regeneration, certain core conditions should ideally be in place, including:

- A legal system, in which property and contract rights in particular are recognized and enforced;
- A stable regulatory structure, in which laws and administrative procedures (for example, obtaining building permits) are transparent and reasonably predictable with respect to cost and timeframe implications;
- A stable national and local fiscal framework, in which the financial responsibilities of various levels of government are known—and in which municipal financial responsibilities are also reasonably predictable;

- Political stability in the form of an established transition process upon changes in municipal administration or political parties in power;
- Market strength, in which market conditions are sufficiently robust to absorb and grow from the anticipated new development.

Given private sector expectations, many cities desirous of attracting private capital have invested time in anticipating and meeting investor demands—all in an attempt to improve local conditions for investment readiness. Typically, until a city has established a proven track record of successful partnership with the private sector, investors may cautiously assume that greater risk is involved and, with it, commensurately higher returns.

An example of government investment in infrastructure and parallel development of planning guidelines can be observed in the revitalization of the Singapore River. The planning authority built a 15-meter-wide continuous riverfront promenade connecting the three zones of the river. Three new pedestrian bridges were also planned and subsequently constructed, linking the three zones together. Urban design and planning guidelines were stipulated by the Urban Redevelopment Authority. Their goal was to enhance the different themes envisioned for each zone by guiding and controlling land use and physical development to be built by the private sector (see chapter 10).

Tool: Defining Early Wins

Early in the process, the scoping exercise would identify potential projects that might be initiated for "early wins" to build confidence in the project. These could be small actions that demonstrate governmental commitment. It is important to also inspire confidence that the visioning and planning process is not just another paper exercise—that it represents a serious commitment to change. Some of these "early wins" might occur early in the planning process to signal the intention and commitment of the government to deliver and dispel mistrust and skepticism. Such "early wins" analysis might include:

- Agreement on criteria for projects, including factors such as generating employment, reducing poverty, improving housing conditions, enhancing the tax base, building community capacity, and so on
- Identification of potential early projects that can produce positive results
- Identification of potential sources of public, private, and community capital that might be accessed to support the planning process and early project stages

While every urban regeneration should include a set of policies and actions that aims at the simultaneous revitalization of social, economic, environmental, and physical conditions of the distressed urban areas, leading the process with "flagship projects" is usually a good strategy to demonstrate the public sector's commitment. Flagship projects lead the process with physical improvements and usually act as a catalyst for the regeneration process, paving the way for private sector investments.

Physical regeneration includes physical enhancement of buildings, lands and sites, public spaces, and provision of infrastructure.

Leading the regeneration process with a physical approach has several benefits, including providing a flagship project that signals to the market the government's intention to invest and change a certain area, reducing the project's cost to the private sector by cleaning up contaminated sites, reassembling fragmented parcels of land or providing certain infrastructure, and acting as a catalyst for private sector investments. In the regeneration of Cheonggyecheon's stream, the government paid for a large up-front investment to remove the elevated highway and to clear up the stream. In return, the private sector compensated for the expenses with a major investment in the urban land along the stream, contributing to the regeneration of the downtown area (see chapter 8).

As an example, box 1.8 outlines the planning process of the Washington, DC Anacostia Waterfront Initiative.

Box 1.8   The Anacostia Waterfront Initiative: Planning process

The Anacostia River in Washington, DC, has long represented a dividing line in the District of Columbia, symbolized by the stark segregation of the city based on race and class. The communities "East of the River" are largely African-American and house some of the poorest neighborhoods in the United States—although this represents only a partial and biased view of these vibrant communities. Nonetheless, in the cognitive map of Washington, DC, the Anacostia River has been seen in stark contrast to the Potomac River along the city's most famous monuments and the affluent Georgetown area.

Against this backdrop, when Anthony A. Williams was elected mayor in 1999, the district was in receivership,[a] and was administered by a federally appointed control board. The powers to run the city were transferred from the control board back to the mayor upon his election. Mayor Williams understood the power and importance of transforming the Anacostia River from a symbol of division in the city to a unifying force that had the potential to bring regeneration to its neighborhoods and environmental restoration to its river and open spaces. He vowed to put the Anacostia River back on the map so that it was no longer ignored or willfully neglected.

In the year 2000, the mayor initiated the Anacostia Waterfront Initiative and enlisted the support of the federal government through the signing of a memorandum of understanding that codified a unique district-federal partnership. It was expected to result in the historic transfer of hundreds of acres of federal land to the district, over US$2 billion of investment, the relocation of a major federal agency to the waterfront with over 7,000 employees, and numerous other community investments.

This remarkable transformation is now seen as a natural evolution of the city's growth. However, at the outset, it was rightfully met with much skepticism. Past efforts to revitalize the Anacostia waterfront were not successful and had faltered for many political, market, and funding reasons. The mayor had to demonstrate that this was not just another planning exercise—even as his administration initiated one of the largest and most ambitious master planning efforts in the history of the city, covering over 2,800 acres, 7 miles of river, and numerous communities on its borders. The mayor understood that one could not simply create plans and hope that the planning process alone would convince people of the seriousness of intent to affect change. Rather, plans had to be coupled

(Box continues on next page)

Box 1.8   **The Anacostia Waterfront Initiative: Planning process** *(continued)*

with projects to provide evidence and give tangible proof that the envisioned urban transformation could become a reality.

The direction the mayor gave to his cabinet was to use any opportunity to fund projects along the waterfront. His idea was to show that the planning process was a reality and that the administration, like the community, was impatient for change.

The first expression of this philosophy was a rapid "charrette process" (see chapter 2) that was organized in the Near Southeast neighborhood of the waterfront where there was a high concentration of public housing. The weekend-long planning process resulted in the consensus that the existing public housing needed to be replaced with a vibrant mixed-income housing community connected to the waterfront with public spaces, quality housing, and—crucially—that every unit of public housing would be replaced on a one-to-one basis. The rapid planning process paved the way for the mayor to apply for a federal Hope VI grant to fund this ambitious project.[b] The grant was awarded based on the federal-district partnership that had been established through the memorandum of understanding, as well as the credibility of the planning process that gained consensus in the Near Southeast community.

The grant award occurred while the larger Anacostia Waterfront Initiative and master plan was underway. It was hugely powerful in demonstrating the sincerity of the mayor and the credibility of the planning process. In addition, it gave hope that genuine change was imminent after years of neglect and decline.

The lesson from the Anacostia initiative was that large-scale transformation must be thoughtfully planned and opportunistically executed. It cannot be a neat sequential process. Rather, it is a dynamic process of change with a constant interplay and integration of plans and projects.

a. The city had outspent its budgets and the city finances were in jeopardy. Therefore, the U.S. Congress appointed a five-member body in 1995 to oversee the district's finances. This body was called the District of Columbia Financial Control Board, and the board had the power to override decisions by Washington's mayor and city council.
b. Hope VI is a policy of the U.S Department of Housing and Urban Development and aims to redevelop the most problematic public housing projects in the country into mixed-income livable communities.

Phase 3: Financing

The types of financing tools used in the regeneration of urban land depend on whether the process is led by the public or the private sector. Transformative urban regeneration projects are typically large, multiuse, and complex. They often require site assembly and construction of (costly) public infrastructure. Therefore, it is quite unusual for a project to be financed solely by the public or the private sector.

The scale of transformative urban regeneration initiatives is typically so large that most cities—with few exceptions[6]—lack the resources to finance the total development cost outright. Typically, therefore, cities deploy a combination of internal resources (including revenues and municipal land), external funding sources (including intergovernmental transfers, grants and, in the case of sovereign cities, borrowing), policy and regulatory tools, and strategic partnerships with the private sector, among other resources.

Financing plans can be highly complex, especially given the multiyear nature of these projects and the difficulty of accurately estimating major infrastructure upgrades and other capital costs years in advance of actual implementation. Depending on the relative size of an urban regeneration initiative, a city may anticipate funding the project entirely through its capital budgeting process. Alternatively, it may seek to do so through a combination of capital budget line-items and off-balance sheet sources, such as a structured partnership with a private sector developer.

How a city finances an urban regeneration initiative depends on the national legal and institutional context within which it operates. Specifically, this involves the amount of control a city has over its fiscal management, especially its ability to raise and allocate revenues. In countries in which cities are highly dependent on transfers from the federal government, such as Malaysia or Mexico, cities must depend on other governmental entities to provide funding and advance large-scale public investments in urban regeneration. In contrast, in countries such as Brazil or China,[7] where national governments have devolved substantial powers to local governments, cities have the authority to impose certain taxes and make capital investments to advance urban regeneration initiatives. In the United States, where municipal governments are responsible for providing a broad range of public services—including police and fire protection, waste collection, public libraries, and often schools—cities typically finance these kinds of services with locally raised revenues that they control. These can include revenues from property taxes, income taxes, business taxes, sales taxes, tourist-related taxes, and other user fees.

A city's approach to financing urban regeneration is tied to its legal and fiscal powers and its ability to utilize additional tools (beyond intergovernmental transfers) to finance urban regeneration. These can include the power (and creditworthiness) to access municipal bond markets and the capacity to utilize innovative financing techniques, such as tax increment financing (TIF), to support specific economic development strategies. Other powers that a city can deploy to capture and direct resources toward urban regeneration include municipal control over local land use, zoning, and urban planning. The design and implementation of these regulatory powers can allow cities to leverage additional funding and resources from the private sector.

The first part of this section will explain the tools available through the municipal finance system of local governments, including capital investment planning and intergovernmental transfers. The second part will explore the primary tools that municipalities have used to finance complex, large-scale, multiphase urban development projects. There are relative advantages and disadvantages to each tool, of course, and those relative benefits and risks vary according to market dynamics as well as institutional factors. Regulatory or financial tools differ in nature as they target regeneration of specific parcels of public or private land. The financial tools directly or indirectly provide financing for urban regeneration, whereas the regulatory tools create an attractive environment for private sector investment. A summary of these tools is featured in figure 1.6.

Figure 1.6   **Financial tools for urban regeneration projects**

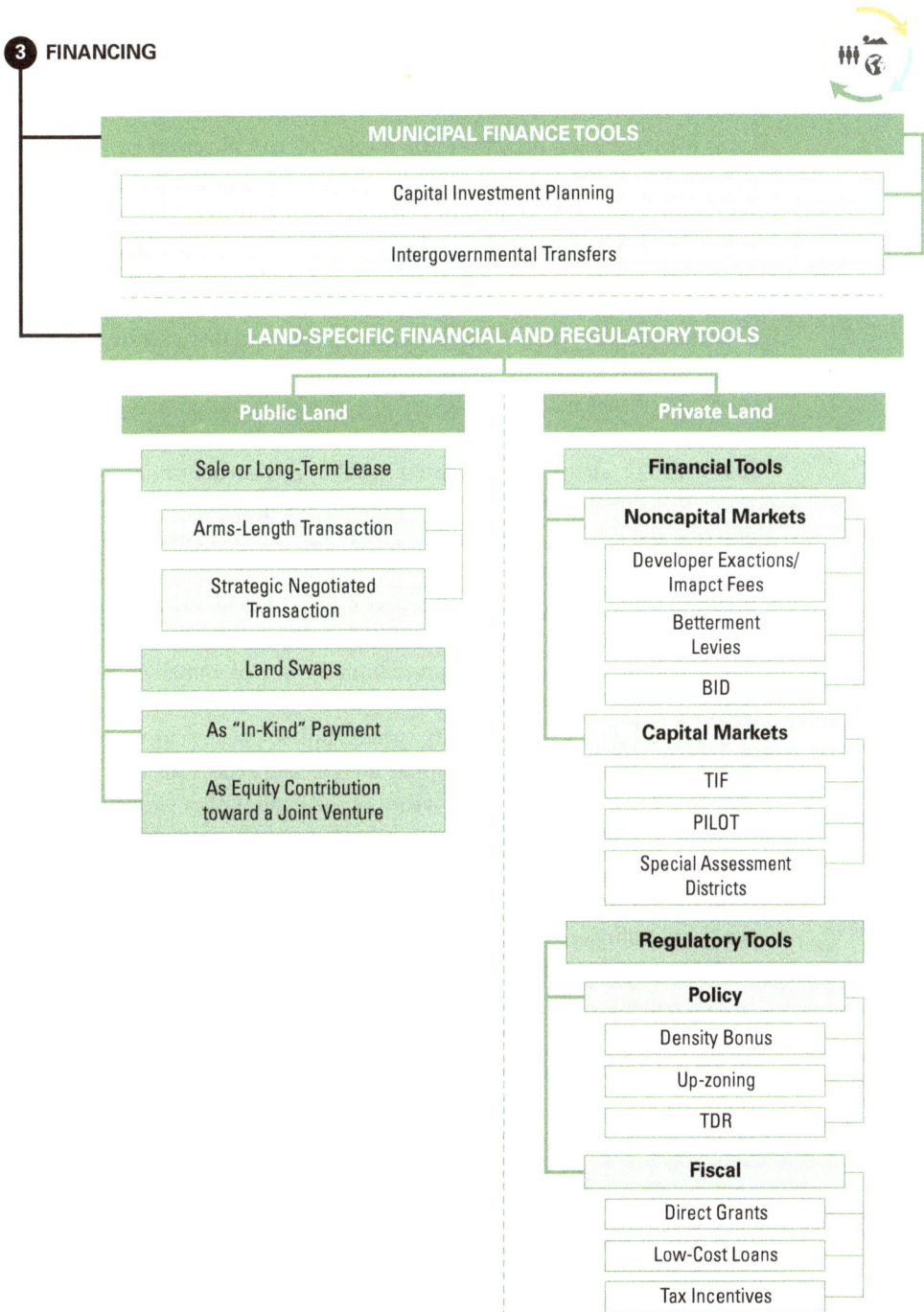

3 FINANCING

MUNICIPAL FINANCE TOOLS

Capital Investment Planning

Intergovernmental Transfers

LAND-SPECIFIC FINANCIAL AND REGULATORY TOOLS

Public Land	Private Land

Public Land

Sale or Long-Term Lease

Arms-Length Transaction

Strategic Negotiated Transaction

Land Swaps

As "In-Kind" Payment

As Equity Contribution toward a Joint Venture

Private Land

Financial Tools

Noncapital Markets

Developer Exactions/ Imapct Fees

Betterment Levies

BID

Capital Markets

TIF

PILOT

Special Assessment Districts

Regulatory Tools

Policy

Density Bonus

Up-zoning

TDR

Fiscal

Direct Grants

Low-Cost Loans

Tax Incentives

Note: BID = business improvement district; TDR = transferable development rights; TIF = tax increment financing.

Municipal Finance Tools

In recent decades, there has been a global trend of devolving more powers and responsibilities to cities. Both industrialized and developing countries employ some form of intergovernmental fiscal transfers. Indeed, there are compelling, practical reasons for doing so, as cities with more financial powers are proven to run more effectively. Therefore, before using various tools for leveraging private sector funds, the city government must investigate the availability of their own resources through capital investment planning and seek the potential of governmental transfers. The section below covers these two important instruments.

Tool: Capital Investment Planning

A capital plan provides a link between the municipality's strategic vision, its urban land use plan, and its annual budget. One recognized best practice in municipal fiscal management is for a city to undergo a typically annual exercise of preparing a multiyear capital improvement plan. This type of plan would identify anticipated public infrastructure and investment projects, as well as a financing approach. A capital investment plan would describe the city's policies and financial abilities to manage the investment needs associated with its spatial development and built environment. Key financial policies might include goals or guidelines for critical fiscal management metrics, such as the percentage of the annual budget to be committed to capital improvements, metrics to limit the size of annual debt service, and limits on total outstanding debt.

A capital plan would identify specific public projects as well as a general schedule. The first year of a capital plan would reflect the city's budget for that fiscal year, and remaining years of the capital plan would represent an estimate of future capital needs to be funded through projected revenue estimates. The timeframe of a city's capital plan is a local decision. For example, some cities prepare four-year plans (coterminous with a mayor's term, for example) whereas others prepare six-year or longer-term plans.

A municipal capital investment plan would likely include a fiscal capacity assessment, in which the city estimates future revenues, future operating expenditures, and the amount of funds available to transfer to capital reserves. Sources of funds for a city's capital plan might include own-source revenues (or "pay as you go" capital reserves); grants or transfers from other levels of government; grants from external sources; and long-term debt (for example, general obligation bonds backed by the full faith and credit of the issuing government). Capital investment plans should be reviewed annually and adjusted to take into account fiscal impacts of capital investments. For example, the construction of an upgraded transit hub increased the value of surrounding commercial uses and stimulated additional private sector construction, thereby increasing municipal property tax revenues.

Comprehensive, multiyear capital plans provide many benefits. They (a) promote the effective management of public capital assets; (b) encourage a municipality to consider funding requirements and the likely timing of major required investments, as well as future costs and timing of major upgrades; and (c) also bundle anticipated projects together, enabling a city to pursue outside funding sources to make up for any possible shortfalls. This can involve borrowing from the capital markets or applying for transfers or external funding sources. In short, capital plans can help cities operate more efficiently and help lower transaction costs.

Most cities lack the resources to fund an entire urban regeneration project from the existing municipal capital budget. It is common for a city to prepare a separate capital investment plan specific to an urban regeneration initiative. This type of plan might include an allocation from a city's overall capital budget, project-specific grant funds from an external source, project-specific proceeds from accessing capital markets for bond-based finance, and other sources. Larger-scale initiatives may be expected to be phased in over a 10–20 year period. As such, not all funds need to be accessed up front. Therefore, a capital plan would need to address the likely timing of when funds would actually be required.

Tool: Intergovernmental Transfers

Intergovernmental transfers can be a useful source of funds for planning and construction. However, a disadvantage of this dependence is that the amount and timing of transfers can be unpredictable. Market cycles, demographic shifts, policy changes by other levels of government, and natural disasters are a few examples of events that can affect government revenues and transfers to lower levels of government. Transfer programs can also distort local decision making. Conditional transfers, for example, generally require municipalities to spend the funds they receive according to state or national guidelines and often require municipal matching funds.

There are generally two types of intergovernmental transfers: unconditional (general) and conditional (project-specific). Many examples exist of cities accessing conditional transfers and grants—sometimes via competitive processes and sometimes requiring matching funds—to advance local urban regeneration plans. One example of a national government providing conditional grants to support large-scale urban regeneration is the U.S. Department of Housing and Urban Development (HUD)'s HOPE VI program. It has provided more than US$6 billion in grants to communities across the country for a specific purpose: namely, to deconcentrate very low-income public housing households and to transform their existing, underinvested neighborhoods into more socially and economically sustainable mixed-use, mixed-income communities. HOPE VI revitalization grants have been used to fund acquisition of sites for land assembly and off-site construction; demolition of severely distressed public housing; capital costs of major rehabilitation of public housing units; and new construction and other physical improvements, such as new public spaces. A successor to the now defunct HOPE VI program is HUD's Choice Neighborhoods Program. It provides implementation grants to cities that have undergone a comprehensive local planning process and are ready to implement their transformation plans to redevelop urban neighborhoods.

Another example of how municipalities access intergovernmental funds for urban regeneration can be found in South Africa, where the National Treasury transfers funds to municipalities to support both operating and capital infrastructure needs. South African municipalities are largely dependent on the central government for capital funds. Indeed, grants represent an average of 80 percent of revenue for capital budgets in rural municipalities and 70 percent of revenue in urban municipalities. According to the National Treasury, since 1999, transfers to local government have grown faster than total government expenditures, consistent with a national policy of fiscal devolution.

However, with few exceptions, South African municipalities have generally struggled to meet the need for public services and reinvest strategically in urban infrastructure. With flat national economic growth projections into the near future, the treasury is offering performance-based incentives in which metropolitan municipalities must meet various metrics. Examples include submission of a "Built Environment Performance Plan," identification of priority urban regeneration projects, and submission of a proposed implementation strategy. These may be required for municipalities to be eligible to access national grants, such as the relatively new Integrated City Development Grant that can be used to finance urban revitalization.

In Chile, there are three sources of revenue for every municipality. These include (a) autonomous income (property taxes, vehicle circulation licenses, building permits, commercial and alcohol licenses); (b) transfer of funds from the Common Municipal Fund (CMF), which is a municipal income distribution transfer system; and (c) transfers from central government agencies' funds. In many cases, the CMF is the main source of funds for municipalities. However, Santiago is among the municipalities that have less economic dependency on the CMF.

Municipalities in Chile have a very restrictive law in relation to budget administration. They do not have borrowing power, which limits their financial management possibilities and reduces the opportunity to embark on larger investments. Municipalities are forbidden to enter into contracts with the private sector and are required to use a bid system.[8] When the amount and length of the contract exceeds both the mayor's electoral period and a certain amount (US$38,000), the allocation of funds would need approval from the mayor and the municipal council (Valenzuela 1997).

Another model of accessing transfers can be found in Mexico, where the federal government provides most of the financial support to states and municipalities on an ongoing basis. It provides support through a mix of unconditional transfers, as well as through transfers that support specific policy areas. Cities that want to invest in major upgrades to their center city core or to their municipal public transit system, for example, petition Banobras, the Mexican Development Bank responsible for promoting and financing infrastructure projects and public services. As the trustee of

Mexico's National Infrastructure Fund, created to increase national and international private investment in this sector, Banobras is the de facto gate-keeper for cities to access grants, as well as low-cost debt financing needed for local capital investments.

Land-Specific Financial and Regulatory Tools

There are various ways by which governments can enable land develop-ment and urban regeneration to occur on private lands without necessarily acquiring ownership. Two distinctive groups of instruments can be used: financial tools and regulatory tools. Financial tools involve direct exchange of funds for a regeneration project. These include various value capture methods such as impact fees, special assessments, and business improve-ment districts. Regulatory instruments include fiscal or nonfiscal (policy) tools, including tax-based and non-tax-based incentives, zoning tools, and use of development rights. In this regard, fiscal tools include any form of monetary assistance (within a city's policy framework) to the private sector, whereas nonfiscal and policy tools involve creating an appealing regulatory environment to attract private companies and individual investors.

A. Noncapital Market Financial Tools

Governments can use a variety of financial tools to capture the value of regenerated land. Some of these tools involve sophisticated public finance institutions and access to capital markets. There are also tools that do not depend on capital markets. This group of tools involves various value capture tools such as developer exactions and impact fees, betterment levies, and structuring the business improvement districts. The tools that require access to capital markets include structuring special assessment districts, tax increment financing, bonds financing, and payment in lieu of taxes (PILOT).

Tool: Developer Exactions and Impact Fees

Development impact fees are required contributions by the private sector to cover the cost of additional public infrastructure and services. Typically, governments levy these fees as a one-time, up-front charge, and receipt of payment is a precondition for public approval to develop land. Developer exactions could assume any of the following forms:

- Dedication of land for public use, for example, a requirement that a project reserve a certain percentage of land in a new development for public space
- Construction of public improvements, for example, a requirement that a developer construct a public road to connect the proposed development with the existing public road network
- Funding, perhaps in the form of a negotiated amount and tied to a broader policy goal such as a contribution toward the cost of a new public day care or recreation center
- Utility connection fees

The concept behind these fees is that development growth brings an increased need for public infrastructure and services, such as sewage capacity, fire protection, and public safety. The fees help protect the existing (tax-paying) local community from having to shoulder the additional cost of added public services by asking the developer and incoming users of new spaces to share such costs. Impact fees and developer exactions are of the same nature. Developer exactions oblige the developer to either build infrastructure or pay for infrastructure elements provided by public authorities. Impact fees cover the external infrastructure costs associated with new development when it brings increased demand for expansion in infrastructure capacity (such as for roads, water supply, public spaces, and so on).

A benefit of impact fees is that they reduce the economic burden on local jurisdictions that may not have sufficient capital funds to keep up with the infrastructure requirements of growth. One of the appealing characteristics of assessing an impact fee is that developers or end users pay the cost of system-wide infrastructure expansion needed to accommodate growth from the urban regeneration project. Another benefit is that up-front impact fees, that is, fees collected prior to or at the time development begins, enable the city to access capital earlier than if a city had to wait for incremental service charges, property tax revenue, or other tax revenue that might be generated by the new development. Further, these fees generally generate a net positive—or in the worst case, neutral—fiscal impact.

It should be noted, however, that the successful use of impact fees requires that a municipality possess a robust analytical framework for how to estimate the infrastructure cost implications of proposed development. Impact fees are most easily estimated for greenfield projects; for urban infill projects, however, estimating the incremental cost of a new development can prove challenging. Among the disadvantages of this financing tool, therefore, is that it can be technically cumbersome to estimate appropriate costs. Indeed, it requires a high level of technical savvy by a municipal team in order to set and negotiate an appropriate amount with the developer. A further drawback is that government discretion regarding assessment amounts can open the door to controversy and perceptions of corruption.

How are impact fees used? The usefulness of these fees as a significant source of financing large-scale transformative urban regeneration efforts depends on the market and regulatory context. In order for a city to tap impact fees as a meaningful source of financing for urban regeneration, a viable private sector developer must be interested in constructing a new or higher density development program. However, many urban regeneration initiatives are located in blighted areas where disinvestment has occurred and private investors have been loath to invest. Whereas an exaction may work as a capital-raising mechanism in an area in which market demand is sufficiently strong to entice a developer to invest, this tool will not be useful as a fundraising instrument for projects whose location or other characteristics (perhaps environmental contamination) make them financially infeasible or unattractive within public intervention.

With the exception of some robust real estate markets (for example, Hong Kong SAR, China), imposing an extra levy can at times have the effect of discouraging, rather than incentivizing, private sector investment. Such fees also do not necessarily take into account—or, better said, may not provide enough funds to achieve—broader policy goals that a municipality might want to effectuate, such as construction of a new park with superior public space design, or the introduction of additional units of low- and mixed-income housing.

Examples do exist of municipalities that have successfully negotiated payment of impact fees that cover more than the incremental infrastructure and property-related city services. The city of San Francisco, for example, has collected impact fees from downtown commercial developments to help pay for public transit improvements, affordable housing, and child care. However, San Francisco (like Hong Kong SAR, China and Manhattan) boasts one of the most robust and expensive real estate markets in the world. Furthermore, new development projects that would increase density or introduce higher-value land uses in central areas (for instance, conversions of former industrial property into residential units) can easily "afford" exactions. However, this tool is subject to the volatility of land markets in that the amount of exaction a project investor can afford to pay varies according to land value.

Tool: Betterment Levies

Betterment levies are a form of tax or a fee levied on land that has gained in value because of public infrastructure investments. They are considered the most direct form of value capture (Peterson 2009). Whereas impact fees and developer exactions work from the cost side of budgets, betterment levies try to capture part of the infrastructure investment already incurred by the government.

There are various ways to implement betterment levies. Indeed, many countries have at one point or another experimented with different variations of this tool. In the United States, many cities used a variant of betterment levies called special assessment districts, which are covered later in this chapter. These districts levy a special assessment on the increment in land values caused by public infrastructure improvements. This assessment is then used to repay the debt incurred from capital markets. For instance, at one point, Great Britain imposed a betterment tax equivalent to 40 percent of the land-value gains that could be attributed to public infrastructure investment (Peterson 2009).

One developing country that has widely—and arguably successfully—used betterment levies to help fund public infrastructure is Colombia. According to a Lincoln Institute study of Colombia's use of betterment levies (known as *contribucion de valorizacion*), in 2011 Bogotá had made about US$1 billion worth of investments in public works from this levy. An additional eight smaller cities combined had obtained another US$1 billion for public infrastructure. The collection of this fee has been generally accepted by taxpayers. Again, according to the Lincoln Institute study (Greenstein and Sungu-Eryilmaz 2004), it had relatively lower default rates than compared with property taxes. Controversies have surfaced, nevertheless, over how the charge is calculated (Borrero and others 2011).

In practice, betterment levies have proven challenging to implement. The main challenge comes from the fact that it is difficult to quantify the land value increment resulting from infrastructure investments. Even in countries with up-to-date property data, recorded land values commonly account for two-thirds or less of the observed variation in the prices of land parcels (Peterson 2009). It is even harder to identify the portion of value increase due to infrastructure investments. Different studies and ex post analyses by academics to determine increment land value increases can differ by as much as 300 percent. These variations are attributable to differences in the way aggregate land value changes are distributed among different parcels. Overall, it seems that the cost of administering parcel-by-parcel betterment levies could be high compared to the collected revenue (Peterson 2009). In sum, this challenge makes it administratively difficult to implement a betterment levy scheme.

For developing countries, in particular, this tool is more problematic. Critics of betterment levies consider this tool to be regressive in nature. They argue that having residents pay for a large portion of public infrastructure results in procurement of infrastructure in the wealthier parts of the city by those who can easily pay for the services. However, evidence from Lima, Peru, suggests that the low-income households are more eager to pay for the public infrastructure and services than the wealthy. In the early 1990s, the city launched a successful program featuring 30 projects that used a contributory tool for financing public services. It was better received by the poor communities than by the higher-income households. Another challenge with betterment levies is the fact that their implementation often meets resistance from public opinion (Greenstein and Sungu-Eryilmaz 2004).

Tool: Business Improvement Districts

BIDs (also known in some countries as city improvement districts or CIDs) have successfully leveraged private funding in cities to catalyze urban regeneration. Indeed, well-managed BIDs have contributed to increased property values, improved sales for local retailers, and decreased commercial vacancy rates.

A BID is a PPP in which property and business owners elect to make a collective contribution to maintenance, development, and/or promotion of their commercial district. A majority of property owners must agree to fund the BID through an extra assessment. The core concept is modeled on the shared maintenance program of many suburban shopping centers. Malls are typically single properties managed by one entity that sublets retail square footage to multiple tenants. Tenants pay a common area maintenance fee to fund services that enhance the appearance of common areas and provide cooperative advertising for the mall and its stores.

Among the benefits of the BID structure is that it creates a reliable funding source for supplemental services and programs, such as public safety, or marketing of a neighborhood brand. Because they are self-managed and funded by the owners themselves, BIDs typically offer the ability to respond more quickly than the public sector to the changing needs of the business community.

Canada, South Africa, the United Kingdom, and the United States are among the countries in which BIDs have been created. In many cases, they have contributed to the turnaround of inner-city areas. Some BIDs have focused on public safety, whereas others have focused on area branding and investment promotion. Among the most dramatic urban transformations that a BID helped facilitate was Bryant Park, a modestly sized, nine-acre site adjacent to the majestic main library located in midtown Manhattan. This site had become a lost urban amenity in the 1970s, going so far as to turn into an open-air drug market. In the early 1980s, several prominent area business executives—including the chairmen of Time Inc. and Rockefeller Brothers Fund—invested in a master plan to reconfigure and upgrade the park. This in turn led the charge to create a BID that would fund and maintain upgrades, such as paths, lighting, fountains, restaurants, and temporary food kiosks. All were designed with the goal of bringing people back to the park. BID members (including land and business owners) benefited from higher office rents and property values. As a result of these infrastructure investments, the area had a significant reduction in crime. With ongoing attention to on-site programming, Bryant Park has become a major social center in New York City, with more than 6 million visitors annually.[9]

Certain conditions must be in place in order for a BID to be an appropriate tool to facilitate regeneration. Most critically, a designated area must have existing local property owners who consider it a worthwhile endeavor to contribute additional funds toward the maintenance and investment in their district. In some cities, public infrastructure and upgrade needs may be so high that a BID would not offer sufficient value. For instance, a BID would not be useful in closing the financing gap for a large-scale development project, as the timing of the revenues it generates would not match the up-front requirements of major capital investments.

The Furman Center (2013) claims that in America where the BID model is used, "bigger means better" in terms of the successful BIDs. Their findings confirm that "large-office BIDs have large and positive impacts on commercial property values, but smaller BIDs have little discernable impact." Regarding property values, BIDs have a significantly more positive impact on commercial property values with an average value increase of approximately 15 percentage points. Given this (and other reasons), the authors suggest that the city should direct its efforts to forming BIDs in larger, denser environments.

In South Africa, Johannesburg's private sector has been a pioneer in using CIDs in its inner city. Specifically, CIDs have been used to finance necessary services and infrastructure. For more information about the Johannesburg experience, see box 1.9.

B. Capital Market Tools

Many cities have looked to private capital markets to help finance urban regeneration projects. Cities and local public service providers, such as

---

Box 1.9   City improvement districts in Johannesburg, South Africa

In Johannesburg, city improvement districts (CID) are defined geographic areas in which property owners agree to pay for supplementary services and improvements in their urban environment. These services can include security measures, urban area upgrades, litter collection, and design and upkeep of public spaces. In addition, some CIDs also take on additional and complementary services including web-based communication and information systems connecting all businesses in the area; programs to attract businesses; environmental upgrades; business retention; branding and marketing of the CID precinct area; or events management to attract more people to the CID area.

In South Africa, a CID can be formed when a petition is filed by at least 51 percent of the property owners in the geographic area and then approved by the municipality. Once a CID is enacted, the property owners are required to pay a CID levy for additional services. The CID levy is compulsory and is calculated based on the value of the individual property and applied pro rata. CIDs are established for an initial period of three years but can extend indefinitely unless members file for a change of the original business plan. The CID levy is collected by the municipal council on behalf of CIDs, and then transferred to the CID without any deductions. In some other cases, the council authorizes the CID to collect the levies on its own.

A board of directors elected from the member property owners governs the CIDs. They control the area within the terms of their original business plan. Although nonvoting members of the board may be included, such as a councillor, tenant, or other stakeholder, property owners must be in the majority. The board usually comprises property owners, business owners, representatives of residents' organizations (if relevant), and representatives of the local authority. The board then selects an urban management company to manage the daily functions of the CID and implement the business plan.

There are three different CID typologies used in Johannesburg. They include legislated CIDs, voluntary CIDs, and special project CIDs. The legislated CIDs' responsibilities and functions have been noted above. Voluntary CIDs and special project CIDs do not fall under the CID legislation. Thus, they are not based on a legally binding agreement between property owners and operate voluntarily.

CIDs are said to have changed the look, feel, and function of a number of areas in Johannesburg's inner city. They have also been subject to both criticism and praise since their inception. Some suggest that little attention has been paid to the growing spatial inequalities that CIDs create, as well as the risk of fragmentation both politically and fiscally—both of which have particular resonance in the post-apartheid context. Some concerns have also been expressed that corporate interests may be promoted to the detriment of addressing social issues (Peyroux 2008). Furthermore, others note that the widening of social and spatial inequalities can occur in the CIDs, given that "property owners in lower-income areas cannot afford the additional fees for privatized services" (Miraftab 2007).

utility companies, may be able to access private capital markets through various mechanisms, including direct issuance of bonds. They can also borrow from an intermediate financial institution, such as a development bank or national municipal development fund.

The primary rationale for a municipality to borrow and invest in public infrastructure and improvement is that such investments would spur economic growth. This, in turn, would create a positive fiscal impact, as well as a secondary economic impact, such as an increase in the number of jobs created. The capital investment needs of an urban regeneration effort can be funded through a city's normal capital-raising efforts through the issuance of municipal general obligation bonds, combining the public investments required to advance urban regeneration with other capital needs.

Although available for most Organisation for Economic Co-operation and Development (OECD) municipalities, access to external funding sources are not as readily obtainable for many municipalities in developing countries. Where subnational borrowing occurs, it often takes the form of loans from multilateral development banks, which are then reloaned by central governments to lower levels of government. These loans may also be heavily subsidized.

Borrowing from the capital markets through a bond issuance is viable and sustainable only if a city can identify a source of funds to pay the anticipated debt service on the borrowed amount. If excess revenues already exist in the city's annual operating budget, then the anticipated annual debt service amount can be serviced. If not, a city would need to either increase existing revenues (for instance, through increasing tax rates) or reallocate other items in the capital budget. This financing approach would make the most sense if a municipality had access to lower cost capital than a private developer, who might use (costly) sponsor equity, seek investor equity, or look for bank financing. The following three tools require cities and municipalities to interact with the capital markets.

Tool: Tax Increment Financing
Cities have accessed capital markets to help fund urban regeneration in a variety of ways. One possibility is through the issuance of TIF bonds. TIF has been used by American municipalities for more than 40 years. This method has provided them with a locally administered redevelopment financing tool that exploits the rise in economic value and associated increase in tax receipts that accompanies successful urban redevelopment.

TIF allows local governments to invest in public infrastructure and other improvements up-front. Local governments can then pay later for those investments. They can do so by capturing the future anticipated increase in tax revenues generated by the project. This financing approach is possible when a new development is of a sufficiently large scale, and when its completion is expected to result in a sufficiently large increase in the value of surrounding real estate such that the resulting incremental local tax revenues generated by the new project can support a bond issuance. TIF bonds have been used to fund land acquisition, sewer and water upgrades, environmental remediation, construction of parks, and road construction, among others. Over the past several decades in the United States, two project variations of TIF have evolved: bond financing and pay as you go.

Bond Financing

This is the most common form of TIF, in which a local government issues bonds backed by a percentage of projected future (and higher) tax collections caused by increased property values or new business activity within the designated project area. In this case, bond proceeds pay for present-day public improvements in the first year. These are projected to create the economic conditions leading to incremental increases in tax revenues, which can take place over a period of 15–25 years. Many bonds are revenue-backed; that is, they are *not* backed by the full faith and credit of the sponsoring government. Others require the backing of a general fund in order to access cost-effective bond terms. This means that the municipality bears the risk of repayment.

To determine the viability and appropriateness of using TIF, a municipality must first determine the market and financial feasibility of the proposed new development. It must also estimate the project's financing gap, that is, the amount of public subsidy required—without which the private sector would not invest. The municipality would identify a geographic area from which a tax increment could be drawn. For a very large project of more than five or six hundred thousand square feet of new construction, for example, the TIF boundaries might follow those of an urban regeneration district; for other projects, the area from which a tax increment would be drawn might be broader and may encompass all of a central business district. Afterward, the city would establish the initial assessed value of all the land and existing tax collections within that designated area. The city would then estimate—based on the proposed development program, market feasibility, and estimated absorption rates—the likely incremental taxes that could be generated within that area over the tenor of the bond. At this point, based on assumed bond terms and estimated transaction costs, the city could assess whether the incremental increase in tax revenues would generate enough to pay for the financing gap.

Pay as You Go

Another form of TIF financing is known as "pay as you go," in which the government reimburses a private developer as incremental taxes are generated. This form of TIF requires a developer to absorb some of the risk, in that the developer is required to invest its own capital in infrastructure costs. The developer can only get repaid (an amount that typically includes interest) after the project delivers and begins to be absorbed by the market.

Advantages of TIFs

Among the advantages of TIF as a source of financing is that it allows governments to invest in improvements without relying on other (more costly) sources of funding, for instance, intergovernmental transfers, capital reserves, or tax increases. Further, a TIF can facilitate the self-financing of a project with minimal negative fiscal impact. By contrast, the up-front timing of when infrastructure funds are made available through TIFs is more attractive than the timing of tax abatements or regulatory tools. Whereas TIFs have been used successfully to stimulate urban regeneration and positive fiscal impacts, this tool has also been poorly used, engendering opposition. One of the criticisms about TIFs as a financing tool is that some cities have deployed it for unnecessary investments, such as offering financial incentives to encourage companies to relocate. Another criticism is that some cities have drawn TIF districts so large that they capture revenue from areas that would have appreciated in value regardless of the TIF designation.

Conditions for Using TIFs

The use of a TIF requires robust real estate and economic conditions. A TIF is most appropriately used when land uses are up-zoned and when there is strong market demand. It is also appropriate in cases when the absence of prior development interest in a site with otherwise excellent attributes is related to a site-specific impediment, such as contamination of former rail yards. In such cases, reducing upfront costs of development can make the site more attractive to developers. An example of this type of TIF case is outlined in box 1.10.

A city must negotiate a realistic time frame with developers for construction and absorption and then determine cost-effective timing for bond issuance. To be most cost-effective, a TIF should be issued at the last possible moment, that is, when the private sector is ready and has committed to construct a negotiated development program. Given high transaction costs (for instance, a bond counsel, or a public finance adviser to help a city size and structure the TIF appropriately), this tool is less appropriate for funding smaller projects. Also, a city must consider how best to mitigate the potential risks of repayment, as well as the potentially negative impact on a city's credit rating as a result of providing a guarantee.

In addition to favorable market conditions, certain institutional and regulatory structures need to be in place. In assessing the attractiveness of a TIF bond, potential bond investors will look to a city's underlying creditworthiness, the project's market viability, the developer's good faith, and any guarantors (perhaps from a higher-level government entity). Investors will expect certainty with respect to the ability of the city to meet its contractual duties. If significant risks exist, investors will want some form of third party guarantee, which can add to the overall complexity and cost of the transaction.

Tool: Payment-in-Lieu-of-Taxes (PILOT)

A cousin of TIF and a variation of local "off-balance sheet" financing is the securitization of anticipated revenues. Payment-in-lieu-of-taxes (PILOT)

Box 1.10 Use of TIF in financing the redevelopment of Atlantic Station in Atlanta, Georgia

One example of a city's successful use of a TIF as a tool to finance urban regeneration can be found at Atlantic Station, a 138-acre (56-hectare) former steel mill site in Atlanta, Georgia. Although the site was centrally located and well positioned along major thoroughfares, because of the significant environmental remediation required, the private sector would not invest. In this case, the public sector decided to finance the up-front costs of required environmental remediation in order to stimulate private sector investment and unlock a positive fiscal economic impact.

The specific policy goals that the city wanted to advance included addressing population growth in a sustainable way through the promotion of a higher-density, mixed-use, transit-oriented community (thereby discouraging urban sprawl); and remediating environmental contamination.

The city and the developers agreed to a redevelopment vision of a smart growth, live/work/play, mixed-use district. The city established a "tax allocation district," and designated a 25-year term from 2001–26 for the project. It was agreed that the funds would be used to help pay for the costs of new roads, utilities, and environmental remediation (reimbursement). In addition, a multistory, below-grade parking structure was planned. Bond offerings were successfully issued in 2001, 2006, and 2007, in amounts of US$76 million, US$166 million, and US$85 million, respectively (Paul 2007).

Typical of TIFs, the bond proceeds covered the costs of issuance and capitalized interest, with the balance utilized to fund infrastructure costs incurred by the developers. In the Atlantic Station case, one of the developers purchased the bonds to finance the improvements, thereby avoiding the need for additional guaranties and credit enhancements.

Prior to the project, the site generated US$300,000 per year in property taxes; by 2013, the site generated more than US$30 million in annual property taxes. The performance of this TIF exceeded initial estimates. Indeed, the formerly blighted site has been redeveloped, and the city has achieved significant positive fiscal, economic, and policy impacts.

bonds are a version of this type of security. PILOT deals, which are typically economic development projects, involve payments from private entities that are used to pay debt service on tax-exempt bonds. A city may issue PILOT bonds backed by, for example, lease payments from a major league sports team over a 15-year period, and then use those bonds to pay for the construction of or upgrades to the stadium.

Another example of this type of financing approach can be seen in the securitization of tobacco settlement revenues. In the years following the Tobacco Master Settlement Agreement, in which the four largest U.S. tobacco companies settled with the attorneys general of 46 states in 1998, a number of state and local governments opted to issue so-called "tobacco bonds." The issuance of this debt security enabled capital-constrained governments to access additional financial resources and transfer some of the risk of declines in future settlement agreement payments to bondholders. For example, Alaska invested a portion of its proceeds into infrastructure projects, and Alabama used them to finance economic development. Although some governments have benefited from being able to access additional resources in this way, a drawback of this tool (depending on the perceived riskiness of the revenue stream) is a potentially high interest rate, which makes the bonds more expensive.

Tool: Special Assessment Districts

Another way for cities to access capital markets to fund their urban regeneration initiatives is through the use of special assessment districts. Unlike a TIF, this type of tool assesses an *additional* tax on the full value of a property, usually paid by property owners within a defined special assessment district that will benefit from specific public improvement(s).

In order to issue special assessment district bonds, a majority of owners must agree to a self-assessment. Special assessment districts have been used to finance major infrastructure upgrades (such as public transport), build roads, and install water and sewer systems. Such upgrades help to enable the construction of new homes and commercial spaces. The appealing aspects of this type of tool are that it expands the available capital budget and aligns incentives of payees and beneficiaries. Further, special assessment districts involve lower repayment risk and are less speculative than TIF because the fees are tied to existing rather than anticipated or future development. The fact that existing owners have agreed to additional self-assessment also makes the option attractive.

Similar to the TIF, this tool requires robust real estate and economic conditions. However, it can also involve high transaction costs. It is best utilized when urgency exists to capitalize on market dynamics such that landowners are willing to commit to an additional assessment in order to access positive economic impact rather than wait for the public sector to identify capital funds. Implementation of this tool is also easier when the majority of land within the designated area is held by a few commercial landowners. This makes it easier to negotiate any required agreements, as opposed to dealing with the organization of hundreds of owners of smaller parcels. See box 1.11 for an example of the use of special assessments in development.

Policy and Regulatory Tools for Financing Urban Regeneration

Cities have significant ability to grow and shape their economies when they have substantial control over local land use, zoning, planning, and enforcement. Whether in partnership with other sources of capital or in the absence of access to external capital, cities can leverage their policy and regulatory powers to create a regulatory framework that promotes the design, building, operation, and maintenance of public infrastructure by the private sector. Policy and regulatory tools enable governments to influence or shape redevelopment in a given area on private land.

Nonfiscal regulatory tools solely depend on the government's land use planning powers and ability to leverage these powers in achieving urban regeneration. Cities that lack the legislative authority or fiscal space to borrow can leverage their limited resources in other ways, such as by exercising regulatory powers. For example, cities can offer zoning

Box 1.11   Financing the Dulles Corridor Metrorail Project through special assessments

One example of a special assessment financing tool is that used for the Dulles Corridor Metrorail Project in Northern Virginia, a fast-growing commercial area within the Washington, DC, metropolitan region. The region is projected to have 45 percent population growth and 60 percent employment growth over the next 25 years. In this context, the US$5.5 billion, 23-mile extension of the existing Metrorail System has been proposed to address public concerns regarding quality of life and the region's competitiveness.

The total project is estimated at US$5.684 billion in capital costs. Part of the estimated cost was covered through various federal grants and loans, as well as from various counties' budgets. As the extension project was conceptualized, it became clear that the transit authority lacked sufficient funds to cover construction costs. Because the Metrorail extension would benefit businesses and their customers located along this corridor, commercial landowners in Tysons Corner, Virginia, agreed to establish a special assessment district to fund a local share of Phase 1 and Phase 2 construction. The share was to be matched by federal dollars and would also help service debt. Commercial and industrial (but not residential) real estate owners in the Phase 1 assessment zone around Tysons Corner agreed to be charged an additional US$0.22 cents per US$100 of assessed value, in addition to normal property taxes, up to US$400 million.

Source: Dulles Corridor Metrorail Project, Metropolitan Washington Airports Authority, Herndon, VA, http://www .dullesmetro.com/.

flexibility and streamline permits or offer more flexible building codes. While arguably a more passive approach than proactive investment of capital or proactive disposition of public land, leveraging land use policy and municipal regulatory powers to encourage or disincentivize aspects of development within a target urban regeneration area can be powerful with respect to advancing an urban regeneration vision.

Tool: Density Bonus

One approach, widely used in the United States, is for a municipality to leverage its regulatory power in order to incentivize private sector investment in a designated urban regeneration area through the offer of a density bonus. A density bonus is an incentive-based tool that permits a developer to increase the maximum allowable development on a site in exchange for either funds or in-kind support for specified public policy goals. This tool works best in cities in which market demand is strong and land availability limited, or for projects or sites in which the developer's financial incentives outweigh alternative development options. Density bonuses have been used to promote, among other policy goals, environmental conservation, public spaces, and production of additional units of low-income (or "social") housing.

The density bonus program was introduced in New York City in 1961. It granted developers the right to build three additional square feet of construction in return for every one square foot of public space improvement they carried out at the street level within their property (usually a setback to create a plaza or the development of an arcade). This density bonus was later revised to 10 square feet for every square foot of public space improvement, up to a certain upper threshold for such a construction bonus. This program was responsible for the development of over 500 privately built public spaces in Manhattan over three decades. São Paulo, Brazil, had a similar program called *outorga onerosa*, which gives property owners an as-of-right construction bonus of up to 20 percent of their existing development if they make a predetermined cash contribution to a city-wide general purpose infrastructure improvement fund.

This tool's usefulness is limited to robust market environments in which a project's developer can "afford" the additional cost of incorporating subsidized housing units. Nonetheless, an advantage of deploying this tool is to encourage creation of a mixed-income community. For example, it allows a municipality to stimulate construction of a public good (in this case, additional affordable low-income residential units) without having to spend precious capital funds.

Tool: Up-zoning

Another approach commonly used by cities in the United States for leveraging regulatory powers is up-zoning, that is, changing the zoning to allow for higher-value (for example, from industrial to residential) or more dense use (for example, increasing allowable FAR). As with density bonuses, up-zoning can be successfully deployed as a kind of financing tool for urban regeneration only when sufficient market demand exists.

An example of how one city used up-zoning to advance its vision for urban regeneration can be found in Washington, DC. The city up-zoned land adjacent to Union Station, the city's major multimodal transit hub, and created a new, 358-acre mixed-use neighborhood, called NoMa. By 2012, NoMa was contributing US$49 million more annually, relative to 2006 levels, in property taxes to the city. In this example, the city did not use capital resources to invest in infrastructure upgrades in the neighborhood; instead, it incentivized landowners and developers to do so. Therefore, the private sector was highly motivated to capture gains made possible by the increase in allowable density. NoMa's success as an urban regeneration story is tied to its unparalleled proximity to the city's major multimodal transit hub, an upswing in market conditions, and a rising trend of people seeking to live near their place of work.

Apart from these examples of successful use of incentive zoning to effectuate urban regeneration goals, the history of incentive zoning generally has been mixed. In New York City, for example, more than three and a half million square feet of public space has been created as part of bonus density programs (City of New York 2014b). However, some spaces are not of high design quality, other spaces are functionally inaccessible, and still other spaces are devoid of the level of design or amenities that can attract public use. One possibility is that it may be more efficient to *require*, rather than to *incentivize*, specific design features (for instance, a civic space whose size is tied to the size of the development) through other regulatory mechanisms, such as a city retaining preapproval rights of open space design.

Tool: Transferable Development Rights

In addition to municipal land, municipalities can also dispose of rights to engage in more intensive land development—a higher floor space index (FSI) or higher FAR[10]—as a way to "finance" and incentivize urban regeneration. Development rights generally refer to the maximum amount of floor area permissible on a zoning lot. When the actual built floor area is less than the maximum permitted floor area, the difference is referred to as "unused development rights," "air rights," or "excess density rights." These excess density rights represent the publicly controlled share of privately owned land. These rights have economic value that can be sold by public authorities, which happened in São Paulo and New York City.

Among the benefits of this financing approach is that the disposition of development rights does not cause a negative fiscal impact. On the contrary, the public sector sale of development rights can generate a positive fiscal impact because cities typically do not include the future possible value of those rights on their balance sheets. If a municipality owns land (for instance, a downtown public parking garage or government buildings below allowable density), it could also sell or transfer its development rights. The sale or transfer of development rights requires a well-designed regulatory framework, for example, for "sending" and "receiving" zones, and for enforcement capacity.

A transferable development rights (TDR) system is a type of local zoning ordinance that allows legal manipulation of the zoning envelope. It is an imaginary 3-dimensional mold that otherwise defines a site's maximum development potential and permits owners of land zoned for low-density development to sell and send their development rights to other property owners. "Transferred" development rights permit purchasing landowners to develop their "receiving" parcel at a higher density than would be legally possible otherwise.

Metropolitan areas have used TDR systems to achieve various policy goals. The city of São Paulo, for example, has used an instrument called Certificados de Potencial Adicional de Construção, or CEPACs (translated as certificates of additional construction potential bonds) as a tool to create development rights for up-zoning. The city then sold these rights to developers to raise funds to finance infrastructure construction. The total number of CEPACs, which is capped by law, is determined by the municipality. CEPACs can be used only in certain designated areas that the city government has targeted for public investments. One attractive feature of CEPACs from the developers' perspective has been that they are not required to undertake their development projects immediately after the acquisition of building rights. Instead, they can decide on the timing of their investments according to market conditions.

A different model of development rights management has been deployed in King County, Washington (the metropolitan area around the city of Seattle, Washington). It has a TDR program that uses market conditions to incentivize preservation of rural land and steer development growth toward urban areas. The program is based on free-market principles and has benefited from robust market prices that have in turn motivated landowner and developer participation. In this example, rural landowners realize an economic return through the sale of development rights to private developers who, in turn, have an interest in building increased density in urban areas where there is strong market demand.

As another example, New York City has a TDR system that allows for the transfer of unused development rights from one zoning lot to another in limited circumstances. This is usually done to promote the preservation of buildings officially designated as historic landmarks, open spaces, or unique cultural resources (for example, the midtown Manhattan theater district). The market for TDRs in New York is market-driven in contrast to São Paulo, which is administered by a public entity. Transactions are "arm's length" commercial transactions between unaffiliated owners. Recently, New York City proposed a special zoning district for Hudson Yards, a mega mixed-use urban redevelopment district under construction on the west side of Manhattan. It would enable owners of lots that meet specific criteria to purchase additional permitted FAR (depending on the lot's location) by making a contribution to a district improvement fund (DIF). The DIF would then be used to finance improvements to the area's transit and pedestrian infrastructure.

Fiscal Tools

Some municipalities have offered financial incentives to help incentivize redevelopment, such as (property) tax abatements and tax credits and grants. These are used as tools to close a project financing gap or stimulate private sector actions consistent with the city's vision for urban revitalization. In contrast to the various tools noted, this approach has resulted in a direct, negative fiscal impact—depending, of course, on whether the incentive is a direct grant or a limited-period tax holiday, and whether the city's tax collections team had already factored in anticipated future tax revenue into annual revenue estimates.

Among the factors that contribute to the usefulness of fiscal incentives as a tool to encourage urban regeneration is the market context. Specifically, a developer or owner needs to be sufficiently motivated—by market demand and anticipation of future returns—to take action. Another factor is the institutional context. The use of fiscal incentives typically requires political support as well as technical capacity to administer and monitor an incentive program. Administering a program—including any up-front negotiations with a developer regarding specific conditions—requires a high level of technical savvy by a municipal team, which translates into a "cost" as well.

Tool: Direct Grants

One common form of fiscal incentive is a direct grant (typically a reimbursement for allowable expenses) to a commercial building owner or space user in exchange for certain actions, such as the hiring of local residents or adopting specified design standards. One way this tool has been successfully used to enhance urban regeneration is through the use of small grants that encourage local residents or business owners to restore, rehabilitate, or repair storefronts and historic buildings. Oregon City, for example, offers a "storefront improvement" program that has provided funding to more than 60 local businesses since 2003. Most are located on or near the historic commercial corridors. The program helps to pay for exterior improvements that foster high(er) design quality and sustainability for properties located within a designated urban renewal area.

Sometimes an urban neighborhood may look blighted due to underinvestment in commercial building facades, a lack of unifying signage for a commercial area, or the lack of a well-designed and well-maintained public space. This type of fiscal incentive is a surgical intervention, appropriate for situations in which a blighted area has many land owners (rather than a few major landowners). Assuming that land assembly is not desirable or possible, it may require a retail rather than a large-scale, transformative approach. In Oregon City, for example, the city's urban development agency offers adaptive reuse grants to businesses and commercial property owners located within the designated urban renewal district. Because the city is trying to encourage a mixed-use neighborhood, the grant program offers funds for the proposed conversion of interior rehabilitation projects.

Tool: Low-Cost Loans

Another form of fiscal incentive is a low-cost loan program. Such programs may be used to encourage businesses to locate in a designated urban renewal area. Small loan programs can also be used to close the gap between vacant properties and more traditional development projects. In this regard, sometimes the costs of rehabilitation (which might include, for example, environmental remediation) along with pre-existing encumbrances (such as tax liens) exceed the market value of these properties. Local government (or a public sector-affiliated financial institution) can offer low-interest loans to encourage rehabilitation of vacant sites or blighted buildings.

Tool: Tax Incentives

Selective and intelligently designed tax incentives can play a major role in absorbing private sector capital for urban regeneration. Unlike the non-tax-based incentives noted (density bonus, up-zoning, development rights transfers), tax-based incentives involve an indirect exchange of funds between the public and private sectors. The tax incentives could be given to private sector developers or to individual residents of a neighborhood to foster area-based regeneration. In order for tax-based incentives to work properly, a city must have a strong and clear planning regulatory framework and tax collection system.

Traditionally many of these incentives (especially in the United States in the 1980s) started to close the gap between the cost of development in inner cities and the value of the development after construction. They have been widely used in the United Kingdom as enterprise zones, which were primarily structured as a job creation tool in distressed neighborhoods. However they have had moderate success in developing vacant and underused land. Enterprise zones allocate tax exemptions and ease some planning regulations to increase business in distressed areas. Another example of this is the urban development zone (UDZ) in South Africa, which is a tax incentive program launched by the Ministry of Finance and implemented by local municipalities. This national-level law allowed the municipalities to designate UDZs around the "areas of priority" listed in their integrated plans, or areas where "significant fiscal measures have been implemented by that municipality to support the regeneration."[11] Johannesburg was one of the first cities in South Africa to start using this program in 2004, and the UDZ included its inner city area. The particulars of this tax incentive are detailed in box 1.12.

Box 1.12 **Urban development zone tax incentives in Johannesburg, South Africa**

The urban development zone (UDZ) tax incentive works in the form of an accelerated depreciation from eligible taxpayer's taxable income—if this income is a result of erection, extension, or improvements of, or an addition to an entire building or part of a building within the central business district (CBD) that is at least 1,000 square meters. The incentive also applies to the purchase of buildings within the CBD with said criteria from a developer, if the developer has not yet claimed any UDZ allowance.

The UDZ incentive distinguishes between construction of new buildings and refurbishment of existing ones. In the case of full or partial improvement of an existing building, the UDZ deductibles are equivalent to

- A five-year straight-line depreciation or 20 percent of the total cost in the year of assessment, during which the building is brought into use by the taxpayer solely for the purposes of trade.
- An amount equal to 20 percent of the cost in each of the four succeeding years of assessment, provided that the person engages in continuous use of the building solely for the purposes of trade.

In cases of erecting or extending an existing building, the deductions follow these rules:

- Twenty percent of the total cost in the year of assessment, during which the building is brought into use by the taxpayer solely for the purposes of trade
- Five-percent of the cost for the 16 subsequent years of assessment conditional to continuous use for the purposes of trade

The UDZ tax incentive is especially attractive to investors because the tax deductibility of costs can be offset against the investors' entire income and not just the income resulting from investment in buildings. For example, assume that a doctor who generates R 500,000 in income purchases a townhouse within the UDZ and spends R 50,000 to rehabilitate the property. He then rents the townhouse and earns R 36,000 a year in rental income, of which R 34,000 are spent on ongoing costs of

(Box continues on next page)

Box 1.12   Urban development zone tax incentives in Johannesburg, South Africa *(continued)*

maintenance, resulting in a net profit of R 2,000. The R 50,000 tax credit would be applied against the entire income of R 502,000—that is, the R 500,000 income received as a doctor plus the R 2,000 town-house rental profit.

The city has praised the UDZ tax incentives as a driving force behind the surge in real estate investments in the inner city in 2005 and 2006. However, it is difficult to analyze the impacts of UDZs independent of all other initiatives that were simultaneously in place. By 2011, more than 200 UDZ applications had been filed with the city of Johannesburg. The city claims to have attracted R 2 billion in private sector investment to the inner city per year and about R 9 billion within the 2010–11 financial year (Garner 2011). Although some smaller-scale development companies have complained about the cumbersome bureaucracy of UDZs, of the 200 UDZs filed, 90 were by smaller development companies. In addition, it is estimated that 65,000 construction-related jobs were created as a result of the UDZ tax incentives (Garner 2011).

The UDZ regulations and conditions have been amended several times since their inception to make them more practical and useful. One important change was the 2005 amendment, which allowed the UDZ benefits to be extended to sectional title ownership. This change resulted in a greater uptake of the incentive by the general public and streamed the benefits from the developers to the buyers of the units. Another amendment has allowed for a 25 percent depreciation (over a period of four years) for the construction of low-cost, high-density affordable housing. Finally, the UDZs are now allowed to include developmental leases by the government to the private sector (Garner 2011).

Source: "Urban Development Zone," City of Johannesburg. Johannesburg, http://joburg.org.za/index.

Financing Tools for Regeneration of Public and Municipal Land

Many cities have successfully leveraged the value of land in their municipal portfolios to advance their urban regeneration vision. Land disposal through the selling, leasing, or transferring of municipal real property assets is one way that cities can leverage their land to help finance urban regeneration. Unlike subnational government debt—the most prominent item on the liability side of a city's balance sheet—subnational governments' management of land assets has been largely unregulated by higher-level government authorities (Peterson and Kaganova 2010). Land is an asset that many cities in the developing world do not take into account in their balance sheets. As such, one of the major advantages of land value as a financing tool is that its use has, in general, had either a neutral or positive fiscal impact on a city's balance sheet.

There are various methods by which a government can dispose of land that it owns (in its private domain) or that it has assembled for this purpose. Such methods vary in terms of transparency of disposition and the way in which the government balances financial and technical considerations (that is, between the price it raises for the land and the quality of the resulting development). There are a variety of methods of land disposition, from the most market-based to the most administrative or discretionary-based methods.

In order for a municipality to leverage the value of public land, certain regulatory and market conditions must be in place. It is preferable if the municipality has a functional, complete, and up-to-date property registry, including book value and market value data (for discussion on land valuation, see chapter 2). The availability of accurate information about recent land sales is critical to a city's ability to negotiate the successful disposition of public land. The absence of such comprehensive information will pose an increased risk to the public sector that it will receive less than fair market value for its assets. In addition, a municipality should possess a keen understanding of real estate market dynamics and the real estate development process. It should also have a sophisticated technical capacity to negotiate agreements with the private sector in which risks are allocated appropriately. The successful use of this financing approach is dependent on publicly owned sites having sufficient market value to enable a financially viable transaction such that a private developer would be able to earn returns appropriate to market conditions and risks.

Tool: Sale or Long-Term Lease of a Municipally Owned Site through an Arm's-Length Transaction

Land assets are an important ingredient of subnational government finance in many developing countries. Direct sales of land by subnational governments are a clear example of "capital" land financing. In this scenario, a municipality's goal is *solely* to maximize the price, or fair market value, it receives for its land. It can then invest the proceeds into urban regeneration and sustainability efforts.

Auctions are the most common form of such disposal of public land and can be used in sales or lease agreements. They are used to generate the highest price of a given parcel of land based on its highest and best use, specifically a predetermined land use or development mix and established building envelope through FAR or a combination of lot coverage and building height. Auctions are not widely used. There are usually concerns among policy makers and the general population that auctions could trigger an uncontrolled increase in land prices. These concerns are unfounded. However, at the same time, when there is no clear medium-term plan for the disposition of public land, auctions can artificially raise prices due to a perceived scarcity of land.

The reality however is that by virtue of maximizing the price that the government receives for the land, auctions are an important market-based land allocation mechanism that reflects real demand. They are also very effective in countering speculation. What is needed in this case is a clearer understanding by developers of opportunities of public land coming to the market over a short- and medium-term horizon to prevent a rapid rise in land prices. The drawback with auctions is that the government receives the maximum price for the land based on demand but is unable to influence the resulting development beyond what the planning and building codes require.

There are many successful examples of the use of auctions as a source for funding city regeneration projects. Auctions were first used in the Arab Republic of Egypt in 2007, when a one-day sale of 2,000 hectares of public land generated US$3.12 billion in revenues—which was equivalent to about 10 percent of the previous year's government revenues. The Mumbai Metropolitan Regional Development Authority auctioned land in the city's new financial center in 2007, and generated US$1.2 billion to help finance projects within the regional transportation plan (Peterson 2009). Singapore has earned billions of dollars by cleaning up parts of its waterfront, selling the reclaimed land, and reinvesting proceeds towards implementing the city's future land use management and investment plans. Beijing, China, too, has used auctions to enter into a land lease arrangement of 50 years for commercial development, and 40 years for industrial development projects, generating revenues that help fund large-scale urban infrastructure.

The sale or lease of land at administratively determined prices to eligible buyers or lessors is a widely used method, including in much of the Middle East (Egypt, Kuwait, and Saudi Arabia, for example). Usually, in such cases, the government sets eligibility criteria (for instance, being a national of the country, not having received prior government assistance) and then either uses prioritization criteria (such as female, single-headed households; young married couples; disaster-affected households; those relocated due to public works, and so on) or alternatively operates on a first-come, first-served basis. In the Republic of Yemen, until 2011, the government would offer public land grants for any investment project beyond a value of US$10 million (World Bank 2009).

Tool: Sale or Long-Term Lease through a Strategic Negotiated Transaction

The government can carry out negotiations directly with developers in a nontransparent form. This prevalent form of public land disposition is often used when the government wants to attract real estate investment for a specific venture. As such, it negotiates directly with large-scale, prominent developers. This type of approach involves mobilizing private capital to help finance urban regeneration through a strategic, negotiated land disposition deal structure that aligns public and private interests.

There are a variety of ways to implement this approach. For instance, a municipality might issue a competitive solicitation inviting developer interest in renovating publicly owned parcels within a specific development program that would advance the city's urban regeneration vision. This might apply, for example, if a city owned a large site, such as a now-defunct rail yard or decommissioned airport. In this case, the public sector might be seeking to maximize the fair market value of the site as well as other policy goals, such as stimulating production of new low-income housing units or construction of a new public park. Through the process of negotiating a disposition and development agreement with a qualified private developer, a city can leverage the value of the public site. It can do so by requiring that the developer take on certain costs and risks that might otherwise fall to the public sector.

A city might have a policy goal of promoting greater density in the form of additional housing units at various price points in an area targeted for urban regeneration. Through a negotiated disposition and development agreement, a city might require a developer to include units of very low-income housing (that would otherwise require a development cost subsidy) along with the market-rate units that the developer would build. By lowering a project's cost basis, discounting land value (if necessary to US$0) can help make an otherwise infeasible project financially viable.

Sometimes such an approach is used in settings with poor governance or one that is prone to corruption both in the identification of the developer(s) in question and in the setting of land prices. Because of the nontransparent approach utilized and the high potential for corruption, such contracts are usually difficult to enforce and often fail to achieve the intended purposes. One of the big rallying cries of the Arab Spring in countries such as Egypt and Tunisia has been corrupt public land management. Indeed, most of the arrests that have taken place in the aftermath of the overturning of the old regimes in 2011 have been of investors who were involved in nontransparent public land deals.

Most land leases are structured based on the concept that a charge is needed for the use of the government's assets (property). Such charges would occur on a pay-as-you-go basis. Usually, the government charges a stream of regular payments (monthly, quarterly, semiannual, or annual) during the entire lease period. Some of the more common lease structures include:

- Equal periodic installments during the entire lease period
- Equal periodic installments, adjusted from time-to-time for inflation
- A low base rate plus some percentage of a tenant's income generated by the leased property (though this form is usually utilized only in the private sector for commercial leases or in unique PPPs)
- A total sum paid up front (Kaganova 2014)

The last case is used mostly in China and Hong Kong SAR, China. In China, this method has created fiscal problems due to an over reliance of the local governments on these one-time revenues. It has also created a false incentive for governments to classify and convert rural land to urban land to be auctioned to developers. Obviously, this situation cannot go on indefinitely as the land supply is limited. See box 1.13 for an example of a direct land deal between the government and the private developers in Shanghai, China.

Tool: Land Swaps

A land swap is a tool that empowers a city to trade a municipally owned site with a privately owned site. Governments can resort to land swaps to enable development and urban regeneration on land that faces other restrictions (for instance, endowment land or land with restrictions such as areas controlled by the military). The city of Rio de Janeiro resorted to land swaps to be able

Box 1.13   Direct land deal between the Shanghai government and developers paved the way for the regeneration of Xintiadi

In China, land became a commodity in the late 1980s, when land use rights were first leased to real estate developers. However, city governments maintained full ownership of the property rights and the power to allocate and utilize land resources through directives rather than through market pricing mechanisms. Land could be leased to developers via administrative designation or public auctions in the secondary land market.

Today auctions are required for almost all types of land leases. In the case of the development of Xintiandi in Shanghai, after the approval of the master plan by the Shanghai municipal government in 1997, the Luwan district government prepared the detailed control plan. It determined the specific floor area ratios, green space ratio, height limits, and other parameters for each block. At this stage, a developer may negotiate the development volume with the district government to guarantee expected returns.

At the end of 1997, Shui On Land Limited, a real estate development company, signed an agreement with the Luwan district government under the supervision of the Shanghai municipal government. The agreement outlined the area and location of the project, as well as the conditions under which the government would provide the land and assist with relocation. Based on this short six-page contract,[a] the developer would pay for the relocation, land, and a portion of infrastructure and redevelopment of the site. This agreement provided the developer with the development rights for the entire Taipingqiao neighborhood (which included Xintiandi), while the title of each parcel within the neighborhood would be negotiated and transferred one-by-one within a 10–15-year time frame. The Shanghai Municipal Urban Planning Administration issued the Location Permission, Land Use and Built Form Permission, and Construction Permission block-by-block in a sequence according to the plan. In this way, the municipal and district government maintained a certain degree of autonomy in their partnership with the investor and developer (Yang and Chang 2007).

Source: Authors' elaboration, based on the case study of Xintiandi, Shanghai (see chapter 6).
a. The team was not able to see this contract first hand and the information is based on interviews with the developers in April 2014.

to assemble the waterfront land it needed for a large-scale development as part of its urban regeneration plan for the 2016 Olympics. The city acquired some waterfront parcels that the Brazilian navy controlled through an exchange or land swap process with other parcels the city owned elsewhere and that were deemed of equivalent value. This land swap approach was used because the Brazilian navy is not allowed to transfer its land. Similarly, *Awqaf* (an Islamic endowment) land is not permitted to be transferred, so land swaps were identified to enable the government in Egypt to acquire strategically located land needed for land assembly and redevelopment.

Urban regeneration efforts generally focus on the qualitative transformation of an *existing* part of the city, perhaps a formerly vibrant but now largely abandoned business district or a once flourishing industrial waterfront area whose allowable land uses no longer match the market. Existing building forms may be slow-changing due to inertia (for instance, perhaps a site has a passive owner who may no longer live in the area) or disinvestment.

Assuming that a city wants to totally transform a targeted area, a sufficiently large scale area or block of land is required in order to do so.

As such, sometimes a city (or project sponsor) has to undertake land assembly in order to amass sufficient land that can be redeveloped to significant scale to enable the achievement of goals related to increased density or the transformation of uses. Land readjustment methods are covered in chapter 2.

In a land swap scenario, a municipality might negotiate with the site owner located within the target urban regeneration area to swap this site for the negotiated fair market value of a city site located elsewhere. This, obviously, would be a one-time, negotiated transaction in which either (a) the existing owner does not want to sell the site but is open to a land swap for the negotiated fair market value of the existing site, or (b) the city does not want to or cannot afford (or legislatively is unable) to pay cash to the existing site owner for the value of the land. In some instances, a swap might be less costly for a municipality than having to come up with precious capital funds.

Public Land as an In-Kind Payment in Return for Construction of Public Infrastructure

This financing approach is viable if a municipality owns a parcel of land that has market value greater than the estimated cost of infrastructure required. One reason that cities may want to consider this approach is that it can be more cost effective for a single entity—the private developer—to coordinate construction. The less attractive alternative would be that the public sector leads the horizontal development process with one construction team. Then, once infrastructure has been completed, a private developer would bring its own construction team to the site to begin vertical development.

Public sector-led construction projects require that contract bidding processes comply with public procurement regulations. Relative to private sector contracting, these involve longer procurement and implementation time frames and higher costs. An additional benefit of this financing approach is that it can help reduce an urban regeneration project's overall capital financing risk because contributions of public land toward infrastructure joint ventures generate funds in an up-front manner. Therefore, it reduces some financing uncertainty, which can make it easier for a developer to secure construction financing. Lastly, this approach is a lower cost source of financing relative to borrowing from the capital markets. Box 1.14 summarizes the land exchange arrangement used in Washington, DC.

Tool: Public Land as an Equity Contribution toward a Joint Venture

A variation of the in-kind payment approach is when a municipality uses the value of its land as an equity contribution toward a joint venture with a developer. In this scenario, a public entity might enter into a partnership with private sector investors for the purpose of redeveloping a targeted urban area. The public sector "invests" the value of its land assets and the private sector partner invests cash. Among the benefits of using a negotiated disposition of municipal land and a negotiated use of land value as in-kind

Box 1.14   Land in exchange for redevelopment: an experiment in Washington, DC

The city of Washington, DC, owned a centrally located downtown site that had previously been home to the city's convention center. Once the city constructed a larger, more modern convention center a couple of blocks away, the former multi-block convention center was demolished, and the site became available for redevelopment.

The city had gone through an extended period of disinvestment, however, with surface parking lots peppered through downtown and a market perception of "crime and grime" keeping potential residents and shoppers away. As such, the city was keen to leverage this site to catalyze a broader reinvestment in downtown through the creation of a mixed-use, more active neighborhood.

Instead of disposing of the city-owned site to the highest bidder, the city decided to negotiate land disposition and development agreements with a competitively selected development team that included the developer committing to construct certain public infrastructure and other project components to specifications as agreed on with the city. In this case, the city negotiated with the development team to establish the site's fair market value. The developer agreed to make ground-lease payments to the city for a 99-year period, as well as to construct a below-grade public parking garage, a new road and pedestrian alleys through the site, and an at-grade civic plaza to the city's specifications. The developer incorporated these elements into its detailed master plan. The city retained approval authority of the site master plan, and the interests of the public and private sectors were aligned in creating high-quality, cost-effective, and timely development.

payment are that this approach allows a city to invest in improvements without tapping other (more costly) sources of funding. Further, this approach causes minimal negative fiscal impact; that is, it does not require a municipality to reallocate a portion of existing operating revenues.

One real-world example of this approach concerns contributing the value of land into a special purpose entity (SPE). One example of an SPE created for the purpose of redeveloping a target area is the Solidere effort in Beirut, Lebanon. Created in the mid-1990s, it was empowered to lead the planning and redevelopment of Beirut's central business district. The implementation concept was that land owners within the target area could exchange their property for shares in Solidere, a company whose shares are now listed on the stock exchange.

Another example is detailed in box 1.15, which describes the case of Puerto Madero, Argentina, where federally owned land was used as an equity contribution to the development corporation in charge of regeneration of the port area. Although this case did not involve a joint venture in its purest meaning, it did involve a public-private corporation.

A Note on Land-Value Capture

The current section on financing presents a comprehensive menu of options for financing urban regeneration. However, many of these tools are also called "land-value capture," or LVC. LVC is an umbrella term for a collection of instruments that are used to enable the financing of

Box 1.15   Federal land as an equity contribution to Corporación Antiguo Puerto Madero Sociedad Anónima in Buenos Aires, Argentina

Corporación Antiguo Puerto Madero Sociedad Anónima (CAPMSA) was established in Buenos Aires following the approval of the Economic Emergency Law (1999), which allowed for the privatization of federal property. The main objective of this quasi-private corporation was the regeneration of 170 hectares of federal land formerly belonging almost entirely to the General Administration of Ports (AGP). According to CAPMSA's first charter, the board would be initially composed of six directors: four representing the federal government and two representing the city of Buenos Aires (see figure 1.7 for the organizational structure). In October 2003, the Statute of the Corporation was amended for the formation of the board to equally represent the nation and the city.

The capital stock was subscribed to by the federal and city governments in equal parts. The company had the ability to issue shares in order to attract private, national, or foreign funds. The decree also transferred the property of the 170 hectares of federal land to the corporation.

The first investment in the area came from CAPMSA itself and consisted of a land survey of the 170 hectares and the mapping of almost 70 users (tenants, irregular occupants) in the former AGP domain, as well as security services to prevent land invasions. After the tenant mapping, a plan was developed to end the concessions and to start charging rent. Apart from these rents, other early resources for CAPMSA consisted of the sale of demolition material, the rental of parking lots, and sets for the television and film industry. The revenues went to cover the costs of office rental, the design of the master plan, and the marketing strategy used to create the conditions for the first tender to sell the warehouses.

CAPMSA then auctioned the land in stages, starting with the area closest to the central business district. It did so by issuing tenders in 1991. The sale of land allowed CAPMSA to generate sufficient funds to finance its administrative expenses and pay for the necessary infrastructure. According to the Lincoln Institute of Land Policy, as of July 2013, CAPMSA had sold property for a total value of around US$300 million. In addition, it had invested US$113 million in public infrastructure with a total operational cost since the creation of the corporation of US$92 million. Public and private investment in 2009 amounted to US$1.7 billion and was estimated to reach US$2.5 billion when completed. By 2010, a total of 2.25 million square meters had been built in Puerto Madero (L. J. Ramos Brokers Immobiliarios 2009).

CAPMSA was established as a temporary corporation to facilitate the development of Puerto Madero. Upon the completion of the project, CAPMSA finalized the first transfer of rights for the infrastructure and public spaces to the Autonomous City of Buenos Aires. However, the largest transfer followed an agreement between CAPMSA and the city of Buenos Aires in February 2011. In this agreement, the parties negotiated a transition period for the free transfer of the domain of public spaces and the responsibility for the provision of maintenance from CAPSMA to the city. CAPMSA registered the areas to the city and then gradually transferred the responsibility for maintenance. In late 2012, the complete transfer of maintenance responsibilities had been accomplished and according to CAPMSA, this eliminated the annual expense of US$3 million from the operating costs of the corporation.

Source: Based on the case study of Buenos Aires in chapter 4.

public infrastructure. Through this approach, the unearned increment accruing to private landowners as a result of the increase in land values due to a land use planning, zoning, or infrastructure delivery decision by the government, is shared between the landowners and the government. In this way, the government can capture part of the increment in land value increase caused by publicly provided planning and infrastructure. It can then use such proceeds for the financing and cost recovery of the infrastructure. The capturing of the added value can be done ex ante (before the infrastructure and development take place) or ex post (through diverse fiscal or tax-based instruments including tax-increment financing and betterment levies), or through development rights-based tools (e.g., the sale of additional construction potential—CEPACs). Some of the financing tools detailed in this section are examples of LVC.

Tax increment financing is an example of an ex ante method, wherein a city borrows against the future flow of property tax increments resulting from a planned infrastructure improvement and urban regeneration project. The city then uses the proceeds to finance the necessary improvements. Alternatively, an example of an ex post LVC tool is the *contribución de valorización* in Bogotá, Colombia, mentioned earlier. The city of Quito, Ecuador, was exploring using the same instrument (called apportionment of benefits and costs) to recover part of the cost of its first metro line.

In addition to the ex ante and ex post instruments, value capture can also be achieved through land development rights. For example, the municipality of São Paulo introduced a development-based land value capture system wherein the city sells CEPACs. (CEPACs are covered in the transferable development rights section in this chapter.) They correspond to additional construction rights in a given zone that the municipal government has replanned and up-zoned. For its part, the city uses the proceeds from the sale of the CEPACs to finance the infrastructure needed to support the higher density development. This ex ante land value capture method has been widely used in São Paulo. Indeed, it was being pursued by Rio de Janeiro for the mixed-use redevelopment of a large waterfront project (Porto Maravilha) that will be used for the 2016 Olympics.

Phase 4: Implementation

The implementation phase entails translating the vision for long-term change into the financial, contractual, and institutional relationships between the public and private sectors. Urban regeneration is by definition a lengthy and complex process that engages the public and private sectors in a diverse set of interrelationships. The public and private sectors are usually intertwined and dependent on each other to deliver infrastructure, land, funding, regulatory approvals, and political support in order for the project to proceed.

The implementation strategy is crucial in ensuring the success of the regeneration program and delivery of intended benefits for the citizenry. It includes developing sound contracts to translate the vision into a tangible partnership between the public and private sectors. This section covers the main categories of issues that need to be carefully thought through as the PPP evolves from idea to action—and as the public and private sectors assume substantial risk, investment, and obligations.

This phase also includes defining public and private objectives and roles, as well as an understanding of what is central to all parties in these complex transactions. It is essential to always keep at the forefront of the process the larger objectives that regeneration will achieve. These should frame and guide contract negotiations.

Time is a critical variable in the PPP: if infrastructure is not delivered on schedule or approvals are delayed, land development can be stymied. This, in turn, can put funding at risk and windows of opportunity in the market may also be missed. The question has to be asked about how the regeneration program will be sustained over its decades-long life, including economic and political cycles. The regeneration program will have to survive many economic and political cycles, some of which could present dramatic swings, such as from a recession to a boom, or from conservative to progressive political regimes.

This section on implementation presents a framework to develop a sustainable partnership between the public and private sectors. It lays out necessary institutional arrangements and contracts that are designed to clearly define roles, responsibilities, and outcomes. It also examines the delivery of regeneration objectives, as well as the protections against changes in political and market circumstances during the project's cycle. Figure 1.7 summarizes the implementation process.

Political Leadership and Continuity

Political leadership is fundamental to the success of urban regeneration. Although this may seem obvious, it is essential to fully appreciate the significance of political leadership if a regeneration project is to be properly conceptualized, implemented, and sustained. The longitudinal test of political leadership is whether the vision is sustained through changes in political and economic cycles—and whether it results not in community division but greater cohesion.

As regeneration is a long-term, transformative process of change that entails disruption and risk, political leadership is essential to managing the change process so that the "city," that is, the multiple constituencies ranging from corporate and business chief executives to local residents, feels engaged in the process, understands its importance to the future of the city, and has genuine outlets in which to participate.

It is in the nature of the regeneration projects that their benefits are often not realized and experienced until much later, whereas the sacrifices (budget trade-offs), risks (investment of public funds), and hardships (such as residential and business displacement) are experienced up front in the early years of the project. Therefore, the political leadership must provide the confidence that the costs and benefits of regeneration are in the best interests of the city. Communicating this effectively and openly is essential.

Figure 1.7   Implementation phase of the urban regeneration process

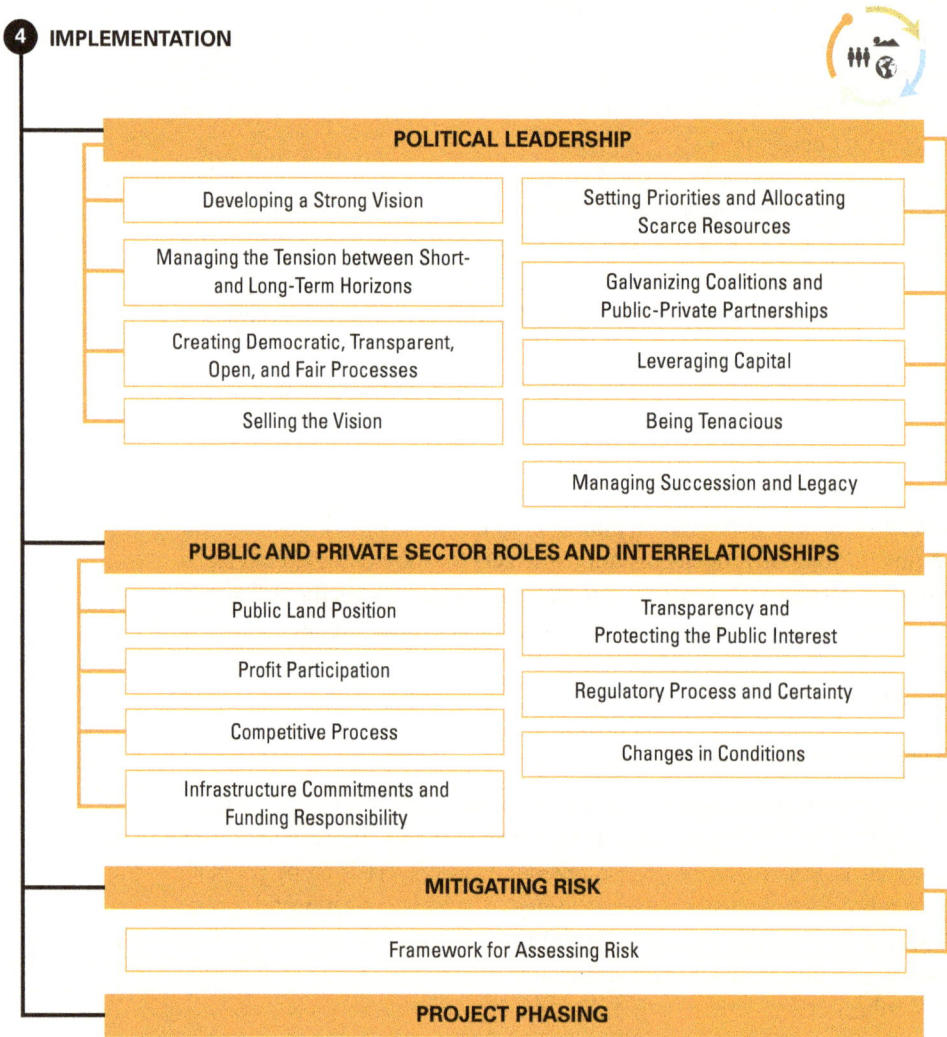

4 IMPLEMENTATION

POLITICAL LEADERSHIP

Developing a Strong Vision	Setting Priorities and Allocating Scarce Resources
Managing the Tension between Short- and Long-Term Horizons	Galvanizing Coalitions and Public-Private Partnerships
Creating Democratic, Transparent, Open, and Fair Processes	Leveraging Capital
Selling the Vision	Being Tenacious
	Managing Succession and Legacy

PUBLIC AND PRIVATE SECTOR ROLES AND INTERRELATIONSHIPS

Public Land Position	Transparency and Protecting the Public Interest
Profit Participation	Regulatory Process and Certainty
Competitive Process	Changes in Conditions
Infrastructure Commitments and Funding Responsibility	

MITIGATING RISK

Framework for Assessing Risk

PROJECT PHASING

Can Political Leadership Help Achieve Consensus?

It is important to recognize that because of the complex and often controversial nature of regeneration initiatives where multiple constituencies are affected, not everyone will agree that they are in the best interests of the city. It is therefore important not to enter into the regeneration process with the expectation that consensus will be possible. Even though consensus is always desirable, it may not be achievable.

Although consensus may be elusive—even in cases where the benefits are clear, the process fair, open, and transparent, and participation encouraged—the lack of consensus should not, in and of itself, be a reason for rejecting the project. At this point, political leadership becomes crucial. The weighing of public benefit, the responsiveness to constituencies, and the articulation of a longer-term vision of the city are the unique responsibility of political leaders. Box 1.16 describes the role of continuous political leadership in regeneration projects in selected cities.

What Can Strong Political Leadership Do?

Some of the key lessons that are important to take into consideration in developing the case for political support for regeneration include:

- *Developing a strong vision.* The importance of developing a strong vision for the regeneration process has been noted. The core idea and aspiration of the regeneration project must be clearly articulated and accepted in the iconography and identity of the city. Political leadership is essential in articulating and promoting the vision. The city leader (mayor, chief planner) represents the interests of the city at large. Indeed, the leader is often seen as the political embodiment of the aspirations of the broader public interest and populace. This is

Box 1.16   Continuous political leadership can ensure the success of regeneration projects

The case study of the Anacostia Waterfront Initiative in Washington, DC, is instructive in demonstrating how a vision conceptualized and launched by Mayor Anthony A. Williams in 2000 has been sustained through two successive mayors. In fact, it has become an accepted feature of any regeneration program for the city. The Anacostia waterfront is now firmly embedded in the cognitive map of the city, where it once was invisible except to those who lived next to the river. It is now almost inconceivable that the future of Washington, DC, can be spoken of without reference to the success of the Anacostia Waterfront Initiative. It is a testament to the power of political leadership in promulgating a vision, galvanizing support, and laying the foundation for generational change.

A similar story has played out in modern Barcelona. Indeed, it continues to build on a vision for the city conceived of over 25 years ago when Mayor Pasqual Maragal envisioned the Olympics as a means of putting the city on the map and transforming it from a decaying, provincial, industrial port into a global city. Since then, through successive mayors, the city has actively engaged in a continuous process of transformation, always finding new ways to innovate. Indeed, it now finds itself again at the forefront of urban transformation as the center of the "smart cities" movement.

The recent successful legacy of the 2012 London Olympics is another example of the power of a political vision to transform one of the most socioeconomically distressed areas of the United Kingdom. The most salient lesson of the London Olympics is that it was born and conceptualized as a means to implement a vision for the growth and regeneration of London that had broad political support. Indeed, it had been in progress for decades. Thus, the legacy of the London Olympics was the driving premise of the bid that London submitted to win. It was the foundation of the master plan, investment program, and institutional structure developed to implement the bid once the city was selected. The vision for regeneration was the starting point for the London Olympic legacy and not an afterthought, as is so often the case in such mega events.

why the role of the city leader is so critical to regeneration and the shaping of the city's future.

- *Managing the tension between short- and long-term horizons.* Regeneration requires a long-term perspective and commitment that is usually beyond the elected tenure of city leaders and officials. Hence, long-term regeneration projects can be complicated given short-term political demands, constituencies, and professional aspirations that have to be satisfied. Mayors, city leaders, governors, and political leaders are in the unique but difficult position of navigating this dynamic.
- *Creating democratic, transparent, open, and fair processes.* Regeneration must be rooted in a democratic process that allows for a diversity of voices, interest groups, and constituencies. Whether regeneration is focused on a small area of the city or is part of a larger city-wide project, the regeneration process must be fair, open, and transparent to have credibility. Although there may not be full agreement on the regeneration project, it is important that there be an opportunity for open participation so that the vision and merits of the project are fully vetted. This must be the case both with respect to the planning and to the implementation phases of the project involving budgets, investments, contracts, and so on. These critical implementation actions must be approved in public processes characterized by open and transparent competition. Political leadership is therefore vital in creating and enforcing these processes if they do not exist, or using existing vehicles for political participation to ensure the process is widely known and advertised.
- *Selling the vision.* Regeneration projects require the patient persuasion of a large group of constituencies in order to succeed. Political leadership and tenacity is essential in selling the vision and building support to make the hard choices regarding allocation of resources. Political leaders are key to building excitement about the future and articulating the benefits of regeneration, as well as any trade-offs that may be required. Such trade-offs often include controversial notions of investing for the future versus satisfying current needs. Without political leadership to articulate the vision and a larger purpose for the regeneration program, it is at risk of dissolving from divided constituencies.
- *Setting priorities and allocating scarce resources.* Political leadership is a prerequisite to the allocation of scarce public resources that are often required to catalyze regeneration. These constitute the down payment and provide confidence to the private sector to invest and take risks. The public sector is normally the first mover in major regeneration projects. As such, it entails leadership to overcome doubts, commit resources, and manage controversies.
- *Galvanizing coalitions and public-private partnerships.* Political leaders play a vital role as facilitators and conveners of constituencies and organizations. The forging of PPPs, particularly in the early stages of regeneration, occurs through the building of relationships

and networks that are persuaded of the value of regeneration and committed to its success. While more formal processes, such as procurement, will be important when land is disposed of or financial incentives are disbursed, the stage has to be set for the participation of private, civic, and community partnerships. This is when political leaders can play a key role, whether the public sector is an instigator of regeneration or a supporter of private efforts.

- *Leveraging capital.* The scale and complexity of most large regeneration projects—and the up-front investment usually required for infrastructure, often before there is a proven market that can guarantee private returns on capital—requires the leveraging of public and private resources and the sharing of risks. This usually entails securing multiple sources of funding from a broad range of sectors. Organizing the early and patient capital is a daunting task unless a city is in the fortunate position and has the rare opportunity to enlist a large, single, well-capitalized backer, such as the state or a large landowner or philanthropist. Political leadership is essential to identifying and obtaining these funds, whether through advocacy, informal relationships, or formal petitions for funds. Mayors, governors, and political leaders play a critical role often as "fundraiser in chief" to kick-start regeneration.

- *Being tenacious.* Regeneration is a long-term endeavor. As such, it requires unusual fortitude and patience. Political leadership is essential to maintaining focus and sustaining the regeneration effort through the inevitable controversies, conflicts, and disagreements among constituencies that occur in any large, transformational effort. Without political leadership, regeneration projects can become stymied and lose momentum, which in turn can result in a loss of confidence and the failure of many efforts. Political leadership must also be deft enough to respond to genuine concerns and critiques of the regeneration effort. Likewise, political leaders should be open to modifications and improvements in response to issues as they arise, thereby making for a better and more-widely accepted project.

- *Managing succession and legacy.* Finally, political succession is very important. It is the rare political leader who will be in office from the beginning to the end of regeneration projects. In most cases, the full realization can often take a decade. The power of the vision, the success in forging coalitions, and the embedding of the regeneration program in the spirit of the city can help build confidence. This requires broad and lasting political leadership during the various tenures of political leaders.

It should also be noted that the success of the regeneration program should *not* be dependent on any one political leader or party. Rather, it should become accepted as a fundamental driver of the city's future, irrespective of political change.

Public and Private Sector Roles and Interrelationships

As regeneration is a long-term undertaking entailing significant interaction between the public and private sectors, the form and content of the PPPs are crucial to ensuring that goals are achieved. Strong PPPs can help ensure that the public interest is protected. In this context, investors and developers can have greater confidence in the integrity of, and commitment to, the program over the long term.

In structuring PPPs, it is important to first be clear about the basics of what the proposed regeneration program will require of both parties and how these requirements may change over time. The key elements that need to be clarified early so that there is no uncertainty as to roles, responsibilities, and obligations include a number of factors listed here.

- *Public land position.* The control of land is a core consideration in the structure of regeneration contracts. It can be a great source of vulnerability and dispute if not skillfully negotiated. The contract needs to define clearly how the public land is being used for regeneration. There are several options for the use of public land, which have been noted. Land can be used in the form of a subsidy or it could be leased or sold to the private sector. Alternatively, the public sector can use the land as an equity contribution and recoup some form of profits at a later date when the project stabilizes. Whichever model is chosen, it is important to spell out the important details of utilizing the public land parcel. A summary of these considerations is detailed in table 1.3.
- *Profit participation.* In structuring contracts, it is necessary to determine whether the public sector wants to receive some amount of land value early as a payment, or whether it would participate in a profit stream if and when the project generates more value over time. Time is a critical variable in how the public sector structures the contracts. Much will depend on how patient the public sector is in receiving returns on its investments, whether in the form of land receipts, loan repayments, or equity contributions to business growth.
- *Competitive process.* It is critical that a competitive process be instituted and rigorously followed for negotiating contracts, selecting development partners, and disposing of land. In this way, the credibility of the regeneration project can be assured, and the best value achieved. The public sector itself must be assured that the process is fair, transparent, and open to competition. It is best if the process is not a closed one favoring "insiders" or a preselected (or politically selected) favored group. However, in some cases like the Xintiandi redevelopment in Shanghai, a tendering process was not initiated due to very special circumstances and the relationship that the government already had established with one developer. To ensure that the competition is successful, there must be clear criteria for selection with objective standards, a selection process that is managed by objective persons with subject matter expertise, and

Table 1.3 **Potential complexities in public land contracting**

Contract item	Action	Potential complexities and problems
Land required and its usage	Determine the amount of land needed.	The public sector has to determine the amount of land needed as efficiently as possible because land is a nonrenewable resource.
The time frame for usage or transfer	The public sector must protect itself from land being transferred to the private sector prematurely, thereby losing control of it.	The public sector needs to guard against land banking whereby large tracts of land are transferred to the private sector before they are actually needed. This would enable the private sector to hold the land and accrue value without actually developing the land.
Phasing of land transfers and identifying parcels to be transferred in each phase	The public sector has to be very cautious in identifying the parcels it will transfer, including the timing and conditions under which they will be transferred. The disposition of land according to a clear phasing plan and clear conditions for the transfer is a core term that must be negotiated.[a]	Without a phasing plan for transfers, the most valuable parcels could be transferred prematurely at discounted values before the larger regeneration program has had time to stabilize and create added value. This will result in financial loss for the public sector.
The price of land	Multiphased regeneration projects require clarity as to the base prices, price escalations, terms, and timing of land transfers between parties.	The land arrangement between the public and private sectors can be subject to arbitrary renegotiation if the contract fails to balance certainty with protection of the public interest.
"Claw-back" clause	It must be clear what the recourse is if parties do not perform, such as not initiating or completing construction, and whether land can be "clawed back."	The risk here is that a private sector party could gain control of the land but without having the necessary capacity or capital to develop it. This would result in stagnation of the regeneration project.

Note: A claw-back clause is a special contractual clause, in which the grantor of the contract reserves the right to limit compensation or other benefits in case the grantee does not deliver on promised services.
a. One example of negotiated transfers can be found in the Shanghai case study, chapter 6.

broad advertisement of the contract process to assure the widest net for participants.

- *Infrastructure commitments and funding responsibility.* Urban regeneration is usually paired with development of a major piece of infrastructure. Funding infrastructure costs is a big determinant in structuring regeneration contracts. It is critical to have clarity as to who is responsible for funding and delivering infrastructure. Whether the public sector has the funding required for the significant up-front investment will determine how financing is structured and whether it will take a more traditional form of direct capital investment or government-backed bonds. If such funding is not readily available, private financing will be necessary. Although private financing of infrastructure may entail higher capital costs, it can supply the resources needed to jumpstart the project. In such cases, contracts should be structured in a way to oblige the private sector to build with maximum quality, best value, and on-time delivery. In order to achieve this, there must be a vigorous and transparent competitive process. Finally, the schedule, obligations, and penalties for not meeting the schedule must also be clear and agreed to in the contract.

In the case of the development of the Navy Yard area of the Anacostia Waterfront Initiative in Washington, DC, the private developer selected for the project was tasked with the adaptive reuse of historical industrial buildings and the construction of new buildings for residential, office, and retail use. The Navy Yard project is worth about US$1.5 billion, and the city's contribution amounted to about US$42 million. City officials justified the subsidy as a way to ensure that the site was redeveloped as a mixed-use project.

- *Transparency and protecting the public interest.* When public-private contracts are developed and negotiated, transparency is vital so that all interests are clear. The contracts should not be subject to allegations of corruption or "soft deals." It is also important for the public sector, which has a fiduciary responsibility regarding the use of public funds or assets, to ensure transparency regarding the financial proposals, funding capacity, and company financial status (accounting reports on its status). In doing so, the public sector will help to guarantee that proper and forensic due diligence is conducted to ensure the soundness of the proposed terms of private sector participation.

But what if the public goals are not achieved and regeneration stalls and is not delivered? It is very important to think through all of the ways in which the project might *not* succeed. The public sector cannot regulate for all these outcomes, as it would create a legal barrier to executing the contract and may preclude private sector participation. However, it is important that key protections are in place, such as phasing and performance conditions for the transfer of public land ownership and protecting against land-banking; claw-backs of funding if not expended; clear definition of profits and when and how the public will participate; adherence to loan terms or financial arrangements; and so on.

- *Regulatory process and certainty.* The time and cost of regulatory uncertainty creates a barrier to investment and can be an impediment to private investment. The contract must clearly specify the timeline, milestones, and incentives to achieve approvals. In London, which is a strong market, many local boroughs enter into Planning Performance Agreements whereby the developer pays a specified amount to fund staff to work on the processing of approvals. In other situations in which the public sector is understaffed or lacks expertise, the government may have to create special regulations or zones with simplified approval processes or delegate the process to a special entity. This was the case in Ahmedabad, India, where the local government delegated the implementation of the Sabarmati riverfront to a local planning consultancy (see box 1.17).

Changes in Conditions

Although changes in market and political conditions cannot be fully anticipated, the contracts must contain provisions for such contingencies, including a process to negotiate changes, should they be required. These provisions cannot be so loose or generic as to render the contract meaningless or without "teeth," but neither can they be so onerous as to prohibit revisiting certain terms, should conditions change. For example, there may be certain expected outcomes that are fundamental to the public sector (such as affordable housing percentages or profit-sharing formulas that can only change if the government passes new legislation). Nonetheless, future governments should be permitted to modify terms if policy changes over time.

Box 1.17 Implementation strategy for the Sabarmati riverfront development in Ahmedabad, India

In redeveloping the Sabarmati riverfront in Ahmedabad, the board of the Sabarmati River Front Development Corporation Limited (SRFDCL) was tasked with developing a project implementation strategy. Initially, there were three broad options for managing the implementation:

- Implement the project by building capacity in-house
- Partner with a private real estate development firm
- Hire private sector consultants for development management services

In their discussions, the SRFDCL considered the merits of all three options. Regarding the first option, it would have been difficult to hire the requisite expertise in-house, and the newly hired staff would have been a liability for the company once the project was completed (which at the time was estimated to be within five years). There was an option to use some of the municipal staff from the Ahmedabad Municipal Corporation on deputation to the company. Deputed municipal staff members would have followed bureaucratic processes, which would have slowed the functioning of the company. Importantly, it would have taken away one of the key advantages of having a special purpose vehicle, that is, the ability to make quick decisions.

The second option of partnering with a private real estate developer was rejected for two reasons. The primary reason was that selecting and appointing a developer partner would have entailed significant political risk. This approach would have left the decision makers vulnerable to criticism that the valuable riverfront land was being sold off to private interests. Secondly, entering into partnership with a private real estate developer may have required an increase in the percentage of land to be set aside for sale. This in turn would have reduced the available land for public amenities and might have negatively affected the public perception of the project.

Instead, the SRFDCL board chose the third option, that is, to outsource the development management services. In 1999, a local planning consultancy was selected as development manager to administer the initial stages of project planning and implementation of the Sabarmati Riverfront Development. The government had worked with this consultancy before and had a positive relationship with them. This allowed the company to leverage its private-sector expertise in managing the project while, at the same time, maintaining full project ownership and decision-making authority.

Source: Authors' elaboration based on the Ahmedabad case study in chapter 7.

The private sector may want the ability to have extensions of time to deliver the project, should market conditions not be favorable to investment. In this context, they do not want to be held responsible for externalities beyond their control. All of these considerations must be carefully weighed so as to provide the flexibility needed to manage change on both sides—without sacrificing the core terms.

In Santiago, Chile, during the implementation of the Repopulation Program, the municipal master plan was modified 29 times. These changes sought to either allow more density and height in some areas, or to restrict and lower the height of the buildings—including the definition of areas of patrimonial protection (Arraigada, Moreno, and Rovirosa 2007). The real estate sector has taken advantage of the flexibility allowed by the master plan. The number of both floors and housing units per building has increased three times. The average number of floors is 13, the number of housing units per building is 176, and the average size of each unit is 69.6 square meters (sq m) (For details, see chapter 5.)

A 2004 World Bank report found that 41 percent of infrastructure concessions in Latin America were renegotiated (mostly in the transportation sector). In all of these cases, the government had to renegotiate the contracts within two years of initiation. This fact undermines all of the benefits of a bidding process, turning it into bilateral negotiations between the selected developer and the government. In these cases, the private sector developer or operator usually has significant leverage because the project has already started. Therefore, it is difficult and inefficient for the government to deny renegotiations and start a new bidding process. World Bank findings (2004) suggest that in order to reduce the risk of renegotiations, contracts should include clauses that forbid renegotiations—except in the case of well-defined triggers. Furthermore, in the case of ostensibly aggressive bids, which may seem better than other submitted bids, the government should develop a detailed analysis before a contract is awarded.

In some cases, the private sector can be obliged to post performance bonds of significant value. It is notable that in some instances, it is the government that initiates renegotiations. This was the case in Shanghai, China, when halfway through the project, the government changed the terms of the contract and the private developer had to comply. For more details, see box 1.18.

Project Phasing

In order to ensure the implementation of large-scale regeneration projects, they need to be broken down into manageable project components. The hand-over process must account for the complex set of interdependencies between the large-scale investments and construction projects, such as major infrastructure (utilities, transport, park systems, brownfields cleanup), and the microdelivery of commercial and residential projects that need to establish a "sense of place" and completion—even though the ultimate build-out of the regeneration project will progress over a long period of time.

Box 1.18   Government-initiated renegotiations in the development of Taipingqiao in Shanghai, China

In the case of the development of Taipingqiao in Shanghai, China, the Shanghai municipal government renegotiated the terms of the contract in 2003 by introducing the policy of "double increase and double decrease." This policy was applied to the central city and required an increase in green open space as part of new developments. At the same time, the gross floor area (GFA) of these developments was decreased to improve the environmental quality of the central city. The change in policy affected many ongoing projects in downtown Shanghai, including the Taipingqiao redevelopment. The allowed GFA was decreased by 16.8 percent.

The original GFA approved by the government in the master plan of the Taipingqiao neighborhood was 1.64 million square meters (sq m). With the new policy, it was decreased to 1.25 million sq m. The private developer, Shui On Land Limited (SoLL) participated in the negotiations with the local government regarding the total GFA. Throughout these negotiations, SoLL reiterated the importance of the location of Taipingqiao to the central city of Shanghai, where a reasonable density was needed. SoLL demanded a minimum GFA to ensure the balance of costs and benefits. The district government was caught between delivering the policy of the Shanghai municipal government while also trying to protect the interests of the developer. A higher GFA meant higher rents and subsequently higher revenues for the district government, which relied on the land rents. The final figure of the decrease was settled in 2005 at 390,000 sq m of floor area, which maintained the 1.25 million sq m as the development volume for the entire Taipingqiao redevelopment area.

Source: Based on the case study of Xintiandi Shanghai in chapter 6.

It is therefore important to clearly map out the life of the project, including the expected project cycle and phases as best as possible, while also accounting for uncertainties. Once mapped, a series of critical questions can be asked that will generate hand-over options as the basis of agreements between the public, private, and other sectors (civic, community) to codify the regeneration process. This will help to ensure project continuity and clarity of roles, responsibilities, and interdependencies. The nature of the hand over differs depending on whether it is a private sector or public sector-led regeneration process. In this regard, it should be noted that these roles can also change and reverse over the life of the project.

Table 1.4 provides an example of the type of high-level summary table that can be created to illustrate the phases, roles, relationships, and organization necessary for a successful regeneration project. This can be expanded and adapted to meet the scope, focus, and local circumstances of the regeneration project.

In many cases, the implementation outline and phasing schedule are major parts of a master plan, highlighting the timetable and phasing for the delivery of the site's development. This will give the government and the community an indication of how development will be staged with infrastructure and services provision and will provide the reasoning for the

Table 1.4   Summary of phases and organization of a regeneration project

Project Phase	Public sector	Private sector	Other sectors	Critical interdependencies
Vision				
Project concept				
Master planning				
Regulations				
Land assembly				
Infrastructure delivery				
Vertical development				
Social infrastructure				
Maintenance				
Design review				

chosen phasing order. The phasing of the development should be described, detailing which elements will be built first and which later, which decisions should be made early, and which should be allowed to evolve in response to future opportunities.

The phasing should be planned around the potential to deliver infrastructure. It should also take into account any relocation of people, sale or rental of land, the property market, possible movement issues, land ownership patterns, funding availability, and relevant planning processes and legislation. It is important to note that phasing a project does not mean that each phase should be done consecutively; in cases of extreme urgency, project phases could be implemented in parallel to each other. However, this arrangement will need better coordination between various actors. An example of this is outlined in box 1.19 and table B1.19.1 summarizes the alternative phasing strategy in the restoration of the Cheonggyecheon stream in Seoul.

A good illustration of the importance of the master plan and phasing is the case of the Taipingqiao development in Shanghai, China. The master plan for the whole area included cultural, entertainment, hotel/retail, office, housing, open space, and other uses, such as education facilities, infrastructure, and other public facilities. Box 1.20 and map B1.20.1 show how the Asian financial crisis changed the phasing strategy of the project. The example also shows that with a robust master plan and clear phasing schedule, various risks and shocks to the process could be mitigated.

Mitigating Risks

Urban regeneration projects are risky by definition. There are many barriers to overcome in building successful PPP models for regeneration areas.

Box 1.19 **Parallel phasing strategy in restoration of the Cheonggyecheon stream in Seoul, Republic of Korea**

The restoration of the Cheonggyecheon stream in Seoul is different from other case studies in this volume in that the planning and construction phases overlapped. The construction work started on July 1, 2003, six months after the "Cheonggyecheon Restoration Master Plan" had started and one year before the plan was completed.

The final design was completed during the construction period, which took two years and three months from the start date. The planning, design, and construction were done simultaneously and not linearly. The process was controversial, but it saved money and time. This was crucial in the process of negotiating with merchants and commercial property owners, as they were concerned about disruption to their businesses and potential financial losses. By combining the planning, design, and construction phases, the time required for completion of the project was minimized. The speed and low cost of the restoration works was outstanding compared to other cases in the world. Table B1.19.1 compares the efficiency of the Cheonggyecheon restoration work with other projects of similar nature and scope.

Table B1.19.1 **Comparing the Cheonggyecheon restoration project to similar projects around the world**

Project	Time	Scale (km)	Cost (US$)	Cost/km (US$)
Cheonggyecheon, Korea, Rep.	2003–05	5.8	345 million	59 million
The High Line, New York City (Section 1,2)	2003–14	1.6	152 million	95 million
Big Dig, Boston, Massachusetts	1982–2007	12	22 billion	1.833 billion
Sanjicheon, Korea, Rep.	1997–2002	0.47	33 million	69 million

Source: Rowe 2010, and the case study of Cheonggyecheon revitalization in Seoul in chapter 8.

The private sector will not invest in regeneration areas without a substantial public sector commitment. The role of the public sector is to create confidence in a regeneration area as an investment location and reduce the level of risk for investors. This can be achieved through various mechanisms, as seen in table 1.5.

Public sector participation in urban regeneration projects is especially key when there is a sizable risk for the private sector. The public sector is able to bring to the table direct kinds of financing, including through land and subsidies. Different types of risks have varying degrees of incidence throughout the project's life cycle. Risks can include (a) project risks (problems that arise during project implementation); (b) commercial risks (linked to economic cycles and expectations of players in the real estate sector); (c) external risks (such as demands from community groups and civil society organizations); and (d) political risks (related to political stability and policy and regulatory changes) (Lindfield 1998).

Table 1.5   Framework for assessing and mitigating risks

Risk	Description/questions to identify risks	Mitigation measures/examples
Political	Political risk can have a negative impact during the entire project cycle and can take a variety of forms, including: • Political instability • Disagreements between various public sector actors involved in the project over technical aspects or plain political opposition • Differences between a mayor and municipal council are common and can affect project implementation • Accusations of corruption from involved officials	Create a broad political consensus based on a long-term vision for the project area. Create a project advisory board for supervision.
Financial	Constraints on economic management can be posed by fiscal and foreign trade imbalances; economic volatility and extremes; health of the country economy; and quality of economic management. Other financial risks include: • Exchange-rate (for foreign capital) risks • Interest-rate risks • Inflation risks • Counterpart risks	The negative impact of some of the risks can be reduced with financial products available on the market. For example, project risks related to the quality of capital investments (such as delays in the delivery of inputs, quality defects of materials and execution of construction, and even the impact of natural disasters) may be covered by insurance. The foreign exchange risk may be covered by financial instruments, such as hedging offered by international financial institutions. The use of these instruments allows for the pricing of risks and including them in the financing plans. Access to insurance and other forms of hedging depend on how developed the financial markets are in the country.
Technical	What is the level of dependence of project design on untested or unfamiliar technologies or processes? Is there a lack of local technical expertise for project management, design aspects, and the structure of PPPs?	Local governments can hire technical experts as needed to support project implementation.
Environmental	One of the main risks affecting economic viability for some urban regeneration projects is that of unknown environmental hazards resulting from former site use(s). Remediation experiences of former industrial sites have shown that the magnitude of these contaminations can be extraordinary, often aggravated by having crossed property boundaries and harmed third parties. In other cases, the proven contamination is much less serious than had been feared. The cost of dealing with past environmental liabilities can be a multiple of property values. Liability is a particularly important issue. It is considered by many to be the main barrier to urban redevelopment, especially in brownfields. Indeed, it can affect the process in several different ways. For the land owner, contamination that is a threat to human health or the environment can potentially bring with it civil lawsuits or government fines. For a developer, liability can mean that future revenues and profitability of redevelopment can be affected by potential legal costs stemming from people's exposure to contamination that was not removed or identified.	Good mitigating practices include (a) incorporating environmental issues in technical feasibility studies and consultation processes with the community and stakeholders; (b) obtaining required approvals by relevant regulatory bodies; and (c) designing an action plan and remediation strategy and identifying sources of financing.

Table 1.5   Framework for assessing and mitigating risks *(continued)*

Risk	Description/questions to identify risks	Mitigation measures/examples
	For a lending institution, potential defaults on loans can mean that the institution will be stuck with a site it cannot easily resell because of environmental issues. For an insurance company, the risks of complicated or unknown pollution are often too high for them to become involved in the process. For a local authority, liability is often what prevents the redevelopment, as private partners become reluctant to get involved.	
Land ownership and regulation	Ownership and legal covenants can bring with them a number of problems. If the site is in private or mixed ownership, the owners might change their minds during the process, bringing the redevelopment to a halt or delaying it. Similarly, an incoherent legal framework can hamper redevelopment goals and can push costs beyond initial assessments. Changes in the land-use plan and/or the development scheme can make the project infeasible for the developer. An unreliable or inconsistent performance by regulators can create inconsistencies that affect project efficiency.	To counter ownership and legal covenant hurdles, good legal specialists should be hired. Solid contracts should be signed with all vested parties. Government rules and regulations may change mid-project (often with a change of government), but conditions at the time of signing should be kept through project implementation—unless new rules prove to be more favorable.
Stakeholders	Project stakeholders' views about how the project meets or conflicts with their priorities and needs is another risk, as is opposition from neighborhood groups. • How do the various categories of stakeholders view the project? • How are their needs or views being taken into account? Are there any outstanding or contentious issues? • Is there any participatory planning mechanism involved? • Is there a possibility that investment benefits will not be shared equally among social groups, especially between women and men, indigenous peoples, ethnic communities, and other disadvantaged groups?	Stakeholder risks can be reduced through a transparent and participatory process to determine the project's goals, components, and investment priorities. The involvement of key stakeholders in program decisions increases the likelihood that their interests will be reflected in project design. It also reduces the incidence of opposition during project execution.
Implementation (fiduciary risk)	What is the extent to which there is a comprehensive and credible budget linked to the project? This includes a sound procurement law and generally good procurement practices and good contract management in the public sector.	Well-planned procurement and a clear plan for implementation are key to mitigating this risk.
Commercial	What is the risk of selling the redeveloped properties? The long development and implementation period of an urban regeneration project faces commercial risks that are difficult to mitigate, particularly those related to changes in the business cycle that affect demand, rate of sale, and real estate prices.	When facing problems that normally lead to falling demand or prices, developers often delay execution, delaying implementation of projects under preparation. Other commercial risks such as late payments by property buyers may be reduced by transferring mortgages to third parties or by obtaining mortgage insurance. This type of risk is difficult to contain. Developers can conduct realistic market studies to try to minimize it. The analysis of different city growth scenarios and their impact on the commercial aspects of the program allows developers to fine tune the sizing and phasing of investments. This helps to minimize the adverse effects of changes in the economic cycle.

Box 1.20   The phasing plan for the Taipingqiao development in Shanghai, China

The Master Plan of the Taipingqiao neighborhood allowed for a 10–15 year development process, starting from the southern residential area. The investment return from housing was supposed to support the construction of the Taipingqiao Lake and Park. However, the Asian Financial Crisis of 1997 caused a dramatic decrease in demand for housing and office space. Therefore, the private developer, Shui On Land Limited (SoLL), adjusted the phasing plan, deferring housing development and giving priority to conservation of the historic fabric. The municipal and district governments decided to initiate the construction of the Taipingqiao Park. The strategy aimed at evading market risk while improving the image of the Taipingqiao area. This preparatory work on the site meant that when the financial situation improved and the crisis was over, investment demand soared as the potential of the area was already being realized.

Map B1.20.1 presents the timeline for development of the Taipingqiao neighborhood, showing projects with public space/use elements (from location numbers 1 to 8) and the remaining 6 phases of totally private development. The redevelopment was implemented from east to west and from north to south. The rationale for the phasing plan was to capture the increasing property value brought by the Xintiandi and Taipingqiao parks. The redevelopment process also followed the logic of block location, market demand, and relocation costs.

Map B1.20.1   Master plan of the Taipingqiao neighborhood and changes in the phasing plan

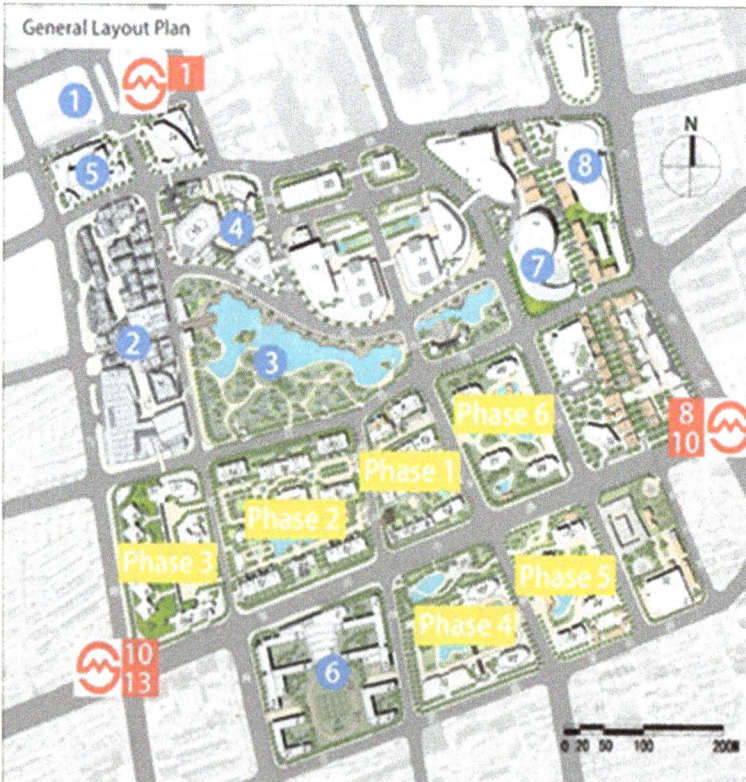

Source: Shui On Land Limited, based on the case study of Shanghai in chapter 6.
Note: The red boxes represent metro lines.

The choice of the components of the regeneration project is an important factor in encouraging private sector participation with regard to financing and implementation. A key element for success is to ensure that the project's components adequately meet the interests of all stakeholders in the process. Ideally, a project should include a combination of public interest investments (improving roads and infrastructure, sanitation and drainage, public parks and playgrounds, cultural monuments, public-use buildings) and commercial investments of interest to the private sector. These can include space for offices, shops, malls, hotels, restaurants, convention centers, and housing. In these cases, mixed-use developments can provide a good design framework for coexistence and complementarity.

Notes

1. For more information on social and environmental concerns, see chapter 2 (Second Asset: Community) and chapter 3.
2. The concept of a creative class was defined by U.S. economist Richard Florida as the socioeconomic class that drives the growth of postindustrial American cities. This classification refers to workers in the so-called knowledge economy as well as the labor force active in creative and innovative industries, including engineers and scientists, designers, artists, architects, and educators. Florida believes that a large part of the postindustrial economy in the United States is driven and will be driven by such creative classes.
3. See chapter 2 for a detailed description of charrettes.
4. Eminent domain is the right of governments to expropriate private property for public use with compensation.
5. We refrain from using the term *joint venture* because in a broader international context there is no single definition of joint ventures. They are more commonly understood as separate legal entities created for a specific purpose (as opposed to contractual relations between parties).
6. Exceptions, of course, exist. Masdar City in Abu Dhabi, capital of the United Arab Emirates, for example, is a planned city in which the majority of its approximately US$20 billion budget has been provided by the Abu Dhabi federal government.
7. It is notable that "local" government may mean different things in different countries. In India, state governments possess much of the decision-making power at the city level. In China, the power is decentralized to the level of district governments, which is one level lower than the city government. In Brazil, the city governments are powerful local entities.
8. There are only three scenarios in which municipalities are allowed to generate private tenders or provide direct contracting, including

(a) in cases of emergency, (b) in cases in which no supplier responded to the public tender, and (c) in cases in which contracts that correspond to the completion or termination of a contract had to be terminated early due to lack of the contractor's compliance or other reasons, and whose remainder does not exceed US$38,000.

9. See Bryant Park, Bryant Park Corporation, New York, http://www .bryantpark.org/.
10. The floor space index is the ratio between the total built-up area and plot area available allowed by the planning department of a city.
11. See government of South Africa, http://www.gov.za/sites/www.gov.za /files/a45-03.pdf.

References

Arraigada, Camilo, Juan Cristóbal Moreno, and Enrique Cartier Rovirosa. 2007. *Evaluación de impacto del subsidio de renovación urbana en el area metropolitana del Gran Santiago 1991–2006* [Evaluation of the impact of the urban renewal subsidy in the metropolitan area of Greater Santiago, 1991–2006]. Santiago, Chile: Ministry of Housing and Urban Development; Pehuen.

Blackmore, Courtenay. 1990. *The Client's Tale: The Role of the Client in Building Buildings.* London: RIBA Publications.

Borrero, Oscar, Esperanza Durán, Jorge Hernández, and Magda Montaña. 2011. "Evaluating the Practice of Betterment Levies in Colombia: The Experience of Bogotá and Manizales." Working Paper, Lincoln Institute of Land Policy, Cambridge, MA.

CABE (Commission for Architecture and the Built Environment). 2008. *Creating Successful Master Plans: A Guide for Clients.* London: CABE.

City of New York. 2014a. "Mayor de Blasio Unveils 'Housing New York': A Five-Borough, 10-Year Housing Plan To Protect And Expand Affordability." Official website for the City of New York. http://www1 .nyc.gov/office-of-the-mayor/news/199-14/mayor-de-blasio-housing -new-york--five-borough-10-year-housing-plan-protect-and#/0.

———. 2014b. Department of City Planning, Zoning, Glossary, Open Space Ratio, http://www.nyc.gov/html/dcp/html/zone/glos- sary.shtml.

Clark, Greg, Joe Huxley, and Debra Mountford. 2010. *Organising Local Economic Development: The Role of Development Agencies and Companies.* Paris: OECD. http://public.eblib.com/choice/publicfullre- cord.aspx?p=540158.

Contrucci, Pablo. 2000. "Repoblamiento del casco central de Santiago de Chile: Articulacion del sector publico y el sector privado" [Repopulation of the center of Santiago de Chile: coordination between the public and private sectors]. In *Desarrollo cultural y gestión en centros históricos* [Cultural development and the development of city management in historical city centers], edited by E. Carrión, 193–210. Quito, Ecuador: FLACSO.

Furman Center. 2013. "Should the Next Mayor Adopt a Mandatory Inclusionary Zoning Program That Requires Developers to Build or Preserve Affordable Housing Whenever They Build Market-Rate Housing?" In *10 Issues for NYC's Next Mayor*. Furman Center for Real Estate and Urban Policy, New York University.

Garner, Gerald. 2011. *Johannesburg: Ten Ahead: A Decade of Inner-City Regeneration*. Craighall Park: Double G Media.

Greenstein, Rosalind, and Yesim Sungu-Eryilmaz. 2004. *Recycling the City: The Use and Reuse of Urban Land*. Cambridge, MA: Lincoln Institute of Land Policy.

Growth Areas Authority. 2009. *Precinct Structure Planning Guidelines: Step 2: Preparing the Precinct Structure Plan*. Victoria, Australia: State Government of Victoria, Australia.

INE (National Statistics Institute, Chile). 2014. *Compendio Estadístico 2014*. [Statistical compendium]. Santiago, Chile: INE.

Kaganova, Olga. 2011. *International Experiences on Government Land Development Companies: What Can Be Learned?* Washington, DC: Urban Institute.

———. 2014. "Land Management as a Factor of Urbanization." Background paper for the Ethiopia Urbanization Review, World Bank, Washington, DC.

L. J. Ramos Brokers Immobiliarios. 2009. "Informe sobre Puerto Madero, el barrio más joven de la ciudad: La segunda globalización en Buenos Aires" [Report on Puerto Madero, the youngest neighborhood in the city: the second globalization in Buenos Aires]. *Informe del Mercado Immobiliario* (June). Buenos Aires: L. J. Ramos Brokers Immobiliarios.

Lindfield, M. 1998. *Institutions, Incentives and Risks: Preparing Markets for Private Financing of Urban Infrastructure*. Monograph 7. Brisbane: Australian Housing and Urban Research Institute.

Lynch, Kevin, Tridib Banerjee, and Michael Southworth. 1990. *City Sense and City Design: Writings and Projects of Kevin Lynch*. Cambridge, MA: MIT Press.

Martinez, R. 2006. "Densificar Santiago: Una receta equivocada" [Densifying Santiago: A bad recipe]. *DU & P: revista de diseño urbano y paisaje* 3 (8).

Miraftab, Faranak. 2007. "Governing Postapartheid Spatiality: Implementing City Improvement Districts in Cape Town." *Antipode* 39 (4): 602–26.

Parra, C., and C. Dooner. 2001. "Nuevas experiencias de concertacion publico-privada: las corporaciones para el desarrollo local" [New experiences and public-private partnership: corporations for local development]. *Medio ambiente y desarrollo* 42: 53.

Paul, Evans. 2007. "Mega-Brownfields Projects Use Tax Increment Financing as the Gap Closer." Northeast Midwest Institute. www.nemw .org/brownfields.htm.

Peterson, G. 2009. *Unlocking Land Values to Finance Urban Infrastructure.* Washington, DC: World Bank.

Peterson, George E., and Olga Kaganova. 2010. "Integrating Land Financing into Subnational Fiscal Management." Policy Research Working Paper, World Bank, Washington, DC.

Peyroux, Elisabeth. 2008. "City Improvement Districts in Johannesburg: An Examination of the Local Variations of the BID Model." In *Business Improvement Districts: Ein neues Governance-Modell aus Perspektive von Praxis und Stadtforschung* [Business improvement districts: a new governance model in view of practice and urban research], edited by Robert Pütz, 139–62. Geographische Handelsforschung [Research on the geography of trade] Series. Passau, Germany: L.I.T. Verlag.

Rowe, Peter, ed. 2010. *A City and its Stream*: The Cheonggyecheon *Restoration Project.* Seoul: Seoul Development Institute.

Sagalyn, Lynne B. 2007. "Land Assembly, Land Readjustment and Public/Private Redevelopment." http://ssrn.com/abstract=1344490 or http://dx.doi.org/10.2139/ssrn.1344490.

Valenzuela, Juan Pablo. 1997. "Descentralización Fiscal: Los Ingresos Muncipalies y Regionales en Chile" [Fiscal decentralization: municipal and regional revenues in Chile]. Politica Fiscal [Fiscal policy] Series 101. UN Economic Commission for Latin America and the Caribbean and Deutsche Gesellschaft für Internationale Zusammenarbeit, Santiago, Chile.

Verdugo, M. 2003. "Programa de repoblamiento comuna de Santiago: Un programa de gestion urbana" [The program to repopulate Santiago commune: an urban management program]. *Urbano* 6 (8): 9.

World Bank. 2004. *Involuntary Resettlement Sourcebook: Planning and Implementation in Development Projects.* Washigton, DC: World Bank.

———. 2009. *Land Tenure for Social and Economic Inclusion in Yemen: Issues and Opportunities.* Washington, DC: World Bank.

Yang, You-Ren, and Chih-hui Chang. 2007. "An Urban Regeneration Regime in China: A Case Study of Urban Redevelopment in Shanghai's Taipingqiao Area." *Urban Studies* 44 (9): 1809–26.

CHAPTER 2

Assets

Urban regeneration involves the interplay of public assets within a process as defined by the institutions and organizational arrangements of the city. The city uses these assets to jumpstart a regeneration project with a potentially immense impact in terms of success, reach, and quality of life. Ultimately, urban regeneration is not an end but a means to an end, namely, economic growth and the upward social mobility of residents.

The assets directly affected by the urban regeneration process are land, community, and the environment. It is important to note that both land and environmental assets could be associated with high public liabilities in cases where they require public spending for decontamination. In some cases, the liabilities could be higher than the land's actual market value, even after cleanup. Furthermore, in extreme cases, these liabilities can result in the formation of negative equity. This section addresses various tools to manage, protect, and leverage these assets for a more successful and over-arching urban regeneration project.

First Asset: Land

Land is the most valuable asset for municipal governments. For the sake of comparison, studies show that revenue generated by land sales can be comparable to urban capital spending or the size of government debt related to financing capital investments (Peterson 2009). An example of this is in Beijing, China, where the government leased public land to finance urban infrastructure. This sale amounted to 45 percent of total fiscal revenue (Y 92.8 billion). Similarly, the city government of Istanbul, Turkey, auctioned and sold an old municipal bus station and administrative building in 2007 for US$1.5 billion. Comparing this with its total municipal capital spending of US$994 million, one can see the potential of land financing. Similarly in Mumbai, India, the city gained US$1.2 billion from the sale of 13 hectares of land in the city's new financial center, totaling 10 times the city's capital spending in 2005 (Peterson 2009).

There are many ways that governments can leverage land for urban regeneration. Many of the tools have been covered in chapter 1. These tools include using land as a collateral for borrowing in capital markets or from local and national banks. They also include auctions and leaseholds. Yet, regardless of how land is used for revenue generation, a strong regulatory framework is usually necessary to maximize these benefits. Local and municipal governments in developing countries usually lack the necessary regulatory framework to manage their land assets efficiently.

Without such a regulatory framework, it is difficult to mitigate the risks associated with municipal level land asset management because the decisions regarding public land are usually long-lived and irreversible. Land is a limited and nonrenewable asset and urban land markets are extremely volatile (Peterson and Kaganova 2010). Furthermore, certain local governments use off-budget land sales to add to their operating expenses. Some other local governments use land assets as a collateral for bank loans, which creates a systemic risk connecting subnational debt to land markets (Peterson and Kaganova 2010). Many land sales and long-term leases are conducted through noncompetitive, nontransparent deals with the private sector, thereby increasing the risk of inefficiency and waste of this valuable public asset. These risks indicate the need for a strong and accountable regulatory system for public land assets, one that can increase fiscal transparency.

The section that follows covers issues related to land and the specific tools that governments can use to ensure that their land assets are managed efficiently. It starts with a summary of various types of land ownership in different cultural and political contexts and goes on to explain some of the common tools used in planning and managing public and private land parcels. Finally, this section describes land regulatory frameworks, which can later become tools for creating vibrant and regulated real estate markets. Figure 2.1 shows the content and hierarchy of the tools covered in this section.

Land Ownership Regimes

Planning for regeneration of under-used urban land starts with developing a clear understanding of the land ownership regime in the city. There are various regimes of land ownership or control. The most common categories are public, private, communal (including customary tenure), and endowments or trusts. A range of formal and informal land tenures can be found within each category. This is especially the case with regard to private tenure, which ranges from formal (whether freehold or leasehold) to a range of informal tenure regimes (for instance, formal land ownership with informal development in violation of planning or building codes, squatter land, and so on). Informal development is associated with a range of legality degrees depending

Figure 2.1 **Land tools**

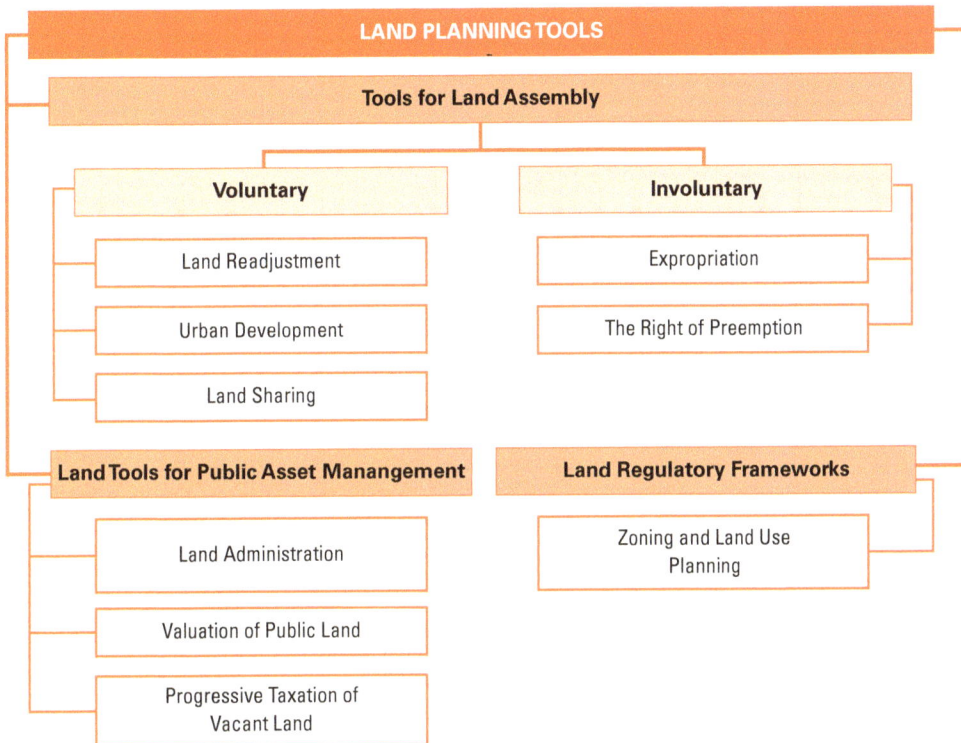

on the country's political and legal context, the length and nature of informal land occupancy, and the presence of adverse possession regulations and property disputes. For example, a study found out that there are seven categories of land tenure in Ahmedabad, India. This is illustrated in figure 2.2.

Public Land Ownership
Public land ownership refers to a government's ownership and control over land, including at the national, federal, and subnational (regional, provincial, and municipal) levels, as well as by state-owned enterprises. Public land controlled by the national or federal government typically falls into two categories: first, *the public domain of the state*, which encompasses land that the government maintains indefinite ownership or control over. This land is not available for alienation to private interests and includes land within cities, typically including bodies of water, public spaces, road rights-of-way, and other land on which government structures are situated, and land outside of cities, including areas that the government intends to preserve, protect, and maintain in their natural state for a variety of reasons. The government may wish to hold this land for environmental conservation (wetlands), public access (beach or waterfront use, security military facilities, and so on). The second category is *the private domain of the state*,

Figure 2.2   **Spectrum of land ownership in Ahmedabad, India**

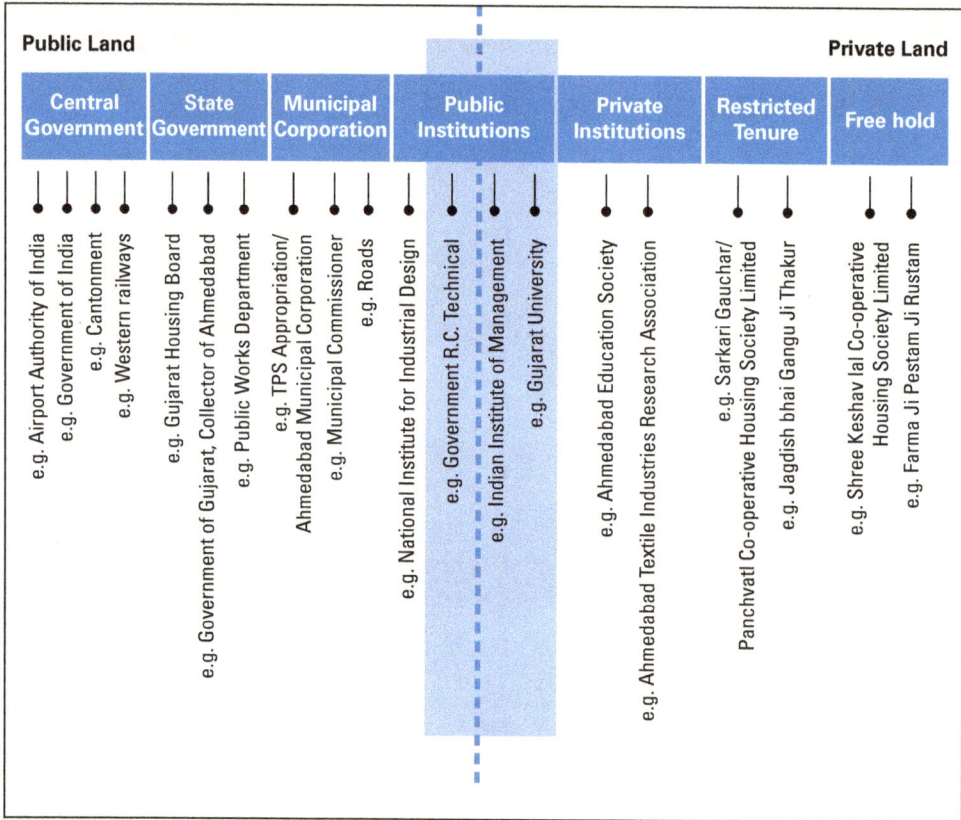

Source: Ballaney and others 2013.

which includes the lands that the state has designated for alienation or transfer to the private sector for exploitation and development into residential, commercial, administrative, or other land use, whether such transfers are through freehold, leasehold, usufruct, or other types of tenure form.

In several countries such as Ethiopia and Singapore, all land is publicly owned by the government. The land is allocated to private interests for use or development through long-term leaseholds or usufruct rights. Lengths of tenure vary between 25, 49, or 99 years and usually come with specific provisions for contract renewal. A similar situation is found in China, which to some extent is covered in the Xintiandi case study in chapter 6. In other countries, including the Arab Republic of Egypt, Kuwait, Saudi Arabia, and other Middle Eastern countries, all undeveloped desert land is controlled by the government. It is allocated to private interests through various tenure forms, including freehold, leasehold, usufruct, or *takhsis* (a form of conditional-use right in Egypt). In addition, various allocation mechanisms are used including auctions of freehold or leasehold rights, sales or leases based on administratively set prices, land grants, and so on.

Private Land Ownership

Private land ownership refers to land owned by private individuals, corporations, or other private interests. Despite the existence of private ownership, the development, use, and exploitation of such land is often subject to government regulations (through master or land use plans, zoning codes, and building codes). These regulations govern (a) the permissible land use(s); (b) the characteristics of the land development, including the applicable floor-area-ratio (FAR) (the total permissible buildable area as a multiple of the land surface area), maximum building heights, maximum plot coverage, minimum setbacks, and so on; and (c) the construction requirements not only to ensure public safety but also to reflect other considerations such as urban and architectural design.

Government regulations may also impose requirements on landowners related to the provision of public services or infrastructure; such requirements are often required in large-scale land developments through the land subdivision process. For example, they may require owners to set aside a share of the land for road rights-of-way and public services. Similarly, local governments may also introduce development impact fees (to require that new land developments contribute toward offsetting the impact in terms of congestion) or inclusionary zoning regulations, which require market rate housing or commercial property developers to contribute cash or in kind toward the development of affordable housing units. These could be used to offset the social impact arising from unaffordable access to land and housing for more limited income groups. Both of these instruments are covered in the finance section (chapter 1).

Against the background of formal or official private land and property ownership, a commonly found situation in a large number of developing country cities is private occupancy of land that is neither formal nor official. This includes squatters who have, at some point in the past, illegally occupied public or private land—but who have often developed and occupied such land for long time frames. In many countries, legislation exists that would allow such individuals to regularize their situation and formalize such squatter land occupancy through a process known as "adverse possession." The government would be authorized to issue certificates of occupancy for those who can demonstrate that they have occupied the land for a given period of time (usually 10–15 years) and that the land is uncontested with no registered dispute(s) in court. This is the case in countries such as Egypt, Tunisia, the Republic of Yemen, and some other Middle Eastern countries. It draws its origins from Islamic jurisprudence, which allows citizens who have valorized "dead" land (nonvalorized desert land, called *mowat*) through planting or building to claim ownership.

Brazil has especially progressive legislation with respect to adverse possession (called *usocapião*). It is codified in the 1988 Constitution and the 2001 City Statute. It allows for the regularization of residential property of no more than 250 square meters (sq m) of land after five years of land occupancy. It then issues usufruct certificates called Certificados de Direito Real de Uso (certificates of real right of use), as long as the occupant does not own other property. The legislation that established Brazil's national housing program "My House, My Life" in 2009 has greatly facilitated the implementation of *usocapião* by transforming the process from a judicial to an administrative procedure. Some governments would allow adverse possession on publicly owned land, but many do not. The state of Rio de Janeiro in Brazil was initially unable to grant long-standing squatters freehold ownership using squatter regularization programs through *usocapião* because it was not allowed to "give away" its land. The transfer of occupied public land took place only after the state's constitution was changed in 2013.

In planning for urban regeneration, the presence of squatters on public land that is tagged for regeneration is a critical issue and has to be dealt with fairly. On the one hand, public land is a public good to benefit all citizens (especially on a waterfront or wetland). On the other hand, the current occupiers of the land are usually the poor citizens without any housing alternatives, who need to be close to jobs within cities.

In the case of the Sabarmati riverfront development in Ahmedabad, India, the presence of squatters on the riverbanks challenged the regeneration process. Most of these squatters were former workers in the mill industry, which was diminishing due to changes in economic productivity patterns. The existence of the squatters affected the flood management system of the river as the squatters were residing in wetlands and catchment areas. The dam supervisors could not release the water from the dam due to the risk that these settlements could be submerged. Many times in recent years, this resulted in severe flooding of these settlements. Over time, the squatter settlements and other private properties reached all the way to the banks of the river, preventing public access along the length of the river. In the process of regeneration, the government found a way to resettle most of the residents through a national-level urban development grant (see chapter 7).

Communal or Customary Land

Communal or customary land refers to land that is collectively owned by a given community or tribe. It is typically managed on behalf of and in the interest of the community by a designated person or entity, frequently the community leader, tribal chief, or a council of elders or community representatives. Customary land tenure is frequently found in many African countries, including Ghana and Zambia. Often in such settings, there are dual land tenure regimes that coexist, which further complicate the management of urban expansion and urban development. In cities such as Accra, Ghana, or Lusaka, Zambia, the coexistence of such systems often leads to distortions in the functioning of urban land markets and causes steep artificial increases in land prices. Communal or customary systems regard the management of the land as a form of stewardship for the interest of future generations. Thus, its allocation to different uses or its transfer to different users needs to be carried out in the overall best interest of society or the community and not that of individuals (Payne 2004).

Endowment Land

Endowment land held in the form of a trust is especially common in the Middle East and in places that follow Islamic jurisprudence (Shari'a). *Awqaf* land in Egypt and *habous* land in Morocco are examples of such special forms of land tenure, wherein the owners of the land have decided to endow the land and its revenue to a charitable or religious cause. Owners have entrusted the management of such lands including its use and the distribution of rents to trustees, individuals, or institutions of a public or private sector nature. Such land can only be used for the purposes and within the restrictions set by the person or entity that endowed the land in the first place. Furthermore, it cannot be sold or indefinitely alienated, and there are often restrictions on uses that contradict religious mores.

Importance of Intergovernmental Cooperation for Land Redevelopment

In many cases, the city does not own the land tagged for regeneration or has no jurisdiction over it. Often states or central governments own significant parcels of land within cities. Several case studies within this volume present challenging situations like this. In the case of Buenos Aires, Argentina, 170 hectares of land belonged almost entirely to the national General Administration of Ports, a central government entity (chapter 4). In Washington, DC, the mayor successfully formed a partnership between the city government and over a dozen federal agencies that owned most of the land along the river (chapter 9).

Efficient cooperation between various levels of government is necessary to take the project forward. Box 2.1 describes one such type of intergovernmental cooperation.

Tools for Land Assembly

Governments use a variety of methods to acquire and assemble land from private interests in order to implement urban development and transformation projects. These land assembly methods for private land fall into two categories: voluntary and involuntary (compulsory) tools. The voluntary tools include purchase at market prices and negotiated settlements (as would be the case with any private market transaction, covered in the financing section), land readjustment, urban development, and land sharing. The involuntary tools include the means by which unwilling owners are forced to part with their land (for which they are compensated). These tools include expropriation and the right of preemption.

Box 2.1   Cooperation between the Serbian central government agencies and local governments in converting surplus military property into civilian use property

In 2006, the government of Serbia adopted a plan for the conversion and "commercialization" of about 450 surplus military properties in 79 locations into civilian use properties. The Ministry of Defense obtained the right to sell these properties and use the proceeds to acquire or build housing for military personnel and retirees. At the same time, local governments were granted a preferential right to buy these properties (based on full market value) before they were publicly auctioned.

The conversion process was stalled for three years (2006–09), during which only 19 properties were sold. The Ministry of Defense and local governments had opposite goals: the ministry wished to maximize the sale prices, whereas local governments tried to minimize the prices they paid. The conflict was exacerbated by a lack of capacity within the ministry, local governments, and the State Tax Administration (STA) to set the price of the land.

This stalemate began to be resolved as a result of technical assistance (TA) sponsored by the United States Agency for International Development in 2009 and 2010. It helped to facilitate a more cooperative relationship between the ministry, the STA, and the local mayors. At the core was a new model that aligned the objectives of the ministry and local governments: it made them cooperating partners in offering the properties to private investors, while at the same time allowing them to share the resulting benefits. In particular, local governments would provide new land use zoning for the military properties for sale, which would make redevelopment financially viable for private investors. Three elements of TA were critical in achieving this progress:

- *Training and a U.S. study tour to learn about "win-win" negotiation concepts and market-oriented property appraisal methods.* A key element of the study tour was the closing event, which included the drafting and discussion of action plans for moving forward with priority conversions within each of the participating municipalities. The appraisal training proved particularly valuable to STA officials.

- *Improvements to the regulatory framework for military property conversion.* As communication was reestablished in a more conciliatory manner, the government formed the Intergovernmental Task Force charged with improving document processing, enhancing the methodology for valuing military properties, and proposing better models for financing property transfers to local governments. Based on the recommendations of the task force, in June 2010 the Serbian government adopted an improved legal framework for the conversion process.

- *Technical assistance for specific cases of military property conversion.* The Ministry of Defense began to engage actively with several municipalities in negotiating the property transfers. Overall, 47 sales took place during 2010–12 (Ilic 2013), including conversion of some military airports into civilian or mixed (military and civilian) aviation and cargo facilities. This transaction volume constituted a fourfold annual increase as compared to the previous four-year period.

Sources: USAID 2011; City of Niš 2012.

Voluntary Tools

After many years of negative experiences with land expropriation for public use, the general policy recommendation is that assembling land through voluntary or negotiated purchase is the most efficient way to undertake urban regeneration without creating severe disagreements with the community. Therefore, many countries have shifted their policies toward assembling land through voluntary purchases, which have proven to be cheaper, faster, and more popular. These purchases are mostly done through negotiations and are based on market value, which is determined by independent appraisal.

If the government does not intend to purchase the private land, it can use several methods to enable land development and urban regeneration on private lands. These include direct intervention methods such as land readjustment, urban redevelopment, and land sharing, as well as methods for financing the public infrastructure components of such developments, which were listed in the financing section.

Tool: Land Readjustment

Land readjustment is an approach that is commonly used in East Asian countries, such as Japan and the Republic of Korea. In addition, it has also been used in Germany to enable the assembly and planning of privately owned land at the peri-urban fringe, as well as the delivery of infrastructure and services on such land. Using this approach, the government pools or assembles the various privately owned land parcels in a given area and prepares a land use plan for the overall area including designating spaces for public infrastructure and services such as roads and open spaces. It then implements the plan and provides the necessary trunk infrastructure. At the end of the process, the government returns to each landowner a land parcel proportional to their original parcel but of smaller size (for instance, 50–60 percent of the original land parcel)—except that the new land parcel is of a higher value because it is now serviced urban land. The government retains selected strategic land parcels that it auctions or sells at market rates for cost recovery of its investment in infrastructure and service delivery (see Lozano-Gracia and others 2013). Land readjustment is a very useful instrument in urban regeneration projects involving private land and fragmented land ownership. Box 2.2 and figure B2.2.1 describe the land component of the Sabarmati riverfront regeneration project.

Land readjustment is an effective tool in allowing local governments to take on regeneration projects through increased land values while engaging and involving the original residents and landowners as stakeholders. Therefore, it is a good tool for stakeholder engagement. It is also beneficial for the government because it does not require a massive up-front investment to buy the land from the owners. However, land readjustment needs strong local institutions and a sound legislative framework to be

Box 2.2   Land and compensation in the Sabarmati riverfront development

In the Ahmedabad, India, case study in this volume, a process of land readjustment called *Melavni*, which means "to match" in the local language, is documented. *Melavni* is a part of the process of town planning schemes by which the records of land ownership are reconciled between paper records and the actual on-the-ground ownership verification of land (Ballaney 2008). The first step of this process

Figure B2.2.1   Melavni-like process for land readjustment in Ahmedabad, India

Source: Various materials provided by HCP Design Planning and Management.
Note: Red lines indicate proposed plot lines. Green lines indicate plot ownership as per official records. Black lines indicate physical survey and on-the-ground ownership of the land.

is to prepare an accurate and detailed survey of the area (see figure B2.2.1). Simultaneously, paper records of land holdings are digitized. The two are overlaid against one another, as well as against the proposed plan for the area. This overlay plan helps clarify the differences between the three and helps identify the owners' compensation rights.

During the Sabarmati regeneration project, the planners used the *Melavni* process to develop an overlay plan. Planners then determined whether a particular land parcel adjacent to the riverfront was impacted by the regeneration project. Impacted land parcels were those whose area was reduced by the new plan.

The project team met with individual landowners of the impacted parcels using this overlay plan and reached an agreement regarding compensation. All impacted landowners were offered two

(Box continues on next page)

Box 2.2   **Land and compensation in the Sabarmati riverfront development** *(continued)*

compensation options. First, they were offered development rights for the lost area of land. Second, if they did not want to be compensated with development rights, cash compensation was offered. Most of the impacted landowners chose to be compensated with development rights, as the value of these development rights would appreciate significantly over time, whereas the value of the cash compensation would diminish over time.

implemented effectively. Another challenge is obtaining the consent of all existing landowners for the regeneration project. Furthermore, the land readjustment process involves valuation of the land. It is generally difficult for the government and the landowners to reach agreements on the true value of the land.

Tool: Urban Redevelopment

Urban redevelopment is conceptually similar to land readjustment, with the exception that it happens in existing urban areas and often involves a rezoning by the government of a given area from a low-density (single-family housing) to higher-density (mixed-use or commercial) development. It is also accompanied by a provision of infrastructure improvements (mass transit, such as metro lines) that can support such up-zoning.

As part of this process, a government assembles the individual private properties and undertakes a new higher development plan and delivers the necessary infrastructure. At the end, the government returns to each landowner a share of the overall new development that is equivalent to their original land or property ownership. It retains a share of the development that it then sells to recover the cost of the infrastructure improvement.

Japan has a comprehensive scheme for implementing this tool under its Urban Redevelopment Law. This scheme allows landowners, tenants, and developers to use the opportunity of new transit development in built-up areas to create development opportunities. The government helps with and benefits from this process by changing zoning codes from residential to mixed-use, while also allowing for up-zoning. For details of this scheme, see box 2.3.

Tool: Land Sharing

Land sharing is a method whereby existing public or private land occupied by squatters is redeveloped in a way that enables the regularization of the existing development through resettlement housing to rehouse squatters. At the same time, new market-rate land uses are co-located and can benefit from these well-located land parcels. This is carried out through a densification of the existing development that can enable a

Box 2.3   A hypothetical scenario using the urban development scheme in Japan

Imagine a hypothetical situation in which a government wants to bring a new metro station to a neighborhood consisting of small land parcels owned by various individuals or rented by tenants. The individual parcels are small and the neighborhood is generally low-rise, consisting of various one- or two-story buildings. A new metro station can create tremendous economic value for the land, some of which could be leveraged to finance the new metro. However, the individual land parcels are too small to be able to use the economic value through densification, and some kind of land assembly is also required. The national government finances a third of the site survey, land assembly, and open space foundation costs using the national general budget, and half of the public infrastructure costs using the roadway special fund.

To use the value created through transit development, the government upzones the site, changes the zoning code from residential to mixed-use, and plans denser development using the assembled land parcels. The development will include a tall building, an underground metro station, and associated public infrastructure (wider roads, public spaces, and amenities). Landowners and tenants are entitled to keep the property rights of floor spaces in the new building that are valued as equal to their original property. However, each landowner can also sell all of their property rights to developers. The "surplus" floor area permitted by the municipal government is then sold to cover the costs of the new development and public facilities. Figure B2.3.1 illustrates this hypothetical situation, and table B2.3.1 summarizes the contributions and resulting benefits of each of the stakeholders in this process.

Figure B2.3.1   Illustration of a hypothetical urban development scheme in Japan

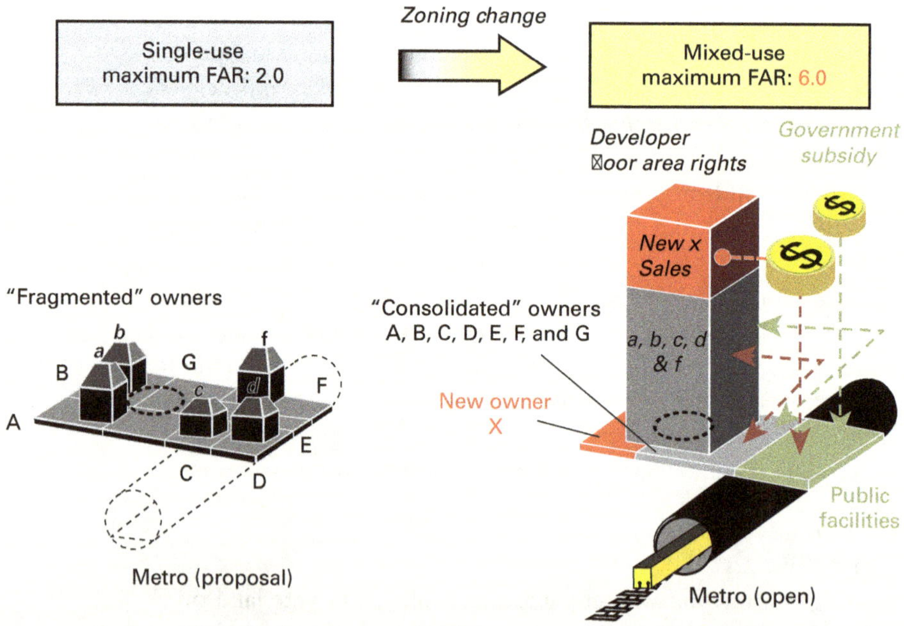

Source: Suzuki and others 2015.
Note: Capital letters indicate the landowners; lower-case letters indicate building owners (building owners could be land owners also). See table B2.3.1 for particulars. FAR = floor area ratio.

(Box continues on next page)

Box 2.3 **A hypothetical scenario using the urban development scheme in Japan** *(continued)*

Table B2.3.1 **Benefits and contributions of various stakeholders in a hypothetical urban development scheme in Japan**

Stakeholders	Contribution	Benefits
Landholders (A, B, C, D, E, F, and G)	Land parcel for the new building	Joint ownership of land for the new building (sections A, B, C, D, E, F, and G) with higher access and better local infrastructure and service provision
Building owners (a, b, c, d, and f)	Old buildings and housing units	Ownership of the new building (sections a, b, c, d, and f) with higher access and better local infrastructure and service provision
Developer	Capital and property development expertise	Profit from section X and from surplus FAR
Transit agency	Construction of transit station	Transit-supportive environment and increased ridership
National government	Subsidies for land assemblage and road construction	Saved road and other public infrastructure construction costs
Local government	Change in zoning code (from single use to mixed use with higher FAR)	Yields higher property tax revenue; promotes local economic development; builds townships resilient to natural disasters

Source: Suzuki and others 2015.

vertical development of existing low-rise or low-density residential uses, thus opening up parts of the land for new development. The land-sharing approach benefits existing occupants who have the right to remain on site (although in new multifamily housing in medium- to high-rise configurations) and existing landowners who can recover and benefit from part of the land. This approach has frequently been used for redeveloping squatter areas in Bangkok, Thailand, and is now being increasingly used in some Indian cities, where it is considered a slum redevelopment scheme.

In Bangkok in the 1970s and 1980s, rapid economic growth resulted in a price hike of urban land. Since many of the slums were located in desirable and accessible urban areas, the government brokered seven land-sharing deals with the slum dwellers to accommodate commercial development without displacing the residents. These deals were struck in cases of longstanding disputed land rights between the landowners and 10,000 slum dwellers. The deal allowed for the construction of high rises to house the slum dwellers so parts of the land could be released for lucrative real estate development. In all of the cases, the slum dwellers paid for a portion of the construction through a loan scheme (Rabe 2010).

Involuntary Tools

It is advisable for governments to avoid using involuntary tools for the purpose of land assembly. The most constructive and efficient way of assembling land is to engage with property owners to ensure an equitable process while facilitating the regeneration project. Many countries have used such tools successfully. However, the voluntary tools can also be used in combination with involuntary tools. For example, if the majority of landowners in a neighborhood agree to sell their land for redevelopment or urban expansion, the government can use expropriation to oblige the rest of the landowners to sell their land as well.

Tool: Expropriation

Expropriation, also known as eminent domain or compulsory purchase, gives the government the right to acquire land in the hands of private ownership even if its owner does not want to sell. To limit potential abuses, the government's use of such power is typically restricted only to cases in which it needs to acquire the land for a public purpose, especially for the provision of infrastructure and public services. However, there are cases when the use of such power is extended to allow land assembly to attract private investment. In this case, the public purpose is to foster local economic development and job creation. This practice was prevalent in countries such as Indonesia prior to 1998 and Tunisia and Egypt prior to 2011. In these instances, it led to a serious backlash. Mandatory land acquisition has also been used in Singapore to facilitate regeneration (see box 2.4 for details).

Tool: The Right of Preemption

Another method for land acquisition involves the right of preemption, which falls between voluntary and involuntary means. In Islamic jurisprudence, this method is called *shu'fa* and it gives a right of first refusal over the sale of a given land or property to its direct neighbors. A similar approach is used in France. Certain zones are declared *Zones d'Aménagement Differé* or zones of deferred development, which are identified by the government for future development. A time frame is set wherein the government has the right of first refusal for any land transaction; owners seeking to sell their land would issue a declaration of intent to sell. The government would have a set period (about two months) to either accept the owner's requested price or, in the case of a dispute over value, agree to a negotiated settlement. Alternatively, the government could also seek a judge-determined price set at the market rate two years before the declaration of the right of preemption. This instrument was introduced to enable the government to avoid the kind of land speculation that immediately follows when future government-sanctioned infrastructure improvement and area development plans become known to developers and the community. Hence, it is a useful instrument in preserving the original residents' rights and controlling gentrification, which usually follows urban regeneration projects.

Box 2.4   Mandatory land acquisition in Singapore

The government of Singapore faced severe urban overcrowding and a slum problem in the decades following World War II. In order to address these problems, the government needed a way to obtain land for urban development at a reasonable cost. Existing legislation did not provide the government with the necessary tools to acquire the land it needed. Therefore, the land ordinance was amended in April 1955 to allow acquired land to be comprehensively redeveloped into new towns. This amendment also stabilized the cost of land for public purposes by awarding compensation based on land prices for the succeeding five years. After the amendment was passed, several land ordinances were also put into place to facilitate the process of land acquisition for the government.

The Foreshores Act was passed in 1963 to allow the government to acquire seafront land (for reclamation use, for instance), without taking into consideration the value of its seafront nature for compensation purposes. This enabled the construction of large-scale public housing such as the Marine Parade on prime, reclaimed seafront land that, in many other countries, would have been exclusively owned by the wealthy.

The most significant land legislation was the Land Acquisition Act of 1966, which had several provisions that enabled the process of land acquisition to proceed in a highly effective manner. Land owners, for example, had no right to challenge the government's right to acquire their land and could only appeal to the appeals board regarding the compensation amount offered. Compensation for the acquired land was also limited to the value *before* the government-led development in the area (Centre for Liveable Cities 2014). The lower than market rate compensation provided for financially sustainable land acquisition exercises by the government and greatly facilitated publicly led developments.[a] Acquired land was used mostly for public development; however, in some cases, it was reassembled and parceled for sale to the private sector for economic development.

The most important, immediate effect of the Land Acquisition Act was that the new government gained the legal authority to acquire large tracts of private land quickly for the development of new towns and industrial facilities. Early acquisitions, after the formation of the Housing and Development Board in February 1960, were primarily used for public housing.

While these measures worked well for some time, land fragmentation was still a problem in cases of private landowners who were not able to reach agreement on land amalgamation. To speed up the redevelopment process, the government started selling small, uneconomical parcels in 1975. A total of 4,000 square feet was used as a guide for assessing parcel sizes, below which independent redevelopment was deemed unviable (Singapore Parliamentary Debates 1966). In what was to be the largest land acquisition exercise to date in Singapore, a total of 215 lots amounting to 31,700 square meters were advertised for acquisition. The government would only pay lower than market rate compensation to the owners. Hence, some owners appealed to the government, presenting plans for amalgamation and redevelopment. Three of the appeals were approved and the land was returned to the owners for redevelopment. The acquired land was cleared, assembled, and reparceled for sale to the private sector developers (see chapter 10).

a. The compensation rate for land acquisition was eventually revised to market rates in 2007.

Methods of Compensation

With regard to compulsory land acquisition, the regulatory framework often sets compensation at market values and assigns the judicial system direct responsibility for setting the value of compensation based on independent expert evaluation. Alternatively, the justice system can serve as an arbitration or grievance redress mechanism in cases of valuation disputes between property owners and the responsible government agency. However, the reality of setting the market value for land is usually very complex for four main reasons: (a) land information systems are typically outdated; (b) land and property rights registration systems are more often than not incomplete; (c) the land valuation profession is underdeveloped in many places; and (d) there is a general dearth of data on land prices—often because of underreporting to avoid land registration fees and property taxes. Even in the developed countries with better data, the assessment of land and property is conducted every decade or so. As such, land taxation is not updated to keep pace with the current value of the property.

When a government acquires land through eminent domain for urban redevelopment purposes, there are different practices involved in determining the compensation for land. These range from *prebetterment values* (that is, at the level of the existing land use prior to the planned redevelopment, as is the practice in France or Sweden where the value is set at its level 10 years prior to the redevelopment and is adjusted for inflation) to *postbetterment values* (that is, at the level of the land use after redevelopment, as is the practice typically in Germany and the Netherlands). The more prevalent approach is the valuation at the level of prebetterment land use. However, in many cases where the conversion of rural to urban land uses entails a differential in price as large as tenfold to fifteenfold, the compulsory acquisition of farmland at agricultural land values often generates significant social unrest on the part of farmers—especially when such compensation is insufficient to help the affected population reconstitute its livelihood.

Tools for Land Management

Implementing urban regeneration projects in countries with less developed property rights and cadastre systems can be very challenging. Land ownership and tenure is a vital source of capital and can open up credit markets and encourage investment in land and development. It can also provide a social safety net for the poor and enable them to transfer wealth to the next generation (Enemark and others 2014). However, it is beyond the scope of this guidebook to suggest developing a land ownership system on a city- and country-wide scale. Even in cities with a decent property registration framework, accessing and using data about vacant land may be difficult or restricted. Many cities in the developing world have paper maps of property lines, often drawn by hand and, in many cases, disputed. Lack of digitized maps and a spatial land administration system limits the power of government in identifying land parcels suitable for development and regeneration. This section covers some of the main tools for land management that are necessary for undertaking urban regeneration.

Tool: Land Administration

Decent systems of land administration that can record tenure and boundaries support the development of efficient land markets and a sound land-use control system. The social benefits of a land administration system are numerous. They include social inclusion, formality, access to credit, management of land disputes, and poverty alleviation. In addition to the social benefits, a sound land administration system helps the government identify potential land parcels for regeneration. It would be extremely difficult, if not impossible, to undertake regeneration projects in cities where more than half the land is outside of the formal land administration system.

Many countries have avoided developing a land cadastre system as it is expensive and requires technically competent staff. However, a newer approach to land administration calls for using methods that are fast, cheap, complete, and reliable. These methods suggest the use of basic large-scale mapping that illustrates land boundaries and parcels. It offers the basis for land administration purposes, including the recording of land tenure, assessing of land values and taxation, identifying and planning land uses, and so on. This system also relies on crowdsourcing and the use of citizen input when necessary. The new approach provides the local governments with the option of upgrading this spatial framework when necessary (Enemark and others 2014). There are four basic principles of the new approach to land administration:

- *General boundaries rather than fixed boundaries.* A "general boundary" of a land parcel could be determined by obtaining satellite imagery. Recording a general boundary is not 100 percent precise, but it is enough for basic land administration purposes, especially in semi-urban areas. If any situation requires determination of fixed boundaries—as in the case of a major development or infrastructure provision—the cost could be paid for by the landowner or other stakeholders.
- *Aerial imageries rather than field surveys.* High-resolution satellite imagery is usually sufficient for most land administration functions.[1] Boundaries are then identified through a participatory approach, and the community helps in interpreting the imageries. The use of aerial imageries is significantly cheaper than field surveys. Furthermore, it does not require that local government have the capacity and technical expertise to undertake fieldwork. Using field surveys for boundary determination is about five times more expensive than using satellite or orthophoto imagery in urban areas. An additional advantage of this method is that it provides planners with a general topography of land use and buildings.
- *Accuracy relates to the purpose rather than to technical standards.* Perfect accuracy in recording parcel boundaries and physical objects is not necessary for all land administration functions. If there is a need for greater accuracy for a specific project or a parcel, then the

technology could be used to achieve that higher level of accuracy. Usually this type of demand exists in dense urban areas and is a result of high land values or implementation of extensive infrastructure work. In such cases, a higher accuracy could be achieved by conducting field surveys and the cost could be borne by the beneficiaries.

- *Opportunities for updating, upgrading, and improvement.* The spatial framework built using satellite imagery is only a starting point. A base should be updated and upgraded as needs arise. The mapping surveys must be linked to a national grid system and also must be updated often so that any changes to the boundaries are recorded. Any opportunity for incremental improvement of the base should be taken so that a spatial framework in line with a modern and integrated land information system can be gradually established over time (Enemark and others 2014).

Tool: Valuation of Public Land

It is helpful if local officials have some kind of an idea as to the value of their public land assets. Many countries use the recorded acquisition value for valuation of land. The downside of this method is that it could lead to assigning a zero value for publicly owned land because it was transferred from the national government to the municipal government. This is problematic, because in the case of leveraging public land for urban regeneration, the true value of this land is unknown. Hence, it can be given away without ever recording a loss on the balance sheets (Peterson and Kaganova 2010).

Market valuation of public land is a costly exercise. Land value appraisals are quite expensive, especially given the large inventories of land owned by governments. The volatility of urban land market values requires frequent updates, most likely on an annual basis. Nevertheless, some countries have started to find solutions to this problem. In South Africa, publicly owned land goes through the same market valuation as privately owned land. In the case that land is used to provide infrastructure, the same rules in valuation apply to the private and public sectors. Another example of this is found in Kuwait, which requires that any public land parcel to be used as an equity contribution for a public-private partnership (PPP) project must be appraised by two independent appraisal companies, and these valuation estimates must be available to the public (Peterson and Kaganova 2010).

While the total valuation of public land stock may be unrealistic and inefficient, at the very least, the city governments can develop methodologies to identify, categorize, and map public land owned by various public entities in their boundaries. It is also important that this public land be categorized in various clusters based on its potential for development and marketability. One example of such inventories is detailed in box 2.5 and map B2.5.1.

It would be difficult to take on any of the land and finance tools described in this volume without at least having a basic land valuation method in place. Sound valuation of land—either public or private—is essential to building a tax system and developing functional real estate markets.

In general and in most parts of the world, land is undervalued. For example, in the United States, properties are assessed on average at 33 percent lower than their market value (Lozano-Gracia and others 2013). In the developing countries the situation is less desirable. In such cases, the bidding process in land auctions is usually used to uncover the true land value.

There must be a clear, fully transparent, and defensible process for determining the value of land. Establishing such clarity is critical so that when land is used for urban regeneration, there are not accusations of corruption, excessive subsidies, or insider deals. In determining the value of land, best practices indicate using outside appraisers so there is an independent basis for land disposition.

The local government may decide to subordinate a certain amount of the value of the land to achieve higher returns at a later stage of the project. Alternatively, it may leverage land value to support the cost of infrastructure or the provision of social benefits, such as affordable housing. However, all the value of these "public goods" should be calculated on the basis of an independently determined assessment. Even for multiphased projects where the future value of land is uncertain, there should be an independently assessed baseline from which to decide on either a

---

Box 2.5   Inventory and valuation of public land assets in Ahmedabad, India

In a unique study, the public land assets in Ahmedabad were systematically inventoried and their value estimated using the geographic information systems (GIS) and land records. This project involved collecting information and consulting with relevant agencies to obtain existing maps and documents related to town planning schemes and cadastral records. It also involved urban planning professionals, GIS technicians, cartographers, and land assessors. It is notable that the land information system created using the GIS was not an end in itself. Rather, it was a means to analyze and build scenarios for policy decisions and land asset management. In this regard, it is important to note that this study was undertaken by a unique team of knowledgeable experts and that India has a well-developed real estate market and related professionals, including skillful appraisers. Replicating this study in some other countries with a less-developed real estate market and industry may not be as successful.

The study classified public land as land owned by the state of Gujarat, the Ahmedabad Municipal Corporation, public institutions, and the central government. The public land resources were identified by the following: (a) town planning schemes, (b) cadastral records, and (c) field surveys. This data was later incorporated into a GIS database to show the geographic distribution. A summary of these findings can be found in maps B2.5.1 and B2.5.2.

(Box continues on next page)

Box 2.5   Inventory and valuation of public land assets in Ahmedabad, India *(continued)*

Map B2.5.1   Public land inventory in Ahmedabad, India, showing land owned by the state and central governments, 2013

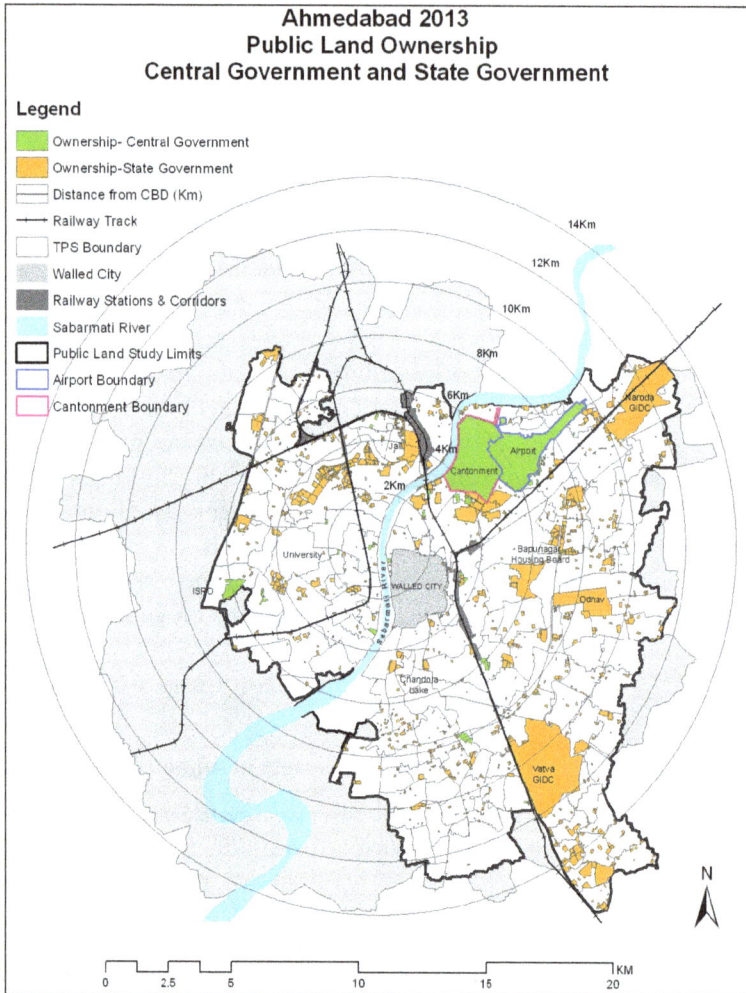

Ahmedabad 2013
Public Land Ownership
Central Government and State Government

Legend
- Ownership- Central Government
- Ownership-State Government
- Distance from CBD (Km)
- Railway Track
- TPS Boundary
- Walled City
- Railway Stations & Corridors
- Sabarmati River
- Public Land Study Limits
- Airport Boundary
- Cantonment Boundary

Source: Ballaney and others 2013.
Note: CBD = central business district; km = kilometers; TPS = town planning scheme.

The study clearly showed that Ahmedabad possesses a sizable amount of public land—amounting to 32 percent of total buildable space in a city known more for its vibrant private sector than for its large government presence. The study found out that the financial resources that could be generated by monetizing public land ranged between rupees (Rs.) 20,000 crores and Rs. 54,000 crores (about US$3.6 billion and US$9.8 billion, respectively).

With a population of nearly 6 million, the amount of public land available amounts to a per capita availability of fiscal resources totaling Rs. 36,000 to Rs. 97,000 (about US$700 and US$1,800,

Box 2.5   Inventory and valuation of public land assets in Ahmedabad, India *(continued)*

Map B2.5.2   Public land inventory in Ahmedabad, India, showing land owned by the Ahmedabad municipal corporation, 2013

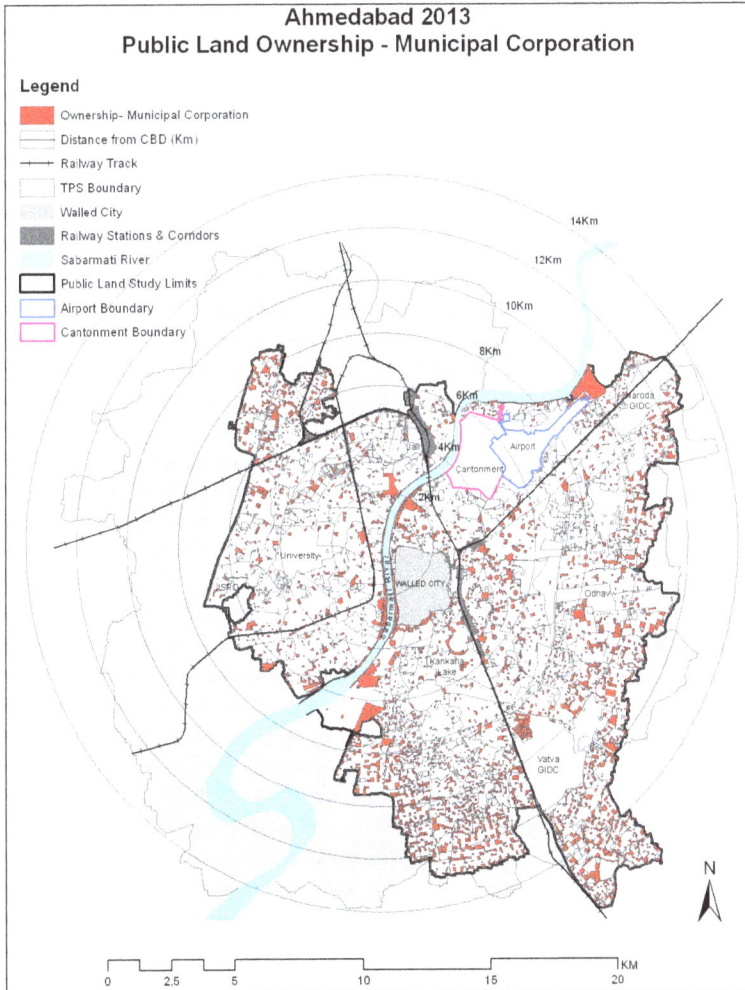

Ahmedabad 2013
Public Land Ownership - Municipal Corporation

Source: Ballaney and others 2013.
Note: CBD = central business district; km = kilometers; TPS = town planning scheme.

respectively). To put this in perspective, a 2005 city development plan estimated capital investment needs for a seven-year period at about Rs. 9000 crores. The minimum value of inventoried public land is over twice this estimate. Therefore, this study clearly establishes that monetizing public land could significantly contribute to investments in infrastructure and other high priority government goals.

Source: Ballaney and others 2013.

fixed value that escalates over time, or a process to revalue land at subsequent stages of development.

The importance of having a transparent and credible method for determining value cannot be over emphasized. It is the basis for all negotiations. It is also critical for the public sector so that it can evaluate the costs and benefits of the key financial and social objectives associated with the regeneration project. For example, the value will determine how much land the public sector is willing to allocate to subsidize higher quality design, small businesses, affordable housing, or public infrastructure.

Although valuation is of high importance, it is unreasonable to expect that all public land assets would be appraised. In this regard, the exercise of valuation of all public land that was done in Australia and New Zealand has been strongly criticized (Kaganova 2012). Instead, local governments can take on valuation of public land when the main public land sites are determined to have potential for reprofiling for private use, when the local government owns or has been given surplus land, and when a specific parcel of land is being used in an urban regeneration project.

Tool: Progressive Taxation of Vacant Land

One of the tools that can be used to discourage speculation and encourage development is taxation of vacant land parcels. Many governments around the world have used this tool to motivate the private sector to develop vacant land. However, governments should not use this tool solely to address budget issues. Rather, they should use this tool to change the behavior of the private sector and block speculation.

A World Bank review of the nine cases of vacant land taxation around the world shows that various governments have different ways of defining, identifying, and prioritizing vacant land; of structuring vacant land fees; of choosing an implementation mechanism; and of deciding who benefits from the fee and how, as well as the various penalties to be imposed in the absence of required payment. There are also differences in prioritizing how to apply the taxation—whether by location, time left vacant, or degree of development. One common denominator among the case studies is the capacity of the local government in implementing the taxation, which proves to be an important factor in the success of this tool. Some observations from the review of case studies are listed below.

- *Motivations for implementing a fee.* Two different traits were observed in this context. In developed countries, the main motivation seems to be addressing disinvestment and blight in cities. However, in developing countries, the focus of this tool is on fighting speculation. This is demonstrated by the examples of Brazil, China, Colombia, Korea, the Philippines, and Taiwan, China.
- *Rate setting (capacity challenges for cadastre and valuation).* Having a property tax system in place is a prerequisite for implementing the vacant land tax. In the cases reviewed, the tax rate structure is based on either the assessed or market value of the property. Without having

a tax collection system in place, governments cannot move to impose a vacant land fee.

- *Implementing agency, fee collection, and revenue uses.* The implementing agency for imposing and collecting the tax is usually the local government. The tax revenues collected are deposited into the city's general fund and are used for public purposes. The Philippines presents a unique case. If a city implementing a tax on idle land is located within Metropolitan Manila, then the tax revenues get split between the city and the Metropolitan Manila Authority.
- *Recourse for nonpayment of vacant land tax.* The nine case studies present a similar course of action in case of delinquency of payment of the vacant land tax. This course usually involves an eventual confiscation of the vacant land by the government after applying an initial interest charge on delinquent landowners and exhausting all other channels of action to receive the vacant land tax (World Bank 2015).

Taxing vacant land parcels has its challenges and problems. Most importantly, it is a costly exercise because it requires a two-rate or split-rate property tax system to assess both improvements to the building site (if any) and the land value. As noted, assessments are expensive and many developing countries lack experienced assessors to perform a sound assessment of land value, regardless of improvements in or around it. Another issue concerns the definition of vacant land, which has to be carefully formulated to ensure an equitable taxation system while also discouraging speculation and blight. For example, comparing a 1-hectare land parcel with a single-family house to a 100-square meter land parcel with no structure on it, which one would be considered vacant and how much tax should be imposed to ensure fairness? See also box 2.6 and table B2.6.1.

Land Regulatory Frameworks

Local governments have many policy and regulatory tools in their hands to determine and control the use of land and the physical shape of the urban environment, while also encouraging the private sector to invest in the city. At the macrolevel, these tools include land-use planning and zoning regulations and on the microlevel, they include master planning (explained in chapter 1). Whereas zoning regulations define the shape of the built environment in the city as a whole, master plans are developed with a specific purpose and site. Zoning and land-use planning are of utmost importance in guiding the participation of the private sector, as well as in setting standards for developers. The following section discusses these tools in greater depth.

Tool: Zoning and Land Use Planning

Zoning is a planning control tool for regulating the built environment and creating functional real estate markets. It does so by dividing land that comprises the statutory area of a local authority into sections, permitting particular land uses on specific sites to shape the layout of towns and cities and enable various types of development. Zoning has a relatively short history as

Box 2.6   International experience on vacant land taxation

Some developing countries have experimented with vacant land taxation. In each case, a specific issue motivated the government to implement a vacant land tax. For example, the postindustrial city of Harrisburg, Pennsylvania, in the United States has been experiencing economic decline for the past several decades. The city started a vacant land tax program hoping that lowering the tax rate on building values and raising it on land values would stimulate new development and conservation of older buildings. In effect, the land value taxation was used as a local policy tool to help reverse economic decline and encourage urban revitalization. In this context, the city of Harrisburg implemented a "two-rate" or "split-rate" property tax system in 1975, imposing a land tax rate that is six times higher than the improvements on the property. The city believes that this tax system has been successful, resulting in the desired reduction in vacant land parcels.

Another example is Seoul, in the Republic of Korea, which experienced a 136 percent increase in land prices in 1978 mainly due to massive speculation. This in turn increased demand for land and decreased market supply, thereby widening the gap between landowners and nonlandowners. This motivated the government to impose a vacant land tax to discourage speculation and promote development. Any land parcel left vacant for two years was considered idle land and was subject to a 5 percent property tax, instead of the normal 2 percent. Similarly, a 7 percent and 8 percent tax would apply for land left vacant for three and five years, respectively. The government would confiscate the land if the taxes were not received. Some other cities in developing countries have also experimented with this tool. Table B2.6.1 summarizes the experience of Bogotá, Colombia; Harrisburg, Pennsylvania, United States; Marikina City, Philippines; and Seoul, Korea, in defining vacant land and structuring tax amounts.

Table B2.6.1   International experience in taxing vacant land

	Government's definition of land subject to fees	Fee structure
Harrisburg, Pennsylvania, United States	A tax on land applied to all properties	• Foreclosure on land = 3% of assessed land value • Improvements = 0.5% of assessed value of improvements
Seoul, Korea, Rep.	Land left vacant for a minimum of two years	• 5% instead of 2% on improved lots • 7% if left vacant for more than 3 years • 8% if left vacant for more than 5 years • 9% if left vacant for more than 7 years • 10% if left vacant for more than 10 years
Marikina City, Philippines	• Land area greater than 1,000 square meters, one-half of which remains unimproved • Residential lots, regardless of land area, one-half of which remains unutilized or unimproved	Additional levy at the rate of 2.5% per year on the assessed value of the property
Bogotá, Colombia	Land that is subject to urbanization but has not yet been developed, and land that has already been urbanized but has had no construction yet	In 2004: • Vacant properties = 1.2–3.3% of the assessed value • For improved properties in urban areas, rates from 0.4% (residential use) to 1.5% (financial institutions) Today: vacant urban land rate has increased to 30%

Source: World Bank 2015.

a tool for land-use planning. It determines the location, size, and use of buildings and decides the density of city blocks (City of New York 2015a).

Why is zoning necessary?

The purpose of zoning is to allow local and national authorities to regulate and control land and property markets to ensure complementary uses. Zoning can also provide the opportunity to stimulate or slow down development in specific areas.

The planning and zoning process functions differently around the world and is controlled by different levels of authority. Most commonly, a local authority such as a municipality or a county controls zoning (as in Australia or the United States) whereas in other cases zoning is implemented at the state or national level (as in France or Germany). Sometimes zoning is governed by a combination of the two approaches. Beyond these immediate controls, additional regulations that affect zoning are often used, such as planning scheme overlays in Australia or impact assessments in Germany.

What constitutes a zoning ordinance?

The zoning regulation is usually developed in the form of a zoning ordinance, which is the text specifying land use of specific blocks and even each individual lot within a city block. Zoning regulations include specifications regarding lot size, density or bulk, height, and floor area ratio (FAR). The zoning ordinance is the formal categorization of land-use policies applicable to land within a municipality. It also sets the legal framework. The zoning ordinance establishes permitted land uses and distinguishes between different land use types. Further, it ensures that incompatible land uses are not located adjacent to one another. Regulations also define setbacks and can build on the city's safety and resilience by setting limitations on building in flood plains and wetlands. The zoning ordinance often also contains information relating to the need for a planning permit for a change of use or development proposal, subdivision of land, construction of new buildings, and other changes to the land (Victorian State Government 2008).

Zoning ordinances usually consist of zoning districts and overlays. For example, in New York City there are three zoning districts: residential, commercial, and manufacturing. Each of these districts is then further broken down to a range of low-, medium-, and high-density residential, commercial, and manufacturing districts. Zoning overlays are special purpose zoning districts that are designed to stimulate a particular set of site conditions and outcomes. They are tailored to the specific needs of certain neighborhoods. For example, a commercial overlay may be allowed on a residential block to provide retail on the ground floor of neighborhood homes. Overlays may also impose height limits or other physical limitations to shape the built environment in a certain way or to protect historic characteristics or waterfront views.

Most zoning regulations also set requirements for the FAR of a development, which often differ from locality to locality. "The Floor Area Ratio is the principal bulk regulation controlling the size of buildings. FAR is the ratio of total building floor area to the area of its zoning lot" (City of New York 2015a). A FAR outlines the intensity of the site use, not the height or site coverage. In New York City, "Each zoning district has a FAR which, when multiplied by the lot area of the zoning lot, produces the maximum amount of floor area allowable on that zoning lot. For example, on a 10,000 square foot zoning lot in a district with a maximum FAR of 1.0, the floor area on the zoning lot cannot exceed 10,000 square feet" (City of New York 2015b).

Can zoning regulations be amended?

The zoning ordinance is a legal framework, but it must also be flexible enough to accommodate and guide development. Amendments can be made to alter it either by the local authority or by the public. An amendment is usually made to "achieve a desirable planning outcome or to support a new policy direction" (Victorian State Government 2008). As such, it must have planning merit and be consistent with the future strategic directions for the local government. Zoning amendments are especially important in urban regeneration projects, as governments can use them to increase the building volume allowed for development to be profitable and attractive enough to the private sector (see chapter 1). In most cases, either a zoning text amendment (changing the zoning regulations) or a zoning map amendment (changing the zoning designation) is necessary to allow for a specific development in a specific location or configuration, currently not permitted.

Making or requesting an amendment is not a simple process. Indeed, it has significant planning implications and will affect the wider community because it "changes the way land can be used or developed in the whole neighbourhood." Making an amendment to most planning schemes is also a rigorous process, often requiring a higher level of government or city council approval. However in some less established planning processes or structures, an amendment may be used more frequently to achieve a planning outcome.

How can zoning be used as a tool for stimulating private sector participation in urban regeneration?

In addition to the three main categories (residential, commercial, manufacturing), the zoning toolkit includes complementary rules that address specific types of development, as well as the design and quality of public spaces. Some initiatives allow for the modification of underlying regulations when developing large sites, whereas others fine-tune those same regulations to address lower-density areas or the particular challenges and opportunities of development projects on the waterfront.

Urban regeneration projects are usually developed on large parcels of land that span several zoning districts and overlays. In order to allow for a better site planning exercise and relationship between buildings and open spaces, the local government may ease the baseline zoning regulation to allow for a more consistent site planning across all lots and blocks.

In addition, to stimulate private sector interest in development, the government can allow for the transfer and merger of development rights. Alternatively, it can fine-tune other regulations to allow for higher density development in exchange for some form of a public good, such as privately financed public spaces or inclusionary housing. In this case, the zoning regulation is amended to allow for more density in exchange for privately financed public space or affordable housing units within a housing complex (see chapter 1).

The push for more affordable housing has led to calls for inclusionary zoning, which is seen as appealing because developers pay for it, and it produces economic integration. However, affordable housing units created by inclusionary zoning require expensive subsidies (Barro 2014). For a full discussion of inclusionary zoning, see the social impacts section in chapter 3. All the case study cities in this volume have well-developed zoning regulations. For example, the evolution of zoning regulation in Ahmedabad is summarized in box 2.7.

Box 2.7 Evolution of zoning regulations in Ahmedabad, India

In Ahmedabad, India, zoning was first established in the development plan prepared in 1954 and approved in 1965. It was based on the Bombay Town Planning Act (1954), which for the first time allowed for the creation of a development plan to manage growth of urban areas. The previous Bombay Town Planning Act (1915) only allowed for the creation of town planning schemes to facilitate the improvement of existing urban areas.

Zoning is included within the development regulations prepared as a part of the overall development plan for urban development areas (UDAs). The UDA is defined in accordance with the Gujarat Town Planning and Urban Development Act (GTPUDA) established in 1970. In accordance with this act, an urban development authority is established for a UDA which is usually greater than the jurisdiction of the city. The Ahmedabad Urban Development Authority has jurisdiction over Ahmedabad's development area (1,866 square kilometers [sq km]), which is much larger than the area of the city (464 sq km). According to the GTPUDA, the development plan for each UDA is to be updated every 10 years.

There are a total of over 20 zones identified in the development plan. However, most of the city development areas are under one of five zones. The core walled city zone includes the old city of Ahmedabad. The Gamtal zone includes various urban villages, which are now part of the greater Ahmedabad development area. The general fabric of the city falls under R1 or R2 zones, which are mixed residential zones. R3 is a more restrictive residential zone usually found on the periphery of the city where higher intensity of development is not encouraged.

Development in the city is mainly focused in the R1 and R2 zones. In these zones, the base floor space index (FSI) is 1.8 and 1.2, respectively—with the possibility of purchasing an additional 50 percent base FSI. This gives a maximum allowable FSI of 2.7 in the R1 zone and 1.8 in the R2 zone. Until the recent development plan, the height restriction for development was 40 meters. With the new development plan, this maximum height has been raised to 70 meters for plots that front on 40-meter wide roads and on all plots in the central business district overlay zone.

(Box continues on next page)

Box 2.7   **Evolution of zoning regulations in Ahmedabad, India** *(continued)*

With the new comprehensive development plan 2021, overlay zones have been introduced. These overlay zones allow a higher FSI of 4.0 in the R1 zone and 5.4 in the R2 zone. In providing for higher FSIs, the base FSI of the underlying zone remains the same. Only the additional purchase is increased. The areas under these zones are expected to be developed in accordance with a local area plan, to be completed soon.

There is a formal process of requesting a variance if a developer wants to build higher or wants to request a relaxation in one of the other regulations (open space, parking, setbacks, allowed use, and so on). Earlier, a variance committee reviewed such requests. However, since the new plan came into effect, the authority to provide variances of certain kinds has been vested with the municipal commissioner and in some cases with the state government.

Second Asset: Community

Participation and public involvement in the planning of development projects are fundamental for project success and sustainability. First, participation is necessary because it is the practical means whereby the public expresses its democratic right to be involved in the public policy process. Second, it allows the communities to express their needs and aspirations, which subsequently feed into the policy-making, delivery, and monitoring process. Third, participation allows for greater efficiency throughout the project delivery process, as projects are more in tune with societal views.

There are also very practical implications for community participation for the successful completion of an urban regeneration project. First, end users add valuable content and information based on local knowledge and personal experience. Public involvement can improve the outcome of the project. Second, participation is a positive way to channel public opinions and interest that can otherwise manifest themselves as opposition and protest. Participation in the planning and design of a project, in particular, gives people the opportunity to influence decisions that affect their daily lives. Third, when people are involved early on in the design and creation of the plan, they are more likely to support the results. Thus, a well-run, inclusive process can improve outcomes.

Tools for Community Participation

This section presents a collection of tools available to the urban regeneration project team to consider when thinking about the community participation strategy. Meaningful participation implies that the communities' views are incorporated into the project's details—and that consultation is not just a step in the process without implications for a project's design and objectives. For this reason, it is important to establish ground rules, define clear targets, and avoid a reactive proforma process.

The process should be robust enough to enable the local community to have a voice in how their local area will be redeveloped, and comments should be welcomed on a wide range of issues—and not just the narrow options offered by professionals. The community engagement format should make consultations widely accessible and ensure effective and continuous feedback, for instance, by allowing communities to see how ideas have developed during the various stages and ensure that everyone is aware of the progress made. A failure to fully engage the community (through workshops, training sessions, visioning sessions, fact sheets, community meetings, and so on) can lead to delays in the redevelopment process, potential litigation, neighborhood backlash, negative media coverage, and disgruntled project partners.

In the case of Washington, DC's Anacostia Waterfront Initiative, the participatory planning approach defined implementation. The District sponsored over 30 community workshops and focus group sessions in six neighborhood target areas. More than 5,000 individuals attended these neighborhood workshops. This extensive consultation process was unprecedented and built the community's confidence in the project. However, while the Santiago Repopulation Program started with an extensive civil society consultation, it was later criticized because the community was not involved during the implementation phase. This led to concerns and oppositions from the local population.

The project team can use different means to communicate and consult with the public. The range of communication techniques used for decision making in an urban project is diverse. In table 2.1, we highlight some of the tools that have been found useful in engaging the public in an urban regeneration project. Further, we present several of these tools in detail.

Tool: Charrettes

A charrette is a type of participatory planning process that assembles an interdisciplinary team—typically consisting of planners, citizens, city officials, architects, landscape architects, transportation engineers, parks and recreation officials, and other stakeholders—to create a design and implementation plan for a specific project. It differs from a traditional community consultation process in that it is design based. In addition, and as opposed to traditional planning exercises that can take a long time to be finalized, charrettes are usually compressed into a short period of time.

For projects focused on community change, charrettes can be used to create a wide range of plans, including master plans within a city's comprehensive plan, town center plans, transit-oriented development plans, affordable housing development plans, and wide-scale redevelopment projects. The charrette process can also be adapted to a range of projects—from constructing an individual building to redesigning an entire neighborhood.

A key component of the charrette is time compression. For four to seven days, participants work together in brainstorming sessions, sketching workshops, and other exercises through a series of feedback loops. Meetings take place with participants coming together as a group at set times or breaking off into smaller working groups. Behind the scenes, the

Table 2.1   **Public participation tools**

Purpose	Technique
Preliminary understanding of situation	Key-person interviews Stakeholder analysis survey
Opinion survey	Questionnaire survey Group interview Focus group survey
Promoting participation	Event (symposium, onsite observation meeting, fair) Mailing list Corporate identity formulation
Dialogue	Briefing Open hearing Open house Workshop/charrettes Task force
Dissemination, understanding of opinions	Public relations documents (brochures, fact sheets, public relations papers) Hotlines, comment cards Website Media Information center

Source: Horita and Koizumi 2009.

core design team works constantly. The entire community, however, does not need to take several days off to participate. Most stakeholders attend scheduled meetings.

The charrette process can be adapted to fit different projects, but all charrette initiatives use the same basic strategy: planners involve as many stakeholders as early as possible in a set of short, intensive design meetings. In these collaborative, hands-on sessions, participants help planners root out potential problems, identify and debate solutions, and create a buildable plan. The charrette compresses the planning process into a matter of days and brings all the stakeholders—and all of the issues—into one room. In the face of so much information, expertise, and expectation, it's hard for developers, designers, and community participants not to pitch in and create a workable plan. (Lennertz and Lutzenhiser 2003). The process of making a good charrette is summarized as follows:

- Charrette participants work collaboratively.
- Team designs cross-functionally.
- Charrettes use design to achieve a shared vision and create holistic solutions.
- Designers work on the big picture and the details.
- Tight time frame for the work schedule facilitates resolution.
- Team communicates in short feedback loops.

- Charrette lasts between four and seven days.
- Charrette is held on site.
- Charrette produces a buildable plan.[2]

Partcipants usually appreciate the charrette format because they see quick results. Another advantage of a charrette is that it can boost creativity. Furthermore, participants can observe the project from an integrated point of view because charrettes bring together all relevant disciplines to create a plan that balances transportation, land use, economic considerations, and environmental issues.

Tool: Using Technology for Public Participation

Social accountability tools (such as online blogs, forums, and discussions) provide a platform for large-scale citizen review, feedback, and dialogue related to public sector policies and services. This can be conducted through up-to-the minute news, meeting notes, postings, data, images, and so on. These multiple-format mechanisms offer new barrier-free models of public participation in which real-time collaboration, experience sharing, and participation are becoming the norm. This enables authorities to constantly remain in touch with some of the people in order to make governance more effective and representative. The various tools that support information and communications technology–based social accountability mechanisms in the framework of urban planning can be found in table 2.2.

Third Asset: Environment

The decision about the location of an urban regeneration project is based on a number of factors such as land availability, market information, an understanding of the city's growth trajectory, available public resources, and access to private sector investment for the project. Urban regeneration mostly takes place in land areas that have some kind of former use (brownfields),[3] including central urban areas or downtown areas, old deprived urban areas around the city center, postwar areas, large high-rise public housing, or old industrial, harbor, military, or railway areas. As a consequence, past land uses and potential contamination need to be investigated and, when necessary, the project team needs to create an environmental cleanup plan including a sound financing scheme. This section provides an overview of the physical environment scoping steps during project preparation that are required when redeveloping brownfields.

There is tremendous variation in the definition and severity of industrial contamination across countries. Countries with the longest history of industrialization and largest number of contaminated sites, such as those in Australia, East Asia, Europe, and North America, tend to have the most well-defined policies and regulations for contaminated sites. However, many other countries—especially those in the developing world—lack such definitions or regulations related to site contamination.

Table 2.2   Information and communication technology tools for public participation

Tool	Uses and characteristics
Surveys (forecast and retrospective)	Citizen surveys are investigations of the behavior, preferences, attitudes, or opinions of a target group sample collected through online questionnaires. Ex ante (or forecast) surveys can help governments and utilities to shape future plans, such as investment or infrastructure plans to expand services, institutional changes, and tariff changes. Ex post (or retrospective) surveys can constitute effective mechanisms for conveying citizen's viewpoints and reviews of public projects and services to authorities.
	Surveys may cover particular subgroups or geographical communities within the service area or the service area as a whole. Ex ante surveys may measure willingness to pay or preferences, for example, such as service levels and tariff structures. Ex post surveys can be used to evaluate and monitor the performance of urban projects and services from the point of view of the citizenry.
	A wide variety of online applications exist for conducting surveys using the Internet. For instance, using mobile phones, respondents can submit their choices using SMS messages, touch-tone number punching, interacting with voice messaging systems, and so on.
Citizen outreach	Outreach can be used to initiate dialogue and consultation, although it is mostly a one-way process, with information flowing from the municipality to the public through SMS messages and alerts or e-mail notifications. This is usually a better option in developing countries where poor communities do not have access to the Internet and computers but widely use messaging. Citizen outreach pertains to efforts by agencies to connect directly with the public for purposes of disseminating vital information and messages pertaining to a variety of issues, such as necessary health precautions, location of skill development workshops, change in tariff levels, tax payment information, and so on. Outreach can also be used to provide information about upcoming meetings or important steps in the project.
Digital publication	An effective way of ensuring the accountability of local governments is by making important documents (designs, plans, and maps) available through online publishing or disseminating relevant information using SMS messages. Such reports provide a mechanism for public review, and a tool to monitor performance.
E-participation	E-participation mediums such as blogs, citizen forums, on-demand information channels (for instance, YouTube, Facebook), online chat rooms, and so on render a virtual feedback, review, critique, and complaint loop between citizens and the concerned authorities and service providers. The goal of such mechanisms in governance is to enable greater citizen participation in the decision-making process. Through e-participation, people can interact with local officials and make their voices heard. It allows citizens to immediately see how and why their representation is functioning the way it is. In addition, it enables citizens to share their comments and views about the functioning and performance of local agencies. Public officials or agencies can judge the prevailing mood of citizens and take a corresponding course of action based on popular sentiment.

Source: Relhan, Ionkova, and Huque 2012.
Note: SMS = short message service.

The Specific Issues Related to Brownfield Redevelopment

Many of the sites considered for urban regeneration are derelict and underused land and may have real or perceived contamination problems.[4] Other major regeneration projects are implemented in waterfront areas, where the water contains pollutants because of prior industrial contaminants or release of sewage. In cases where contamination is substantial, it is essential to conduct an environmental assessment very early in the process, specifically during the scoping period, to get a first notion of the potential cleanup costs. This is extremely important because contamination cleanup costs may make the project unviable.

The initial environmental site assessment and investigation can provide information pertaining to environmental hazards, the extent of pollutant exposure, and the impact on neighboring communities, as well as on the public's perception of the site. This can be done in a fairly cost-effective way by making use of readily available data. In this section, we look at simple tools that planners can use to start the environmental assessment of a possible redevelopment site. It is however important to note that environmental assessment is a technically savvy task that needs to be delegated to specialized companies.

Tool: Site Assessment

The purpose of this step is to evaluate the potential for contamination at a particular site by collecting and reviewing existing information. The site assessment is an initial investigation and is usually limited to a search of historical records and a review of existing data. The review and collection also includes information about past and current environmental conditions and historical uses of the site. The site assessment is a crucial step in the regeneration of brownfield sites because any further environmental investigation and cleanup will hinge on whether potential environmental concerns are identified during this phase.

Tool: Site Investigation

The site investigation phase focuses on confirming contamination, locating any such contamination, and characterizing its nature and extent. It is essential that an appropriately detailed study of the site be performed to identify the cause, nature, and extent of contamination, as well as the possible threats to the environment or people living or working nearby. The results of the site investigation are used in determining goals for cleanup, quantifying risks, determining acceptable and unacceptable risks, and developing effective cleanup plans that minimize delays or costs in the redevelopment and reuse of the property. To ensure that sufficient information is obtained to support future decisions, the potentially applicable cleanup measures and the proposed redevelopment of the site should be considered when identifying data needs.

A site investigation is logically based on the results of the site assessment. The site investigation phase usually includes the analysis of soil and soil gas samples, groundwater, groundwater vapor, surface water, and residual substances on the brownfield site (for example, in old tanks, barrels, and on trash heaps). The potential migration pathways of contaminants are also examined during this phase, and a baseline risk assessment is conducted to determine the risk to human health and the environment. The results of the site audit will strongly influence the immediate follow-up action for site development. Obviously, the larger and more complex the contaminants found on the site, the more time and money will be required to bring the site into a condition fit for redevelopment. Further, there may also be more residual restrictions on site use as a result.

One of the challenges in brownfield management may be the lack of local expertise in site assessment and investigation. Different technologies are available, but access to them is often limited to more developed regions and countries. It is therefore important to hire experienced environmental consultants for all of the technical preparatory work. In this context, a job initially done well can save a lot of money later on. The high quality of information collected helps with better understanding the liabilities and estimating the true value of the land. See box 2.8 for some examples of river cleanup efforts in the case studies.

In the planning phase, remediation and redevelopment plans are defined with precision. An environmental impact assessment and a mitigation plan are also developed as a way of describing, quantifying, and analyzing the environmental impact of the proposed redevelopment. In addition, PPP roles are negotiated, as are the sharing of risks and benefits among participating parties (based on a thorough development appraisal by the developer, and a clear impact analysis performed by the local authority). Finally, incentive schemes and sources of cofunding are identified.

Following close consultations with involved stakeholders, the preferred remediation and redevelopment options are chosen and further elaborated to define the project content, budget and timeframe. This serves several purposes: (a) obtaining the construction permit, (b) securing the funds required for investments from private and public sources, (c) providing detailed solutions to technical problems (for instance, the required cleanup technology), and (d) creating the basis for tender design and documents for procurement. In this phase, the contamination pattern will be characterized with high precision, the site development elaborated in detail (including all main quantities and dimensions, areas and volumes, layouts and appearances of structures and infrastructure), and a site remediation plan will be readied for implementation.

Tool: Environmental Impact Assessment and Site Remediation Plan

The environmental impact assessment (EIA) will address two types of contamination: first, those materials that need to be removed because

Box 2.8 **Environmental river cleanup in three cities: Ahmedabad, Singapore, and Washington, DC**

Three case studies in this volume illustrate the centrality of dealing with environmental issues in waterfront urban regeneration projects. Indeed, the environmental aspects of the projects were a defining theme in respect to the vision for the sites, as well as during project implementation.

In the case of Sabarmati in Ahmedabad, India, the project was envisioned as a multidimensional environmental improvement, social uplift, and urban rejuvenation project. One of the key objectives was to stop the flow of sewage and keep the river clean and pollution free. Untreated sewage from the informal settlements and nearby developments opened directly into the river, which resulted in extreme and constant pollution. By providing an interceptor sewer line along the entire length of both sides of the river, the project eliminated the direct flow of sewage into the river. In the process, it also helped to clean up the quality of the water and enhance the possibility for improving ground water recharge.

The cleanup of the Singapore River was a massive operation, which involved extensive multi-agency action and coordination to relocate shipping activities, polluting industries, street hawkers, and squatters to alternative accommodations. These were to be constructed and allocated by the government. Riverbeds were dredged to remove the debris, and infrastructure, such as modern sewers, had to be constructed by the government.

Finally, in the case of the Washington, DC's Anacostia Waterfront Initiative, concern about the river's pollution was central to the original vision, which focused on providing opportunities and environmental justice to an extremely poor community. To this end, the District's Water and Sewer Authority formulated a strategy to bring the city's sewer infrastructure into compliance with standards at an estimated cost of over US$1.3 billion to be implemented over a 20-year period.

of planned construction activities (for instance, because a foundation will be placed in contaminated soil, or waste heaps on the surface need to be cleared for landscaping or structures); and, second, those that need to be removed or remediated in situ due to their environmental impact or their hazard to public health and safety or for the common good. Examples include a contamination plume in the groundwater that could threaten the water supply; highly contaminated materials that lie under proposed foundations to be remediated with microbiological methods; and hazardous substances close to the surface that could pose a hazard through direct human contact or ingestion of dust.

The initial remediation and redevelopment plans are sharpened by performing an EIA. The EIA takes into account the environmental baseline of the site (investigated and characterized during site assessment and investigation). It also analyzes the environmental impact of the planned redevelopment on neighborhood and surrounding jurisdictions. New legislation in most countries is strict about avoiding potential negative impacts on people but is often less clear on how environmental impacts can be mitigated. The technical investigation activities related to an EIA are similar to the initial investigations for the environmental site audit. In fact, much of the information generated at the initial phase may subsequently be used for the EIA. Gaps may need to be closed, for example, due to new aspects of the development concept. However, these could be addressed through supplementary investigations. The information generated can in turn be used to encourage sustainable redevelopment practices.

Remediation Options

Choosing remediation technologies is contingent on availability and cost-effectiveness. Often, in projects with significant contamination, public entities finance much of the environmental investigation and remediation, especially if no other owner can be held responsible. These entities may also cover at least part of the site's environmental, financial, or legal liabilities. This helps to lower the threshold for private enterprises to take on projects with potential environmental risks.[5]

Financing Remediation

Historical models for contaminated site remediation place the financial burden upon the companies whose operations led to the contamination.[6] This so-called "polluter pays" principle, although economically fair, does not take into account the lack of knowledge regarding environmental releases underlying earlier decades of the industrial age (Cordato 2001). In addition, many contaminated sites are products of companies that no longer exist or do not possess the capital to remediate the sites to legal standards. Some of these sites have been transferred to the ownership of a bank or a government entity, whereas others may remain in the ownership of an extant corporation. A site could still be operational, but the presence of contaminants in certain areas may require remediation to ensure compliance with government regulations. A variety of possible ownership and occupancy conditions may exist, and applying the polluter pays principle may not be entirely feasible. In such cases, the surrounding community often suffers from unfavorable economic and environmental conditions. In the absence of a clearly identifiable and financially capable polluter, the burden of financing industrial site remediation typically falls on the public sector.

Government entities frequently prioritize abandoned sites to receive public financing for remediation. Most targeted remediation programs are specific to abandoned industrial sites, and the bulk of resources referenced herein will necessarily be limited to the remediation and redevelopment of vacant contaminated sites. Table 2.3 summarizes a variety of financing mechanisms for remediation, providing some examples for further research. The mechanisms presented in this section overlap somewhat with the guidebook's financing section in chapter 1. However, here the information is limited to remediation financing.

Table 2.3   **Mechanisms for financing site remediation**

Definition	Example	Global application
Bond finance programs		
Bonds are one of the most prevalent financial mechanisms for addressing brownfield redevelopment through a variety of structures and schemes.

The two types of bond issuing entities are governments and the private sector. In the United States, government bonds are exempt from federal income taxes.

One of the key strengths of bond financing is the relative flexibility in using this tool. Bonds can be used for directly financing the cleanup of certain contaminated sites. However, bond proceeds are also frequently used by communities to seed brownfield-specific loan programs, or in conjunction with other tools such as tax increment finance and tax credits. | In the United States, the city of Chicago established the Chicago Brownfields Initiative in 1993 to acquire, assemble, and rehabilitate properties, returning them to productive use. The Initiative links environmental restoration with economic development by cleaning up and redeveloping brownfields and improving policies to promote private redevelopment.

The city funded the Brownfields Pilot Program with US$2 million in general obligation bonds, expecting it would pay for environmental testing on the five selected properties and remediation on two properties. In fact, the city was able to return all five sites to productive use for a total of about US$850,000.

The city's experience with these sites laid the groundwork for continued innovation with an aggressive large-scale cleanup program. | In countries that lack a well-established bond market, the effort required to first create one may not be practical for the purpose of brownfield redevelopment or site remediation alone.

In addition, the cost savings associated with tax exemption may not be available in countries that lack taxation on interest income.

Ultimately, bond finance works most efficiently in countries with existing bond markets and a sufficient density of contaminated sites and potential developers to make pooling projects worth the investment for the community. |
| **Loan fund programs** | | |
| A revolving loan fund (RLF) is a self-replenishing pool of money, utilizing interest and principal payments on active loans to issue new loans.

An RLF provides access to a flexible source of capital that can be used in combination with more conventional lending sources. Often, the RLF fills a gap between the amount a borrower can obtain in the private market and the amount needed to start or sustain a business. | In the United States, the state of Washington's Department of Commerce manages an RLF targeting urban and rural brownfields that present an immediate danger to human health and the environment. Eligible applicants include government entities, site owners, and developers— provided that private sector applicants are not responsible for the initial site contamination. | Revolving loan funds can be created and sustained through nearly any economic structure. Public funds may be required to capitalize an RLF, but thereafter the fund can be designed to provide a sustainable stream of revenue for the funding of future projects.

Loan recipients can be public or private entities, provided that the ultimate borrower is capable of repayment. |

(Table continues on next page)

Table 2.3   Mechanisms for financing site remediation *(continued)*

Definition	Example	Global application
Loan fund programs		
Eligible uses for RLF loans can include: working capital, professional fees, acquisition of land and buildings, site remediation, new construction, facade and building renovation, landscape and property improvements, and machinery and equipment.	Loan funds do not cover pre-remediation site assessments, as site assessments form an important piece of the underwriting for these projects. Washington's interest rates are fixed "at or below the prevailing prime interest rate" and determined on a borrower-by-borrower basis. Loans range in size from US$10,000–450,000, with no listed minimum requirement for an equity contribution.	Individual project structures can be designed strategically—such as interest-only payments through construction, and either a lump sum due at the sale of the property or amortization upon occupancy of the site—to suit underlying economic conditions within a given region.
Tax increment and special assessment finance programs		
Tax increment finance (TIF). TIF is a financing tool that allows local governments to invest in infrastructure and other improvements. They pay for them by capturing the increase in property tax revenues (and in some areas, other types of incremental taxes) generated by the enhancements. Environmental remediation can be an explicitly approved improvement, making TIF particularly applicable to contaminated site cleanup.	In the United States, the city of Dearborn, Michigan, commonly uses TIF to finance brownfield projects. As one example, the city of Dearborn used TIF to finance the cleanup and renovation of an abandoned 150,000-square-foot building formerly occupied by Sharon Steel. In 1996, Dearborn commenced redevelopment of this large, abandoned parcel. First, the city formed a commission to perform several site tests. Test results revealed significant environmental problems with the property.	To use TIF for the remediation of site contamination, the country must already have a property tax, sales tax, or other reliable stream of municipal income in place. Without the proceeds from these taxes, there can be no revenue stream such as a TIF would require. As a country develops its TIF infrastructure, it must be cognizant of the total development to take place on the contaminated site. It must establish security measures that protect against the development not taking place. Guarantees from developers, credit enhancements from state governments, reserve funds, or insurance must be sought to protect against potential losses. Legislative policy must be carefully crafted to govern the use of this tool and limit its applicability to projects that benefit the public sector.

Table 2.3   **Mechanisms for financing site remediation** *(continued)*

Definition	Example	Global application
Special assessment financing. Often, special districts may be formed to finance certain project costs. In the United States, most special districts can impose by a vote of the residents or property owners within the district's boundaries, one of the following types of taxes: sales tax, property tax, or special assessment. When new sales taxes and property taxes are imposed within a special district, 100 percent of those taxes, the net of collection fees, can be contributed to paying the costs of project improvements.	To finance environmental remediation and the subsequent improvements, Dearborn established a TIF district. TIF proceeds reimbursed entities that were able to make the property a safe location. Once the site was clean, the city took steps to make it a family-oriented area. The city rezoned the property and built a school where the Sharon Steel facility once stood.	

Tax credit and incentive programs

A tax credit is a monetary reduction of a taxpayer's tax liability. It is a governmental vehicle designed to encourage investment in certain socially or economically favored industries or activities. Tax credits accomplish important public policy objectives by encouraging the private sector to provide social benefits through projects that probably would not have been developed without such credits.	In the United States, the Brownfields Tax Incentive reduces an investor's tax burden by lowering the investor's taxable income. The incentive allows the investor to claim up to 100 percent of the eligible costs of cleaning up brownfields land as current expenses— rather than capitalizing these expenses as long-term assets. This is the only federal brownfield incentive targeted for private site owners. It has attracted new owners to abandoned and contaminated brownfield sites. The incentive program, which provides an immediate incentive to offset short-term project costs, encourages the cleanup and development of polluted land. The true value of the incentive is the ability to level the economic playing field between shovel-ready and brownfield sites through the favorable tax treatment of cleanup costs.	Tax credits are strictly performance-based, meaning developers and project partners receive virtually nothing if they do not perform. Since tax credits are awarded after cleanup, they encourage nearly flawless execution. If project developers do not perform, they do not benefit from the incentive. An existing corporate taxation regulatory framework is a prerequisite to the implementation of tax credit incentives for contaminated site remediation programs.

(Table continues on next page)

Table 2.3   Mechanisms for financing site remediation *(continued)*

Definition	Example	Global application
Grant financing programs		
Grants are the distribution of funds to remediation projects generally without any requirement of repayment. They can fund 100 percent of project costs, but typically contribute a percentage, with the developer required to make up the difference through equity or debt financing. Historically, brownfield remediation has been typically heavily subsidized through grants. However, direct grants to private entities are increasingly rare in some countries, as government budgets strain under economic conditions and public officials increasingly demand a higher return on investment. Grants from higher levels of government to lower levels, such as the national government to the city, are common methods of seeding other contaminated site remediation financing programs, such as revolving loan programs, forgivable loan programs, or technical assistance services.	When the U.S. Environmental Protection Agency (EPA) issues grants from one level of government to a lower level of government, these grants are expected to leverage significant outside financing or funding. The EPA administers a robust and diverse set of grant funding programs, providing annual competitive subgrants to cities and counties for leveraged brownfield cleanup programming.[a]	Grant programs can be implemented at any level of government, regardless of economic structure or market conditions. Grant programs can also be combined with other financial mechanisms, such as revolving funds, to provide support for up front studies or other aspects. The only caveat to the implementation of a grant program would be the lack of sustainable capital to maintain fund operations. All grant funds and administrative costs must be contributed by the grantor entity and replenished periodically. Grant programs must be carefully structured to reduce opportunities for political influence and to ensure that funds have a reasonable opportunity to target only feasible site remediation projects with a legitimate financial need. The structure of a successful grant program will depend largely on the goals and economic climate of the government implementing it.

Source: World Bank 2014.

a. See http://www.epa.gov/swerosps/bf/index.html.

Notes

1. High resolution satellite imagery of 50 cm pixels or better, or orthophoto imagery on the scale of 1:2,000 for rural and low density areas, and 1:500 scale for dense urban areas.
2. "NCI Charrette Start-Up Kit: Key Tools for Getting Smart Growth Built." CD-ROM, 2003.
3. The definition of *brownfield* is a formerly developed industrial site whose future development prospects are impaired by real or perceived contamination. Brownfield may include operational or abandoned factory sites, dumping sites, or any structures containing (or perceived to contain) substances hazardous to human health.

4. This section is heavily based on "The Management of Brownfield Redevelopment. A Guidance Note" (World Bank 2010). For more details on Brownfield redevelopment, see http://www-wds.worldbank .org/external/default/WDSContentServer/WDSP/IB/2010/06/14 /000333037_20100614004032/Rendered/PDF/550090WP0P118011 PUBLIC10brownfields.pdf.

5. For an overview of remediation technologies, see: *The Management of Brownfields Redevelopment*, Annex 5, World Bank.

6. This section is based on the World Bank Working Paper "Financing Mechanisms for Addressing Remediation of Site Contamination." October 2014.

References

Ballaney, S. 2008. *Town Planning Mechanism in Gujarat*. Washington, DC: World Bank Institute.

Ballaney, Shirley, M. Bertaud, P. Clarke Annez, C. K Koshy, B. Nair, B. Patel, V. Phatak, and V. Thawakar. 2013. *Inventory of Public land in Ahmedabad, Gujarat, India*. Washington, DC: World Bank.

Barro, J. 2014. "Affordable Housing That's Very Costly, The Upshot." *New York Times*, June 7. http://www.nytimes.com/2014/06/08/upshot /affordable-housing-thats-very-costly.html?abt=0002&abg=0.

Centre for Liveable Cities. 2014. *Urban Systems Studies: Land Acquisition and Resettlement: Securing Resources for Development*. Singapore: Centre for Liveable Cities.

City of New York. 2015a. http://www.nyc.gov/html/dcp/html/zone/zonehis .shtml.

———. 2015b. http://www.nyc.gov/html/dcp/html/zone/glossary.shtml.

City of Nis. 2012. *E-Newsletter* 37 (January).

Cordato, R. 2001. *The Polluter Pays Principle: A Proper Guide for Environmental Policy*. Washington, DC: Institute for Research on the Economics of Taxation.

Enemark, Stig, Keith Clifford Bell, Christiaan Lemmen, and Robin McLaren. 2014. "Fit-For-Purpose Land Administration." FIG and World Bank, Copenhagen.

Horita, M., and H. Koizumi. 2009. *Innovations in Collaborative Urban Regeneration*. New York: Springer Publishing.

Ilic, Danijela. 2013. "An Initiative to Solve the Issue of Military Brownfield Properties in Underdeveloped Municipalities." Standing Conference of Towns and Municipalities, Belgrade.

Kaganova, Olga. 2012. "Valuation and Pricing of Government Land and Property: A Tip of a Growing Iceberg." *Real Estate Issues* 37 (1): 9.

Lennertz, B., and A. Lutzenhiser. 2003. "Charettes 101: Dynamic Planning for Community Change." Building Blocks 4 (1). http://community-wealth.org/content/charrettes-101-dynamic-planning-community-change.

Lozano-Gracia, Nancy, Somik V. Lall, Cheryl Young, and Tara Vishwanath. 2013. "Leveraging Land to Enable Urban Transformation: Lessons from Global Experience." Policy Research Working Paper 6312, World Bank, Washington, DC.

Payne, Geoffrey. 2004. "Land Tenure and Property Rights: An Introduction." *Habitat International* 28 (2): 167–79.

Peterson, George E. 2009. *Unlocking Land Values to Finance Urban Infrastructure*. Washington, DC: World Bank.

———. 2013. "Unlocking Land Values for Urban Infrastructure Finance: International Experience: Considerations for Indian Policy." Policy Research Working Paper 6683, World Bank, Washington, DC.

Peterson, George E., and Olga Kaganova. 2010. "Integrating Land Financing into Subnational Fiscal Management." Policy Research Working Paper, World Bank, Washington, DC.

Rabe, Paul E. 2010. "Land Sharing in Phom Penh and Bangkok: Lessons from Four Decades of Innovative Slum Redevelopment Projects in Two Southeast Asian 'Boom Towns'." http://www.worldbank.org/content/dam/Worldbank/document/urban/places-we-live-competition-Rabe.pdf.

Relhan, Gaurav, Kremena Ionkova, and Rumana Huque. 2012. "Good Urban Governance through ICT: Issues, Analysis, and Strategies." Working Paper 71512, World Bank, Washington, DC.

Suzuki, Hiroaki, Jin Murakami, Yu-Hung Hong, and Beth Tamayose. 2015. *Financing Transit-Oriented Development with Land Values: Adapting Land Value Capture in Developing Countries*. Washington, DC: World Bank.

USAID (U.S. Agency for International Development). 2011. *Municipal Economic Growth Activity (Serbia): Final Program Report*. Washington, DC: USAID.

Victorian State Government. 2008. Planning: A Short Guide: Department of Planning and Community Development. http://www.dtpli.vic.gov.au/__data/assets/pdf_file/0009/228672/Planning_-_a_Short_Guide.pdf.

World Bank. 2010. "The Management of Brownfields Redevelopment: A Guidance Note." World Bank, Washington, DC.

———. 2014. "Financing Mechanisms for Addressing Remediation of Site Contamination," Working Paper. World Bank, Washington, DC.

———. 2015. "Ethiopia Urbanization Review: Urban Institutions for a Middle Class Ethiopia." Report 100238, World Bank, Washington, DC.

CHAPTER 3

Social Impacts

Social Equity Aspects of Regeneration

The main objective of urban regeneration projects is local economic development. Urban regeneration projects can have a number of direct positive social impacts on the population living in the vicinity. In fact, many urban regeneration projects are conceived as integrated approaches that go beyond the physical aspects of improving the environment. A set of social interventions should be designed to respond to the community's needs and priorities that the team has identified throughout the project scoping phase.

The social initiatives related to the regeneration project might be instigated by the public sector, by the civil society through nongovernmental organizations (NGOs), or even by the private sector through corporate social responsibility initiatives. The key is to generate synergies and complementarities between the physical regeneration part of the project and the social initiatives.

The main purpose of this guidebook is to present methods to finance urban regeneration initiatives through attracting private sector funds and leveraging public assets. It does not intend to list all of the social components that could be part of a regeneration project. However, we provide a short introduction to the idea that including social equity components in regeneration is possible, desirable, and can have a very tangible impact on the original population living in the regeneration area.

Social equity components usually refer to activities related to training, access to social services, early childhood education, health, crime and violence prevention, and access to quality public spaces, to name a few. Some social components that could be included in a regeneration project follow, although the list is not exhaustive, just illustrative.[1] These programs are mainly applicable to neighborhoods with poverty concentration, which have been disconnected from job and growth opportunities in the past (see table 3.1).

Table 3.1   **Interventions for a more socially equitable regeneration project**

Intervention option	What it entails
Public safety for crime and violence prevention	This is applicable to communities with high crime rates and public safety threats. Regeneration, which improves physical living conditions in neighborhoods, can reduce levels of crime and violence. Basic services and simple environmental design interventions such as street lighting, public telephones, closed-circuit television, and improved street layouts can create safer urban spaces and enhance community integration. Neighborhood watches can also be established. These types of interventions can include mediation and conflict resolution programs. They can also be complemented by social prevention programs that address the causes of crime and violence.
Early childhood education and parenting programs	Higher student performance is associated with the involvement of parents in their daily activities. The support of parents in the first years of childhood development (preschool and primary education) has a significant impact on children's future opportunities. Parenting education can be provided with a strong emphasis on parent-child communication. In neighborhoods where there is a shortage of preschool services, mothers can also be recruited and trained to develop learning activities for children below primary school age.
Job training (soft and hard skills)	Training can be provided to increase the skills and employability of the unemployed. Life skills courses on motivation, work life, social skills, and job search skills can also be included in the skills enhancement programs to increase the employability of the unemployed. The curriculum can also be complemented by mentorships, internships/apprenticeships, or job trial opportunities to provide work experience. Training and technical assistance can also be provided to increase both the skills and knowledge of entrepreneurs to create and run businesses (such as obtaining licenses, accounting, and marketing).
Job search assistance	Comprehensive local employment services, including employment counseling, mentoring, and job search assistance can be provided to job seekers who may not have adequate information, networks, or the necessary job search skills to find jobs. It can help to improve the job search effort by providing information about vacancies and by assisting with the preparation of job applications. Given that location discrimination is often a barrier to employment prospects, the employment service can also serve as a liaison between employers and prospective employees by providing brokering services.
Youth programs: before- and after-school, arts and sports for youth	In collaboration with schools, communities can introduce additional activities or learning materials to make the learning experiences of the children in the community more relevant and meaningful to their family and community life. Additional activities and materials could include after-school assistance to help children complete homework or catch up with after-school recreation activities, such as sports, music, and arts. These activities can help to nurture social and life skills.
Employment opportunities for residents through construction projects and new businesses	When a local project involves the creation of new jobs for the construction or the operation or maintenance of social services or infrastructure, people from the local community can be simultaneously trained and hired to fill the new jobs.

Table 3.1   Interventions for a more socially equitable regeneration project *(continued)*

Intervention option	What it entails
Community health clinics	Awareness-raising events or materials can be prepared to promote healthy lifestyles and deter risky behaviors. The importance of accessing health care services, such as prenatal checkups and vaccinations, should also be emphasized. Such information can be provided as part of a broader life skills education.
New social infrastructure (schools, health centers)	As part of the initial assessment of the project, the team should determine if the neighborhood's growth, which is meant to be triggered by the regeneration project, will require additional social services, such as schools, health centers, and public transportation.
Microfinance	A scheme can be developed (through a partnership with a microfinance institution) to provide small loans to help homeowners improve their housing, or to help local small businesses make start-up investments (for example, for facilities, equipment, raw materials, and other inputs).
Civil registration	In the event that a lack of civil registration, such as a birth certificate and residential address, is constraining community members' eligibility to access social and financial services, an intervention can be designed to facilitate and assist civil registration.
Community social workers	Some communities can benefit from an on-the-ground presence of community social workers who actively engage with community members and monitor their needs and issues on a day-to-day basis. Community social workers, especially when permanently based in a community, can serve as an open channel of communication between the community members, service providers, and local project planners. They can help enhance the provision of services and relevance of interventions by facilitating the identification of needs, while also gathering the most current information about the conditions of existing infrastructure, services, and development opportunities.

Continued and direct communication with community members, including local NGOs and government representatives, is also essential to monitoring project implementation, keeping track of project priorities and results, and initiating course correction, as necessary. When community social workers come from the communities they serve, it enhances partnerships and communication through trusted relationships with community members built over the years. |
| Land registration and titling | When the regeneration project takes place in an informal area of a city characterized by illegal occupation of land or unregistered subdivisions, the regeneration project should be complemented with a land-titling component.

Land regularization interventions vary considerably depending on local regulations but generally include inventories of land ownership and a titling program. Inventories of land ownership generally involve cadastral audits that enable government agencies and partners to quantify the exact number of parcels eligible for titling and assess the requirements for transferring ownership of public lands. Titling programs typically involve the completion of land surveys, completion of register and cadastre searches, verification of occupancy information, and provision of technical assistance to eligible beneficiaries. When dealing with vulnerable communities, project developers need to identify mechanisms to surpass existing barriers (such as lack of personal identification documents and illiteracy) to access property titles, or to regularize land. |

(Table continues on next page)

Table 3.1 **Interventions for a more socially equitable regeneration project** *(continued)*

Intervention option	What it entails
Historic preservation/ cultural heritage	Conservation of urban heritage should be an important part of any regeneration project, as these irreplaceable assets belong to all generations. Moreover, cultural heritage assets have an actual economic value that can be quantified with contemporary assessment methods.[a]
	The scoping and planning phases of any urban regeneration project should take account of cultural heritage, both landmarks and historic urban cores and downtowns. When these assets are accounted for, their location and potential usage should be included in the master plan. If the monument does not have a current use (as a tourist destination, for instance), its adaptive reuse should be considered. If in fact such monuments do have a current use as a destination, they should be incorporated into a tourism and activity circuit, which also includes other attractions in the area. In this way, the spending-per-visitor will be distributed in a larger geographic area than just the vicinity.

a. For a list of these methods, see Licciardi and Amirtahmasebi 2012.

Managing the Potential Undesirable Impacts of Urban Regeneration: Gentrification and Loss of Social Capital

One of the unintended consequences of urban regeneration is gentrification. Gentrification is a shift in an urban community toward wealthier residents and businesses, with consequent increases in property values. Gentrification is typically the result of investment in a community by real estate development businesses, local government, or community activists. It can and often does spur economic development, attract businesses, and lower crime rates. In addition to these potential benefits, gentrification can lead to some adverse population migration trends in which poorer residents are displaced by wealthier newcomers. In a community undergoing gentrification, the average income increases and the average family size decreases. Poorer pre-gentrification residents who are unable to pay the increased rents or property taxes may be driven out. Consequently, new businesses arrive to the area, which can afford the increased commercial rent. They cater specifically to a more affluent base of consumers—further increasing the appeal to higher-income migrants and decreasing accessibility to the poor.

When designing an urban regeneration project, the social aspects of the initiative should be as important as environmental and economic considerations and should be fully taken into account at the outset of project preparation. Community engagement is one way to discover, define, and address social issues pertaining to the regeneration project. As such, people with the right skill set are needed for the job.

Gentrification is a very complex matter and there are numerous arguments for and against it, as well as its social consequences for the community. It should be noted that whereas some scholars have negative views about gentrification, others simply accept it as a market reality.[2] Some others have criticized it as social restructuring by the state or even "displacement" (Snel and others 2011). Gentrification could be led by the market or the state. Indeed, urban regeneration policies implemented by central or local governments can have a tremendous impact on gentrification, as well as on the lives of the original residents. In this section, we focus on a variety of tools that cities have used to address the problem of gentrification and access to affordable housing.

A second unwanted consequence of regeneration projects—related to gentrification and out-migration of the original population—is the loss of social capital, or community ties. Broadly speaking, social capital can be defined as a set of social norms of conduct, knowledge, mutual obligations and expectations, and reciprocity and trust that are widespread within a given region or community. The concept is also connected with social networks (Colantonio and Dixon 2011).

Social capital refers to the collective value of all "social networks" (who people know) and the inclinations that arise from these networks to do things for each other (norms of reciprocity). The term "social capital" emphasizes a wide variety of specific benefits that flow from the trust, reciprocity, information, and cooperation associated with social networks. Because social capital creates value for the people who are connected, the urban regeneration team should be concerned about how out-migration and relocation will impact economic opportunities for the population. For example, the loss of access to information flows can disrupt the relocated population by reducing opportunities to learn about jobs.

The case of Anacostia in Washington, DC, offers a good example of how to manage gentrification in the targeted neighborhood. For example, the Arthur Capper/Carrollsburg development guaranteed one-for-one replacement of demolished public housing units in the same footprint as the original development. At the Southwest Waterfront, the planning effort was crystalized in an agreement between the developer and the long-term residents by which the tenants received affordable units in the new housing development. The Yards project also includes affordable housing units.

Tools to Mitigate the Undesirable Social Impacts of Urban Regeneration

How can project managers avoid these undesirable social outcomes? This section outlines some tools that have been used in different contexts to minimize the negative impacts of urban regeneration projects.[3]

Successful urban resettlement requires attention to density and diversity, usually in a context of rapid change. High population density is an obvious hallmark of urban life. Although population density in the urban landscape creates opportunities (such as concentrated demand for goods and services, employment, and land and other natural resources), it also creates problems, such as pollution and waste disposal. Resettlement in urban areas is often expensive because public infrastructure must be built, rehabilitated, or upgraded in an area where people are already living and working. As a consequence, even projects acquiring little land in urban areas can generate a fairly large displacement. Furthermore, even a temporary loss of land or other assets can cause severe and costly impacts.

When Is Resettlement Justified?

Even though population displacement should be avoided when possible, some urban regeneration projects might require resettlement in order to be implemented. The need for resettlement should be looked at from a cost-benefit point of view. Project planners should attempt to understand the project's potential winners and losers. Potential gains can be manifested in terms of property value increases, tax revenues, and private investment in the area that might not otherwise occur. Potential losses may involve displaced populations and businesses, as well as hardship in accessing jobs due to distance. Some positive aspects of the regeneration projects may be hard to quantify. This includes improvements in the quality of life, quality of urban environment, and an improved image for the city. But the negative impacts, such as resettlement, will be observed by the community. The point is that resettlement is only justified if the regeneration project brings large enough gains for the city to outweigh the losses of the impacted population. In many cases, project teams can develop win-win situations, whereby the resettled population lives in improved conditions. See, for example, box 3.1 on vertical resettlement in India.

Early resettlement planning is always advised. This is especially important as resettlement costs can escalate quickly in urban areas. A good practice is to base the initial project design on an assessment of social and demographic conditions and then revise it to incorporate information from public consultations. Timing is crucial, because resettlement mistakes can be especially costly in urban projects. Careful, early, and participatory planning is necessary to later avoid major revisions in respect to investments during implementation. It also helps to ensure that the displaced populations accept resettlement conditions.

Resettlement itself is invariably complex. The many tasks to be performed range from urban planning to the issuance of land acquisition notices, to provision of resettlement-site infrastructure, to payment of compensation, to provision of employment or other forms of economic rehabilitation. A substantial number of governmental agencies scattered horizontally across several jurisdictional levels are therefore likely to be involved in any operation.

Resettlement can be an opportunity for low-income communities, as it can help them gain titles to properties they occupy. Resettlement of low-income informal communities often provides opportunities for moving

Box 3.1   Vertical resettlement: A tool for urban regeneration

As part of the World Bank's India Mumbai Urban Transport Project, about 100,000 residents of urban slums and shanty towns were resettled in high-rise buildings. The displaced persons (DPs) were living along railway tracks and roads that needed to be upgraded as part of the project. Most of the DPs did not have any titles to the land they occupied.

After consultations with the World Bank, local NGOs, and the DPs, the Maharashtra State and Indian Railway Authorities designed a program to relocate the DPs to apartment buildings, each with seven floors, as close as possible to their current locations. Given the importance of social mobilization and the difficult task of getting DPs to adapt to new residential patterns, the task of designing and implementing the resettlement program was given to two reputable NGOs, SPARK and National Slum Dwellers Federation. Both organizations had already been working actively with the DPs. Given the time needed to acquire and develop some of the urban sites, provisions were made for temporary housing close to the permanent resettlement sites.

In order to reduce the total cost of the resettlement program, the government helped establish a market in tradable development rights. This enabled builders who had constructed buildings for resettlement at subsidized rates to construct additional commercial space—beyond what would otherwise be allowed under development regulations in other commercial locations in Mumbai.

More than 50,000 people were resettled under the program and have expressed high levels of satisfaction with the resettlement program. The success of the resettlement program was evident from early indicators. For instance, there were no defaults on the loan components of housing assistance. Residents worked together to form cooperative societies for maintenance and other activities. Electricity and water tariffs, as well as maintenance fees, have been paid regularly. Women-led savings and loans' groups have been established in every building. Finally, the DPs have adapted quite well to living in high-rise buildings.

Source: World Bank 2004.

beyond the narrow mitigation of adverse impacts to promoting community development, security of tenure, and rational land use.

The Principle of Minimizing Displacement

Technical considerations are fundamentally important in project design, but they are not the only factors to consider. Environmental and social factors are also important. In dense urban settings, minimizing displacement is likely to reduce overall project costs and make project implementation easier. From the social perspective, resettlement costs may not simply be directly proportional to the number of displaced people. Costs depend on the type and degree of impacts. Compensating a large number of people for minor or partial land acquisition may cost far less than physically relocating a few people and providing them with income-restoring alternatives.

In urban projects, minimizing both the number of displaced people and the severity of resettlement impacts—especially residential relocation and changes in employment—is necessary. Another good practice is to minimize the distance of any necessary relocation: families moving less than a kilometer in the city often find that their lives, community ties, and livelihoods are much less disrupted than those moving greater distances. The following are some of the steps normally taken in the early stages of project design:

- Send out information about project objectives and potential impacts within the project area. Given the diversity of tenure arrangements, a good practice is to supplement legally required notification with other public announcements to ensure that renters, owners, and others are informed about the project.
- Conduct a census of project impacts and publicly display the results.
- Solicit information from potential displaced persons regarding valuation of losses and preferences for possible resettlement options.
- Send out information regarding compensation rates and other entitlements. Also include the resettlement implementation schedule.
- Form a community-based committee to coordinate with the project resettlement agency.
- Require careful coordination of several layers of government and multiple line agencies for successful design and implementation of urban projects.

Compensation Methods

The rules for compensation will be formulated by each country and should follow existing rules, laws, and procedures. The general notion is that compensation should be fair, which means that it should cover both the expropriated assets and rehabilitation measures to help restore incomes or standards of living (including foregone income). It is key to have in place a set of procedures for asset valuation. The World Bank policy for resettlement establishes that compensation should be paid at replacement cost. The alternative of replacing at market cost may not be fair in countries in which land markets do not function well and prices are distorted.

The census of affected people should identify residential and commercial tenure arrangements for people with and without formal rights, such as residents claiming ownership of private land but lacking legal title. Other individuals and groups to consider include tenants, squatters on public lands, squatters in public safety zones, owners of enterprises lacking licenses or property titles, marketers, and mobile and itinerant vendors. Consideration also needs to be given to issues involving drains, riverbeds, and rights-of-way. Furthermore, urban residential and commercial areas in most developing countries often have informal (unauthorized or unlicensed) economic activity. The displacement of informal enterprises can be disastrous for people who derive their incomes from them. The loss of such information enterprises may also deprive communities of access to products or services. Potentially displaced formal and informal enterprises should be identified and appropriate remedies devised.

In many urban projects, the identification of replacement land and provision of replacement housing are serious constraints. Regarding land, the calculation of replacement cost is made more complex by gross disparities in land prices or, in some cities, the absence of a functional land market. The provision of replacement housing is often a crucial ingredient in urban resettlement planning. Remedies usually take some variant of two basic forms. In some cases, those losing their housing are relocated to newly developed housing sites. In other cases, projects follow "fill-in" resettlement strategies, in which displaced people obtain existing vacant housing. Alternatively, new housing is constructed on vacant lots scattered throughout several areas. Land replacement, whether in kind or in cash, recognizes not only the quantity of land acquired but also its characteristics, such as location and productive capacity. For land in urban areas, location accounts for great differences in value. Because of its centrality, a parcel of land in the inner city may be worth many times the same sized plot in a peripheral area. Such an inner-city plot may also have advantages of location that cannot be compensated by a larger plot in a more distant area.

The Ahmedabad case study provides good lessons about how *not* to deal with resettlement. The Ahmedabad Municipal Corporation, the agency in charge of project implementation, proposed that the relocation of the project-affected households be done on municipal-owned land sites far from the riverfront, where the affected households were located. This was justified on the basis of project costs because the land used for relocation would come from the municipality through its land bank and not the project itself. This saved the Sabarmati Riverfront Development Corporation a considerable amount of resources. However, many of the informal settlements were relocated to residential complexes far from the city center. The project was also accused of not providing resettlement compensation to all affected parties.

Tool: Inclusionary Zoning

Another approach that has been used by many cities to reduce gentrification and protect the rights of the most vulnerable population around the regeneration site is inclusionary zoning (IZ). IZ is a means of using the planning system to create affordable housing and foster social inclusion by capturing resources created through the marketplace. The term refers to a program, regulation, or law that requires or provides incentives to private developers to incorporate affordable or social housing as a part of market-driven developments. This can be achieved either by incorporating the affordable housing into the same development, building it elsewhere, or contributing money or land for the production of social or affordable housing in lieu of construction.

The IZ concept is becoming more popular among developers because local governments usually offer a number of incentives, including low-interest financing tools, cash subsidies and grants, free or low-cost land, density bonuses, tax abatement programs, rehabilitation assistance, fast-tracking of plan reviews and permits, and reduced or waived fees. IZ is a useful tool for urban regeneration projects that have the explicit goal of creating diverse neighborhoods that include various socioeconomic, racial, and age groups.

IZ regulations vary, but they typically require that a certain percentage of units be affordable to certain low-income families. For example, in California, most ordinances target very low, low, or moderate incomes: "very low" is usually classified as up to 50 percent of the county's median income, "low" as 51–80 percent of the median, and "moderate" as 81–120 percent of the median. Depending on the ordinance, builders must sell or lease 5–25 percent of the new homes at below-market rates.

In many cases, the below-market units must be of similar size and quality as the market-rate units. They must also be spread throughout the project in order to create integration and avoid creating ghettos. Some jurisdictions allow off-site construction or enable developers to pay a fee in lieu of building a below-market unit. However, the intent of IZ is to have the below-market units mixed among the market-rate units. Some ordinances are mandatory, meaning builders must participate in order to obtain permission to build, but a few ordinances are voluntary in that they offer incentives in exchange for a builder selling at price-controlled rates. Jurisdictions may also offer compensating incentives, such as density bonuses, fast-track permitting, or fee waivers.

Reviews of the impact of IZ policies highlight that even though IZ regulations are intended to add to the supply of affordable housing, they tend to produce small numbers of homes, and at potentially substantial cost. To date, IZ programs have played a relatively small role in meeting the needs for affordable housing in the United States. It is estimated that IZ programs nationwide have led to the creation of approximately 150,000 units over several decades (Calavita and Mallach 2010). In contrast, the U.S. Department of Housing and Urban Development's largest rental assistance program—housing choice vouchers—serves approximately 2 million households, and the Low-Income Housing Tax Credits program has created more than 2 million affordable homes. Low production obviously limits the potential of IZ to promote social inclusion for low-income recipients (Schwartz and others 2012).

Precisely because IZ programs are intended to provide affordable housing within high-cost housing markets, they can require large cost offsets to developers or direct subsidies to IZ dwellers—or both. The size of the price discount decreases as the income-eligibility of the target IZ population increases. This trade-off has direct implications for the potential of IZ programs to target low-income recipients and promote social inclusion. Jurisdictions with high demand for market-rate housing may be able to offset the substantial loss a developer would incur on an IZ home that is sold at, say, 40 percent of market value to a low-income purchaser by offering a substantial benefit, such as a large density bonus. Indeed, for IZ programs to produce homes, they must offset developers' potential losses or even enhance the overall profitability of the housing project (Calavita and Mallach 2010).

"In-Lieu of" Options and Cost Offsets Available to Developers
The types of incentives provided to developers can affect their willingness to participate in voluntary IZ programs. Some forms of incentives can affect the extent to which the programs succeed in promoting social integration. Of course, the underlying housing market conditions also drive developers' choices—strong housing markets with high demand for market-rate dwellings are much more conducive to acceptance of more demanding IZ design criteria. These can include smaller incentives, fewer opt-outs, lower minimum project sizes, and higher set-aside provisions. The most common form of incentive provided to developers is a density bonus, which allows them to build more square feet than would otherwise be permitted under zoning provisions. Other common incentives include fee waivers, reductions in parking spaces required by zoning and building codes, and expedited permitting (Calavita and Mallach 2010). Two other types of incentives are the availability of alternative means of compliance (for example, paying a fee rather than building IZ units) and the option to build the IZ units off-site—which may defeat the goal of mixed-income neighborhoods depending on where the units are built.

For example, the IZ ordinance in Boulder, Colorado, allows developers to pay in-lieu fees rather than build IZ units. The goal is to have 50 percent of the ownership units built on-site. Affordable rental units can be constructed either on- or off-site, provided they meet size requirements. The IZ ordinance of the city of Irvine, California, provides a menu of alternative compliance options, including converting market-rate units or extending the affordability period on existing affordable units; in-lieu fees; transfer of existing units to a nonprofit housing agency; transfer of off-site credits for affordable units (that is, a developer can provide more than the minimum number of units at one site and count those against another site); alternative housing (such as special needs, single-room occupancy, and shelters); and land dedication for affordable housing.

Developers can also fulfill affordable housing goals by trading credits with other building sites. The types of opt-out offerings, if any, should be aligned with program goals. If the intent is to enforce the maximum degree of social inclusion, in-lieu options are less likely to be effective. If the intent is to maximize the supply of affordable housing in the jurisdiction regardless of specific locations, opt-out provisions could be useful. Box 3.2 summarizes IZ practices in New York City.

Tool: Housing Vouchers (or Demand-Side Subsidies) as an Alternative to Inclusionary Zoning

Critics of the inclusionary housing approach often cite housing vouchers as a better alternative to provide subsidies for affordable housing. The alternative choice to IZ—or project-based housing assistance—is tenant-based assistance, which operates on the demand side of the housing market. Demand-side aid most commonly takes the form of government provision of housing vouchers to eligible households. If and when a voucher recipient

Box 3.2 Inclusionary zoning practices in New York City

The Department of City Planning of the City of New York has been implementing an Inclusionary Housing Program since 1987. This program aims to promote economic integration for low-income households by offering an optional floor area bonus to developers in exchange for the creation or preservation of affordable housing. All bonus floor area must be accommodated within the height and setback provisions of the underlying zoning district. The program "requires a percentage of the dwelling units within a building to be set aside or new or rehabilitated affordable units to be provided off-site within the same community district or within one-half mile of the bonus development. All affordable residential units created through the Inclusionary Housing Program must remain permanently affordable" (City of New York 2014).

There are currently two programs for IZ housing in New York City. The original is the R10 Program that provides a floor area bonus of up to 20 percent in applicable residential and commercial districts. The other program, the Inclusionary Housing Designated Areas, allows a bonus of 33 percent of floor area that can be obtained for providing 20 percent as affordable housing. These designated areas, 16 in total, are located in four of the five boroughs of New York City, with a large majority of locations in Manhattan and Brooklyn (Association for Neighborhood and Housing Development Inc. 2013; City of New York 2014).

The output and impact of IZ in New York City indicates the following: 2,769 affordable housing units have been generated between 2005 and mid-2013; on the West Side of Manhattan and on the Brooklyn waterfront, the IZ program has proven to be an effective and efficient means of generating affordable housing units; outside of these two areas, very few IZ housing units were created, even where there was significant development; and overall, IZ represents less than 2 percent of all multi-family building permit applications in New York City during these years (Lander, Freedman-Schnapp, and Ullman 2013).

The push for more affordable housing has led to calls for IZ to be made mandatory. The mandatory versus voluntary topic is a whole debate on its own. It was summed up in a 1994 study by the California Coalition for Rural Housing that found that "mandatory programs produce the most very low- and low-income affordable units compared with voluntary programs, both in terms of absolute numbers and percentage of total development" (Furman Center 2013). From the developers' perspective, if the costs of a mandatory IZ program mean a less than profitable outcome, it will also affect the developers' ability to undertake the project. Ultimately, it may actually decrease housing supply and increase overall housing prices (Furman Center 2013).

finds a private landlord willing to participate in the program, the tenant pays a set percentage of the household's monthly cash income toward the monthly rent, and the government pays the remaining balance directly to the landlord.

Section 8, the principal housing voucher program in the United States, fixes the recipient's share of the rent at 30 percent of monthly income. Housing vouchers typically are portable in the sense that the benefit travels with the recipient. Vouchers are designed to give recipients more choices among the dwellings within the stock of existing housing. IZ, by contrast, attempts to influence the design and distribution of dwelling units in the relatively small flow of newly constructed and substantially rehabilitated buildings.

Final Words

The transformation of urban areas is a political process that requires mobilizing and coalescing resources and constituencies behind a common vision for change. As we know from the experience of urban renewal in the United States and Europe, as well as other cities around the world, urban regeneration has generational consequences with respect to urban form, social cohesion, and the economic foundation of the city. Any program of change has to be carefully considered, and great care must be taken to not hastily destroy communities in the name of progress—only to result in longer-term deleterious consequences. Throughout the case studies presented in this book, a series of lessons has emerged. They are compiled below, with the goal of provoking serious thought for developers and city leaders who are about to start a city regeneration process.

- *Staying the course.* Regeneration is a long-term proposition. As such, it requires unusual fortitude, tenacity, and patience. Political leadership is essential to maintaining focus and sustaining the regeneration effort through the inevitable controversies and conflicts among constituencies that occur in any large, transformational effort. Without political leadership, regeneration projects can become stymied and lose momentum, resulting in a loss of confidence and failure of many efforts. Political leadership must also be deft enough to respond to genuine concerns and critiques. Leaders may need to modify and improve aspects to respond to public concerns, resulting in a better, more widely accepted project.
- *Establishing a line of succession and a legacy.* Political succession is very important. It is the rare political leader who will be in office from the beginning to the end of a regeneration initiative because the full realization of results and benefits can often take a decade. Broad and lasting political leadership will be required to maintain the power of the vision, achieve success in forging coalitions, and embed the regeneration program into the essence of the city. So too political leaders help to establish momentum and ensure the delivery of early results that help to build the confidence of all stakeholders.
- *Creating an appropriate institutional structure.* The establishment of an administrative structure tasked with leading the regeneration process is key to the project's success. Several different types of administrative and financial structures have been created around renovation projects. However, there is not one model that works for every case. The institutional arrangement should also include a clear and coherent decision-making structure that private actors and civil society can trust.
- *Using a combination of financing options.* Likewise the project team should study the different financing options and use the most suitable

to the regeneration challenges. Depending on the institutional structure used for the project, market conditions, and the legal context, there are several financing options that may be available for project implementation. A menu of options provided in this volume shows how creative governments have been in leveraging their regulatory powers and incentivizing private sector investment in the regeneration of urban land.

- *Promoting connectivity.* Many urban regeneration projects are located in deteriorated urban areas, which do not have access to public transportation systems. One of the strategies commonly used for these types of developments is transit-oriented development. It is based on the principle of integrating land use in the planning of transport systems to ensure that mobility connections are grounded in public transport. This approach has the advantage of generating synergies for investment whereby public investment in infrastructure creates the confidence and momentum for private investment to follow.

- *Creating a new local spatial identity.* Urban regeneration is based on the principle of changing the identity of the project's location. For this reason, design becomes a fundamental element in creating a unique and memorable sense of place based primarily on the human dimension of urban space. In addition, urban design is essential to ensure pedestrian access and connections, contributing to a low-carbon development impact.

- *Aligning the incentives.* In all regeneration projects, there are conflicting priorities and demands with regard to land use. Public and private owners, developers, residents, and government agencies may have very different ideas about the vision for the regenerated city. Yet, all actors are central to the success of the initiative. They must come together and agree on issues such as the environmental, cultural, and financial impacts of the renovation. The project structure should therefore include a thorough understanding of all voices and seek to align incentives for each of these stakeholders to contribute positively to the development of the project.

- *Building in flexibility so the project can be adjusted over longer-term market cycles.* Urban regeneration projects tend to be expensive processes that extend over long periods of time, in part because many are located in dilapidated urban areas with low levels of infrastructure and services. A long implementation time frame exposes projects to political and economic changes. These conditions require that projects be conceived in a flexible manner and include possibilities for adaptation to changes and externalities over the life of the project cycle.

Notes

1. The list of social interventions is based on a 2014 World Bank book, *Handbook for Improving the Living Conditions of Roma*. http://documents.worldbank.org/curated/en/2014/01/20356975/handbook-improving-living-conditions-roma.
2. For example, a study on Dutch inner-city districts showed that while regeneration results in out-migration of the original residents, many of them are content with their current living situation and unwilling to return to their original residences (Kleinhans 2005). Another study about London argues that the declining number of working class households in London is not due to gentrification. Rather, it is the result of the transition from an industrial economy to a postindustrial one (Hamnett 2003).
3. Some of this section is based on World Bank (2004), including the World Bank's principles and rules for resettlement and compensation, which can differ from specific national contexts.

References

Association for Neighborhood and Housing Development Inc. 2013. *Guaranteed Inclusionary Zoning: Ensuring Affordability Is a Part of New York City's Future*. New York: Association for Neighborhood and Housing Development Inc.

Calavita, Nico, and Alan Mallach. 2010. *Inclusionary Housing in International Perspective: Affordable Housing, Social Inclusion, and Land Value Recapture*. Cambridge, MA: Lincoln Institute of Land Policy.

City of New York. 2014. "Zoning Tools: Inclusionary Zoning." Department of City Planning, City of New York. http://www.nyc.gov/html/dcp/html/zone/zh_inclu_housing.shtml.

Colantonio, A., and T. Dixon. 2011. *Urban Regeneration and Social Sustainability: Best Practice from European Cities*. Oxford, UK: Wiley-Blackwell.

Furman Center. 2013. "Should the Next Mayor Adopt a Mandatory Inclusionary Zoning Program That Requires Developers to Build or Preserve Affordable Housing Whenever They Build Market-Rate Housing?" In *#NYC Housing: 10 Issues for NYC's Next Mayor*. New York: Furman Center for Real Estate and Urban Policy, New York University. http://furmancenter.org/files/fact-sheets/FurmanCenterNYChousingSeries.pdf.

Hamnett, Chris. 2003. "Gentrification and the Middle-Class Remaking of Inner London, 1961–2001." *Urban Studies* 40 (12): 2401–26.

Kleinhans, Reinout J. 2005. *Sociale implicaties van herstructurering en herhuisvesting* [Social implications of housing diversification in urban renewal]. Sustainable Urban Areas Series 6. Delft, the Netherlands: Delft University of Technology.

Lander, B., M. Freedman-Schnapp, and S. Ullman. 2013. "Inclusionary Zoning in New York City: The Performance of New York City's Designated Areas Inclusionary Housing Program since its launch in 2005." Office of Council Member Brad Lander. http://bradlander.nyc/iz.

Licciardi, Guido, and Rana Amirtahmasebi. 2012. *The Economics of Uniqueness: Investing in Historic City Cores and Cultural Heritage Assets for Sustainable Development.* Washington, DC: World Bank. http://public.eblib.com/choice/publicfullrecord.aspx?p=1048958.

Schwartz, H., L. Ecola, K. Leuschner, and A. Kofner. 2012. "Is Inclusionary Zoning Inclusionary? A Guide for Practitioners." Technical Report, RAND Corporation, Santa Monica, CA.

Snel, Erik, Salome Aussen, Fense Berkhof, and Quirine Renlo. 2011. "Views of Gentrification from Below: How Rotterdam Local Residents Experience Gentrification." Paper presented at the International RC21 Conference, "The Struggle to Belong. Dealing with Diversity in 21st Century Urban Settings," Amsterdam, July 7–9.

World Bank. 2004. "Resettlement in Urban Areas." In *Involuntary Resettlement Sourcebook: Planning and Implementation in Development Projects.* Washington, DC: World Bank.

Part II
Case Studies

Map 4.1 **Puerto Madero, Argentina**

a. Puerto Madero metropolitan area

b. Project location

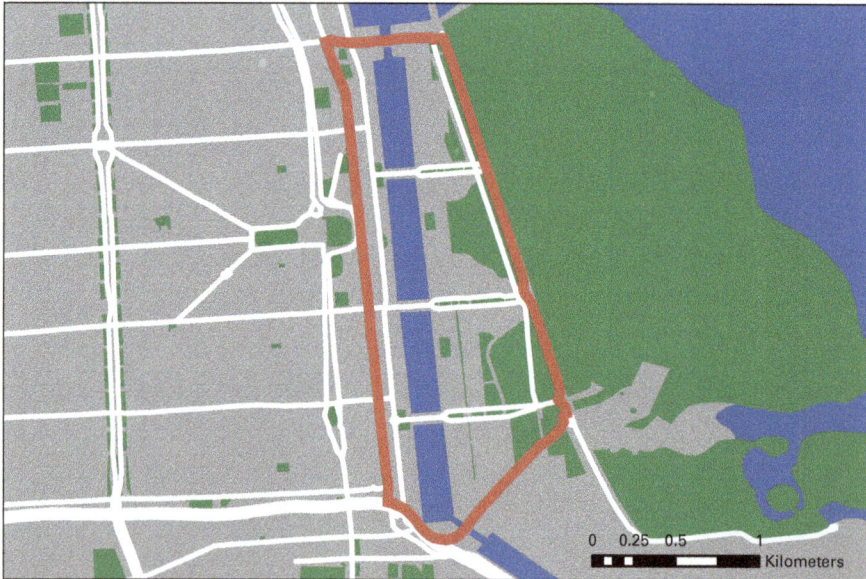

Source: World Bank using Open Street Map data, 2015.

CHAPTER 4

Puerto Madero: Regenerating a Port Area in the Historic District of Buenos Aires

Introduction

Buenos Aires is the capital and largest city of Argentina and the second-largest metropolitan area in South America after São Paulo in Brazil. Based on the last national census (2010), almost 13 million people reside in what is considered the Buenos Aires metropolitan area. The greater metropolitan area comprises approximately one-fourth of Argentina's population. The Autonomous City of Buenos Aires (Ciudad Autónoma de Buenos Aires, CABA) has maintained a stable population since 1940, while the greater metropolitan area has grown considerably during the same period. CABA, which is the national capital of Argentina, is a 200 square kilometer (sq km) territory that is part of the 4,500 sq km of the Buenos Aires greater metropolitan area (GBA).

During the 1980s and 1990s, the city's central business activities shifted away from the downtown area toward the north and northwest axis of the city. This outward sprawl, together with the development of gated communities 30–50 km away from the downtown area, was considered a threat to the metropolitan area's economic viability and sustainability. Indeed, from 2001 to 2010, the population grew 14 percent, reaching 10 million. At the same time, CABA's share of the national population actually decreased from 20 percent in 1914, to 10 percent in 1980, and 7.2 percent in 2010.

The Puerto Madero project played a key role in the regeneration of the traditional administrative and central business district (CBD) of Buenos Aires (map 4.1). In this regard, the scope of the Puerto Madero regeneration project went beyond the transformation of the formerly industrial port area. From the project's conceptualization, the goal of political leaders and city planners was the revitalization of Buenos Aires' southern area, which includes the national administrative area (Casa Rosada), and some of the oldest neighborhoods of the city. Leaders considered the project a strategic investment for the area that would catalyze other private investments in surrounding neighborhoods.[1]

The project was also conceived of as an economic stimulus and employment generation strategy for the construction sector. One of the leading proponents of Puerto Madero, Alfredo Garay,[2] defined the project's goal as "rescuing Buenos Aires' downtown area," including through the creation of new housing demand, thereby bringing renewed vitality and changing popular perceptions about the area. The project also created new public spaces for general enjoyment and served as a growing tourist attraction for the city. A real estate developer and key supporter of the revitalization effort asserted: "We had tremendous success in developing the Puerto Madero District from an abandoned stretch of property into one of the most valuable pieces of real estate in Buenos Aires."[3] Indeed, there is general agreement among stakeholders that the project has revitalized an underutilized area of the city.

Puerto Madero's characteristics and the attendant political and socioeconomic conditions that allowed for the successful implementation of the project are very particular—even unique—and hard to replicate. These include the prime waterfront location, adjacent to the federal administrative buildings and the central business district; the historical industrial buildings; the relative simplicity of the land tenure system; and the political and regulatory environment that facilitated the approval of the required laws and regulations. These initial conditions, coupled with the centralization of the decision-making process, the regulatory environment that permitted the sale of public property, and the simple institutional arrangements allowed for quick project execution. Finally, the speed of the decision-making process also implied that public consultation and the debates around the area were few and limited, thereby facilitating quicker implementation.

Context and Background

History of the Site

Built behind a man-made barrier, Puerto Madero was Buenos Aires' first port. A series of four docks[4] parallel to the coastline were built in front of Argentina's federal administrative center (Plaza de Mayo) and the president's residence (Casa Rosada). As with so many examples of industrial architecture that were abandoned as outmoded, the repetitive sturdy red brick fabric with protruding iron utilitarian elements once again became fashionable in the late 1970s and 1980s.

The port was inaugurated in 1889, when the rustic pier to the wide River Plate (Rio de la Plata) was replaced by Puerto Madero. The port was rendered useless a decade later because it lacked access to deep water and had a faulty design, which generated operational difficulties. Not long after, a new port was opened further north, and Puerto Madero began to decline. Access to the area was fenced off from public use from the very beginning.

In 1918, the municipality of Buenos Aires started the construction of a public promenade along the shore that would become the Costanera Sur. The Costanera Sur functioned as a popular public beach up until the 1950s, when the pollution of the River Plate became so pervasive that the boardwalk area deteriorated. At the end of the 1970s, a new urban highway program reclaimed the land that was to be destined for the new administrative center of the city (see box 4.1). However, in 1984 the project was abandoned. Puerto Madero and Costanera Sur lost the open view

---

Box 4.1   Chronology of plans for the Puerto Madero area: The resilience of planning ideas

Buenos Aires Master Plan 1940

In his visit to Buenos Aires in 1929, the famous, influential Swiss architect Le Corbusier sketched a Cité des Affaires (administrative district) with offices located on an artificial island. A strong access route would cut in half the old Puerto Madero area. This island was to house the administrative center in tall skyscraper buildings. Along with local architects' Juan Kurchan and Jorge Ferrari Hardoy, Le Corbusier's ideas were captured in the 1940 Buenos Aires Master Plan. The purpose of the old harbor was slated to shift to cultural and recreational uses.

The Regulatory Plan (1962)

The subsequent regulatory plan,[5] approved in 1962, examined in detail the legal structure and ownership of the port land and proposed to decommission the almost obsolete Puerto Madero. Virtually all of the land east of the docks would be turned into public recreational areas. Only one small portion would be used for administrative and cultural purposes. A small area east of dock 4 was reserved for port functions, an area that is today used for the boat terminal.

The Master Plan for 2000 (1969)

The 1969 Master Plan for 2000 (Esquema Director para el Año 2000) took a regional approach. The importance of the central business area (including Puerto Madero) in the Buenos Aires Metropolitan Region was highlighted. The plan recommended expanding the city's business district by reclaiming land in front of Puerto Madero district. The plan also kept the recreational uses of the previous regulatory plan, as well as a small port area on the coast. Notably, it included residential uses for the first time.

The Urban Renewal Plan for the South Area of Buenos Aires, 1971

The municipality, in consultation with public and private service companies, sponsored and published the Urban Renewal Plan for the South Area of Buenos Aires in 1971.[a] Kurchan, who had worked with Le Corbusier, led the preparation of the plan. The plan focused on two specific areas, including the Puerto Madero.

The Puerto Madero would accommodate the expansion of the central business area and would include a ferry terminal and cultural and recreational areas (including sports grounds, exhibition

(Box continues on next page)

Box 4.1   Chronology of plans for the Puerto Madero area: the resilience of planning ideas *(continued)*

areas, parks, and space for aquatic sports). Many of these proposed uses would recur with subsequent project plans.

It should also be noted that, at that time, the architectural value of the warehouses was not considered. Indeed, the plan entailed the demolition of the red brick buildings located at the west side of the dock. The plan also included a highway that would have cut through the existing city center and the docks. This idea would continue to be discussed in subsequent plans.

The regulatory tools proposed in the urban renewal plan were the basis for the planning code later approved in 1977. Part of the proposed regulations for the Puerto Madero area was resumed by the current U11 district (zoned for residential, administrative, commercial, financial, and institutional facilities to the highest density). These would later be identified as a particularly relevant measure for the viability of Puerto Madero's urban project.

a. Consultations were made with public companies, such as the Compañía de Servicios Eléctricos del Gran Buenos Aires, Gas del Estado, Empresa Nacional de Telecomunicaciones, Administración General de Obras Sanitarias de la Nación, Subterráneos de Buenos Aires, Dirección Nacional de Transportes Terrestres, Ferrocarriles Argentinos, and la Dirección General de Puertos; and the private electricity company, Compañía Ítalo-Argentina de Electricidad.

of the river and, in 1986, the reclaimed area was declared a nature park and ecological reserve (Ordinance 41.247/86).

These efforts were part of a much longer history of many plans formulated to redesign and redevelop the entire Puerto Madero area. In fact, beginning in the 1940s, there were a series of plans designed to build and improve upon the area—some initiated by local and international architects, and some by regional, municipal and city officials (box 4.1).

In 1981, the Buenos Aires Municipality prepared a land use plan for the expansion of the central business area which proposed to utilize the reclaimed river area for the extension of the city's CBD. A supergrid would advance into the river. The channel between the Costanera Sur (which is part of the Puerto Madero area) and the reclaimed area would be filled. As a result, the area would increase to a total of 800 hectares (ha). The plan included uses directly related to the CBD, as well as for residential use. There was also a metropolitan park closer to the waterfront for recreation.

Puerto Madero covers a total area of 170 ha, 40 ha of which constitute the water bodies that comprise the dock. Costanera Sur divides the dock area from the ecological reserve. The 16 old red brick port warehouses with iron railings and exposed interior columns had a total area of 140,000 square meters (sq m) and are considered an excellent sample of the English architecture of the Industrial Revolution.

Buenos Aires' Organizational Structure and Demographics

CABA, with only 5.2 percent of the total metropolitan area (3 million inhabitants), is five times denser than the metropolitan region as a whole. Furthermore, the population of CABA represents less than 8 percent of the total Argentinian population (40 million, according to the last national census) but generates 25 percent of the total national gross domestic product (GDP).[6]

CABA is an independent district established by a 1994 constitutional amendment. It is neither officially part of Buenos Aires Province nor the Province capital. At the time of the development of the Puerto Madero project (1989), Buenos Aires was a federal district led by a chief of government directly appointed by the president of the republic. In 1996, after the amendment was enacted, the first Mayor was elected with the appointment going to the opposition party.

The relevance of the initial administrative arrangement for Puerto Madero is that the city administration had a direct connection to the federal government during the conception of the project, as well as during the very first critical tasks such as the transfer of land to the administrative body. This arrangement changed because since 1996, CABA's administration has been in the hands of the political opposition.

The administrative organization of CABA changed several times throughout the life of the regeneration project. Two years after the 1994 constitutional amendment, the city approved its own constitution. As such, the city was divided into 16 participation and management centers (Centros de Participación y Gestión, or CGP). The CGPs constituted a new administrative layer by grouping two or three neighborhoods in each CGP.

In 1996, Puerto Madero was incorporated with the status of *barrio* (neighborhood) by Ordinance 51,163. In 2005, with Law 1,777, the CGPs were replaced by 15 *comunas*, the city's smallest political administrative division. Each comuna is in turn subdivided into neighborhoods. Puerto Madero belongs to comuna 1 and is grouped together with the Constitución, Monserrat, Retiro, San Nicolás, and San Telmo neighborhoods (map 4.2). Comuna 1 encompasses Buenos Aires' historic center and CBD. Puerto Madero comprises some 210 ha (including the 40 ha water surface of the docks), plus 350 ha of the ecological reserve, Costanera Sur.

Phase 1: Scoping

Political and Socioeconomic Context

The political and socioeconomic backdrop and context are key to understanding Puerto Madero's redevelopment. Indeed, the project was initiated within the overall context of a Washington Consensus-type Structural Adjustment Program in Argentina. The program started following the socioeconomic crisis that prompted the early ending of President Raúl Alfonsín's administration (1983–89)—and the onset of the accelerated implementation of privatization policies of public services and state property—which were key to the redevelopment project.

By mid-1989, during the first administration of President Carlos Menem (1989–95), two contentious laws—the Administrative Emergency Law and the Economic Emergency Law—provided the legal context and enabling

Map 4.2   **CABA's jurisdictions: 15 comunas and 47 neighborhoods**

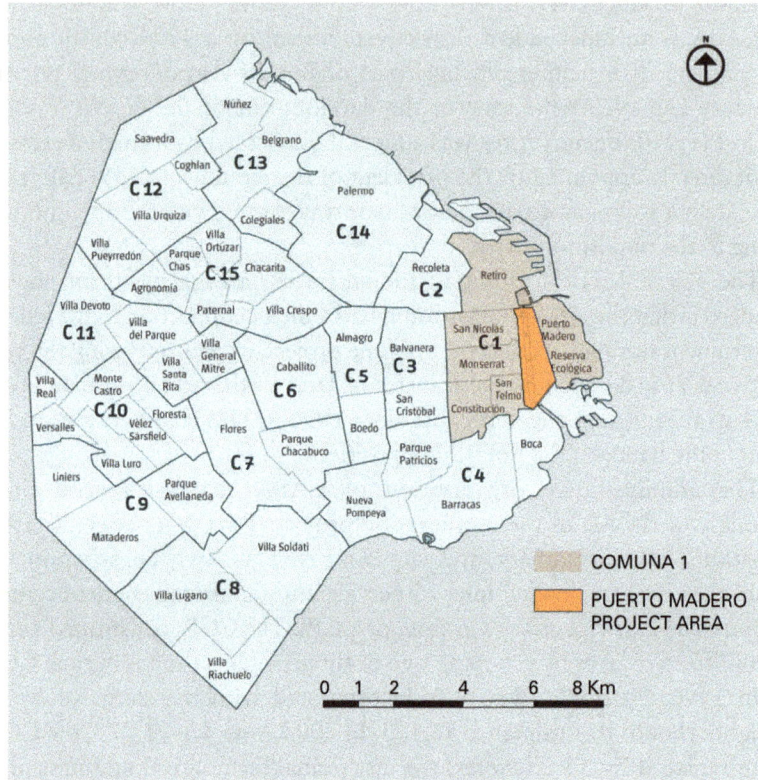

COMUNA 1

PUERTO MADERO
PROJECT AREA

Source: Based on Ciudad de Buenos Aires 2012, coloring added.

regulations to make possible the quick implementation of the Puerto
Madero Project. The Economic Emergency Law allowed for the privatization of federal property. In the case of Puerto Madero, it enabled a simplified transfer of the ownership of national land to the recently created
Corporación Antiguo Puerto Madero Sociedad Anónima (CAPMSA), the
quasi-private corporation created to implement the project. Notably, this
was accomplished without requiring normal legislative approval procedures (see box 4.2).[7]

The project began to move forward when, less than three months later,
the presidential decree 1279/89 established CAPMSA.[8] The main objective
was to urbanize 170 ha of land formerly belonging almost entirely to the
national General Administration of Ports (AGP). The regeneration of
Puerto Madero was then presented by the administration to the media as a
demonstration project for Argentina's state reform. It was to symbolize the
new, modern, and financially integrated Argentina. The area was extremely
visible and the project had been in the works for a long time. President

Box 4.2 **The 1989 economic crisis and public sector reform**

Argentina had a major debt crisis in the 1980s. The Argentinian economy was in a precarious state. The growth of real output stagnated, financial markets collapsed, prices rose as the currency steadily depreciated, and capital fled the country in pursuit of safer havens. Most public enterprises were running large deficits, and the external debt kept mounting.

The banking system and inflation rate were particularly impacted during the crisis as the government resorted to desperate measures to rescue the economy. The central government, hampered by low tax collection and desperate for revenues, turned to the central bank for finance through the taxation of deposits and money printing. Inflation, which had risen gradually over the previous three decades, soared—reaching average annual rates of 2,600 percent in 1989 and 1990. The banking system practically disappeared. Although it tried a number of times to bring inflation under control, the central government was unable either to balance its budget or to escape its reliance on inflationary financing.

The hyperinflation of 1989 and 1990 provided the impetus for reform, which began with the Convertibility Plan of 1991. The reforms of the 1990s also included financial system reforms, liberalization of trade and the capital account, and far-reaching public sector reforms.

Public sector reform, which substantially reduced the size of the public sector, entailed privatizing almost all of the major public enterprises. It had three main results: (a) public subsidies to the enterprises were reduced or eliminated, (b) enterprise efficiency and the provision of services improved dramatically, and (c) funds became available to cover a substantial part of the government deficit (while other reforms, including those pertaining to the tax system, were also under way).

Furthermore, during the first months of President Menem's administration, the Congress delegated to the executive vast legislative powers through the Ley 23.696 de Emergencia Económica and the Ley 23.697 de Reforma del Estado. The first of these laws, the Economic Emergency Law, dismantled the main institutions related to the state-centered, inward-looking development model including subsidies, industrial promotion regimes, and so on. The second law, the State Reform Law, conferred vast powers on the executive to define the details of the reform policies, including the privatization of state-owned enterprises.

Sources: Pou 2000; Bambaci, Saront, and Tommasi 2002.

Menem would say, "Puerto Madero is the showpiece of a new city and integrated country which all Argentineans deserve."[9]

Project's History

The team behind the Puerto Madero project had a grand vision: the project would regenerate the port area into higher-value land uses and would also help revitalize the CBD. Puerto Madero was conceived as a catalytic project that would overcome years of disinvestment in the Buenos Aires CBD and change the public's perception of the downtown area.

As noted, the idea of developing Puerto Madero's vacant area was not new. All planning efforts for the city since the 1960s had included ideas about new uses for this centrally located land. However, none of these plans had ever been executed because there were too many administrative and financial challenges that prevented implementation, most notably, with regard to transfer of federal land to the private sector. With the creation of CAPMSA, the area would include a mix of uses, with overlapping residential, commercial, educational, and recreational aspects (see box 4.2).

International Influences

The conceptualization and implementation of the Puerto Madero Project was also influenced by some key international city experiences and exchanges. One major influence was Barcelona's Port Vell. Two of the key actors in the implementation of Puerto Madero, Alfredo Garay (head of the CAPMSA, and Buenos Aires's secretary of urban planning) and Buenos Aires's mayor, Carlos Grosso (1989–92),[10] visited Barcelona's Port Vell[11] and met with its mayor, Pascal Maragall (1982–97). They witnessed the opening of Barcelona's port after years of neglect and abandonment. During their visit, Mayor Maragall removed the iron bars of Barcelona's port area during a public event. It is not a coincidence then, that in 1990 President Menem and Mayor Grosso organized a similar public event in which part of the fence surrounding the old docks along Huergo Avenue in Puerto Madero was removed.

A second international reference involves London's Canary Wharf Project. President Menem was photographed operating a crane in a similar manner as Margaret Thatcher at the time of the ground-breaking opening of the Canary Wharf in London in 1988. These symbolic events highlight the importance that the national government gave to the Puerto Madero project, as well as the use of the media to portray it as a symbol of Argentina's modernization.

Finally, Garay himself cited many international influences in his work, for example, with regard to his academic training in Belgium, his thesis about French planning instruments for mixed public-private operations in the urban renewal of the Les Halles market in Paris, and his research about the Barcelona and the London Docklands projects. American influences on the project were also noteworthy and included the cases of festival marketplaces and the American boardwalks of the late 1970s and 1980s, in particular the Baltimore Harborplace urban revitalization (1977–79), and Battery Park City in New York.

Another bridge between the international urban regeneration projects was Mayor Grosso's experience as manager in Macri Holdings Limited. Grosso participated in the development of Lincoln West in New York during the 1980s, which included 30 ha of the rail yard formerly owned by Penn Central located along the Hudson River.

Project Prerogatives

The Puerto Madero project was founded on a set of simple principles and on (mostly) existing administrative and financial tools. First, it benefited from the exceptional circumstances created by the profound socioeconomic and institutional crisis at the end of Raúl Alfonsín's presidency.[12] Specifically, newly passed Administrative Emergency and Economic Emergency Laws enabled the speedy creation of an administrative entity with real proprietary rights over the Puerto Madero land. Second, expeditious negotiations helped to neutralize the project's detractors. Finally, sought and used international expertise helped to overcome the lack of local expertise for a project of this magnitude.

Regarding project financing and assets, CAPMSA financed the project by the sale of the port land. The municipality did not contribute any financial resources. The only asset that CAPMSA possessed was the land itself. Therefore, the CAPMSA team had to resort to creative uses (such as renting the land to TV crews) to cover initial years' operating expenses. The corporation did not issue debt, use public housing subsidies, or tax incentives to attract private sector investment. All of the project's expenses, including administrative expenses and infrastructure, were financed by the land proceeds.

The most attractive feature for private sector developers was the high rent potential of centrally located waterfront land. The existence of some infrastructure (Huergo Avenue, Costanera Sur, the port turnaround yards, the water supply and drainage system, and the power network) was also key for attracting prospective investors. Finally, the fact that the CAPMSA had clear proprietary rights over the land and a very high degree of decision-making autonomy was also extremely important for development of the site. In the beginning, Puerto Madero's team did not pursue international investments.[13] The goal was to work with local, medium-scale developers who were willing to take risks.

Local, surrounding communities were not involved in the planning process through any participatory consultations, because at the time Puerto Madero's area was not residential, and it was bisected by high-speed, fenced-off roads. The first notifications of the project were released to the local media after the presidential decree in November 1989. However, consultation and project discussion took place with the professional Chamber of Architects.[14]

Institutional Structure

The legal creation of CAPMSA was established three months after the adoption of the Administrative Emergency Law in 1989 and the presidential decree 1279 issued on November 23, 1989, by President Menem.[15] The federal government was represented by the Ministry of Finance, the Ministry of Public Works, and the Interior Ministry. Puerto Madero's land was owned by the General Administration of Ports, which was part of the Ministry of Public Works.[16]

Under Decree 1279, CAPMSA was formed by the spin-off of the AGP and the municipal enterprise Autopistas Urbanas Sociedad Anónima/Urban Highways SA (AUSA).[17] The AGP represented the national government and contributed the land. The city was responsible for land use planning and project design. According to CAPMSA's first charter, the board initially would be composed of six directors: initially four on behalf of the federal government and two representing the city of Buenos Aires. Each member had one vote, and only in the event of a draw could the president's vote count as double.[18]

Because CAPMSA was created as a public limited corporation, it was regulated by the country's commercial code. The financial and administrative provisions for public entities are not applicable to this type of corporation. As a result, CAPMSA functions as a private company. This allows CAPMSA to buy, sell, exchange, rent, or lease assets, create joint ventures with other companies, and engage in any kind of union or lawful cooperation. The charter also enables the corporation to carry out any necessary or convenient lawful act for the accomplishment of its objectives. The statute set forth the duration of the company as 100 years from the date of registration in the Public Registry of Commerce.

CAPMSA has a six-member board in charge of leadership and management of the corporation. The board positions were unpaid during the time that CAPMSA did not have resources. CAPMSA's shares are equally distributed between the federal government and the CABA. The company has the ability to issue shares in order to attract private national or foreign funds.

The decree also transferred the property of the 170-ha Puerto Madero area to the corporation. It declared all existing concessions and leases terminated and set a deadline to make the possession effective. The board had 90 days to process the deed transferring titles and to register the lands in the National Property Register. CAPMSA was enrolled in the Supervisory Board of Companies (Inspection General de Justicia) in February 1991. After the land survey was finalized, it was entered in the National Public Property Registry under the corporation's name.

The statute of the corporation set the capital stock at Arg$40 million (australes) represented by 40,000 common shares. Each share is entitled to one vote. The capital stock could be raised to five times the amount previously set by means of a resolution of an ordinary shareholders' meeting. The national and city governments contributed with Arg$20 million each.

An article published in the national newspaper, *La Prensa*, on May 23, 1990, questioned the land transfer and considered it undervalued. The article claimed that the Arg$20 million was the equivalent of US$4,000.[19] It also asserted that the appraisal of the properties was not performed by a competent authority, in this case, the National Appraisal Board (Tribunales de Tasaciones). See figure 4.1 for an updated organizational structure.

Feasibility Studies

Feasibility studies are an important part of city regeneration projects. In this case, two studies finalized before the beginning of the implementation of the project laid out some ideas for the future use of the area. The first study done by the Center for Transatlantic Sailings (Centro de Navegaciones

Figure 4.1   **Current CAPMSA organizational structure**

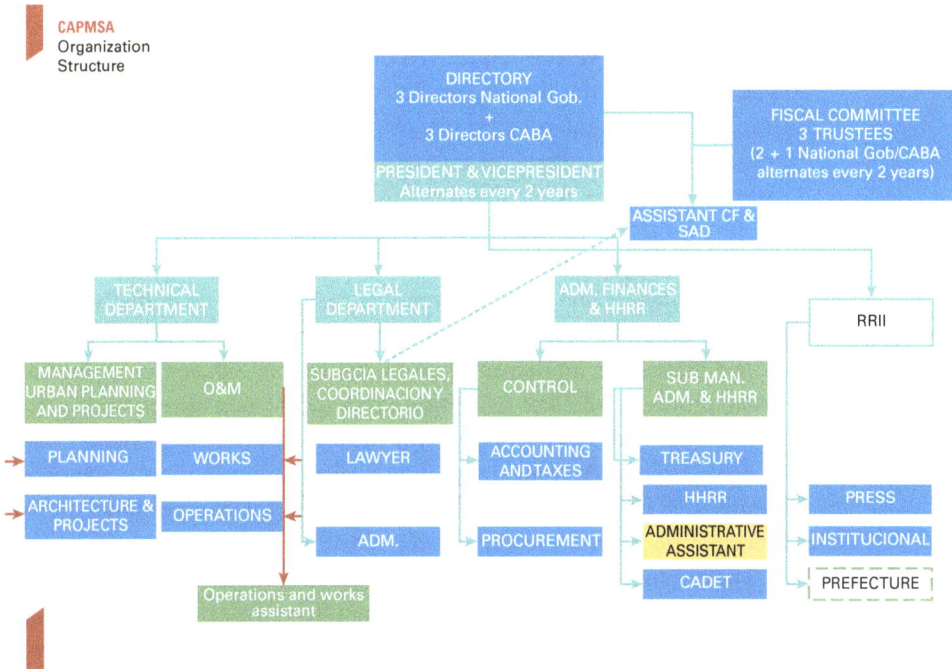

CAPMSA
Organization
Structure

DIRECTORY
3 Directors National Gob.
+
3 Directors CABA

PRESIDENT & VICEPRESIDENT
Alternates every 2 years

FISCAL COMMITTEE
3 TRUSTEES
(2 + 1 National Gob/CABA
alternates every 2 years)

ASSISTANT CF & SAD

TECHNICAL DEPARTMENT

LEGAL DEPARTMENT

ADM, FINANCES & HHRR

RRII

MANAGEMENT URBAN PLANNING AND PROJECTS

O&M

SUBGCIA LEGALES, COORDINACION Y DIRECTORIO

CONTROL

SUB MAN. ADM. & HHRR

PLANNING

WORKS

LAWYER

ACCOUNTING AND TAXES

TREASURY

ARCHITECTURE & PROJECTS

OPERATIONS

ADM.

PROCUREMENT

HHRR

ADMINISTRATIVE ASSISTANT

PRESS

INSTITUCIONAL

Operations and works assistant

CADET

PREFECTURE

Source: Reproduced by permission from Corporacíon Antiguo Puerto Madero 1999. © Corporacíon Antiguo Puerto Madero.

Transatlánticas) in 1985, the Study of the National Bureau of River and Maritime Transportation, was done for the AGP. It evaluated the area of the Old Puerto Madero from an operational perspective. The study concluded that the design of the docks was too small in size for the ships-in-service, deeming some 75 percent of the area as unsuitable from a capacity perspective.[20]

The second study done by the University of Buenos Aires (UBA) in 1986 was an urban planning analysis commissioned by the Ministry of Public Works and the Department of Transport (Borthagaray 1987). It included the area of Puerto Madero, the strip by the river known as Costanera Sur, and the reclaimed area of the Ecologic Reserve.[21] CAPMSA considered the study to be one of the main documents for due diligence and feasibility. It described the uses proposed by successive plans and mapped the tenancy to date. In addition, it gathered information on the heritage buildings (docks and institutional and recreational buildings of the Costanera Sur). This research delved into the preliminary ideas and program definition for land development. Furthermore, it outlined alternative access routes and a connection to the 25 de Mayo Highway.

Phase 2: Planning

The Development of the Master Plan

The development of the master plan took place in stages, building on previous initiatives. CAPMSA conceived of the master plan as an instrument of negotiation with the developers. In this regard, it was used as more than simply a strict regulatory framework. The plan was loosely based on all previous planning efforts for Puerto Madero that had never reached implementation (see box 4.1). When the new administration took over in 1989, CABA's Secretary of Urban Planning, headed by Alfredo Garay, started to lay out the master plan. The first plan was drafted by Garay and Architect Jorge Moscato[22] and was presented to the minister of public works, José Roberto Dromi and President Menem to introduce the idea.

The first plan's implementation model was set up as a corporation that would represent all 24 of Argentina's provinces (state governments), requiring the approval of the Congress for the land transfer. This model was discarded when the Administrative Emergency Law was passed, which made the transfer of land possible without the need for congressional approval. Indeed, it facilitated and expedited the process.

The original plan was broad and simple and consisted of a basic subdivision and a general shape and size of buildings. It included mechanisms to allocate parcels to different types of private partners to be developed for various residential, commercial, and other uses. The master plan was defined by a series of iterations that saw additional adjustments made as the result of dialogue with new partners such as international consultants and local professional associations and organizations representing the users of the port area. The master plan was finalized in 1992.

The first draft, the Catalan Strategic Plan for the Old Puerto Madero, was done in 1990. The team behind the development of Barcelona's Port were invited to provide advice for the design of Puerto Madero's master plan. Their plan was the first to define a high-density residential zone in the eastern section in front of Costanera Sur with buildings of up to 25 stories. An intermediate area comprised rows of buildings perpendicular to the docks and a strip of commercial 20-story buildings facing the docks (including offices, hotels, and the cleaning industry). The plan's total built-up area was 3,500,000 sq m for the 42 ha intended for subdivision, with an average density of 500 inhabitants per ha (see figure 4.2).

In July 1990, the mayor of Buenos Aires officially received the strategic plan for the Old Puerto. However, it was accompanied by the start of a public and media debate. The presentation of the plan at the Central Society of Architects (SCA) spearheaded a public confrontation with the corporation in the public media. On August 7, 1990, a public debate was organized on the premises of SCA. The criticism focused on the narrow vision proposed by the plan without considering surrounding areas (the waterfront from the New Port to Costanera Sur). The loose zoning

Figure 4.2   **The strategic plan of the Antiguo Puerto Madero, 1990**

Source: Borja 1990.

proposed as one of the strategies in the Catalan plan was seen as a mistake, as well as the loose guidelines for residential uses. Even the timing and the necessity for the project were questioned. For Odilia Suarez, an eminent university professor in urban studies and leader of the opposition to the plan, the vacant land should have been assigned for administrative uses. The ultimate objective of SCA was to slow the course of action and call for a national competition for a master plan to secure the participation of local professionals.

The calls of protest were eventually heeded by the corporation, and the national contest for Puerto Madero's master plan took place in 1992. At first, the corporation resisted the idea of a national call for proposals, arguing that time was short.[23] A strong opposition continued for several months and in June 1991, the Buenos Aires Municipality commissioned the SCA to organize a national competition to produce a master plan for Puerto Madero. A consultative body, composed of members of the corporation, municipality representatives, and the SCA was formed to write the terms of reference for the competition (CAPMSA, 1989–99).

The consultative body called for the redevelopment of the derelict area and set a maximum land occupancy of 1.5 million sq m (the lowest of all the preceding urban plans). It also emphasized the development of green spaces and direct access to the river. The area would be mixed use, including residential, commercial, and office space. In addition, the plan established the need to preserve the warehouses because of their patrimonial value.

The competition proceeded apace, while CAPMSA continued to move forward with land and building sales and rezoning. Firms entering the competition had 120 days to finish and submit their proposals. In the meantime,

CAPMSA started selling the land on which the industrial warehouses on the west side were located. There were 100 entries for the competition, among which three finalists were selected to work together and produce the final master plan. Meanwhile, the city rezoned the warehouse area to allow for mixed use (Ordinance 44945 of July 1991).

The negotiations proved that the corporation was resourceful enough to handle the public opinion and opposition while continuing to implement the project in a timely manner. Furthermore, the municipality agreed to approve the necessary regulatory framework for the resulting plan. According to Garay, the agreement between the municipality and the SCA was the turning point for the Puerto Madero project to become a reality.

The winning proposals were published in January 1992.[24] It soon became clear that the corporation wanted to retain the ability to fine-tune the final plan. The jury specifically selected contrasting layouts. Two of the entries had the same arrangement emphasizing the strong axis from the city to the river with three wide boulevards. The third entry focused more on the small urban scale by bringing the monumental scale of the site down to a neighborhood level. One of the entries proposed the advancement of a high rise toward the waterfront and then a recession of penetrating green open spaces back into the city. This was the massing scheme maintained in the final plan.

The winning teams and CAPMSA finally came together in the formulation of the master plan, with all sides achieving their aims. For nine months, three members of each winning team worked together on the master plan. The preliminary urban plan for Puerto Madero was presented in October 1992. Not surprisingly, CAPMSA managed to increase the total built-up area back to 3 million sq m, which was much closer to the total estimated density proposed by the Catalan plan. Another significant strength of the final plan was that it was based on the existing regulatory framework. In this way, Puerto Madero finally had its master plan, backed by the local professional community. In April 1994, the plan was formally approved through Ordinance 001/94. However, it was not published in the official bulletin until July 1997 when another ordinance amended the existing zoning. See map 4.3 for the final master plan and table 4.1 for an evolution of the master plan's main features.

Land Ownership and Negotiations

Land issues were somewhat simplified by the fact that most of the land was already in government hands. Ninety-five percent of the land in the Puerto Madero area was publicly owned by the AGP. There was only one private company,[25] Molinos Rio de la Plata, that had full ownership rights (since 1935) over six lots in docks 2 and 3 (see photograph 4.1). Aside from this property, there were two cases for which CAPMSA had to negotiate acquisition: the AGP and Colegio Nacional de Buenos Aires.

Map 4.3   **CAPMSA illustration of the master plan, 2014**

Source: CAPMSA 1999. Reproduced by permission from Corporacíon Antiguo Puerto Madero.

Table 4.1   **Summary of evolution of main features of master plan**

	Catalan plan, 1990	Central society of architects competition, 1991	Final master plan, 1992
Built-up area (square meters)	3,500,000	1,500,000	3,033,505
Public parks (hectares)	10.98	18.84	28

Source: Rua 2014, 188.

The AGP was the public authority in charge of administering all ports in Argentina. Using the Administrative Emergency Law, the Puerto Madero land was transferred from the AGP to the CAPMSA. The AGP wanted to preserve some of the land for port use. Finally, an agreement was signed by which CAPMSA relinquished the east part of dock 4 as a container yard against the payment of rent. This income represented some of the first funds received by the corporation.[26]

Despite the fact that most of the project land was already publicly held, there were still legal disputes, specifically pertaining to a plot of land that belonged to the Colegio Nacional de Buenos Aires, part of the UBA, the largest public university in Argentina.[27] In 1914, the school had received two ha of land for its sports field but failed to register the property in the National Property Registry. When the boundary of Puerto Madero was drawn in 1989, the land was inadvertently included and registered in the

Photograph 4.1   Molinos Rio de la Plata grain storage, elevator, and mill complex in Puerto Madero, 1999

Source: http://www.wikiwand.com. Reproduced by permission from Corporacíon Antiguo Puerto Madero CAPMSA. ©1999 by Corporacíon Antiguo Puerto Madero.
Note: The complex was renovated and converted into the Faena hotel, apartment, and office complex and reopened in 2004.

National Registry in the name of the corporation. The school initiated legal proceedings.

Zoning issues also arose during the dispute. In 1997, when the new zoning was approved, an agreement had not been reached with the institution. The zoning for the disputed plot was kept with the highest development ratio of floor area ratio (FAR) 6 and extremely flexible uses,[28] whereas the lot that had been assigned for the relocation of the sports field had a lower value zoning of FAR 2 with uses restricted to special community facilities and public education use.

The negotiations were ultimately unsuccessful, worsened by the value the approved regulations attributed to the land. In February 2012, after more than 15 years of disputes, the final ruling determined the ownership of the disputed plot of land to the UBA and ordered the rectification in the Property Registry.

Preparing for Implementation

The implementation strategy for Puerto Madero was simple and the development rollout proceeded in three stages:

- *First stage: The launching and anchoring of the project (1989–93).* This included the preparation of the land (regularization of land ownership, surveys, security guarantee for the area, and call for proposals for the master plan) and the sale of the 16 port warehouses on the west side of the docks.
- *Second stage: consolidation of the west side and first sale on the east side (1993–97).* The second phase began with the sale of a narrow strip of land opposite the docks. The commercialization of the land on the east side was initiated with the very first sale. However, the new zoning had yet to be approved.

- *Third stage: consolidation of the east side (1997–2012).* The Urban Planning Code was amended in 1997 to allow for the new zoning of the east side. In 1998, a US$40 million investment in infrastructure was publicly announced. The project muddled along during the *Corralito Crisis* (bank freeze) in late 2001 and subsequent recession. As a consequence of the crisis, residential use increased and demand for commercial/office space decreased. The implementation ended with the sale of the majority of the land and transfer of ownership and maintenance of public roads and parks to the city. The transfer was completed by the end of 2012.

Project Risks

Risks—and the perception of risk—changed over the 25-year project life cycle. For instance, the situation at the outset of project implementation was quite different from the third stage. The prices of the land captured the improvement in project conditions. However, the sale of Puerto Madero's parcels also reflected the fluctuations in the Argentinian economy throughout the life of the project. Once the initial uncertainties lessened, the general risk of failing to stimulate economic activity and reverse the suburbanization process diminished. The perceived success of the warehouse sale in less than three years and the inauguration of the first buildings in September 1992 also moderated this risk.

The initial risks identified by the planners—even before the creation of the corporation—were political, economic, and administrative in nature. The regulatory challenges concerned the inability of the government to dispose of the public land that resulted in decades of failed plans. Two key national laws changed this instantly (see box 4.2).

The larger macroeconomic and market risks would prove to be more difficult to overcome. In particular, the 1989 hyperinflation at the beginning of project implementation and the Corralito crisis in late 2001 had significant negative impacts on project implementation. In 1989, market confidence was very low. The general perception was that Puerto Madero was extremely dilapidated and the city did not have the required expertise to complete such a complex redevelopment project. Eduardo Gianna, one of the directors of the corporation from April 1991, recounted that the directors "had to explain what the corporation was and communicate a feeling of trust both to the public institutions and private sector, which were watching us with close attention….When we [the directors] took potential investors to see the area, it was hard to convey the potential for development" (CAPMSA 1999).

The main risks during the first stage were regulatory, financial, social, and technical. Regulatory risks included the necessary normative adjustments that would be needed to implement the project, such as the creation of the corporation, land transfer, zoning changes, and development of the master plan. On the financial side, CAPMSA had no operational budget assigned. However, there were a number of expenses, such as the land survey, that required funding before the land could actually be sold. With regard to social risks, the structural adjustment measures triggered a confrontation with some media and community representatives. Furthermore, as the project was seen as a demonstration project for state reform, opposition could arise more easily. Finally, there were technical issues because no project of this scale had ever been attempted in Argentina. Likewise, the board of the corporation and CABA did not have similar previous experience.

During the second stage, some political and economic risks were considerably diminished. With the inauguration of the first buildings, the perception of success began to be reflected in a more positive public opinion. Also, the political and economic situation was much more stable. The major risk at this stage was the threat of inactivity produced by land speculation and the regulatory uncertainty with regard to the east side. The commercialization of the land in this area began with the first sale. However, the new zoning had yet to be approved. No residential or commercial plots were sold.

Regarding the third stage, some political, economic, and financial risks re-emerged. However, there was one major breakthrough with the passage of the Urban Planning Code amendment, which allowed for new zoning on the east side. CAPMSA had accumulated the required resources for the major infrastructure investment needed to develop the east side. Demand rose and between 1997 and 1999, CAPMSA sold the majority of the land. Nonetheless, the risk of pacing the demand, calibrating the sales, and retaining the land was not well understood—and no preparations were made to mitigate this risk. The project muddled through the political instability and economic slowdown at the end of President Menem's second term in office (1999), which extended to the Corralito crisis (2001). The construction industry activity was virtually halted for two years. As a result, the corporation had a negative balance sheet for three years.

Phase 3: Financing and Implementation

During the first stage of implementation, the project advanced incrementally by converting the port's warehouses on the west side of the docks into residential, commercial, and educational buildings. CAPMSA did not have sufficient resources to invest in a major upgrading of public infrastructure. However, it needed to show commitment to execute the project and the warehouses served that purpose. As the west had almost all of the required infrastructure, the expenses of the corporation were minimal. The critical path consisted only in applying to the secretary for urban planning for regulatory change. CABA's Ordinance 44945/91 modified the zoning for the western area from "Future Urbanization" to

"Old Puerto Madero Heritage Protection Area" (U32), a special category that complements the C1 zone (central area district). This change enabled the development of warehouses on the west side for commercial and high-density residential use but also restricted the scope of development rights in the buildings and surrounding areas. Any change in the character of the buildings would have required the approval of the city's assembly.

The first investment in the area came from CAPMSA itself and consisted of a land survey of the 170 ha, the mapping of almost 70 users (tenants, irregular occupants) in the former AGP domain, and security services to prevent land invasion. After the tenant mapping, a plan was developed to end the concessions and begin charging rent. Aside from these rents, other early financial resources for CAPMSA consisted of the sale of demolition material, the rental of parking lots, and space to be used as television and film sets. The revenues were allocated to cover the costs of office rental and the design of the master plan, as well as the marketing strategy to create attractive conditions for the first tender to sell the warehouses.

By November 1990, the CAPMSA received expressions of interest from several investors, including multinationals such as the Bunge & Born Group, Alto Palermo, Enrique Capozzolo, the architect Cesar Pelli, Raymond Studio (United States), Dumey (France), Mont Coccol (United Kingdom), and the construction company Odebrecht (Brazil).[29] The largest proposals came from Olympia & York and Donald Trump. These companies were seeking to buy and develop all of the 170 ha of land, arguing that local investors and planners lacked the required experience for an enterprise of this scale. However, as Garay recounts, President Menem "was pretty confident that we could solve it."

Once Ordinance 44945 passed, the corporation decided to sell the warehouses in stages, starting with the area closest to the CBD and the national government buildings. CAPMSA published the tender documents for the first five warehouses closest to the downtown area, (see map 4.4) in July 1991. Two envelopes were requested. The first envelope would describe the architectural project for the recycling of the buildings, the date of completion, and the bidder credentials and financial capacity. The second one would contain the economic offer. Project proposals were considered before economic offers. The envelopes were screened first, and only those considered acceptable were considered in the second round.

Execution, completion, and sale conditions were specified in the bidding process. The clause of completion meant that if the completion date was not met, the property would return to CAPMSA. The execution of the project could not take more than 48 months (Levy-Hara, Faierman, and Sanguinetti 2014). The penalties for delays were significant. Such conditions also prohibited the reselling of the structures to discourage speculation. Gonzalo Bunge, the commercial manager of CAPMSA at the time,

Map 4.4   **First stage: Sale in stages of 16 west side warehouses**

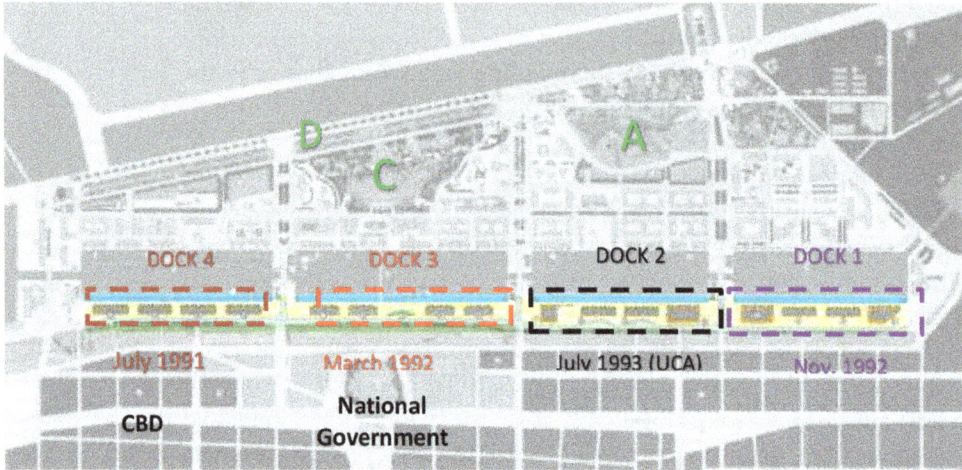

Source: Based on CAPMSA's most current illustration of the area.
Note: Dates indicate when tender documents were published. CBD = central business district;
UCA = Universidad Católica Argentina.

stated that "the aim was to finish the redevelopment of an area which would, in turn, attract future investors. Construction took precedence over sales because building was the measure of success; the objective was to urbanize the area, not to generate profit" (CAPMSA 1999). The sale conditions included a 20 percent down payment, with a five-year mortgage and full payment within five years.[30] The same bidding mechanism would be used and perfected throughout the project. It became more sophisticated by adding a third stage.

The first batch of sales in 1991 was concentrated on docks 3 and 4, the area closest to the Buenos Aires CBD, and amounted to US$19 million. The buyers were mostly local and included the Cia del Plata–Kocourek and the Consortium for Antiguo Puerto Madero. The land sales moved gradually southward to docks 2 and later to dock 1 (see map 4.4).

The Catholic University (Pontificia Universidad Católica Argentina) played an anchoring role by buying the four warehouses in dock 2. In 1993, it acquired warehouses 9–12 for approximately US$6 million. In May 1994, it inaugurated the first building, which housed the schools of economics and law. The redevelopment of warehouse 12 began in 2003 with an art pavilion dedicated to cultural activities. Ultimately, the university occupied a total of 35,000 sq m in Puerto Madero.

The second stage started with the sale of the east side plots in 1993. In November 1993 the corporation sold a 20-ha block located on the east of dock 1 to the developer, Newside S.A., for a price of US$9 million (Reporte Inmobiliario). The zoning for the east side had not yet been amended, and the land was still labeled for port operation uses. According to the final master plan published in October 1992, the plots east of dock 1 would be planned for use as fairgrounds, an exhibition and convention center, a hotel, and other uses.[31]

In October 1994, the SCA carried out a second national design competition for the new green areas of Puerto Madero and the revitalization and enhancement of the Costanera Sur. In 1998, the Telecom Tower opened in dock 4. It was the first corporate building developed by the American architectural firm Kohn, Pendersen & Fox.

During the third stage, Puerto Madero was officially incorporated into the city with the status of a *barrio* (district).[32] In 1997, Ordinance 51675 amended the Urban Planning Code and regulated the subdivision of land, urban area, and land use in the eastern sector of the CAPMSA polygonal. The U11 area was allocated for residential, administrative, commercial, financial, and institutional facilities to the highest degree of density. A strip of residential park was also created against the Costanera Sur, corresponding to green open spaces. In September 1997, the opening ceremony of the neighborhood was held in the presence of President Menem and the newly elected head of government, Fernando De La Rua.

With the administrative jurisdiction defined, the zoning approved and financial resources obtained through the sale of property, the program for major infrastructure investments was publicly launched. In September 1998, the corporation announced a US$40 million infrastructure investment for the east side comprising potable water, sewage and storm water pipes, electricity, telephone, cable television and data transmission. It also included the construction of 15 km of new roads and street lighting.

The phasing for infrastructure investment maintained the north-to-south roll out, with phase A, the area in front of dock 4; phase B for the area in front of dock 3; and phase C, corresponding to dock 2. However, the area in front of dock 1 represented an exception. At a very early stage, the land was sold in block to Newside S.A. for the purpose of developing the fairgrounds and a convention and exhibition center. In this area, the infrastructure was constructed by the developer.[33] In 2011, CAPMSA estimated that it had spent US$113 million in public works (see table 4.2) (Garay and others 2013).

The implementation of Puerto Madero's regeneration project did not rely on direct subsidies to promote private sector participation. Further, at project inception, there was no international investor interest, given the project's many perceived risks. Therefore, the team behind the project decided to adopt a self-financing scheme led by a public corporation (that is, CAPMSA) that would manage the land to be developed.

Table 4.2   CAPMSA's infrastructure investments

Type	Detail
Roads and bridges	Replacement of five existing (1880s) pivot bridges and 15 kilometers of roads, including a 38-meter-wide boulevard with three lanes in both directions Horizontal and vertical signage Underground ducts for a traffic light system
Sewage	Pumping station; main and secondary lines, inspection chambers
Potable water	Main network
Fire	Distribution network and hydrants
Gas	Gas station; gas distribution network
Communications	Installation of telephone, cable TV, and data transmission lines
Power	Tunnels for medium- and low-tension power lines; Street lighting system
Public open space	Micaela Bastidas Park, 7.2 hectares; Mujeres Argentinas Park, 6 hectares; Maria Eva Duarte de Perón Park, 4 hectares; refurbishment of the Old Costanera Sur; pedestrian sidewalks; other public squares
Street furniture	Street lighting, benches, and railing
Mooring	Bollards for Fragata Presidente Sarmiento Museum Ship

Source: CAPMSA: Un modelo de Gestión Urbana 1989–99; and CAPMSA annual balances 2001–12.

Outcomes and Impacts

The project outcomes can be viewed through the perspective of land sales, volume of construction, amount of investment in the area, and profits for the private sector. Other important outcomes that have not been measured in this case study include the increase in property tax collection and the availability of new public facilities (parks).

Land Sales

The sale of land allowed CAPMSA to generate sufficient funds to finance its administrative expenses, as well as pay for all of the necessary supporting infrastructure. As risks diminished and the first results were seen on the ground, the price of land started to increase. Indeed, the sale price of sq m of land multiplied by a factor of eight during the 25-year lifespan of the project.

Between 1991 and 1993, CAPMSA received US$54 million for the sale of the warehouses, plus the first lot on the east side. The peak of sales would come in the third stage, with the zoning in place and the infrastructure investment plan published. Between the years 1997–99, CAPMSA recorded 19 sales for more than US$173 million—over 50 percent of total sales in the life of the entity (see figure 4.3).

According to the master plan, there were 60 ha of land available for sale. During the life of the project, CAPMSA recorded sales amounting to

Figure 4.3 **CAPMSA land sales, 1989–2013**

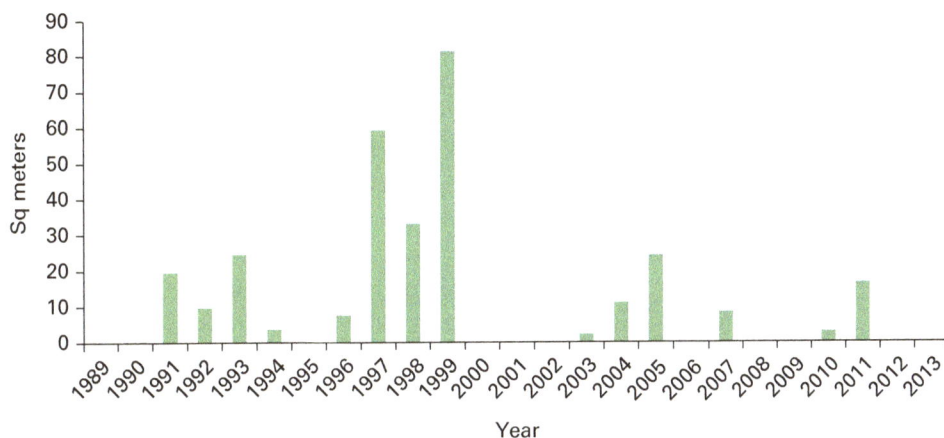

Source: Based on CAMPSA land sales internal information.

Table 4.3 **Comparative land prices: In several Buenos Aires neighborhoods, 1993–2012**
US$ per square meter

	1993	1996	2001	2002	2003	2004	2005	2006	2007	2008	2009	2010	2011	2012
CABA	n.a.	n.a.	555	274	388	534	722	905	1,038	1,148	1,171	1,460	1,681	1,844
Comuna 1	n.a.	n.a.	940	538	380	1,408	1,408	1588	1,719	2,407	1,616	2,322	2,152	2,161
Centro	n.a.	n.a.	n.a.	n.a.	n.a.	n.a.	n.a.	n.a.	2,916	3,089	3,750	3,235	n.a.	4,331
Retiro	n.a.	n.a.	n.a.	n.a.	n.a.	n.a.	n.a.	n.a.	2,065	n.a.	n.a.	n.a.	n.a.	n.a.
San Telmo	n.a.	n.a.	n.a.	n.a.	n.a.	n.a.	n.a.	n.a.	n.a.	1,408	1,588	1,344	n.a.	1,373
Constitucion	n.a.	n.a.	n.a.	n.a.	n.a.	n.a.	n.a.	n.a.	n.a.	1,613	1,264	1,036	n.a.	846
Puerto Madero	45	116	375	n.a.	n.a.	1,125	1,711	n.a.	2,006	2,266	n.a.	n.a.	5,427	n.a.

Source: Based on data from Real Estates Survey Report 2014.
Note: n.a. = not available.

US$300 million,[34] with an average of US$500 per sq m. This represents less than the value for one sq m of land in CABA in 2001. Table 4.3 shows the evolution of land values in U.S. dollars per sq m in CABA, the average of comuna 1, and a decomposition of the comuna 1 neighborhoods. Comuna 1 has historically recorded higher values than the average of CABA, with the exception of the postcrisis years of 2001 and 2002. Most of the land under the project was sold before 2000. It was not until 2005 that the prices rose above *comuna* 1 averages.

Construction

By 2010, a total of 2.25 million of sq m had been built in Puerto Madero (L. J. Ramos Brokers Immobiliarios 2009). The acceleration in the construction occurred during the third stage of the development roll out, once the east side had been regularized. After the 2001 economic crisis, real estate was considered a safe investment, and construction picked up again in Puerto Madero between 2005 and 2009. According to an article published by the Lincoln Institute of Land Policy in July 2013, CAPMSA sold property for a total value of around US$300 million. It invested US$113 million in public infrastructure, with a total operational cost since the creation of the corporation of US$92 million. Public and private investment in 2009 amounted to US$1.7 billion and was estimated to reach US$2.5 billion when completed (Cuenya and Corral 2011).

Profits

The value of a sq m for residential use almost doubled between 2005 and 2013 (US$2,647 per sq m in 2005 and US$4,948 in 2013) (Real Estate Survey Report 2014). This fluctuation in the price of land and sales value implies millions in profits from commercialization in an extremely short period of time. A detailed study of the sale and subdivision of land in the dock shows the following profits. In 1993, a local company bought 20 ha on the east side of dock 1 for US$9 million (US$450 per sq m). After 12 years, they had sold 30 percent of the initial plot for US$53 million (US$883 per sq m). However, with the resale of some plots, prices rose to US$1,125 per sq m after only three years (between 2001 and 2004). The study's authors point out that in a period of 10 years, people paid for one acre of land as much as they used to pay for 20 ha of land (Real Estate Survey Report 2014) (see figure 4.4).

Sustainability and Maintenance of Public Space

The maintenance and sustainability of project infrastructure was transferred over time from CAPMSA to CABA. In February 1999, CAPMSA finalized the first transfer of rights for the infrastructure and public spaces to CABA. Some streets, piers, and pedestrian areas were transferred to the city for maintenance. However, the largest transfer followed an agreement between CAPMSA and CABA in February 2011. In this agreement, the parties negotiated a transition period for the free transfer of the domain of public spaces and the responsibility for the provision of maintenance from CAPMSA to CABA. In this regard, CAPMSA was to first register the areas to CABA and then gradually shift the responsibility for maintenance. In late 2012, the complete transfer of maintenance had been accomplished. According to CAPMSA, US$3 million in annual expenses were eliminated from the operating costs of the corporation.

Figure 4.4   Average residential price in Puerto Madero, 2000–13

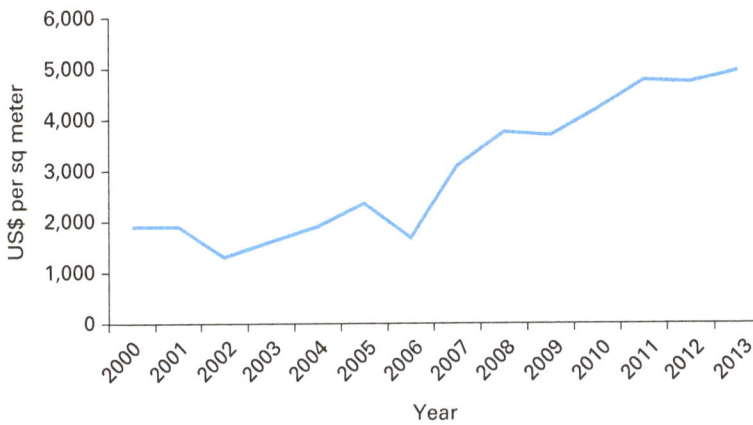

Source: Real Estate Survey Report 2014.

Lessons Learned

The impact and success of the Puerto Madero project can be analyzed at two levels: the project level and the city level. The general consensus is that at the project level, Puerto Madero was a success. Some administrators also recognized that in order to maximize profits for CAPMSA, land sales could have been paced more strategically after all the regulatory framework was in place. Having paced the sales better (releasing land more gradually), the project could have yielded much greater profit for the corporation. Instead, much of the profit went to private developers. However, looking at the project's original objectives—to revitalize the Buenos Aires CBD, catalyze investment in the surrounding areas, provide an economic stimulus, and generate employment in the construction sector—the project did well. The Buenos Aires CBD is now buzzing with activity, and the Puerto Madero area itself has become a new city destination for both local residents and tourists.

From the city perspective, the results are more nuanced. Puerto Madero has helped increase housing supply but only for a very small high-income market, although in Buenos Aires, there is a chronic demand for middle- and lower-income housing. Project design could have included mixed-income housing and utilized innovative inclusionary zoning tools or provided fiscal or regulatory incentives for developers to go down market. Public financing is a good mechanism for making middle- and low-income housing financially viable and for achieving the goal of mixed-income neighborhoods.

Finally, from a practical perspective, Puerto Madero provides other lessons for implementation:

- *Fast implementation.* Speed gave project sponsors discretionary powers to execute the project without extensive political interference.[35] Decision making was concentrated within a small number of stakeholders, mainly CAPMSA's board of directors.
- *Simple development instruments.* Maintaining the proposals within the existing zoning and only modifying what was strictly necessary helped facilitate project implementation and minimized confrontation with other affected interests. The project adopted adjacent land use zone parameters such as the CBD (C1) that allowed for high densities and multiple uses.
- *Skillful incorporation of decades of urban planning into a single, long-lasting master plan.* The final master plan for Puerto Madero had a long-term vision for the neighborhood, building on the history of the area, as well as on past plans. The quality of the plan and the high design standards speak to the durability of the master plan.
- *Flexible zoning allowed for mixed-use developments (residential, retail, offices, recreational uses) and medium to high densities.* The plan advocated for commercial uses on the ground level to create an active pedestrian area.
- *The lack of public financing gave credibility to the corporation with the private sector and reduced continuous scrutiny and reporting.* The fact that Puerto Madero implementation was independent of public sector budget allocation made it more appealing for private sector investors, given Argentina's recent history.
- *A flexible approach to negotiating with investors, especially during economic downturns.* This allowed for the adjustment to contractual terms, the negotiation of extensions, and alterations in land uses when market conditions rendered project financial feasibility difficult.[36] The strategic use of the political and economic opportunities provided by the economic crisis and regulatory reform helped to facilitate project implementation.

Notes

1. National Decree N°: 1279/1989, published in Boletin Oficial N° 26767 on November 23, 1989, "Convenio de constitución y estatuto social Corporación Antiguo Puerto Madero S.A."
2. Architect Alfredo Garay was the secretary of urban planning during Carlos Grosso's administration of the city. Later Garay would be part of the first CAPMSA board of directors.

3. Alan Faena, the main investor in the area and founder of Faena Properties, the real estate division of Faena Group, was a high-visibility developer of hospitality, retail, and residential property in Puerto Madero.

4. In the Puerto Madero project, the word *dock* (used in English) is used to include the historic red brick warehouses. However, in the literature related to port and maritime structures, it is more commonly used for an enclosed area of water for loading, unloading, building, or repairing ships. This chapter uses the latest definition of *dock*.

5. The Plan Regulador was also known as the Plan Director OPRBA (Oficina del Plan Regulador de Buenos Aires de la Municipalidad de la Ciudad) between 1957 and 1962. It was approved by Decree 9064/1962 and published in 1968.

6. http://www.buenosaires.gob.ar/areas/hacienda/sis_estadistico /boletin/buenosaires/economia.html.

7. The Administrative Emergency Law (23.696, August 17, 1989) and the Economic Emergency Law (23.697) were two fundamental measures used to execute the structural reform. With these laws, approved in cooperation with the opposition, Congress delegated broad powers to the executive branch to reform the state. These included the ability to privatize public enterprises.

8. National Decree N°: 1279/1989, published in B.O. N° 26767 on November 23, 1989: "Convenio de constitución y estatuto social Corporación Antiguo Puerto Madero S.A."

9. Author interview, January 12, 2014, with Alfredo Garay, secretary of urban planning from 1989 to 1992 and director of the corporation after its creation.

10. Mayor Grosso resigned in October 1992 after a series of corruption allegations. Later, most of the lawsuits that had been filed were dismissed for lack of merit or because they had received acquittals. However, this series of scandals ended his political career.

11. Port Vell is a waterfront harbor in Barcelona, Catalonia, Spain, and is part of the Port of Barcelona. It was built as part of an urban renewal program before the 1992 Barcelona Olympics. Prior to this, it was a rundown area of empty warehouses, railroad yards, and factories.

12. In 1989, Argentina was shocked by hyperinflation. Prices would increase several times a day. Hyperinflation brought instability and social arrest.

13. At the beginning of his presidency, part of President Menem's constituency (the Peronist Party) defended national protectionist measures.

14. An article entitled "An Entity to Recycle Puerto Madero" appeared in the daily newspaper *Clarin* on November 21, 1989, a day after the presidential decree.

15. The Sociedad Anónima Antiguo Puerto Madero was enrolled in the Supervisory Board of Companieson February 25, 1991.

16. The National Decree 1456 of September 4, 1987, provides for the transformation of the General Administration of Ports (AGP), a public company pursuant to the terms of Article 9 of Law 20705.

17. AUSA was only used as a front to formalize the contribution of the city. It was a Spanish capital equity company, which had gone bankrupt and been absorbed by the CABA.

18. In October 2003, the statute of the corporation was amended to equally represent the national government and CABA in the board.

19. Because of hyperinflation in Argentina from 1989 to 1992, it is difficult to estimate accurately the dollar equivalent to the austral. In January 1989, Arg$1 amounted to approximately US$18. In November of that same year, around the time of the signing of the decree that created the corporation, US$1 was equivalent to Arg$1015. At the peak of its value before the change of currency to the peso, one dollar reached Arg$11,000 in February 1991. This means that at the time of the appraisal, they were given a nominal value of 170 ha of Puerto Madero of US$19,704.

20. The study referenced in annex 1 of Decree 1279/1989 was published on November 23, 1989. It concerns the agreement that established the Corporación Antiguo Puerto Madero S.A.

21. Later on, Costanera Sur and the ecological reserve were left out of the corporation's boundary. The polygonal demarcation line was drawn excluding the old coastal boulevard and the reclaimed area adjacent to the historic promenade.

22. Jorge Moscato is an architect and professor of Diseño Arquitectónico I and V (Architectural Design I and V) at the University of Buenos Aires. From 1991 to 1993, he was a member of the Buenos Aires Planning Board.

23. Interview with Alfredo Garay (2014): "We [members of the CAPMSA board] were pressed with time. The trade-off between public consultation, participation and political time was apparent with this discussion. We used the national master plan completion as an instance to close the public discussion and be able to start implementation and delivering results."

24. The three winning entries were by Architect Cristián Carnicer & others; Architect Garcia Espil & others; and Juan Manuel Borthagaray, Pablo Dobal & Associates.

25. The holding Bunge y Born owned 15 ha of land including the mill, elevator and grain storage Molinos Rio de la Plata.

26. Interview with Alfredo Garay (2014).

27. The Administrative Emergency Law excluded the universities. See box 4.1.

28. The land occupancy factor equal to six permits in a built-up area is equivalent to six times the plot area. According to the code, it was set up as "an area for locating administrative, financial and institutional facilities at the national, regional and urban scale."

29. "La polémica sobre el futuro de Puerto Madero recién comienza" [The controversy over the future of Puerto Madero is just beginning], *Página 12*, November 28, 1990.

30. In Argentina, real estate is most commonly sold with a 30 percent down payment, with the rest due over 30 days before deed signing.

31. After several failures of the proposed uses, this nomenclature would be changed to allow for commercial development and housing.

32. By Ordinance N° 51.163 of December 5, 1996, and officially published on February 13, 1997.

33. *Clarin* newspaper, September 28, 1998, "Las venas del nuevo barrio de Puerto Madero. Construyen la infraestructura del lado este de los diques."

34. The benefits estimated at the creation of the corporation were US$150 million (Garay 2001).

35. Interview with Alfredo Garay (2014).

36. Interview with architect Marcela Suarez, CAPMSA Urban Planning and Project Manager, Technical Department, from 1992 to the present (2014).

References

Bambaci, Juliana, Tamara Saront, and Mariano Tommasi. 2002. "The Political Economy of Economic Reforms in Argentina." *Journal of Economic Policy Reform* 5 (2): 75–88.

Borja, Jordi. 1990. "Presentación." In Plan Estratégico de Puerto Madero [The strategic plan for Puerto Madero], Consultores Europeos Asociados, Buenos Aires.

Borthagaray, J. M. 1987. "Propuesta para la recuperación y Desarrollo del Área de Puerto Madero, Costanera Sur y Relleno sobre el Río" [Proposal for the regeneration and development of Puerto Madero, South Waterfront and river infill]. Ministerio de Obras y Servicios Públicos, UBA, Buenos Aires.

Ciudad Autónoma de Buenos Aires. 1986. Municipal Ordinance 41.247/86.

———. 1991. Municipal Ordinance 44945 of July 1991.

———. 1994. Municipal Ordinance 001/94.

———. 1996. Municipal Ordinance 51.163 of 5 December 1996.

———. 2000. Urban Planning Code.

———. Auditoría General. 2003. *Survey Report for Puerto Madero Corporation.*

———. 2012. Annual Statistical Data.

Ciudad de Buenos Aires, Dirección General de Estadística y Censos. Buenos Aires en Números. Producto Bruto Interno. http://www.buenosaires.gob .ar/areas/hacienda/sis_estadistico/boletin/buenosaires/economia.html.

Corporación Antiguo Puerto Madero. 1999. *Corporación Antiguo Puerto Madero, Un Modelo de gestión Urbana: 1989–1999* [Antiguo Puerto Madero Corporation: a model for urban management: 1989–1999]. Buenos Aires: Ediciones Lariviere.

Corporación Antiguo Puerto Madero. 2012. Annual balances 2001–2012.

Cuenya, B., and M. Corral. 2011. "Empresarialismo, economía del suelo y grandes proyectos urbanos: el modelo de Puerto Madero en Buenos Aires" [Enterprises, land economics and big urban projects: the Puerto Madero model in Buenos Aires]. *EURE* 37 (111): 25–45.

Garay, A. 2001. "The Management of Urban Projects: Learning from Puerto Madero." In *Case: Puerto Madero Waterfront*, edited by J. F. Liernur. New York: Prestel. http://www.itemciudad.org/boletin/boletin3-acerca-de -la-gestion-de-pus-las-ensenanzas-de-puerto-madero-alfredo-garay.pdf. Accessed March 2015.

Garay, A., L. Wainer, H. Henderson, and D. Rotbart. 2013. "Puerto Madero: A Critique." *Land Lines*. July. https://www.lincolninst.edu/pubs/2257 _Puerto-Madero--A-Critique. Accessed March 2015.

Instituto Nacional de Estadistica y Censos. 2010. National Census.

L. J. Ramos Brokers Immobiliarios. 2009. "Informe sobre Puerto Madero, el barrio más joven de la ciudad: La segunda globalización en Buenos Aires" [Report on Puerto Madero, the youngest neighborhood in the city: the second globalization in Buenos Aires]. *Informe del Mercado Immobiliario* (June). Buenos Aires: L. J. Ramos Brokers Immobiliarios.

Levy-Hara, F., E. Faierman, and P. Sanguinetti. 2014. "Puerto Madero and the Valorization of Urban Land." Unpublished research provided to the author by CAPMSA.

Pou, Pedro. 2000. "Argentina's Structural Reforms of the 1990s." *Finance and Development* 37 (1). http://www.imf.org/external/pubs/ft/fandd/2000 /03/pou.htm. Accessed March 2015.

Presidencia de la Nacion. 1989. National Decree 1279. "Convenio de constitución y estatuto social Corporación Antiguo Puerto Madero S.A." *Boletin Oficial* 26767. November 23.

Real Estate Survey Report. 2014. "Puerto Madero, the WTI Square Meter Withstands." Reporte Inmobiliario. 2014. www.reporteinmobiliario .com.ar.

Rua, Sandra. 2014. "Estrategias del marketing urbano y su impacto en la revitalización económica de un área: El caso de Puerto Madero" [Urban marketing strategies and their impact on the economic renewal of a location: the case of Puerto Madero]. Master's thesis, Universidad Torcuato di Tella, Buenos Aires.

People Interviewed

Alfredo Garay, secretary of urban planning at the time of the conception of the project; director of CAPMSA; board member; architect, UBA

Roberto Converti, CAPMSA president 2000–2002; architect, UBA

Rodrigo Martinez Daveño, Síndico de la Comisión Fiscalizadora de CAPMSA; Consejo del Plan Urbano Ambiental; lawyer specializing in administrative law, UBA

Marcela Suarez, CAPMSA urban planning and projects manager; architect working at the corporation, 1992–present

Eduardo Albanese, CAPMSA technical manager, 1997–present

Map 5.1 **Santiago, Chile**

a. Santiago metropolitan area

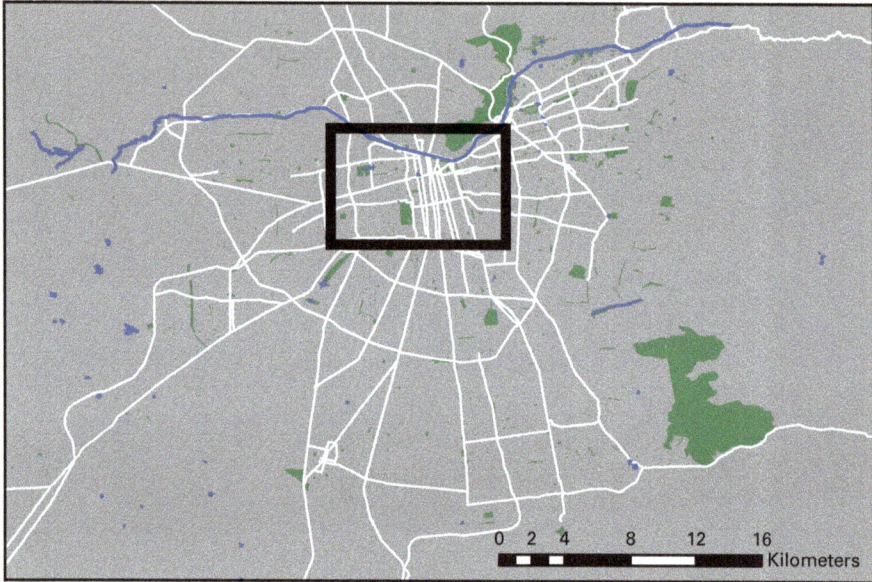

b. Municipal district of Santiago

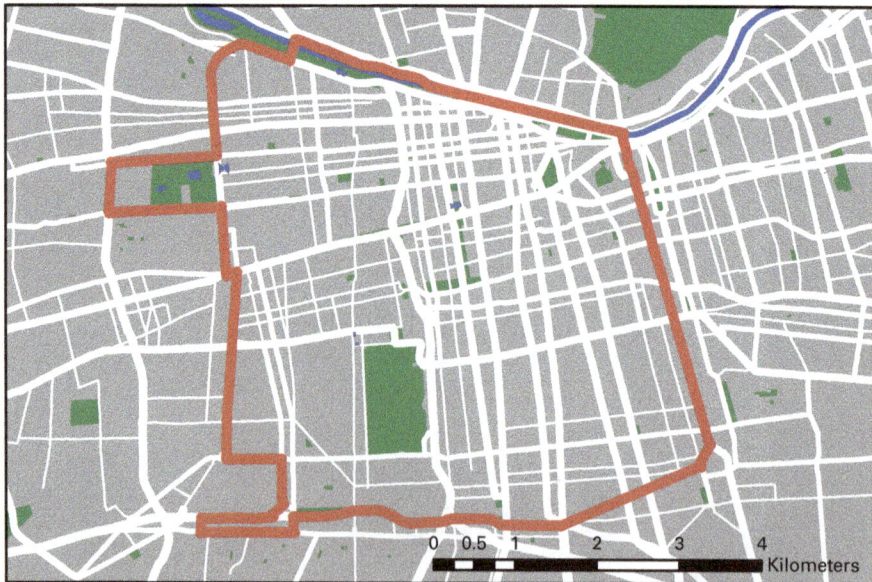

Source: World Bank using Open Street Map data, 2015.

CHAPTER 5

Santiago's Repopulation Program: A Successful Strategy for Regenerating a Shrinking City

Introduction

Santiago's Repopulation Program (SRP) came at an auspicious historical moment in Chile (see map 5.1 for its location). After 17 years of dictatorship, a newly elected democratic government took office in 1990. This more conducive political and economic environment proved to be essential in launching the repopulation program. Indeed, the transition to democracy was marked by a spirit of cooperation, optimism, and will to make things happen among those working in both the private and public sector.

The SRP formed the core of a broader strategy for urban regeneration established by the municipality of Santiago that same year. The goal was to reestablish the central, historical role that Santiago had always played in the past as the capital city—not only as a business and cultural hub but also as an attractive residential destination.

The Santiago Municipal District (SMD) had been facing strong urban deterioration trends for several decades. Between 1950 and 1990, SMD lost almost 50 percent of its population and 33 percent of the housing stock. The housing stock was later replaced by warehouses for industrial activities, small workshops, motels, and parking lots, among other uses. Like many large Latin American cities, the population loss of the central areas was mainly caused by new housing demand favoring lower-density housing developments located in the outskirts of the cities. This trend was accelerated by steady economic growth during the 1990s that increased household incomes, as well as mass access to mortgage credits from the private banking sector (Gonzales 2005).

In 1990, the municipality of Santiago initiated the SRP, which sought to stop the loss of both population and housing stock. Santiago's mayor, who was committed to boosting Santiago's regeneration, led the process. The SRP aimed to attract middle-income residents to relocate to the inner city.

From the initial stages of the process, it was clear to the mayor and his team that the participation of the private sector was necessary for the success of the program. Therefore, the Santiago Development Corporation (SDC) was tasked with implementing the program because of its capacity to convene and mediate between private and public actors. Between 1990 and 2000, the SDC mainly promoted private housing development in the SMD.

The municipality designed several strategies to stimulate increased demand and supply of housing in the SMD. On the one hand, the municipality attempted to improve Santiago's quality of life and change its negative crime-ridden and unattractive public image. The goal was to demonstrate to potential homeowners the value and the benefits of living in the center of the city, which would offer services, proximity to employment, and large public spaces. On the other hand, there were efforts to persuade real estate developers that investing in Santiago would pay off, as there was a large demand for housing in the center of the city.

The SRP has been widely recognized as a successful experience in Chile. It has resulted in boosting the national interest in infill development in other municipalities that face similar problems of urban decay and population loss. Various municipalities are learning from and working with the SDC to implement such repopulation programs.

This case study describes the process of regeneration of Santiago's inner city. It outlines various elements that contributed to attracting the private sector to develop downtown housing units. It also illustrates the way in which both the public and private sector worked together in the implementing the SRP.

Context and Background

The Santiago metropolitan region (SMR) comprises 40 percent of Chile's population (6 million) and generates 44 percent of the country's gross domestic product (GDP). The district of Santiago (with around 300,000 inhabitants) is one of the 52 municipal districts that comprise the metropolitan region (see map 5.1).

Founded in 1541, Santiago is the capital city of Chile and is located in the geographical center of the metropolitan region. Santiago municipality is the oldest district in the region. It hosts all of the government offices and is ranked second within the region in the market for office buildings. In addition, 22 percent of retail businesses are located in Santiago City (Galetovic and Poduje 2006). Santiago also hosts 13 percent of all companies in the region.

In the past two decades, it has become a university hub as well. Indeed, 53 percent of the national institutions of higher education are located in the SMD, primarily concentrated in the University Neighborhood (Trivelli 1998). Such a diverse mix of uses has resulted in a large daily transient population in the SMD (1.8 million), which is almost six times larger than the actual number of local residents (Contreras 2011).

The average annual growth in land prices in the SMR for the past 30 years was 13 percent. The average price of the land in the region is US$320 per square meter (sq m) and US$688.69 per sq m in the SMD. In 2012, Santiago's Province had 4,197[1] vacant plots of land, of which 51 were in the SMD (MINVU 2012) (see maps 5.2 and 5.3).

Map 5.2   **Distribution and size of vacant land in the metropolitan area of Santiago, 2012**

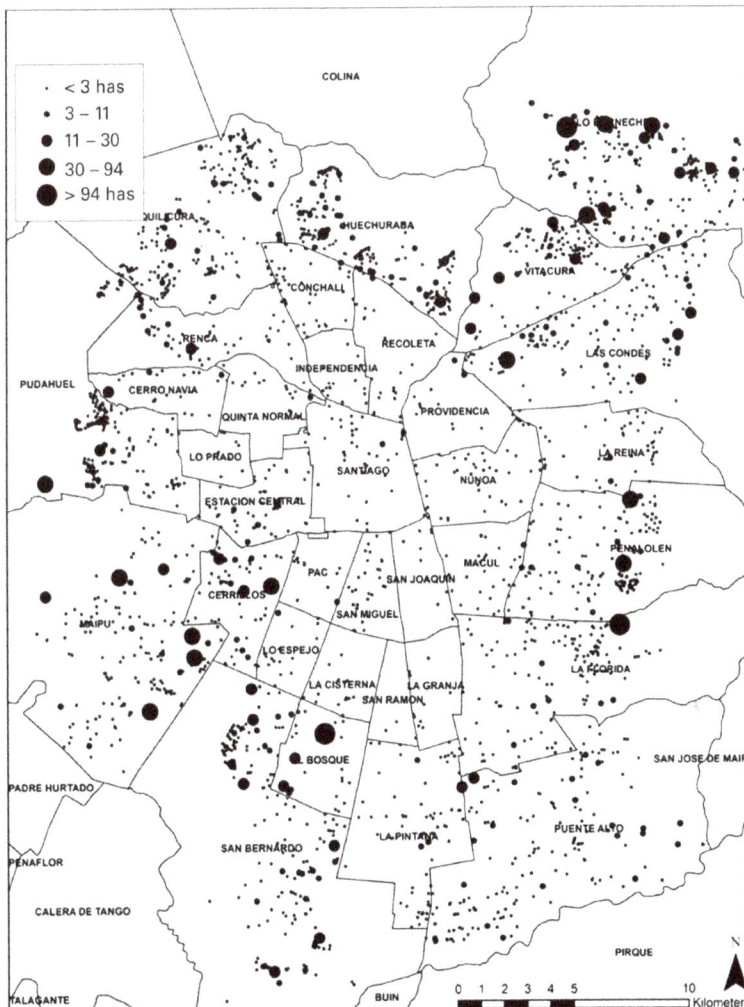

Source: MINVU 2012. Reproduced by permission of Ministry of Housing and Urban Development, Santiago, Chile.
Note: The dots indicate the size of vacant land in hectares (see legend.)

Map 5.3   Land value in Santiago's municipal district, 2011

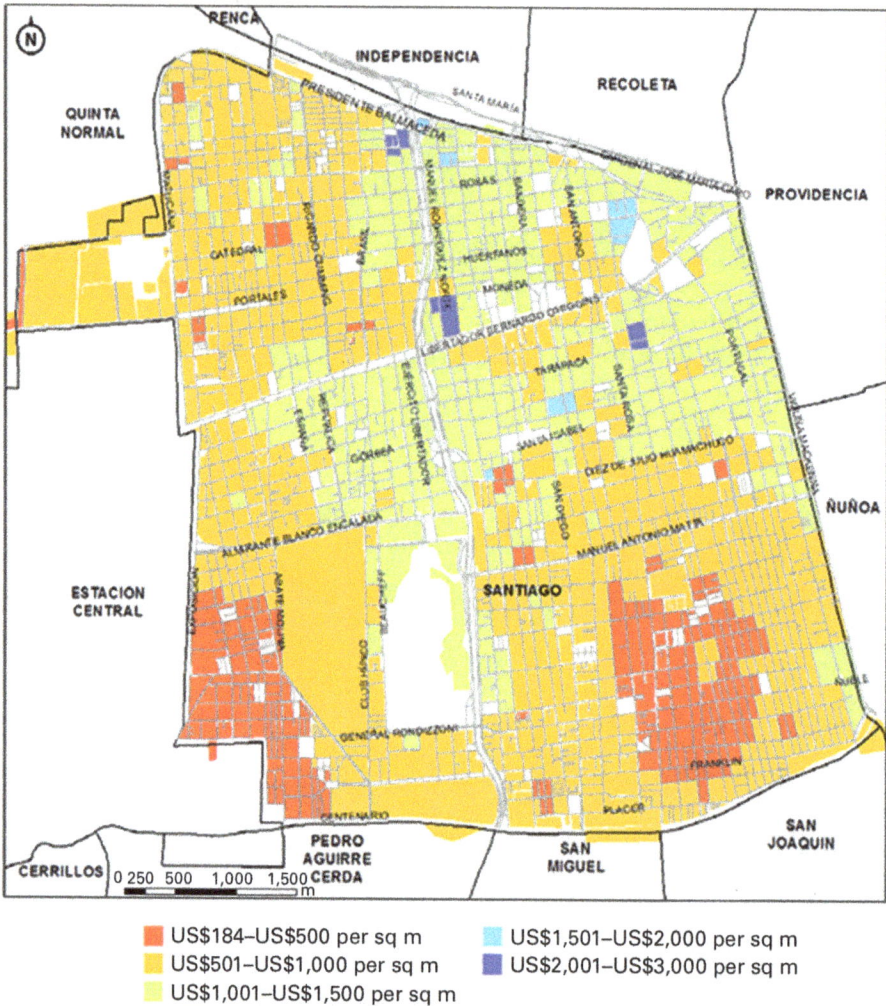

■ US$184–US$500 per sq m	■ US$1,501–US$2,000 per sq m
■ US$501–US$1,000 per sq m	■ US$2,001–US$3,000 per sq m
■ US$1,001–US$1,500 per sq m	

Source: CCHC 2013a.

Santiago Municipal District

The SMD is divided into six zones comprised of 20 neighborhoods. The mayor and the city council are popularly elected every four years and are in charge of the city administration.[2] There is also a Communal Council of Civil Society Organizations elected from representatives of all organizations in the district. The council advises the mayor's administration, suggests public voting for some special investment projects, and participates in the discussions of master and zoning plans.[3]

Municipalities are enabled by law to create corporations, which are private, nonprofit organizations governed by private law.[4] A maximum of

7 percent of the municipal budget can be assigned to such corporations. These organizations are accountable to the municipality every six months for their activities and use of resources. Directors of corporations do not receive any compensation for their performance, and municipalities cannot be the guarantors of commitments subscribed to by these entities. Corporation employees are also governed by private sector labor law.

Currently there are six corporations operating in the Santiago municipality: four of them are related to the administration of cultural spaces, including, the municipal theater and museums; art centers;[5] and one supports small and medium-size enterprises. The SDC is in charge of implementing investment and renovation plans—one of the most important being the SRP between 1992 and 2010.

There are three sources of revenue for every municipality in Chile: (a) autonomous income (from property taxes, vehicle circulation licenses, building permits, and commercial and alcohol licenses); (b) transfers of funds from the Common Municipal Fund (CMF), which is a municipal income distribution transfer system; and (c) transfers from central government agency funds.[6] In many instances, the CMF is the main source of funds for municipalities. In this context, it is important to note that Santiago is among the municipalities that have less economic dependency on the CMF.[7]

Municipalities in Chile have very restrictive constraints regarding budget administration. They do not have the legal authority to borrow, which reduces their capacity to undertake larger capital investments. Municipalities are also forbidden from entering into contracts with the private sector without using a bidding system. For contracts exceeding a ceiling of US$38,000 and the mayor's electoral period, the allocation of funds would need approval from both the mayor and the municipal council (Valenzuela 1997).

Urban Context

Toward the end of the 1980s, several ongoing problems began to give rise to significant urban deterioration in SMD. First, between 1952 and 1992, Santiago's population decreased by 50 percent (table 5.1). This was primarily due to the ongoing trend of suburbanization in the region, as well as the relocation of informal settlements in other municipalities within the metropolitan region (see figure 5.1).

Not surprisingly, the loss of population was coupled with a decrease in the housing stock and deterioration of the environment. The 1985 earthquake exacerbated this situation, causing major structural damage to many buildings that were never repaired. In many cases, they became warehouses, parking lots, automobile repair shops, furniture shops, and motels. As a result of this shift, the housing stock decreased by 30 percent from 90,949 units in 1940 to 63,727 units in 1992 (Trivelli 1998). The shortage of housing stock affected both low- and middle-income households in the district. Middle-income households preferred to move out of the SMD, as the housing supply was insufficient and did not meet their standards. Low-income

Table 5.1 Population trends in the Santiago metropolitan region and municipality of Santiago, 1952–2012

Year	1952	1960	1970	1982	1992	2002	2012
Metropolitan region	1,754,954	2,437,470	3,154,000	4,316,133	5,220,732	6,045,532	6,683,852
Santiago municipality	439,979	375,000	300,931	232,667	230,977	200,792	311,415

Source: INE 2014a.

Figure 5.1 Growth trends in the Santiago metropolitan region, 1990–2002

1890	1940	1970	1980	1990	2002

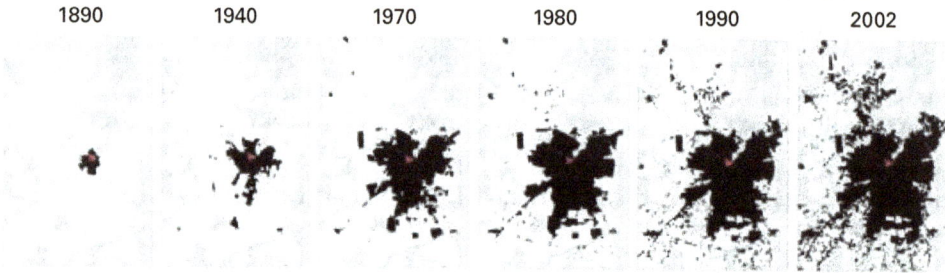

Sources: Galetovic and Poduje 2006. Reproduced with permission of the Centro de Estudios Publicos, Santiago, Chile.
Note: The red dot corresponds to the Santiago municipal district.

households were willing to stay because they did not have an alternative housing solution.

Over this same time frame, investment in residential development was minimal. The rate of issuance of construction permits in the district of Santiago represented merely 2 percent of the total permits authorized in Santiago's metropolitan area during the 1980s (Contreras 2011). The SMD did not offer housing solutions that met the expectations of low- and middle-income groups. In addition, the urban environment was not attractive for housing because of unregulated industrial and commercial activities.

Other elements, such as high crime, pollution, and lack of investment in public areas, also contributed to the depopulation of Santiago. The rate of crime was high and informal street vendors had taken over the downtown area. There was no investment in the creation and maintenance of public spaces by the local government. In addition, the industrial/commercial activities in the area generated negative externalities, such as noise and congestion, which contributed to significant deterioration of the quality of life in the district. As such, the city's public reputation and image suffered, resulting in further decay and depopulation.

Changing Political and Economic Conditions

The SRP was established in the beginning of the 1990s and reflects the country's larger economic and political context. First, the 1990s saw the transition to democracy and the first popularly elected democratic government after 17 years of dictatorship. The transition to democracy generated a new spirit of optimism. Second, the country started to experience unprecedented economic growth at the end of the 1980s. In this period, the Chilean economy grew faster than any other time. Indeed, the growth rate was three times higher than in other countries in Latin America and the Caribbean (LAC) region.[8] Poverty rates also decreased from 38.4 percent in 1990 to 14.4 in 2011 (UNDP 2013).

Housing Subsidy Programs

Chile has had a well-established housing subsidy program for some time. Housing assistance programs in Chile are comprised of three components: subsidies, savings, and mortgage credits. The access to subsidized housing requires that applicants have a formal savings account in a financial institution, complemented with a mortgage credit (provided by a private or public bank). The amount of subsidy depends on the household income. This mechanism has led to a very dynamic housing market whereby the private sector, including developers and financial institutions, play an important role in the provision of housing.

In the 1990s, three of four houses in Chile were constructed with public subsidies—for an annual average of 116,500 units. The subsidy ranged from 8 to 10 percent of the value of the housing unit for middle-income households and up to 94 percent of the housing value for very low-income households (Gonzales 2005). The proportion of housing units built *without* subsidies also increased from 15 percent in 1990 to 45 percent in 1997 (Gonzales 2005). These housing assistance programs paved the way for access to housing for middle- and low-income households and were a key factor in the success of the SRP. Indeed, the program relied on the capacity of the middle class to buy housing units in the private market.

Phase 1: Scoping

Despite its difficulties, the SMD still had enormous potential for growth given its comparative advantages over other recently developed areas in the metropolitan region. Indeed, the SMD had excellent urban infrastructure that was underutilized, including sewage, water pipes, lighting, pavement, public schools, and hospitals. It also offered many benefits related to the centrality of its location, especially proximity to workplaces, commercial areas, and public transport, including buses and the subway system. Moreover, it was endowed with a rich cultural legacy and heritage and large public green spaces.

Regardless of these advantages, however, the private sector had stopped investing in the district due to a perceived low demand for housing and an estimated low rate of return on investments. At the time, the real estate industry primarily invested in larger developments in the peripheral areas of the metropolitan region.

In 1990, after assessing the challenges of the municipal district, the municipality of Santiago developed a clear strategic vision with the goal of recovering the prominent residential role of the SMD.[9] The SRP's objective was to attract 100,000 new residents to the district over the course of 15 years. The strategic analysis concluded that in order to stop the exodus of residents and attract new ones, the municipality needed to work on three fronts simultaneously. First, it needed to attract private investment in housing. Second, it needed to improve the deteriorated physical environment of the district through public investments. Third, it required changing people's perception of SMD through public campaigns.

The Strategic Planning Framework

The SRP was anchored in a participatory exercise led by Santiago Mayor Jaime Ravinet (1990–2000).[10] It resulted in the development of a plan for the renovation of Santiago. This plan had three components: (a) restoring the residential character of the district; (b) strengthening the commercial, industrial, and service activities; and (c) improving the quality of life by providing better public spaces, redesigning private and public transport, increasing residents' security, and protecting the environment.

Previous city and municipal administrations had conducted diagnostic studies to assess the SMD's urban and socioeconomic structure (see box 5.1). Mayor Ravinet's administration shared the assessment's recommendations with the community through a participatory strategy called "Municipality and Participation." The plan was indeed participatory as more than 16,000 residents took part in council meetings under the slogan, "Santiago, a Task of All." The outcome of this dialogue with the community was the clear demand of residents to stop the exodus of inhabitants and to restore the quality of life in Santiago. As a result of this process, the Plan for the Renovation of Santiago was prepared and launched at the First Convention of Santiago.[11] Notably, it included the participation of 1,200 community leaders and organizations.

The implementation of the Plan for the Renovation of Santiago resulted in the creation of two programs, namely SRP and the Housing Rehabilitation Program (REHA). The SRP's goal was to attract new residents and activate the housing market in the municipal district by utilizing a public-private partnership (PPP) structure. The REHA's aim was to reconstruct 500 tenement halls[12] composed of 7,500 housing units. These tenements are old collective condominiums[13] that were originally built to serve the housing needs of the most vulnerable population (see photograph 5.1). The mayor assigned the responsibility of these programs to the newly created SDC.

Box 5.1   **Background studies for Santiago's renovation plan**

The Plan for the Renovation of Santiago, initiated in 1990, was based on a series of studies that had been developed during the previous administration. These studies are listed below.

The Imperatives of the Urban Renovation of Santiago: the Costs of Expansion. This study compared the costs of developing housing solutions in consolidated areas of the city versus areas of urban expansion. The results demonstrated that building in peripheral areas was almost 18 times more expensive than in consolidated areas of the city.

Plan for the Municipal Development. In 1988, the former mayor of Santiago, Gustavo Alessandri, asked the Catholic University to undertake a complete assessment of the economic and social situation of the district in order to design a development plan for Santiago. The report found that the intensive industrial activity in the district had caused a decrease in the quality of life and led to the increased flight of residents. The report recommended reactivating the housing market within the municipal district, regulating industrial activity, rehabilitating tenement halls, and investing in public spaces. Mayor Ravinet used the recommendations from this study to begin the dialogue about urban renewal with the community.

Sources: SDC 1987.

Photograph 5.1   **Tenement halls in Santiago's municipal district**

Source: Chiang 2005. Reproduced by permission of Alfonso Raposo Moyano, *Revista Diseño Urbano y Paisaje.*

Phase 2: Planning

The SRP targeted the entire municipal territory. The goal was to focus on infill development and attract new residents to the inner city of Santiago. The SDC initiated the work in the northwest area of the district because there were large parcels of land available for redevelopment.

A Strong Institutional Arrangement: The Santiago Development Corporation

The implementation of the SRP was delegated to the SDC. The SDC was conceived as the executive arm for the implementation of the Plan for the

Renovation of Santiago (see box 5.2). This flexible institutional structure enabled it to negotiate and develop partnerships with the private sector. As noted, municipal corporations in Chile are governed by private law. As such, they are authorized to enter into contracts with public or private institutions, receive contributions, and borrow from private banks or financial entities.[14]

This institutional feature allowed SDC's executive directors to play the role of public entrepreneurs, working on behalf of the community while using the financial instruments available to the private sector. The PPP agreements between SDC and other actors were regulated in the same manner as contracts between two private actors. However, beyond its managerial attributes, the SDC worked closely with the municipality, as the mayor was the president of the corporation (see table 5.2).

The SRP's Initiative to Boost Private Sector Investment

The scale of the repopulation program was so huge that it would not have succeeded without the active participation of the private sector. However, in the beginning, private developers did not believe that the rate of return on their investment would be as high as building in peripheral areas of the city. After meeting with developers and private sector players, the mayor and the SDC realized that there was a need for a paradigm shift to convince the developers to invest in the inner city and stimulate demand of the residents. Hence, attracting private investment and residents to the inner city had to go hand-in-hand with changing their image of the city. Therefore, the SRP focused on four main tasks.

On the planning side, SRP focused on (a) identifying available land for redevelopment; and (b) redefining the national housing subsidy to fit Santiago's needs. On the financing front, the SRP aimed at (a) demonstrating the existence of high demand for housing in the district; and (b) collaborating with private developers through special agreements. These steps are detailed below.

Identifying Available Land for Redevelopment

The SDC began its mission by conducting a land market assessment using the updated 1987 cadastre of vacant or highly deteriorated or underutilized properties. The process of updating the cadastre included identifying 90 hectares of land owned by private entities and public bodies (the municipality and other national ministries) that qualified for redevelopment and whose owners were willing to sell their properties. The SDC also compiled a list of potential interested developers to buy the land. The lists were created through two tenders: the first, the *Tender for Landowners,* aimed to capture landowners willing to sell their lands. The result was quite modest, and just a few sites were offered at high prices.[17] The second tender, the *Tender for Developers,* asked developers to present projects for the sites obtained in the previous tender. However, not a single proposal was received by the SDC.

Box 5.2   **The Santiago Development Corporation**

The Santiago Development Corporation (SDC) was created in 1985 to foster economic and urban development in the Santiago Municipal District (SMD). Its role is to liaise and mediate among the private sector, public sector, and the community. SDC's responsibilities focus on planning, coordinating, and executing projects for the urban, economic, and social development of the municipal district. In addition, the SDC is responsible for developing visions for the city and conducting research and analysis to determine the city's growth trends. On the evaluation side, the SDC is mandated to conduct impact assessments of its projects.

Most of the SDC's budget comes from transfers from the municipality of Santiago (72 percent).[15] In fact, the SDC is the largest receiver of funds among municipal corporations in Santiago. The rest of its budget comes from the lease of real estate properties that it owns.[16] The budget is used to cover the administrative and human resource costs of the Santiago Repopulation Program (SRP).

The SRP team reached a maximum of 15 staff during the 1990s. The SDC's Board of Directors comprises representatives from the public and private sectors, as well as universities, architects' associations, nongovernmental organizations (NGOs), and the chamber of commerce.

The projects and programs administered by the SDC are developed jointly with the municipality. Specifically, their aim has been to change the general negative public perception of Santiago. The SDC focused on attracting the interest of private investment in the district. All the different lines of work that SDC managed were aligned with the Plan for the Renovation of Santiago, and later the SRP (see table B5.2.1).

Table B5.2.1   **The Santiago Development Corporation: Areas of work, 1990–2000**

Areas of work	Units or activities
Repopulation of Santiago Housing Unit	*Objective:* Stimulate housing demand (potential buyers). *Actions:* • Promote the program among potential buyers (future residents). • Help buyers in the application process for housing subsidies. • Promote the idea of living downtown. • Link housing applicants and developers.
Real Estate Management Unit	*Objective:* Organize the housing supply (developers). *Actions:* • Search land suitable for housing development. • Advise real estate developers. • Promote residential projects. • Prepare files with FARs, regulations, guidelines and designs for developers. • Produce reports with information about real estate activity in the district.
Housing Rehabilitation Program	*Objective:* Rehabilitate 500 tenements (6,700 housing units). *Actions:* • Organize the residents of tenements and alleyways. • Prepare betterment projects. • Tender the projects. • Partially finance the projects (operations). • Search for funds through donations, credits, and subsidies. • Oversee project development. • Organize the savings and fee payments of residents.

(Box continues on next page)

Box 5.2   **The Santiago Development Corporation** *(continued)*

Table B5.2.1   **The Santiago Development Corporation: Areas of work, 1990–2000**
(continued)

Areas of work	Units or activities
Complementary actions (SDC + municipality)	*Objective:* Improve quality of life in the inner city. *Actions:* • Create development committees in nine neighborhoods. • Improve public spaces including, walkways, renovation/redevelopment of old buildings and parks, and recovery of building facades with historic value. • Renovate and redevelop seven cultural buildings. • Improve resident security, public space illumination, street vendor eradication, and surveillance in tenements. • Reformulate local ordinances that regulate charge/discharge hours; noise, traffic, circulation, and parking of taxis, rationalize garbage removal, and so on. *Objective:* Support economic activities. *Actions:* • Regulate commercial and industrial activities in public spaces. • Implement innovation programs and tax incentives. • Increase the number of underground parking spaces. Create legislation to allow for the use of the underground areas of public-use.
Emblematic projects (SDC + municipality)	*Objective:* Change the public perception of the SMD and trigger private investment. *Actions:* • Construction of Los Reyes Park in 1992 (31 hectares) was financed by a donation obtained from the Spanish Crown. • Renovate the former prison of Santiago into modern office buildings (developed under a PPP project). • Reconstitute the former railway station of Santiago into a large cultural center (for which the Cultural Corporation Estacion Mapocho was created). • Renovate and restore historical areas, Concha y Toro Neighborhood, Paris Londres Neighborhood, Cousiño Palace, and Matta Avenue, among the most relevant.

Sources: Based on Trivelli 1998; Contrucci 2013; Chiang 2005. SDC = Santiago Development Corporation.
FAR = floor area ratios; ha = hectares. PPP = public-private partnership.

The lack of interest from private developers was a wake up call for the SDC. In order to attract private investment, the SDC would first need to demonstrate actual housing demand. The SDC pursued different strategies to prove the existence of a significant middle- and low-income housing demand in the SMD.

Redefining the National Housing Subsidy to Fit Santiago's Needs
In 1992, the Ministry of Housing and Urban Development (MHUD) designed and implemented a program called the Subsidy for Urban Renovation (SUR) to support the repopulation program. The aim of the SUR was to provide subsidies to middle- and lower-middle income households to buy properties located in high-priority urban renovation areas.[18] This subsidy provided tax

Table 5.2   **The Santiago Development Corporation organizational chart**

Office or entity	Officers and organizations
Presidency	President (mayor) Vice president (municipal secretary of planning)
Executive director	Director Vice director Manager of administration and finance
Directors (five elected members)	Representative of universities President of the architects' association Representative of the chamber of commerce of Santiago Representative of NGOs Representative of firms of Santiago
Assembly of Associates (35 members with urban interests)	Guilds (architects' association, engineers' association, Chamber of Commerce of Santiago, developers' association, small- and medium-enterprises' association) Representatives of banks Representatives of universities Representative of Ministry of Housing and Urban Development Housing cooperatives Representatives of real estate developers Representatives of neighborhood development committees Representatives of the neighbors' association

Source: Based on Parra and Dooner 2001; Contrucci 2013.
Note: NGOs = nongovernmental organizations.

benefits to properties constructed or renovated in areas classified for urban renovation, effectively freezing their valuation for tax purposes for 20 years (starting in 1987). In cases in which properties were subdivided, the land tax would be apportioned among the various housing units.

Santiago's SUR built upon an existing national subsidy with the goal of reinvigorating the housing market in the district. Santiago's mayor personally requested the support of the MHUD in 1990.[19] He argued that a greater incentive was needed to encourage private developers to invest in housing projects in the district. The petition included an understanding that the SUR program would be applied to the municipal district. The SDC also asked the MHUD to increase the subsidy amount for Santiago's SUR.

The SDC demonstrated to the MHUD that providing services and infrastructure for social housing developments located in the periphery was much more expensive than in the city, including the SMD, which had existing infrastructure and services. In consolidated areas, the average cost of infrastructure (water pipes, sewage, electric power networks, and access and circulation roads) and services and equipment (health and education services, police surveillance, sports and recreational equipment) for each housing unit was US$363 as compared with US$6,487 in areas of peripheral expansion (see table 5.3).

Based on the argument about cost differentials, the MHUD agreed to support the repopulation program. The housing subsidy (SUR), originally launched in 1990,[20] was modified and approved in 1994.[21] The subsidy amount approved by the MHUD was US$8,347.62 (200 unidades de fomento [UF], financial units of account indexed for inflation) and was fixed, regardless of housing value.[22] The required savings varied by housing price. The MHUD authorized the SDC to apply to SUR on behalf of the beneficiaries (see table 5.4).

The creation of the SUR was an important political signal that demonstrated the commitment of both the national and local governments to

Table 5.3 **Cost of incorporating a new residential unit in the city center versus the periphery**

Item	City center (US$)	City outskirts (US$)
Infrastructure	178	740
Water pipes	45	236
Sewage	12	98
Rainwater drainage	0	12
Electric power networks	112	161
Access and circulation roads	9	234
Urban equipment	185	5,747
Health	0	237
Education	0	4,100
Police surveillance	133	1,361
Sports and recreation	72	49
Total	**363**	**6,487**

Source: SDC 1987.

Table 5.4 **Housing subsidy for urban renovation**

	Original SUR (1991–93)		Current SUR (1994–present)	
	UF[a]	US$	UF	US$
Housing value[b]	Up to 500	20,869.05	—	—
Subsidy	200	8,347.62	—	—
Credit (max.)	250	10,434.53	—	—
Saving (min.)	50	2,086.91	—	—
Housing value	Up to 1,000	41,738.11	Up to 1,000	41,738.11

(Table continues on next page)

Table 5.4   **Housing subsidy for urban renovation** *(continued)*

	Original SUR (1991–93)		Current SUR (1994–present)	
	UF[a]	US$	UF	US$
Subsidy	200	8,347.62	200	8,347.62
Credit (max.)	700	29,216.67	700	29,216.67
Saving (min.)	100	4,173.81	100	4,173.81
Housing value	Up to 1,500	62,607.16	Up to 2,000	90,740.00
Subsidy	200	8,347.62	200	8,347.62
Credit (max.)	1,000	41,738.11	1,000	41,738.11
Saving (min.)	150	6,260.72	150	6,260.72

Sources: Based on Contrucci 2000; MINVU 2014a.
Note: SUR = Subsidy for Urban Renovation; UF = Unidade de Fomento; — = not available.
a. UF = US$41.74 (March 3, 2014); UF is a financial unit indexed for inflation as measured by the Consumer Price Index (CPI).
b. This housing value range was eliminated in 1994.

support the SRP. The subsidy was very innovative in its allocation criteria, moving away from previous notions. For the very first time in Chile, subsidies could be targeted based on a geographical or urban definition of the area—instead of income criteria. See map 5.4 for an example of the number of SURs allocated to the SMD in 2008.

Phase 3: Financing and Implementation

Demonstrating the Existence of High Demand for Housing in the District

To stimulate and demonstrate significantly high demand for housing in the inner city, the SDC used two strategies. First, it developed a mechanism to organize potential buyers within the SMD. Second, it initiated pilot projects to demonstrate housing demand. In doing so, the SDC could speed up the process of allocation of the units developed in the pilot projects and offer real estate developers access to this list.

Compilation of Housing Demand
The SDC and Santiago's housing unit generated a list of potential housing buyers in the district of Santiago. The list included employees of the municipality and its service arms (hospitals, schools, and others), employees of large firms located in Santiago, and residents invited by the neighborhood associations, among others. This list started with 1,500 applicants and reached a maximum of 8,000 persons. Until 1992, only residents of the SMD were included in the list of potential buyers managed by the municipality.

In 1993, the list was further expanded to include relatives of SMD residents, and in 1994 it was enlarged to include anyone interested in

Map 5.4   SUR allocated in the Santiago municipal district, January–September 2008

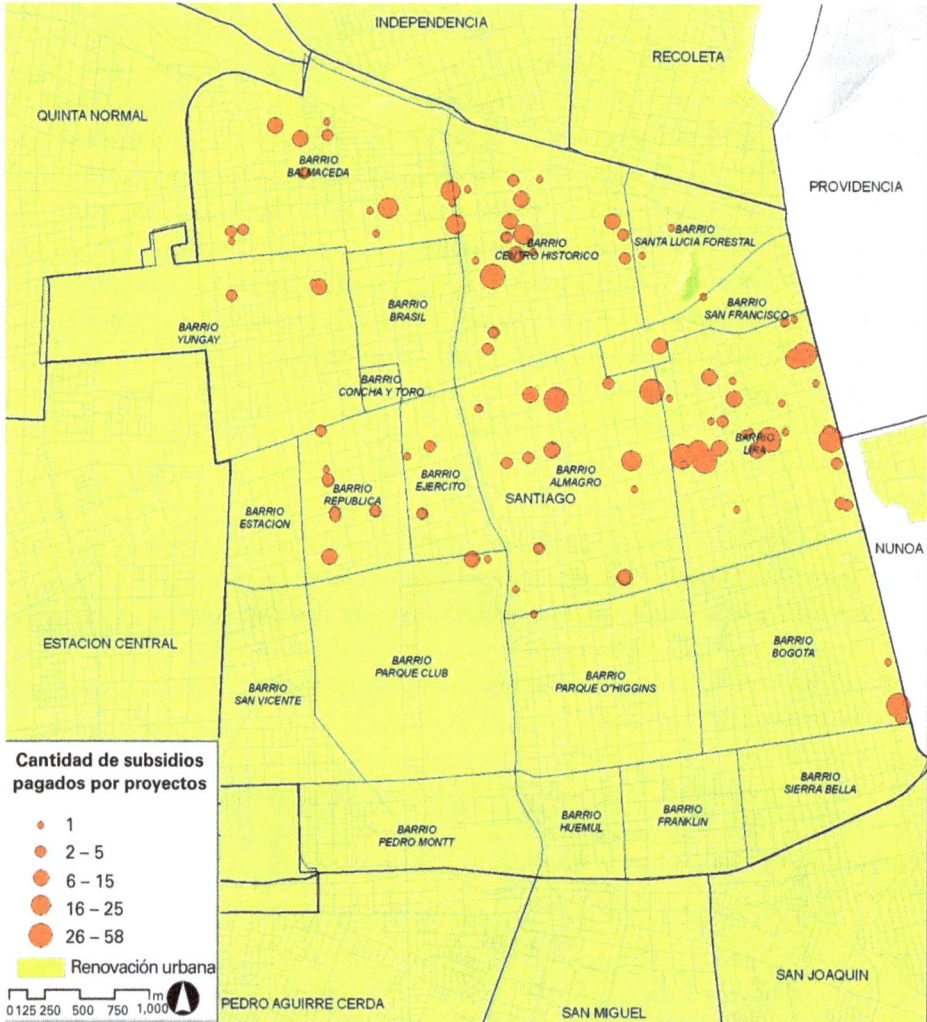

Source: Observatorio Habitacional MINVU 2014b. Reproduced with permission from Observatorio Habitacional, Ministerio de Vivienda y Urbanismo, Santiago, Chile.
Note: SUR = Subsidy for Urban Renovation. Red dots represent the number of SURs per housing project.

buying a housing unit in Santiago. The SDC organized various dissemination strategies to advertise the new line of housing credit, including: neighborhood workshops, presentations to workers of large firms both in the SMD and other municipal districts, newspaper articles, municipal billboards, radio presentations by developers, and brochures.[23] Additionally, the SDC provided developers with the preapproved SUR beneficiary list, which allowed them to more easily access credit for the housing projects.

Pilot Projects to Demonstrate the Existence of Demand

The projects developed by the SDC and the municipality were implemented with a private housing cooperative, HabitaCoop, that had previously developed projects in the SMD. This was the first PPP signed by the SRP. The terms of the agreement included the following responsibilities:

- *Municipality*: Creating a list of potential buyers and sharing it with HabitaCoop overseeing the construction process.
- *SDC*: Consulting, advising, and property management for the acquisition of land suitable for housing; participation in project design and procurement of construction in conjunction with HabitaCoop.
- *HabitaCoop*: Preparation of the SUR application, due diligence for applicants, including checking savings and mortgage credit requirements; land acquisition; and procurement of architectural and construction tenders.

After the completion of the demonstration projects, which were quickly sold to the buyers identified by the Santiago municipality, the interest of real estate developers increased. Between 1991 and 1995, ten projects with a total 2,561 housing units were developed.

The first two SDC-HabitaCoop PPP housing projects included a total of 344 apartment units. (See box 5.3 for details).

Collaborating with Private Developers through Special Agreements

After the pilot projects were implemented and the housing subsidy approved, more private developers started to show an interest in investing in the district. In response, the SDC created a mechanism to formalize the cooperation with private developers called repopulation agreements. These were formal letters of collaboration between the SDC, the municipality, and private developers.

Box 5.3   **Two pilot projects**

First pilot project: ESPERANZA I, 1991
Neighborhood: Balmaceda
Year: 1991
Housing units: 78
Floors: 4
Project total sq m: 4,192.40
Budget: US$265,118

The first pilot project was developed on a 3,000 sq m site located on the west side of the municipal district, which had been used for storage of abandoned vehicles and trash. The Ministry of National Assets donated the site to the municipality of Santiago at a nominal value.[a] The design of the building was assigned to an architectural firm that had previously developed projects in Santiago

(Box continues on next page)

Box 5.3   Two pilot projects *(continued)*

(Taller Norte). The resulting model, including 78 apartments in a four-story building, was presented in the city hall building.

The people interested in the apartments had to complete a form with contact information that was placed near the project model. The value of the housing units was US$25,000. The Santiago Development Corporation (SDC) then tendered the construction of the housing project. The housing unit in the municipality of Santiago managed a list of 1,500 potential buyers. In this case, the decision was to allocate the apartments to teachers from public schools in the municipality. Teachers represented the type of demand for housing in the district that had not been covered, that is, middle-income households with steady incomes, working in the district, and without access to proper housing to suit their needs and preferences.

In this case, the buyers applied for a special housing subsidy called the Special Program for Employees, which was provided by the Ministry of Housing and Urban Development for formal employees.

Second pilot project: RONDIZONNI, 1993
Neighborhood: Pedro Montt
Year: 1993
Housing units: 289
Floors: 5
Project total sq m: 18,265
Budget: US$4,640,000.00

The second pilot project was developed on an 11,000 sq m site located on the southwest side of the municipal district. It belonged to the municipality and was sold to HabitaCoop for US$930,000 (US$85 per sq m). The funds obtained from the sale by the municipality were re-invested in the project in order to improve the construction standards. Apartment sizes varied between 45 sq m and 92 sq m and the value ranged from US$21,200 to US$38,300.

In this case, HabitaCoop tendered the construction of the project to another developer. Therefore, HabitaCoop's role was focused on overseeing the construction process, as well as in finding the buyers and conducting duediligence. The buyers applied to the newly created Subsidy for Urban Renovation (SUR) launched by the Ministry of Housing and Urban Development (MHUD) in 1992.

a. With the transition to democracy, this kind of collaboration between institutions was quite common at the time.

In these agreements, the SDC pledged to play the role of a broker mediating the demand and supply of land and housing. The SDC and private developers made commitments as follows:

The SDC committed to

- Coordinating the demand (potential buyers) with the Housing Unit of the municipality of Santiago. This included helping buyers apply for the housing subsidy and providing a list of buyers willing to pay for housing costing up to US$85,000.
- Providing access and information to the available land bank, which included a total of 90 hectares of land suitable for redevelopment.
- Providing developers with information for every site of interest, including a fact sheet with location, landowner contact, approximate

value of the land, gross building area, floor area ratio (FAR), density allowed, and master plan regulations, among other items.

- Providing advice about the project design by analyzing the housing market, as well as suggesting sites and setting up meetings between landowners and developers.[24]
- Accelerating the process of municipal approval of housing projects by assigning a point person at the municipality's Construction Management Office (CMO) to review the preliminary design of projects developed under the SRP. In this way, developers could save time and change the project as needed before submitting the final version to the CMO director approval.
- Promoting the projects and the benefits of living in the Santiago Municipal District.
- Allowing developers to use the logo of both the SDC and the municipality. Developers appreciated this official imprimatur as it helped to instill buyer confidence.
- Developing quarterly market analysis reports which included the number of potential buyers (and other information, such as their municipal district of origin), available land, value of the sites, description of all the projects/units being developed, and so on. These reports were then certified by the Chamber of Developers.

Developers committed to
- Sharing with the SDC all information about the project development (number of units, costs, buyers, and so on), which was then compiled by the SDC and distributed back (or sold) to developers.
- Paying a commission to the SDC, which amounted to 0.2–0.5 percent of each unit sold.

Investor Incentives

Investors became interested in the SMD after realizing that Santiago offered a combination of three important elements. First, the pilot projects demonstrated that there was a high demand for housing. Second, the new subsidy covered a significant part of the housing value. Third, the master plan allowed greater flexibility and high FARs. Developers realized that the rent that could be obtained from the land was very attractive, given the master plan's features and existing housing demand.

The first project built was essential in generating confidence in the rest of the industry. As soon as the project was completed, more than 300 interested buyers showed up at the sales office to buy the units. The developer (Paz-Froimovic) understood the great opportunity and immediately bought three other sites and started five new developments.[25]

Paz-Froimovic saw the business potential immediately, but also favored the idea of increasing the density of Santiago's central business district (CBD), instead of contributing to sprawl and developing projects on the periphery. Having worked in other dense urban areas such as Barcelona,

Spain, urban life was a core value for the company. They assessed Santiago's potential as any other central city (and capital) in the developed world, where high density and proximity to amenities is positively valued (see box 5.4).

The SDC's role has evolved significantly during the 20 years of SRP implementation. As noted, the SDC's leadership was key to creating the conditions and putting the incentives in place for the private sector to meet the demand and start investing in Santiago. However, once the demand was proven, the SDC's role diminished. Table 5.5 summarizes the activities undertaken by SDC during the last 25 years to achieve its goal of repopulating Santiago.

Outcomes and Impacts

Housing Stock and Demographic Impact

The most important outcome of the SRP was to boost the housing market and repopulate the SMD, which has now become one of the most vibrant residential areas in the metropolitan region. Between 2002 and 2012, the population increased by 55.1 percent and the housing stock almost doubled. The goal of recovering the residential role of the district has been achieved through effective PPPs. The merit of the SRP was in foreseeing the

---

Box 5.4   Private developer's testimony

"Cities should be densified not expanded, that is how every city in the developed world grows. Santiago must be raised, built in height so that people do not have to travel one hour to get to work....

When we started working in the area, we had to attract people to come to live in Santiago. Our target market was people that liked living in the city and appreciated the proximity to services and work, like young professionals, students, young couples with one or two kids, divorced people, and retired people that sold their houses and wanted to live in a smaller place....

In terms of the business, our gains came from the volume of units sold. Given the high FAR and density allowed by the master plan, we bought the land at prices that were higher than other districts. But, as we had the capacity to build a larger number of apartments, we sold the units 15 to 20 percent cheaper, which made it very attractive for buyers....

When we started, our concern was to verify whether people had purchasing power. SDC played an important role because they presented a list of preapproved buyers, which gave us certainty to start a project. The SUR also played an important role to make the projects profitable."

Source: Interview with Benjamin Paz, president PAZCorp. Ltd.
Note: SDC = Santiago Development Corporation

Table 5.5   Evolution of Santiago's Repopulation Program, 1990–present

Initiation, 1990–95: process primarily driven by SDC

- The SRP devised different strategies, including a Land Bank, a list of preapproved buyers, and a pilot project with a housing cooperative (HabitaCoop). It also obtained official permission to apply on behalf of housing buyers to obtain the housing subsidy, SUR.
- At the same time, the SDC and the municipality implemented a set of multiple complementary investments together with promotional activities. These actions sought to renovate deteriorated spaces and buildings in the SMD.
- The strategy implemented in this phase sparked the interest of other private developers in signing cooperation agreements with the SDC for the construction of new housing, as well as to access the list of preapproved housing applicants.
- The housing applicants initially looked for housing units costing up to US$42,000, whereas at the end of this phase, the housing applicants were looking for housing costing up to US$82,000, which was very attractive for private developers as well.
- The SRP helped with access to credit and housing subsidies, specifically: (a) a US$8,347 (UF200) housing subsidy granted by the MHUD to families buying in areas of renovation; and (b) a new line of 25-year mortgage loans from private banks for middle-income households to finance the cost of housing not covered by household savings and subsidies.

Consolidation, 1996–2002: collaborative action among the SDC, the municipality, and private developers

- The SDC started to sign new repopulation agreements with private developers.
- The SDC worked on accelerating the SUR subsidy application process, advising real estate developers about the design and location of their projects, selling project units, and so on.
- In 1996, the MHUD allowed the use of the SUR for housing costing up to US$90,000 (2,000UF). On average, 750 SUR were allocated each year to housing applicants in the SMD, which represented 23 percent of the housing units built per year in Santiago.
- In this phase, housing demand grew faster than the supply of apartment units.
- To preserve the provision of social housing in the district, the collaboration agreement with HabitaCoop continued. However, the change in the SUR led to an increase in the price of land, making it unfeasible to develop social housing. In 1997, HabitaCoop went bankrupt.
- The municipality and the SDC developed a strong campaign to improve the image and highlight the advantages and benefits of living in Santiago.

Expansion, 2003–10: process primarily driven by the private sector

- The repopulation process became autonomous. The housing market in the SMD became the most vibrant in the metropolitan region and was the preference of apartment buyers.
- The SDC's role in the Repopulation Program decreased, and it shifted its focus to other programs. Although it continued working under the aegis of the repopulation agreements, its role became secondary. At this time, sales commissions were eliminated. The process of organizing the housing applicants became the most valuable work of the SDC in the PPP process.
- As demand increased, more developers entered SMD's housing market without the assistance of the SDC.
- The proportion of people buying a housing unit using the SUR housing subsidy decreased significantly and represented less than 10 percent of the total units sold in this period.
- In 2003, the master plan reduced the FAR and gross building area in Santiago's west side because of the high concentration of projects in that area that resulted in opposition from the current residents.

(Table continues on next page)

Table 5.5   Evolution of Santiago's Repopulation Program, 1990–present *(continued)*

Redefinition, 2010–present: rethinking the future role of the SRP

- In 2010, the SDC reoriented its focus to respond to the needs generated by the earthquake that occurred in February 2010.
- Today, the SDC and the municipality of Santiago face the challenge of responding to two different kinds of residents: the *traditional residents*, the majority of them elderly, who claim that the apartment building towers have worsened their quality of life; and the *new residents* who live in the apartment towers, generally young professionals, demanding more green areas, and services such as daycare, better administration of the buildings, and so on.
- The municipality plans to address the new challenges by redefining the role of the SDC and the SRP in the future. In this context, the municipality has requested a complete assessment of the impact that the repopulation has had in the SMD.

Note: MHUD = Ministry of Housing and urban Development; SDC = Santiago Development Corporation; SMD = Santiago Municipal District; SRP = Santiago Repopulation Program; UF = Unidades de Fomento.

opportunity and generating the strategy to accelerate the process of repopulation. Although the SUR was applicable to many other districts in the metropolitan region, because of the SRP, the SMD was the only one that actually benefited from its use (see map 5.5).

Although it was ultimately successful, the repopulation process took 10 years to reverse the decreasing population trend in the capital region. From 1992 to 2002, the SRP managed to activate the housing market in SMD. However, housing demand was not strong enough to reverse the depopulation trend. The positive outcome only became evident after 2002, when the steady growth in the housing market was coupled with a massive increase in the number of new residents.

According to census data, between 1992 and 2002, the housing stock in the SMD experienced an increase of 21.6 percent (13,787 new housing units). In the same period, the population decreased by 13 percent. This occurred because 40 percent of the new units produced were bought by residents of the SMD (Trivelli 1998). In addition, the average size of households decreased from 1992–2002. Therefore, despite the fact that the number of households increased, the absolute number of new residents did not compensate for the population loss (see table 5.6).

By contrast, from 2002 to 2012, the housing stock almost doubled and the population grew 55.1 percent. This trend stands out when compared with the surrounding districts that still lost population (see map 5.6). The reduction in household size by 21 percent was not offset by population growth. Furthermore, the proportion of housing buyers from SMD was similar to the previous decade. During this time, 56.6 percent of the buyers came from other municipal districts, and 43.4 percent were residents of the district of Santiago (CCHC 2013a; MINVU 2014a; Contrucci 2013).

The new housing stock has changed the structural and demographic configuration of the capital region, where most new developments are high-rise apartment buildings that have attracted young professionals and students.

Map 5.5 **Housing market stock average annual growth rate, 2002–12**

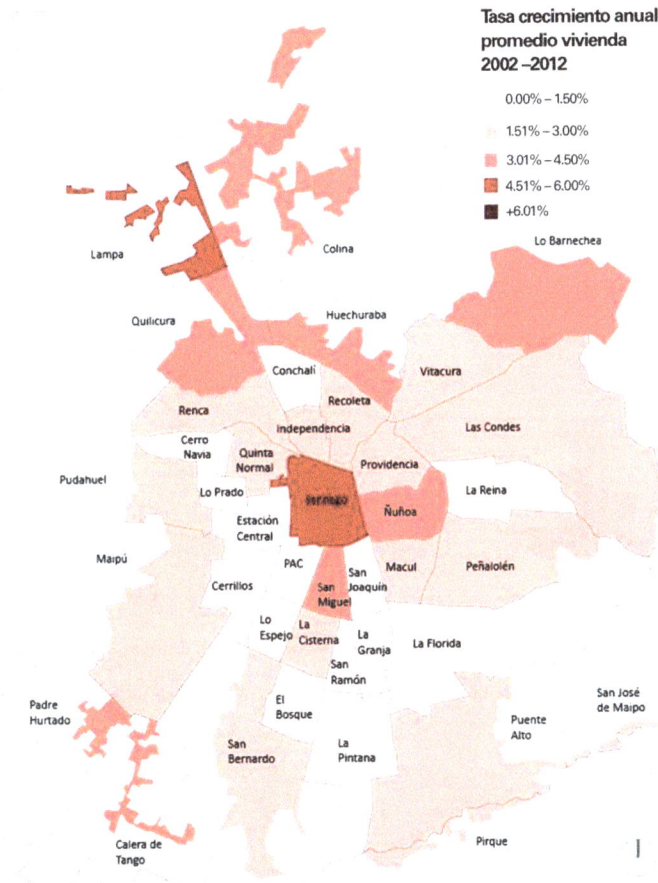

Tasa crecimiento anual
promedio vivienda
2002–2012

- 0.00% – 1.50%
- 1.51% – 3.00%
- 3.01% – 4.50%
- 4.51% – 6.00%
- +6.01%

Source: Cámara Chilena de la Construcción 2012. Reproduced by permission from Cámara Chilena de la Construccíon.

Table 5.6 **Evolution of housing stock, population, and household size in SMD, 1992–2012**

Census year	Housing stock	Variation (%)	Population	Variation (%)	Household size	Variation (%)
1992	63,727	—	230,977	—	3.6	—
2002	77,514	21.6	200,792	-13.1	2.6	-27.8
2012	149,592	93.0	311,415	55.1	2.1	-20.8

Source: Based on CCHC 2013a; INE 2014; Rojas 2004.
— = not available.

Map 5.6   The SMR's population annual growth rate for two census periods, 1992–2002 and 2002–12

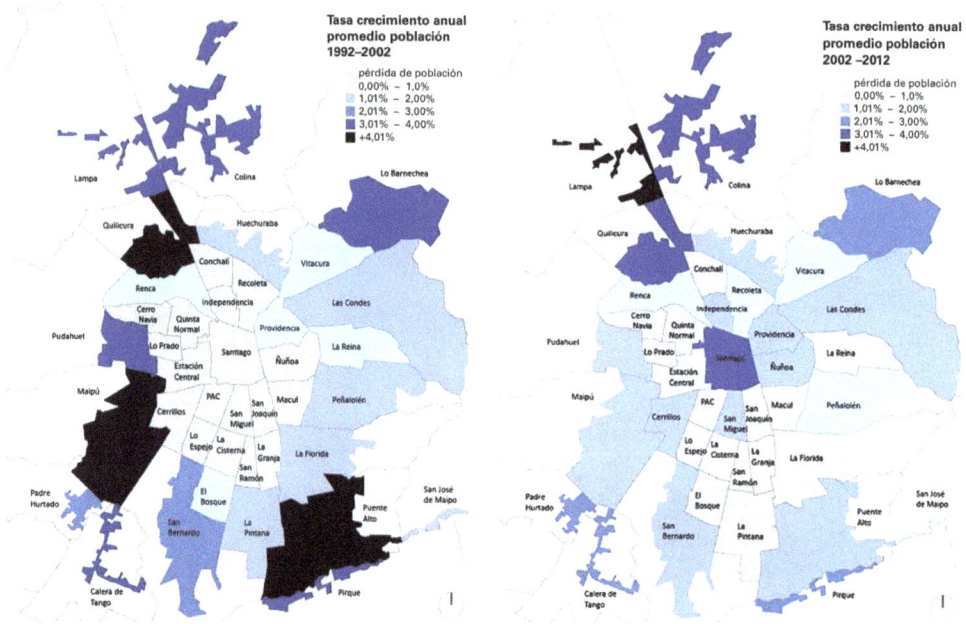

Source: Cámara Chilena de la Construcción 2012. Reproduced with permission from Cámara Chilena de la Construcción.
Note: The color gray indicates loss of population; blue indicates population growth. SMR = Santiago metropolitan region.

Currently, of the total number of residents over 15 years old, 52.3 percent study and 40.7 percent work within the district. This demographic fact also explains the high amount of renters in SMD (50 percent, compared to 33 percent in the metropolitan region) and the typology of the housing stock, which is concentrated in apartments (62 percent) instead of single-family units (33 percent). In contrast, in the metropolitan region, the typology includes 20 percent apartments and 78 percent single-family units (CCHC 2013b).

Since the SRP began, 646 building projects have been constructed. The share of Santiago's housing permits within the metropolitan region grew from 2 percent between 1980 and 1998 to 4 percent between 1990 and 1999, and then to 17 percent between 2000 and 2009 (Contreras 2011). This positioned Santiago to become the hottest apartment market in the metropolitan area, with a share of 35 percent (CCHC 2013a; MINVU 2010) (see table 5.7 and map 5.7).

Over the years, the housing market has become more autonomous and competitive. Around 10,000 units were developed under collaboration agreements between developers and the SDC from 1990–2012. Until the

Table 5.7   **Annual average percentage of apartments sold by municipal districts, 2009–12**

Tramo	2009	2010	2011	2012
Providencia/Ñuñoa/La Reina	16,4	17,2	8,3	13,4
Las Condes	7,5	9,4	9,5	9,4
Lo Bamechea	0,7	1,1	1,9	2,6
Vitacura	1,7	2,6	2,1	1,6
Macul	3,7	2,0	2,8	3,9
Santiago Municipal District	**37,8**	**35,3**	**36,5**	**42,0**
San Miguel	4,1	2,6	6,4	5,3
Puente Alto/La Cistema/El Bosque	3,3	3,1	3,1	1,6
Huechuraba/Independecia/Quilicura	5,7	6,0	6,9	3,8
Recoleta	3,1	3,1	4,6	2,2
La Florida/Peñalolén/San Joaquín	4,0	5,0	10,0	7,7
Estación Central/Pudahuel/Maipú/Cerrillos	12,0	12,7	7,8	6,4

Source: Cámara Chilena de la Construcción 2012. Reproduced by permission from Cámara Chilena de la Construcción.

Map 5.7   **Distribution of building permits in the Santiago municipal district, 1990–2012**

1990 – 1994 > building permits

1990 – 1999 > building permits

1990 – 2004 > building permits

1990 – 2012 > building permits

Source: Based on SDC 2014.

year 2000, around 40 percent of the housing projects were the result of PPPs between real estate developers with the SDC and the municipality of Santiago. However, since then, the housing market in the district of Santiago has started to work autonomously. More than 200 real estate developers have invested in housing projects from 1990 to 2012, and the number of projects grew from an annual average of 19 projects in the 1990s to 35 projects from 2000 to 2012, manifesting of a very dynamic and competitive market.

During the implementation of the repopulation plan, the municipal master plan was modified 29 times. These changes sought to either allow more density and height in some areas or to restrict and lower the height of the buildings. The changes also included the definition of areas of cultural heritage protection (Arraigada, Moreno and Rovirosa 2007).

The number of both floors and housing units per building has increased by a factor of three (see map 5.8). The average number of floors is 13. The number of housing units per building is 176, and the average size of each unit 69.6 sq m. Densities in many projects vary between 3,200 hectares (ha) and 7,000 ha (Martinez 2006). SMD's density has increased 2.4 times in the past decades, from 90 ha in 1992, to 143 ha in 2002, to 220 ha in 2012 (INE 2014a).

The new housing stock developed since 1990 not only has changed the SMD's urban landscape, but it also has prompted many criticisms. The area is now characterized by the preeminence of high-rise apartment buildings. However, the quality of these buildings in terms of architectural design and construction materials is one of the weaknesses of the repopulation program. The critics have complained about the flexibility allowed by the master plan, as well as the mild regulations, considering the dynamism of the housing market. From the residents' standpoint, the critiques are focused on the significant contrast that the projects have with respect to the old residential buildings and traditional neighborhoods. The new buildings are not well integrated with the existing environment. In many cases, this situation has generated opposition from residents. Residents started to oppose new projects and demanded that the municipality freeze building permits and reduce the FAR and heights allowed in their neighborhoods.

In general, the financial outcomes of Santiago's renovation plan have been significant. The total municipal revenues increased 55.2 percent in the period from 2001 to 2013. The revenues obtained through property taxes[26] increased 85.1 percent in the same period. The increase in the municipal revenues from licenses (77.1 percent) can be attributed in part to the increase in economic activity that the repopulation of the district has generated (see table 5.8).

These revenues are significant considering that almost 65 percent of the residential units in the SMD are exempt from property taxes[27] and a

Map 5.8   **Number of apartment units per building in the Santiago Municipal District, 1990–2012**

Units per building
- 600 – 1200
- 350 – 600
- 200 – 350
- 100 – 200
- 4 – 100

Source: Based on SDC 2014.

Table 5.8   **Sources of revenue for Santiago municipality, 2001 and 2013**

	2001 (US$ millions)	2013 (US$ millions)	Variation 2001–13 (%)
Total municipal revenues	157.35	244.17	55.20
Revenues from taxes	48.84	88.41	87.40
Municipal licenses[a]	26.34	46.76	77.10
Property tax	22.50	41.65	85.10
Revenues from waste collection fee[b]	6.18	10.07	62.90

Source: Based on SINIM 2014.
a. Revenue sources include vehicle registration permits and municipal licenses (for selling alcohol, building permits, commercial and professional activities, and industrial activities).
b. Every property is obliged to pay two monthly tax units (unidad tributaria mensual) UTM (approximately US$90–100) to the municipality for what is called the "right to waste collection."

significant proportion of those who pay property tax receive a considerable tax deduction on the total appraised value of their property (850 UF).[28] Therefore property owners actually pay tax only for the portion of the property value over the tax exemption.[29]

Total private investment, municipal revenues, and natural subsidies highlight the financial success of the SRP. Since the start of the SRP, private investment in Santiago has reached almost US$3 billion. The municipality has collected US$43.5 million from building permits, increasing 45 times since 1990, and reaching two percent of the annual municipal budget. The central government contributed to the program through the SUR subsidies; an annual average of 750 subsidies was allocated to Santiago in the period from 1992 to 2002, for a total of US$138.8 million.[30]

The value of the land has remained stable in the past decade at between US$450 and US$1,000 per sq m. The major changes in prices took place in the 1990s. The average value in 1990 varied in the range of US$140 per sq m to US$328 per sq m, whereas in 1997, the range increased to US$421 to US$562 per sq m. Then, in 2012, the average increased again to US$688 per sq m (Contrucci 2013; Trivelli 1998; MINVU 2012).

Figure 5.2 shows both the amount of land offered (sq m) and land prices (UF). The trend shows that in the 1990s, the activation of the market created an increase in the supply of land and prices. In the 2000s, as the land supply decreased, prices went up. The most expensive areas are those in which the CBD, universities, and national administrative buildings are located.

The SUR has been crucial in stimulating the housing market in SMD. Indeed, around 70 percent of the total SUR allocated in renovation areas within the metropolitan region are being used in the SMD. During the 1990s, almost 50 percent of the housing units were bought using the SUR. Since 2000, however, this decreased to 10 percent (Arraigada, Moreno, and Rovirosa 2007). Today the housing market has become less dependent on the SUR although, in some cases, it still serves as a stimulus.

Housing prices in Santiago have steadily increased since the beginning of the SRP. In the first half of the 1990s, housing values ranged from between US$25,000 and US$38,300, to between US$40,000 and US$60,000 in the second half of the 1990s. In the 2000s, the range widened again from US$40,000 up to US$90,000.

According to data from the MHUD, in the period 2005–09, the SMD concentrated 55 percent of the housing offered in the value range of US$40,000 and US$90,000 (the maximum allowed by the SUR). The steady growth in the housing value has created a very restrictive scenario for the provision of housing for low-income households in the SMD. To illustrate this situation, of the total housing built in the SMD between 2007 and

Figure 5.2 Price variation and area of land offered, quarterly periods, 1982–2013

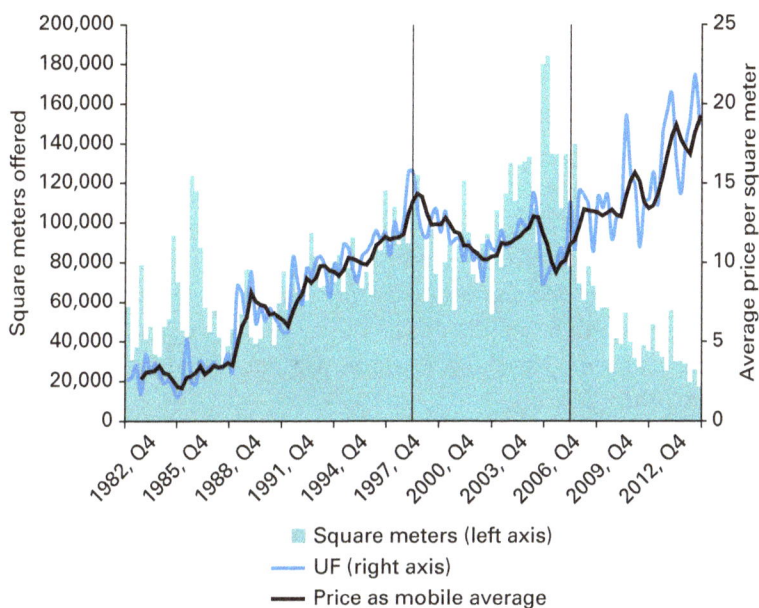

■ Square meters (left axis)
— UF (right axis)
— Price as mobile average

Source: Trivelli and Cia. Ltda.
Note: UF = financial unit indexed for inflation (Unidades de Fomento).

2010, less than 1 percent were affordable housing units (Casgraine and Janoschka 2013).[31]

The SUR has also played a role in the increase in housing prices. In 1994, the SUR was modified by the MHUD to allow for the purchase of higher priced units, that is, 25 percent more expensive, from 1500 to 2,000 UF. This pushed up both the price of the land and the housing. For the SDC, it became very difficult to ensure the provision of affordable housing for low-income households within the district.

Although the SMD has seen a large supply of housing for middle- and middle-low-income households in the past decades, supply for low-income households has been very limited. In this regard, the SDC developed a program called REHA to renovate 500 existing tenement halls, where a considerable number of low-income households live. This program initially helped to compensate for the lack of housing availability for this income group. However, the rehabilitation of tenements then resulted in gentrification. Hence, although a group of these tenements remained affordable, others were restored to meet the demand and preferences of middle- and high-income households.

Social Impact: Gentrification Considerations

The decrease in housing for lower-income households has led to a discussion about whether SMD repopulation has resulted in gentrification. The SRP did not include a proactive strategy to prevent gentrification. The few actions taken, such as the affordable housing constructed by HabitaCoop, have been reactive rather than proactive. In spite of the efforts, the economic feasibility of building affordable housing for low-income households turned out to be very low.

There is no agreement among analysts as to whether the SMD has indeed undergone a process of gentrification. Those who argue that there is an ongoing gentrification process in the SMD believe that the current situation has been driven by the real estate sector, which has taken advantage of higher rents that can be obtained from the land, thereby generating indirect displacements rather than direct evictions (Casgraine and Janoschka 2013; Lopez and others 2013).

The arguments rejecting the idea of gentrification focus on the fact that new housing has been acquired by middle- and middle-low-income households. Furthermore, the change in the social composition of SMD residents is also related to a process of economic development that has occurred nationwide, with the consequent increase in income and reduction in poverty rates (Arraigada, Moreno, and Rovirosa 2007; Contreras 2011).

In fact, it is hard to argue that gentrification has occurred given the availability of land for development and the socioeconomic characteristics of the population that bought the newly developed apartments. Before the start of the SRP, the district had underutilized capacity to host more population. The housing market generated a housing supply for an income group that would not have had the possibility of renting or buying in the SMD given the cost of the land. The high densities enabled people who could not normally afford a well-located housing unit to have that option. The SMD master plan made it feasible for middle-income households to live in the capital area. However, the situation for low-income households is different. Supply for this income group is almost nonexistent since land has become expensive, making it difficult to build social housing.[32]

Final Considerations

Twenty years after the start of the SRP, the impact has been substantial. The last census showed that the SMD's population grew 55.1 percent between 2002 and 2012 (INE 2014b). Since 1990, 646 building permits have been issued and 123,855 housing units have been built. The private sector has invested around US$3 billion in residential developments (SDC 2014). The SMD has the largest number of housing units built in the country. It also ranks first in buyers' preferences in the whole SMR.

The significant population growth that SMD has experienced in the last decade can be explained by the convergence of several elements that were present at the beginning of the process in the 1990s. First, there was a clear vision for the city that was sustained through the years under the active leadership role of Santiago's mayor. Second, the SDC worked with both private and public entities, acting as a broker between supply and demand of land and housing. Third, the execution of complementary actions included emblematic projects that aimed to change the public perception of quality of life in the city. Fourth, the active participation of the private sector as the main executor of the repopulation process was key. Fifth, the MHUD supported the provision of a targeted housing subsidy assigned to areas in need of urban renovation. Finally, the project had the necessary set of preconditions that facilitated the execution of the plan, that is, a conducive macroeconomic and political situation, access to credit, and a strong and active national housing policy, among others.

Future Challenges

Critics of the repopulation process of Santiago focused on the lack of control the municipality had over the process. There is a general agreement regarding the benefits of repopulating the SMD. However, the costs of leaving the housing market lightly regulated, without sufficiently specifying the construction standards and design criteria, led to a negative perception of the regeneration effort. The criticism points to the passive role of the SRP and the municipality once the housing market took off. The city did not think strategically about the costs of the repopulation (pressure on green spaces) or about the opportunity to use good design frameworks to make the city a destination. Today, the challenge posed to the municipality of Santiago rests in managing the impact of the housing stock already built, as well as in guiding the new housing production in the municipal district—without restraining the private investment.

In response to neighborhood association requests, Santiago's municipality and the SDC have limited the FAR and height allowed in the southeastern area of the Municipal District, where most of the new real estate investment has been taking place. Meanwhile, the master plan is under review, with the purpose of fostering a sustainable equilibrium between new housing projects and the quality of life of current SMD residents.

Lessons Learned

- *Maintain proactive municipal leadership.* A repopulation process does not occur in a short period of time. Rather, it takes time to reactivate a housing market that has been stagnant for decades. The process of repopulating Santiago took 20 years to complete—although such results would not have been possible without the strategies generated by the SRP during the 1990s. In this regard, institutional and political stability are very important when creating major change through a long process lasting decades. In the case of SRP, the mayor's leadership and vision was a central element in the project's success. His vision and capacity for negotiation were important in not only empowering the SDC but also in gaining support from the national government and the private sector.

- *Create institutional arrangements to support public and private cooperation and partnerships.* The SDC created the conditions for establishing a PPP with real estate developers that would have been impossible under the normal municipal organizational structure. The features of the new entity leading the process were also important in terms of the flexibility and adaptability it offered to stakeholders. The team involved in the regeneration project needs to be able to adjust and innovate with respect to standard public sector procedures. In the particular case of the SDC, the team in charge had the opportunity to combine the advantages of the public sector—the possibility to set up the rules and generate the conditions of redevelopment—with the flexibility of the private sector to negotiate and take risks.

- *Adjust incentives and regulations for private developers to respond to changes in market dynamics.* Both the SUR subsidy and the flexibility of Santiago's master plan were key to making the repopulation plan a success by attracting private investors and low- and middle-income household buyers. However, the SUR, which was crucial at the beginning of the repopulation plan, was not adjusted to new market conditions. Today, it no longer plays an important role. It is important for the government to make periodic assessments of the instruments and regulations in place to ensure that they remain relevant. For example, the SUR could have been modified to allow for the construction of social housing for low-income residents within the district. Likewise, the master plan that was fundamental to attracting the interest of real estate developers should have been redefined in order to ensure the quality of the projects generated.

- *Continuous community participation.* Participation and engagement should be a permanent part of city regeneration processes, as the changes brought by urban renovation generate tangible impacts for the residents. Therefore, it is not enough to limit the participation to the design phase. The community should also be involved during project implementation. Poor access to information and the impact that the new buildings had in the regenerated neighborhoods led to distrust in the community. Even though the SDC made some efforts to involve the community through the advancement committees,[33] at the beginning of the 2000s, some communities created neighborhood associations to stop the real estate developments that affected the neighborhood's quality of life. Meaningful participation can prevent these types of negative reaction.

- *Holistic approach to collaboration and renovation by all stakeholders.* The SRP was part of a major strategy for Santiago's revitalization, which included actions to improve the quality of life in the city, make investments in emblematic projects, and improve the district's image. All parts of the strategy worked together in a complementary fashion to achieve the goal of repopulating the city. Investments in housing were key for the effort and would not have been possible without financing from the private sector. However, the public sector investments were the catalytic element in getting the whole process started.

Notes

1. Twenty percent of the land (1,184 sites) was larger than one hectare.
2. Organic Constitutional Municipalities Law 18.695.
3. See Santiago's municipal organizational chart. http://www.municipali daddesantiago.cl/categorias/home/municipio-2/organigrama.
4. This legal entity was incorporated in the Civil Code in 1981. In 1988, the law restricted the creation of corporations only for the promotion and dissemination of art and culture. Recently, it has allowed the creation of corporations that aim to promote sports, municipal development, and economic productivity.
5. Santiago's Cultural Corporation administers the municipal theater: www.municipal.cl; Santiago's Mapocho Station Corporation: www .estacionmapocho.cl; the "Balmaceda 1215" Cultural Corporation: www.balmacedartejoven.cl; and the "ARTEQUIN" Space for the Art Corporation: www.artequin.cl.
6. This mechanism is defined in the Constitution (Article 122). The way in which the CMF works is by collecting the revenues of all the municipalities: 60 percent of the property taxes, 50 percent of the vehicle circulation permits, 55 percent of commercial and alcohol licenses, and 50 percent of the tax over vehicles transfers. It can also be complimented by funds provided by the central government. The distribution of CMF funds is estimated using different indicators; among the most important is the poverty rate, the proportion of land exempted from property tax, and the municipal income per capita. The municipality of Santiago has to allocate 45 percent of this specific source of revenue, and the other three municipalities in the metropolitan region have to allocate 55 percent (Vitacura, Las Condes, and Providencia). They pay a higher percentage because they are among the richest municipalities in the country (Law 18695; Art.10).
7. In 2012, 38 percent of municipalities were financially dependent on the CMF in the range of 50–75 percent, whereas the municipality of Santiago received only 1.6 percent for its annual budget from the CMF.

8. The annual rate of growth of GDP per capita in the 1980s was 1.3 percent, whereas in the 1990s it was 4.8 percent (De Gregorio 2005).

9. The diagnosis of the problem was clear before the mayor took office in the municipality in 1990—although it was under his administration from 1990 to 2000 (two electoral periods) that a clear strategy was designed to start a process of regeneration and redevelopment of the municipal district as a whole.

10. In 1990, as the transition to democracy in Chile was just starting, the mayor of Santiago, Jaime Ravinet, was first appointed by the new president. In 1992, he was popularly elected and reelected in 1996, until the year 2000.

11. After 10 years, in the year 1999 at the end of Mayor Ravinet's second term, the "Second Convention of Santiago" took place. During the Second Convention, the results obtained from the strategies designed after the First Convention were presented.

12. Tenement halls are a group of houses, usually with continuous facades that face a private common area that has access to a public street through one or more doors. The average number of housing units in each tenement is 15. The size of the sites ranges from 500 sq m to 2,000 sq m; the size of dwelling units varies from between 50 sq m to 100 sq m (Chiang 2005).

13. Around 33 percent of Santiago's tenement halls were built in the late nineteenth century, and 50 percent between 1900 and 1940 (Chiang 2005).

14. The SDC can receive contributions or donations, and it can sign contracts with institutions, agencies, firms, and workers. It can also borrow money, acquire, sell or lease assets or real estate properties and, in general, enter into any contract needed to meet its objectives. Given that the private law governs corporations, the SDC can do everything that the law does *not* forbid, whereas municipalities, governed by public law, can only do what the law allows. It is precisely this institutional feature that facilitated the participation of the private sector in the SRP (Articles 1 and 6 in SDC's Bylaws, 1985).

15. In 2013, the SDC received US$5.5 million, which was equivalent to 29.2 percent of the total municipal budget allowed by law to be transferred to corporations.

16. The most important lease corresponds to a commercial center of small traders that was relocated from streets to this commercial center as part of the SDC's actions to improve the security and quality of public spaces in the district.

17. The references regarding land prices are generally obtained from the registration of previous transactions of land and properties in the district managed by the Office of Property Registration. The National Internal Revenue Service (IRS) uses it as a reference to calculate the appraisal value of the properties.

18. Currently the SUR targets primarily middle-income households.
19. Both Santiago's mayor and the minister of MHUD at that time were from the same political party. The political atmosphere after the reestablishment of democracy in Chile was one of great confidence and collaboration among governmental agencies.
20. Supreme Decree 44 No. 136 09-14-1990, MINVU.
21. Supreme Decree 44 No. 136 09-14-1994, MINVU (MINVU 2003).
22. UF is a financial unit indexed for inflation as measured by the consumer price index (CPI).
23. The municipality used many innovative ways to advertise the program: newspaper articles covering the process; municipal billboards located in public spaces across the municipal district; a radio program called "Topics about the City," in which the guest speakers were generally real estate developers (developers also paid for the advertisements in the program); and an information newsstand (kiosk) located in the busiest downtown corner in the district (Huerfanos/Ahumanda), which also distributed 70,000 brochures per year.
24. The SDC charged both the landowner and the developers a broker fee, which varied from 1-2 percent of the land value.
25. After almost 20 years, this developer has built more than 30 projects in the SMD.
26. This is the only tax collected by the National Internal Revenue Service (IRS), and returned to the municipalities, whereupon each municipality has to contribute to the CMF. In the case of the SMD, this corresponds to 65 percent of its revenues.
27. Since 2014, the rate of property tax corresponds to 0.98 percent of the value of the property. All properties with a value up to 850 UF (approximately US$36,000) are exempt from paying property tax.
28. Before 2014, the property tax rate was one percent of the total property value, and the tax exemption threshold was for properties appraised at up to 800 UF (approximately US$34,000).
29. For instance, a property that has an appraised value of US$50,000 has the possibility to discount US$36,000 (property tax exemption value). Therefore, it pays the 0.98 percent of US$14,000 annually.
30. Estimates done are based on Arraigada, Moreno, and Rovirosa 2007; SDC 2014; and INE 2014a.
31. A social housing (*vivienda social*) in Chile corresponds to housing units devoted to very low-income households for which the housing subsidy covers almost its total value. For middle- and middle-low-income households, the housing units are called "affordable housing" (*vivienda economica*) and the housing subsidy has to be complemented with savings and mortgage loans.
32. Social housing refers to units financed entirely by the public sector for very low-income households, whereas affordable housing refers to housing units that have some amount of subsidy (such as the SUR).

33. Advancement committees are groups of representatives from the community, entrepreneurs, and universities that discuss and plan community investments.

References

Arraigada, Camilo, Juan Cristóbal Moreno, and Enrique Cartier Rovirosa. 2007. *Evaluación de impacto del subsidio de renovación urbana en el area metropolitana del Gran Santiago 1991–2006* [Evaluation of the impact of the urban renewal subsidy in the metropolitan area of Greater Santiago, 1991–2006]. Santiago, Chile: Ministry of Housing and Urban Development, Pehuen.

Cámara Chilena, de la Construcion. 2012.

Casgraine, A., and M. Janoschka. 2013. "Gentrification and Resistence in Latin American cities: Santiago de Chile Example." *Andamios: Revista de Investigación Social* 10 (22): 19–44.

CCHC (Chilean Chamber of Construction). 2013a. Real Estate Activity in Santiago 7, Cámara Chilena de la Construcción, Santiago, Chile.

———. 2013b. Analysis and conclusions. Preliminary results of 2012 Census. Edited by A. Valenzuela.

Chiang, Pamela. 2005. "Ciudad horizontal, un espacio dinámico: alternativas para la reconversión de pequeños bolsones urbanos" [Horizontal city, a dynamic space: alternatives for restructuring small urban spaces]. *Revista Diseño Urbano y Paisaje* 2 (4). http://www.ucentral.cl/du&p/pdf/0002.pdf.

Contreras, Y. 2011. "Urban and Residential Regeneration in Downtown Santiago: New Inhabitants, Significant Socio-Spatial Changes." *EURE* 37 (112): 89–113.

Contrucci, Pablo. 2000. "Repoblamiento del casco central de Santiago de Chile: Articulacion del sector publico y el sector privado" [Repopulation of the center of Santiago de Chile: coordination between the public and private sectors]. In *Desarrollo cultural y gestión en centros históricos* [Cultural development and the development of city management in historical city centers], edited by E. Carrión, 193–210. Quito, Ecuador: FLACSO.

———. 2013. *Santiago de Chile, Repopulation Program: Achievements and Challenges*. International Seminars Quintandinha +50. "Esvaziamiento Dos Centros: A dinâmica urbana e a expansão incontrolável." Salvador Bahia, Brazil.

De Gregorio, J. 2005. "Economic Growth in Chile: Evidence, Sources and Perspectives." *Estudios Publicos* 98. http://www.cepchile.cl/dms/archivo_3536_1762/r98_degregorio_crecimi-economic.pdf.

Galetovic, A., and I. Poduje. 2006. "Santiago: dónde estamos y hacia dónde vamos [Santiago: where we are and where we are going]." *Revista eure* 32 (97): 113–17.

Gonzales, G. 2005. "Mortgage Loans and Access to Housing for Lower-Income Households in Latin America." *Revista de la Cepal 85* (April). http://www.cepal.org/publicaciones/xml/7/21047/lcg2266egonzales.pdf.

INE 2014a. (National Statistics Institute, Chile). Census. 2014. *Compendio Estadístico 2014*. Santiago, Chile: INE.

———. 2014b. *Censo*. www.censo.cl.

Lopez, E., C. Arriagada, D. Meza, and I. Gasic. 2013. "First Metropolitan Survey to Neighborhood Residents of Regeneration Neighborhoods in Great Santiago: Towards an Integral Measurement of Socio-Spatial Impacts of Regeneration and Real State Market." *Seminario Fau*, Fau U Chile.

Martinez, R. 2006. "Densificar Santiago: Una receta equivocada" [Thickening Santiago: A bad recipe]. DU & P [Urban and landscape design]: revista de diseño urbano y paisaje 3 (8).

MINVU (Chile, Ministry of Housing and Urban Development). 2003. "Construction Regulation." http://normativaconstruccion.cl/Instrumentos /Ds44.

———. 2010. "Private Real Estate Market Greater Santiago 2005–2010." Santiago: MINVU, Observatorio Habitacional.

———. 2012. "Survey for Characterization and Valuation of Land Tracts in Valparaiso and Santiago." MINVU and Observatorio de Ciudades [city observatory] UC, Santiago, Chile.

———. 2014a. "Title II Territorial Subsidy." http://www.minvu.cl/opensite _20070223102916.aspx.

———. 2014b. Urban Observatory: Median Households." http://www .minvu.cl/opensite_20070223102916.aspx.

Parra, C., and C. Dooner. 2001. "Nuevas experiencias de concertación público-privada: las corporaciones para el desarrollo local, estudio de casos en las comunas de Santiago y, Area Metropolitana de Santiago de Chile" [New experiences of private-public partnerships: local development corporations: case studies of the communes of Santaigo and Huechuraba, metropolitan area of Santiago, Chile]. *Medio ambiente y desarrollo* 42: 53.

Rojas, E. 2004. *Coming Back to Downtown: Regeneration of Urban Central Areas*. Edited by G. Giannoni. Washington, DC: Inter-American Development Bank. https://publications.iadb.org/bitstream/handle/11319 /202/Volver%20al%20centro.pdf?sequence=1.

SDC (Santiago Development Corporation). 1987. "Imperativo de la recu-peración urbana: algunos costos de la expansión" [Imperatives for urban regeneration: some costs of expansion]. Unpublished paper.

———. 2014. Permits 1990-2012. ExcelSheet. Santiago Development Corporation.

SINIM (Sistema Nacional de Información Municipal, Chile). 2014. National System for Municipal Information. http://www.sinim.gov.cl/indicadores /serie/.

Trivelli, P. 1998. *Present and Future Santiago: Challenges and Proposals for the XXI Century.* Santiago: P. Trivelli Ltd.

UNDP (United Nations Development Programme). 2013. "Poverty Reduction and Inequality." http://www.pnud.cl/areas/ReduccionPobreza /datos-pobreza-en-Chile.asp.

Valenzuela, J. P. 1997. "Fiscal Decentralization: Municipal and Regional Revenues in Chile." Santiago: CEPAL/GTZ. *Serie Politica Fiscal* 101.

People Interviewed

Designers and Implementers of the SRP from the public and from municipal Agencies

Pablo Contrucci, architect; director of the Santiago Municipal Development Corporation

Gustavo Carrasco, architect; member of the Department of Municipal Public Works since 1988

Pablo Trivelli, economist; project manager of emblematic projects (parks, cultural center, old prison)

Hernán Caceres, public administrator; director of the Santiago Municipal Development Corporation from 2000 to 2011

Verónica Serrano, architect; director of the Regional Housing Department of the Ministry of Housing and Urban Development from 2000 to 2006; adviser to the mayor of Santiago (1996–2000); current director of INOVAL branch of SALFA real estate firm

Private sector, community, and researchers

Francisco Vergara, architect; first real estate developer to establish a project under Santiago's repopulation plan

Herman Chadwick, lawyer; vice president of CORDESAN; chair of different real estate firms

Benjamin Paz, architect; president of PazCorp Real Estate Corporation; developer with the largest number of projects (residential towers) developed in Santiago

Pablo Allard, planner; dean, Department of Architecture, Universidad del Desarrollo

Julio Poblete, planner; president, Polis Office of Architecture and Planning; professor, Department of Architecture and Urban Studies, Catholic University

Rosario Carvajal Araya, head of Our Patrimony Foundation

Current developments

Claudio Maggi, engineer; director of the Santiago Municipal Development Corporation, 2012–present

Bernabe Aravena, asset manager, Santiago Development Corporation

Mauricio Valenzuela, research area, Department of Municipal Planning 2012–present

Map 6.1 Shanghai, China

a. Shanghai metropolitan area

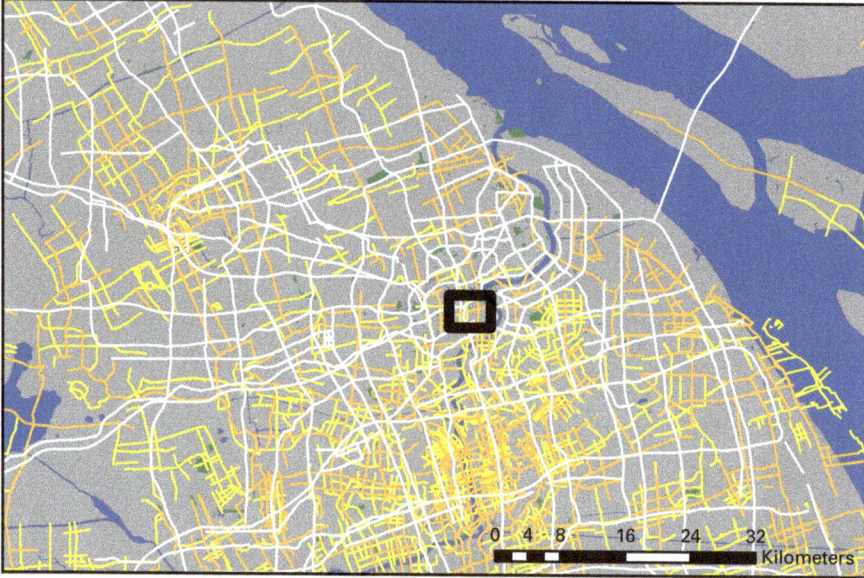

b. Project location

Source: World Bank based on Open Street Map data, 2015.

CHAPTER 6

Shanghai: Regenerating a Historic Neighborhood through Commercial Development

Introduction

The city of Shanghai, one of the major economic and population centers of China, has undergone a dramatic urban expansion and redevelopment of its downtown precinct since the 1990s. Much of this change can be attributed to the demolition of entire dilapidated neighborhoods, the relocation of communities, and rebuilding of new modern high-rise towers. This profit-driven redevelopment model proved easy to implement but had little regard for the preservation of the traditional urban fabric or historically significant structure. The Xintiandi area, located in the neighborhood of Taipingqiao within the former Luwan District of Shanghai, was the first neighborhood *not* to blindly follow this model of urban regeneration. This chapter explores this model of development and the role of various actors. Map 6.1 shows the map of Shanghai and the project site.

The redevelopment of the Xintiandi area aimed to preserve the two blocks of existing Shikumen buildings[1], while also realizing the commercial value of historic neighborhoods and preserving a sense of place. Indeed, the redevelopment of Xintiandi could be regarded as the first successful case of historic downtown redevelopment in China. The city of Shanghai subsequently initiated programs to preserve and rehabilitate more of historic neighborhoods, discarding old plans to demolish such places. Furthermore, the Xintiandi model had an important demonstration effect and has been used as an example by other city governments in redeveloping their own historic areas.

The Xintiandi area consists of two blocks within a neighborhood known as Taipingqiao (Peace Bridge). The site was developed according to a master plan, with the goal of commercial development based on conserving and using a certain portion of traditional Shikumen style architecture, as well as a neighborhood layout known as Li-Nong to maintain the local character. Xintiandi was redeveloped by Shui On Land Limited (SOL), a real estate development and construction company based in Hong Kong SAR, China.

Although Xintiandi was in poor condition, as was much of downtown Shanghai, it had a number of significant geographical, historical, cultural, and commercial characteristics that attracted the private sector to its redevelopment. These features included close proximity to famous commercial streets and public transport, important landmarks and heritage sites, such as the riverfront area or the Bund,[2] and the People's Square. More important, the two blocks called Xintiandi include the First National Congress Building of the Communist Party of China. The name Xintiandi (new heaven and earth) was given to memorialize the historical significance of the location. Xintiandi and Taipingqiao were also unique in terms of their urban fabric, street life, and commercial and cultural services and activities.

The two blocks that comprise Xintiandi cover an area of 3 hectares (ha) within the larger 52 ha of the Taipingqiao neighborhood. Given that the potential returns from development of the entire Taipingqiao area were an incentive to finance the high cost of the conservation of Xintiandi, this report discusses the development of both the Xintiandi and Taipingqiao neighborhoods.

This case study first describes Shanghai's geographic and demographic composition, as well as the city's organizational structure and financial arrangements. It then provides a description of the regeneration project, including costs, revenues, and sustainability elements. The case study concludes with a description of the project's outcomes, impacts, and lessons learned.

Context and Background

Shanghai is the largest metropolis in China in terms of total population. According to the 2010 Chinese Census, its population is approximately 23 million. Shanghai's population increased by approximately six million between 2000 and 2010—equivalent to an annual growth rate of 3.24 percent. Shanghai's urban population has the highest annual disposable income per capita in the country, averaging around Y 40,188 (US$6,350) in 2012, as compared to Y 24,565 nationally (NBS 2012).[3] The administrative area of Shanghai covers over 6,340 square kilometers (sq km), and the central city, defined by the so-called Outer Circle Highway, covers approximately 600 sq km.

Most of the urbanized land is owned by the state in China, and land leases are based on the sale of the right to use the land. This has become the main source of revenue for local governments in China. The land market in Chinese cities began to take off in the late 1980s, while the ownership of urban land remained with the state. The price of land rentals has soared since the 1990s and continues on an upward trajectory. Shanghai, which is ranked number one in Chinese cities collected Y 82 billion (US$12 billion) in rents in 2009 (according to the statistics from China Real Estate Index System Databases).[4] For the first four months of 2014, the land turnover in Shanghai was about 3.6 million square meters (sq m), increasing by 24.6 percent. The total land rent received was Y 57.3 billion (US$9.3 billion)—increasing by 75 percent compared to the same period in 2013.[5] Indeed, with the revenues that local governments are accruing from such rental arrangements, they are increasingly promoting urban redevelopment at sites with good locations.

The City's Organizational Structure

Shanghai is one of four municipalities directly under the control of the central government of China. It adopted a two-level government structure, plus a three-level administrative structure (see figure 6.1). The two levels of government include the Shanghai municipal government and the district government. Each has its own urban planning administration. The third level of administration is the community or street office. Whereas in most countries, local government means the city government, in Shanghai there are two levels of local government with various levels of authority and financial responsibility.

The Shanghai municipal government has responsibility for planning approvals, and the district government and its planning administration are responsible for developing the detailed plans. The district government usually works in collaboration with land owners, including state-owned corporations and semi-public developers, such as development corporations

Figure 6.1   Organizational structure of the Shanghai government

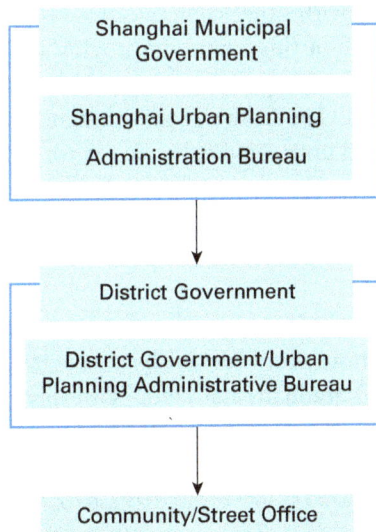

Two-level government/Three-level administration

Source: Wang and Hoch 2013.

(which, in turn, are supported by the district government and private developers). Each development project must obtain three permits from the municipal planning administration to complete the statutory process. The first permit is for location permission and is approved by the planning administration of the project location according to the master plan or detailed control plan (DCP). The second permit, the land use and building form, is approved by the planning authority and related government departments of the project. Finally, the third permit is the construction permission, which is the approval by the planning authority and related government departments for the actual construction of the project. The three permits are approved in the order outlined.

The municipal government has always been in charge of providing permits to development projects in designated areas of special significance, such as the Taipingqiao neighborhood. As for the third level of administration within Shanghai's institutional structure, the street office, it does not have the authority to develop plans or approve developments. Rather, leaders of the street office usually provide opinions and share visions, representing local residents when participating in active consultative meetings during the planning process. They also assist the district government in organizing communities with regard to relocation and compensation negotiations.

Evolution of Urban Development Policies

The extent of the authority of the district and municipal governments in Shanghai is related to the evolution of urban development policy in the city, which took place over two specific time periods. The first began in the late 1970s and the second in the 1990s. Since 1978, the vision for Shanghai has been focused on developing a multicultural and cosmopolitan city that competes with other centers of trade and commerce around the world. On the basic of this vision, improving the urban environment in central Shanghai and solving the housing problem became a major goal of the local government. Thus, the city government worked on developing green public spaces and upgrading urban areas to make for a more desirable urban environment. To this end, the authority to make decisions was transferred to the district government, allowing it to lease land and encouraging Mainland Chinese property companies to get involved in urban redevelopment projects.

This district government's authority was further strengthened in 1988 when land-use regulations were revised by the central government and a system for leasing land gradually matured. With this reform, the Shanghai government successfully encouraged investors, especially from Hong Kong SAR, China, and Taiwan, China, to build in Shanghai on the leased land, resulting in a construction boom. From 1992 to 1997, 23 million sq m of low-quality housing were demolished—three times the amount that occurred during the 42-year period of 1949 to 1991 (Yang and Chang 2007).

A siginificant era of urban redevelopment in Shanghai started in the 1990s with the 365 Program, which called for the renovation of approximately

3.65 million sq m of shanty houses by the end of the twentieth century. The plan was to provide a living area of 10 sq m per person. To meet the targets of this ambitious plan, the Shanghai city and district governments began to closely collaborate on land rental processes, mostly executed by the district government. On the basis of the 365 Program, approval for building demolition and land use for all land plots was to be collected by the district government and then submitted to the municipal government's Housing and Land Bureau.

The authority for the demolition and redevelopment was transferred by the municipal government to the district governments, which marked the beginning of the rising authority and influence of the district governments. Indeed, in the 1990s, the district government started to take responsibility for the examination and approval of site plans, as well as for negotiating land rents. This trend in devolving greater authority to the district levels continued into the 2000s, when district governments were able to sign agreements for renting certain land parcels to foreign investors, without the approval from the Shanghai municipal government.

The district and municipal governments jointly engage and cooperate with developers/investors in the process of land rental and redevelopment. First, the district government issues a permit for the development of a particular land parcel. It then prepares a "detailed control plan" in collaboration with the developer/investor to outline the rate and extent of infrastructure and property development to be presented to the municipal government. After the municipal government's approval, a "land acquisition fee" is agreed upon, which includes the cost of infrastructure and the relocation (if any) of the original residents. When the contract terms are finalized, the district government then asks the municipal government to approve the plan and permits. Lastly, the district government issues site plans and permits, and the project is launched.

Because of changes in urban policies in the 1990s, district governments had a major incentive to make development projects work for two reasons. First, the districts were under pressure to achieve certain financial gains through land leases and other means. Furthermore, 85 percent of the gains would remain with the district government and the remaining 15 percent would be transferred to the municipal government (Yang and Chang 2007). Second, every year the districts (and their leaders) were assessed and rated by the municipal government based on various criteria, including the extent of public-private collaboration with regard to urban redevelopment. This in turn put some pressure on district level leaders to achieve more financial autonomy by attracting private funds.

Beginning in the 1990s, the Shanghai municipal government announced a series of policies to redevelop dilapidated neighborhoods, including shanty housing. In 1985, the residential floor area per capita of Shanghai was 4.4 sq m; some 16,700 households had less than 2 sq m of living space.[6] In 1992, the Shanghai municipal government initiated the 365 Program. A total of 337,800 sq m of shanty houses in Luwan

District were listed in the 365 Program for redevelopment (*Luwan District Chronicle* 1994–2003). This was a trigger for the redevelopment of Xintiandi, among other neighborhoods.

The Luwan District of Shanghai, where Xintiandi is situated, was one of the focus districts for the government's regeneration program in the 1990s. Each district government in the central city of Shanghai was asked to propose sites for regeneration to the municipal government. Once the site was approved, the municipal government would include it in the mentioned regeneration program. To facilitate quicker implementation, a deduction of fees and a shortening of the approval process were then applied to the projects on selected sites.

The Luwan District was one of the most densely populated districts among the 16 districts of Shanghai until 2011, when it was merged into the Huangpu District. The total land area of the Luwan District was about 8 sq km, with a total population of 248,779 residents, as of the 2010 census. The first leasing of land for export sale housing (land that could only be sold to foreigners) took place in the Luwan District in 1992. It was developed as a pilot project to attract foreign investment into urban regeneration projects. In 1993, the municipal government developed specific rules and procedures for regulating and promoting land leasing, real estate development, and infrastructure construction. These new regulations were a part of the "Shanghai Temporary Regulation for Adopting Foreign Investment in Domestic Market Housing Program," formalized in 1995. This set of regulations aimed at integrating foreign investments in housing that were then sold to local residents. As a result, 1.8 million sq m of dilapidated and shanty housing were demolished to make way for new, market-rate housing projects.

In 1997, the Asian financial crisis resulted in a slowdown of foreign investment, including in redevelopment projects. In response, the Shanghai municipal government announced new preferential tax policies and the provision of particular types of financial support to the remaining sites of the 365 Program. Overall, between 1991 and 2000, a total of 28 million sq m of dilapidated housing were demolished and 640,000 households relocated. Compensation methods for relocated residents varied from case to case. They included providing existing housing or construction of new housing and/or monetary payments and buyouts.

Relocated residents usually obtained housing units with more floor space but on the periphery of the city. The location usually did not compare to the original site in terms of facilities for education and health and proximity to jobs. However, residents may have chosen to relocate due to the increase in living space, number of rooms, and better infrastructure. As a result of the redevelopment efforts in Shanghai, the average floor area of dwellings increased from 6.7 sq m per capita in 1991 to 11.8 sq m per capita in 2000.[7]

Financial Aspects of Redevelopment in Shanghai

The Chinese municipal finance system has undergone constant revisions since 1949. However, it has been relatively stable since the implementation of the tax distribution system in 1994. Under this new system, the local tax revenue is mostly equally divided between the central government of China and the local governments. In this context, local governments now have more responsibility in urban development matters, such as the provision of infrastructure and public facilities. In fact, the district and county governments of Shanghai now obtain a greater percentage of local tax revenues than the municipal government.

Since the implementation of the 1994 tax distribution system, city governments have played a major role in urban development, providing funding, drafting plans, and implementing construction projects. With limited tax revenues, city governments started to search for new sources, such as land rents and domestic loans, as well as loans from international organizations. Subsequently, land rents have gradually become the main source of financing for city governments.

Land became a salable commodity in the late 1980s, when land-use rights were first rented to developers. However, city governments maintain full ownership of the property rights and the power to allocate and use land resources through directives rather than through market pricing mechanisms—thereby giving governments control of the primary land market. At this time, land could be leased to developers via administrative designation or public auctions. It is now a requirement that almost all types of land go through an auction and bidding process for redevelopment.

The Redevelopment Site

The Xintiandi area covers two blocks within the Taipingqiao neighborhood that were redeveloped as part of a larger package by SOL, the Shanghai-based property development company of the Shui On Group. The entire neighborhood is now usually referred to as Xintiandi because its redevelopment anchors the regeneration of surrounding neighborhoods as well (see map 6.2 and photograph 6.1). In this case study, we differentiate Xintiandi from Taipingqiao. We discuss the development of Xintiandi as a historic conservation and rehabilitation project and Taipingqiao as an urban regeneration project.

The Taipingqiao neighborhood (including the two blocks of Xintiandi) experienced many social changes throughout China's long history, gradually falling into decay over the decades. In 1997, it was 52 ha in size and comprised 23 blocks with a population of 70,000 people, constituting more than 20,000 households prior to the redevelopment initiative. It was located in the former French Concession area and was once inhabited by middle-class Chinese families. But beginning in the 1940s, the original owners left the area, and buildings were occupied by low-income households. Over the years, living conditions declined and eventually, after many appropriations

Map 6.2 **Location of Xintiandi**

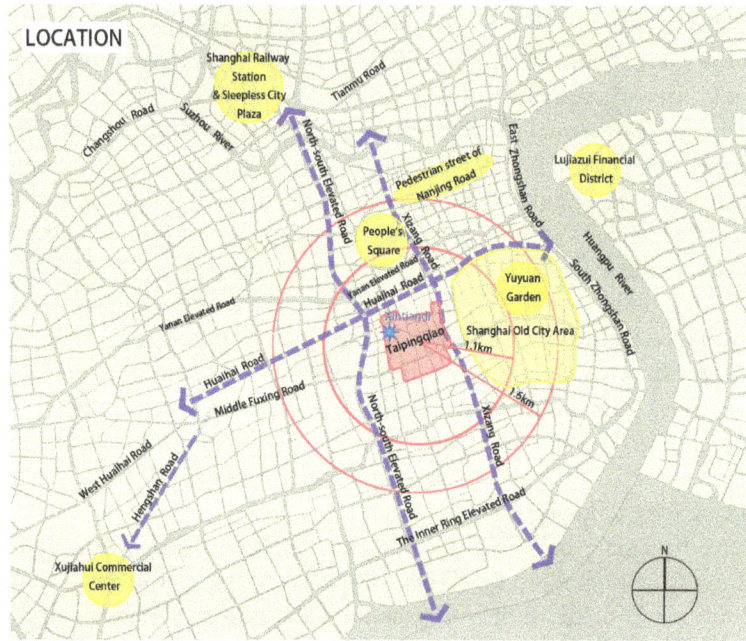

Source: Shui On Land Limited 1997.

and relocations, it became an area inhabited by lower-middle-class residents. By 1993, after decades of socialist housing policy, 88 percent of the dwellings in the district fell under public housing. For instance, a public flat of around 40 sq m could be rented for Y 10–20 per month in 1998, or around US$1.25–2.50 at the time (Yang and Chang 2007).

The Taipingqiao area consists of alleyway housing style unique to Shanghai. It is a hybrid of the traditional Chinese courtyard house and the western terraced house with winding lanes known as *Shikumen*, which trace back to 1860 (Bracken 2013). Shikumen buildings with decorated stone gates were organized along the main lanes and sublanes that formed an urban vernacular specific to Shanghai. This model of urban design became known as *Li-Nong*.

Over the next century, residential buildings with a similar design and layout were constructed. However, they were poorly maintained. By the 1990s, most of the buildings were dilapidated and living conditions were both unsafe and unsanitary. The layout of these buildings and the existing infrastructure could not support increasing living standards and lacked public amenities. Residents expected improvements in living conditions, which provided the initial impetus for the local government to redevelop this area. The dilapidated conditions meant that the unique characteristics of the Shikumen buildings and special urban fabric of the Li-Nong were not

Photograph 6.1   Li-Nong scene before redevelopment

Source: Shui On Land Limited.

recognized or appreciated at the time. Indeed, large numbers of Shikumen buildings were demolished and redeveloped as office and residential high-rise buildings. No historic preservation plan for the area existed. The only building required to be preserved was the site of the First National Congress of the Communist Party of China, which brought with it a series of height controls to the area.

Phase 1: Scoping

The redevelopment project for the Taipingqiao neighborhood was planned at a time when the large-scale demolition and construction in Shanghai was at its peak. In the 1990s, the establishment of the land market provided the legal framework to lease land for real estate development to private developers. High-rise office buildings emerged as a means of revenue generation for governments. The lack of investment between the 1950s and 1980s had caused serious residential shortages and poor living conditions in many of Shanghai's neighborhoods, which, in turn, provided a window of opportunity for the large-scale redevelopment of Shanghai. The last decade of the twentieth century, therefore, witnessed a rapid and extensive urban redevelopment, mostly for the building of residential and commercial towers.

Under these circumstances, the Taipingqiao neighborhood with its poor living conditions, high population density—but good location—became a priority for redevelopment under the 365 Program. In the early 1990s, the local government of the Luwan District identified the Taipingqiao neighborhood as a key site for redevelopment and began searching for private developers. However, because of the high relocation costs and complicated ownership of the buildings, few developers were interested.

SOL was one of the few property companies to enter the Chinese market in the 1980s. At the time, the founder and owner of SOL launched a US$23 million venture to build the City Hotel in Shanghai. With this project, a good relationship and sense of trust developed between the company and the local government of Luwan District. In 1996, SOL completed the development of a high-rise office building, which was located adjacent to the Taipingqiao neighborhood. After this project, the Luwan District government directly approached SOL with the idea of developing a plan for the Taipingqiao neighborhood. The two entities began to explore the possibility of creating a vision for the redevelopment of the area.

In 1996, SOL hired the American architectural firm Skidmore, Owings, and Merrill (SOM), to develop a master plan for the entire Taipingqiao neighborhood. The master plan was developed by SOM with inputs from SOL and the Luwan District government. It was then submitted by the district government to the Shanghai municipal government's Urban Planning Administration Bureau. The planning officials at the municipal level reviewed the plan and brought together a cross section of stakeholders to discuss and reach an agreement on the proposed redevelopment vision.

The master plan of Taipingqiao Redevelopment Project was finished in 1996, and approved by the Shanghai municipal government in 1997. A total of 1.6 million sq m in floor area was designated within the 52 ha Taipingqiao area, of which 890,000 sq m would be allocated to housing (Yan 2012). The Luwan District Government then started to prepare a DCP to define the specific floor area ratios (FARs), green space ratio, height limits, and other parameters and specifications for each block.[8]

At the end of 1997, SOL signed an agreement with the Luwan District government under the supervision of the Shanghai municipal government. The agreement outlined the area and location of the project and the conditions under which the government would provide the land and assist with relocation of affected households. On the basis of this short six-page contract,[9] SOL would pay for the relocation, land, and a portion of infrastructure and redevelopment costs of the site. There were no penalties or restrictions contained in the agreement, which signaled a level of confidence and willingness of the government and private developer to work together.

This agreement provided SOL with the development rights for the entire Taipingqiao neighborhood. The title of each parcel within the neighborhood would then be negotiated and transferred one-by-one within a 10–15 year time frame. The Shanghai Municipal Urban Planning Administration issued the necessary permissions, including the location, land use, and built form, and construction permissions on a block-by-block sequence according to the plan. In this way, the municipal and district governments maintained a certain degree of autonomy in their partnership with the investor and developer (Yang and Chang 2007).

Opposing the popular real estate development model of the time, the developers of Xintiandi rejected the single-use, high-FAR model. During the development of the plan, the parties decided to preserve the block containing the site for the First National Congress of Communist Party of China and the block to its south. At the same time, SOL had its own vision for the site. At the International Business Leaders' Advisory Council for the Mayor of Shanghai, the company representative said that "it is necessary for Shanghai to create a good living environment to attract, train, and retain the most excellent domestic and foreign talent. As an international financial and commercial center, it should also construct active venues in [the] downtown area so as to provide entertainment places for local and foreign professionals" (Sha 2010). Therefore, the Taipingqiao neighborhood was targeted as an integrated international center with office, residential, and entertainment development. Within the 23 blocks of the Taipingqiao area, the two blocks consisting of the Shikumen buildings would be preserved and redeveloped for world-class entertainment and commercial venues.

In 1997, the Asian financial crisis hit and foreign investors withdrew in droves from Mainland China's real estate market. Consequently the demand for both office and luxury residential space dramatically decreased. Many development projects were postponed and eventually abandoned. SOL was also confronted by this crisis. However, it went against the prevailing trend and decided to maintain its investment in the Taipingqiao area. Furthermore, as a sign of confidence, it transferred most of its capital assets to Shanghai. This helped to strengthen the partnership and trust between the company and the municipal and district governments (Yang and Chang 2007).

Since there was no precedent for Shikumen redevelopment in Shanghai, SOL asked its staff to conduct a worldwide search for architects who could advise on the urban design. An American architect was appointed to undertake the detailed design of the two blocks. Experts and professors from the College of Architecture and Urban Planning, Tongji University in Shanghai were also invited as consultants to participate in the design process. In addition, the Singapore office of Nikken Sekkei Ltd, a Japanese consulting company, contributed to the design process.

Planners at both the municipal and the district levels supported the idea of preserving the two blocks of Xintiandi. However, the Fire, Sanitation, and Infrastructure Departments had their own sets of regulations, which the Xintiandi project was not able to follow. The ordinary regulations had strict requirements for setback, green coverage, and density, which fit well for new developments but not the traditional Shikumen architecture of Xintiandi. The review and approval procedures had to be revised to make the preservation of the historic buildings feasible. For instance, the Shanghai Urban Planning Administrative Bureau transferred the authority to review the transportation and construction permits from the municipal level to the committee at the district level, which facilitated the approval process.

Within the 23 blocks of the Taipingqiao area, the two blocks containing the Shikumen buildings were to be well preserved, renovated, and redeveloped into world-class entertainment and commercial venues, following the original master plan design. However, only the north block of Xintiandi and the northern section of the south block were preserved. In addition, a shopping mall was developed in the southern section because of the financial pressures on SOL and the need to guarantee adequate profit.

The public and private sectors collaborated on many public infrastructure projects in the area. For example, the Taipingqiao Park on the east side of Xintiandi received some financial support from the municipal and district governments. This allowed for the development of the original vision of large-scale green spaces and an artificial lake, thereby providing public amenities at the municipal level. The construction cost of the park was divided among the municipal and district governments and SOL. However, SOL was required to provide developer contributions to fund the ongoing operation and maintenance of the park and lake (interview with SOL 2013). With the completion of the Xintiandi and Taipingqiao Park, this amenity raised the potential of the area as a popular destination for tourists and real estate investors.

The Master Plan of Shanghai (1999–2020) called for the development of a world-class city. However, to achieve this, the quality of life needed to be improved to attract international talent and human capital. Xintiandi was planned to accommodate commercial, retail, catering, and entertainment spaces with special historic characteristics. It was also designed to meet the needs of Shanghai in this new development stage (see map 6.3 and photograph 6.2).

Phase 2: Planning

Phasing and Timeline

The land uses of Taipingqiao were many and varied. They included cultural, entertainment, hotel/retail, office, housing, open space, and others. The area would also include education facilities, infrastructure, and other public facilities. In this regard, the master plan had conducted prior analyses related to market demand.

Xintiandi consists of the two blocks located on the west side of the Taipingqiao area developed as a cultural/entertainment precinct. Office space was planned in the north, close to the Shui On Plaza. Prior to the

Xintiandi project, residential space was mainly designated to the southern section of the plan, connecting with office space through the Taipingqiao Park. To the far east side, hotel and retail spaces were planned. A horizontal mixed-use precinct was intended to create an office-residential balance within the 52 ha (see table 6.1).

Map 6.3   Urban fabric before and after redevelopment

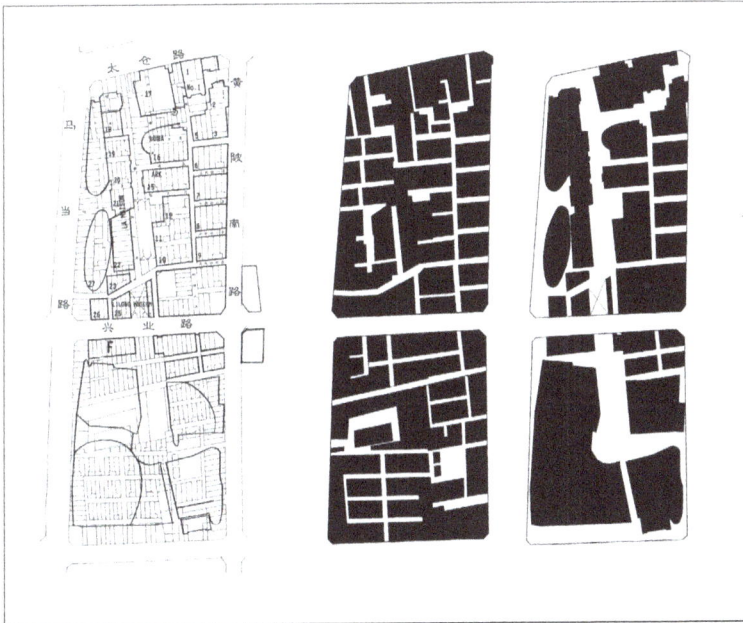

Source: Shui On Land Limited. Reproduced by permission of the Shui On Land Group.

Photograph 6.2   Aerial view of Xintiandi before redevelopment and after redevelopment

Source: Shui On Land Limited.

Table 6.1   **Land-use balance, master plan, 1997**

Land use	Land area (hectares)	Floor area (square meters)	Average floor area ratio
Residential	17.30	902,448	5.22
Education	3.30	38,500	1.17
B1 (commercial, business, and entertainment)	12.02	625,867	5.21
B2 (hotel)	0.96	65,400	6.80
Green space	4.68	n.a.	n.a.
Other (street office, parking)	0.99	8,600	0.87
Subtotal (nonroad)	39.26	1,640,815	4.18
Road	13.60	n.a.	n.a.
Total	52.86	1,640,815	n.a.

Source: Shui On Land Limited 1997.
Note: n.a. = not applicable.

The Master Plan of the Taipingqiao Neighborhood allowed for a 10–15 year development process, starting from the southern residential area. The investment return from housing was supposed to support the construction of the Taipingqiao Lake and Park. The redevelopment around the site of the First National Congress of the Communist Party of China would be implemented at a later stage, according to the plan. The Xintiandi project officially started at the beginning of 1999, and the construction of the Taipingqiao Park was launched later in 2000. Both projects were completed in 2001 when former National President Jiang Zemin visited the site of the First National Congress of the Communist Party of China for its 80-year anniversary. The site was also the venue for the Asia-Pacific Economic Cooperation (APEC) Summit in 2002.

After the visit of former National President Jiang Zemin in 2001, the site quickly caught both national and international attention. The construction of the office complex, the corporate avenue, and a luxury residential building called the Lakeville were initiated. Later, as the adverse effects of the Asian financial crisis diminished, the whole project entered into an accelerated development phase.

Although the original plan was to start with the development of housing and office complexes, the Asian financial crisis initiated a dramatic decrease in demand for residential and office space. In response, SOL adjusted the phasing of redevelopment, deferring the housing development and instead starting the conservation of historic structures. In the meantime, the municipal and district governments initiated the construction of the Taipingqiao Park. In modifying the phasing, the strategy aimed to mitigate market risks and improve the reputation of the Taipingqiao area. While early investment concentrated on the redevelopment of the historic area and urban public space, the postcrisis investments could proceed at an accelerated pace as the potential of the area had already been realized.

The detailed development timeline is presented in map 6.4 and figure 6.2, with sequential numbering for each project. Figure 6.3 presents the timeline for the development of the Taipingqiao neighborhood. The redevelopment has been implemented from east to west and from north to south. The phasing process rationale is to capture the increasing property value brought about by the new Xintiandi development and the Taipingqiao Park. The redevelopment process also follows the logic of block location, market demand, and relocation costs.

Regulatory Framework

The DCP serves as a legal interface between planning officials and developers. Initially, the DCP lacked legal authority under the City Planning Act of 1989. Then, the Law of the People's Republic of China on Urban and Rural Planning was adopted at the 30th Meeting of the Standing

Map 6.4 **Project map and phasing plan for the redevelopment of the Taipingqiao neighborhood, 2005 version**

Source: Reproduced by permission from Shui On Land Limited.
Note: The phases refer to development stages in the plan, identifying the order of parcels to be developed. The blue numbers are project numbers listed in figure 6.2 as components of the Taipingqiao project development.

Figure 6.2   Components of the Taipingqiao project development

1. Shui On Plaza	• Shui On Plaza, a world-class office tower located to the north of the Taipingqiao neighborhood, was not officially included in the master plan. However, it initiated the redevelopment of the Taipingqiao neighborhood and connected the area with the city-level commercial street, Huaihai Road. Shui On Plaza now hosts the headquarters of SOL.
2. Xintiandi	• The Xintiandi area is composed of two blocks in the west of the Taipingqiao area totaling 3 hectares of land area and 60,000 sq m of floor area. It was the first project to be completed within the Taipingqiao neighborhood.
3. Taipingqiao Park	• Taipingqiao Park covers approximately 4.4 hectares in the center-north part of the Taipingqiao area. Taipingqiao Lake covers 1.2 hectares. The construction of the artificial lake, green space, and underground garage with a total of 200 parking spaces commenced at the end of 2000 and was completed in June 2001.
4. Corporate Avenue	• Corporate Avenue is a project of office towers located northwest of the Taipingqiao area and to the east of Xintiandi. This enterprise park covers over 350,000 sq m in gross floor area. The construction of phase 1 approximately 78,000 sq m in gross floor area took place after the completion of the Taipingqiao Park in 2001 and was finished in 2004. The second phase is ongoing.
5. Xintiandi Hotels	• The Langham and Andaz Xintiandi Hotels are located in the northwest of the Taipingqiao area and to the north of Corporate Avenue. Construction of the two 6-star hotels started in 2009 and was completed in 2012.
6. International School	• An international school is located in the southwest corner of the Taipingqiao area. The land area is about 3.5 hectares. Construction was planned to start in 2012. However, at the time of developing this case study, it had not yet commenced.
7. Magnolia Building	• The Magnolia Building is located in the northeast of the Taipingqiao neighborhood. It will be a landmark for the entire area and is planned for 2020.
8. Arts Center	• The Arts Center is located in the northeast corner of the Taipingqiao neighborhood and shares the same block with the Magnolia Building. Construction will start in 2020, according to the plan.

Figure 6.3 Timeline for the Taipingqiao neighborhood redevelopment, 1996–2020

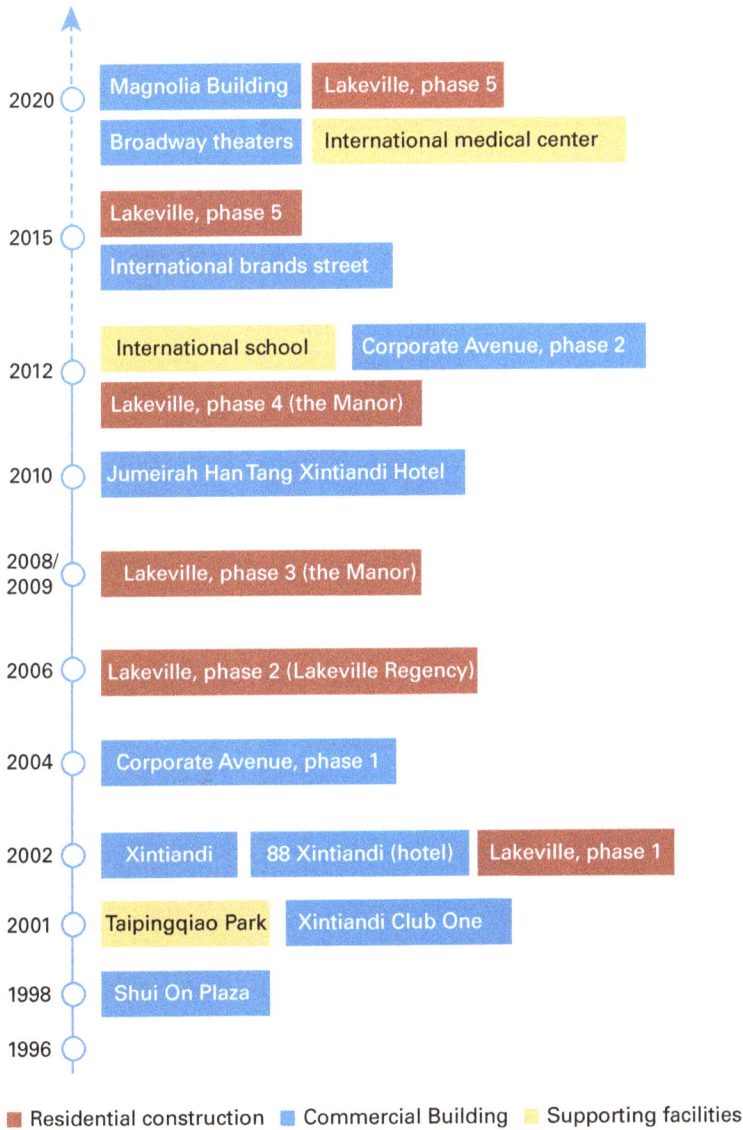

- 2020: Magnolia Building | Lakeville, phase 5
- Broadway theaters | International medical center
- 2015: Lakeville, phase 5
- International brands street
- 2012: International school | Corporate Avenue, phase 2
- Lakeville, phase 4 (the Manor)
- 2010: Jumeirah Han Tang Xintiandi Hotel
- 2008/2009: Lakeville, phase 3 (the Manor)
- 2006: Lakeville, phase 2 (Lakeville Regency)
- 2004: Corporate Avenue, phase 1
- 2002: Xintiandi | 88 Xintiandi (hotel) | Lakeville, phase 1
- 2001: Taipingqiao Park | Xintiandi Club One
- 1998: Shui On Plaza
- 1996:

■ Residential construction ■ Commercial Building ■ Supporting facilities

Committee of the Tenth National People's Congress in 2007 and was enacted in 2008. The Town and Country Planning Act was also enacted.[10] This ensures that the DCP complies with more strict requirements. The DCP also takes into account the planning and development parameters and specifications for every land plot. It identifies development indicators for parcels and provides specific statutory site regulations, including land use, FAR, building height, entrance locations, lot coverage ratios, green spaces, setbacks, and parking. A detailed construction plan is also required for submittal alongside the DCP.

The DCP of the Taipingqiao neighborhood considered the specific characteristics of historic preservation, local character, and renovation needs, and subsequently provided statutory planning exceptions to ensure the viability of the development. The Taipingqiao neighborhood redevelopment had an average FAR of 3.1. Height controls were applied around the site of the First National Congress of the Communist Party of China. The green space requirement was calculated across the entire Taipingqiao area, as opposed to a specific requirement for each block. This helped maintain the historic fabric of the two blocks of Xintiandi. The existing setback of Xintiandi was maintained for heritage reasons, even though it did not meet the standard planning regulation of a 3–5 meter setback. The underground garage of the Taipingqiao Park and the new buildings within Xintiandi provided sufficient space for automobile parking.

To facilitate the Xintiandi development, the Shanghai Urban Planning Administration Bureau eased certain review and approval processes, which usually involved lengthy cross-departmental, multi stakeholder engagements. For instance, an endorsement was required from the Transportation and Construction Committee at the municipal level in order for the Shanghai Urban Planning Administrative Bureau to provide building permits. In this case, the Shanghai Urban Planning Administrative Bureau decentralized the review from the Transportation and Construction Committee at the district level, which streamlined the approval of building permits. The municipality and districts also adopted many measures to facilitate urban redevelopment, such as helping with relocation, decreasing land lease prices, and offering financial subsidies.

The standard building codes for fire safety, infrastructure and sanitation requirements were not appropriate for the Li-Nong neighborhood style construction and layout. For Xintiandi, the Shanghai Urban Planning Administration Bureau again decentralized the construction permit process to the Transportation and Construction Committee at the district level. This decentralization of authority sped-up the review and approval process and also decreased strict construction requirements at the municipal level. Another regulatory adjustment was to apply permit requirements to each building individually. In particular, this loosened the green-space requirement for the historic neighborhood, which would have otherwise been difficult to achieve.

Local governments usually provided direct assistance and financial support for public infrastructure—especially associated transportation systems—and parks, which also helped to attract private investors. For instance, all costs of the Taipingqiao Park were equally funded by the Shanghai municipal government, the Luwan District government, and SOL. The two metro stations around Taipingqiao could also be regarded as a form of indirect support from local government. Metro Lines 1, 8, and 10 connect this project to the major urban areas of Shanghai. Metro Line

13 is currently under construction and will connect Xintiandi to the suburbs of Shanghai. The government's full commitment helped ensure the construction of these key metro lines and stations.

The city of Shangahi offered a number of new favorable policies to attract domestic and foreign investment in the area. In doing so, it sought to accelerate redevelopment and meet the social needs of residents.[11] In order to encourage real estate companies to participate, a series of favorable policies—including reduction and deferred payment of land use fees—were offered by the Shanghai municipal government to projects developing commercial housing with either domestic or foreign capital.

The policies adopted by the city of Shanghai waived many administration fees for urban redevelopment of neighborhoods specifically identified as dilapidated and filled with shanty housing. In some cases, land rents were completely waived for those identified areas. For the uncompleted 125 ha of dilapidated and shanty housing in the 365 program, municipal and local governments provided a subsidy for redevelopment at the rate of Y 300 (US$36)—or Y 112 (US$150) per sq m for specific identified areas.[12]

Land-Use Rights

The land that comprises the Taipingqiao neighborhood was not offered through a public auction in the 1990s.[13] Instead, with the assistance of the Luwan District government, the Shanghai municipal government signed an agreement with SOL, which designated the land to the company as long as they agreed to pay for estimated relocation compensation, infrastructure development, and local amenities.

A series of regulations was announced to provide operational guidance and calculate compensation entitlements. It is estimated that SOL paid local government relocation compensation by as much as Y 650 million (about US$78 million at the time) (Yang and Chang 2007). A relocation company was put in charge of negotiations and relocations. Once the relocation was done, land title would then be given to the developer with a separate payment as land rent. For land with potential residential uses, the rent tenure is 70 years. For commercial uses, the land rent period is 40 years. In terms of office usage, land is usually rented for 50 years. Land title for the Taipingqiao neighborhood was transferred to SOL block by block, as the relocation and demolition of each specific block was completed.

Institutional Structure

With regard to the public-private partnership arrangement in Taipingqiao, a subordinate real estate development company of Luwan District, the Fuxing Construction Development Company, established a joint venture with SOL. The share of the Fuxing Construction Development Company ranged from 1 percent to 3 percent, depending on the specific phase of the project for each block. The company's main functional role was to assist with the paperwork and approval process from different departments of the municipal and local governments. This institutional setup with a nominal partner also ensured transparency, facilitated the process, and made private investment easier. In addition, it gave the district government the ability to participate in the dialogue throughout the entire development process.

The district government of Luwan developed a collaborative relationship with the private developer based on informal institutional arrangements. SOL provided estimated relocation compensation to the Luwan District government, and a specialized company was hired to operate the demolition and relocation. This arrangement enabled the local government and private developer to avoid negotiating directly with residents. The process of relocation went smoothly and efficiently for the projects of Xintiandi and Taipingqiao Park.

This type of relocation company has caused social tension in other redevelopment neighborhoods of Shanghai when residents realized the extent of property value appreciation after the redevelopment projects. In the Taipingqiao neighborhood redevelopment, the relocation company is still helping SOL and the Luwan District government to negotiate with local residents about the remaining blocks. The compensation increased to correspond with the property value in Taipingqiao. This created challenges and difficulties in convincing residents to relocate, thereby postponing redevelopment.

According to the approved master plan, a community center was built by SOL and then transferred to the Taipingqiao Street Office. Another public facility, an international school, was planned to be transferred in 2012 to the local education bureau. Although this construction has not yet commenced, this construction-transfer arrangement helped governments without sufficient revenue to provide public facilities.

Social and Distributional Impacts

Urban redevelopment in China has involved the relocation of households and jobs. With regard to the Xintiandi project, 2,300 households including about 8,000 residents were eventually relocated as a result of the redevelopment plan. The overall compensation fee was as high as Y 650 million (Luwan District Chronicles 1994–2003). Similarly, the development of the Taipingqiao Lake involved the relocation of 3,800 households and 156 working units,[14] as well as the demolition of a 870,000 sq m area. These were relocated in just 43 days, setting the fastest record for relocation in the history of redevelopment in Shanghai (Xu 2004). It should be noted that the average residential area per household was only 22 sq m in this neighborhood.

The development of world-class and diverse restaurants, clothing stores, and entertainment venues in Xintiandi attracted domestic and international tourists. It has also created a dynamic nightlife in the neighborhood. Lakeville, a luxury residential project, was launched after the construction of the Xintiandi and Taipingqiao Parks. According to SOL's Annual Report for 2012, the initial average selling price (ASP) in 2002 was Y 20,000 per sq m (US$2,400). In 2012, the ASP increased to Y 158,100 (US$25,000) per sq m.

The reputation and property prices of the Taipingqiao neighborhood significantly improved and increased because of the redevelopment program. Residents about to be relocated asked for higher compensation because of the increased property values—captured primarily by developers and local governments. This created social tensions and challenges for the relocation.

Efforts have been made to alleviate the conflicts. For instance, local governments increased the compensation rates but still cannot meet the growing housing prices. Certain financial support and policies from the government also encouraged the developer to help the original residents resettling in the redeveloped site. However, even with compensation, it was difficult, even impossible, for low-to-middle income households to purchase the redeveloped housing in the Taipingqiao area. At the same time, the in-kind compensation with replacement housing had become unattractive with deficient facilities and locations far from downtown.

The Xintiandi project and its surrounding redeveloped areas were clearly targeted to higher-income groups. The original residents in the Xintiandi and Taipingqiao Park blocks have been relocated and did not benefit from new amenities and public spaces created. The remainder of the residents stayed in the dilapidated areas waiting for redevelopment. The redevelopment of the Taipingqiao neighborhood is still ongoing. The distribution of profits generated from the urban redevelopment are now being handled through negotiations between representatives of local governments and residents, because the residents have realized the value of the land they occupy.

Project Risks

A number of internal and external risks were associated with the project. A major risk to the project in general, and to the Xintiandi blocks in particular, was the complexity of preserving the historic urban fabric. Historic preservation would impact the development due to higher costs and longer time frames. Because of this heightened risk, the board of SOL initially objected to investing in the preservation and redevelopment of Xintiandi because of the expected longer term process of review and approval for historic buildings and the unclear investment return.

Legal and political risks were also prevalent, particularly concerning land acquisition and relocation, as well as shifting policies within China as a whole. For instance, the relocation of residents became more challenging due to the revision of legal procedures, which aimed at a more equitable development. When the Taipingqiao project was first initiated, relocation was not an issue as residents were willing to relocate to a new residential area with more floor space and better infrastructure. However, with the increasing property prices in downtown Shanghai and China's 2007 property law, the relocation was faced with a more complicated process and stricter requirements. For example, 90 percent of local residents needed to agree to move in the first round of relocation consultations before the redevelopment and relocation plans could begin. Of the local residents, 85 percent needed to agree on when the demolition and relocation would commence. Thus, the revised legal policy of land acquisition and relocation caused increased delays and costs. In the Phase four of Taipingqiao, further relocation consultations for the remaining 496,000 sq m of gross floor area (GFA) for various lots have yet to commence (SOL 2012).

The external financial shocks that resulted from the global financial crisis of 2008–09 meant that the austerity measures taken by the Chinese government had spillover effects on the property market—bringing along with it major challenges to SOL. For the year 2012, SOL generated a revenue of Y 4.821 billion (about US$760 million), down by 43 percent from Y 8.484 billion (SOL 2012).

The central government of China started imposing new property ownership policies[15] to curb the over-inflated economy. These policies, which aimed at curbing speculation, also exposed SOL to financial risks. Housing purchase restrictions, for instance, raised the down payment from 20 to 30 percent for first-time home buyers to 60 percent for the purchase of a second housing unit. The interest rates were also raised to avoid further speculation. Indeed, this affected the entire housing market in China. As a result, the housing turnover in the Taipingqiao project decreased.

Another policy change was a new legal requirement by the Chinese central government to hold public auctions for land over 20 ha. Even though the original agreement in 1997 gave the development rights for the 52 ha of Taipingqiao to SOL, the rest of the undeveloped land within this area now needs to go through a process of public auction. SOL may have a good chance to obtain contracts, because they have worked in the area before. However, certain risks are now raised due to this procedural revision.

Phase 3: Financing and Implementing

Project Costs

The total cost of the project amounted to about Y 1.4 billion (about US$175 million) in design, construction, and resident relocations for the two historic blocks of Xintiandi. The cost included the development of infrastructure, such as a separate, self-operating underground sewage treatment system in Xintiandi. The estimated compensation paid from SOL to the local government for relocation was about Y 650 million for 2,300 households (about 8,000 residents).

Twenty years after the opening of the redeveloped Xintiandi area, the rental and related income from Shanghai Xintiandi is Y 297 million in 2014 (SOL 2014). The Xintiandi development project costs were considered a large investment for an area with a physical footprint of only 3 ha. SOL broke even on its investment by balancing its costs and benefits within the Taipingqiao redevelopment area as a whole.

Another important project within the Taipingqiao redevelopment area was the Taipingqiao Park. The Shanghai municipal government and the Luwan District government decided to improve the environment through the provision of public green space. The idea of the artificial lake was put forward by SOL. The total cost of the Taipingqiao Park was approximately Y 1 billion, and it was funded by the Shanghai municipal government, the Luwan District government, and SOL. The estimated total investment by SOL in the redevelopment of the Taipingqiao area was Y 25 billion.

Project Revenues

Regarding the Taipingqiao neighborhood redevelopment project, it was agreed that all residential properties included in the master plan would be sold to generate cash flow. Almost all of the office, retail, and cultural facilities would be held by SOL for management convenience and property quality.

The master plan allotted a specific GFA for various uses. The total leasable and salable GFA of the Taipingqiao redevelopment project in the master plan is about 1 million sq m. Of this amount, the total residential GFA portion allocated in the plan is 256,000 sq m, or about 25 percent of the total GFA. The total office space allocation is for about 390,000 sq m, or about 39 percent of the total GFA. The retail GFA portion is about 278,000 sq m, and about 76,000 sq m are reserved for hotels or serviced apartments (SOL 2013).

The residential average selling price (ASP) has grown dramatically since 2002. The ASP for the Lakeville Phase 1 was Y 20,000 per sq m. In the Lakeville Phase 2, the ASP rose to Y 55,000 per sq m in 2006. The ASP of the Lakeville Phase 3 rose even higher from Y 85,000 (US$12,100) per sq m in 2008, to Y 158,100 per sq m in 2012. The contracted sales of Shanghai Taipingqiao for the whole year of 2012 was Y 166 million (US$26.35 million), a total GFA of 1,050 sq m was sold and presold (SOL 2012).

The Xintiandi development has not been offered for sale. SOL collects rental income in order to maintain the quality of the developed property for the tenants. This type of low-density historic preservation and redevelopment project took a long time to come to fruition. In fact, it reduced the developer's profit margins and lengthened the payback time. The reason SOL could afford to invest in Xintiandi was because it was able to balance the costs and benefits within Taipingqiao area as whole.

Xintiandi improved the quality of urban space, which resulted in higher real estate prices in the surrounding area.

Contract Renegotiations: Double Increase, Double Decrease

A contract renegotiation was required in 2003 when the Shanghai municipal government introduced the policy of "double increase and double decrease," which was applied to the central part of the city. The "double increase" required an increase in green and open spaces to improve the quality of life in the central city. The "double decrease" meant a decrease in the density and FAR of these developments. The change in policy affected many ongoing projects in downtown Shanghai, including the Taipingqiao redevelopment. For example, a decrease of 4.05 million sq m GFA was required for the 376 already approved projects which exceeded the new GFA.

The new policy decreased the allowed GFA. SOL participated in the negotiations with the local government regarding the total GFA. Throughout these negotiations, SOL reiterated the importance of the location of Taipingqiao to the central city of Shanghai, where a reasonable density was needed. It maintained that the private developer required a minimum GFA to ensure the balance of costs and benefits. The Luwan District government was caught between delivering the policy of the Shanghai municipal government, while also trying to protect the interests of the developer. At the same time, the revenue of the local governments relied heavily on these land rents. The higher the FAR for each site, the higher rent and more income would be generated for the local governments.[16]

The final figure was settled in 2005, decreasing the allowed GFA from 1.64 million to 1.25 million sq m as the development volume for the entire Taipingqiao redevelopment area.

Handover and Sustainability

The Xintiandi project rejuvenated a dilapidated neighborhood and transformed it into a mixed-income community, including opportunities for entertainment, retail, office, and residential uses. It became a venue for significant events, such as the annual meeting of APEC and the Shanghai Annual International Fashion Show. Indeed, Xintiandi attracted diverse enterprises from 80 countries and districts around the world. The number of daily visitors to Xintiandi reaches 30,000 during holidays. With the development of the Xintiandi and Taipingqiao Parks, property values in the surrounding areas have also increased and brought sufficient benefits to balance the costs.

The Xintiandi project had important demonstration benefits. Now that the Xintiandi brand has been established, public officials from other Chinese cities have approached the developer to create other Xintiandi-type projects. As a result, SOL has started similar projects in other major cities, including in Wuhan, Chongqing, Foshan, and

Dalian. These would follow and improve on the established model (see table 6.2 and box 6.1). These projects improved the reputation of SOL as a popular, high-level developer able to identify and promote the unique character of historic areas and preserve the urban fabric and buildings for reuse with modern functions.

Table 6.2 **Scale-up of Xintiandi model**

Tiandi project	Type	Residential GFA (sq m)	Office and retail GFA (sq m)	Hotel/Service apartments GFA (sq m)	Total (million sq m)
Shanghai Taipingqiao (Xintiandi)	Inner city and heritage	594,400	589,700	33,500	1,283,800
Wuhan	City center riverfront	699,700	848,200	35,800	1,630,200
Chongqing	Central business district	1,503,400	1,239,600	66,500	2,910,600
Foshan Lingnan	Inner city and heritage	691,100		83,000	1,541,200
Dalian	Knowledge community	1,495,200	2,359,700		3,941,600

Source: Shui On Land Limited internal documents.
Note: The numbers in the table refer to approved masterplan GFAs. All GFA numbers only refer to above-ground areas, and do not account for any underground areas. GFA = gross floor area; n.a. = not applicable; sq m = square meters.

Box 6.1 **Tiandi projects**

Four subsequent, mixed-use projects were planned for Tiandi (re)-development. The land-use template for the Shanghai Taipingqiao area was applied to all of the Tiandi projects around China. In the delivery of these projects, it was essential for the developer to conduct a thorough socio-economic, cultural, and environmental analysis in putting together a master plan. In addition, it was also important to ensure ongoing communications with the government, while also understanding the role of the project as part of the local government's larger plans.

The Wuhan Tiandi project is located in the city center of the Hankou District on the Yangtze River waterfront. The Wuhan municipal government approved plans for the area to be developed as a Riverside Business Zone in 2008. It was initially designed to be one of the city's financial business centers, an innovation hub, and a cultural destination. Wuhan Tiandi was eventually planned as a large-scale, mixed-use redevelopment. The residential average selling price of Wuhan Tiandi almost tripled from Y 13,400 per sq m in 2008 to Y 37,300 per sq m in 2012.

The Chongqing Tiandi project is situated in the Yuzhong District, a traditional central business District of Chongqing. The master plan includes the creation of a lake with pavilions and

(Box continues on next page)

Box 6.1   **Tiandi projects** *(continued)*

a promenade along the waterfront, as well as a commercial core comprising office buildings, hotels, retail, and entertainment facilities. The mixed-use ratio of these functions is similar to that of the Shanghai Taipingqiao project. However, the scale of GFA is twice that of the Taipingqiao project. The residential ASP in Chongqing Tiandi rose from Y 7,100 per sq m in 2001 to Y 12,700 per sq m in 2012.

The Foshan Lingnan Tiandi project will be the most similar in nature to that of the Shanghai Xintiandi project. It is located in the central Chancheng District, Foshan's traditional downtown area and public transportation hub. It is a large-scale urban redevelopment and integrated community project and is comprised of office, retail, hotel and cultural facilities, and residential complexes. The cultural heritage in Foshan is centered around the *Zumiao* ancient temple. The master plan for this area follows the template of Shanghai Taipingqiao in rejuvenating it as a business and commercial zone focusing on business, culture, and tourism development. The residential ASP was around Y 20,000 per sq m for apartments and Y 40,500 per sq m for town houses in 2012.

Dalian Tiandi is the largest mixed-use development of all Xintiandi-type projects, expanding across 12.5 sq km. To date, a total of 207,000 sq m of office GFA has been developed by established technology companies. The residential ASP was around Y 10,000 per sq m for apartments and Y 23,800 per sq m for town houses in 2012. In terms of the financial aspects, all residential properties in the master plan will be sold to generate cash flow. However, almost all of the office space and retail and cultural entertainment centers will be held by SOL as the property manager.

In most of these Tiandi projects, the private developer worked together with the public sector to reshape dilapidated neighborhoods in locations with potential to generate profits. The physical appearance, infrastructure, function, and reputation of the neighborhood are promoted through the redevelopment with substantial investment, efficient operational mechanisms, and elaborate designs (He and Wu 2005). Thus, the redevelopment project of Xintiandi has provided a prototype for public and private partnerships in redeveloping run-down historic neighborhoods with significant cultural and historical value.

Source: Based on SOL annual reports and literature.
Note: To clarify, each U.S. dollar was Y 8.3 in 2001, Y 7.1 in 2008, and Y 6.3 in 2012.

Outcomes and Impacts

The redevelopment of the Xintiandi and Taipingqiao areas generated significant socioeconomic, political, and cultural benefits. The Xintiandi project and the surrounding Taipingqiao area fulfilled the development goals of promoting and internationalizing the city by attracting and retaining professionals in Shanghai. This integrated international community is a successful political and economic achievement and also helped to raise revenues for local governments.

Although the Xintiandi project did not sufficiently balance overall costs and benefits, it did catalyze the process of transformation for the whole area, changing it into a unique location with world-class amenities. The project has been immensely successful in value generation from a historically significant but dilapidated neighborhood. Its success has interested public officials from other cities, motivating them to adopt similar redevelopment models.

However, neither the value created nor the amenities developed have directly benefited the original residents. Although local residents were not involved in the decision-making process, their demands for improved living conditions were basically met by relocating them to new modern residential buildings. However, these new buildings are located far from jobs and economic opportunities. The public benefits of the project include the construction of the Taipingqiao Park and Lake, which increased green, public spaces in the central city of Shanghai.

The project has called attention to the need for greater historic and cultural preservation in Shanghai and China as a whole. In cultural effects, Xintiandi has introduced a new way of using public spaces, promoting a vibrant street life. The commercial and cultural success in redeveloping the Shikumen buildings proves the value of rehabilitating and reusing historic neighborhoods.

This project introduced the concept of adaptive reuse of the historic and cultural fabric at the same time as the city was going through a construction boom. This is especially valuable because it demonstrated that a balance could be achieved between preservation and profit maximization from real estate development projects. It also proved that cultural heritage is a form of capital, which can be leveraged to attract tourism and visitors to generate economic return. Overall, even though the rehabilitation of Xintiandi may have some critics who would have preferred the complete preservation of the buildings and way of life, it does present one kind of successful model of rejuvenating historic buildings and neighborhoods.

Lessons Learned

The redevelopment of Xintiandi and the surrounding Taipingqiao neighborhood has been economically, politically, and culturally successful. On the basis of the lessons learned in Xintiandi, future redevelopment initiatives should consider the following:

- An initial draft master plan or urban design framework will provide an appropriate discussion tool. It can enable the developer to reach a consensus with local public officials, as well as other stakeholders from the outset. A clear, well-designed, and deliverable master plan is of utmost importance. However, it should also allow for flexibility and changes in design or phasing to ensure a desirable urban environment that is also respectful of cultural and historical aspects.
- Ongoing implementation of the plan—despite unfavorable or unforeseen circumstances—can help to reassure developers and investors in their expectations about profits and/or property values.
- Integrating the redevelopment of a special area within a larger area can be helpful in balancing the long-term costs and benefits. It may

also help to allay short-term considerations of investment returns and an unwillingness to contribute to public facilities. Indeed, in the case of Xintiandi, the scale of the redevelopment made the historic preservation and development of public facilities possible.

- Cultural heritage should be considered an asset and a form of capital that can enhance the identity of a place, generating and even raising property values.
- Consistency in local government ideas and priorities for the project is important, especially in longer-term redevelopment efforts.
- The development of a good relationship between private sector developers and local governments is paramount. It was such trust and confidence that made the Xintiandi development possible with the use of a simple agreement. Although solid contracts and institutional frameworks are necessary to form a partnership between the two sectors, the possibility of innovation and maneuver may be limited if these contracts are structured too rigidly.

Notes

1. Shikumen is the name of the traditional architecture of Shanghai, which combines the traditional Chinese architectural elements with western motifs. This style dates back to the 1800s and comprises 2- to 3-story housing units with high brick walls encircling a narrow yard. A group of Shikumen houses along an alley shapes the traditional Shanghainese urban fabric called Li-Nong. The entrance to the alley is usually through a specially-decorated stone arch.
2. The Shanghai Bund has dozens of historical buildings lining the Huangpu River that once housed numerous banks and trading houses from various contries.
3. The exchange rate between U.S. dollars and the yuan is adjusted throughout the document based on historical exchange rates.
4. "Goverment Land Transferring Rent Reasearch Report." http://fdc.fang.com/news/zt/200911/crj.html.
5. "Land Transferring Rent Amounted to 57.3 billion in Shanghai, 75% Higher than Last Year." http://news.sh.fang.com/2014-05-16/12802971.htm.
6. http://www.shtong.gov.cn/node2/node2247/node4602/node79792/node79814/userobject1ai104526.html.
7. See http://shfg.gov.cn/2013/rdjj/ggfzsl/. The relocation programs have been controversial, with many scholars advocating both for and against them. In this report, we do not suggest any relocation be implemented or recommend any particular method of relocation. We simply state the practices found in the case studies, acknowledging that some are controversial.
8. The master plan for Taipingqiao was developed by SOM in collaboration with the developer and planning officials. The detailed control plan was

in turn based on this master plan. Once the detailed control plan was approved by the municipal government, the development index needed to be adjusted. After 2008, the process of revising the detailed control plan became more strict because the approval and revision process of the plan needed to follow certain legal processes.

9. The authors were not able to read the contract. The information is based on interviews with Mr. Lo, Mr. Cheng, and Mr. Chan of SOL conducted in April 2014.

10. Law of the PRC on Urban and Rural Planning. http://www.china.org.cn /china/LegislationsForm2001-2010/2011-02/11/content_21899292 .htm.

11. Shanghai Municipal Goverment Chronicle, Section 4 Redevelopment of Dilapidated Buildings. http://www.shtong.gov.cn/node2/node2245 /node72907/node72915/node73052/node73070/userobject1ai85891 .Htm. In April and September 1992, the former mayor of Shanghai, Huang Ju, held two working conferences regarding land leasing. The focus was on land parcels mainly composed of dilapidated buildings and shacks. The Mayar sought to explore paths to accelerate the rejuvenation of the old town which would be financed by domestic and foreign capital.

12. For more information see the text of the regulation, "Implementation Method of Fasten Shanty Housing Redevelopment in the Central City of Shanghai," issued by Shanghai Municipal Government. Source: http:// www.law-lib.com/law/law_view.asp?id=32861. In the 365 Program, there remain 1.25 million sq m of dilapidated housing, which are subsidized by both the municipal and district governments. For the 400,000 sq m of dilapidated housing listed in the 1998 Plan of Shanghai, the municipal government would allocate a subsidy of Y 300 for each sq m of demolition. For the remaining 850,000 sq m of dilapidated housing, the municipal government would subsidize Y 900 for each sq m of demolition.

13. This law has since changed, which means that SOL now has to compete for each new block with other developers.

14. These are called *danwei* in pinyin; it is a Chinese term that covers orgnizations, enterprises, and so on.

15. A series of housing policies is now in place to slow the increase in housing prices. The housing purchase restriction is the major policy change. People usually engage in speculation by purchasing multiple housing units with mortgages. They make a limited down payment and then rent the remaining unit(s) to cover the monthly payment. The restriction policy increases the down payment on the second home to avoid multiple purchases.

16. The basic land rent or price for public bidding is usually calculated by an assessment company based on location, site condition, and FAR. And then the land will get into the market for auction with this basic land price.

References

Bracken, Gregory. 2013. *The Shanghai Alleyway House: A Vanishing Urban Vernacular*. Routledge Contemporary China Series. New York: Routledge.

He, Shenjing, and Fulong Wu. 2005. "Property-Led Redevelopment In Post-Reform China: A Case Study of Xintiandi Redevelopment Project In Shanghai." *Journal of Urban Affairs* 27 (1): 1–23.

Luwan District Chronicle. 1994–2003. "Redevelopment of 337,800 Square Meter Shanty House." http://www.shtong.gov.cn/Newsite/node2/node4/node2249/node85092/node85099/node85160/node85170/userobject1ai124990.html.

NBS (National Bureau of Statistics of China). 2012. National Data (database). http://data.stats.gov.cn/search.htm?s=2012%20%E4%B8%8A%E6%B5%B7%20%E4%BA%BA%E5%9D%87%E5%8F%AF%E6%94%AF%E9%85%8D.

Sha, Yongjie. 2010. *Towards A New Chinese Urbanity: Urban Design Concept of Shui On Land Developments*. Beijing: China Architecture & Building Press.

SOL (Shui On Land Limited). 2012. *Annual Report 2012*. Shanghai: SOL.

———. 2013. *Annual Report 2013*. Shanghai: SOL.

———. 2014. *Annual Report 2014*. Shanghai: SOL.

Wang, L., and C. Hoch. 2013. "Pragmatic Rational Planning: Comparing Shanghai and Chicago." *Planning Theory* 12 (4): 369–90.

Yan, Huaming. 2012. "Public-Private Partnership in China's Urban Regeneration: A Case Study of Xintiandi Project in Shanghai." *Urban Development Studies* (8): 41–48.

Yang, You-Ren, and Chi-hui Chang. 2007. "An Urban Regeneration Regime in China: A Case Study of Urban Redevelopment in Shanghai's Taipingqiao Area." *Urban Studies* 44 (9): 1809–26.

Xu, M. 2004. "Study on the Renewal and Development Patterns of the Old Settlements in the Inner City of Shanghai." [In Chinese.] Doctoral thesis, Tongji University, Shanghai.

People Interviewed

Mr. Albert Kain Bon CHAN, Director of Development Planning and Design, Shui On Land Limited

Mr. Vincent Hong Sui LO, CEO, Shui On Land Limited

Mr. Benjamin WOOD, Chief Architect, renovation designer for Xintiandi

Mr. Yaliang CHEN, Former Director of Urban Planning Administration Bureau of Luwan District

Ms. Lin WANG, Former Director of Historic Preservation and Landmark Division, Shanghai Urban Planning Administration Bureau

Mr. Henry CHENG, Former Project Manager of Taipinqiao Redevelopment Project

Mr. Meitang YE, Chief Planner, Shanghai Urban Planning Administration Bureau

Map 7.1 **Ahmedabad, India**

a. Sabarmati Riverfront area

b. Ahmedabad Municipal corporation area

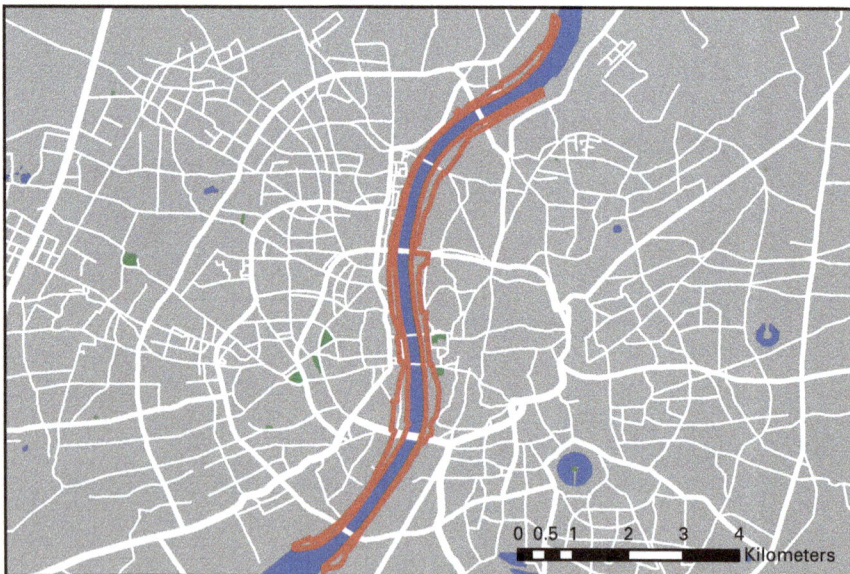

Source: World Bank based on Open Street Map data 2015.

CHAPTER 7

Ahmedabad: Reclaiming the Sabarmati Riverfront

Introduction

The Sabarmati Riverfront development in Ahmedabad, India, is a self-financed project, backed by funds from the future sale of a portion of reclaimed land. The project was initiated in 1997 with the formation of a special purpose vehicle (SPV), the Sabarmati Riverfront Development Corporation Limited (SRFDCL), to undertake the development of the riverfront and to return developed land and public amenities to Ahmedabad Municipal Corporation (AMC) in order to recover the project costs (see map 7.1).

The project has been funded via loans from the Housing and Urban Development Corporation (HUDCO)—a large national level infrastructure funding agency—and from the AMC. According to the original proposal, a portion of the developed reclaimed land was to be auctioned after the completion of the project to cover the cost of development. In the past few years, because of various contingency factors, the pace of implementation of the project has slowed. At present, since the entire project has not yet been completed, the auction of the land for sale has yet to take place. It is also unclear what the long-term maintenance and upkeep strategy for the project will be. Therefore, the SRFDCL is exploring alternatives to finalize a strategy.

To date, a significant portion of the project and a number of public amenities associated with the riverfront have been completed and offered for public use. This includes the pedestrian promenades near the water and street level. Large fairgrounds to the west are being used year round for various events, such as different festivals, the annual Ahmedabad marathon, and the cyclothon, among others. The informal market *Ravivaari* (Sunday market) is now open every day, and a Dhobi Ghat (informal laundry facility) has also been functional since 2013. Two new parks—one a community park and the other a large city-level amenity—have been opened and are being used extensively. A small portion of the project has yet to be completed.

This chapter outlines important aspects of the planning and implementation of the project. It ends with an analysis of key findings from the project, as well as the potential for replication in other cities with a similar context.

Context and Background

Ahmedabad was founded in 1411 as a walled city on the eastern banks of the Sabarmati River at 49 meters (m) above sea level (Gillion 1968). It is the largest city in the state of Gujarat and the fifth largest in India (Census 2011). Situated on the banks of the Sabarmati River, the city occupies 464 square kilometers (sq km) with a total population of approximately 5.5 million (Census 2011). During the early- to-mid-twentieth century, Ahmedabad was the epicenter of the textile industry in India. During this period, several notable and prestigious institutions were also established in the city, making it an important center for higher education, science, and technology. Today, it is one of the better managed cities in India, and it has pioneered many urban development innovations (Spodek 2011).

Population Growth

Until the early twentieth century, the growth of the city of Ahmedabad was restricted to the eastern side of the city. The opening of the Ellis Bridge in the early twentieth century connected the western bank, which allowed the ongoing development of the city in this direction. The 1970s saw significant growth in the city's population because of the rapid expansion of industry. Since the 1980s, western Ahmedabad has expanded more rapidly than the eastern parts of the city. The population of the city has increased from 3.5 million in the year 2001 to 5.6 million in 2011 (AUDA 2013).

The Project's Organizational Structure

Ahmedabad's local government first came into existence in the year 1857.[1] This governing body was recognized by statute and designated as a city municipality in 1874 (Gillion 1968). The current structure of the AMC was constituted in 1950 under the Bombay Provincial Municipal Corporation (BPMC) Act, 1949 (AMC 2014). In accordance with the act, the city governance comprises elected representatives and administrative staff.

The entire area of the city is divided into smaller governance units called wards and zones. The AMC area is divided into six zones. The zonal system envisages decentralization of activities and a more responsive administration at the zone level. Each zone is headed by a deputy municipal commissioner who has the responsibility for public health and infrastructure provision for the respective zone. The city administration is further decentralized to 64 administrative wards. Each ward is represented by three elected municipal councillors.

The AMC is governed by a general body comprising these councillors, and it in turn appoints the mayor and the deputy mayor. It also selects members for the three statutory committees (Standing Committee, Transport Committee, and School Board), as well as 14 other committees. The Standing Committee is responsible for all of the policy decisions, the approval of the budget, and appointments and expenditure estimates sent by various departments. The municipal commissioner is the administrative head of the AMC.[2] The municipal commissioner is usually an Indian Administrative Service (IAS) officer who is appointed to this role by the chief minister of the state. (See box 7.1 for a description of the IAS.) The tenure for the position is usually restricted to three years, after which the commissioner may be transferred to a different role or given an extension in the same role.

Box 7.1   **The Indian Administrative Service**

The Indian Administrative Service (IAS) is the administrative civil service of the government of India. The IAS has its roots in the Imperial Civil Service initiated during the British rule in India after 1857. The officers of the IAS are recruited and trained by the union government and serve in various state governments, the union government, and public sector undertakings. IAS officers are trained to handle government affairs. Their key responsibilities include policy formulation and implementation, implementation of development programs, and monitoring and supervision of projects. They are generalists who assume a diverse array of responsibilities and work closely with their respective ministers.

On the state level, the chief secretary is the highest position at the state level of government. An IAS officer of the level of principal secretary or higher heads each department of the state government, such as the urban development department, the revenue department, the transport department, and so on.

On the city level, the municipal commissioner is the de facto executive head in cities with populations over 500,000. The commissioner is responsible for the provision and maintenance of various municipal services, such as the water supply, drainage, solid waste management, roads and public transport according to the provisions of the relevant state municipal services act (for example, the Bombay Provincial Municipal Corporation Act of 1949). Additional municipal commissioners and deputy municipal commissioners assist the municipal commissioner in this role.

The government of Gujarat appoints the municipal commissioners and occasionally the deputy municipal commissioners from the IAS cadre. The chief officers in smaller cities are appointed from the Gujarat Public Service Commission, which is a state-level civil service organization. In this regard, there is no functional specialization within the IAS and appointment, as head of a municipal corporation requires no prior experience in urban management.

Most states in India have also constituted urban development authorities to ensure planned development of areas falling outside the periphery of municipal corporations. The important functions of development authorities include the preparation of a physical master plan for the urban agglomeration and development of essential urban infrastructure, such as roads, public housing, parks, gardens, and so on in their jurisdiction. The chief executive officer of the development authority is usually an IAS officer, and the authority is governed through a board comprising some political representatives and senior officers from state and city governments.

The AMC has the authority to levy taxes, development charges, impact fees, user charges, and other such means of raising revenue for internal expenditures as well as capital expenditures. The city also has the ability to obtain loans from a variety of sources. For details of the governance system of Ahmedabad, see figure 7.1.

Figure 7.1   Organizational chart, Ahmedabad municipal corporation

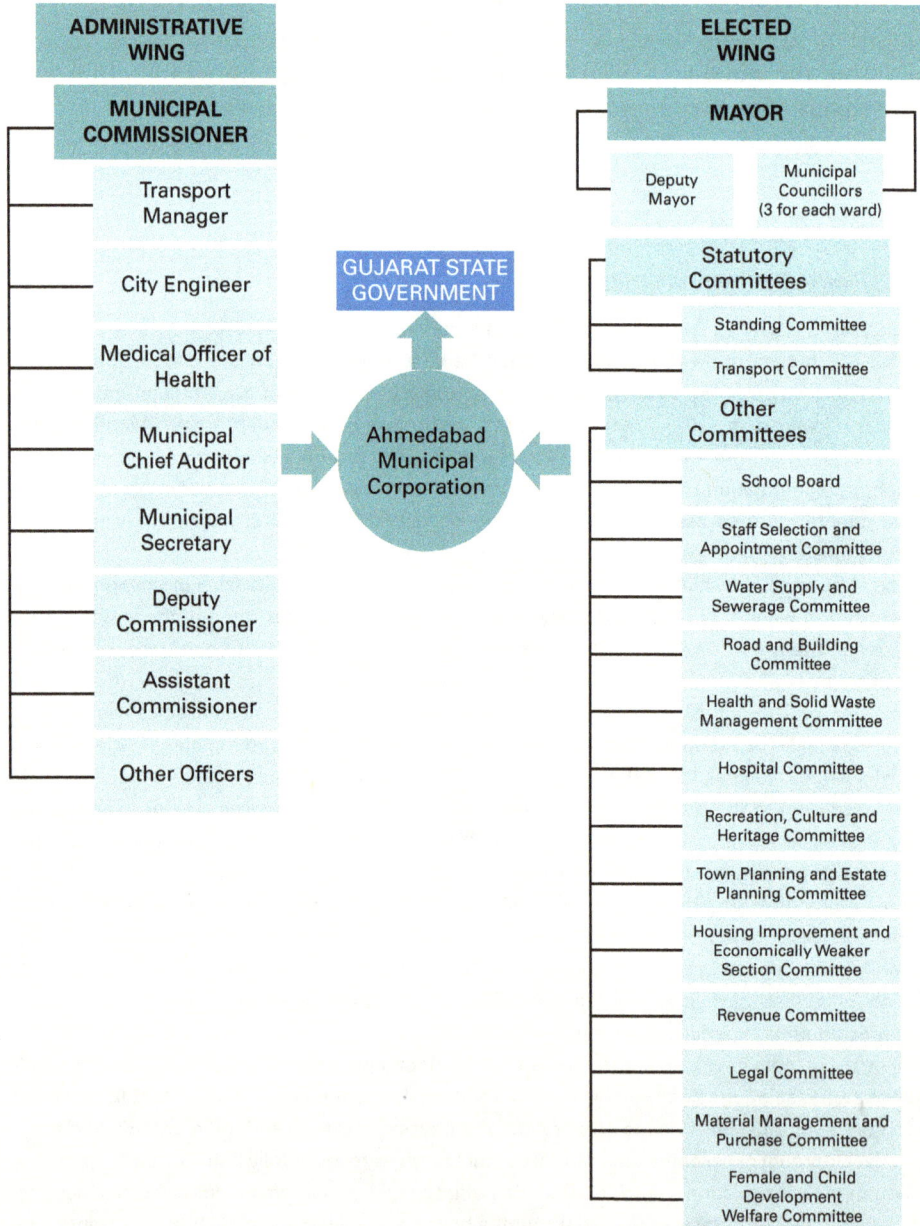

ADMINISTRATIVE WING	ELECTED WING
MUNICIPAL COMMISSIONER	**MAYOR**
Transport Manager	Deputy Mayor / Municipal Councillors (3 for each ward)
City Engineer	**Statutory Committees**
Medical Officer of Health	Standing Committee
Municipal Chief Auditor	Transport Committee
Municipal Secretary	**Other Committees**
Deputy Commissioner	School Board
Assistant Commissioner	Staff Selection and Appointment Committee
Other Officers	Water Supply and Sewerage Committee
	Road and Building Committee
	Health and Solid Waste Management Committee
	Hospital Committee
	Recreation, Culture and Heritage Committee
	Town Planning and Estate Planning Committee
	Housing Improvement and Economically Weaker Section Committee
	Revenue Committee
	Legal Committee
	Material Management and Purchase Committee
	Female and Child Development Welfare Committee

GUJARAT STATE GOVERNMENT

Ahmedabad Municipal Corporation

Sources: Based on BPMCA 1949, and www.egovamc.com.

Apart from the AMC, the Ahmedabad Urban Development Authority (AUDA) is responsible for planning and managing growth on the periphery of the city. The AUDA was formed in 1978 and was authorized as the urban development agency charged with planning and managing growth of peripheral areas of the city of Ahmedabad, including an additional 300 villages and nine adjoining municipalities. The planning of areas within the city limits is the responsibility of the AMC. However, in recent years, AUDA and AMC created a joint urban planning unit to prepare the Revised Development Plan for Ahmedabad 2021. This unit is staffed by professionals from both agencies and is housed in the AUDA. The goal is to promote a more integrated planning approach to areas under the jurisdiction of both entities.

The main task of AUDA was to prepare and implement the development plan of the area under its jurisdiction (currently 1,866 sq km). The development plan, at the strategic macrolevel, provides a broad framework for future growth of the city and surrounding areas. It is to be revised every 10 years and implemented primarily through the mechanism of town planning schemes. The statutory process of the development plan involves the following main stages: (a) creation of a base map to identify existing conditions, (b) creation of a draft development plan; (c) consultation with stakeholders, and (d) creation of a final development plan, which is then sent to the state for approval.

The most recent development plan was updated in 2012 and is valid until 2021. Like many Indian cities, Ahmedabad is experiencing a rapid growth in population. Therefore, one of the key features of its development plan is to outline the area identified for expansion of the city. This area is then planned in more detail with streets and utilities, after a readjustment of land ownership to carve out land required for public use. This process of detailed planning and implementation along with readjustment of land is known as the town planning scheme (TPS).

The TPS is a statutory planning tool that allows for the readjustment of land and levy of betterment charges in lieu of improvement of services and infrastructure (Ballaney 2008). The AUDA is an agency of the state and, although it is not directly under the control of the state, it relies on the state for approval or direction for all significant decisions. Reflecting the nature of its relationship with the state, the structure of AUDA consists of the elected wing, led by a political appointee nominated by the chief minister, and the administrative wing, led usually by an IAS officer who is also appointed by the chief minister. Since the Gujarat Town Planning and Urban Development Act of 1976 does not grant AUDA the power to impose taxes within its jurisdiction, it relies on financial support from the state for its day-to-day functioning. However, AUDA is allowed to use the levy betterment charges (through the TPS process) toward the cost of infrastructure and planning process within its jurisdiction. Likewise, it can also use development charges for projects.

Finances

The finances of the city are managed through annual budgets prepared by the AMC. The budget is prepared by the administrative wing and approved by the standing committee of the AMC. Revenue sources include property taxes, service charges, grants, and loans. Revenues are in turn spent on capital and operating expenses.

Historically, during the 1930s, the Ahmedabad municipality raised funds to provide affordable housing to workers by using increased import taxes on cotton. During the 1990s and 2000s, because of rampant municipal tax evasion, the AMC was severely impoverished (Spodek 2011). At the time, *octroi*[3]—a local tax imposed on goods entering the city—was the major source of municipal income. Thus, during the 1990s to improve municipal income, the city initiated strict enforcement of tax and octroi collection.

By 1995, the AMC had a budget surplus and began several new project works. To undertake capital improvement projects, the AMC initiated the process of receiving a credit rating to issue bonds. In 1997, the AMC received a credit rating of A+ from CRISIL (a financial management firm). Bonds were issued in the amount of Rs 100 crores (US$16 million; 1 crore = 10 million). Ahmedabad became the first Indian city to issue bonds. Since then, the AMC has had three more successful issuances of municipal bonds for financing city infrastructure.

Project Context

The Sabarmati River in the Aravalli Hills of Rajasthan is one of the four major rivers flowing through Gujarat before joining the Gulf of Khambhat in the Arabian Sea. Today the Sabarmati River flows right through the center of the city, bisecting the city into its western and eastern halves. There are nine bridges across the river connecting east and west Ahmedabad (see map 7.2).

Ahmedabad has always had a strong association with the Sabarmati River. In the initial years from the early to the mid-twentieth century, Ahmedabad was the epicenter of the developing textile industry in India (Spodek 2011), and the city grew organically. During this period, the river offered a tranquil background to palaces, religious structures, gardens, and recreational spaces. However, growing industrialization resulted in environmental degradation of the river. Industrial waste and sewage from nearby neighborhoods was being discharged directly into the river. Later Mahatma Gandhi built his ashram on the western bank of the river in 1915.

The city's major thoroughfare, Ashram Road, runs parallel to the river. Prominent institutional buildings are located on the banks of Sabarmati, such as the Mill Owners' Association building and Sanskar Kendra, both designed by the famous architect, Le Corbusier. Since Sabarmati was a seasonal river, it ran practically dry for nine months of the year and carried water mostly during the monsoon season. The dry river bed and river banks were used for farming and a regular weekly market, Ravivaari, as well as

Map 7.2   **Sabarmati Riverfront context**

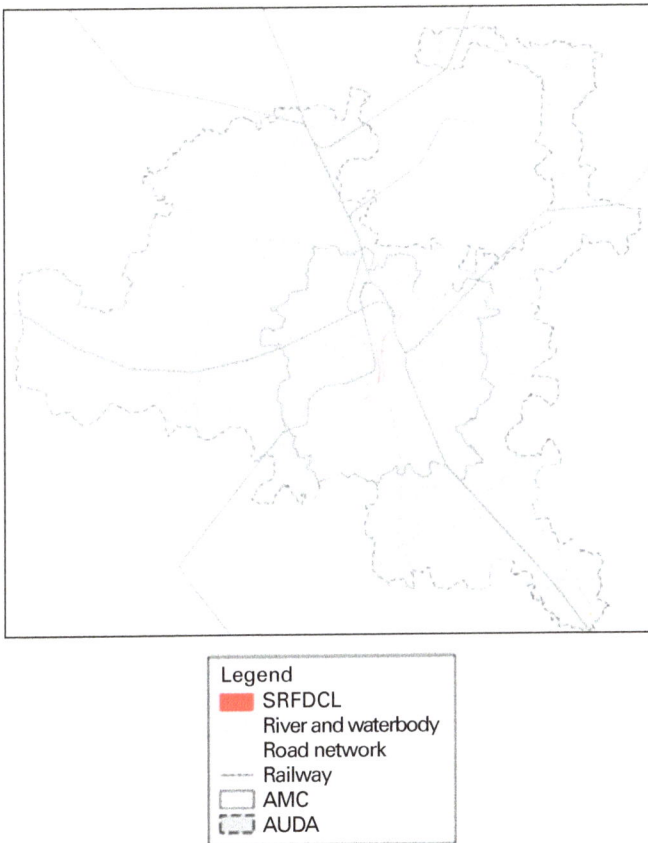

Legend
- ■ SRFDCL
- River and waterbody
- Road network
- ---- Railway
- ☐ AMC
- ☐ AUDA

Source: HCP Design Planning and Management 2014.

other activities such as the circus. Until about the 1970s, the river was also the city's prime source of water.

Today, Ahmedabad receives the majority of its water supply—more than 65 percent—from the Narmada Canal. However, several French wells dug in the Sabarmati bed still remain an important source (more than 12 percent) of drinking water for the city.

With the declining ecological health of the river and the city's association with it, a number of informal settlements arose along the riverbanks,[4] further reducing direct access to the river. Most people living in these settlements originally worked in the mills nearby. As the mills started to close, a number of their workers had to find alternative employment, which was not always in close proximity to these settlements.

These encroachments affected the flood management on the Sabarmati River. In case of heavy rainfall in the catchment area of the river and attendant flood management/prevention, water needed to be released from Dharoi Dam. Fear of these encroachments being submerged due to release of excess water from the dam prevented dam supervisors from releasing the water intermittently (as it should have been). Instead, they waited until it was absolutely critical to release the water for the safety of the dam. This resulted in severe flooding many times. Indeed, in recent years, it has become an annual phenomenon. Although attempts were made to relocate some of these riverfront settlements in the past, it was found that as the relocation sites were too far, the strategy was unsuccessful in curbing the growth of slums along the river (Patel and Kansal 2011).

Apart from housing a section of mill workers, the informal settlements were also home to a number of other people. A section of these informal settlements included people engaged in farming on the riverbed, as the river was dry for most part of the year. Another section included the Dhobi Ghat, an informal laundry place. In addition, there were also many other smaller groups of informal vocations, such as fruit and vegetable vendors, flower vendors, *agarbatti* (incense stick) rollers, and so on. Some of these informal settlements were also havens for certain illegal activities such as bootleg liquor.

Over a period of time, these encroachments and the private properties grew to the banks of the river. Therefore, there was no more public access possible along the length of the river. As a consequence, the only place from which the expanse of the river could be enjoyed by the citizens was the bridges. Sabarmati redevelopment was initiated to restore the public access to the river and reduce the risk of flooding. Photograph 7.1 illustrates the extent of the project.

Phase 1: Scoping

The revitalization of the Sabarmati Riverfront has been attempted at least twice in the past. Bernard Kohn, a French architect living in Ahmedabad during the early 1960s, prepared one of the earliest proposals for redevelopment of the riverfront. He visualized a linear development for predominantly recreational uses along either bank of the river between the Gandhi and Sardar Bridges. The proposal included a series of parks and open spaces with intermittent access to the river via a series of steps. The government of Gujarat then set up a special committee to examine the proposal, which concluded that the project was technically feasible after a slight modification of the design. However, the project did not move forward, allegedly because of a lack of political stewardship.[5] Kohn, disappointed with the poor response to his proposal, eventually left the country in the late 1960s.

In 1973, a major flooding led to a renewed interest in the river and management of its seasonal flow. One initial outcome was the creation of the Dharoi Dam in 1976, approximately 200 km upstream of the Sabarmati River. Around the same time, and as an unrelated development, a barrage

Photograph 7.1   Original condition with an overlay showing the planned redevelopment area

Source: HCP Design Planning and Management 2010.
Note: The photograph shows the defined waterway and reclaimed land along 12 km on both banks of the river.

was built on Sabarmati near Vasna, just south of the then boundary of the city of Ahmedabad. The idea was to provide irrigation for agricultural areas downstream. In the same year, a group of architecture, planning, and engineering professionals formed the River Front Development Group. This group proposed an incremental approach to creating a public riverfront along the river banks (EPC 1998). Without significant interest in the proposal from the government, possibly because of the unclear approach to financing and implementation of the proposals, this plan also remained on paper only.

After 1975, Ahmedabad went through a period of economic downturn from the closing of many textile mills, which had been the key economic drivers of the city. Growth resumed again only decades later in the mid-1990s following the economic liberalization initiated in 1991. In this context, one of the prominent local politicians convinced the municipal commissioner of Ahmedabad to enable the AMC to undertake this ambitious project. At the time, the redevelopment of Chimanlal Girdharlal Road

Box 7.2   C G road development

C G Road is one of the key north-south connectors in the western part of Ahmedabad. It derives its prominence from its proximity to Ashram Road, which was the main commercial corridor in the city. As the city grew westward, a section of businesses moved to C G Road. By the mid-1990s, C G Road had become a key retail and commercial corridor in Ahmedabad. The new municipal commissioner realized the potential significance of the project as a symbol of revitalization for the city and decided to move forward.

The plan was to implement a street design program for a 2.5 km stretch of C G Road, complete with a service lane, paid parking, sidewalks, street lighting, crosswalks, and more. Although the AMC management was convinced about the importance of the project, it was struggling with finances and its political independence from the state. Hence, it was decided that the project would be implemented through private financing.

The project was funded by a private corporate group, which implemented the project in return for seven-year advertising rights along the entire stretch of the redeveloped C G Road. To facilitate this, the design of boards and street advertising was included as a part of the overall design of the street. This approach of privately financed infrastructure improvement provided a great boost to AMC's image and its ability to undertake future projects.

Three key lessons can be drawn from the successful implementation of the C G Road project. First, the outsourcing of project development and project management services helped the project to benefit from private expertise and facilitated the swift implementation of the project. Second, it was one of the first examples of self-financed projects in the city, which provided a public good without using public funds. Finally, the project made the political benefits of visible urban improvement very tangible and laid the path for political support for similar projects later.

The lessons from the C G Road project guided the planning of the Sabarmati Riverfront project. For example, the decision to undertake the project through an SPV was greatly influenced by the success of the C G Road project as a privately financed, managed, and implemented venture by the AMC. The commissioner was convinced that municipal bureaucracy and a slow decision-making process would hamper the timely execution of this project.

(C G Road), which was one of the first street redevelopment projects in the state, had just been completed as a self-financed project. The successful completion of C G Road and the lessons learned from its planning and implementation proved to be very valuable for scoping and initiating the riverfront project (see box 7.2).

Special Purpose Vehicle

The SRFDCL was established as a wholly owned company by the AMC (and a few other minority shareholders). The company was conceived as a development company with a mandate to plan and implement the Sabarmati Riverfront development project.

While setting up the leadership of this SPV, the proponents of the project were also aware that a project of this scale and complexity could not be implemented under the sole leadership of the municipal commissioner. Hence, it was decided that the board of directors of the SRFDCL would comprise a coalition of stakeholders. The board included important members of the bureaucracy, such as the municipal commissioner and district collector. The board also included political representatives from the AMC—the mayor of Ahmedabad, the opposition leader, and the standing committee chairman. Having these local politicians from both the ruling and opposition parties helped to ensure that the project was perceived as a civic project rather than a project aligned with a particular party's agenda. Finally, the board included professional leaders and technical specialists. An unsuccessful effort was also made to include a representative from one of Ahmedabad's many strong nongovernmental organizations (NGOs).

During the early stages of the project (from initiation until the mid-2000s), the political leadership behind the project was instrumental in ensuring that people with strong independent reputations were recruited to the board, and a collaborative spirit of decision making was maintained at all times. This ensured that the technical, financial, social, and aesthetic management and operational factors were considered in making decisions for the project.

Along with having a diverse representation from among the bureaucracy, political leadership, and private sector, the combination of long-term board members versus shorter-term ex officio members helped balance the interests in favor of the long-term continuity of the project. Project champions and long-term members of the board have been able to keep the project going in spite of turnover in the ranks of the ex-officio members (Patel and Kansal 2011).

A key factor in the early success of the project was the presence of both the ruling and opposition parties on the SRFDCL board. In 1997 when the riverfront corporation was established, the ruling party mayor and opposition leader were both inducted to its board, which ensured the continued political leadership over the project when the parties changed places in the 2000 elections. This was a very important factor in the success of the project, because changes in political leadership are a major risk in urban regeneration and capital improvement projects.

Proposal and Feasibility

Once the SPV was in place, the first task the board undertook was to commission a feasibility study. This task was entrusted to a not-for-profit urban planning and urban development management firm, Environmental Planning Collaborative (EPC), which was also involved in the development of C G Road. EPC put into place a diverse team of experts to undertake this feasibility study within a matter of months. The scope of this study was to prepare a new proposal for development of the riverfront and assess preliminary feasibility of the project.

The proposal, as outlined in the 1997 study, called for training the width of the existing river to 275 m. Its untrained width varied from 340 m to 600 m between the Subhash Bridge in the north and the Vasna Barrage in the south. The land reclaimed through this river training was approximately 162 hectares (ha) or 400 acres (which subsequently increased to 200 ha or 494 acres) spread along 9 km (which subsequently expanded to 12 km) along the west and east banks of the river. According to the proposal, 20 percent of the reclaimed land was to be sold to finance the entire cost of the project while the rest was to be used for new streets, parks, and development of other civic amenities. A key feature of this proposal was a continuous promenade along the east and west banks of the river. The study also proposed implementation mechanisms and financing strategies (EPC 1998).

Phase 2: Planning

At the outset, the project was envisioned as a multidimensional environmental improvement, social uplifting, and urban rejuvenation project. Key objectives were as follows:

- *Make the riverfront accessible to the public.* Over the years, the city had ignored the river. Most of the east and west banks of the river were privately owned. Citizens only had access to the bridges. The proposal created a continuous public promenade on the east and west banks, thereby making the river accessible to the public.
- *Stop the flow of sewage, and keep the river clean and pollution free.* Untreated sewage from the informal settlements and nearby developments opened directly into the river, which resulted in extreme and constant pollution. By providing an interceptor sewer line on both sides of the river along the entire length, the proposal eliminated the direct flow of sewage to the river. In the process, the quality of the water improved, enhancing the possibility for improving ground water recharge.
- *Provide a site for the permanent rehousing of informal settlements along the riverbed.* The proposal acknowledged the presence of informal settlements along the riverbed and adjacent areas. The project planned for the relocation of existing informal settlements and improving their livelihoods through access to more permanent and better quality housing.
- *Reduce the risk of erosion and overflow to flood-prone neighborhoods.* Over the years, the banks of the river had witnessed unplanned development. Property owners, who could afford to, built private embankments along the river's edge to protect their properties from floods and erosion. Those who could not afford such embankments experienced almost annual flooding and erosion of the banks. The plan fixed this problem by providing a continuous public embankment along both banks of the river.
- *Create riverfront parks, promenades, and* ghats *(steps leading to the river) to enjoy the water.* The proposal for the development of reclaimed riverfront land set aside a large portion for new city and neighborhood-level parks and gardens as an amenity for the local residents. Moreover, the continuous promenades and *ghats* would be open for public access, bringing the river back to the city.

- *Provide Ahmedabad with new cultural, trade, and social amenities.* Along with other improvements, a new convention and trade facility was proposed, one of the larger public amenities suggested along the riverfront. The land reclaimed through the riverfront project made this possible for Ahmedabad.
- *Generate resources for paying project costs.* The proposal included a well-defined and detailed assessment of project costs, as well as a revenue model to ensure that the development was self-financed and would not need additional investment from the AMC or the state.
- *Enhance connections between the east and west sides of Ahmedabad.* The proposal includes new east-west connections across the river to connect both sides.
- *Create a stronger identity for Ahmedabad.* By creating well-defined urban design guidelines[6] for the development along the riverfront and the surrounding areas, the proposal envisions creating a stronger identity for the city.
- *Revitalize riverfront neighborhoods and rejuvenate Ahmedabad.* This was not a part of the original proposal. However, during a presentation to the-then chief minister, this issue was highlighted and became one of the significant features of the land use plan that was subsequently prepared. When implemented, the riverfront project would lead to improved attractiveness for new development and redevelopment in the neighboring precincts. Hence, the overall plan included a proposal for creating development guidelines for the neighboring precincts. Typically, in the planning process, such development guidelines are created at the time of creation or revision of the development plan by the urban development agency responsible for the given area.

Compared to previous proposals, the one prepared by the EPC was comprehensive in its scope and addressed all the important aspects of the redevelopment project, albeit in a preliminary manner. The report included a study of river hydraulics and the effect of land reclamation on flood levels, impact on existing bridges, impact on neighboring areas, and so on. The report also contained a study on the ownership of land surrounding the development and how it would be affected by the project. Since the project did not rely on the use of land acquisition as a means of creating a public realm, it reduced the possibility of opposition from the landowners in the development area.

Managing Feasibility and Other Studies

Whereas the feasibility report outlined a broad strategy for planning and implementation, a number of specific studies needed to be conducted before the actual implementation could be planned. Even before these additional studies could be initiated, the board needed to agree on a strategy for implementing the vision of the project. At the outset, as identified in the EPC plan, there were three broad options for managing the implementation: (a) implement the project by building in-house capacity, (b) partner with a private real estate development firm, or (c) hire private sector consultants to oversee development management services.

The SRFDCL considered the merits of all three options. In the case of the first option, it would have been difficult to hire the requisite expertise in-house, and the hired staff would have been a liability for the company once the project was completed (which at the time was estimated to be within five years). An option was presented to use some of the municipal staff from the AMC, seconding them to the company. But, seconded municipal staff members would have followed bureaucratic processes, which would have slowed the functioning of the company and would have taken away one of the key advantages of having an SPV, that is, the ability to make quick decisions.

The second option of partnering with a private real estate developer was rejected for two reasons. The primary reason was that selecting and appointing a developer partner would have entailed significant political risk. This approach would have left the decision makers vulnerable to criticism that the riverbed was being sold off to private interests. Secondly, forging a partnership with a private real estate developer may have required an increase in the percentage of land to be set aside for sale. This would have reduced the available land for public amenities and may have affected the public perception of the project.

Instead, the SRFDCL board chose the third option to outsource the development management services. In 1999, EPC was appointed as development manager for the initial stages of project planning and implementation of the Sabarmati Riverfront development. The role played by the private sector development management in the C G Road project around this time also helped to make this approach credible. This allowed the company to leverage private sector expertise in managing the project, while maintaining full ownership of the project.

It would have been difficult for the SRFDCL to assemble an in-house team of diverse experts to execute all of the required tasks. Outsourcing the expertise required proved to be more effective, while still retaining the right to oversee all operational and financial aspects of the project. There were also a number of additional studies and plans that needed to be prepared before the project could be realized. After the commencement of the project, there was more interest within the AMC to be part of the project team. Hence, AMC staff were either seconded to the project or given this task as an additional responsibility. Although this helped to build a coherent team within the SRFDCL, it has taken away some of the earlier entrepreneurial private sector spirit of the company.

A Note on Project Risks

As mentioned, one specific instance of risk identification and mitigation was the creation of a multistakeholder presence on the board of SRFDCL—more specifically, the involvement of senior leadership from the political opposition. At the time the project was initiated, the Bhartiya Janta Party was in power at the municipal level. However, with the leader of Congress Party, their main opposition being on the board of SRFDCL from the beginning, there was a smooth transition when the Congress Party came back into power a few years later. This allowed the project to be viewed as a pure city improvement project rather than that a particular political agenda.

Phase 3: Financing and Implementation

Stage 1: Laying the Groundwork, 1999–2003

The first stage of the project between 1999 and 2003 laid the initial groundwork for project implementation. During this period, various studies were conducted to build a solid analytical and technical base for the project. These studies included soil testing, financial feasibility, infrastructure, construction technologies, and so on. Parallel to this process, the project team also vigorously pursued the issue of land transfer clearance from the Irrigation Department for Reclamation. This land transfer was a critical element without which the project could not proceed further, as the majority of the funding for the project was to be drawn from the sale of a portion of this reclaimed land. Although the application for the land transfer was made in February 1999, it was only in 2003 that the land transfer process was finally completed.[7]

Stage 2: Launch and Project Delay

In 2003, the project was formally launched by the chief minister of state. Soon after, the municipal commissioner of Ahmedabad (who was also the chair of the board of SRFDCL) decided to move the project further northward. The reasons for this move were not entirely clear. By moving upstream, the whole project would have been outside the city. The purpose of the project was to act as a catalyst for revitalization of the city as a whole, and it would not have been as meaningful to locate it between Ahmedabad and Gandhinagar.

The commissioner moved forward with appointment of new consultants and quickly awarded contracts. But before the idea of moving the project northward could materialize, the commissioner was transferred to a different role. The new commissioner subsequently revoked the earlier decision and refocused on the original project design.

Stage 3: Pilot Project and Key Infrastructure, 2004–10

In 2004, the construction of the pilot project was initiated in order to finalize the technology to be used for the construction of the majority of the retaining walls. Whereas one alternative might have been better suited for this role, the logistics of managing the material needs for this alternative would have made it unfeasible. Therefore, the standard concrete technology was selected for the construction of the retaining walls of the riverfront.

After this pilot process was completed, contractors were selected from several rounds of proposals and construction was initiated in 2007.

Stage 4: Significant Completion and Use, 2011–Present

Between 2007 and 2009, major infrastructure improvements were undertaken. These included the construction of underground interceptor sewer lines along both banks and construction of diaphragm walls, as well as a lower promenade and main retaining walls. Given that the construction posed little threat to the informal settlements in the vicinity, no significant relocation was undertaken at this time.

From 2010 onward, the relocation process started as the upper level promenade and streets needed to be developed. The project team implemented this according to a phased strategy. After the relocation of the dwellings occupying the land, ongoing construction was phased in based on the availability of land. At times, the complexity of this jugglery—of constructing the alternative accommodation, relocating the households to the alternative accommodation, demolishing the old informal settlement and then initiating construction—led to increasing delays in the construction schedule.

Then, from 2011 onward, sections of the riverfront development started to open to the public after completion of construction activity. To date, a majority of the lower promenade and two public parks have been opened for public use, and the alternative site for the Ravivaari has been opened as has the Dhobi Ghat. A city level exhibition and conference facility, which has been planned and is ready for implementation, awaits a fresh infusion of funds or a private partner that could manage the construction and operation of this facility for a period of time. Similarly, a proposal for construction of a large Ferris wheel—along the lines of the London Eye—has been put forth. Applicants have been invited from interested parties to design, construct, operate, and maintain this significant structure along the riverfront.

Relocation of Informal Settlements

At the time of the preparation of the project feasibility study, the Vikas Center for Development, an NGO based in Ahmedabad, was engaged in preparing resettlement and rehabilitation plans. Their intention was to take a human approach to resettlement. Inputs were also sought from the Self-Employed Women's Association and a quick assessment of the number of affected households was undertaken. This resulted in the affected households being relocated to sites within the boundary of the SRFDCL reclaimed land. Ideally, it may have been better to relocate the project-affected households to sites in close proximity to the river. First, because the project was at a very nascent stage, it was difficult to identify parcels of publicly owned land in nearby locations that could be used for relocation of project-affected households. Second, the AMC would have had to commit the land for the project to make credible proposals that would be acceptable to the NGOs involved in the process. And third, at this early stage of the project when the future success of the project was not yet visible, it was difficult for AMC leadership to entitle a few of the informal settlements in the city to be relocated outside the reclaimed land of SRFDCL. Residents of other informal settlements of the city would have seen such an approach as inequitable.

Furthermore, political leaders in the AMC were some of the biggest opponents of the project because they saw the informal settlements within their jurisdiction being disintegrated (through relocation outside the project area and therefore, outside of their jurisdiction). This would have had a significant effect on reducing the number of voters in their jurisdiction. Hence, it was decided that these households would be relocated to sites within the reclaimed land area of SRFDCL.

The inauguration of the project in 2003 at the hands of the chief minister caused significant concern among the project-affected households in the informal settlements. As a result, they initiated a series of discussions with officials at the city and state departments. Failing to find any convincing answers to their queries, they decided to take legal recourse by filing a public interest litigation against the state and the project. This legislation, filed in mid-2005, made a thorough and detailed plea regarding adequate and just resettlement. They argued that the new location should be in proximity to their existing place of livelihood. The court placed a pause on any eviction until a full relocation and rehabilitation plan was placed in front of the court. However, the court was silent on the timeline for submitting this plan and on the location of such resettlement sites (Desai 2014).

The AMC submitted a final relocation and rehabilitation plan in 2008. It identified more than 8,000 households in the Socioeconomic Survey of 2002 as directly affected and another 4,000 as partially affected by the relocation. By this time, the national government had initiated a scheme to provide a national housing subsidy to people below the poverty line or those in economically weaker sections.[8] Through this scheme, the AMC proposed that the project-affected households be relocated to municipal-owned land far from the riverfront. This allowed the burden of one of the significant components of the relocation cost—land for the resettlement units—to be taken off the SRFDCL and be borne by the AMC through its existing land bank.

The bulk of the resettlement of the project-affected households was carried out according to the relocation and rehabilitation plan under the supervision of a committee established by the High Court. Although this ensured that a majority of the relocation was implemented properly, certain households were not provided with relocation housing and, as a result, have been adversely affected by the riverfront project. As the relocation process moved forward, this process became politicized. The committee was besieged by claims from various fronts that some households from the riverfront area had not been included in this list. There was a threat that the list was going to keep expanding and that there would be no end to the relocation process. Subsequently, the High Court decided to clamp down on such additional claims and referred them to be substantiated. However, the committee then stopped processing further claims.

As many of the relocation sites were farther from the original location of the informal settlements along the riverfront, many families found it difficult to become acclimated to their new environment after their move (Spodek, Bass, and Munas 2013). However, the same families, over a two-year period, have now settled into their new surroundings and seem to be satisfied with the current situation.[9] This situation was especially harder for the segment of the relocated population who were settled farther from the city center and jobs. Another segment of the informal settlements were relocated much closer to the city center.

After significant criticism from the media throughout the process of relocation, the AMC has now engaged NGOs to work with resettled families to help support local community organizations and day-to-day management of their new surroundings. NGOs were not engaged during the actual relocation process. However, their engagement now has helped improve satisfaction of residents in their new surroundings.[10]

Land

One of the critical issues involved in the successful implementation of this project was the approach to land. This was clearly understood by the project champions and planners. Early on, the project planners discarded the use of land acquisition as a means to appropriate the land necessary for redevelopment of the riverfront. However, to streamline and organize the boundaries of private lands adjacent to the riverfront development, some land panels would have to be realigned. For this, an accurate map was needed, and to arrive at this, the project team decided to use a method similar to *melavni*.

Melavni—which means "to match" in the local language—is a part of the process of town planning schemes by which the records of land ownership are reconciled between paper records and the actual on-the-ground ownership of land (Ballaney 2008). The first step of this process is to prepare an accurate and detailed survey of the area. Simultaneously, paper records of land holding are digitized. The two are overlaid against one another and against the proposed plan for the area. This overlay plan helps clarify the differences between the three and helps identify the owners' rights for compensation.

Through this melavni-like process, the project arrived at a final overlay plan. Using the plan, it became clear whether a particular land parcel adjacent to the riverfront land was affected by the riverfront development. Such land parcels were those whose area was reduced by the new plan. The project team met with individual landowners of those parcels and arrived at a negotiated agreement regarding compensation, if any.

All affected landowners were offered two options for compensation. First, they were offered development rights of the lost area of land that could be used on the remaining land area. Second, if they did not want to be compensated with development rights, cash compensation was offered. Most of the affected landowners chose to be compensated with development rights, as the value of these development rights would appreciate significantly over time, whereas the value of the cash compensation would diminish over time.

Outreach

The earliest outreach and consensus-building efforts began during the preparation of the design of the riverfront plan and soon thereafter. At the time, the plan was a framework for implementing redevelopment of the Sabarmati Riverfront through a self-financed model. The political and technical leaders of the project wanted the project to be endorsed by senior leaders from their respective parties. The project was presented to the chief minister and to all Ahmedabad region members of the legislative assembly. A number of presentations were also made to various NGOs in the city. The private development managers, EPC, led this entire initial outreach and consensus-building effort.

Various government departments had key roles in the implementation of the project. The revenue department controlled the riverbed land to be reclaimed by the project, which needed to be transferred to the AMC for the project to move forward. The urban development department needed to amend the city's development and building regulations at the appropriate time based on the recommendations of the proposal. The Gujarat Infrastructure Development Board was an important stakeholder as SRFDCL was seeking seed funding to undertake critical technical studies to improve the details of the proposal. The irrigation department was responsible for approval of all river hydraulics and related studies. A design workshop, anchored by the development managers of EPC, was also organized in 2000 to engage with Ahmedabad's community of architects and planners.

In late 2009, the chief minister again emphasized the significance of the project in stimulating revitalization of the city. As a result, a series of presentations depicting plans for integration of 18 precincts delineated along the riverfront were prepared. The project team then conducted a number of focus group discussions to identify key development issues and opportunities in each precinct.

In early 2010, the project had garnered significant negative publicity. Many newspaper articles suggested that the project was designed to generate substantial financial profits for large developers at the cost of taxpayer money to be spent on infrastructure. To rectify this false impression and to understand the origins of this public perception, the project team conducted informal surveys through conversations with residents from diverse backgrounds across the city, including with many of the NGOs that were involved in working with the informal settlements near the river.[11]

In addition, later that year, the private firm that served as project planners prepared an exhibition of large size renderings of the riverfront development (Patel 2013). These renderings depicted a vision of the life on the riverfront in the form of large and engrossing life-size images. The purpose was to counter the perception that the project was elitist, benefiting only a small section of the society. This exhibition was successful in making the point that the project was a multi dimensional city revitalization project, including benefits for every part of the society (photograph 7.2).

Institutional Structure

From the outset, the SRFDCL was conceived as a development company with a mandate to plan and implement the Sabarmati Riverfront development project. The concept plan prepared by SRFDCL would need to be approved by the state government. The AMC would simultaneously ask the state government to transfer the ownership of the riverbed land to the AMC. Subsequently, the AMC would make an agreement with the SRFDCL to reclaim and develop all land in return for 20 percent of the reclaimed land. This land would then be transferred (after public auction) to its final purchasers at the request of the SRFDCL, thus saving on multiple transactions and associated taxes while remunerating SRFDCL adequately for its costs.

There were many reasons for such an arrangement. First, the SRFDCL would be able to use the agreement and the pledged land as collateral to borrow funds commercially as needed. Second, by keeping the land under the ownership of the AMC, the SRFDCL was prohibited from becoming an asset-rich company. At the time, it was also understood that once the project was implemented and completed, the company would be dismantled and the AMC would take ownership of all public areas and maintenance responsibilities.

Photograph 7.2 **Exhibition of riverfront renderings in 2010**

Source: HCP Design Planning and Management 2010.

The board and project leaders were continually concerned about the scope and risks of the SRFDCL. If the SRFDCL were to develop the land for sale and then sell the developed property, there would be huge associated commercial risks. This would also paint a different image of the SRFDCL as a profit-oriented real estate developer rather than a nonprofit developer of large environment improvement projects.[12] Hence, this alternative was never proposed. Instead, it was agreed that the SRFDCL would sell the land marked for commercial and residential developments and act as master planner and regulator (Patel and Kansal 2011). In accordance with the Gujarat Town Planning and Urban Development Act, the SRFDCL has been named as the planning authority for development of the area under its control.

As a special planning authority, the SRFDCL is responsible for preparing development plans and regulations for the entire riverfront area. This responsibility was also recognized in the Revised Development Plan of Ahmedabad prepared in 1999 (and approved by the state in 2002), and a clause was included to this effect.[13] Subsequently, during its revision of the development plan, the AUDA has recognized the redevelopment potential of areas around the riverfront. It has identified an area for intensified development on both banks adjacent to the riverfront development. Development guidelines for these areas are currently being prepared by AUDA. Specifically, these plans are being prepared by the joint urban planning unit,[14] comprising staff members from AUDA and AMC, rather than being undertaken by SRFDCL because these areas do not fall under its jurisdiction.

Although there is adequate overlap and oversight by AMC on SRFDCL's board, the agreement to be prepared by AMC charging SRFDCL with the specific mandate of developing the riverfront has not yet been implemented. There are many unclear areas in ongoing maintenance and long-term sustainability of the project. These issues are currently under discussion and will likely be resolved soon.

Leveraging Land for Financing the Development

At the time of the concept plan and feasibility study, the cost of the project was estimated to be Rs 361 crores (US$60 million). It was estimated that sale of 20 percent of the total reclaimed land would generate Rs 458 crores (US$76 million)—enough to cover the cost of all capital improvements, resettlement, organization, and interest on loans.

After the preparation of the feasibility study, the Gujarat Infrastructure Development Board was approached for a small Rs 1.31 crores (US$218,000) project development loan. These funds were used for engaging a financial consulting firm to prepare a detailed and convincing project financing strategy (see box 7.3).

With the help of this strategy, a number of commercial financial institutions were approached for loans. However, because of the changed political and financial scenario and AMC having access to

Box 7.3   Financial feasibility plan

Based on the concept plan, in 2000, the SRFDCL hired a consultant to prepare a financial feasibility plan and help identify and act as a liaison with large financiers to provide loans for the project. For the most part, the report confirmed the basic premise of the project as self-financed through the sale of a portion of the land, including a detailed time line for recovery of costs over 10 years (as opposed to the five years originally mentioned in the concept plan).

Major cost components included land development costs, contingency costs, and preliminary/ preoperative expenses. Revenue components included the sale of a portion of the reclaimed land, advertising income, tolls on portions of the roads, and increases in property tax.

The report outlined implementation of project construction in four phases beginning in 2000 and ending in 2006. Revenues were projected to start from the year 2003, and the sale of high-value commercial development plots was placed in the last phase. The cost increase was anticipated at a conservative 7 percent a year (at the time, average 10-year inflation was at 9.6 percent), and an increase of 5 percent a year was estimated on revenues.[a] The entire project was to be completed by the year 2008–09. The projected internal rate of return was 17.23 percent. Whereas the report served as a high-level strategy direction, many of the specifics of the report deviated from the actual course of project development.

Along with preparation of the report, the consultants were also charged with initiating and facilitating talks with large financiers for funding the project development. However, at the time, private financiers were skeptical of such large projects due to the significant support and buy-in required from the government for their implementation. Hence, it was found that the interest rates demanded by them were significantly higher than prevailing market rates.

Eventually, by the time project construction took off (in the mid-2000s), the majority of the board members were not so keen on soliciting private financing. One of the board members initiated talks with HUDCO. Eventually, HUDCO provided the financing for the project after placing AMC-owned land parcels as collateral.

a. Though the report mentions detailed estimates on property values worked out by Ayojan engineers and valuers as annexes to the report, these details were not available with the report.

additional funds, it issued loans for commencing pilot project construction. In 2004, before larger stretches of construction began, HUDCO, a central government financial institution, was also approached for a loan. As collateral toward the loan, existing serviced land under ownership of AMC was pledged to HUDCO (see map 7.3). This was a rather expedient arrangement. This reduced the financing risk because collateral land was not affected by the timeliness or success of the riverfront project. Had the collateral been the actual riverfront land, whose existence and value depended on the timeliness and success of the project, there might have been a greater collective push to complete the various stages of the project more expeditiously.

SRFDLL obtained a loan of Rs 417 crores (US$69 million) from HUDCO against a total expense of Rs 1,103 crores (US$184 million). A total amount of Rs 900 crores (US$150 million) has already been approved.

Apart from the HUDCO loan, AMC has also been granting loans to the project on an ongoing basis. To date, the amount loaned by AMC to the

Map 7.3   **Land placed as collateral against the HUDCO loan**

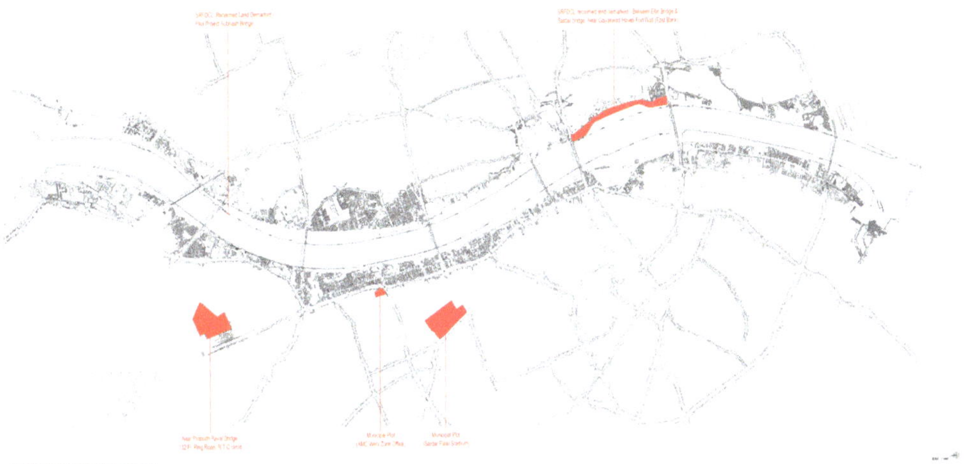

Locations_Mortgage of Properties with HUDCO

Source: HCP Design Planning and Management 2014.

project totals Rs 445 crores (US$74 million). The remaining sources of funds, approximately Rs 240 crores (US$40 million), have been in share capital sold by the SRFDCL. As a wholly owned subsidiary, the shares are under the ownership of AMC. Table 7.1 summarizes the sources and uses of funds for SRFDCL. Figure 7.2 shows a diagrammatic representation of these arrangements.

Some Rs 219 crores (US$36 million), or approximately a fifth of the total expenses of Rs 1,103 (US$184 million) crores has been spent so far toward interest on loans. Resettlement costs have been minimal at Rs 6 crores (US$1 million). However, this is primarily because of the availability of the nationally funded housing program of Jawaharlal Nehru Urban Renewal Mission, which subsidized the entire construction of the resettlement housing.[15] Without this, the resettlement costs would have been substantially higher. Apart from this, Rs 8 crores (US$1.3 million) have been placed as fixed deposits.[16]

In overall capital revenue, the main source of income identified was the sale of land of up to 29 ha or 14.5 percent of the total reclaimed area. The sale was expected to generate significant revenue for SRFDCL. Current estimates by the Sabarmati Riverfront development team show that the sale of this land, with its prime location in the center of the city, could yield an amount that adequately covers the current estimates of the total costs with a small buffer. However, it is notable that some of the large public amenity projects (such as the convention and exhibition center, the city museum, and the recently announced Ferris wheel project by AMC) yet to be completed,[17] there are apprehensions in some quarters that the land sale may not adequately cover the construction of these large projects. However, these fears are unsubstantiated and there is no evidence either way.

Table 7.1   **Uses and sources of funds for SRFDCL**

Uses of funds (Rs)		Sources of funds (Rs)	
Development cost	870 cr	Loan from HUDCO	417 cr
Interest cost	219 cr	Loan from AMC	445 cr
Relocation and rehabilitation	6 cr	Share capital (equity and preference shares)	240 cr
Fixed deposits and balance	8 cr	Credit reserve ratio	1 cr
Total	1,103 cr	Total	1,103 cr

Source: SRFDCL 2014.
Note: AMC = Ahmedabad Municipal Corporation; HUDCO = Housing and Urban Development Corporation; N/A = not applicable.

Figure 7.2   **Land collateral and development rights**

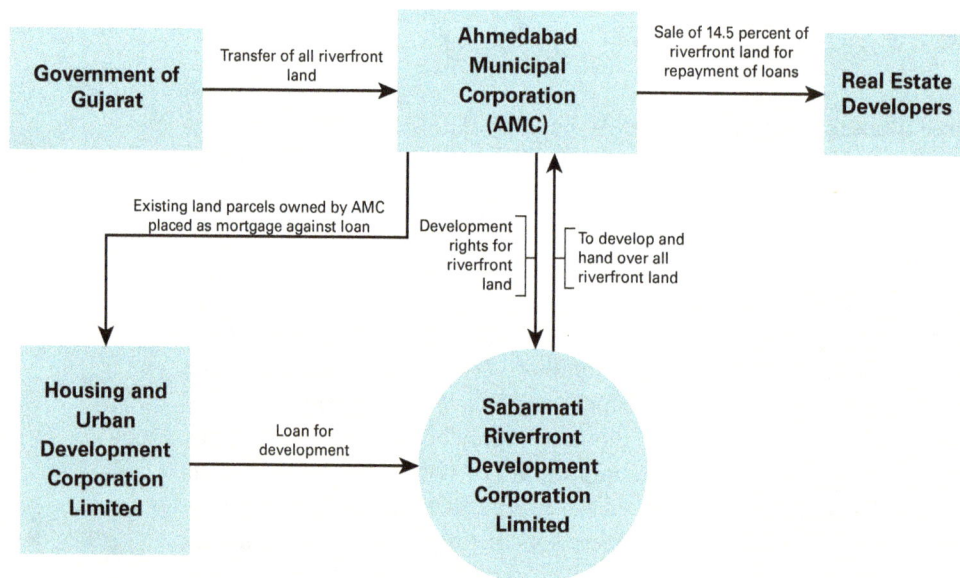

Source: Patel 2013.

In the meantime, the SRFDCL team is also simultaneously exploring other alternatives, such as public-private partnerships specifically for these large projects. The project team is also currently developing the ideas related to ongoing maintenance and upkeep of all public areas and regulating mechanisms for development on the land for sale.[18]

Apart from capital revenues, a number of avenues of operating revenues have been identified during the course of the project. One such avenue is to charge user fees for accessing parks and gardens. This was first used at the Kankaria Lake Park for a fee of Rs 10 (US$0.16) per person. The revenue raised was used to maintain the parks and create better amenities for the users. A similar approach is being used for the two riverfront parks currently open to public. There are also concession agreements for food and other stalls, which contribute to the operating revenues. Lease revenue is also realized from the lease of currently undeveloped grounds on the riverfront, which are being used for citywide events such as the kite festival, the flower festival, the Sabarmati Marathon, and so on. All of these are being reviewed as part of an overall strategy for ongoing upkeep and maintenance for the SRFDCL. Photograph 7.3 shows some of the parks and amenities in the redeveloped waterfront.

Outcomes and Impacts

As of June 2014, 85 percent of the entire stretch of the Sabarmati Riverfront project has been completed. This includes the entire stretch of the lower promenade, the majority of the interceptor sewer lines on both banks and the pumping stations, as well as the majority of the fill portions of land. Sections of the upper promenade are being sequentially completed. The north-south street along the riverfront is mostly completed on the west side, but large sections remain to be completed on the east side. Two public parks have been completed and are opened for public use. The informal market near the east end of the Ellis Bridge has been opened for public use, as is the Dhobi Ghat. In addition, the relocation of all project-affected households has been completed, albeit to varying degrees of success. The planning for redevelopment of adjacent areas has also been initiated through a development plan prepared by AUDA.

There are also many pieces of the project that have yet to be completed. The sale of land parcels, which will pay for this project, has been delayed. There are various factors responsible for the delay. However, the primary reason concerns the calendar of state and national elections, which have preoccupied the government in the last two years. The sale of land will be undertaken after completion of all works in order to maximize the value realized through the sale.

A number of large citywide amenities planned or considered, such as the convention center, city museum, and so on have not yet been implemented. Whether these will be implemented through additional loans from AMC, HUDCO, other lenders, or development partners, remains to be seen.

The strategy for ongoing maintenance and operations of the public areas of SRFDCL is still under discussion. Two main options are being discussed. First, the company would be dissolved and the area under the jurisdiction of the company would then be merged with the AMC for future maintenance. Second, the company would continue to maintain the existing area under its jurisdiction. However, these ideas are at a preliminary stage and await a final decision.

Finally, planning for areas surrounding the riverfront project is currently under way in two sections: North Central Business District (CBD) on the eastern bank and the main CBD on the western bank along Ashram Road. Remaining areas need to undertake similar planning exercises to fully integrate with the riverfront development and benefit from its proximity and access.

Photograph 7.3   **Views of the waterfront park along the Sabarmati Riverfront**

a. Lower Promenade

b. Riverfront Park, Shahibaug

c. Riverfront Park, Shahibaug

d. Riverfront Market

source: 7.3a. Dinesh Mehta for HCP Design Planning and Management 2014
7.3b. Chirayu Bhatt, 2014
7.3c. Niki Shah for HCP Design Planning and Management 2014
7.3d. Dinesh Mehta for HCP Design Planning and Management 2014

Lessons Learned

A number of key lessons emerge from the planning and implementation of the Sabarmati Riverfront development project:

- *The existence of a strong, diverse and vocal board of directors.* One of the key lessons of the project has been the importance of having a strong and diverse board of directors. Proponents of the project clearly understood the importance of having a diverse board that represented not only a variety of interests, but also, more significantly, a variety of specific experience and skill sets that helped steer the project effectively during the critical period of its development.

- *The importance of portraying the project as a civic improvement project rather than a partisan political project.* This was evident in the presence of both the ruling and opposition parties on the board of the SRFDCL. Without the presence of the opposition party on the board, the project could have been viewed as a party agenda rather than a civic project. Having the opposition party involved in the project from the beginning meant that they had a stake in the project. Thus, they were able to support this project even when political power changed hands during an interim period. Many other projects of this kind have failed at this level because the ruling party chose not to involve the opposition, and the project stalled after the political tide turned against them.

- *The decision to take external managerial support along with other technical and professional inputs.* Over the years, many cities accepted technical support from external consultants. However, one of the differentiating factors of this project was that the SRFDCL chose to take external managerial support from a consultant in the very early stages of the project. The early stages of the project can be highly challenging as there is very little tangible outcome while the land is being transferred or the implementation and financing strategy is being worked out. Moreover, at this early stage there are very high risks that threaten the project implementation. Therefore, it is not always feasible to expect an internal managerial team to rally behind a project whose future is uncertain. This important decision helped in using external managerial support, which in turn helped them stay focused in the early stages of uncertainty (Patel 2013). The SRFDCL now relies on a set of internal management expertise that was possible because of the early groundwork laid by professional management consultants.
- *The importance of an experienced and able city resource team.* It is no coincidence that this project is based in Ahmedabad. For a long time, Ahmedabad has had a unique tradition of strong civic-minded leadership from the private sector that would help support the development of the city. Along with this tradition, the city has benefited from a number of reforms and capacity enhancement leading up to this project. In the 1990s, for example, the United States Agency for International Development played a role in reforming municipal finance through its FIRE-D project. The city issued its first set of public bonds, which was very successful. Subsequently, the implementation of the C G Road redevelopment as a completely self-financed project helped bolster the city's confidence in being able to consider and successfully deliver large-scale upgrading projects. Hence, the success of the riverfront project stands on the shoulder of many small and incremental improvements over a long period of time in Ahmedabad. Thus, the city had prepared itself over time to be able to undertake such a large and relatively risky project.

Along with these lessons that contributed to the successful implementation of the project, there are a few aspects of the project that could have been improved:

- *The communication with the public and other stakeholders could have been improved.* The communication strategy for the project has been a challenge since the very beginning. Despite the strong reputation of the municipal government, most officers and political leaders have been wary of engaging with the public. This is true even today. This stems from a general distrust of the public, including a distrust of NGOs, who champion their cause. Over the course of the project, project planners have attempted to improve communication and consensus building. However, this is one area that could be improved if there is adequate political support.

- *The process of relocation of project-affected people could have been more equitable.* There were a number of challenges with the way the process of relocation was conducted. Funding from the Jawaharlal Nehru Urban Renewal Mission made the relocation possible. Certain sections of the board were wary of rehousing the project-affected households from the informal settlements within the riverfront land—citing impact to the neighboring development as one of the issues. Whereas relocating the households to wherever vacant land was available had a lower cost and ensured a publicly available waterfront for the people of Ahmedabad, it led to some resistance from the occupants who were being moved. The company also did not engage in high quality verification of previous surveys until the issue of relocation had become very prominent, and the relocation process went to the High Court for supervision. There is significant potential to improve this process through the sharing of information in a timely and transparent manner, acknowledging the rights of informal settlements, and providing just compensation. Early and consistent engagement of NGOs to facilitate the process of relocation would have also helped improve the process.
- *Implementation during the later stages suffered because of political election timetables.* More recently, the implementation has slowed down and decision making has become difficult. Partially, this is due to the fact that the state government has been deeply engaged in preparation for state and national elections over the past two years. Also, changes in the board of directors based on the state government's decisions have affected the decision-making process. Keeping the decision-making process of the SRFDCL board local in nature may have prevented such a significant effect.

The project has since become a model for the development mantra, popularly known as 'the Gujarat Model of Development."

Notes

1. The first local government in Ahmedabad was the Municipal Commission established by Act XXVI of the Bombay presidency. This was a continuation of the earlier Town Hall Committee, established in 1831 (Gillion 1968).

2. On reading the BPMC Act, it may seem that the true power is in the hands of the elected representatives. The reality of most Indian cities including Ahmedabad is that the commissioner is quite powerful. The commissioner acts as representative of the state government. In the actual functioning of the AMC, the commissioner has a disproportionately higher importance vis-à-vis the elected representative because of the dependence of the municipal corporation on the state government for finances, as well as a number of statutory procedures to be followed in the day-to-day functioning of the corporation, which are controlled by the state.

3. *Octroi* means a levy on the entry of goods into the limits of a city for consumption, use, or sale therein (BPMCA 1949).

4. The feasibility study estimated approximately 10,000 families to be living in informal settlements along the riverfront.

5. Although there were some indications that Kohn's proposal included a mechanism to implement and finance the development of the Sabarmati Riverfront, there has been no evidence to support this. It could have been one of the reasons for the poor response to the proposal.

6. The proposal and concept plan for the riverfront included a vision for development that would provide for a memorable image and identity of the city. SRFDCL would eventually prepare development guidelines within the development boundary that would promote such an identity.

7. The key factor that caused the delay in the transfer of land concerned its valuation. Since the land in question was riverbed land, it was difficult to arrive at an appropriate valuation. The appraiser proposed the value of the land to be equivalent to the nearby developed land on the riverbank, resulting in a greatly inflated land value of the riverbed. This would have resulted in the project becoming unviable. Thus, the SRFDCL proposed to the state government that, in the public interest (since the majority of the reclaimed land parcels were to be allocated for public use), a political decision be made to transfer the land at a negligible price to the AMC. This political decision-making process took a long time.

8. As a part of Jawaharlal Nehru National Urban Renewal Mission, funding was available for construction of permanent housing for households from an economically weaker section of the society. Under this scheme, the national government would fund 50 percent of the total cost of construction, the state government would bear 20 percent of the cost, with the remaining 30 percent to be borne by the local government. In this case, the AMC chose to split this amount. It was to be borne in two parts, one to be borne by AMC and another to be borne by the beneficiary of the new housing. The beneficiary would pay a one-time deposit of Rs 17,000 (to be paid over one year in 12 equal installments) at the time of allotment of the house and an additional Rs 70,000 (US$1170) to be repaid over 10 years (Desai 2014).

9. Interview with Howard Spodek, 2014.

10. Interview with Bharati Bhonsale, 2014

11. The purpose of this survey was to better understand the causes and context of the public perception of the project. On the basis of the findings, the project team was then able to improve their communication strategy and prepare a new project brochure, which highlighted the multiple dimensions of the project (SRFDCL 2011).

12. Although SRFDCL is not a nonprofit entity in the true sense, it is a wholly owned subsidiary of the AMC. In this sense, it inherits AMC's goal of furthering public purpose rather than a goal of wealth generation, which may be valid for any other regular private sector company.

13. In the Revised Development Plan of 1999, a clause was included, which recognized that the development regulations for the sabarmati development land would be prepared by SRFDCL based on their concept and detailed plan.

14. The planning cell was initially established to prepare the Revised Development Plan 2012. However, AUDA and AMC have agreed to continue this joint urban planning unit for undertaking further planning work in a coordinated manner.

15. Considering approximately Rs 450,000 (US$7,500) per house in construction costs, including the cost of land, resettling 11,000 families would cost approximately Rs 495 crores (US$82 million) (Desai 2014).

16. Fixed deposits are term deposits placed with the bank. These are secured deposits and do not carry any risk of capital.

17. As the project has evolved and the AMC board members and leadership has changed, ideas about projects along the riverfront have also changed. Hence, there is no real complete list of projects for the riverfront development. The overall allocation of land and its uses remains as is, but new ideas for projects continue to be added and removed as the SRFDCL tries to arrive at a workable long-term self-financing plan for the maintenance and upkeep of the development.

18. Currently, maintenance of SRFDCL areas is managed by AMC through various departments, which also manage the maintenance in the neighboring precincts. These maintenance costs are currently not available as they are spread between departments.

References

AMC (Ahmedabad Municipal Corporation). 2014. *AMC Diary 2014*. www.egovamc.com/corporation/AMC_DIARY.pdf.

AUDA (Ahmedabad Development Authority). 2013. *Revised Development Plan for Ahmedabad 2021*. Ahmedabad: AUDA.

Ballaney, S. 2008. *Town Planning Mechanism in Gujarat*. Washington, DC: World Bank Institute.

Bhonsale, B. 2014. Interview conducted by Chirayu Bhatt, March 5. 2014.

BPMCA (Bombay Provincial Municipal Corporation Act). 1949. (Act no LIX of 1949). https://www.suratmunicipal.gov.in/downloads/acts/bpmcact/bpmcact1.pdf. Accessed on June 23 2014.

Census of India. 2011. Primary Census Abstract Data Tables (India & States/UTs — Town/Village/Ward Level). http://censusindia.gov.in/pca /pcadata/pca.html. Accessed on June 23 2014.

Desai, R. 2014. *Municipal Politics, Court Sympathy and Housing Rights: A Post-Mortem of Displacement and Resettlement under the Sabarmati Riverfront Project, Ahmedabad.* Ahmedabad: Centre for Urban Equity, CEPT University.

EPC (Environmental Planning Collaborative). 1998. "Proposal for Sabarmati Riverfront Development". Unpublished report.

Gillion, K. 1968. *Ahmedabad: A Study in Indian Urban History.* Berkeley, CA: University of California Press.

Patel, B. 2013. Interview conducted by Chirayu Bhatt and Rana Amirtahmasebi, November 21.

Patel, B., and T. Kansal. 2011. "Bringing a City Back to Its River: Why the Sabarmati Riverfront Development Project Has Come Thus Far". Unpublished report.

Sabarmati Riverfront Development Corporation Ltd., 2014, Sabarmati Riverfront, Available at: http://www.sabarmatiriverfront.com/funding [Accessed 10 March 2016]

Spodek, H. 2011. *Ahmedabad.* Bloomington, IN: Indiana University Press.

———. Interview conducted by Chirayu Bhatt, March 29.

Spodek, H., W. Bass, and Z. Munas. 2013. *The Urban World: A Case Study of Slum Relocation.* Motion picture. Screened at CEPT University in Ahmedabad on Jan. 6 2014. http://cept.ac.in/events/the-urban-world -a-case-study-of-slum-relocation.

People Interviewed

Dr. Bimal Patel, Director, HCP

Mr. Surendra Patel, Director, SRFDCL

Dr. Guruprasad Mohapatra, Managing Director / Municipal Commissioner, SRFDCL / AMC

Mr. Thennarasan, Exececutive Director / Deputy Municipal Commissioner, SRFDCL / AMC

Dr. Vatsal Patel, Chief Town Planner, AMC

Ms. Aparna Joshi, Urban designer, HCP DPM

Mr. Jignesh Mehta, Urban planner, HCP

Mr. M S Swaminarayan, Engineer, EPC

Mr. Niki Shah, Urban designer, HCP DPM

Mr. Howard Spodek, Historian

Ms. Bharati Bhonsale, Community organizer

Ms. Nilima Rawat, Consultant

Map 8.1 **Map of Seoul, Republic of Korea**

a. Map of Seoul

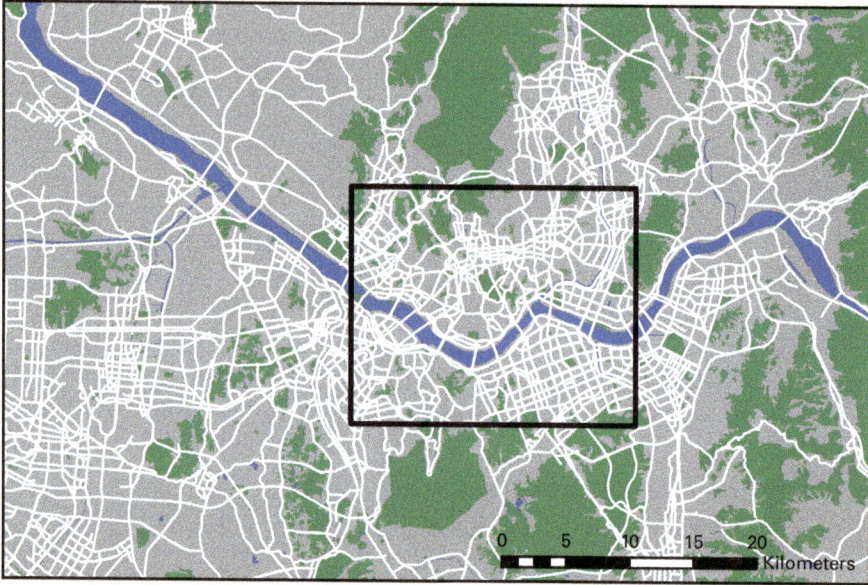

b. Three business districts in Seoul

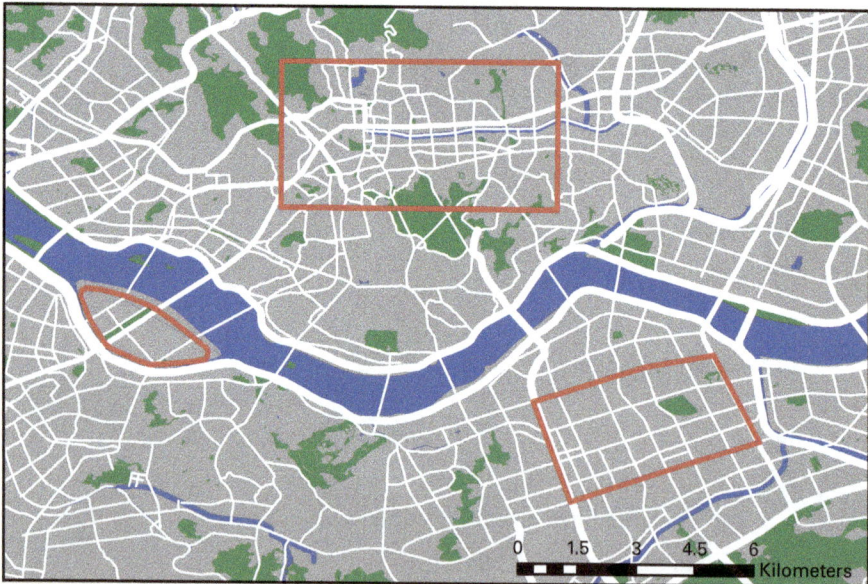

Source: World Bank based on Open Street Map data 2015.
Note: The business districts from left to right are Yeouido Business District, Central Business District, and Gangnam Business District.

CHAPTER 8

Seoul: Downtown Regeneration through Restoration of the Cheonggyecheon Stream

Introduction

The Cheonggyecheon restoration project involved revitalizing an old stream that had been covered for decades by an overpass, which included an 18-lane highway. By enhancing the urban environment, the city of Seoul used its own resources to bring new life to the downtown. In doing so, the Seoul government triggered regeneration in three main areas in downtown Seoul. (map 8.1 shows project areas.) The restoration of the Cheonggyecheon was a means to an end. It was a key project that led to the revitalization of central Seoul. The project significantly benefited from an unleashing of Cheonggyecheon's potential as a green public space. Leveraging such historical and environmental values was critical in creating a new future for the heart of Seoul.

The Cheoggyecheon restoration project was a catalyst for the broader regeneration of Seoul's inner city areas. The project was regarded as an opportunity to develop a new framework for the regeneration of the inner city, prompting the establishment of a Downtown Development Plan (2004), a Seoul Master Plan 2020 (2004), and an Urban Renaissance Master Plan (2007). It also gave momentum to Seoul's public transportation reform. Today, the story of Cheonggyecheon can serve as a model for other global cities.

At the beginning of the twenty-first century, regenerating the heart of Seoul was seen as a crucial step for transforming Seoul into a sustainable, livable, and global city. Restoring the Cheonggyecheon and offering access to its underexploited cultural and environmental values was therefore a necessary step.

In the 1960s, the Cheonggyecheon stream had already gone beyond its capacity to accommodate all the needs of Seoul's 2.4 million population. It had also become seriously polluted and prone to flooding as well.

However, with the current population swelling now to 10 million—and with increased climate challenges—simply restoring Seoul's industrial past was no longer relevant. Cheonggyecheon had to be transformed to fit into Seoul's newly envisioned future. "The new Cheonggyecheon was not just restored. It was recreated" (Rowe 2010).

Context and Background

The decline of the old downtown area of Seoul had been a persistent problem over the years manifesting itself in persistent population decline. In the two decades from 1975 to 1995, Seoul's population increased by 44 percent, from 6.88 to 9.89 million residents. However, during the same time period, the population in the downtown[1] area decreased by 52 percent from some 620,000 to 300,000 residents. This decline was also evident with respect to construction and real estate development. The total floor area of Jung-gu, the borough containing the Cheonggyecheon Stream, changed little. In fact, the area declined slightly from 790 to 787 hectares (ha) between 1985 and 1995, whereas in Seoul, it increased by 81.5 percent from 13,747 to 24,946 (ha).

Regarding the socioeconomic and demographic status of residents, the proportion of households with an education level lower than middle school in the downtown area was 40 percent, compared to 25 percent in the city of Seoul. Substandard housing types (mostly rentals or squatters) accounted for 35 percent of downtown housing—2.5 times the average of Seoul. In this regard, about 48 percent of people moving out of the downtown area were young people in their 20s or 30s (Yang 2001; Lee and Jun 2002).

The number of businesses and workers in downtown Seoul significantly decreased during the 1990s. For instance, the number of enterprises in the downtown area declined by 24.1 percent from 1991 to 2000. By contrast, in the city of Seoul, the number of enterprises actually increased by 24.6 percent. The number of downtown businesses as a share of the overall number of businesses in Seoul also declined to 10.8 percent from 1991 to 2000. An attendant decrease in the number of downtown workers was also observed (Seoul Metropolitan Government 2006a).

Historically, the city government's efforts to regenerate the downtown area came to naught because of the small-scale nature of the initiatives. Previous regeneration strategies were limited to improving dilapidated individual houses and enlarging plot size. Other efforts were made to widen roads and improve infrastructure in the old downtown blocks with small plots[2] and poor traffic conditions. Subsequent downtown redevelopment projects extensively promoted in the 1980s aimed to transform the downtown area into a central business district. The approach was to raze older buildings and start anew.[3]

Since the 1990s, the municipality tried in vain to promote residential redevelopment and transit-oriented development to counteract the decline of the downtown area. It also made substantial efforts to sustain economic vitality and conserve the historical environment of downtown through a new Seoul Downtown Management Master Plan in 2000. However, the scope was restricted to improving buildings and facilities within a few blocks.

Phase 1: Scoping

There were some unique and difficult challenges in regenerating the downtown area of Seoul. Among the most significant was an 18-lane elevated highway that stood over the Cheonggyecheon Stream. Since removal of this massive highway did not seem feasible, most plans did not have any real impact on the area. It was not until the early 2000s that plans to restore the stream finally emerged.[4] Earlier plans such as the 1997 Seoul Urban Master Plan 2011, did not include Cheonggyecheon restoration. Likewise, the Master Plan for Seoul's Downtown Redevelopment published in 2001 focused on improvement of small lots, minor streets, and dilapidated buildings and facilities within a few blocks. Again, though, it did not include the Cheonggyecheon Stream area.[5]

The restoration idea was not included in the official urban planning documents because the idea was seen as too ambitious or beyond the imagination or capacity of the local government. Furthermore, since Cheonggyecheon was located in the center of an old downtown filled with business activities, the area suffered from chronic, massive traffic volumes and high levels of congestion. Seoul's key sewage and drainage facility for flood prevention[6] was also located under the stream. The upper part of the stream housed the elevated highway, with traffic volume exceeding some 170,000 vehicles per day. In the event of rainfall, rainwater was discharged through the Cheonggyecheon to the Han River.

Restoring Cheonggyecheon would have been of great value, as it would have conserved the natural environment, enhanced the urban environment, and catalyzed development in downtown Seoul. However, as noted, this would have required eliminating a total of 18 traffic lanes in the downtown area and could have caused unprecedented damage to Seoul's overall traffic flow. Further, the restoration imposed technical challenges, such as sewage treatment and flood preparation difficulties. Furthermore, it could have caused substantial disturbance to business activities in the neighborhood: "At the time, people thought of the idea of restoring Cheonggyecheon as just a hollow dream" (Seoul Metropolitan Government 2006a).

Discussions regarding the restoration—including plans for the elevated highway—suddenly reemerged as the mayoral candidate, Myungbak Lee, established as his major campaign pledge the Cheonggyecheon restoration and downtown regeneration.[7] At the time, the safety issue of covering the elevated highway was raised, and the city's plan to demolish and reconstruct the elevated highway was announced. The safety of the Cheonggye highway had been an issue of concern since the 1990s. An in-depth investigation was conducted by the Korean Society of Civil Engineers in 1991–92. They found corrosion in the highway's steel frame construction, as well as structural flaws in its upper plate. Thorough repair work was then conducted for a two-kilometer sector of the upper stream. At this point, it was evident that the 30-year-old road covering the Cheonggyecheon would cost substantial sums of money just for normal, continuing maintenance and repair work.[8]

Another in-depth safety check was conducted in 2000–2001 and revealed that cracks and exfoliation persisted in the upper slab. In addition, the load-carrying capacity was insufficient to handle traffic because of worn-out concrete beams. As a result, a full-scale reconstruction was inevitable.

The reconstruction issue became bound up in politics in the early 2000s. In 2001, the city government of Seoul announced plans to demolish and reconstruct the elevated highway, beginning in August 2002. It was estimated to cost ₩93 billion (US$78.2 million equivalent) over three years (Seoul Metropolitan Government 2006a). However, the debate about restoration versus reconstruction was vigorously pursued during the mayoral election scheduled for June 2002, a few months before the reconstruction start of the Cheonggye highway. In this context, the Cheonggyecheon restoration project had an inextricable connection with the mayoral election and politics because the two strongest mayoral candidates had differing views about it. Hence, politics played a major role in seeing the revitalization of Cheonggyecheon come to fruition. Indeed, had the opposing candidate been elected, the project would have not been realized.

The successful mayoral candidate believed that the Cheonggyecheon restoration project was sensible given that the elevated highway was old, unsafe, and in need of major repairs. He also believed that the restoration would help with revitalizing the declining downtown area and economy. The mayoral candidate announced that the city would invest ₩360 billion (US$302.8 million) to revitalize the stream with clean water flow. It would also demolish six lanes of roads, including three lanes on each side of the stream. As a countermeasure, traffic would be detoured and two or three roads would be secured along each shopping district. This plan made sense as the highway repair alone would cost ₩100 billion (US$84.1 million), without any added value. Restoration of the stream was expected to attract private investment totaling ₩11 trillion (US$9.2 billion), resulting in an added value of ₩30 trillion (US$25.2 billion) (Seoul Metropolitan Government 2006a).

The opposing mayoral candidate believed that demolishing the elevated highway would result in extreme traffic disturbance and congestion—and would result in an additional cost of ₩530 billion (US$446 million)[9] each year. He believed that funds must instead be spent on more urgent items, such as education. He also expressed concerns that if the new transportation plan was not carefully developed, the arterial roads connecting downtown from east to west would experience unmanageable traffic. Another concern was the objection of the neighboring merchants and commercial property owners regarding business interruptions that would adversely impact them for years during the construction process (Seoul Metropolitan Government 2006a).

Phase 2: Planning

The Cheonggyecheon restoration project was initiated on July 1, 2002, as the new mayor took office. Upon inauguration, the Cheonggyecheon Restoration Headquarters, the Cheonggyecheon Research Group, and the Cheonggyecheon Citizens' Committee were established to handle research activities related to the restoration. They were also to work together to develop basic plans and establish an organizational structure to jumpstart the process.

With the restoration gaining momentum, the Downtown Development Plan was announced in June 2003. The plan's stated aim was the systematic reorganization of the Cheonggyecheon neighborhood and the long-term development of the downtown area. The plan also included (a) strategies for downtown development, (b) urban plans for the Cheonggyecheon neighborhood and other major target areas, and (c) the revitalization of downtown industries. In short, it was the Cheonggyecheon restoration that led to broader urban regeneration efforts to create the new downtown Seoul.

The initial period for developing the restoration plan was estimated at 10 months. However, it actually took two years to plan and build a social consensus. It was done using an institution called the Cheonggyecheon Revival Academy, which was established in the early 2000s. As noted, there were also extensive public discussions about the project that helped to inform public opinion during the mayoral election. Table 8.1 outlines through a series of newspaper article titles the restoration issues that were considered and publicly discussed. Citizens were exposed to major issues such as the direction of development, potential economic impact, traffic congestion concerns, the environment and ecology, water supply, neighborhood development, historic preservation, and the like. The political electoral process enabled active communication and social consensus formation between the government and its citizens, as well as among the citizenry.

Along with the downtown development plan, the master plan for the Choenggyecheon restoration was completed in 2004. The master plan included specific measures to restore the Cheonggyecheon's natural environment and create a more human-oriented public space. Specifically, it included plans to restore and landscape the stream, secure water resources, treat sewage, handle traffic, construct bridges, restore historical assets, and manage social conflicts.

What distinguishes the case of Cheonggyecheon from other case studies in this volume is the fast moving process and that the planning and construction phases overlapped. The construction work started on

Table 8.1   Newspaper articles: Bringing new life back to Cheonggyecheon, 2002

Date	Newspaper article
April 4	"Restoration Discussion on Track: Remove the Scourge of Development and Help Nature Breathe"
April 23	"Restoration Costs and Economic Effects: 360~640 Billion Won Is Required, Excluding the Canal"
April 30	"What Happens to the Traffic Flow: The Restoration's Effect on Transportation Will Not Be Serious"
May 7	"How Will the Environment and the Ecological System Change?"
May 14	"How to Supply Water and Manage Water Quality... 65 Thousand Tons a Day... with Enough Groundwater and Water from the Han River"
May 31	"Design of a Neighborhood: Low or High Density in the Cheonggyecheon Neighborhood"
June 7	"Revived Streams: Malodorous Stream Turned into Rest Area for Citizens"
June 14	Old Bridges of Cheonggyecheon: 14 Bridges 100 Years Ago, Most of Which Have Disappeared"
June 21	"Cheonggyecheon Restoration Materialized: Private and Public Joint Committee Formed and the Project on Track"
June 28	"Who Dreamed It First? Professor Heedeok Lee's Dream 11 Years Ago"
July 3	"Interview with Seoul Mayor Myungbak Lee: Eco-Friendly Restoration to Be Finished within the Term"

Sources: Seoul Metropolitan Government 2006a; *Hankyoreh Newspaper*, various issues.

July 1, 2003, six months after the process of the "Cheonggyecheon Restoration Master Plan" had started, and one year before the plan was completed. The final design was made during the construction period, which took over two years from the start date. Thus, the plan, design, and construction were done simultaneously and not linearly. The process was controversial, but it proved effective in terms of savings with regard to both time and cost. The simultaneous work was crucial in the process of negotiating with merchants and commercial property owners, as they were concerned with the potential for business disruptions and subsequent financial losses. The combination of planning, design, and construction minimized the time required for completion of the project.

The pace and low cost of the restoration project is commendable compared with other restoration or regeneration projects around the world. The projects listed in table 8.2 represent different scope and content. However, the table shows the financial efficiency of the Cheonggyecheon restoration work in comparison with some other well-known projects.

Stream Restoration Plan and Downtown Regeneration Strategy

For large-scale undertakings such as the Cheonggyecheon restoration project, both a long-term vision and a short-term action plan should be

Table 8.2 **Comparisons of similar city regeneration projects in the Republic of Korea and the United States**

Project	Time period	Scale (kilometers)	Cost (US$)	Cost per kilometer (US$)
Cheonggyecheon	2003–05	5.8 km	345 million	59 million
High Line, New York City (sections 1 and 2)	2003–present	1.6 km	152 million	95 million
Big Dig, Boston, Massachusetts	1982–2007	12 km	22 billion	1.8 billion
Sanjicheon, Jeju-do, Korea, Rep.	1997–2002	474 m	33 million	69 million

Source: Based on Rowe 2010.
Note: km = kilometers; m = meters.

prepared simultaneously. Urban regeneration is inevitably a long-term task because various issues including historic preservation, ecological concerns, neighborhood residents, and local businesses all have to be considered and planned for. To realize the long-term vision, short-term practical tasks first have to be defined and implemented. While the longer-term vision should establish the overall direction—with flexibility to adapt to future changes—the short-term action plan will have to be specific and feasible. With regard to restoring Cheonggyecheon, the short-term action plan had to be doable within a limited budget, as well as within the mayor's four-year term in office. With this in mind, the first phase of the project went well.

Establishing the broad direction to regenerate the downtown by restoring the stream was only the beginning of the plan. Major details had to be decided in the planning phase. There were many differing opinions about what the restored stream should look like and what it should represent (figure 8.1). Some prioritized the historical value, whereas others wanted to minimize construction-related inconveniences. Transportation and flood prevention were also important considerations, as were the practical issues of construction time and cost.

The decision processes regarding the budget, phasing of implementation, project boundary, water supply, and technical level of construction were not easy. There was also the possibility that differing opinions might push the project in different directions—or even break apart the project. This is where the project leadership played a crucial role in pushing the project forward.

Building Consensus

The most powerful opposition to the restoration concerned the issue of transportation planning, because of the removal of the highway. It was also among the toughest issues that the government had to address in the restoration effort. Since the very first stage of the project, traffic congestion was one of the primary concerns because the busiest roads in the downtown would

Figure 8.1   Differing ideas about restoration and regeneration

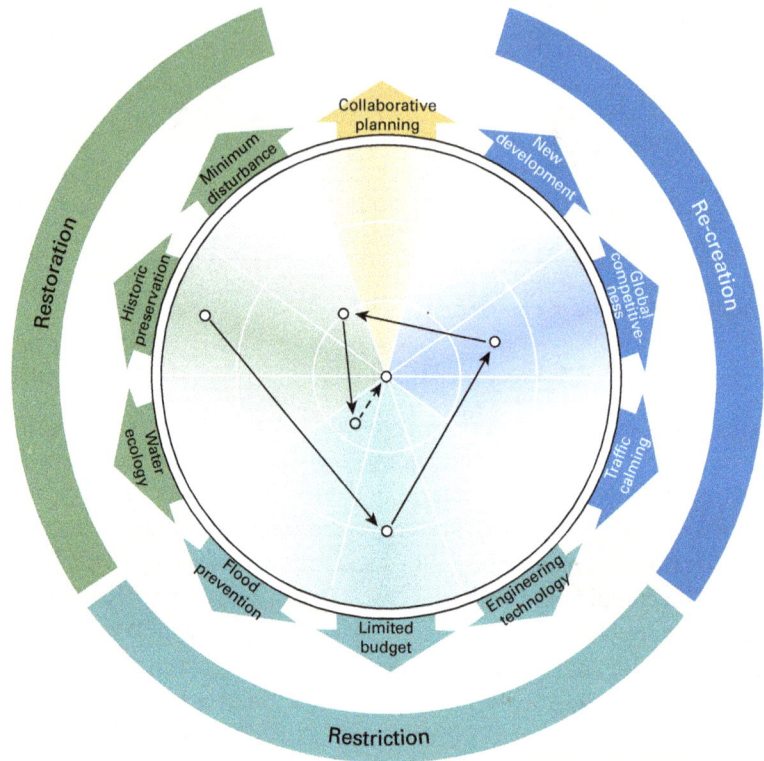

be removed. Many were concerned that eliminating the 18 traffic lanes by demolishing the elevated highway would generate serious traffic inconveniences. In response, the city government created circular-route buses, increased parking fees to discourage traffic, put a strict stop to illegal parking, and introduced reversible and one-way lanes to address such concerns. In addition, measures to promote citizen participation such as car-free days were also devised. However, these measures were insufficient and would not be the fundamental solution to the downtown transportation problem.

The city then accelerated its efforts by introducing a more comprehensive solution in the form of a mass transit–oriented system. This was achieved by increasing the capacity of buses and subways. Consequently, the restoration of Cheonggyecheon triggered a fundamental transition to a public transit system. The share of private cars in the total downtown traffic volume decreased from 21 percent (Seoul Metropolitan Government 2006a) before the restoration to 15 percent in 2007, and the share of public transport, walking, and bike-riding increased.[10]

The strongest opponents to the restoration of Cheonggyecheon were the merchants operating in the vicinity of the elevated highway. They worried about traffic congestion and the attendant negative effects, such as noise, dust, and other inconveniences that would occur during the demolition and construction.[11] Some 4,200 meetings in various forms were held between city officials and merchants. Some local merchants also protested against the project (see photograph 8.1).

The city's strategy was to adhere to the principle of no direct compensation.[12] The municipality promised to complete the construction work as soon as possible. It also established parking lots at the Dongdaemun Stadium and provided free shuttles during the construction phase to minimize inconvenience to the merchants. In addition, the city sought to attract new businesses to the downtown area. As such, it provided financial and administrative support and incentives for businesses that wanted to relocate and gave them favorable rights to move into a new commercial complex to be created in the Munjeongdong area. The city also moved the street vendors to the Dongdaemun Stadium and then to a folk market in Sinseoldong after the stadium was demolished for redevelopment.

Conserving History and Heritage

The discord over the spatial and historical aspects of urban revitalization was substantial. Some insisted that the small plots and lower-height buildings should be prioritized to preserve the small alleys and the historical values of the downtown area. Others argued that taller building construction in the larger plots should be allowed to generate a modern appearance for the downtown area and also provide more spacious public areas. This

Photograph 8.1   Demonstration by merchants against the project, 2003

Source: Seoul Metropolitan Government 2006a.

dispute is still ongoing. In fact, there are a variety of opinions about how to define the identity and design of the downtown area. Achieving a balance between preservation of the past and accommodating new land uses presented an ongoing challenge. To this end, various redevelopment strategies were applied to adapt to distinctive land use patterns and identities for each block.

The government tried to address the many concerns related to historical preservation. Indeed, the restoration of historical value was important in justifying the project and ensuring the support of the citizenry. With this recognition, the Seoul Municipality set a principle to preserve all of the heritage items excavated during the construction—but only to the extent to which citizen safety from flood and other risks could be ensured.[13] However, some members of the citizens' committee and some civic associations insisted that the stream be restored entirely to its original state. Such differences sharpened during the construction phase. As specific concerns emerged with regard to flood control, transportation and neighboring businesses, some of these considerations became incompatible with the preservation of historical remains.

One of the biggest issues of contention concerned the restoration of the Gwangtonggyo Bridge, originally built in the early Joseon Dynasty. There was a strong argument to restore it to its original shape in the original location (see map 8.2). To secure enough cross-sectional area for the water flow (into the discharge area), it was necessary to purchase private land in the vicinity. However, this was practically impossible. The city eventually decided to restore Gwangtonggyo at a spot 150 meters away from the original location toward the upstream area. The belief is that restoration at the original location will be possible in the future when better conditions can be prepared.

Map 8.2   Placement of original Gwangtonggyo Bridge and relocated bridge

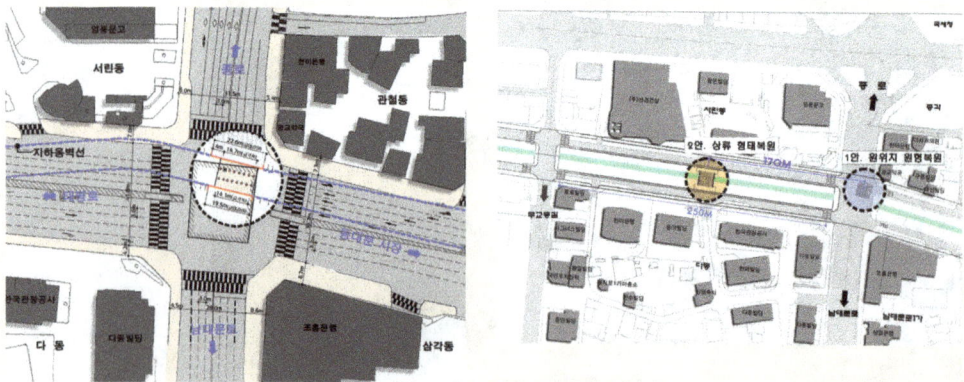

Source: Seoul Metropolitan Government 2003.

Phase 3: Financing and Implementation

The Cheonggyecheon restoration project differs from past practices in that it created a triangular implementation system composed of the citizens' committee, the project headquarters, and a research group. Each of these entities comprised government officials, experts, and citizens. This framework was designed to simultaneously promote efficient project implementation, collect public opinion, and build public relations. Figure 8.2 illustrates this triangular arrangement.

The project headquarters office served as the main implementation arm of the project. It was launched in July 2002 within the city hall to ensure efficient communication and project implementation. Initially, it consisted of three departments for managing, planning, and implementation. The organization was modified continually to adapt to the evolving stages of work.

With the objective of focusing strictly on the actual site works, the headquarters office conducted a weekly meeting hosted by the mayor to maximize efficiency and collaboration. All high-level staff attended the meeting to discuss the major planning and implementation issues. They made decisions in a speedy and determined manner. The Saturday meeting in particular contributed to resolving potential conflicts within the municipality and ensured the consistency of the work (Seoul Metropolitan Government 2006a, 106).

The Cheonggyecheon Research Group was established under the auspices of the Seoul Development Institute to support the restoration project.

Figure 8.2   **Triangular implementation system of the Cheonggyecheon restoration project**

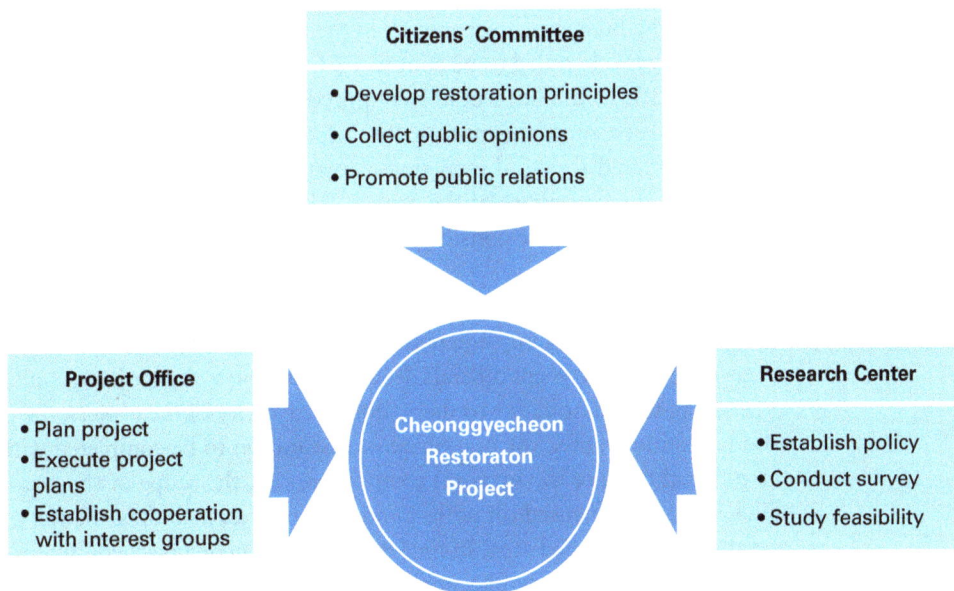

Citizens' Committee

• Develop restoration principles

• Collect public opinions

• Promote public relations

Project Office

• Plan project
• Execute project plans
• Establish cooperation with interest groups

Cheonggyecheon Restoraton Project

Research Center

• Establish policy
• Conduct survey
• Study feasibility

Its assignment was to conduct research projects related to basic data and blueprints for the Cheonggyecheon restoration. Specifically, it contributed to the project by researching issues such as transportation, land use, urban planning, the environment, and culture. It also organized a variety of seminars and meetings with experts and conducted many activities to promote the restoration through academic events, public relations, and media outlets.

Finally, the Cheonggyecheon Citizens' Committee was established to serve as an official channel to collect the opinions and concerns of the citizenry with regard to the project. Experts of the Cheonggyecheon Revival Research Group joined the committee, along with other experts and citizen representatives of various backgrounds. The committee's primary role was to set the direction of the restoration project. It was given rights to provide advice, conduct audits, and monitor the project. The committee also had legally binding rights with regard to enacting ordinances. In addition to deliberation and assessment, the committee conducted a series of hearings and briefings to garner public opinion, build a public consensus, and encourage citizens to participate in the project.

The budget and financing aspects of the project were, of course, key issues—mostly involving government decisions and public finance. The city wanted the project recognized as a public project, for which a government budget would be secured. As such, it was important to obtain the approval from the Seoul Metropolitan Council. To secure the budget of ₩384 billion (US$323 million) for the restoration, the municipality utilized the ₩100 billion (US$84.13 million) that was initially assigned for the overall renovation of the Cheonggye elevated highway. It also saved some ₩100.4 billion (US$84.47 million) by downsizing less urgent projects and introducing creative work procedures to enhance the efficiency of the city administration. The rest of the budget was secured from the city's general accounting. Since the project was scheduled to be conducted from 2003 to 2005, some ₩130 billion (US$109.3 million) would be required each year. This only amounted to about one percent of the municipality's total budget. This budget funding was appropriated to avoid incurring a financial burden, and it influenced the scope of the first phase of the project.[14] Box 8.1 describes other financing possibilities that were considered for the project but ultimately rejected.

Phasing Plan

Since prolonged project implementation would increase costs and disturbance to merchants, government officials decided to complete the project as quickly as possible. In addition, due to the political sensitivity of the project, the city administration wanted the first phase of restoration to be completed within the political cycle of the mayoral term. Therefore, the scope of the restoration's first phase focused on more limited objectives, including the riverbed and the publicly owned area. In the later phases, Cheonggyecheon would be developed into a green, public, and ecologically friendly space, which would in turn help drive the regeneration of the broader downtown area.

Box 8.1   **A note on project financing: Missed opportunities**

The entire project budget of US$345 million was financed by the Seoul metropolitan government. However, a number of discussions took place to consider various financing methods for the project. One of the most commonly used methods for private-public infrastructure projects was an impact fee which is imposed on a new development project to pay for the increased infrastructure demand it will entail. However, for Cheonggyecheon, this was not an option as it was a public-led project.

Since the project was public, the city sought alternative funding methods. One of the options considered was tax increment financing (TIF). It is a method that utilizes future gains from the increased land values as a result of development. TIF uses the anticipated real estate tax revenue increases to subsidize the project.

After the restoration of Cheonggyecheon, land values in the adjacent area increased by about 25 percent to 50 percent. If TIF had been adopted at the average effective tax rate of 0.5 percent in Korea, the cost of the project would have been recovered within approximately 20 years. At higher effective rates that are used in Japan and the United States,[15] for example, the recovery period could have been less than 10 years. However, the TIF method was not adopted, as it had not been introduced in Korea. Furthermore, Korean laws did not allow for its usage at that time.

The urban regeneration project adopted a phased strategy in which the public and private sectors assumed their respective roles in turn (see figure 8.3). The idea was that the improvement of key public space by the public sector would lead to a better urban environment and would then be followed by private sector regeneration efforts. First, the city government was to demolish the coverage and the elevated highway, create an eco-friendly waterfront, and restore the historical value of the stream through public investment. The ripple effect of the restoration would then help revitalize the downtown and neighboring area, which would be conducted in partnership with the private sector. Furthermore, it would be done in such a way as to benefit both the public and private sectors.

Stream Restoration and Technical Issues

The main concern of neighboring merchants was the potential loss of business during the construction period. Therefore, the government made it a priority to complete the work as soon as possible to minimize the inconvenience to merchants and citizens. In addition, it was critical to complete important foundation works between rainy seasons.[16] As Cheonggyecheon had a large basin area, construction tools and materials in the stream were vulnerable to flooding damage. Such an incident actually occurred in 2004, and the project was on the verge of sustaining serious damage. Therefore, city officials decided that the construction works should be completed as quickly as possible in preparation for the seasonal floods in the summer.

To shorten the construction period and accommodate a diversity of creative ideas from the private sector, the contract for the project was processed as part of the "fast-track, design-build" system. The project was divided into three zones, which were meant to be built simultaneously.

Figure 8.3 **Phased strategy for the urban regeneration of downtown Seoul initiated by the restoration project**

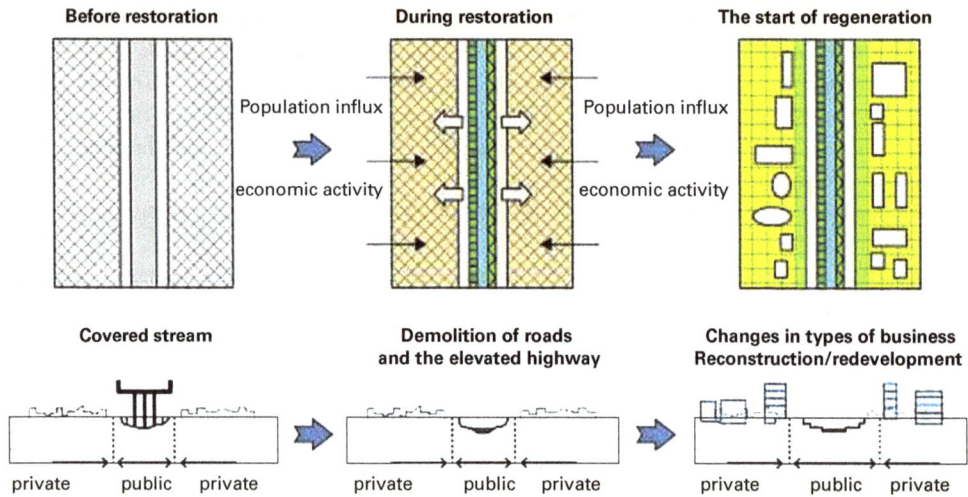

Contractors were selected from among the companies that participated in the bidding process, which was based on the basic design guidelines developed by the city government of Seoul. Since three different entities designed each zone separately, the city government intervened to ensure consistency and solve problems, such as those involving concept differences or errors in sewage pipeline connectivity between each zone (Rowe and others 2010).

Construction did in fact proceed with due haste and regard for flooding considerations. The construction started in July 2003, and major structures were demolished by October (figure 8.4). During demolition, the detailed design for construction works in the stream was developed simultaneously, and the construction was completed in early 2005. After a series of test runs during the rainy season, the new Chenggyecheon was opened to the public in September 2005–27 months after the beginning of construction. Ninety-six percent of the waste generated during the construction was also recycled.

One of the priorities in the restoration process was safety, which included taking appropriate flood prevention measures. The target flood recurrence was set at an interval of 200 years. Given that other 2nd-grade local streams were managed a 50-year interval assumption, the decision was taken to better ensure citizen safety by securing sufficient stream capacity to deal with local torrential rainfalls (figure 8.5). The city also strove to secure the discharge area by excavating underneath both banks of the stream.

The municipality made special provisions to deal with sewage problems during project implementation. A substantial number of sewage pipes were buried near the Cheonggyecheon because the sewage water of downtown Seoul traditionally gathered along it. Finding ways to treat such sewage was

Figure 8.4   **Construction process of the Cheonggyecheon restoration project, July 2003–September 2004**

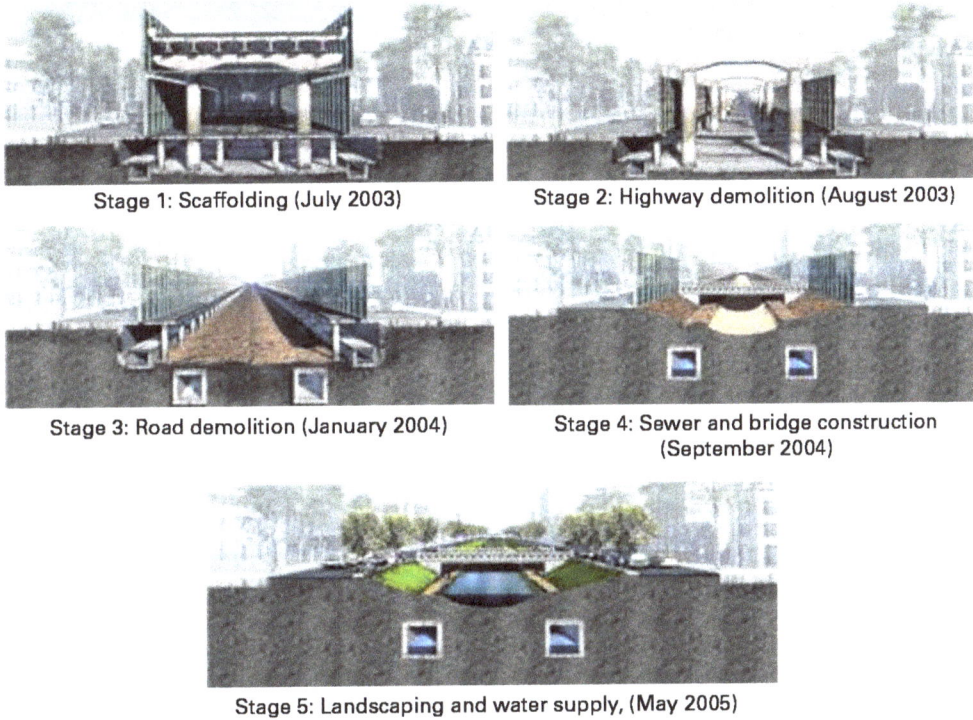

Stage 1: Scaffolding (July 2003)

Stage 2: Highway demolition (August 2003)

Stage 3: Road demolition (January 2004)

Stage 4: Sewer and bridge construction (September 2004)

Stage 5: Landscaping and water supply, (May 2005)

Source: Seoul Metropolitan Government 2005.

a precondition to the restoration. Since the existing sewerage system was often combined with the rainwater collection system before it reached the stream, it was practically impossible to segregate sewage from rainwater. Separation between them was also inappropriate because the downtown rainwater flowing into the Cheonggyecheon was highly polluted. Therefore, the municipality adopted a double-box system (figure 8.6). The sewage would be treated in a combined system. However, the highly polluted initial rainfall (less than 5 milometers/hour) would be segregated into a separate pipeline to be treated at the treatment facilities and would not flow directly into the stream. In the event of abundant rain, it would exceed the capacity of the treatment facilities and the pollution particles would be diluted. Thus, it would be discharged into the stream.[17] This system proved to be cost efficient and effective in treating the initially highly polluted rain water.

Cheonggyecheon was historically an ephemeral stream. Over time, the underground water level became lower because of urbanization, making it difficult to maintain the water flow. Given that there was no valley water coming from upstream, an artificial supply of water was required to maintain

Figure 8.5 **Cross-section of the Cheonggyecheon stream**

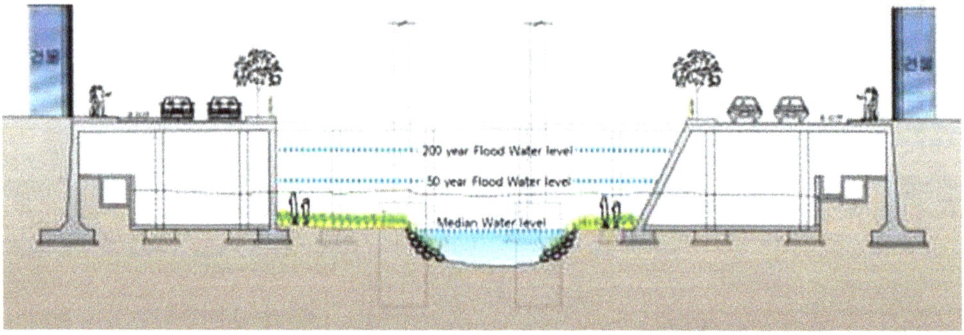

200 year Flood Water level
50 year Flood Water level
Median Water level

Source: Based on Seoul Metropolitan Government 2006a.

Figure 8.6 **Double-box sewage treatment system**

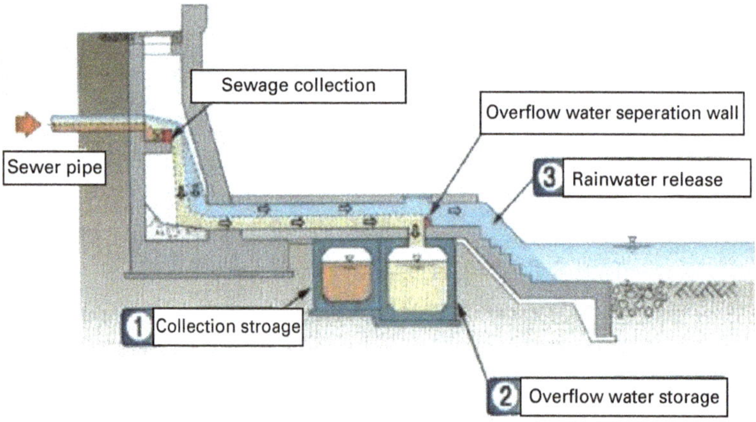

Sewage collection
Overflow water seperation wall
Sewer pipe
3 Rainwater release
1 Collection stroage
2 Overflow water storage

Source: Seoul Metropolitan Government 2006a.

the stream. Therefore, the Seoul Municipality pumped up water from the Han River and used the groundwater discharged from nearby subway stations. The water supply capacity was 120,000 cubic meters (m^3) per day with a total of 98,000 m^3 per day coming from the Han River and another 22,000 m^3 per day coming from subway stations (Seoul Metropolitan Government 2006a).

Outcomes and Impacts

The impacts of the Cheonggyecheon Restoration project are twofold: direct impacts resulting from the restored stream and indirect impacts involving the effect of the stream's regeneration, which created higher real estate values for the adjacent area. The direct impacts of the restored stream included the provision of public spaces and a natural environment, a green public network in the downtown area, and the restoration of the ecosystem that lowered the temperature in the city. In addition, the restored stream greatly contributed to revitalizing the once-stagnating downtown Seoul, rendering it a highly attractive place. The restored downtown area has been revitalized and now attracts people and business activity. More broadly, the restoration resulted in changes to civic consciousness as well as to urban planning strategies for downtown and public transportation reform. Contrary to popular expectations—remarkably—traffic congestion after the completion of the project did not worsen.

Until early 2002 when project discussions began, the approach and perspective of regenerating downtown Seoul did not diverge from previous practices. However, the paradigm shift initiated by the Cheonggyecheon restoration and downtown regeneration projects demonstrated new ideas and possibilities for the future of Seoul. In some city regeneration cases, popular opinion drives a city's transformation. However, this case shows that it was the vision of the city and municipal leaders that led to the paradigm shift in urban planning, as well as the shaping of citizenry perceptions.

Direct Impacts

The project included the creation of new green public space totaling 16.3 ha. This new space hosts pedestrian and cultural activities, provides habitats for animals and plants, and benefits the environment by lowering temperatures. From the perspective of the citizenry, the biggest contribution of the restoration was the creation of a pleasant place to relax (see photograph 8.2). In a 2013 public opinion survey, 59.6 percent of respondents indicated as such (Cheonggyecheon Citizens' Committee 2014). Cheonggyecheon also became a venue for diverse cultural events, with 259 events hosted there in 2005–07—helping to firmly position the stream as a place for culture and recreation.

Apart from its significance as a pleasant place, the Cheonggyecheon stream provides an important connection between various city attractions. With the restoration of the Cheonggyecheon, other attractions in the downtown area—such as Gyeongbokgung, Changdeokgung, and Myeongdong—were linked through pedestrian roads, enhancing the overall value of the public spaces. Thus, Seoul's downtown has become a more attractive tourist spot as well. The enhanced attraction of the downtown area has also led to an increase in the transient population.

Surprisingly, the downtown traffic conditions did not worsen as much as previously feared. The vehicle speed in the major downtown routes showed little change, before and after the restoration.[18] Even though the bus ridership (transportation card usage) change was subtle immediately after the restoration, it increased by 15.1 percent after the public transport reform was completed. In addition, subway ridership increased by 3.3 percent in Seoul and by 9.0 percent in the downtown area.

The Cheonggyecheon stream

Source: Authors.

Private car users switched to public transportation because it proved to be more convenient and less costly. The change in citizen awareness and better public transportation helped to improve the overall Seoul transportation experience.[19] In sum, the restoration experience made citizens realize the value of having available public space for a variety of uses.

Environmental improvements and reduced traffic volumes in the Cheonggyecheon area enhanced the quality of living in the downtown area. Air pollution decreased in the project area. Shortly after the restoration project, the concentration of fine dust and particle pollution (PM-10), nitrogen dioxide (NO_2), volatile organic compounds, and other air pollutants was significantly reduced (Seoul Metropolitan Government 2006b).

The project also had a positive impact on temperatures and the surrounding ecosystem. The heat island effect in the downtown area declined. The temperature of the Cheonggyecheon area before the restoration was 2.2 degrees centigrade higher than the average temperature of Seoul, which declined to 1.3 degrees centigrade after the restoration, dropping by 18 percent (Seoul Metropolitan Government 2006a). As the air-blocking elevated highway disappeared, a wind corridor was established and the creation of a stream positively affected the neighboring environment. The ecosystem was also restored and the population of fish species, birds, insects, and plants increased.

Flood control in the downtown area also improved significantly as a result of the restoration. The Cheonggyecheon is the lowest-lying area in the old downtown with an extensive basin to collect rainwater and gently sloped banks, which make it highly prone to floods. Since the proportion of the built-up area near Cheonggyecheon is higher than in other regions of Seoul, the possible disaster damage to population and economic activities also becomes greater. Flood damage has been reported during heavy floods in the last 20 years. Furthermore, an increasing number of torrential rainfalls due to recent abnormal climate conditions would likely cause even greater damage.

Most of the low-lying area around Cheonggyecheon had been subject to inundation before the restoration. However, since the restoration—which included provisions for flood prevention—most of the neighboring areas are now free from flood damage. Whereas overflows occurred for two consecutive years before the restoration began, causing damage in the downtown area, no flood damage has been reported since the restoration.

Indirect Impacts

Impact on Real Estate Values

The most notable indirect impact of the Cheonggyecheon restoration has been the increased real estate values and new variety of uses in the surrounding downtown area. Before the restoration, land prices within a 100-meter radius of the Cheonggyecheon were only 15 percent higher compared to those within a 600-meter radius. However, after the transformation, the gap in value increased by 30 percent. Office rents also increased by 20 percent (Kang 2009). The surrounding area experienced a construction and renovation boom (figure 8.7 and map 8.3). Land use changes were implemented primarily for commercial and business uses.

According to the Seoul Metropolitan Facilities Management Corporation, about 49,000 people on average visit the Cheonggyecheon area per day. Since the restoration, an impressive total of 163 million people have visited the area (see map 8.4a and 8.4b). Pedestrian volume in the vicinity has also generally increased, especially on weekends.[20] Previously, the downtown area was not popular with tourists, but this has changed since the restoration.

Impact on the Economy

Before the project, the economy of downtown Seoul was mainly characterized by manufacturing (19 percent) and wholesale, retail, and transportation businesses (32 percent). But industries were declining. The urban core of Seoul was struggling with comparatively higher unemployment rates than that of the Seoul area as a whole. The downtown area was also losing its share of employment to the Seoul metropolitan area, from 16 percent in 2000 to 14 percent in 2012.

The restoration of the stream and consequent development helped shift the downtown area economy toward financial and professional services. This shift was in keeping with Seoul as a whole, where the share of service industries rose from 41 percent in 2000 to 58 percent in 2012. This

Figure 8.7   Physical changes in building stock and location choices in the 10 years since the restoration, 2003–12

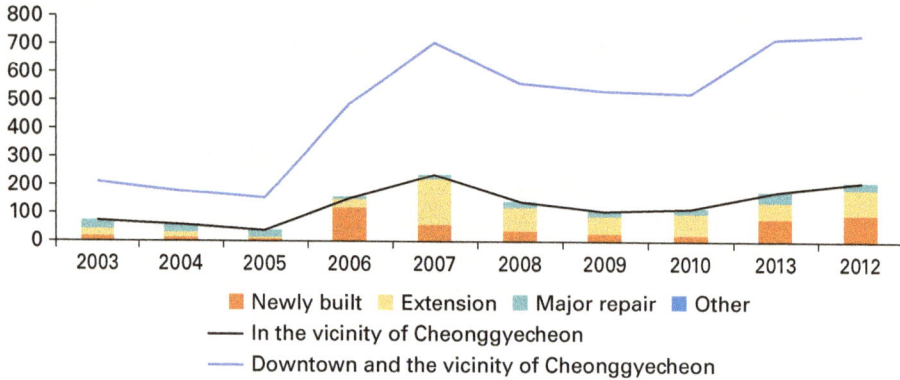

Source: Seoul Institute 2014.

Map 8.3   Changes in the development patterns near the Cheonggyecheon stream after project completion

Source: Seoul Institute 2014.

phenomenon could be attributed to the restoration project in downtown. Indeed, 60 percent of the downtown's economy derives from the service industry, soaring from the preproject rate of 38 percent. In particular, the size of the financial and professional services sector nearly doubled from 20 percent (2000) to 38 percent (2012). In 2012, the financial and professional sector became the leading industry in central Seoul.[21]

Impact on the Population

In the early 1990s before the new towns were built, the population of Seoul was on a steady increase. Despite sharp population increases, however, the population in downtown Seoul was shrinking fast. When there was a minor decrease in Seoul's population between 1990 and 2000, the downtown Seoul area experienced an even sharper decline. Corresponding to the restoration of the stream, the population decrease slowed in downtown while

Map 8.4   **Changes in pedestrian volume in the Cheonggyecheon area, 2003–06**

a. Weekdays

b. Sundays

Source: Seoul Metropolitan Government 2006a.

the population of Seoul as a whole continued to decrease as people were moving to the new towns (see figure 8.8).[22] The number of employers in the downtown Seoul area rose by around 50,000, from approximately 570,000 (2005) to 620,000 (2012). During the day, the number of people in downtown Seoul is escalating, considering that it is a transient population.

The restoration of the Cheoggyecheon brought about a significant increase in the transient population in the area. The waterway became a centerpiece of Seoul as a result of the improved accessibility and amenities in the area. This in turn led to increased land values and rents in the surrounding area.

Impact on Citizens' Environmental Awareness

One significant legacy of the Cheonggyecheon project was that it raised the environmental awareness of the citizenry. Environmental concerns were

Figure 8.8   Population changes in Seoul and downtown, 1975–2010

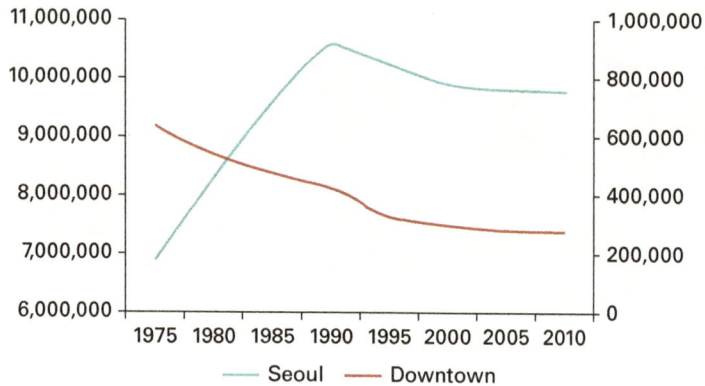

Source: Korea Statistics Bureau 2011.

already on the rise, but after the restoration of Cheonggyecheon the awareness became far greater. According to a willingness-to-pay survey after the restoration of the Cheonggyecheon, the price that citizens were willing to pay for an environmentally friendly stream greatly increased from ₩20,226 (US$16.50 equivalent, based on an exchange rate of US$1 = ₩1,225) per person to ₩37,724 (US$30) per person per household (Sohn, Cho, and Kim Hong-suk 2012). This positive improvement in public recognition of the importance of the environment is a crucial asset in Seoul's transformation to a more sustainable city, including the public transportation reform.

Lessons Learned

- *A clear and strong vision must lead urban regeneration.* As Cheonggyecheon had been covered by elevated concrete highways for almost half a century, the river underneath it was forgotten. In fact, many of Seoul's citizens had not seen the river throughout their lives, especially because more than half of the current population migrated to the city after the construction of the motorway. Therefore, restoring the Cheonggyecheon was deemed a major undertaking because it would potentially cause serious traffic issues and force local businesses to close to allow the demolition to proceed.

  Under these circumstances, an imaginative vision was instrumental in uncovering the buried assets of the Cheonggyecheon and in creating new opportunities for Seoul's downtown core. The efforts not only integrated the forgotten historical values but also overcame practical difficulties. The idea of losing 18 vehicle lanes in the busiest part of the city was initially unimaginable. With the ever-increasing urban traffic congestion, the plan involving the removal of lanes was deemed simply absurd and it faced strong opposition. However, the resuscitated river and previous road space has now been turned into a vibrant waterfront area that attracts citizens and wildlife, substantially enhancing the quality of life of the citizens and the downtown landscape. It took real leadership, determination, and direction to initiate this transition and overcome the difficult realities of execution (see photograph 8.3).

• *Political leadership matters.* Such a radical transformation would not have been possible without strong political leadership, which presented a clear vision, utilized institutional and human recourses efficiently, built internal trust, and resolved external conflicts. To combat the inertia that can occur in urban development, a leadership style characterized by vision, drive, and managerial and communication skills is imperative.

• *Along with long-term vision, short-term action plans need to be developed.* Another significant quality that political leaders should have is the ability to translate the long-term vision into effective short-term implementation plans. For the Cheonggyecheon project, the long-term goal to establish a vision for a people-friendly and sustainable urban environment could easily have been lost. A concrete action plan that defines how to achieve goals can facilitate the process toward realizing the larger vision. If necessary, it can be defined by targets in specific phases.

Making connections between the long-term vision and short-term actions can sometimes be difficult. The Cheonggyecheon project had an ambitious long-term vision, but its first phase goal was reached within three years. Achieving such progress can help build momentum for subsequent phases.

Photograph 8.3   Cheonggyecheon before and after its restoration

a. Before restoration   b. After restoration

Source: Seoul Metropolitan Government 2003, 2005.

- *Partnership structure matters.* The tripartite arrangement established in the initial stage of the project was key to facilitating the restoration process. The city's partnership with expert groups and citizen's committees proved to be successful. In particular, the civic committee's role in consolidating public opinion was integral in setting the right direction and making the project better understood by the public.

- *Technical details are as important as financing and planning details.* The Cheonggyecheon restoration was a complex project beyond the reach of any single sector or actor. It required coordination across areas encompassing water engineering, civil engineering, landscape, architecture, urban planning, economics, and social welfare, among others. The cross-sector approach was effective in consolidating different interests and views that could have otherwise conflicted. However, there were also numerous challenges involved in engaging citizens and interest groups. In this regard, sound management is important in maximizing the benefits of collaboration.

- *Public-private partnerships were an indispensable component in promoting a positive upgrade of the urban core.* By easing height regulations (to some extent) for the private properties along the Cheonggyecheon, the city could secure public space with environmental value for its citizens. This in turn allowed for private sector participation in transforming the urban core but with reduced risks. This successful collaboration led to the wider introduction of participatory planning in Seoul. Finally, the project also required a highly skilled work force and dedicated full-time staff to move the project forward.

Notes

1. Downtown refers to Jung-gu and Jongno-gu.
2. Fifty-two percent of the plots in the downtown area were less than 66 square meters (sq m), and more than 80 percent were less than 165 sq m (Yang 2001).
3. Other than dismantling buildings and infrastructure, other approaches such as rehabilitation were introduced as well. However, in practice, the dismantling approach was commonly used.
4. From the early 1990s, a small group of scholars and writers started to discuss restoration of the stream. However, the discussion never resulted in any concrete action. The discussion at the time was primarily focused on stream restoration, not the urban regeneration strategies to revive the declining downtown area.
5. In the redevelopment plan, the environs of Cheonggyecheon were excluded because of the negative effects of the elevated highway on the neighborhood. In other words, the Cheonggye elevated highway that once promoted the development of the neighborhood by providing greater accessibility actually hindered its later regeneration.

6. Since Cheonggyecheon occupied the lowest ground in the downtown area where the water flow of the downtown basin was collected, flood prevention has always been an important issue. For example, King Yeongjo (1752–1800) established a special organization called *Juncheonsa*, and mobilized some 210,000 workers to dredge the Cheonggyecheon over a 57-day period. (Given that Seoul's population at the time was estimated at about 200,000, the scale of dredging was very large.) In addition, stone embankments were established on both banks of the stream to prevent soil erosion.

7. There was discontent about the imbalance between old downtown (the so-called Gangbuk) in the north and the new urban area (the so-called Gangnam) in the south. The Cheonggyecheon restoration and downtown regeneration was suggested as a measure to solve the imbalance.

8. From 1985 to 1992, the Cheonggye overpass required five to six repair rounds every year, with each round lasting from 50 to 90 days. The average annual repair cost was ₩900 million and went up to as high as ₩2.9 billion in 1991. The overpass also underwent an emergency repair in 1995 that cost ₩5.7 billion (US$4.8 million; when applied with the conversion rate US$1 = ₩1,225). For four years, from August 1994 to July 1998, renovation works were conducted during which the overpass traffic had to be completely controlled from the Namsan Tunnel 1 to the Cheonggyecheon 4-ga street.

9. The exchange rate US$1 = ₩1188.60 was used as of August 12, 2015, and was applied for all other conversions, too.

10. The Metropolitan Household Travel Survey 2006, cited in Seoul Metropolitan Government 2010, 74.

11. The solidarity among 200,000 merchants near Cheonggyecheon was strong, as most had been there for more than 20 years (Hwang, Byun, and Nah 2005, 99–100).

12. As the Cheonggyecheon project involved only public properties and no private properties in the vicinity, there was no need for land compensation. However, merchants demanded direct compensation for their financial losses because of inconvenience.

13. The target flood recurrence was set at an interval of 200 years. Given that other second-grade local streams were managed on a 50-year interval assumption, the decision was made to better ensure safety by securing sufficient stream capacity to deal with local torrential rainfalls. The city also strove to secure the discharge area by excavating underneath of both banks.

14. The Seoul Municipality's total budget in 2003 was some ₩13 trillion (US$10.94 billion). The construction funds for some bridges such as the Samilgyo, Mojeongyo, Gwangtonggyo, and Jangtonggyo bridges were donated, allowing the municipality to save ₩8.2 billion (US$6.90 million) from the budget.

15. Korea's effective tax rates are about one-third of the rates in the United States and one-half of the rates in Japan (Ministry of Strategy and Finance 2007).

16. Korea has a rainy season, and 50 percent to 60 percent of annual precipitation occurs between July and September. Floods also tend to occur in this season (Korea Meteorological Administration 2011).

17. There was a plan to move sewage pipes underneath the Cheonggyecheon. However, it required a total change of the sewerage network, which was already tightly woven into the downtown area. Since the change would have cost an enormous amount in expense and time, city officials decided to treat the sewage and rainfall and retain the previous sewerage network.

18. The average travel speed of Cheonggyecheon-ro is 17 km/hour in the morning, and 12 km/hour in the afternoon.

19. Broadly speaking, the improvement in transportation and larger ridership generated positive effects, both socioeconomically (a shorter commuting time) and environmentally (air pollution improvement).

20. The pedestrian volume investigation was done at the ground level, and sidewalks of the stream at the underground level. The pedestrians along the sidewalks are estimated to have walked to enjoy the Cheonggyecheon rather than simply using it for exercise. The analysis in maps 8.4a and 8.4b was based only on the survey of ground-level pedestrians. If sidewalk pedestrians are included, the pedestrian volume change would have been even larger.

21. After the restoration, the number of employers in the manufacturing sector has been on a sharp decline, and those working in the financial and professional services sector have increased. Hardware and metal manufacturing, Cheoggyechon's dominant industry before the restoration, has been pushed to the outskirts of the city when it lost its market competitiveness after the motorway was removed. There are two contradicting views about this transition. One view sees the gentrification-induced displacement of the people in the manufacturing businesses as a violation of human rights, whereas the other view considers the decline in the urban manufacturing industry as something unavoidable for a city like Seoul, which is heading toward becoming a world-class city.

22. Seoul is a metropolis of 10 million residents. Cheonggyecheon and its vicinity, a small area situated in the urban core of Seoul, do not necessarily have to house a great number of residents. For example, the residential population of Manhattan, one of New York City's five boroughs, is 1.6 million (U.S. Census 2010), much less than its daytime population of 4 million (Moss and Qing 2012). Seoul's downtown area (Jongro-gu, Jung-gu, Yongsan-gu, Dongdaemun-gu, Seongdong-gu, Mapo-gu, Seodaemun-gu), is comparable to Manhattan and has a population of 1.8 million.

References

Cheonggyecheon Citizens' Committee. 2014. "Historic Preservation and Ecology Restoration of Cheonggyecheon." Seoul Metropolitan Government, Seoul, Republic of Korea.

Hwang Kiyeon, Miree Byun, and Taejun Nah. 2005. *Cheonggyecheon Project: Conflict Management Strategy*. Seoul: Nanam.

Kang, Chang-Deok. 2009. "Land Market Impacts and Firm Geography in a Green and Transit-Oriented City: The Case of Seoul, Korea." PhD diss., University of California, Berkeley.

Korea Meteorological Administration. 2011. "Rainy Season of Korea." White Paper, Korea Meteorological Administration, Seoul.

Korea Statistics Bureau. 2011. *Population Census 1975–2010*. Seoul: Korea Statistics Bureau.

———. 2013. *Census on Establishments 2000–2012*. Seoul: Korea Statistics Bureau.

Lee, Myeong-Hun, and Byung-Hye Jun. 2002. "A Study on the Spatial Characteristics of Inner-Urban Area in Seoul." *Journal of Korea Planners Association* 37 (2): 289–98.

Ministry of Strategy and Finance. 2007. State Affairs Briefing. March 15.

Moss, Mitchell, and Carson Qing. 2012. "The Dynamic Population of Manhattan." http://wagner.nyu.edu/files/rudincenter/dynamic_pop _manhattan.pdf. Accessed on March 24, 2014.

Rowe, Peter, ed. 2010. *A City and Its Stream: The Cheonggyecheon Restoration Project*. Seoul: Seoul Development Institute.

Seoul Institute. 2014. "Historic Preservation and Ecology Restoration of Cheonggyecheon." Seoul, Republic of Korea.

Seoul Metropolitan Government. 2003. "Feasibility Study of Cheonggyecheon Restoration." Seoul, Republic of Korea.

———. 2005. "Back to a Future." Seoul, Republic of Korea.

———. 2006a. "Cheoggyecheon Restoration." Seoul, Republic of Korea.

———. 2006b. "Change in Urban Structure and Pattern after the Cheonggyecheon Restoration." Seoul, Republic of Korea.

———. 2010. "Urban Management Plan." Seoul, Republic of Korea.

Sohn, Min-soo, Woo-young Cho, and Hong-suk Kim. 2012. "Change of Willingness-to-Pay after Cheonggyecheon Restoration." *Regional Studies* 28 (2): 23–37.

U.S. Census. 2010. *2010 Decennial Census of the United States*. Washington, DC: Bureau of the Census.

Yang, Jae-Seob. 2001. *Investigation of Residential Conditions and Proposal for Preserving Residential Use in Downtown Seoul*. Seoul: Seoul Development Institute.

Map 9.1 Washington, DC

a. Project area

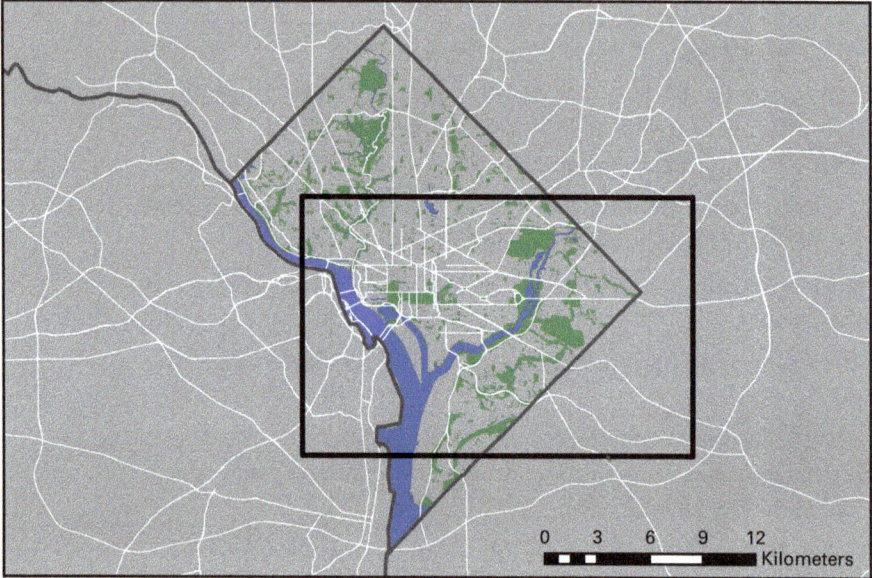

b. Site for redevelopment

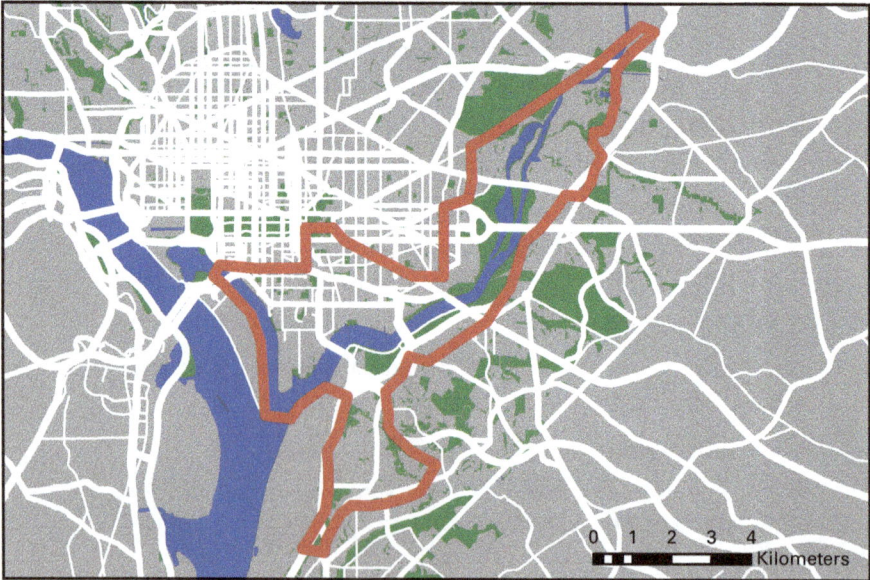

Source: World Bank using Open Street Map data 2015.

CHAPTER 9

Washington, DC's Anacostia Waterfront Initiative: Revitalizing the Forgotten River

Introduction

Washington, DC, has traditionally been viewed as a prime example of urban planning. The nation's capital is a model of urban revitalization, from the 1791 L'Enfant Plan that created the well-known city grid to the 1901 McMillan Plan, which established the city's park system, to more contemporary planning exercises, such as the Pennsylvania Avenue Development Corporation, which attempted to revitalize the area between the Capitol and the White House using a public private partnership model. Being an innovator in planning, the District of Columbia (DC) has also become a test case of ideas about cities and a reflection of intellectual currency regarding urban conditions and interventions at key moments in history.

The city is defined geographically by two important rivers, the Potomac and the Anacostia. Whereas the Potomac River is well known, home to many famous landmarks, and attractive to both residents and tourists, the Anacostia River is less widely known and has traditionally served mainly as the working waterfront for government facilities in Washington, largely without attractive public spaces.

Washington is a racially and socioeconomically segregated city and the Anacostia Waterfront always reflected the stark division of the city as one of the poorest census tracts in the United States. The Anacostia Waterfront Initiative (AWI) became both a concrete project and a symbol to attempt to bridge this psychological, economic, social, physical, and civic divide (see map 9.1). The AWI was seen as an opportunity along the banks of the Anacostia to create a dynamic live/work/play environment, one that would build on the appeal of Washington as a world-class city with extraordinary, diverse gathering places.

Context and Background

The Anacostia River forms a tributary to the Potomac River that drains 176 square miles of land in Maryland and the District of Columbia.[1] It flows for 11 kilometers (km) through Washington on the eastern side of the city. The river's watershed is the most densely populated subwatershed in the Chesapeake Bay, and it has been identified as one of the bay's three primary toxic hotspots. The river's water quality has been described as one of the most endangered in the nation.

Within the district, the shoreline is overwhelmingly owned by the federal government. Major facilities include the National Arboretum, the National Park Service's Anacostia Park, the Washington Navy Yard, and the United States Army's Ft. McNair. The district leases or has jurisdictional control over several federal parcels, including RFK Stadium, the DC General Hospital, the DC jail, and the main sewage pump station, as well as all of the streets and bridges that form the city's transportation system. The district also owns several sites, including the Southwest Waterfront. Two electricity power plants along the river are owned by the Potomac Electric Power Company (PEPCO). In total, more than 90 percent of the river's shoreline is in public ownership.

The river—initially the commercial lifeline of Washington and the upstream port of Bladensburg, Maryland—had already been compromised by erosion and siltation by the time of the Civil War. During the nineteenth century, weapons manufacturing and shipbuilding activities at the Navy Yard provided enough jobs to encourage the first residential community on the east side of the river, originally named Uniontown and today referred to as Historic Anacostia. When the United States Army Corps of Engineers began implementing the vision of the MacMillan Plan in the 1910s and 1920s, hundreds of acres of tidal estuary were filled and the river's configuration was reengineered, but the proposed damming of the river proved infeasible and was never implemented.

The highway building era of the 1950s took advantage of the reclaimed lands to construct new regional infrastructure, thereby reducing the need to take private lands in existing neighborhoods. The newly created lands along the river were eventually transferred to the U.S. Department of the Interior with the designation of park use, but with the land crisscrossed by regional infrastructure, the great park building effort envisioned by landscape architect Frederick Law Olmsted Jr. never came to pass.

In the mid-twentieth century, the neighborhoods along the river became one of the primary targets of Washington's urban renewal actions, in which existing residences and businesses were torn down and replaced with housing projects. The Southwest became the nation's largest urban renewal project. Many residents were relocated into neighborhoods further east, with a resulting concentration of public housing along the river and a legacy of social disruption.

Several legal actions have defined the recent history of the river. Using the Clean Water Act, several nonprofit organizations have pursued litigation regarding the Combined Sewage Overflows.[2] The District of Columbia's Water and Sewer Authority (DC Water) has recently formulated a strategy to bring the city's sewer infrastructure into compliance with Environmental Protection Agency standards at an estimated cost of over US$1.3 billion over the next 20 years.[3]

The area targeted by the AWI, which can be broadly described as the four wards (5, 6, 7, and 8) that border the Anacostia River, was characterized by a concentration of poverty, public housing, deteriorated housing conditions, and an African American population. This area of the city stands in contrast with the other four wards (the west of the city) where most of the white and better-educated populations live. (See the statistical annex for a quick comparison of poverty, income, crime, and housing value indicators by wards.)

Phase 1: Scoping

Even though the AWI's start date can be placed with the signing of the memorandum of understanding (MOU) in 2000 (see below), there are several key milestones prior to the MOU that helped to set the stage for a successful project implementation. Among them were the National Capital Planning Commission (NCPC)[4] Legacy Plan and the decision of the U.S. Navy to move NAVSEA (the purchasing unit of the U.S. Navy) to the Southeast Washington Navy Yards.

In 1997, the NCPC published a report "Extending the Legacy: Planning America's Capital for the 21st Century" that helped to set up the stage for the AWI. The Legacy Plan departed from previous federal plans that concentrated facilities and investment around the National Mall. It shifted the perceived center of the city to the Capitol and directed federal development outward into all quadrants of the city. By channeling new museums, memorials, and office buildings outward, along the ceremonial corridors radiating from the Capitol, the Legacy Plan sought to ease congestion in the monumental core; help revitalize neighborhoods; expand the reach of public transit; eliminate obsolete freeways, bridges, and railroad tracks that fragmented the city; reclaim Washington's historic waterfront for public enjoyment; and add parks, plazas, and other amenities. The Legacy Plan built upon the capital city's most important historic plans—the 1791 L'Enfant Plan and the 1901 McMillan Plan.

The plan's most crucial depiction was a simple axial diagram showing the Capitol as the center of Washington, with bold lines radiating north, south, east, and west. This single move redefined the plan, pushing it east and south toward the Anacostia River and enlarging the traditional boundaries of the Monumental Core Framework Plan. Unlike earlier plans, extending the Legacy goes beyond the Mall to include adjacent neighborhoods, waterfronts, parks, and gateways.

Election of New Mayor and Development of a New Powerful Vision for the City

The local political context, largely defined in the 1990s by the takeover of Washington, DC's finances by the congressionally legislated control board, became the backdrop for the 1998 election of Anthony A. Williams as mayor of DC.[5] Building on his personal interest in ecology and rivers and his political commitment to social justice in neighborhoods throughout the city, Williams raised the challenges associated with the river to the highest level of attention.

The mayor's vision for the future of the city was bold and clear. He believed that the Anacostia River represented a huge opportunity for revitalization and also had a symbolic significance for an economically and racially segregated city. The revitalization of the Anacostia River could help to reunite the capital city economically, physically, and socially. The revitalization would reinvigorate the river with new resident-stewards; reclaim the waterfront's parklands for community use; reconnect neighborhoods with new bridges and roads; create new museums and monuments; and expand opportunities to live, work, play, and learn in an urban setting. The vision for the Anacostia was one of vibrant and diverse settings for people to meet, relax, encounter nature, and experience the heritage of Washington. The clarity of his vision was based on his understanding of the history of the district, which provided a context for the future. The Anacostia River could be used as an organizing framework and, as a means to heal the city, a return of leadership, and a new control of its destiny.

Key to the vision and to the implementation was also the idea that the historical residents would benefit from the economic growth. The AWI tried to ensure that the social and economic benefits derived from a revitalized waterfront were shared in an equitable fashion by those neighborhoods and people for whom the river had been distant, out-of-reach, or unusable.

The idea of growing to the east was also based on the natural growth pattern of the city. With Washington's downtown nearly built out, the city's pattern of growth was moving steadily eastward toward and across the Anacostia River. The team behind the vision understood that the capacity of the capital city to grow was inextricably linked to recentering its growth in the coming decades on the Anacostia River. The Anacostia's long-neglected parks, natural environment, and urban infrastructure become a top priority for both the local and federal governments responsible for land stewardship in the nation's capital.

Phase 2: Planning

The Creation of the Anacostia Waterfront Initiative

In 2000, Mayor Williams successfully forged a partnership between the city government and the federal agencies that owned most of the land along the river (see map 9.2). Conceived as the Anacostia Waterfront Initiative, the

Map 9.2   **Land ownership in the Anacostia area**

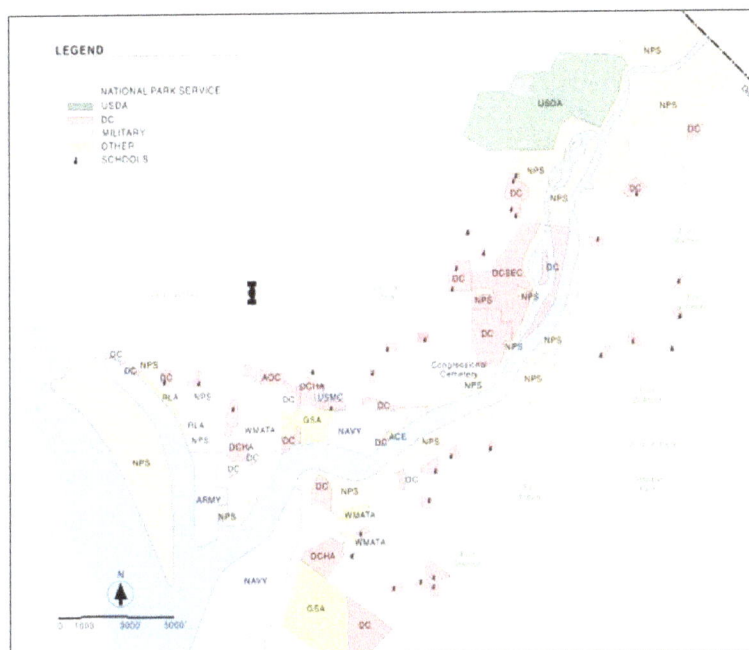

Source: World Bank 2014.
Note: Nearly all the Anacostia shorelines are held by public agencies.

partnership was memorialized in an MOU that was signed by the mayor and more than a dozen federal agencies in March 2000 at the Navy Yard. The initiative joined the district and federal agencies in a participatory planning process to form a common policy and development vision for the river and its public lands. This process was unprecedented for the Anacostia River and unprecedented in the history of urban planning in the district and was described by Williams as one of the most important partnerships ever created between the district and the federal government.

The Planning Process

In addition to providing guiding principles, the MOU contained a number of innovative provisions that made the AWI an unprecedented planning process in the history of Washington. First, by identifying the District of Columbia Office of Planning (OP) as the lead agency in the process, the city was put in a leadership role to coordinate the vision for the river, including the federal lands; second, it established a joint steering committee composed of OP, the National Park Service, and the General Services Administration (GSA) to oversee the planning progress; and third, it established a mandate to proactively engage the citizens of the district in the planning process.

In consultation with city council members, the OP established a 150-person citizens steering committee that included opinion leaders representing individual neighborhoods, environmental advocacy groups, and the business and design community. This committee was formed to provide a baseline of support for the planning process as well as a forum to discuss the major public policy disputes related to the river. Concurrent to the quarterly meetings of the steering committee, OP sponsored more than 30 community workshops and focus group sessions in six neighborhood target areas. More than 5,000 individuals attended these neighborhood workshops or the well-publicized progress presentations at the National Building Museum or at the Arena Stage, a regional theater.

Learning from Successful International Experiences

The process of creating the AWI also benefited from other successful international riverfront revitalizations experiences. In particular, the team developing the AWI learned from the city of Barcelona, spain, which had successfully gone through a similar conceptualization exercise. One of the lessons learned from Barcelona was that master plans and vision were important, but to simplify the ideas, the plan needed to be grounded in a specific project. Planning and implementation would then go hand in hand in the case of AWI.

AWI Framework Plan

Growing out of the dialogue fostered between citizens and the federal agencies, OP produced the Anacostia Waterfront Framework Plan to guide the river's redevelopment over the course of the next generation (Government of the District of Columbia 2003). To achieve the goal of a great waterfront along the Anacostia River, the Framework Plan identified five planning themes, which formed the basis for the five chapters of the plan (see box 9.1). Each of these themes responded to citizen concerns or public policy debates focused on the river corridor.

Neighborhood-Level Plans

While the Framework Plan explored riverwide issues, target area plans were prepared to chart redevelopment strategies on a neighborhood scale (see neighborhoods in map 9.3). Six target area plans applied the five waterfront planning themes to a site-specific context. Each was completed with direct involvement of community stakeholders and then brought to the city council for approval as a supplement to the city's comprehensive plan.

Each target area plan opened planning issues specific to its neighborhood that were resolved in the context of river-wide goals outlined in the framework. Conflicts and trade-offs between river-wide goals and local plans required balance, with each neighborhood expressing their own set of challenges. Height and density impacts of proposed high density development were most pronounced at the Southwest Waterfront, where existing residents were likely to have river views affected by new buildings. Housing affordability and the management of public housing assets, were most pronounced in the Near Southeast, where the planning process included actual public-private development proposals to redevelop the Arthur Capper Carrollsburg housing project; issues of

Box 9.1   **AWI's framework planning themes**

A Clean and Active River (Environment): Charting the Environmental Restoration of the River over 25 Years

The voice of community and environmental advocates was clear and unambiguous: the river needs to be restored to a "fishable and swimmable" level of water quality. This was, and continues to be, one of the most controversial recommendations of the Framework Plan, given that billions of dollars were needed to fund the implementation of the Sewer Long-Term Control Plan as well as watershed restoration. Furthermore, given the significance of ongoing non-point source contaminant loading, and the fact that the majority of the river's watershed is in Maryland, the Framework Plan highlighted Washington's political predicament—it is downstream—and the fact that Washington had no way to force the state of Maryland to prioritize this watershed restoration effort.

Breaking Down Barriers and Gaining Access (Transportation): Reconstructing Transportation Infrastructure to Better Serve Neighborhoods and the Region

While neighborhood groups had recently halted the expansion of the city's freeway network, few stakeholders offered a positive vision for the future of traffic around the river. One issue that the planning process helped articulate was that the river itself was not the primary barrier, but rather it was the poorly designed freeways that were constructed alongside the river to usher workers from the downtown to the newly emerging suburbs.

A Great Riverfront Park System (Public Realm): Transforming over 1,800 Acres of Public Open Space into an Interconnected River Parks System

The steering committee played an important role in elevating the discourse on parks and advocated for design and environmental excellence to match the standards of other parks in the capital. From the outset of the planning process, the mayor championed the idea of a continuous river walk on both sides of the river. The river walk captured the public and media's imagination and the district government was able to fund several demonstration segments of the river walk, which made the notion of continuous public access to the river a concrete and widely accepted goal.

Cultural Destinations of Distinct Character (Culture and Institutions): Introducing New Museums and Monuments That Emphasize the Civic Importance of the Anacostia

The waterfront planning process was preceded by a citywide Museum and Memorials Plan completed by the National Capital Planning Commission (NCPC). Given that memorial sites on the National Mall are growing scarce, NCPC completed this plan to highlight opportunities to locate monuments off of the National Mall. Waterfront sites represented many of the most promising locations. The Framework Plan sought to flesh out strategies whereby new memorials would reinforce existing river attractions, as well as existing, underappreciated historic resources. The effort to locate the new major league baseball park was guided by the desire to transform a segment of the river into a citywide and regional destination, in an attempt to attract tourist dollars and celebrate the river's civic importance.

Building Strong Waterfront Neighborhoods (Economic Development): Increasing the Vitality of Waterfront Neighborhoods by Adding over 20,000 Households and up to 40,000 New Jobs

As the planning process proceeded, the issue of residential gentrification and potential resident displacement was even more passionately debated than the need to restore the river's environmental quality. Ultimately, the Framework Plan recommended adding 15,000 new units of housing along the river, justified by the opportunity to grow mixed-income neighborhoods without displacing existing residents.

Source: Government of the District of Columbia 2003.

Map 9.3   **Neighborhoods in the Anacostia Waterfront Initiative area**

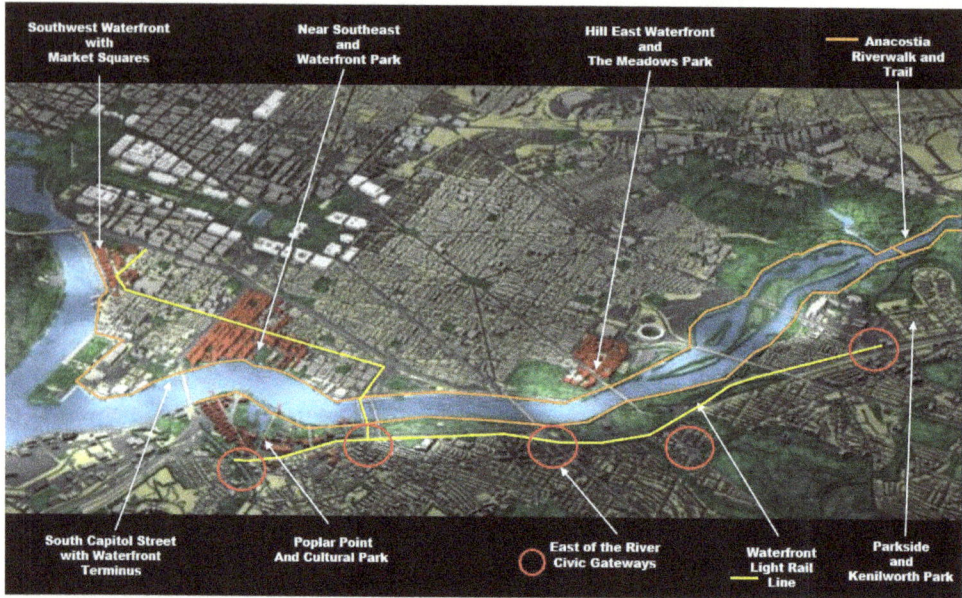

Source: World Bank 2014.

proposed land uses were most pronounced at Hilleast, where the district had recently closed the public hospital and where the need to accommodate municipal services, such as health care clinics and correctional uses, was balanced with the expansion of the residential uses to connect Capitol Hill with the river; open spaces issues pertaining to park and recreation versus the restoration of habitat were balanced in the Anacostia Park.

In summary, issues of environmental restoration and gentrification were discussed on a city-wide scale, while neighborhood quality-of-life issues such as parks, traffic, and retail development were advocated for on a neighborhood-by-neighborhood basis.

The Institutional Structure: The Anacostia Waterfront Corporation
The Framework Plan proposed a new dedicated municipal entity to coordinate the implementation process. Land parcels along the river fell under the jurisdiction of multiple federal and local authorities and agencies, not one of which had a clear mandate for revitalizing the waterfront. A new institution would ensure that the resources necessary to implement the plan were advocated for and wisely and equitably invested for the river as a whole. The corporation's role would be to oversee implementation of the plan, ensure sustained public participation by acting as a design "clearing house," and be responsible for promoting waterfront activities and in some cases managing public spaces.

In considering how the Anacostia Waterfront Corporation (AWC) would be organized, several models were explored based on federal-local actions in other cities. Among those evaluated were the Pennsylvania Avenue Development Corporation in Washington, DC, Presidio Trust in San Francisco, and the Southern Nevada Land Act. Each of these redevelopment projects were initiated with federal legislation, with each having significant localized outcomes as its purpose. In the case of the Southern Nevada Land Act, the proceeds from federal land disposition were reinvested in federal lands but in a partnership arrangement with local jurisdictions.

Ultimately, federal legislation was dismissed for the AWC for three primary reasons. First, the tools to creatively finance public-private partnerships resided with the District of Columbia; second, given that the district continues to be under the oversight of Congress, the opportunity for a unique federal partnership was de facto in place; and third, the initiative itself had always been focused on reconnecting the citizens of the district to their river. A locally chartered organization appeared most effective in raising the awareness of the city's citizenry of the river's assets. In summary, the structure that emerged took advantage of the city's own powers of creative financing but formed a semi-autonomous municipal entity with which land owning federal agencies and Congress could easily partner.

The District of Columbia Anacostia Waterfront Corporation Act passed by the city council in 2004 created a district government–chartered corporation charged with the development, promotion, and revitalization of the Anacostia River Waterfront. With a board that included both mayoral appointees as well as ex-officio members from both the district and federal agencies, the corporation was a city-created entity poised to become a development partner for both municipal and federal agencies.

Other cities, such as London, San Francisco, Barcelona, and Pittsburg were successful examples of waterfront development that used a single-purpose, dedicated public entity and strategic coordination between many government agencies—often involving state, municipal, and federal jurisdictions over long periods of time—in order to complete projects that have physical challenges unique to waterfronts.

The idea behind the corporation was that a single development corporation was the best institutional architecture to make sure that all the various components of the AWI—residential development, maritime uses, recreational uses, transportation infrastructure, commercial and retail development, cultural uses, and environmental restoration—were coordinated to maximize the benefit of the river as a natural asset to the district.

This case study also shows that even though the AWC was successful at launching the developments in the area, the initiative was strong enough to survive institutional and political changes.

Phase 3: Financing and Implementation

The financing and implementation of such an ambitious plan was possible
through smaller projects that were part of the overall framework and that
contributed to the vision. In this case study, we will focus on one particular
area, the Capitol Riverfront (see map 9.4), that concentrates most of the
investments at the beginning of the AWI's implementation and is also an
excellent example of a wide variety of tools available for local governments
when dealing with urban regeneration.

The Capitol Riverfront (which includes the Near Southwest and
South Capitol Street Corridor) is the first neighborhood within the AWI
where significant results can be observed. A series of public and private
investments have transformed the area into a thriving neighborhood.
Developing the Capitol Riverfront became a reality in 1995 when the
U.S. Navy decided to move NAVSEA Command to the Navy Yard in
Southeast Washington, which in turn moved 10,000 employees to the
area and created demand for three new private office buildings on

Map 9.4   **Capitol Riverfront area**

Source: Capitol Riverfront Business Development Area 2014.

M Street (navy contractors). Investment and development efforts began in earnest when the U.S. Department of Transportation (DOT) headquarters site was chosen; GSA selected the private developer Forest City for the Yards; the district received a US$35 million HOPE VI[6] grant for the redevelopment of Arthur Capper Carrollsburg public housing; and Maritime Plaza Phase I completed construction.

Since 2001, Forest City has developed the Yards; a new major league baseball stadium was constructed on the waterfront; and the DOT headquarters building generated US$100 million in tax increment financing to help fund multiple public infrastructure and parks projects. In all, between 2000 and 2010, US$1.2 billion in district and federal investments have been made in the Capitol Riverfront, matched by US$1.8 billion in private investments (Government of the District of Columbia 2010). Public funds were used to pay for multiple infrastructure needs, fund a significant entertainment attraction, and create affordable housing options.

The Southeast Federal Center: A Model of Federal Public-Private Partnership and the Growth of the Near Southeast Waterfront

In 2000 Congress passed the Southeast Federal Center (SEFC) Public Private Redevelopment Act, which granted GSA, the federal agency in charge of administering federal land, the authority to enter into various types of agreements with private entities in the SEFC area. Further, GSA was authorized to sell or exchange property in the 55-acre area that included the Navy Yard.

This legislation opened all kinds of possibilities for the Southeast area of the AWI, including nonfederal use of the land and partnering with private developers. In turn, this would lead to the creation of the Yards Park and real estate developments that surround it through a partnership with Forest City and to the move of DOT to the area.

The Relocation of the Federal Department of Transportation to the Southeast Waterfront: An Anchor for Change

One of the first manifestations of the SEFC Act was the building of the DOT headquarters, an 11-acre area along M Street Southeast that is home to 5,000 employees. The innovation in the financial structure for the project was that instead of just building a new federal facility that would be owned by the federal government, the building was privately developed and rented to the DOT for 15 years.

The new DOT headquarters is located on an 11-acre parcel along M Street Southeast and provides identity and definition to the area. This project is the first new cabinet-level headquarters to be designed and constructed in the district in more than three decades. The new complex is home to the agency's 5,000 employees. The building boasts several sustainable development features, including the district's largest green roof at 68,000 square feet (sq f). Construction also required remediation of more than 100,000 cubic yards of contaminated soil from the site because it was previously a factory for fabricating battleship gun barrels for the Navy.

Navy Yards and the Yards Park: Creating Public Spaces through a Public-Private Partnership

The development of the Yards project is an excellent example of collaboration of the public and private sectors under complex conditions.[7] It illustrates how some projects may take time to materialize and how the persistence of the actors involved in its implementation is necessary (see figure 9.1).

First steps—ancillary investments that helped the neighborhood get started. The Navy, with the oldest continuously operating Navy Yard in the country, played a lead role in this reinvestment through its efforts at its waterfront facilities by consolidating regional employment at the Navy Yard through the Base Realignment and Closure Act in 1995. Over US$400 million was invested in rehabilitating historic industrial buildings into a Navy administrative space, and employment nearly tripled to almost 11,000 enlisted and civilian employees. This was the first step in the revitalization of the area. The passing of the SEFC Act was also a prerequisite for the development of the Yards project, allowing GSA to negotiate a contract with Forest City.

Characteristics and cost of the project. The Yards, which is located by the Navy Yard, is a waterfront project created as the centerpiece development along the water's edge. The Yards project includes reopening several public streets to better access the waterfront and construction of a 5.5-acre park, which is one of the centerpieces related to the vision of creating public spaces for the citizens to enjoy in the Anacostia Waterfront. The construction of the Yards by Forest City, the private developer selected for the project, includes the adaptive reuse of historic industrial

Figure 9.1   **Rendering of the Yards project**

Source: Forest City.

buildings and the construction of new buildings for residential, office, and retail use. The Yards project is worth about US$1.5 billion and the city's contribution amounted to about US$42 million. City officials justified the subsidy as a way to ensure that the site was redeveloped as a mixed-use project.[8]

Number of actors involved. The development of the Yards involved numerous actors in the public and private sectors, including historic preservation groups, the GSA, the DOT, the Navy Department, the NCPC, DC Water, and the Anacostia Waterfront Corporation. "It's hard to imagine any place in America with a more complicated set of issues around a property," said Stephen Goldsmith, chair of AWC. "You have to have the right set of political and business skills to get through something as complicated as this."

"We tend to focus on underutilized urban areas, where we believe the demographics are poised for growth," said Forest City President Deborah Ratner Salzberg. "When we looked at how close the Capitol was to this site and the fact that it was on the river, the combination made for a perfect long-term site. It is very rare in a major metropolitan area where you could control this much."[9]

Need for a public subsidy to attract private developers. The need for a considerable public investment in the area to trigger the private investment was justified on the following grounds: (a) the cost of infrastructure (the site was not connected to the public utilities and city street grid, and it needed new sewers, streets, public lighting, and public parks); (b) the distance to traditional residential and commercial areas (even though the site is located two metro stops away from the downtown area, the psychological distance from traditional residential and commercial areas is greater than that); and (c) cost of environmental remediation for the land that had been utilized as an industrial site for 200 years (this cost was covered by the federal government, which is responsible for cleaning up the land that it has contaminated in the past).

PILOT Bonds. To make the investment profitable for the private developer, the city utilized a US$230 million Payment in Lieu of Taxes (PILOT) bond to pay for the infrastructure investments (roads, parks, and sewers) for both the Yards and the DOT's headquarters development (which is located north of the Yards development and is also part of the SEFC area).[10]

Winning a HOPE VI Grant to Redevelop Arthur Capper Carrollsburg Public Housing and Turning a New Page in Urban Renewal

The redevelopment of the Arthur Capper Carrollsburg public housing complex was perhaps the most innovative and highly leveraged housing project to be completed under the U.S. Department of Housing and Urban Development's (HUD's) HOPE VI program. The project guaranteed a 1:1 replacement of all public housing and increased land densities to double the amount of housing units by supplementing 700 units of public housing with 400 units of subsidized housing and 400 units of market-rate housing. This was one of the projects under the initiative that seek to reduce gentrification.

The Capper Carrollsburg dwellings, a 23-acre development also in the Capitol Riverfront neighborhood, was once two public housing complexes with a total of 707 units. The properties were old and obsolete with a high concentration of low-income units in barracks-style architecture. In October 2001, the District of Columbia Housing Authority (DCHA) received a US$35 million HOPE VI grant award from HUD for the revitalization of the Capper and Carrollsburg site. With the addition of private and public investors, this initial grant grew to more than US$750 million to form one of the largest urban redevelopment areas in the country.[11]

When completed, the Capper Carrollsburg development will be the first HOPE VI project in the country to provide one-for-one replacement of demolished public housing units in the same footprint as the original developments. The development plan calls for more than 1,600 new rental and home ownership units to create a thriving mixed-income community of apartments, town homes, and a seniors' building, which was completed and occupied in 2007.

The project's economic stimulus plan included 50,000 sq f of retail space and nearly 700,000 sq f of office space. DCHA secured commitments to provide at least 1,130 jobs over a three-year period for public housing residents. The project also addressed the social and educational needs of residents and included the construction of an 18,000-square-foot community center and a new public park (Canal Park) adjacent to the site. In conjunction with the DC Public Schools, DCHA is building a new school in the Capper and Carrollsburg neighborhood as well.

Another critical component of the Capper Carrollsburg redevelopment project is the replacement of the public infrastructure at the site. DCHA signed an agreement with the district government to coordinate the installation of new underground utilities, sanitary and water lines, and a new storm management system. The district agreed to reimburse DCHA for the work by funding a US$55 million PILOT bond.

The Capitol Riverfront Business Improvement District

The Capitol Riverfront area has also benefited from the additional services provided by the business improvement district (BID).[12] The Capitol Riverfront BID goal is to make the Capitol Riverfront clean, safe, friendly, and vibrant by focusing on cleaning and maintenance (pickup and remove trash from the public realm and provide maintenance and beautification of the public space); safety and hospitality (provide public safety as additional "eyes and ears" and provide a welcoming environment by greeting passersby, answering questions, and providing directions); marketing, branding, and special events (raise awareness of the district, promote its emerging identity, brand it as a destination, market its assets, and produce special events); economic development (support current and attract new office tenants, residents, retail, restaurant, and entertainment uses); coordination and advocacy (coordinate and advocate for improvements in the public realm, streetscape, infrastructure, transportation, parking); and community building (assist in developing a sense of community, while addressing issues of local employment and homelessness).

The BID keeps track of different indicators in the area to determine the neighborhood's success in securing investments. One such indicator is the residential inventory. According to BID data there were 250 residential units in 2004, 3,550 in 2014, and a projection of 6,450 for 2017.[13] Office space, retail stores and hotel units have increased considerably in the area too. Table 9.1 shows projections for inventory growth in office, retail, residential, and hotel spaces.

Baseball Comes to Washington and the Anacostia Waterfront

The construction of the Nationals Park is perhaps the defining element of the revitalization of the Anacostia Waterfront. The process to bring the Nationals baseball team to Washington, DC, was long and generated considerable resistance from some members of the city council who believed the city should not use public financing for a sports facility. The mayor's vision was that the Nationals was not only an economic development tool for the city but also an instrument to increase the city's sense of community and people's shared experience of Washington. It was also a critical project for the AWI area, a catalytic investment that could help the AWI became a reality. The construction of the ballpark in the area would bring 2 million people south of the highway per year and expose them to a part of the city that was not used or known by most of the population.

In 2004, the district approved US$611 million to construct a Leadership in Energy and Environmental Design (LEED)–certified ballpark to be able to bring the Nationals to the city.[14] Besides the district's investment, the principal owners spent tens of millions of dollars in additional upgrades to the 41,000-seat ballpark. This was a key outcome for the success of AWI: the Nationals attract between 2.0 and 2.5 million patrons to the Capitol Riverfront each year and are the defining feature of the neighborhood.

Table 9.1 **Annual inventory growth by product type in the Capitol Riverfront, 2004–17**

Inventory growth trends	Office (square feet)	Retail (square feet)	Residential units	Hotel keys
Average annual growth, 2004–14	275,467	19,820	331	20
Projected average annual growth, 2015–17	75,667	47,925	969	178

Source: Capitol Riverfront BID.

The district agreed to fully fund a stadium as part of the deal that brought the former Montreal Expos to Washington. The city council capped "hard expenditures" for the ballpark (including construction and land acquisition costs) at US$611 million. The city owns the ballpark, and it is operated by the Washington, DC, Sports and Entertainment Commission. The ballpark was paid for by the sale of US$535 million in municipal bonds, which will be repaid by stadium-generated revenues and by a tax on businesses within the city. No money was spent from the city's general fund to pay for the stadium. Certain upgrades at the park that would break the cost cap are being paid for by the team's owners.

In reality the ballpark ended up costing more than originally planned, as shown in tables 9.2 and 9.3,[15] but the special purpose collection is higher than the amount necessary to repay the bond.

The Historic Land Transfer Act That Returns the Waterfront to the District

In 2006 Congress passed a key piece of legislation to unlock more development in the AWI area.[16] The land swap (Washington also returned some land to the federal government) included roughly 200 acres of federal land,

Table 9.2   **Spending on Nationals Park and expected revenue, 2008**
US$ millions

Spending	Amount
Stadium agreement (construction, legal and architectural fees, parking, financing, land acquisition)	611.0
Contribution from Major League Baseball per stadium agreement	20.0
Additional contribution from Nationals	11.0
Land cost overrun (eminent domain settlements and environmental remediation) paid by the city	43.0
Federal contribution to Navy Yard Metro station upgrade	20.0
Artwork contribution from DC Commission on the Arts and Humanities	2.0
South Capitol Investments (signage installation, sidewalks, roadway construction, and wastewater updates)	31.6
Frederick Douglas Bridge rehabilitation	31.0
Total cost of stadium project	769.6
Expected revenue	
Taxes on business with gross receipts over US$5 million	14.0
4.25% special sales tax on food, concessions, tickets, and parking at the ballpark	20.0
Rent from the Nationals	3.5
Taxes on utilities and telecommunications paid by nonresidential taxpayers	12.5
Total expected revenue 2008	50.0

Source: Washington Post 2008.

Table 9.3 **Nationals Park revenue fund collections and debt service, fiscal 2005–11**
US$ millions

	FY 2005	FY 2006	FY 2007	FY 2008	FY 2009	FY 2010	FY 2011	Total
Ballpark sales taxes	8.5	8.9	8.2	12.1	9.4	10.0	9.5	66.6
Ballpark fee	16.2	15.4	23.7	24.7	28.2	23.7	33.3	165.2
Utility taxes	9.0	12.5	12.7	12.8	13.0	12.2	11.2	83.4
Rent	n.a.	n.a.	n.a.	n.a.	7.3	4.0	4.5	15.8
Total collections	33.7	36.8	44.6	49.6	57.9	49.9	58.5	331.0
Debt service	n.a.	6.0	34.4	30.1	31.8	31.2	31.2	164.7

Source: Washington City Paper 2012.
Note: FY = fiscal year; n.a. = not applicable.

much of it valuable waterfront property, key to the city's plans to transform areas bordering both sides of the Anacostia River. The biggest parcel was Poplar Point, a 100-acre site on the eastern side of the Anacostia. Also transferred to city control is Reservation 13, a 66-acre site on the western edge of the river that houses the former DC General Hospital campus and is slated for mixed-use development and health-related facilities. The land transfer is the biggest hand off of federal property since the city achieved home rule in 1973.

This was a great achievement for the city, since the land transfer placed the land on tax rolls, which would produce significant revenue when the land is redeveloped. For years, district officials have argued that the federal government's presence here creates a "structural imbalance."

Southwest Waterfront

The Southwest Waterfront is the portion of the waterfront along Water Street between 6th and 10th Streets Southwest. Given the proximity of the Southwest Washington community to the entire waterfront, the redevelopment progress for this target area of the AWI Framework Plan also includes redevelopment efforts for Waterfront Station, Arena Stage, the new Mandarin Hotel, and planning for Buzzard Point and 10th Street, Southwest. These additional efforts contribute significantly to the quality of this unique stretch of waterfront near the National Mall.

In 2009, the Land Disposition Agreement was executed by the district and its master development partner. The district contributed US$198 million in tax increment financing to offset infrastructure costs and catalyze the US$1.3 billion project. The planning effort for those areas was successful and was crystallized in an agreement between the developer and the long-term residents of the Southwest Waterfront. The long-term tenants were scheduled to receive affordable units in the future development. The implementation of the development required the approval of multiple congressional actions to resolve title and other encumbrances on the property.

Some of the key projects in the area include the following:

- *The Waterfront Station.* For 50 years, Southwest Washington was divided in half by a shopping mall and an office complex that were withered with age.[17] Like the freeway that isolates the neighborhood from downtown, Waterside Mall left its community without a center. The new pedestrian-friendly, mixed-use project at the Metro's door, Waterfront Station, is the first of a US$800 million redevelopment project. The project includes 1.2 million sq f of offices, the same amount of residential space, and at least 110,000 sq f of retail and restaurants. The area also includes government buildings.

- *Mandarin Hotel.* Built in 2003, the Mandarin Hotel is the district's newest five-star hotel. It has 400 suites and rooms and overlooks the Southwest Waterfront and Washington Channel. The hotel received US$40 million in tax increment financing.

- *Arena Stage at the Mead Center for American Theater.* Arena Stage is the second largest performing arts complex in Washington after the Kennedy Center and will be one of the country's leading centers for the presentation and development of American theater. The new center features the new Kogod Cradle, a 200-seat space with flexible seating and state-of-the-art technical capabilities. The renovation strove to preserve significant elements of the original center's character through the preservation of the round, 680-seat Fichandler Stage, and the 500-seat Kreeger Theater.

- *Buzzard Point.* Buzzard Point is a nearly hidden area within the AWI that is currently home to a power plant, U.S. Coast Guard headquarters, automobile impound lots, and low-density housing. Interest in the site increased as a result of the removal of the South Capitol Street viaduct and improved access to Nationals Park. In 2009, a planning assistance team from the American Planning Association reviewed the potential for the site and provided recommendations for building a new mixed-use and high-density neighborhood that contains parks and cafés on the river.

Outcomes and Impacts

Even though the results of the AWI directly affect the lowest-income communities in the city (Wards 5, 6, 7, and 8), in reality the project was envisioned to improve the city as a whole. When comparing data from 2000 to 2009, all major indicators for the advancement of environmental, economic, and community goals within the Anacostia Waterfront Development Zone are positive. The AWI, when complete, will require an estimated US$25 billion in private and public investments and is projected to yield US$1.5 billion in additional tax revenues for the district per year (see box 9.2). Photograph 9.1 shows the area before and after redevelopment.

Box 9.2 **Summary of AWI's outcomes**

Restore: Environment

- To date, the DC Water and Sewer Authority has reduced combined sewer overflow (CSO) by 36 percent and is implementing the Long Term Control Plan, a US$2.6 billion endeavor to replace 17 CSOs and build tens of miles of new underground wastewater tunnels.
- The district has achieved an approximate 50 percent decrease in the concentrations of the oxides of nitrogen and sulfur that lead to acidification of water bodies.
- The district approved the AWI environmental standards for sustainable development in 2007.
- Five acres of new wetlands have been planted throughout the district's portion of the watershed.

Connect: Transportation

- The District Department of Transportation (DDOT) awarded its largest construction project, the US$300 million 11th Street Bridge project, in August 2009.
- Scheduled for three years of construction, DDOT instead was able to remove the South Capitol Street viaduct and improve surrounding streetscapes in nine months to coincide with the opening of the new Nationals Park.
- Of the 20 miles planned in the Anacostia Riverwalk Trail, more than 10 miles are complete; the remaining segments of the trail are in design.
- The district published the Anacostia Waterfront Transportation Guidelines, which guide low impact development standards in the public streetscape.

Play: Parks

- Over US$100 million in public investment has been made to create and renovate parks, including the Yards Park, Canal Park, Diamond Teague Park, Kingman Island, Marvin Gaye Park, and the Anacostia Riverwalk Trail.
- The Yards Park is the centerpiece for the Capitol Riverfront neighborhood, with 5.5 acres of public gathering spaces, an award-worthy pedestrian bridge, and retail pavilions.
- Watts Branch Park has been transformed from a grassy field and drug-infested park to a renovated series of amenity parks dedicated to musician Marvin Gaye, a Washington native who grew up in the nearby neighborhood.

Celebrate: Destinations

- In 2004, the district successfully recruited Major League Baseball back to Washington and, in 2008, opened the US$611 million, state-of-the-art, LEED–certified baseball stadium for the Washington Nationals.
- Opened in 2004, the Mandarin Hotel is the newest five-star hotel in the district, perched on 12th Street Southwest overlooking the Tidal Basin and the Southwest Waterfront.
- In October 2010, Arena Stage opened its doors to the US$135 million, renovated, and expanded Mead Center for American Theater.

Live: Neighborhoods

- The total population of the AWI has increased from 16,675 to 23,280 (40 percent increase).
- The total number of households has increased from 8,021 to 11,324 (41 percent increase).

(Box continues on next page)

Box 9.2   **Summary of AWI's outcomes** *(continued)*

- Annual real property tax revenues increased from US$35 million in 2005 to US$109 million in 2009 (211% increase), which outpaced the district's overall property tax revenue growth.
- The Capitol Riverfront is the first new waterfront neighborhood to evolve and now boasts 10 million square feet of new residential, office, and retail space; it is also home to the Washington Nationals.

Source: Government of the District of Columbia 2010.

Lessons Learned

Transforming 2,800 acres of neglected waterfront land and restoring one of the nation's most polluted rivers is a complex and long-term undertaking, as is coordinating among multiple federal and district agencies to achieve a shared goal. Some of the lessons that emerge from the implementation of the AWI are explained in this section:

- *Vision is the crucial foundation.* The success of AWI can be traced to the boldness of the initial vision of Mayor Anthony A. Williams. It is critical that complex regeneration projects are rooted in a powerful, well-thought-out, and inspiring vision for the city and the areas that will be the focus of regeneration. The vision should be bold enough to inspire action, to challenge the status quo, and to have identified some initial seeds of success to demonstrate its potential and build confidence.

  The vision should have a sufficiently long-term perspective to allow it to survive political and market cycles, yet be grounded in short-term projects that can show tangible results that build civic support and generate resources and investment.

  The vision should be rooted in an appreciation of the history of the city that can be called on to inspire the future. In Washington, DC, this was recalling the history of great plans that had transformed the city in the past.

  Plans should understand the DNA of the city: the formulation of plans should be grounded in an appreciation of the positive aspects of the city's physical form and social and economic issues. Where does the city work well and where does it break down? The vision and plan must honestly confront those areas where the city is not functioning. This ranges from confronting shortcomings in its urban form, to social divisions and economic inequalities. The Anacostia Waterfront was an area of the city where the powerful urban form of the city—its street grid, sequencing of open spaces, and building fabric—had been ruptured through successive and destructive waves of urban renewal, highway building, and a lack of planning. And the city had severe divisions by race, class, and economic position that

Photograph 9.1   Before and after photos of the riverfront and Navy Yard area

a. July 2008

b. May 2015

Source: Jacqueline Dupree. Used with permission. Permission required for re-use.

segregated the city. If these issues were not addressed, they would continue to affect the city.

- *Understanding the basics—market position, land ownership, and existing conditions—is critical.* In embarking upon a regeneration project it is important to have a clear understanding of the "base position" of the proposed regeneration area. Establishing the base position is critical to assessing the scale and scope of the challenge, the barriers that will need to be overcome, and the opportunities that can be created.

A firm understanding of the market position of the area and its relationship to the broader market position of the city and region is essential to assessing the viability of the proposed project and the level of public and private support that will be required. It is also important to be clear about the true market position of the site. If it is a low demand, weak market, the strategy will differ greatly than if it is a growth market.

The AWI vision was able to have a level of confidence in its goals because the growth of the city was constrained and the logical direction of growth was to move toward the river where land values were lower, transportation access was in reasonable condition, and the river was close to the core of the city. While success was far from assured, at least the prerequisites for growth seemed clear so that if the substantial barriers to growth could be unlocked there would be a market to take advantage of the opportunity.

Also important is gaining a clear understanding of land ownership. It is quite often the case that government does not have an accurate understanding of its land assets. For example, at the time AWI was initiated, the city did not have a comprehensive database of its publicly owned land or the status of existent land development agreements and title. As public land is often a critical asset to spur regeneration, this basic information is essential to have from the outset.

- *Success depends on an integrated framework and approach.* AWI has been successful because it was conceptualized from the start as a comprehensive and integrated approach to urban revitalization. It recognized the interdependencies between the physical, social, economic, cultural, and environmental regeneration of the area. Urban regeneration can only be successful when the "silos" that traditionally divide professional disciplines and narrowly focused bureaucracies are overcome and transcended.

Cities are complex phenomena that cannot be neatly disaggregated and therefore require comprehensive approaches. This is not to say that all problems can be solved, or solved simultaneously, but that there has to be an approach that takes into account the multiple dimensions of urban regeneration.

It is important to create a framework plan that articulates the vision, is comprehensive in scope, sets clear goals and targets to measure success, and illustrates the types of actions and projects that the plan envisions. The "art" of developing a successful framework plan is to combine clarity and flexibility. When the vision is clear and the basic principles of what constitutes success are set forth, the plan can be more successful. The plan must be flexible in how it is implemented because conditions will change and it must adapt. With clear vision and principles, the plan can survive political and market cycles and can be "refreshed" as needed to address the changing circumstances of the city. Fifteen years after its publication, the AWI Framework Plan continues to serve as a foundational document.

- *Process matters: the community must "own" the project.* AWI invested enormous energy and resources to engage the myriad constituencies that were required to support the effort; the highest political levels of the Office of the President of the United States; Congress; the dizzying maze of federal, regional, and local governmental agencies; community groups on all sides of the river; the private sector; and the city at large. Thus the broad, multifaceted, and exhaustive engagement process was designed and implemented. This was essential to the plan's success.

  The vision for AWI, while emanating from the mayor, had to be shared and, more important, "owned" by the broadest possible cross-section of the political, business, civic, and community leadership.

- *Leaders must create and sustain a sense of urgency.* Because the challenges of urban regeneration can seem overwhelming and the time horizon for seeing results can appear distant, it is important to generate an urgency to act and to create momentum. Otherwise the project risks being perceived as "yet another plan." Recognizing this from the start, it is important to identify why the regeneration is of utmost importance to the city and why it demands attention when there are so many competing and pressing demands in the city.

  At the same time, decisions should not be made too hastily—such as selling parcels or approving poorly conceived projects—that could foreclose future opportunities.

- *The "time" dimension, expectations, and phasing must be well managed.* One of the greatest challenges is to manage public expectations that changes will happen "overnight." At the same time, there will always be concerns that the project is going too slowly. It is therefore important not to succumb to the pressure of overpromising results that cannot be achieved. It is important to educate both the broader public and the markets early on about the timeline for the project so they have a realistic understanding of how the project might unfold.

AWI, as is typical in most complex regeneration projects, is a 20- to 30-year effort that will unfold over time and in phases. Even with the success of AWI, today there is still a vast effort to be undertaken that will take a generation to fully complete. This does not mean it has failed. But it is critical to set progress against a realistic understanding of the length of time in which urban redevelopment occurs.

- *Intimidating barriers to success must be overcome.* At the beginning of AWI many counseled the mayor not to be so ambitious in his plans, if for no other reason than that the majority of the land along the waterfront was owned by the federal government. The mayor was undaunted by this and believed that a powerful vision could transcend jurisdictional boundaries and that it was his duty as mayor of the city to have a vision for the city irrespective of land ownership. This example illustrates the simple point that in every regeneration undertaking there will be challenges that will appear overwhelming and discouraging. But these should not necessarily dissuade one from action or pursuing the vision if there is an underlying belief in both the power of the idea and the possibility for change.

  Instead of deferring from pursuing the vision or acceding the vision to the federal government, the mayor engaged the federal government in the pursuit and support of his vision. The first action was to organize the MOU, which began the process of tackling the challenge head-on. It is therefore important to identify and understand the challenges facing the project and to devise strategies to engage these issues in the best forum and manner.

- *Leaders must identify anchors and seize opportunities by planning and doing.* As part of the strategy of instilling urgency in the regeneration project from the outset, it is critical to identify anchors and catalytic actions that send a strong message that the project is "for real." Simply put, it is important to demonstrate real commitments to the vision as early as possible and to be opportunistic and aggressive in securing commitments to the regeneration project. AWI learned from the Barcelona project the value of planning and acting concurrently and not sequentially. Anchors such as the relocation of the federal DOT and the Hope VI grant for the Capper Carrollsburg housing complex were essential in giving AWI credibility even as the AWI Framework Plan was still being developed.

Anchors or catalysts do not have to be large and capital-intensive projects. Smaller, community-based initiatives are equally valuable, such as support of the work of the Earth Conservation Corps in building the early segments of the Anacostia riverwalk.

- *Public and private resources must be leveraged effectively.* All regeneration projects require the leveraging of public and private resources in the most effective manner. The key is to understand when, and to what extent, public resources are required to unlock and incentivize private capital and when the market is sufficiently robust to operate without public financial support.

  The synchronization of public and private capital must be carefully managed to inject public capital and land to catalyze development while protecting the public investment (through future profit sharing) and not overinvesting once the market is established. AWI needed early and significant public investment to establish the viability of, and confidence in, the market potential of the area. Without the investment in key anchors and infrastructure, and the disposition of key publicly owned parcels in the first phases of AWI, the development of the Near Southeast area would not have happened.

- *Leaders must show tenacity and focus for success in the "long game."* In every speech, in every municipal budget, in every request of the federal government, the mayor would advocate for investment in AWI. This unrelenting tenacity and focus, not to the exclusion of other priorities, but as a primary emphasis of his vision for the city, sent a powerful message that AWI was not a fleeting interest but a foundation of his agenda for the city. With each success, such as obtaining a Hope VI grant, or funding for the South Capitol Street bridge, Mayor Williams would build on the momentum to request the next critical investment rather than claim victory and turn his attention elsewhere. He understood the "long game" of regeneration and the need for a tenacious focus on the AWI if the foundation was to be secured.

  This is an important lesson for all regeneration projects and political leaders and urban administrators who undertake them. It must become widely and popularly known that the regeneration project is the priority. Governments and markets respond to these messages and will test the level of commitment by the depth and tenacity of the commitment of leaders. If at the first sign of controversy or failure, the process falters or is abandoned, the regeneration effort will be doomed.

- *Planners must embed success by following a strategically forward-looking organizational strategy.* It is important to plan for how best

Statistical Annex

| | Ward 1 | Ward 2 | Ward 3 | Ward 4 | West of the river | | East of the river | | Near Southeast/ Navy Yard Cluster 27 | City |
					Ward 5	Ward 6	Ward 7	Ward 8		
Population 1980	70,124	56,986	68,919	83,237	89,145	81,715	91,496	96,707	6,273	638,328
Population 1990	71,005	59,457	74,271	78,010	83,198	75,556	78,966	86,437	5,040	606,900
Population 2000	71,711	63,408	75,375	75,001	71,604	70,912	70,011	74,037	4,633	572,059
Population 2010	74,492	76,883	78,887	75,773	74,308	76,000	71,748	73,662	5,705	601,723
Black non-Hispanic 1990 (%)	60	19	5	79	86	66	96	92	85	65
Black non-Hispanic 2010 (%)	33	10	6	59	77	43	95	94	46	51
White non-Hispanic 1990 (%)	20	65	84	15	11	30	2	6	13	27
White non-Hispanic 2010 (%)	40	70	78	20	15	47	2	3	44	35
Poverty rate 1980 (%)	22	17	8	9	18	22	22	27	43	19
Poverty rate 2010 (%)	15	18	8	12	20	21	26	36	34	18
Unemployment rate 1980 (%)	8	4	3	6	7	8	9	10	16	7
Unemployment rate 2010 (%)	7	4	4	11	15	8	19	22	14	10
People without HS diploma 1980 (%)	38	17	10	30	42	39	43	41	62	33
People without HS diploma 2010 (%)	16	6	3	16	18	10	17	19	17	13

Anacostia Waterfront Initiative

| | Ward 1 | Ward 2 | Ward 3 | Ward 4 | Anacostia Waterfront Initiative | | | | | City |
| | | | | | West of the river | | East of the river | | Near Southeast/ Navy Yard Cluster 27 | |
					Ward 5	Ward 6	Ward 7	Ward 8		
Avg. family income 1980 (2010 US$)	57,495	125,535	153,822	93,673	65,842	66,659	58,428	47,582	37,171	77,355
Avg. family income 2010 (2010 US$)	99,428	222,345	240,044	115,482	79,153	129,674	57,387	43,255	77,952	118,384
Violent crimes 2000 (per 1,000 people)	16	16	3	9	18	20	18	22	40	15
Violent crimes 2011 (per 1,000 people)	14	9	2	8	13	12	17	19	10	12
Property crimes 2000 (per 1,000 people)	55	125	31	37	49	70	44	34	135	55
Property crimes 2011 (per 1,000 people)	50	67	21	30	46	49	42	38	53	43
Median price of single family homes 1995 (2012 US$)	169,000	502,000	469,000	194,000	146,000	161,000	127,000	126,000	109,000	184,000
Median price of single family homes 2012 (2012 US$)	576,000	1,160,000	915,000	475,000	395,000	621,000	231,000	212,000	776,000	541,000

Source: Washington, DC, Office of Planning (2012), based on U.S. Census Bureau data.
Note: Avg = average; HS = high school.

to create an organizational strategy to give the regeneration project the best chance for success in the long term. There is no one answer or way to do this, and this can change over time. It is very dependent on the local context, political circumstance, and the strength and relative positions and roles of the public and private sectors. AWI tried to embed success through the creation of a public development corporation, the Anacostia Waterfront Development Corporation. As we saw, this was dissolved when a new mayor was elected who wanted AWI within the mayor's office. In New York City, a city–state development entity, the Battery Park City Authority exists to this day and was instrumental in guiding one of the most successful urban waterfront regeneration projects in the United States.

Thus whereas there is no single organizational model to follow, it is critical that the issue of institutional and professional capacity to support the long-term regeneration project needs to be developed as part of the planning process and cannot be an afterthought. This may require legislation, new financing mechanisms, and building a professional team that may not currently exist within the government.

Notes

1. This section draws heavily on Brandes (2005).
2. Kingman Park Civic Assoc. vs. U.S. Environmental Protection Agency, 84 F. Supp. 2d 1 (D.D.C. 1999)
3. District of Columbia Water and Sewer Authority (now DC Water), WASA's Recommended Combined Sewer System Long Term Control Plan (2002).
4. NCPC is a U.S. government agency that provides planning guidance for Washington, DC, and the surrounding National Capital Region. Through its planning policies and review of development proposals, the commission seeks to protect and enhance the extraordinary resources of the nations capital. The 12-member commission includes three presidential appointees, one of which must be from Virginia and one from Maryland; the mayor of Washington, DC; the chair of the city council; two mayoral appointees; and the chair of the House and Senate committees with review authority over the district. Other commission members include the heads of the three major land holding agencies, which are the Department of Defense, the Department of the Interior, and the General Services Administration. The commission is supported by a professional staff of planners, architects, urban designers, historic preservation officers, among others.
5. Williams first rose to prominence as DC's chief financial officer during the final term of Mayor Marion Barry in September 1995. By that

time, however, Washington was in the midst of a fiscal crisis of such proportion that Congress had established a financial control board charged with oversight and management of the district's finances. The same legislation had created the position of chief financial officer, who had direct control over day-to-day financial operations of each city agency and independence from the mayor's office; whereas Barry had the authority to appoint Williams, only the Control Board had the authority to fire him. This gave Williams an unusual level of political strength in dealings with the mayor, with whom he had a number of very public battles; Williams, who had the support of the Control Board as well as Congress, tended to win these battles, even gaining power in 1996 to hire and fire all budget-related city staffers. Given this political clout, Williams began steering DC's finances toward financial recovery, moving from a US$355 million deficit at the end of 1995 to a US$185 million surplus in the city's fiscal year 1997.

6. For a brief description of the HOPE VI program, see chapter 1.

7. "Developer Chosen for Southeast Federal Center," *Washington Post*, January 29, 2004. http://www.washingtonpost.com/wp-dyn/articles /A62028-2004Jan29.html.

8. "Mayor Proposes $230M Jump-Start for SE Fed Center, "*Washington Business Journal*, June 5, 2006. http://www.bizjournals.com/washington /stories/2006/06/05/story1.html?page=all.

9. "A Neighborhood Arises at the Yards," *Washington Post*, May 28, 2007. http://www.washingtonpost.com/wp-dyn/content/article/2007/05/27 /AR2007052701000.html.

10. For more information on PILOT and TIF, see chapter 1.

11. See District of Columbia Housing Authority. http://www.dchousing. org/?docid=9, and "Frontin'," *City Paper*, November 28, 2012. http:// www.washingtoncitypaper.com/blogs/housingcomplex/2012/11/28 /frontin/. Accessed March 2016.

12. A BID is a defined area within which businesses pay a self-imposed additional tax in order to fund projects within the district's boundaries. The BID is often funded primarily through the levy but can also draw on other public and private funding streams. BIDs provide services, such as cleaning streets, providing security, making capital improvements, constructing pedestrian and streetscape enhancements, and marketing the area. The services provided by BIDs are supplemental to those already provided by the municipality. For more information, see chapter 1.

13. "Up to 825,000 RSF in the Heart of Washington's Capitol Riverfront District," *Washington Business Journal,* September 19, 2014. http:// www.capitolriverfront.org/_files/docs/capitol-riverfront-bid_new.pdf. Accessed March 2016.

14. Leadership in Energy and Environmental Design is a system for rating the design, construction, maintenance, and operation of green homes, other buildings, and neighborhoods. The rating system has been

developed by the U.S. Green Building Council, a private nonprofit membership organization that promotes sustainability in green building design, construction, and operation.

15. "Paying for the Ballpark," *Washington Post*, March 24, 2008. http://www.washingtonpost.com/wp-dyn/content/graphic/2008/03/24/GR2008032400073.html. Accessed March 2016.

16. "The District Is One Signature Away from 200 Acres of New Land," *Washington Post*, November 17, 2006. http://www.washingtonpost.com/wp-dyn/content/article/2006/11/16/AR2006111601605.html. Accessed March 2016.

17. "Southwest Neighborhood in D.C. Takes a Turn for the Better," *Washington Post*, April 27, 2010. http://www.washingtonpost.com/wp-dyn/content/article/2010/04/26/AR2010042601676.html. Accessed March 2016.

References

Brandes, Uwe Steven. 2005. "Recapturing the Anacostia River: The Center of 21st Century Washington, D.C." *Golden State University Law Review* 35 (3).

Capitol Riverfront BID. A Health market for growth. Special advertising supplement for the Washington Business Journal. September 2014.

Government of the District of Columbia. 2003. "The Anacostia Waterfront Framework Plan." Office of Planning. https://www.anacostiawaterfront.org/awi-documents/the-anacostia-waterfront-framework-plan-2003/. Accessed March 2016.

———. 2010. "Anacostia Waterfront Initiative: 10 Years of Progress." http://ddot.dc.gov/publication/anacostia-waterfront-initiative-10-years-progress. Accessed March 2016.

Washington, DC, Office of Planning. 2012. Data from U.S. Census Bureau. http://planning.dc.gov/node/616252. Accessed March 2016.

Washington City Paper. 2012. "Those Greedy, Greedy Nats."August 28. http://www.washingtoncitypaper.com/blogs/looselips/2012/08/24/those-greedy-greedy-nats/. Accessed March 2016.

Washington Post. 2008. "Paying for the Ballpark." March 24. http://www.washingtonpost.com/wp-dyn/content/graphic/2008/03/24/GR2008032400073.html. Accessed March 2016.

World Bank. 2013. "Best Practices for Urban Regeneration: The Case of National Administrative Center CAN." World Bank, Washington, DC.

———. 2014. Informal Presentation by AWI's Planning Team. World Bank, Washington, DC.

People Interviewed

Uwe Brandes, Director of Capital Projects for the Anacostia Waterfront Corporation and Associate Director of the District of Columbia Office of Planning

Stephen Green, Director of Development, District of Columbia, for former Mayor Anthony Williams

Alex Nyhan, Senior Vice President – Development, Forest City

Michael Stevens, President, Capitol Riverfront Business Improvement District

Tammy Shoham, Vice President of Economic Development and Research, Capitol Riverfront Business Improvement District

Brett Banks, Project Executive, General Services Administration

Barbara Smith, Project Manager, US Environmental Protection Agency

Map 10.1 **Singapore**

a. Singapore's city center

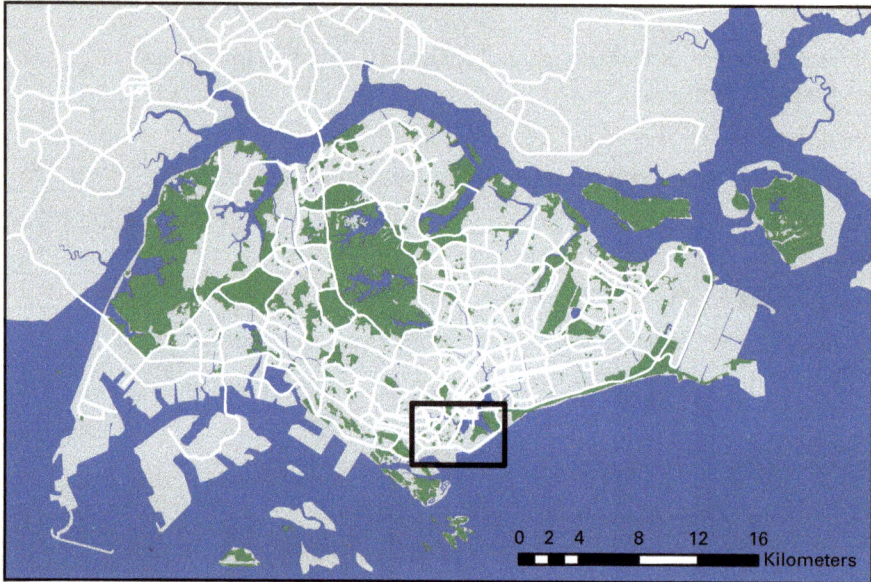

b. Singapore's redevelopment area

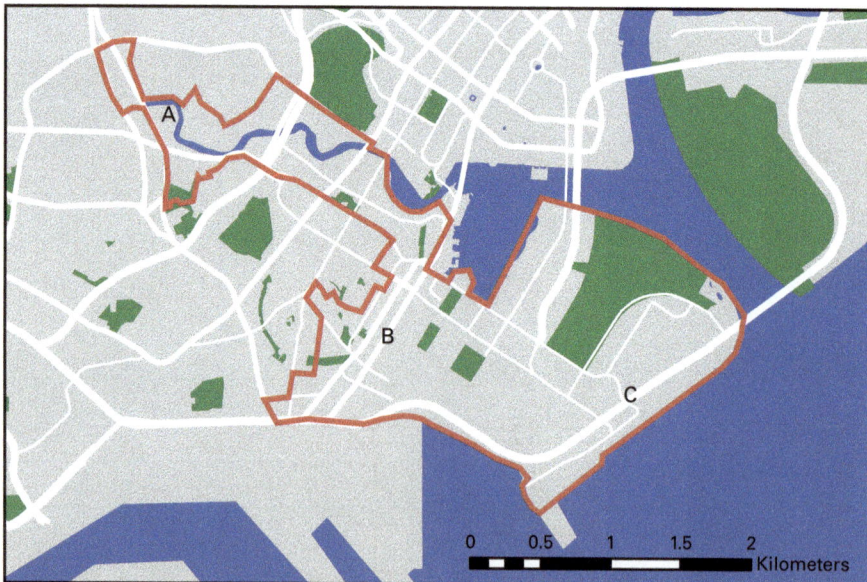

Source: World Bank using Open Street Map data 2015.
Note: A is the Singapore River area, B is the Golden Shoe area, and C is Marina Bay.

CHAPTER 10

Singapore: Urban Redevelopment of the Singapore City Waterfront

Introduction

The redevelopment of Singapore's city center from an overcrowded, slum-filled decrepit urban core during the beginnings of self-governance in the 1960s to the modern global financial center it is today is often held up as one of the most visible manifestations of the city-state's success. Along the urban waterfront stretching from Singapore River to Marina Bay, the juxtaposition of modern skyscrapers against the traditional sloping roofs of the historic conserved districts highlights Singapore's unique approach to urban revitalization. This approach combined urban renewal, conservation, and new growth areas on reclaimed land.

This case study provides an overview of how the urban renewal process worked through a process of legislative, policy, and government organizational reforms. The study consists of three selected areas along the waterfront in Singapore's city center: the Golden Shoe District, the Singapore River, and the Marina Bay (see map 10.1).[1] Each of these areas was representative of how urban redevelopment was carried out in different periods. The transformation of these areas also illustrates how extensive state intervention combined with active private sector participation successfully enabled urban redevelopment in Singapore.

Context and Background

Singapore today is a densely populated metropolis with 5.4 million people living on 716 square kilometers (sq km) of land. This represents more than a three times increase from the population of 1.7 million in the 1960s, when Singapore was plagued with economic woes, poor infrastructure, and squalid conditions. Within the same period, the total gross domestic product (GDP) grew from S$2.1 billion in 1960 (about US$1.5 billion) to S$390 billion in 2014 (about US$304 billion) (Department of Statistics 2015), illustrating the rapid growth and development during the past five decades.

Urban Structure

The urban areas in Singapore are organized along the southern coast of Singapore's main island, together with a "loop" of built-up areas around the Central Catchment Area—a "green lung" consisting of reservoirs and nature reserves in the heart of the island. Anchoring the urban areas along the southern coast is the city center, often referred to as the Central Area. The Central Area is the historic heart of the city. It now houses most of the commercial functions in Singapore within a high-density compact area, with a good mix of retail establishments, hotels, and entertainment amenities.

Most of the housing is located in public housing towns constructed across the island along major transport corridors over the past five decades, a result of an extensive and successful public housing construction program initiated since 1960. Industrial areas and port functions are concentrated to the west of the island, while the international airport, Changi Airport, is located to the east.

Unlike most other cities in the world, Singapore is both a city and a state. This means that Singapore also has to accommodate land for defense and water catchment purposes within the 716 sq km. Doing so requires effective governance and integrated long-term planning to strike a balance between economic, social, and environmental goals.

Organizational Structure

Being a city-state, Singapore has a centralized, single-tier government. Planning and development policies are generally made at a national level without a separate layer of local government. The Ministry of National Development (MND) is the key ministry responsible for national land-use planning and development. Several autonomous government agencies or statutory boards support it, each with their own specific missions and area of purview. The key agencies under MND are the Urban Redevelopment Authority (URA), the national land-use planning and conservation authority, and the Housing and Development Board (HDB), the public housing authority. The agencies also work together with other agencies from different ministries, such as the Singapore Land Authority (under the Ministry of Law) and the Public Utilities Board (under the Ministry of Environment and Water Resources). Specifically, they work through a range of structures (both formal and informal) to deliver an integrated and coordinated approach to planning and implementation.

A unique aspect of Singapore's urban development approach is the extensive public ownership of land, comprising some 70 percent. Most of the developments in Singapore today are on leasehold land—typically 99 years for residential and 60 years for commercial. These are developed through a combination of land sales programs to the private sector for a stipulated lease term according to sales conditions, and public construction programs, in particular for public housing.

Financial Structure

Financing and budgeting is done as part of a "whole-of-government" approach in Singapore. In contrast to most other city governments, urban infrastructure and development programs are not financed solely through land sales or development charges. Rather, they draw from a broader pool of operating revenues known as the Consolidated Fund, which includes direct and indirect taxes, licenses, and permits, as well as other user fees and charges. Similarly, other ministries such as education and defense would also derive funding from the Consolidated Fund.

Fiscal prudence is the central principle guiding Singapore's approach to sustainable infrastructure financing. Government expenditure is categorized into operating and development expenditures. The Development Fund in particular provides funding for the government's direct development expenditures undertaken by the ministries. In addition, it provides for grants and loans to, or investments in, public agencies or corporations for development projects. The Development Fund draws from a few sources, including the Consolidated Fund, proceeds of loans made for the purposes of the fund, interest, and other income from investments of the fund, as well as repayments of any loans made from the fund. Some statutory boards such as the URA, which operate on a self-financing basis, are excluded from the government budget but may seek government funding for development projects.

The 1960s and 1970s saw economic expansion at GDP growth rates in excess of 8 percent. Supported by efficient collection machinery, the government could then leverage these growing revenues to meet rising expenditures. In the early years following self-government and later independence, the government prioritized funding for key national priorities, such as building physical infrastructure for economic and social development, particularly housing. In those years, Singapore also borrowed from the World Bank and the Asian Development Bank to finance the construction of infrastructure, such as power stations, reservoirs, the Changi Airport, and so on. However, the Singapore government was also clear that external borrowing would be used primarily to develop the economy and for productive purposes, rather than for consumption. Since 1989, the Singapore government has not had to raise loans for development expenditures. Indeed, the country has ceased to carry any public external debt since 1995.

As the economy matured toward the late 1980s, the Reserves Protection Framework was put into place in 1991 to foster fiscal prudence and financial sustainability. Singapore's reserves are divided into two portions: "past reserves" refer to reserves accumulated in previous terms of government, and "current reserves" refer to those that accumulated by the current term of government. Hence, some government revenues and collections, such as land sales and capital receipts are secured as reserves and cannot be spent by the current government.

The constitution contains two key rules that promote fiscal responsibility and sustainability: (a) the current government cannot draw on past reserves unless agreed to by the president, and (b) the current government is only allowed to use up to 50 percent of the net investment returns from past reserves. These rules oblige the current government to balance its budget over its term of office, typically five years. Singapore has enjoyed budget surpluses in most years since 1988, running relatively small budget deficits in a few years when the global economic environment was particularly difficult. In fiscal 2012, the government's operating revenue was about S$55.2 billion (US$38.86 billion, based on the 2012 exchange rate), with total expenditures of S$50.1 billion.

Overall Context: Laying the Groundwork for Urban Renewal, 1959–1960s

When Singapore achieved self-governance in 1959, the housing shortage in the city center was severe because of the post-war population boom, an influx of immigrants, and the destruction of housing stock during the war. Overcrowding was acute, with some areas in the city accommodating well over 1,000 persons per acre (Housing and Development Board 1963). The increasing population and high unemployment rates also generated immense pressure on the government to create more jobs through economic growth. Indeed, these pressures forced the newly elected government to initiate swift, extensive, and often radical urban interventions to improve the well-being of the population.

Despite the acute urban problems, the new government did not immediately embark on an urban renewal program. Instead, the first five years or so of self-governance were used to establish an effective system of urban governance, which eventually enabled the success of ensuing urban renewal initiatives.

Institutional Reorganization

Singapore began by reorganizing the planning and housing development agencies. Within weeks of taking office in 1959, the new government absorbed the various departments of the city council into the government ministries (Dale 1999). This created a centralized, single-tier government, which helped expedite decision-making. This fact sets the Singaporean case apart from other urban regeneration experiences because the decision-making process was set at the *national* level.

Two new authorities—the Planning Department and the HDB—were subsequently set up in 1960 to take over the Singapore Improvement Trust's core responsibilities of land-use planning and public housing provision, respectively. The establishment of such action-oriented agencies, each with their dedicated missions and objectives, helped to translate government policies into results. Indeed, they proved to be fundamental to Singapore's urban development. Moreover, key planning and development agencies such as HDB and the Planning Department, were part of the MND, which helped to successfully coordinate and implement projects.

Legislative Reforms

Several legislative changes were implemented in the early 1960s, contributing significantly to subsequent urban renewal efforts by both the public and private sectors. The most significant was the Land Acquisition Act (1966), which had several aspects that enabled the process of land acquisition to be highly effective. The act allowed the state to secure private land for public benefit, without excessive financial cost. Its four key features were (a) the ability to acquire private land for an extremely broad variety of purposes, (b) the lack of any process for landowners to challenge the government's decision to acquire their land, (c) the below-market rate compensation paid to landowners, and (d) the establishment of an Appeals Board to adjudicate the amount of compensation paid (see box 10.1).

Box 10.1   **Singapore's resettlement policies**

Land acquisition and resettlement were jointly conducted in Singapore and played a fundamental role in making land available for redevelopment, particularly in the early days. Once a piece of land was acquired by the state, existing residents and activities needed to be relocated before development could commence. The cleared land would then be vested in the state on an unencumbered basis. It could then be aggregated to enable comprehensive planning and the construction of modern buildings and infrastructure, either by the state or by private developers.

Resettlement was new to most people in the 1960s and was initially viewed with great hostility and suspicion. Resistance and even violence against public officers were not uncommon. After the land had been acquired, those who remained on state land were deemed to be squatting. Squatters who refused to move were called to court after being notified and paid compensation, after which a police warrant would be granted to evict the occupants.

Whereas former landowners and other "interested parties," such as long-term leaseholders were awarded compensation under the Land Acquisition Act, informal dwellers without legal entitlements to the land (for example, short-term tenants-at-will or squatters)—which formed a substantial group of people to be resettled—were awarded ex gratia compensation under the resettlement regime. Ex gratia compensation was generally based on "land improvements" to such things as shacks, vegetable plots, and livestock. These dwellers were also given priority allocation of new land (for farmers) or HDB flats.

The government established a meticulous compensation formula. Resettlement officers were sent out to measure the height of fruit trees; the number and age of pigs, chickens, and ducks; the size of prawn and fish ponds; and the size and height of dwellings. These were valued at market rates— although many squatters still attempted to inflate their compensation claims. Some would plant "instant trees," move livestock and plants from one plot to another to be recorded multiple times, or even partially uproot their existing trees and plants to make them seem taller and therefore deserving of higher compensation. Others moved quickly onto the sites to take advantage of the compensation. To thwart these efforts, a prompt census and photographic record of the squatters' assets had to be taken by resettlement officers, once the land acquisition was announced.

(Box continues on next page.)

Box 10.1   **Singapore's resettlement policies** *(continued)*

Despite these challenges, resettlement was necessary due to the unsanitary and overcrowded living conditions in many slums. The government quickly learned from earlier resettlement experiences and carefully planned and calibrated the process together with its public housing policies, contributing to eventual success. For instance, many squatters and farmers were initially resettled into HDB flats in Toa Payoh, formerly a swamp with few existing residents. Crime levels, such as theft, rose significantly in these resettlement areas, and the northeast part of Toa Payoh became known as "the Chicago of Singapore."

These social problems were addressed when many of these early emergency and one-room apartments were rebuilt in the late 1970s and early 1980s. The concept of an HDB precinct—a 2–3 hectare public housing area—was introduced then and ensured that the newly resettled residents did not comprise more than one-third of the total precinct population. This was necessary to create a mixed-income neighborhood. In so doing, HDB managed not only to avoid creating a vertical slum but also to help family members, particularly the children of the resettled households, to learn good habits and lifestyles from other urban dwellers in the same precinct.

Source: Centre for Liveable Cities 2014a.

The state pays compensation for all land acquired from landowners. The formula for calculating the compensation amount has evolved over the years. The 1966 act determined compensation by taking the market value of the property and discounting it through various conditions and exclusions. In 1973, the concept of a statutory date of acquisition was introduced for the purposes of determining market value. This meant that when properties were acquired, compensation would be awarded using the estimated market value at the historical statutory date, rather than the current market value of the property. From 2007 onward, the state used current market value as the primary basis for compensation.

The most important immediate effect of the 1966 Land Acquisition Act was that the new government gained the legal authority to acquire large tracts of private land quickly to develop new towns and industrial facilities. After the formation of HDB in February 1960, early acquisitions were made primarily for public housing.

The 1964 Planning Bill amendment also incorporated several changes to support urban renewal. One of the changes was the introduction of a development charge system, which required developers to pay to the state a part of the benefit arising from the grant of development permission, as well as the increase in land value brought about by public development (mainly infrastructure improvements, roads, sewage, water, and public housing) in the vicinity. The development charge would in turn contribute to the financial resources required for public infrastructure and development. Another change introduced in the 1964 bill was the requirement for developments to be completed within two years of granting development permission. This helped to reduce land hoarding and speculation within the private sector, especially after planning permission was granted.

Until 1980, the development charge was implemented based on fixed rates determined by two parameters: land use and geographical location of the site (Central Area/Town Map [for urban areas outside of the Central Area]/Island Map [rural areas]). From 1980 to 1984, the development charge levied was either a prescribed percentage of the appreciation in land value as assessed through spot valuation by the chief value official, or a value calculated using a schedule of fixed rates, whichever was higher. In 1985, fixed rates were dropped for spot valuation only.

From 1989 until today, fixed rates based on permitted land use and geographical location were reintroduced, albeit with a more sophisticated schedule including 47 geographical areas and 8 use groups. This helped to strike a balance between achieving reasonable accuracy in land valuation and transparency for the private sector.

Establishing a Comprehensive Planning Framework

The government also recognized the need for a comprehensive planning framework to guide the redevelopment of the city (see box 10.2). However, the planning framework at that time was based on the conservative 1958 Master Plan. It generally served as an instrument of development control and was severely inhibitive and inadequate for guiding urban growth and development. In addition, the new Planning Department was severely understaffed and had insufficient capabilities to formulate a fresh approach to master planning that could coordinate the future public and private developments that Singapore needed.

Singapore sought urban planning technical assistance from the United Nations (UN). This was carried out in three phases, starting in 1962 with a six-month study by a UN town planning expert, Erik Lorange. He recommended that the Central Area (Singapore City center) be divided into 21 precincts according to development priority, based on factors such as the availability of land for redevelopment and the stage of deterioration of existing buildings. Lorange also initiated the idea of private participation through the sale of development sites by the government, with appropriate incentives and guidance from the public sector.

A second UN team of three experts—Otto Koenigsberger, Charles Abrams, and Susumu Kobe—collectively referred to as the "KAK team," followed up on Lorange's recommendations in 1963. The team recognized that Singapore could not afford to wait for a new master plan to guide its future development, thereby replacing the 1958 Master Plan. They advocated a strategy of urban renewal, as a "movement from negative and restrictive planning to actual implementation" (Abrams, Kobe, and Koenigsberger 1980).

The recommendations by the KAK team paved the way for the first urban renewal initiatives in Singapore in 1966. In the meantime, the UN involvement in planning continued into a third phase as part of the

Box 10.2   Singapore's planning process

Singapore's planning system brings together the policies and programs of various government agencies and incorporates them into a common national urban policy document, known as the *concept plan*. The concept plan is a strategic integrated land-use and transportation plan that sets out the directions for the next 40–50 years. It takes into consideration all projected land use demands for housing, industry and commerce, recreation and nature areas, and transport and utility infrastructure, as well as defense requirements. For instance, when the HDB, Singapore's public housing authority, ramped up its development program to meet public housing demand in 2012, land had already been safeguarded in various parts of Singapore for housing development under the 1991 Concept Plan. The concept plan is revised once every 10 years to ensure that it keeps abreast of changing demographic, social, economic, and technological trends.

The emphasis on having tight coordination among the different stakeholders in government is not just at the strategic level of the concept plan but also at the level of the master plan. The master plan translates the broad and long-term strategies of the concept plan into detailed plans for implementation over 10–15 years and guides the exercise of development controls. This high level of coordination has been important to Singapore, for instance, in ensuring an adequate transport network. The transportation corridors for the development of Singapore's Mass Rapid Transit system had been identified and safeguarded since the 1971 Concept Plan, ensuring that when new housing estates are developed, they are adequately served by public transport.

Singapore's experience has also shown that insisting on a high degree of coordination has another practical outcome—it allows for conflicts among different agencies to be resolved early and for trade-offs to be dealt with in constructive and innovative ways. For example, during the review of the 1991 Concept Plan, the Ministry of National Development, the Ministry of the Environment, and the Ministry of Trade and Industry made a proposal to lift both the urbanization cap and population density limit within protected water catchment areas. These had previously been put in place to minimize the risk of contaminating Singapore's water resources. Following the proposal, future developments would no longer need to be curtailed as long as pollution control measures were rigorously implemented.

Source: Centre for Liveable Cities 2014b.

four-year state and city planning project from 1967. This project eventually produced Singapore's first concept plan in 1971, setting out the development needs for a projected 4 million population by 1992. The key idea in the 1971 Concept Plan was the decision to develop Singapore along a Ring Plan, which addressed both land-use and transport system planning. Today, much of Singapore's built-up areas—particularly the ring-cum-linear shape—is based on the 1971 Concept Plan.

Addressing the Housing Shortage through the Public Housing Program

The most critical task that Singapore had before launching its urban renewal process was to address the acute housing shortage in 1959. The government fully recognized that alternative accommodation for families and businesses affected by urban renewal initiatives had to be planned for and built to minimize the negative social impacts of urban renewal.

The newly created HDB wasted little time in addressing the housing shortage problem (see box 10.3). To relieve the overcrowding in the Central Area, the HDB's first five-year building program was concentrated within the vicinity of the city center to allow easy access to jobs in the city, including Singapore's first public housing estate, Queenstown (Housing and Development Board 1963). Subsequent development of housing estates on the rest of the island was planned together with economic projects where jobs were located. The Jurong Industrial Estate and the Jurong New Town were good examples of colocation of jobs and public residential developments.

In contrast to many cities that were carrying out urban renewal during that time, resettlement activities due to urban renewal generally did not face opposition from the displaced communities. Many of the families that were resettled were living in rent-controlled properties that had not been

---

Box 10.3 The prominent role of the Housing and Development Board in Singapore's urban development

The Housing and development Board's (HDB's) achievements are impressive in light of the high-profile failures of other large-scale public housing projects worldwide. About 9 percent of Singapore's residential population lived in HDB flats in 1960. This proportion grew steadily to 87 percent by around 1990.

Since its inception, the HDB has been more than a provider of public housing. Indeed, it was responsible for the development of entire new towns of about 100,000–250,000 population. The HDB was involved in a multitude of different functions over the decades, including town planning and estate management; architectural design; engineering work; the quarrying and production of bricks, granite, and tiles; the provision of housing loans; the rental of commercial and industrial premises; the provision of spaces and facilities for recreational, educational, and social activities; land reclamation; road planning and construction; car park management; and landscape design within HDB estates.

To meet the demand for public housing, business space, and amenities from 1960 to 2011, HDB constructed more than 1,011,000 dwellings, 19,460 commercial premises, 15,230 industrial premises, more than 1,500 schools and community facilities, and 110 recreational sites, as well as bus interchanges, civil defense shelters, and numerous car parks.

Upon internal self-governance in 1959, this extensive construction program was enabled by placing housing as a top national priority alongside defense and economic development. Indeed, it was given clear priority in the government budget. At the same time, HDB made continual efforts to keep the housing program affordable to the government and flats affordable to homebuyers. For example, the HDB dismantled uncompetitive tendering practices which had restricted tendering to a small group of registered contractors.

In the early 1980s, HDB introduced prefabrication technology to reduce construction costs. The Land Acquisition Act was another key instrument that enabled the government to keep a ceiling on development costs by allowing the government to acquire land for public purposes at lower than market compensation.

Source: Centre for Livable Cities 2013.

maintained and that had become extremely deteriorated. The public housing offered to them was of much higher quality. The government was also proactive in its approach with the community. For instance, resettlement officers were sent to the areas identified for redevelopment to talk with the community, explain the process, and show them the new area where they would move. The government also ensured that the people would be resettled together with their neighbors in the new public housing estates. This was done to address concerns about the loss of community ties after resettlement.

Beginnings of Urban Renewal

By 1965, the government had achieved a breakthrough in public housing. The HDB had completed 54,430 units from mid-1960 to mid-1965, exceeding the target of 51,031 units for HDB's first 5-Year Building Program. In contrast, Singapore Improvement Trust had constructed only 23,019 units from 1927 to 1959. This new-found confidence was reflected in HDB's Annual Report for 1965, which announced that HDB had then achieved "a position to tackle the twin problems of urban renewal and the provision of housing to keep pace with the rapid rate of population growth" (HDB 1966).

Having established supporting legislative mechanisms, development strategies based on action programs, and an effective public housing program by the mid-1960s, the government started to focus on urban renewal. The Urban Renewal Unit was created in 1964 under the Building Department of HDB to take charge of the urban renewal program in the Central Area (see box 10.4).

Box 10.4   History of the Singaporean Urban Redevelopment Authority

The Urban Redevelopment Authority (URA) began as the Urban Renewal Unit (URD) in 1964. At the time, it was part of the Housing Development Board (HDB). As the URD, its first task was to undertake the comprehensive urban renewal and redevelopment of the Central Area. The goal was to redevelop the Central Area as a vibrant and modern commercial center. This required the resettlement of affected residents and businesses.

In 1974, the URD was converted to an autonomous statutory board—the Urban Redevelopment Authority—under the Ministry of National Development. It focused on the comprehensive redevelopment of the Central Area. Between 1967 and 1989, the URA vacated and sold a total of 184 hectares of land. The resulting 155 development projects transformed the Central Area into a modern financial and business hub. These achievements were possible because of the greater autonomy and flexibility in implementing urban renewal programs as a statutory board.

In 1989, the URA merged with the former Planning Department and the Research and Statistics Unit of the Ministry of National Development to form the new URA. With the combined expertise of

(Box continues on next page.)

Box 10.4 History of the Singaporean Urban Redevelopment Authority *(continued)*

these agencies, the URA was able to plan and facilitate the physical development of Singapore with greater efficiency. In this regard, it was able to meet land demands while balancing economic and social development. At the same time, URA was also established as the national conservation authority, undertaking the crucial responsibility of conserving Singapore's heritage.

With the approval of the Planning Act in 2003, the URA was recognized as the national land planning authority. The act was amended to include land planning and development control as URA functions.

The government's goal of making Singapore a more competitive city led to the URA's new mission in 2002 — "To make Singapore a great city to live, work and play in." Over the years, the URA's role has expanded in tandem with the changing needs of Singapore — from the early days as a unit focused on the urban renewal of the Central Area, to the multifaceted role it has today, which includes land-use planning, land sales, place management, conservation, and urban design, as well as promoting architectural excellence.

Source: URA (http://www.ura.gov.sg/uol/about-us/our-organisation/ura-history.aspx).

Pilot Urban Renewal Precincts, Precincts N1 and S1

The redevelopment strategies developed by UN experts in 1962–63, which divided the entire Central Area into 21 precincts, was soon implemented by the government, starting with Precincts N1 and S1 at the northern and southern ends of the Central Area, respectively. These precincts were identified for priority in redevelopment, mainly due to the availability of "soft" areas consisting of reverted properties[2] or state properties, such as Outram Prison in Precinct S1, where redevelopment could be more easily initiated by the government.

Early urban renewal efforts in Precincts N1 and S1 saw the government continuing the extensive public construction program within these precincts—not only to resettle displaced residents but also to accommodate the affected businesses in public mixed-use complexes known as "resettlement centers." The "resettlement centers" helped maintain spatial proximity between homes and businesses, mimicking the traditional shop-house setting in the urban areas of Singapore, where residents would live directly above their businesses. This helped to minimize the hardship of resettlement typically experienced by the displaced population in urban renewal programs. Indicative of the social objectives of such resettlement centers, the first annual report by the URA (established by the Urban Renewal Department [URD]) in 1974–75 highlighted that these centers were built to "ensure that the small entrepreneur retains his place in the commercial heart of the Republic" (URA 1975). Photographs 10.1 and 10.2 show some of the improvements in these precincts.

Whereas redevelopment was extensive, Precinct N1 also saw some of the first efforts in heritage protection. The historic Fatimah Mosque was

Photograph 10.1   **Precinct N1 before redevelopment and after**

Source: ©Urban Redevelopment Authority. Chua 1989.

Photograph 10.2   **Precinct S1 before redevelopment and after redevelopment**

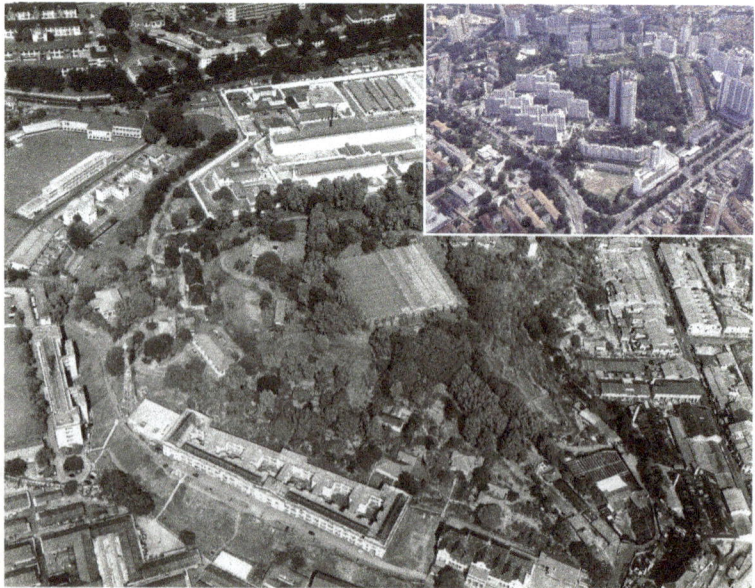

Source: ©Urban Redevelopment Authority. Chua 1989.

preserved as part of the precinct plan, paving the way for subsequent comprehensive urban conservation initiatives in Singapore in the 1980s.

Government Land Sales: Private Sector Participation in Urban Redevelopment

Whereas the urban renewal of Precincts N1 and S1 saw extensive public
action, the government also recognized the need for both the public and
private sectors to cooperate and complement each other's efforts in order to
achieve the intended balance between social and economic goals for the
urban renewal program. The Sale of Sites program, also known as the
Government Land Sales program, was established in 1967 to offer state
land through public tender to the private sector for development within a
stipulated lease period, usually 99 years for residential uses (Housing and
Development Board 1968). The program eventually became highly successful and played a crucial role in the redevelopment of the Central Area, with
25 percent for office space, 68 percent for shopping space, and 22 percent
for hotel rooms completed from the sale sites by 1983 (URA 1984). The
location of the sites sold through this program is illustrated in map 10.2.

In general, sale sites were identified by the government and took into
consideration several factors including (a) overall land use and development
plans, (b) acquisition and clearance programs, (c) supply and demand

Map 10.2   **Locations of sites sold under the Sale of Sites program, by 1983**

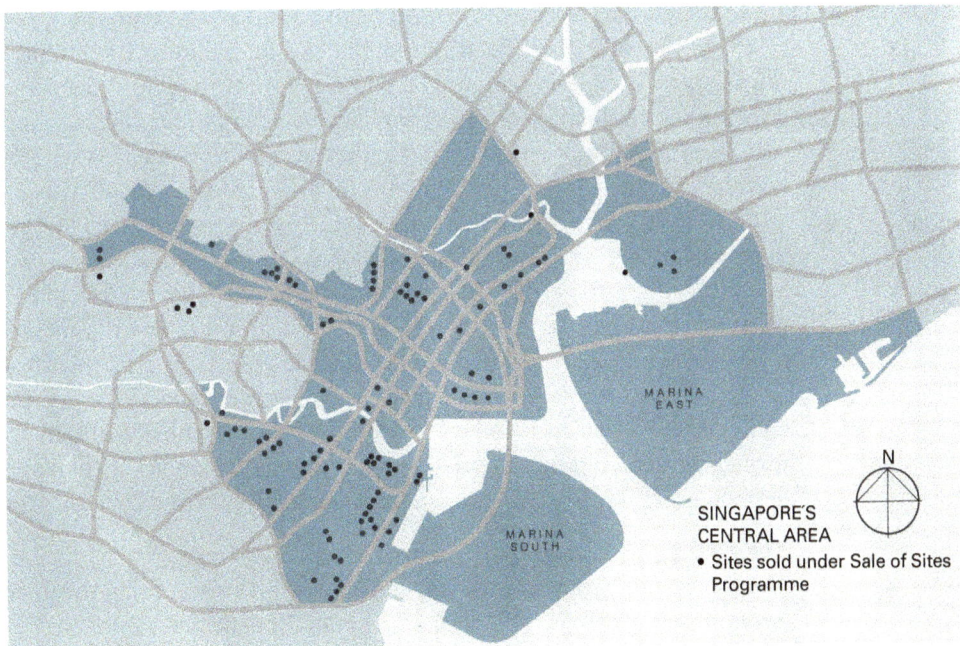

Source: ©Urban Redevelopment Authority. URA 1983.
Note: Dots mark the locations of the sites sold under the Sale of Sites Program.

projections for various types of developments, (d) feedback from private developers, and (e) policy directives from the Ministry of National Development (URA 1983).

Planning and Implementation of Sale of Sites of program

Comprehensive planning and preparation works for each site were to commence once sites were identified for sale under the program. This was expected to take about four to six months. Preparation works included the checking of infrastructure and utilities provisions; drawing up tender conditions, parceling and finalizing site boundaries, and other technical information, such as carrying out soil surveys.

Tender conditions included planning parameters (such as allowable uses; development intensity, height control, and so on) and urban design requirements (including setback requirements, pedestrian connectivity, and so on), as well as general terms and conditions of sale. These conditions stipulated clearly what developers could or could not do. At the same time, they ensured that developments met the planning objectives by complying with planning, urban design, and other technical requirements by public agencies. Over the years, safeguards were built into tender conditions. These were implemented to prevent land hoarding and speculation, as well as to ensure the timely delivery of the planned supply of spaces.

Bidding Process

The tender mechanisms for the Sale of Sites program have evolved since the program was first launched in 1967. In general, the tender mechanisms aimed to achieve transparency and integrity in the bidding process.

Under the Singapore Constitution, the elected president has the discretionary power to decide on the use and disposal of the government's past reserves, which includes land and buildings owned by the state. To implement these constitutional safeguards, a set of rules to protect past reserves was agreed on between the government and the president. These rules would require land transactions to be conducted through a competitive and open tender process and to be disposed of at fair market value.

Most of the sites in the Government Land Sales program are sold today via the "price only" tender, in which concept and design are usually not taken into account. Tender approaches that use price as the sole criterion for award include open tenders and auctions. For tender processes that require concept and design to be taken into consideration, various methods were formulated according to the different requirements demanded by the planned developments for the land parcels, for example, the Marina Bay sale sites.

The First Sale of Sites

The first sale of Sites was launched in 1967, with 14 sites within the Central Area, including Precincts N1 and S1. The sites for the first sale ranged from 19,300 square feet (sq ft) to 408,700 sq ft and were mostly on state-owned land or land that had been acquired under the Land Acquisition Act (1966). The sale sites were also "preapproved"[3] for technical planning permissions, with the URD seeking planning clearances from the various technical departments in the government prior to the sales. This was especially significant given the lack of transparency in the planning framework during that time, when developers had no way of obtaining assurance for allowable developments on their land parcels, other than going through the protracted process of formal planning submissions. Developers could then proceed with their investments on the sale sites with certainty.

Information packages including full details and simulated plans for each sale site, known as "Developer's Packets," were sold to prospective developers. The simulated plans and building designs were prepared by the URD to demonstrate the available development potential. The developer who successfully tendered for the site, however, was free to propose alternative building designs for the sale site development within the stipulated development guidelines.

The types of developments in the First Sale ranged from hotels to office buildings, with total capital investment cost estimated at S$90 million (1967 prices) (Housing and Development Board 1968). The government also introduced Incentives in the First Sale to encourage private sector participation in the program. These include the following:

- A property tax rate set at 12 percent instead of the usual 36 percent for a period of 20 years
- Exemption from property tax payments for six months, plus one month per story of the building to be constructed
- Waiver of development charges
- Successful tender with a down payment of 20 percent (inclusive of the 5 percent deposit for each tender) on signing the relevant building agreement; the remaining 80 percent of the tendered premium could be paid over 10 years without interest
- Priority in clearance of layout and building plans given to ensure that building operations start on schedule
- Possession of vacant sites given within three months of the building plans being approved

The incentives were eventually repealed over time as the confidence and demand from investors proved resilient. The tax concession was removed in 1974 and the down payment and installment scheme ceased in 1988.

Redevelopment of the Golden Shoe District

Scoping

The Golden Shoe area housed the traditional commercial heart of Singapore since colonial times. It is centered on Raffles Place, which used to be known as Commercial Square. Prior to redevelopment, the area consisted of low-rise but densely laid out commercial and retail establishments, as well as overcrowded shop-houses sitting on highly fragmented land parcels. Along the waterfront at Shenton Way, there were warehouses, jetties filled with "bumboats," and car parks where street hawkers plied their wares on empty lots. This highly fragmented land ownership meant that comprehensive redevelopment could not take place and the potential of the most prime real estate in Singapore could not be maximized.

The rapid modernization of Singapore's economy created significant demand for commercial development by the late 1960s. This was largely due to the establishment of the Asian Dollar Market in 1968 on the advice of Singapore's economic adviser, Albert Winsemius. At the same time, the successful industrialization program also increased the demand for office and commercial spaces. To fuel growth in the commercial sector, the government started the redevelopment of the commercial heart of Singapore around Raffles Place, which was to become the Golden Shoe District.

Although the earlier urban renewal efforts in Precincts N1 and S1 saw an extensive role undertaken by the state, the redevelopment of the Golden Shoe was planned with incentives for leveraging private sector funds. The government was involved in the planning of the area, carrying out site clearance and resettlement, building infrastructure, and social amenities. The private sector then would provide the financial resources and entrepreneurship to undertake development on lands cleared and released by the government for sale.

Planning

During the 1960s, the government recognized that Singapore lacked a focused financial center to support a burgeoning finance industry. Although several banks were located in Raffles Place, their presence was diffused among commercial and retail activities. However, the area was already beginning to redevelop by the mid-1960s, with two major state financial institutions—the government-financed Development Bank of Singapore and the Central Provident Fund—constructing high-rise head quarters at the location. Building on these efforts, the government then decided that the area should be redeveloped into a financial center similar to Wall Street in New York City.

Plot ratios were established in view of the road capacity in the area, as well as the pedestrian and vehicular traffic generated. Site coverage was generally maximized at 100 percent because of the urban context. The URD also drafted urban design guidelines for the redevelopment of the area, generally specifying a podium and tower configuration to maintain visual uniformity and human scale. The URD planners were also careful in planning for the actual placement of each tower to allow buildings on both sides of Shenton Way, the main thoroughfare, to have views of the harbor. To activate the ground floor, a continuous link of all buildings for pedestrian and shopping activities along sheltered walkways integrated with the podiums was planned. In addition, a minimum of 2 percent of the total development costs were to be spent on landscaping as stipulated in the land sale conditions (Chua 1989).

Financing and Implementation

Redevelopment of the Golden Shoe began with the second Sale of Sites in 1968, with 14 sale sites consisting mostly of state land. Five of the parcels were along the waterfront at Shenton Way, where public warehouses, car parks, and jetties previously served as a port area for bumboats. With the rise of large-scale container ports, which were to be constructed at Tanjong Pagar, further away from the city, such traditional ports were left under-used and were eventually phased out for redevelopment. After consultations with the Economic Development Board, the URA launched the 1968 land sale. It was focused on office developments, with a total of 163,881 square meters (sq m) of available office space. This was a substantial increase from the first sale, which focused mainly on hotel developments and created only 56,723 sq m of office space.

Whereas the Land Acquisition Act and Sale of Sites program provided the government with a powerful mechanism to make land available for comprehensive redevelopment by the private sector, state intervention in the form of land acquisition was generally reserved as a means of last resort. To the extent possible, the government tried to facilitate comprehensive redevelopment by the private sector through other market-friendly policies.

Lifting of Rent Controls

Other than the issue of fragmented land ownership, the key obstacle to comprehensive redevelopment by the private sector at that time was the Rent Control Act. The act was imposed in 1947 to protect tenants from rising rents due to a housing shortage in the aftermath of World War II. It prevented rent from rising beyond the 1939 level on any kind of premises. However, rent control had two detrimental effects on the urban condition. First, artificially suppressed rents made it uneconomical for property owners to conduct proper building maintenance. Second, the redevelopment of properties was severely restricted, as property owners could only repossess properties under certain limited conditions. Furthermore, the 1961 amendment prevented the owner from repossessing the house for new developments (Chua 1989). This effectively deprived the city of available land for redevelopment.

To address the negative effects of rent control, the government passed the Controlled Premises (Special Provisions) Act in 1969, empowering the Ministry of Law and National Development to phase out rent control for advertised areas. Owners of properties were allowed to recover their premises through the payment of compensation to their tenants as determined by the Tenant Compensation Board under the Ministry of National Development.

The government was mindful of the negative consequences of rent decontrol. These included the need to resettle affected households that could then overtax the housing supply and sharply increase land values, thereby leading to inflationary pressures. Therefore, rent decontrol was limited only to designated areas to study the effects. The area defined by Telok Ayer Street, Maxwell Road, Shenton Way, Cross Street, Raffles Quay, Collyer Quay, Boat Quay, and Market Street was selected as a pilot area for rent decontrol in February 1970. This area not only encompassed the traditional commercial heart of Singapore at Raffles Place but also included within and around its vicinity eight of the sites from the second Sale of Sites in 1968. Map 10.3 shows the location of areas impacted by rent decontrol regulation.

The area was coined by the media as the "Golden Shoe," after the "Golden Mile" at Beach Road and the shape of the advertised rent-decontrolled district, which resembled an upturned shoe. This phase of redevelopment was generally undertaken by the private sector, including the assembly of land and the resettlement of affected tenants. For example, the developer of the Clifford Centre project bought an adjacent parking lot and adjoining developments, creating a parcel with two frontages facing the prestigious addresses of Raffles Place and Collyer Quay. About 38 tenants ranging from the Stock Exchange of Singapore and Malaysia to private law and medical professionals were resettled by the developer. They were offered either priority for spaces in the newly completed development and/or cash compensation (Chua 1989). By 1974, within five years of rent decontrol, 13 projects were completed in the Golden Shoe, with another 14 projects under construction and nine approved (Chua 1989). Photograph 10.3 illustrates the change made by the urban regeneration efforts in Golden Shoe District.

Compulsory Land Acquisition

Land fragmentation still proved to be a problem, particularly in instances in which private land owners were unable to come to an agreement on

Map 10.3 **Plan showing extent of rent decontrol, according to the Controlled Premises (Special Provisions) Act of 1969**

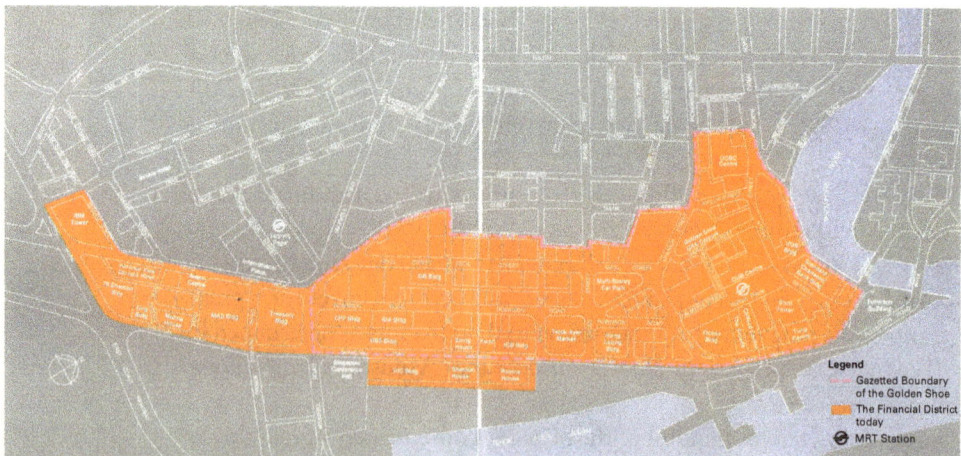

Source: ©Urban Redevelopment Authority. Chua 1989.
Note: Orange areas indicate those affected by rent decontrol.

Photograph 10.3 **The Golden Shoe District before regeneration and after regeneration**

Source: ©Urban Redevelopment Authority. URA Annual Report 1977/78.

land amalgamation. To speed up the redevelopment process, the government started advertising small, uneconomical parcels for acquisition in 1975. The area of 4000 sq ft was used as a guide for assessing parcel sizes, below which independent redevelopment was deemed unviable. In what was to be the largest land acquisition exercise to date in Singapore, a total of 215 lots amounting to 31,700 sq m were advertised for acquisition.

To avoid compulsory acquisition by the government which would provide only lower than market rate compensation, some owners appealed to the government, presenting plans for readjustment and redevelopment. Three of the appeals were approved and the land was returned to the owners for their redevelopment. The acquired land was subsequently cleared and reconfigured by the government. It was sold in the eighth and ninth Sales of Sites in 1980 and 1981, respectively, for development by the private sector.

By 1979, the government again felt that redevelopment in the Golden Shoe District was slowing down. Once again, the MND issued guidelines regarding the minimum sizes of proposed developments (an 8,000 sq ft site area) and situations whereby small land parcels should be acquired either by the state or by the private sector. The threat of compulsory acquisition was further emphasized, with the imposition of a three-month deadline for compliance. Eventually, 16 lots amounting to 4,226 sq m were acquired in 1980.

The low compensation rates for public land acquisition served different purposes for different types of developments. On the one hand, it ensured that land acquisition by the government was kept financially sustainable particularly for public infrastructure and developments. On the other hand, compulsory acquisition was used as a threat to force the private sector to amalgamate their land for comprehensive private redevelopment. However, this was enforced only as a last resort to overcome market encumbrances.

Public Infrastructure Works

In addition to land acquisition and amalgamation, the public sector also facilitated the urban redevelopment process through public infrastructure works. These included road improvement projects, which involved rationalizing the street network, road widening, and conversion of streets into one-way traffic pairs, where feasible. Additional parking facilities were required because of technical difficulties in providing car parking within developments as per the plan guidelines. These were provided through construction of public car park stations in the area. A prorated levy was then charged to the developer for the insufficient provision of car parks required with the development.

Public food centers termed as "hawker centers" were also constructed in the district, offering inexpensive food for the working population. Environmental improvement works including construction of pocket parks and landscaping of the waterfronts along the Singapore River and the harbor waterfront were also implemented from the early 1970s to enhance the living environment of the district.

Singapore River: Urban Revitalization through Environmental Cleanup and Conservation

Scoping

The comprehensive redevelopment of the Golden Shoe District was well underway by the mid-1970s. At the same time, the nature of the Central Area also changed drastically by the late 1970s due to public development programs and the successful Sale of Sites program, which generally focused on the Central Area. The latter contributed significantly to the redevelopment of the Central Area, with 25 percent for office space, 68 percent for shopping space, and 22 percent for hotel rooms completed from the sale of sites by 1983.

The change can be most keenly observed from the residential population figures for the Central Area. At the start of the urban renewal process in the 1960s, the Central Area had about 360,000 residents. By 1980, the population decreased to 155,800. So too the percentage of the total population living in the Central Area decreased accordingly from 30 percent to 6.5 percent. The Central Area had therefore transformed from a traditional, mixed-used urban core to a predominantly commercial hub with modern developments.

The government began to turn its attention toward the Singapore River area, which together with the other major water body in the city center, the Kallang Basin, suffered from heavy pollution. The Singapore River, located adjacent to the Golden Shoe District, was at that time still choked with trading bumboats that polluted the water with garbage and oil spills. Sewage from the squatters, street hawkers, and industries along the river further contributed to the pollution problems. The heavily polluted environment occurred despite the fact that the Singapore River was located strategically within the Central Area. In several ways, it also defined the historical center of the city.

Key Planning Reforms in the Late 1980s
During the late 1980s, a number of reforms were implemented to improve the transparency of the planning system. These reforms were aimed at impacting how urban redevelopment in Singapore would be carried out and, in the greater scheme of things, facilitate greater efficiency with regard to private sector participation in urban development.

Development Charge Tabulation
The Development Charge system used prior to the reforms was highly inefficient and lacked transparency, especially for the private sector. Following the last review in 1980, the determination of development charge rates was based on either prescribed rates or valuation from the chief value official, whichever was higher. The property boom in 1980–81 meant that the chief value official's valuation was often the higher amount. This not only required the time and effort for the chief value official to conduct numerous case-by-case valuations for each development application but also created uncertainty for the developer in terms of how development charges would be levied.

The convoluted Development Charge system spurred the MND to review the system in 1989. After the review, it was decided that the Development Charge rates would be based on a standardized table detailing the use and geographical sector. The table would be revised by the chief value official and publicly announced every six months, thereby allowing developers to calculate the amount of charges expected to be levied for their proposed developments. Private developers could then estimate the amount of resources required and assess the risks even before the development application was approved.

Creating a Future-Oriented Master Planning System
The 1958 Master Plan and the subsequent master plan reviews until the 1990s served only to update developments that existed or had already been approved. In assessing plan submissions, planners were guided by a separate set of internal "drawer" plans on future developments for their respective areas of purview. This meant that the private developer could only submit a development application in order to ascertain the allowable development for his property.

The URA sought to address this soon after the completion of the 1991 Concept Plan, widely regarded as Singapore's watershed plan. The Development Guide Plans (DGPs) translated the broad intentions of the concept plans to detailed local plans with the whole island divided into 55 DGP areas. Future land use, development control, and road network information were shown for each of the DGP areas, together with planned supporting public amenities. This brought about a more systematic and transparent means of communicating future planning intentions to the public.

The intention was to create DGPs for the entire island and to form a new forward-looking statutory master plan.

The precursor to the DGPs was the detailed guideline plans that the URA had been preparing for the Central Area. These DGPs were eventually completed by 1998, following which the new master plan was advertised. The DGPs and the subsequent master plans were a radical departure from the previous master plans in terms of clarity and resolution of details. This gave the private sector greater certainty about their developments and contributed to a more efficient urban development system.

The Great Singapore River CleanUp

The story of Singapore's River transformation began with the environmental cleanup of the river. The government recognized the negative impact of poor environmental conditions on the city-state's image, as well as the Singapore River's historical importance and potential for redevelopment. In addition, as with the port area in front of Golden Shoe, the Singapore River would eventually be rendered unsuitable for trading port activities using the traditional bumboats, given the increasing importance of large-scale container ports.

Most important, the government recognized the need to conserve and protect water resources in the city-state to work toward water security. Then prime minister of Singapore, Lee Kuan Yew, eventually launched a campaign in 1977 for the government to cleanup the Singapore River and the adjoining Kallang Basin within 10 years.

A master plan was drawn up for the cleaning up of the river, highlighting the need to resettle squatters, farmers, backyard trades and industries, as well as street hawkers within the entire catchment area of the Singapore and Kallang Rivers. The massive cleanup involved extensive multiagency action and coordination to relocate affected activities and people to alternative accommodations constructed and allocated by the government. Riverbeds were dredged to remove the debris and infrastructure, such as modern sewers, had to be constructed by the government.

The cleanup was eventually completed in 1987. This involved resettlement of more than 26,000 families, the majority of whom were resettled into public housing by the HDB. It also involved the phasing out of 610 pig and duck farms, as well as the resettlement of 2,800 backyard trades and small industries into industrial estates built by the HDB and the Jurong Town Corporation (the public agency that develops and manages industrial estates and related facilities). Finally, it required the relocation of 4,926 street hawkers into food centers built by the HDB, URA, and the Ministry of the Environment.

The cleanup cost the government nearly S$300 million, excluding resettlement and compensation costs. This initial investment in infrastructure and coordination work by the government clearly demonstrated the government's commitment to revitalizing the Singapore River area. It was to eventually pay off, as the private sector played its respective role in conserving the properties and implementing new developments through the Government Land Sales program.

Planning

As the cleanup of the river was underway, the URA began drafting new plans for the river. The resettlement of the activities along the river involved the clearing of dilapidated and vacant buildings in several areas. Additional physical infrastructure such as roads, bridges, and pedestrian walkways also had to be planned and constructed to support new developments.

A different approach for the Singapore River was undertaken. It involved preservation of the heritage along the river, in contrast to the redevelopment in the adjacent Golden Shoe District, which transformed the traditional low-rise commercial district into a modern financial center of skyscrapers (see box 10.5). This came about at a time when Singapore started considering urban conservation on a comprehensive scale in the early 1980s. This followed the large-scale redevelopment of the city center in the 1960s and 1970s by both the public and private sectors.

Box 10.5   Urban conservation in Singapore

Conservation in Singapore was not considered on a comprehensive scale until the 1980s. This was largely due to the pressing need for land for redevelopment to address social and economic needs during the 1960s. By the early 1980s, the context began to change drastically, and the URA started to proceed with conservation activities on a comprehensive scale (Singapore Institute of Architects 2013).

The Central Area Structure Plan
With the decision made in 1982 to construct the Mass Rapid Transit system, the Central Area Planning Team—an interagency planning committee for the Central Area headed by the URA—seized the opportunity to earmark areas well served by transport infrastructure for intensification. These would then be balanced out by the creation of major green spaces and lower-rise historic districts "to be conserved as the lungs that breathe life into the city" (Kong 2011). With room for growth accommodated within the intensive development areas, the Central Area Planning Team was able to strategize and rationalize the extent of areas for conservation.

The conservation plan was prepared and eventually announced to the public in 1986 as part of the Central Area Structural Plan. The plan was also supported by the Tourism Product Development Plan study commissioned by the Singapore Tourism Promotion Board, which provided the economic justification for Singapore to enhance its unique identity as a tourist destination.

Achieving Conservation Objectives through Public-Private Efforts
Urban conservation was a relatively new concept in the 1980s. The government had to play a significant role in ensuring the success of conservation efforts in Singapore. As then Minister of National Development, Suppiah Dhanabalan, explained, "the role of the Government in conservation was to designate areas, set guidelines, initiate pilot projects and provide infrastructure" (Straits Times 1988).

(Box continues on next page.)

Box 10.5   **Urban conservation in Singapore** *(continued)*

Private-sector participation was also considered a "key requirement," as the private sector owned three-quarters of the conservation areas (*Straits Times* 1988). The advertising of the conservation districts was therefore only half of the battle. Over the following years, the URA had to work hard to convince the shop-house owners of the importance and value of conservation. To demonstrate to the private sector the government's commitment to the conservation program, the URA successfully implemented a pilot project in Tanjong Pagar in 1987. This project showed how the dilapidated shop-houses could be restored into charming properties (Singapore Institute of Architects 2013).

A great emphasis was placed on the economic viability of conservation initiatives. A strategy of adaptive reuse was chosen, following a carefully planned and phased lifting of rent controls, as announced by Minister Dhanabalan in 1988. This was combined with incentives for private sector developers to address development constraints faced by conserving buildings. These included incentives such as the waiver of the car park deficiency charges[a] and the waiver of development charges for change of use.[b]

The economic value of conserved properties was soon realized with greater private sector interest in conserved buildings. The Conservation Initiated by Private Owners Scheme launched in 1991 further boosted private sector participation by providing incentives to private owners to offer their properties for conservation.

Flexible Framework to Balance Conservation and Development

To balance conservation and development needs, the URA formulated a flexible framework for the conservation program. Conservation of the advertised areas was to be implemented in phases and prioritized according to their historic importance and development pressures.

Whereas the oldest urban districts would be conserved fully in the Central Area, new developments were allowed to be mixed among conserved buildings outside of the Central Area. The URA also allowed the back portion of the relatively younger conserved buildings outside of the Central Area to be redeveloped within stipulated guidelines—without compromising on the scale of the streetscape. This allowed for greater development intensity for the conserved land parcels belonging to shop-house.

a. Conserved shop-houses faced limitations in providing adequate car parking spaces to comply with development guidelines. They would have attracted car park deficiency charges if not for the waiver.
b. Conserved shop-houses were then zoned as residential, which would have attracted higher development charges should they be converted into commercial use.

The URA's 1985 Singapore River Concept Plan was drafted in line with the overall conservation approach that combined economic viability with heritage preservation. The plan formed part of the Central Area Structure Plan in 1985 that laid out the conceptual structure of the future development of the entire Central Area. The concept plan had three key objectives, including (a) give the river a new economic role by repositioning it as a commercial and activity corridor in the Central Area, (b) initiate a sustainable revitalization process by balancing economic viability with conservation, and (c) optimize land use along the river while preserving rich architectural heritage and retaining old buildings with architectural and historical merit while developing new buildings at a compatible scale.

The plan identified suitable uses (for living, working, and playing) for the three distinct development zones along the river, namely Boat Quay, Clarke Quay, and Robertson Quay (see map 10.4). Different focal themes were developed for these zones, thereby leveraging the selective conservation of historical buildings.

A 15-meter-wide continuous riverfront promenade connecting the three zones and three new pedestrian bridges was planned and subsequently constructed by the government. Urban design and planning guidelines were also stipulated by the URA to enhance the different themes envisioned for each zone. This was to be done by guiding and controlling the land uses and physical developments to be built and introduced by the private sector.

The planning for Singapore River continued to be refined. Following the completion of the 1991 Concept Plan, which set out the overall vision for urban development in Singapore pulling together everything from transport to recreation, a detailed DGP was developed for the Singapore River planning area. The DGP set out the vision to transform Singapore River into "an exciting activity corridor that capitalizes on the river frontage and reflects its unique historical character" (URA 1992a).

At the same time, the government was also actively engaging the private sector through public exhibitions and consultations. This helped to secure buy-in/ownership from the people and the private sector for the government's plans. The public engagement efforts—which were targeted more toward the professionals in the private sector—contributed to the DGP for Singapore River, which was published in 1994.

Detailed planning strategies for Singapore River identified since the DGP included the following:

Land use

- Develop the area into a vibrant mix of residential and commercial uses by stipulating allowable land uses and development intensities for each parcel of land. Activity-generating uses such as retail were required to front the river to create an active waterfront.
- Encourage phasing out of existing industries and warehouses by planning for land uses of higher values (for example, commercial or residential) (see map 10.4).

Urban design and conservation

- Conserve buildings of architectural and historical value.
- Develop urban design guidelines to create appropriate building scale and character for infill developments to contribute to a sense of place and maintain a human scale. To achieve the human scale for the area, blocks fronting the promenade were limited to a maximum height of four stories; buildings set back from the water were allowed to be as

Map 10.4 **Locations of Robertson Quay, Clarke Quay, and Boat Quay in the Singapore River planning area**

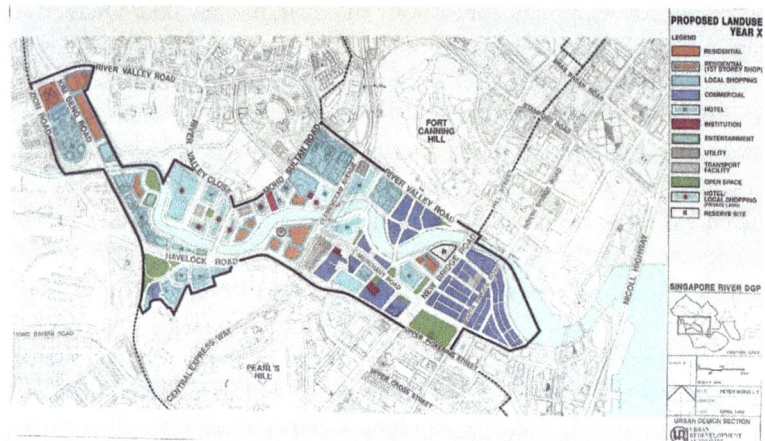

Source: ©Urban Redevelopment Authority. URA 1994.
Note: Colors in the map indicate different types of land use. This is a mixed-use neighborhood with residential (orange), commercial (blue), institutional (red), entertainment (light blue), and open space (green), among other uses.

high as 10 stories. Buildings were also required to abut the promenade to create a sense of place along the waterfront.

- Construct public-space amenities, including pedestrian malls, promenades, and bridges for better accessibility to the waterfront.

Transport

- Provide boat landing points to facilitate water activities.
- Widen roads and extend works to cater for anticipated increase in traffic volume from redevelopment.

Financing and Implementation

Public Construction Efforts

The government demonstrated its commitment to the public to revitalize the river with a plan to improve the environment along the river, following the completion of the cleanup. The public implementation efforts focused on the construction of public amenities planned by the URA. These were mostly implemented by the Public Works Department under the MND. They included a 6-kilometer (km) long riverfront pedestrian promenade completed in 1999, restoration of historic bridges, and three new pedestrian bridges constructed across the river in the Robertson Quay area. The river wall was also reconstructed from 1992 to 1999, which involved damming and dredging the river bed. River boat landing points were integrated with the river wall construction, allowing river taxis to ferry tourists along the length of the river.

Implementing the Conservation Program

The implementation of the URA's conservation program along the Singapore River was not without problems. The release of the first phase of plans for restoring the 108 shop-houses at Boat Quay was met with skepticism by the existing private owners. They were not convinced that restoring the shop-houses would bring about adequate returns. The problem was further exacerbated by the fragmented ownership of the Boat Quay properties, which made coordination among the private sector challenging.

Despite the difficulties in implementing the conservation program, the URA tried various means of encouraging the owners to restore their shop-houses, including workshops, public dialogues, and seminars with the owners (see box 10.6 for an example). After four years of lackluster progress in conservation at Boat Quay, the government decided to package a cluster of 54 state-owned shop-houses at the adjacent Clarke Quay as a single parcel for sale. The successful tender and announcement of the redevelopment plans at Clarke Quay, in which the successful tenderer committed US$75 million to develop the site, helped convince the Boat Quay property owners to restore their properties. The government did not offer additional tax or other types of incentives. To prevent the use of arson as a means of bypassing the conservation plan, however, the government threatened the owners of Boat Quay with acquisition. By the early 1990s, the conservation of Boat Quay and

Box 10.6   Blending the old and the new in China Square

The China Square was one of the earliest urban areas in Singapore, dating back to the early nineteenth century. Similar to Chinatown itself, the area was bustling with traditional trades and activities. China Square also occupied a prime location between Chinatown, the financial district in the Golden Shoe, and the Singapore River—presenting significant development potential (see map B10.6.1).

China Square's historical significance naturally led the URA to include it in its conservation proposals in 1989 for the MND's approval. However, due to Singapore's limited land supply and the site's strategic location, the MND requested that the URA review its proposal.

The URA remained determined to conserve as much of China Square's character, charm, and heritage as possible. Several development options were studied to formulate solutions that could achieve high density on the site, while conserving most of the buildings. High-density developments were planned to be concentrated at the periphery of the site along the main roads, with the rest of the site retained as conserved shop-houses.

Through careful urban design considerations, an interesting mix of new and old building forms and roofscapes, as well as a network of pedestrian streets and open spaces were incorporated in the revised proposal. This innovative concept that combined development needs with heritage conservation was eventually supported by the MND. The URA then proceeded with the land sales tender for the China Square sites, which were sold separately to seven developers.

(Box continues on next page.)

Box 10.6   Blending the old and the new in China Square *(continued)*

Map B10.6.1   Location of China Square URA planning subzone

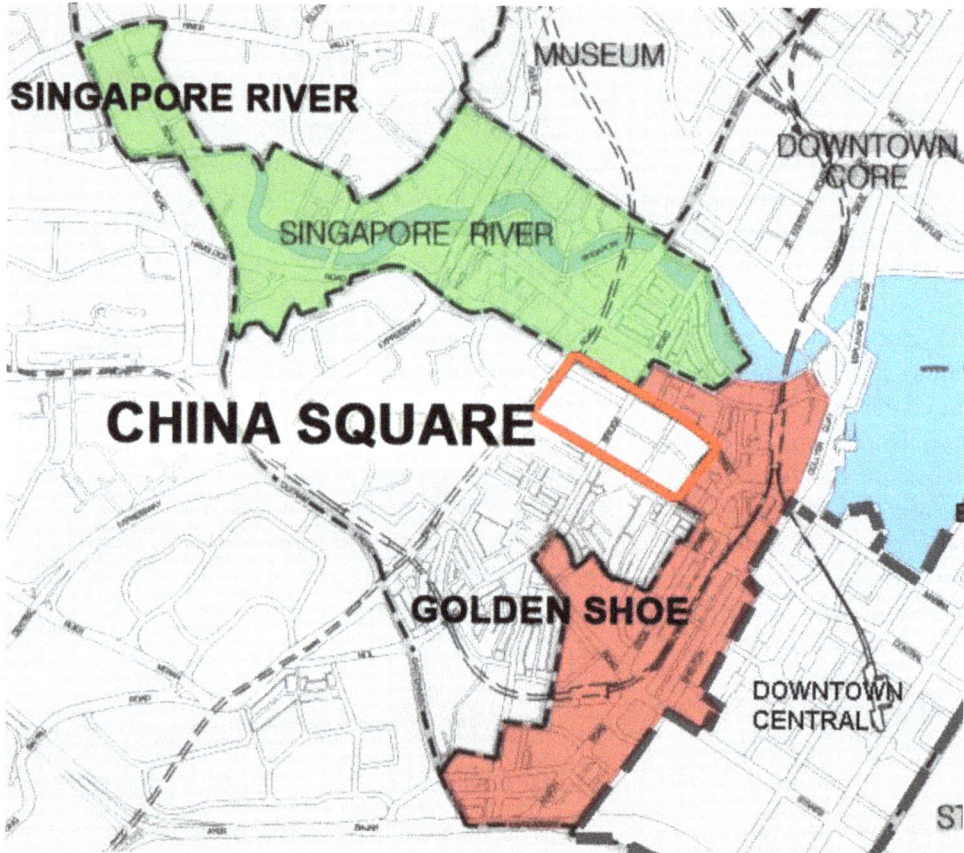

Source: Adapted from URA (http://www.ura.gov.sg/dc/plng_area/images/plng-area-map-a.gif).

The innovative planning approach was followed by private developer participation during the implementation stage. The Far East Organization, one of the developers that tendered successfully for one of the parcels, led the private sector in generating creative concepts for the development. Although the tender conditions stipulated that the new infill blocks were to have facades that harmonized with the conserved buildings, the developer proposed a bold modern glass structure that contrasted with the shop-houses. This was eventually supported by the URA and approved by the MND, as the architectural design was considered to present an interesting contrast between the new and the old.

Another deviation from the tender conditions was the proposed high-level glass canopy above the pedestrian walk on Amoy Street. The walk was to be retained as open to the sky according to the tender. The canopy would provide protection from the elements, especially during inclement weather, and enhance comfort without the use of air conditioning. The URA again showed flexibility by approving the canopy and recognizing the benefits of weather protection for outdoor areas in Singapore's tropical climate. The creativity of the private sector and the flexibility of the public authorities contributed to a largely successful product in the Far East Square. The development won the prestigious FIABCI Prix d'Excellence award in 2001 and was to inspire similar developments overseas, including Xintiandi in Shanghai (Kong 2011).

Clarke Quay was successfully completed and attracted both locals and tourists with their concentration of waterfront restaurants and entertainment establishments.

Seeding Developments through Land Sales

Land sales for new residential and commercial developments at the other parts of the river were also launched as catalysts to seed developments along different parts of the river. In order to ensure successful sales and subsequent development of the sale of sites, the URA incorporated feedback through consultation with the private sector. Specifically, they discussed parcel sizes as well as the timing of the sales tender according to market demands. The initial parcels were sold over three tender exercises between 1991 and 1994, which helped attract subsequent private-sector-investment interest in the Singapore River area.

The partnership between the public and private sectors also went beyond land sale tenders. Implementation of public infrastructure such as the riverfront promenade had to be coordinated. In this regard, the private developer was required, according to the land sales conditions, to build the stretch of the river promenade in front of its development, while the other stretches were to be built by the government. The guidelines for the promenade were stipulated by the URA, ensuring consistency in the materials used, as well as in tree planting and night lighting. The coordinating role played by the URA in terms of design guidelines and phasing and timing contributed greatly to the successful integration of private developments and public spaces.

The Singapore River is in many ways a product of a successful public-private partnership, with the government demonstrating its commitment to urban revitalization through extensive upfront investment in infrastructure and cleanup. This effort was followed by publicity and consultation with the people and the private sector. This collaborative approach helped the government to realize the vision laid out for the Singapore River area as "an exciting activity corridor that capitalizes on the river frontage and reflects the unique historical character of the area" (URA 1994).

Marina Bay: Building a Global City

The rejuvenation of Singapore's urban waterfront extends beyond the original shoreline where the financial district of the Golden Shoe and the historic Singapore River area are situated. In recent years, the realization of the vision for Marina Bay as the icon of Singapore's ambitions as a global city has placed the country on the world map for international investors and tourists alike. With about 360 hectares of prime waterfront real estate reclaimed from the sea, Marina Bay allows for the seamless expansion of the existing central business district (CBD) centered at the Golden Shoe District.

Scoping

Plans for reclamation along the southern waterfront off of Singapore's traditional CBD were initially introduced in 1971 as part of Singapore's first concept plan. The reclamation was then planned as part of the construction of a coastal expressway, the East Coast Parkway, together with an accompanying green belt along the southern coast of Singapore. This would link the eastern part of the island to the west, diverting through-traffic away from the city center.

It was not until 1977 that the government decided to expand the scale of reclamation works at Marina Bay to create a large parcel of reclaimed land to enable the development of a new urban area. This development was seen as providing a significant competitive advantage for Singapore, with a substantial land bank right next to the city center to allow for a seamless expansion of the financial district. Furthermore, the large tracts of undeveloped land at Marina Bay created opportunities for development of modern financial complexes that would require increasingly large floor plates and integrated amenities—something which the traditional CBD at the Golden Shoe District could not accommodate due to spatial constraints (see photograph 10.4).

Planning

Providing the capacity for future developments alone was insufficient to create the distinct character and identity that Marina Bay needed. The anticipated economic potential of Marina Bay was balanced with, and enhanced by, a strong emphasis on urban environmental quality.

As early as the 1970s, URA started planning for extensive greenery in the Marina area as part of the "blue and green" strategy for Marina Bay. Basically, it involved a planning strategy to maximize the potential of

Photograph 10.4   Reclaimed land at Marina Bay, with insert of map of Marina Bay

Source: ©Urban Redevelopment Authority. URA 1985/86.

parks and water bodies and enhance the quality of life. The creation of Marina Bay as an iconic water body in the city center was also a conscious decision by the government that was planned in tandem with the rejuvenation of Singapore River. The plan was formed in recognition of the potential of urban water fronts to enhance the quality of life. Although more land could have been made available for the development by filling up the bay area, the enhanced land value was estimated to make up for the loss of the developable land area because of the resulting higher quality of the environment. The decision to construct the 101-hectare "Gardens by the Bay" project in 2005 was similarly made after careful consideration of the benefits to the public and enhancement to the urban environment, which also outweighed the opportunity cost related to the loss of developable land.

Creating a Unique Water Front Development

A heavy emphasis was placed on the urban planning and design of Marina Bay. In 1983, two internationally renowned architects, I. M. Pei and Kenzo Tange, were engaged in developing conceptual master plans for the bay. Pei's flexible grid layout was generally adopted. The URA also studied similar urban waterfronts around the world, such as Sydney's Circular Quay and Baltimore's Inner Harbor, before deciding on the final profile and size of the bay's design.

The plan for Marina Bay continued to be revised through the years. It was drafted as part of the overall Master Plan for Urban Waterfronts in 1989, which identified distinct development characters for each of the prime waterfront areas in Singapore—the Singapore River, Marina Bay, and the Kallang Basin (URA 1989).

Detailed plans were drafted for Marina Bay and the Kallang Basin (map 10.5). These plans further refined the development directions for Marina Bay and complemented the 1985 Singapore River Concept Plan.

Another key master plan review for Marina Bay was conducted in 2003. The renowned architectural and planning consultancy from the United States—Skidmore, Owings and Merrill—was engaged to review the master plan for Marina Bay. One of the key recommendations was to further refine the grid road network to allow flexibility in parcel sizes. This was done to enable land to be sold in smaller or bigger parcels, depending on market conditions. Ideas proposed by the consultancy firm were subsequently incorporated into the URA's 2003 Statutory Master Plan.

Financing and Implementation

Land Sales: A Targeted Approach

As Marina Bay consists of reclaimed land belonging to the state, developments are generally initiated through government land sales to the private sector. By the 1990s, the Government Land Sales program had evolved since the first Sale of Sites in 1967. It had evolved into a sophisticated system with land sales for important sites specifically designed to achieve the intended development objectives for the site. This could be illustrated through three

Map 10.5   **Two master plans that were part of the 1989 urban waterfront master plan**

a. Marina Bay

b. Kallang Basin

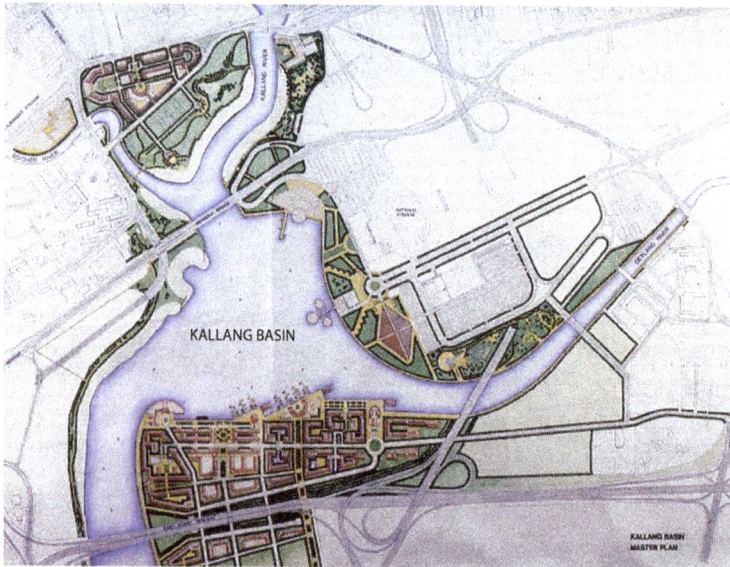

Source: ©Urban Redevelopment Authority. URA 1989.

of the major land sales in Marina Bay: the Marina Bay Financial Center, the Marina Bay Integrated Resort, and the Collyer Quay development.

The Marina Bay Financial Center

The concept of an integrated financial center development was proposed in the early 2000s, when the URA required a catalyst to spur the future growth of Singapore as a financial center, such as Canary Wharf in London. Such developments required large floor plates for huge trading floors. At the same time, the development should also have integrated residential and entertainment components to support the lifestyle demanded by the top tiers of the global financial industry. A detailed study was conducted by the URA to establish the development requirements for such financial centers. These requirements could not be accommodated within the old financial district of Shenton Way. Marina Bay, being adjacent to the financial district, became a natural choice for the location of the new financial center. The selected site also had the necessary infrastructure in place for the development to be implemented upon sale.

Due to a series of economic downturns between 2001 and 2004, the sale of sites was only launched in 2005. The site could accommodate a salable floor area of 438,000 sq m, almost three times the size of the first sale site in Marina Bay, with a minimum of 60 percent to be dedicated to office use. This ensured that the vision for the development as a major financial center would be realized, while at the same time allowing the master developer to coordinate the different mix of uses URA had envisioned for the sale site.

Because of the uncertain market conditions during the time of the sale as well as the unprecedented size of the development, URA formulated an options payment scheme. This allowed the successful tenderer to buy and develop the site in phases. The developer was required to purchase and develop the land for the initial phase and was offered the option to buy and develop the remaining land within specified option periods. The prices for the options were fixed by a formula that shared the risk with the government with regard to future price fluctuations. This innovative options-based tender approach not only helped to limit the risks faced by the developer in reducing the upfront financial commitment but also ensured that the transparency and integrity of the Government Land Sales program would not be compromised. With market conditions eventually improving, the developer could exercise the option to purchase and develop for a second phase. The entire development was fully completed by mid-2013.

Marina Bay Integrated Resort

During the same period, Singapore also began to look into introducing integrated resorts in the country. These were resorts that would include casinos and world-class attractions helping to further promote Singapore as a global business and tourist destination. The location of the Marina Bay integrated resort was decided on the basis of the URA's recommendation. It was to allow close integration with the city center and would tap into existing infrastructure available in the city.

Because of the requirements for a top-notch architectural design to create a substantial effect at the prominent location, as well as the critical development objectives the integrated resort had to meet, the site could not be sold in the normal way using the usual highest-price-tender method. Instead, the fixed-price method was chosen, by which the land price was fixed during the tender and the developers would compete on the basis of their design and concept proposals. The site was eventually awarded to Las Vegas Sands Corp. It was awarded on the merits of its proposals in design, as well as its effect on meeting Singapore's economic and tourism objectives.

Collyer Quay Development

The Collyer Quay site adopted yet another tender approach for its land sale in 2006. The site comprised the historic Clifford Pier and Custom Harbour Branch, which were conserved and allowed for new infill developments to complement the conserved buildings. Although a good concept was required for the site, the Collyer Quay development was not as significant as the Marina Bay Integrated Resort development requiring a fixed-price approach. The two-envelope concept and price tender method was used instead. It required the tenderer to submit two envelopes for evaluation, one containing the concept proposal and the other containing the land price. The concept proposals were assessed first, and only the tenderers with a good concept would move on to the second stage of tender, which would then be based purely on price.

Urban Design Requirements for Sale Sites

A rigorous set of urban design guidelines was formulated by the URA for all the developments in Marina Bay, as was done with the Singapore River. These guidelines ensured that the developments were well designed and related and integrated well with the overall built environment—including other developments as well as public spaces. In this way, the overall vision and objectives for Marina Bay could be achieved through private sector participation. These guidelines were then translated into detailed urban design requirements in the sales conditions for each development.

The Marina Bay Financial Center, for example, had detailed urban design requirements within the sales conditions that ensured connectivity with other developments by stipulating connections to a comprehensive underground pedestrian network planned for Marina Bay, as well as for vertical connections to the ground level. Open space and landscaping requirements were also incorporated to safeguard views from the development toward the waterfront. At the same time, the guidelines catered to the desire for a seamlessly integrated development by stipulating public open spaces at the ground level, while at the same time allowing for the development to be linked through extensive underground connections.

Marketing and Branding

Beginning in the early 2000s, the URA made concerted efforts to market the Marina Bay to international investors through international marketing platforms, including real estate trade shows such as Cityscape. International events held at the Marina Bay, such as the Formula One Grand Prix—the first city night race in the world—further raised the global profile of Marina Bay not only as an investment destination but also as a place for business, work, and leisure.

Marketing efforts by the URA were also complemented by a strong branding for Marina Bay. The URA engaged a consultant to help with the branding of Marina Bay by establishing the "heartware" to complement the "hardware" infrastructure that had been put in place. A new tagline for Marina Bay—"explore, exchange, entertain"—was created in line with the overall "live-work-play" proposition for Singapore.

Place Management

To further strengthen the "heartware" of Marina Bay, the URA also focused on place management to generate activities within the area for public participation. The URA initiated seed funding for public events such as running events at the Bay, particularly in the earlier years. Local stakeholders such as the Esplanade-Theatres by the Bay, and private developments such as the Marina Bay Sands were also involved in creating diverse activities for the public. A calendar of events throughout the year was created together with other regular annual public events, including annual nationwide celebrations including the National Day and Marina Bay New Year's Eve Countdown. These activities helped generate vibrancy in the new development area and supported Marina Bay's role as the focal point for Singapore as a nation.

Public Infrastructure Investments

The reclamation works demonstrated the long-term approach to planning and development in Singapore. This emphasis on up-front infrastructure investments by the government was continued in recent years. The construction of comprehensive road and rail networks in the yet-to-be developed reclaimed land, a common services tunnel to provide key utilities for the developments, as well as public space infrastructure such as the waterfront promenade and pedestrian bridges, all contributed to facilitating future quality developments by the private sector. Infrastructure investment by the government totaled about S$2 billion (URA 2006). Some of the key infrastructure in Marina Bay are highlighted here.

The Common Services Tunnel (CST) was a strategic piece of infrastructure implemented up front before development came to Marina Bay. The CST houses telecommunications and utilities networks as well as the District Cooling System in a "plug and play" format. It also has full emergency backup services and capacity for expansion for future needs. The CST would not only enhance reliability of these services but also result in land savings as land previously set aside for underground services can be used for development. The implementation of the CST exemplified the long-term approach to planning and development, laying the groundwork for future urban growth.

The Marina Barrage is a dam built across the Marina Channel to create a freshwater reservoir from the Singapore River (Kallang Basin) to the Marina Bay water body. This followed the concerted cleanup efforts in Singapore River and Kallang Basin and doubled as a tidal barrier to prevent flooding of the low-lying flood-prone areas within the city center. The stabilization of the water levels with the barrage also enabled a wider range of water-related recreational activities to take place in the Marina Reservoir.

Lessons Learned

The redevelopment of Singapore's urban waterfront was illustrated by the three case studies of the Golden Shoe District, the Singapore River, and Marina Bay. Together, they encapsulate Singapore's unique approach to urban development in balancing economic, social, and environmental goals within a land-scarce context. While the process had evolved since the early days, fundamental principles have been consistently maintained through the years. Some of the lessons learned from this experience are listed here.

- *Think long term.* Urban redevelopment required forward thinking and planning and was initiated in tandem with formulating a comprehensive master plan framework for Singapore. A systematic approach to long-term planning was eventually established, involving a review of the concept plan every 10 years to set out development directions for the next 40–50 years. The approach also included the drafting of a master plan to translate the broad and long-term strategies of the concept plan into detailed plans for implementation over 10–15 years. Similarly, the development of the Marina Bay was the result of several decades of planning and infrastructure investment before the need and opportunity for developments actually surfaced.
- *Execute effectively.* What differentiates Singapore's integrated planning regime from other cities is that its plans do not exist merely on paper. They are coordinated, implemented, and executed effectively through dedicated government agencies, with attendant expertise and resources. These action-oriented agencies include the Urban Redevelopment Authority, the Housing and Development Board, and the former Public Works Department. The case of Singapore River demonstrated how the agencies worked together to effectively translate plans into action, transforming a decrepit urban waterway into a thriving waterfront destination within a couple of decades through a combination of public sector initiative and private sector investments.
- *Work with markets.* The transformation of Singapore's urban waterfront is very much a product of the government working successfully with the markets. In many ways, this partnership is manifested in the Government Land Sales program, with the government providing up-front public infrastructure and a clear, transparent framework for the

development in the form of land sale conditions and tender processes. For its part, the private sector contributed the creative expertise and financial capital. This created an effective system of urban redevelopment that combined public initiative and vision with private sector interest.

• *Lead with vision and pragmatism.* Leadership has an important effect on planning and implementation. One important aspect of leadership is having the political will to push through policies or projects that are considered unpopular or politically difficult—if leaders are convinced that such policies or projects are for the long-term benefit of the city. For example, the extensive land acquisition program since the 1960s required strong leadership to push through policies to support urban redevelopment in the long run. At the same time, the government was mindful of the social implications commonly associated with urban redevelopment in other countries. An extensive resettlement program for affected residents and businesses was not generated as an afterthought. Rather, it was built into the land acquisition process, contributing immensely to the redevelopment of the city in the long term. Long-term vision also needs to be balanced with a good dose of pragmatism. Singapore's conservation framework exemplified how the URA achieved its conservation objectives with innovative yet pragmatic policies to balance conservation with development needs.

Notes

1. For the purposes of this case study, the geographical definitions of the three case study areas are as follows: The Golden Shoe District is defined by the boundaries for lifting of rent control under the Controlled Premises (Special Provisions) Act of 1969. The Singapore River is defined by the URA Singapore River Planning Area. The Marina Bay is defined by URA planning areas Marina South and Straits View, and URA subzones Bayfront and Downtown Central.
2. Reverted properties refer to plots with expired 99-year leases with ownership "reverted" back to the state.
3. Preapproval was targeted at cutting red tape for developers, as well as providing more certainty for them. Master plans drafted at the local level were not released publicly. They were used as internal "drawer plans" for development coordination purposes. This was partly because the master plan then generally captured existing uses only. It was used as a basis for calculation of development charges at that time; authorities would run into problems of "conferring" land value to land owners if future plans were released.

References

Abrams, C., S. Kobe, and O. Koenigsberger. 1980. "Growth and Urban Renewal in Singapore." *Habitat International* 5 (1/2): 85–127.

Centre for Liveable Cities. 2013. *Urban Systems Studies: Housing: Turning Squatters into Stakeholders*. Singapore: Cengage Learning Asia Pte Ltd.

———. 2014a. *Urban Systems Studies: Land Acquisition and Resettlement: Securing resources for Development*. Singapore: Centre for Liveable Cities.

———. 2014b. *Liveable and Sustainable Cities: A Framework*. Singapore: Centre for Liveable Cities, Civil Service College.

Chua, B. H. 1989. *The Golden Shoe: Building Singapore's Financial District*. Singapore: Urban Redevelopment Authority.

Dale, O. J. 1999. *Urban Planning in Singapore: Transformation of a City*. Singapore: Oxford University Press.

Department of Statistics. 2015. *Annual GDP at Current Market Prices*. Department of Statistics, Singapore. http://www.singstat.gov.sg/docs /default-source/default-document-library/statistics/browse_by_theme /economy/time_series/gdp2.xls.

Housing and Development Board. 1963. *Housing and Development Board Annual Report 1960*. Singapore: Housing and Development Board.

———. 1966. *Housing and Development Board Annual Report 1965*. Singapore: Housing and Development Board.

———. 1968. *Housing and Development Board Annual Report 1967*. Singapore: Housing and Development Board.

Kong, L. 2011. *Conserving the Past, Creating the Future: Urban Heritage in Singapore*. Singapore: Urban Redevelopment Authority.

Singapore Institute of Architects. 2013. *RUMAH 50*. Singapore: Singapore Institute of Architects.

———. 1988. "*Conservation: Ideas Needed from S'poreans*." March 17.

URA (Urban Redevelopment Authority). 1975. *Urban Redevelopment Authority Annual Report 1974/75*. Singapore: URA.

———. 1978. URA Annual Report.

———. 1983. *Chronicle of Sale Sites*. Singapore: URA.

———. 1984. "Planning for a Better City: A Challenge for URA." *Skyline* 11 (July/Aug.): 6–7.

———. 1985/86. *Urban Redevelopment Authority Annual Report 1985/86*. Singapore: URA.

———. 1989. *Master Plan for the Urban Waterfront at Marina Bay and Kallang Basin*. Singapore: URA.

———. 1992a. "Singapore River Development Guide Plan: Draft." URA, Singapore.

———. 1992b. "Downtown Core and Portview: Planning a Downtown for the 21st Century, Development Guide Plans." URA, Singapore.

———. 1994. *Singapore River Planning Area: Planning Report 1994.* Singapore: URA.

———. 2006. "State-of-the-Art Utility Infrastructure in Place in Marina Bay." *Skyline* (July/Aug.): 6–7.

———. 2013. *Urban Design Guidelines for Singapore River Planning Area.* Singapore: URA.

Map 11.1 Johannesburg, South Africa

a. Johannesburg

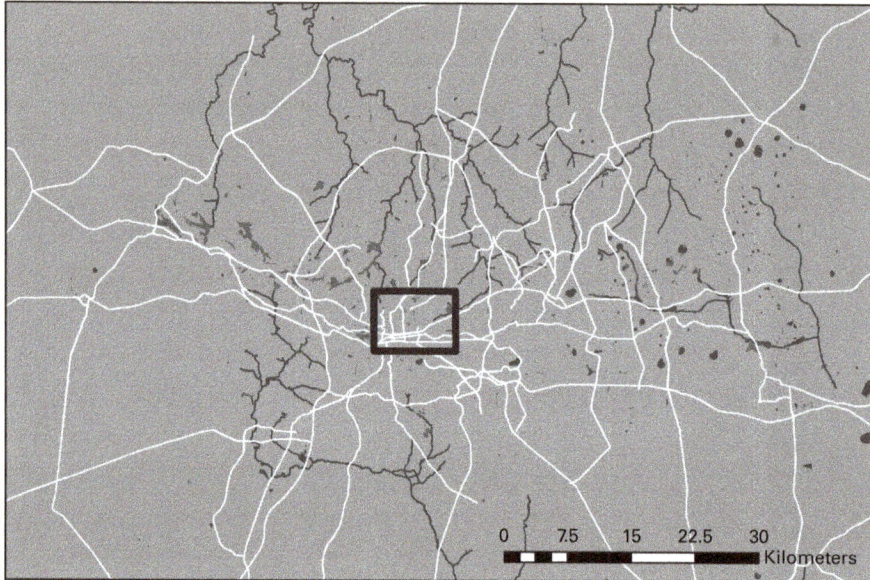

b. Boundaries of Johannesburg inner city

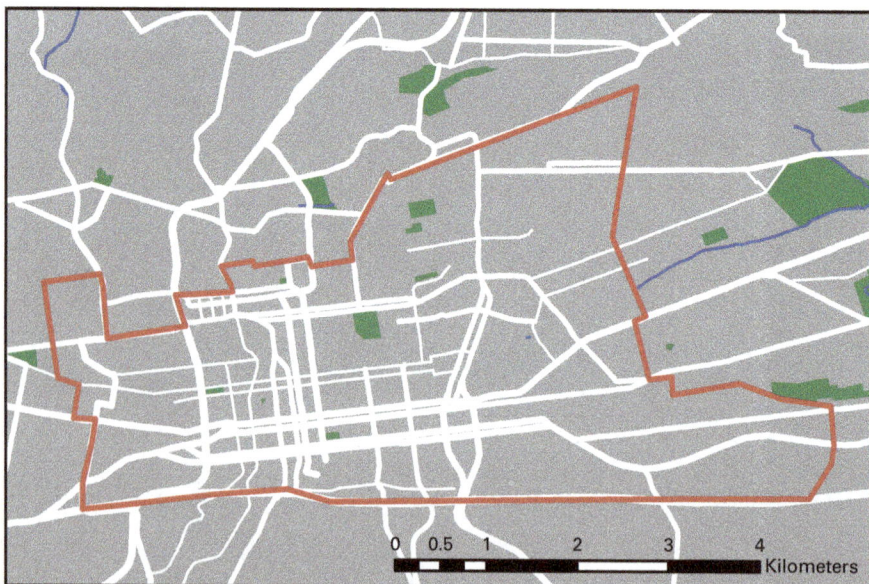

Source: World Bank using Open Street Map data 2015.

CHAPTER 11

Johannesburg: Aligning Diverse Prophecies for Revitalizing a Declining Inner City

Introduction

The site of the original mining camps, Johannesburg was formed in 1886 and grew steadily until it became the most populated city in the African continent in 1936. The city's spatial structure was developed under the segregation policies that had started long before but were made explicit during the apartheid era. These policies resulted in a divided and spatially segregated city, which was governed by a minority white group. Despite this, the city prospered economically in the first three quarters of the twentieth century as many companies and financial institutions moved to Johannesburg throughout the years to benefit from its location as the center of commerce in Africa.

The Johannesburg metropolitan area is the largest metropolitan area in South Africa. The Johannesburg inner city, which is the subject of this study, is part of the Johannesburg metropolitan area, situated in the southeast section and spanning over an area of 18 square kilometers. It is the historic core of the city where the original mining town started. Today, the inner city is the hub of commercial, residential, and entertainment activities. It can be divided into five segments: (a) the commercial core or central business district (CBD); (b) the office satellite center of Braamfontein; (c) the lower-density residential suburbs to the east of the city center, including Yeoville, Bertrams, Troyeville, and Jeppestown; (d) the higher-density residential areas of Berea and Hillbrow; and (e) City Deep, with Newtown, Fordsburg, Pageview, and Vrededorp to the west. The extent of the Johannesburg inner city is shown in map 11.1.

The Johannesburg inner city is the core of economic activity in the metropolitan area, contributing 21 percent of the overall metropolitan economy (Fraser and Cox 2011). Four hundred thousand people reside in the area, and about 1 million people commute to and from the inner city every day. The inner city hosts the headquarters of major banks and companies, in addition to the Gauteng provincial government and the Johannesburg metropolitan government. It also hosts many small businesses and local retailers, owned mainly by the lower income segment.

Context and Background

The Decline of the Inner City

Understanding Johannesburg's decline would not be possible without an understanding of the impacts of apartheid and attendant segregationist policies over the decades and the consequent political transition, which changed the spatial demographics of the inner city. Although most believe that the process of decline in Johannesburg started during the political transition in the late 1980s, the core reason for decline actually began in the early 1950s, when the city council decided to move out to the Braamfontein neighborhood in the north of the inner city. In the1960s, the parking regulations changed to restrict the usage of cars—but without any corresponding improvement in public transport. This parking plan was coupled with developing major roads to transport traffic to the periphery of the city, which also encouraged out-migration.

Others have argued that the decline of Johannesburg started because the existing landowners in the inner city shifted their investments to the peripheries in the period of economic decline, undermining their existing inner-city real estate portfolio and contributing to the decline. Another major reason for disinvestment in the inner city was the oligopolistic nature of the investment markets. Twenty institutions owned most of the land, while six institutions controlled the investment market in the CBD (Tomlinson 2003). The excess capital held by these institutions was used to drive the new decentralized development, which seemed more attractive than the decaying inner city. These investors mostly got in a false competition with one another as opposed to responding to actual development demand (Tomlinson 2003). Another view also exists, which attributes the disinvestment in the inner city to racist tendencies, when the black community finally was given the right to leave the townships and live in the inner city after the end of apartheid.[1]

After businesses and commerce moved out of the inner city, the city's tax base started to decline. Many buildings were left vacant and services and infrastructure started to deteriorate (see photograph 11.1). Crime rates started to rise to high levels, to the degree that it was considered the single most important barrier to investment. Meanwhile, the trade sanctions imposed on South Africa by the international community weakened the financial and banking sector. One additional problem was disinvestment in mass transit infrastructure, which resulted in the development of the minibus taxi industry, causing unmanageable congestion in the inner city. By the early 1990s, informal traders were also taking over the streets of the inner city, causing even more traffic and congestion.

Photograph 11.1   Examples of abandoned buildings in the inner city

Source: © Tanya Zack. Used with permission. Further permission required for reuse.

The decline of the inner city worsened in the late 1980s. Between 1982 and 1994, 17 of the top 100 national public companies located in Johannesburg moved from the CBD to other areas within the Johannesburg metropolitan area. Likewise, only 27 percent of the 104 top national business enterprises were located in Johannesburg in 1994. In addition, merely 2 out of the top 10 retail companies in the country kept their previous headquarters in the CBD (Tomlinson and others 1995). The financial institutions and banks started redlining the inner city properties and invested in suburban properties in the north of the inner city.

It is important to understand that the case of the inner city decline in Johannesburg was different from other declining postindustrial cities (Garner 2011). In this case, the inner city was not abandoned completely. New residents from faraway townships moved in as the apartheid regime was replaced with the first democratic regime in South Africa, which allowed integration of different races into one neighborhood. The property owners saw an opportunity in this new wave of in-migration and flooded their buildings with lower-income tenants. In other cases, illegal tenants moved into abandoned buildings and stopped paying their municipal bills and taxes. In this context, the inner city found itself struggling with many "bad" buildings, declining public spaces, lack of service delivery, high crime rates, and a subsequent sharp decline in investment.

The Project Cycle

The regeneration of the Johannesburg inner city is the result of many initiatives, collaborative organizations, and individual inputs. In this sense, the Johannesburg case study is different from other cases in this volume, as the various phases of the regeneration strategy overlap and intersect at different points of time. Although the process of regeneration of the inner city of Johannesburg was not linear, based on the unified format of all case studies and in order to facilitate comparison among them, the process has been broken down into phases.

Phase 1: Scoping

During apartheid and up until the 1980s, there were not many meaningful efforts or effective initiatives for regenerating Johannesburg's inner city. During the years prior to the change of the regime in South Africa in the late 1980s and early 1990s, most civil society institutions were reluctant to get involved or collaborate with the city council and the local government. The very first attempt to create a vision or a plan for revitalization of the inner city was launched in 1986 by the Johannesburg City Council. The result was a small booklet that proposed involving the private sector in the regeneration process. The political change in the council and the changes in the leadership of the city government prevented the proposed plan from being implemented. However, the vision to include the private sector as a major player in regeneration efforts was initiated from the time of this very first plan.

Key Developments in the Early 1990s

In early 1991, the inner city's private sector occupants—mainly property owners who were concerned with increased urban blight, crime, and vacancy rates—planned a multisectoral, multistakeholder workshop in an attempt to find solutions to these problems. In a "vision" document published called the "Strategic Initiative for Central Johannesburg," the private sector expressed acute concern about a "desperate security problem, lack of cleanliness, traffic congestion, expensive and inadequate parking, and the fact that a perceived lack of amenities were driving investors away" (City of Johannesburg 1992). The document suggested the creation of a tripartite partnership between the public sector, the private sector, and the community. It also suggested that such a partnership form an "independent, non-profit development agency, which would unite all key players in facilitating, planning, and effectively implementing action programs designed to address current problems as well as the future" (Bremner 2000). This institution was established in 1992 and was called the Central Johannesburg Partnership (CJP). The CJP's purpose was to represent the interests of inner city businesses.

The CJP was established as a nonprofit organization. From 1992 to 1995, the period when a nondemocratically established city council was still in place, the CJP faced difficulties in planning and implementing actions. Therefore, CJP engaged instead in research about urban regeneration in various parts of the world, as well as reasons for the decline of the inner city. After 1995 and the establishment of a democratic government, the CJP's structure was altered to accommodate the changes. At this time, there did not seem to be any need for the three sectors to cooperate within one organization. Hence, CJP's structure changed to represent the business sector only.

The community's interests were represented by the newly established Johannesburg Inner City Community Forum, and the public sector was represented through the city council. This was an important change in the structure of the partnership, that is, a move toward trilateral engagement rather than a parallel presence represented in one single organization. Then the role of the CJP as the representative of the business community was transformed again into a newly established Johannesburg Inner City Business Coalition, a private nonprofit organization managed by the CJP. Today, the CJP focuses only on the establishment and management of city improvement districts (Fraser and Cox 2011).

The main effect of the CJP was the introduction of the concept of business improvement districts or, as they are called in South Africa, city improvement districts (CIDs) in 1993. In collaboration with the United States–based International Downtown Association and the British Association of Town Centre Management, the CJP also organized a study tour in 1996 to the two countries for members of the city council, the community, and provincial government officials to study the effectiveness of CIDs. This tour resulted in the establishment of the first CID in South Africa in the CBD of Johannesburg. However, because there was no existing legislation for structuring CIDs, the first ones had to be structured on a voluntary basis. The success of the first CID was so positive that the CJP was asked to establish more CIDs in the inner city—leading to the creation of five more between 1994 and 2000. In 1997 as needs arose, the Gauteng Provincial Government drafted the legislation for the establishment of CIDs, which became effective in 1999.

The role and responsibilities of the CJP started to change after a democratically established city council started to work in 1996 and a single metropolitan government was established to govern all of the suburbs and townships under a single budget. Therefore, another coalition was formed to take on the "visioning" exercise for Johannesburg. The Johannesburg Inner City Development Forum (JICDF) was established in 1996 with the participation of diverse stakeholders, including the provincial government, local government, the Inner City Business Coalition, and the Johannesburg Inner City Community Forum. The mandate of the forum was to formulate a vision for the inner city that would "encompass both policy formulation and the identification and facilitation of projects.

These will be guided by the long term vision for the city which must be broad based and needs driven" (Fraser and Cox 2011).

Johannesburg: The Golden Heartbeat of Africa

As discussed in the first section of this volume, the scoping phase of a regeneration project usually involves crafting a "vision." The "visioning" process for the regeneration of the Johannesburg inner city has been a long and collaborative process. It started in 1996, when inner-city stakeholders came together in the JICDF and crafted a vision through an inclusionary process.[2] The private sector led the process. Four separate groups of stakeholders submitted their visions for the city, including the metropolitan government, the provincial government, the community, and the business sector. These four visions were then combined and consolidated into one vision during a workshop, which brought together all four groups.

This vision, "Johannesburg: The Golden Heartbeat of Africa," called for a city that is "livable, safe, people-centered, accessible, dynamic, well managed"—in short, a city for all. This vision was different from previous efforts because it focused on the global status of Johannesburg as an African city, with an emphasis on trade as a driving force for economic development (Bremner 2000). The vision also emphasized participation and partnerships to achieve these goals. The strategies outlined in the vision were focused on environmental upgrades; development of infrastructure; reducing crime, congestion, and homelessness; and improving public services through public-private partnerships, among other things.

The implementation process of this strategy proved to be slow due to political, administrative, and budgetary issues. On the political side, the governance body for metropolitan Johannesburg consisted of transitional metropolitan council members and subregional council members who did not have any formal decision-making powers, because they were still considered to be in transition. On the administrative side, the inner city fell under the jurisdiction of three different councils. No single official entity was responsible for its regeneration. The same problem existed with regard to budget allocation, as there was no consolidated budget for the inner city as a whole.

Initiatives by the Provincial Government

In parallel to private sector efforts, the provincial and local governments started initiatives to revive the inner city. In 1994, the provincial government moved its offices from Pretoria to the CBD, showing its commitment and support for the regeneration efforts in the inner city (Fraser 2007). Consequently, the Executive Committee of the Gauteng Province initiated an urban renewal strategy for the inner city. This plan focused on three pillars, including local economic development, residential development, and social development. In 1996, the provincial government led the development of a four-point plan for the regeneration of Gauteng inner cities, including Johannesburg. The four-point plan's objectives were to

(a) promote clean and safe centers, (b) foster compact development, (c) encourage vibrant commercial centers, and (d) build regeneration partnerships (Fraser 2007). This plan had the support of both provincial and local governments and was presented to the civil society at a conference (Fraser and Cox 2011).

At this time, several other plans, strategies, and visions were developed by the municipal and provincial governments, which are not covered in this volume.[3]

Establishment of Johannesburg Development Authority and Subsequent Visions

As noted, although the JICDF was a core working group for developing a vision for the inner city, it did not have the authority or resources to implement this vision. Therefore, an "Inner City Committee" was established in 1998, which was a subcommittee of the Johannesburg Metropolitan Council. It consisted of private sector representatives, city officials, and nongovernmental organizations. The committee then commissioned a report on the future of the inner city, which recommended the establishment of an organization with a similar mandate to urban development corporations in the United States and the United Kingdom. The proposed entity would be responsible for urban regeneration and for involving the private sector in these efforts.

Based on this recommendation, an Inner City Office (ICO) was established in 1998 as a specialized project management arm of the greater Johannesburg Metropolitan Council. The responsibilities of this office were to coordinate all activities and projects related to the inner city and to implement the inner city strategy developed by the JICDF. Later in 2001, the ICO changed its name to the Johannesburg Development Agency (JDA). Since then, the JDA has been instrumental in coordinating and implementing regeneration efforts in the inner city.

When established, the ICO developed a spatial and economic framework for the inner city. This framework also promoted the participation of the private sector in regeneration efforts. Specifically, the framework focused on promoting investment opportunities in the inner city, while ensuring an inclusive, attractive, and well-managed environment for residents and businesses.

iGoli 2002

The iGoli 2002 was developed in parallel to the creation of a single metropolitan authority for Johannesburg, which by itself was a major success measure in its regeneration (City of Johannesburg 2002). It was a three-year strategic plan for the structural transformation of the city (City of Johannesburg 2006a). The iGoli 2002 mostly focused on collecting data and creating an organizational framework for regeneration of the inner city. It also focused on service delivery by creating and revising public agency mandates and privatizing many of the public utility provisions for the city (Mabin 2007). Several "arms-length" municipal-owned service delivery entities (utilities, agencies, and corporations) were established and some were completely privatized (City of Johannesburg 2006a). This plan was later dropped because of its short-term vision. The subsequent plan was called iGoli 2010.

iGoli 2010

The iGoli 2010 Plan was developed and published at the end of 2000, at the time when a new political administration was coming in after the local government elections. While iGoli 2010 was revised early on in the process, it worked on research and data collection through a participatory process. In a way, the city built and restored the partnership with various stakeholders through this process. The iGoli 2010 focused on economic growth, private sector development, human development, and service delivery (City of Johannesburg 2004). Unfortunately, while the scope of iGoli 2010 was broader than the 2002 or even the upcoming 2030 vision, it got pulled into the political turmoil of the 2000 elections, which resulted in its passive reception within the ruling party (Segbers, Raiser, and Volkmann 2007).

iGoli 2030

The iGoli 2030 was a response to increased poverty and decline in the quality of life in Johannesburg in general, and the inner city in particular. The major difference between iGoli 2030 and the two previous strategies was that it had a longer time horizon and was an outward-looking strategy, whereas the iGoli 2002 and 2010 plans were more focused inward to determine a direction for the council. Another difference was that this plan launched a comprehensive economic development strategy that was lacking in the two previous plans (Fraser and Cox 2011). It emphasized a poverty reduction strategy that was based on sustained economic growth, rather than through direct government spending (City of Johannesburg 2004). It suggested that sustained economic growth in Johannesburg could be achieved by fully exploiting the agglomeration economies resulting from urbanization as the city's economy changed from a mining/manufacturing economy to a service-based one. This plan built on various strategies developed in the years before to provide a synthesized version along with an implementation plan.

iGoli 2030 envisages that in 2030, Johannesburg will be a global-scale, service-based economy and "a world-class City with service deliverables and efficiencies, which meet world best practice." Further, it plans for a city with a strong tax base and an active private sector. The foundation of iGoli 2030 is to leverage urbanization for growth in Johannesburg. It aims at putting Johannesburg's economy on a growth path from the present 0.1 percent per capita gross domestic product growth to a required minimum of 5 percent. It also notes that because of a high crime rate, businesses invest 61 percent less than their potential. The city also suffers from a lack of skilled labor, which has led to official unemployment. However, it has resulted in the growth of the informal sector employment from 9.6 percent to 16 percent (City of Johannesburg 2004; Fraser 2007). In this regard, the foundation document lays out not only urban planning measures but also macroscale industrial and labor policies. In addition, it includes plans to develop various sectors, such as transportation, tourism, and others to foster economic growth.

To implement this grand vision, iGoli 2030's strategy is to establish a conducive environment for growth by reducing crime and addressing the mismatch of skills. The second strategy is to address spatial planning issues by creating an urban growth boundary area to prevent further sprawl and transportation problems. It also encourages infill development and urban regeneration initiatives. Another priority set of actions supports a growth level of 6–8 percent and an acceleration of the "economies of localization" by establishing a sound data and information system, supporting small and medium enterprises, and implementing catalytic projects. As we will see later, these catalytic projects had a major role in accelerating growth in the inner city and leveraging private sector investment.

Other Visions and Strategies

The Human Development Strategy was created in 2004 to address inequality and social inclusion issues in the inner city in order to ensure more of the Johannesburg inner city residents would benefit from economic growth. In 2006, the city developed its Growth and Development Strategy, which included a long-term strategy for development of the city as a whole. The strategy found many aspects of iGoli 2030 relevant; however, it aimed at a more comprehensive strategy based on more recent data and newly formed priorities announced by the president of South Africa. For example, some of the strategies of iGoli 2030 were based on a projected 1 percent population growth rate at that time. However, later it was reported to be over 4 percent per year. In addition, the strategy integrated national- and regional-level priorities and strategies to align them with a vision for the inner city.

Phase 2: Planning

The regeneration process for the inner city of Johannesburg started from the very first vision exercise and continued in parallel for years. However, a major plan was developed only after iGoli 2030 and the subsequent growth and development strategy. It was called the Inner City Regeneration Business Plan, developed by the Economic Development Unit of the city of Johannesburg in 2004 for the period 2004–07. The goal was to "locate and synchronize the efforts of all agencies, led by the city of Johannesburg Metropolitan Council, who are actively working for the regeneration of the inner city" (City of Johannesburg 2004). The plan called for the cooperation of various agencies including local, provincial and national government, the private sector, nongovernmental organizations, and the civil society.

The business plan aimed at capturing and synthesizing all major existing initiatives in a single document, as agreed upon by all involved sectors and agencies to foster better coordination and use of resources. The plan had five pillars, each with a designated set of programs and activities. These pillars were as follows (a) addressing sinkholes, (b) undertaking intensive urban management, (c) maintaining and upgrading infrastructure, (d) promoting ripple pond investments, and (e) supporting economic sectors.

Although this plan was very extensive and well-thought-out, it was still subject to some criticism. Some argued that the five pillars of the plan were too broad and neglected to include critical issues of the inner city, such as informal trading, safety and security, and lack of social inclusion (Fraser and Cox 2011). The business plan included 63 initiatives and programs, all to be completed by 2007. However, 44 percent of the programs and initiatives did not have an allocated budget. Therefore, the whole plan was not properly realized.

Institutional Structure

One unique and interesting fact about the inner city of Johannesburg is the multitude of institutions, actors, and sectors involved in regeneration efforts. After the new political system was established, the existing municipalities were dismantled and the city of Johannesburg's metropolitan municipality was established in 2000 as a single-tier municipality with committees and an executive mayor. One of the most effective institutional changes, which affected the inner city, was that the city fell under the jurisdiction of a single municipal council. The new municipal structure was significant in that it created three sets of service delivery entities: utilities, agencies, and municipal corporations. A core administration entity was in charge of the three sets of delivery entities, while also overseeing 11 regional administrations (City of Johannesburg 2004). All of these new functions were under the umbrella of the new political governance system.

Political Governance

The city of Johannesburg has two related organizational streams: one that provides political governance and leadership and the other that is in charge of administrative functions. The political governance system of the city is led by the council and the mayoral committee (see figure 11.1). The mayoral committee consists of 10 members and acts as a city-level cabinet. The council is the city's highest decision-making body and consists of 217 elected members. It is in charge of approving bylaws, budget, and the integrated development plan, as well as electing the executive mayor. The executive mayor's role is another key institutional innovation in addressing the issue of fragmentation in political governance. The executive mayor has executive powers to run the city, including the power to appoint the members of the mayoral committee.

Under the political governance system, two important bodies were formed by the council members. Section 79, or the Inner City Advisory

Figure 11.1   **Johannesburg's political governance system**

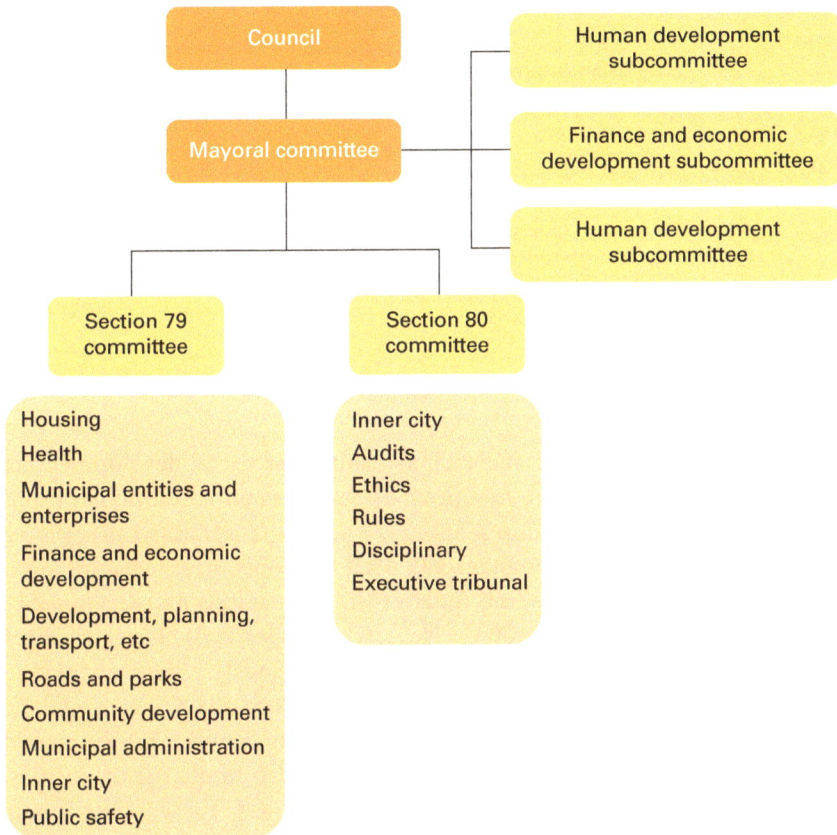

Source: Adapted from City of Johannesburg 2005.
Note: Section 79 = Inner City Advisory Committee. Section 80 = Inner City Portfolio Committee.

Committee, was established to "promote the realization of the Vision for the Inner City of Johannesburg" and to "develop, and monitor the implementation of, appropriate policies, strategies, programs and projects for the economic and social development of the inner city" (City of Johannesburg 2004). The Section 80 committee (Inner City Portfolio Committee) was established with the objective of "promoting the development of the Johannesburg inner city in line with the Inner City Vision" (City of Johannesburg 2006a). Table 11.1 summarizes the institutional arrangement, duties, and differences between the Section 79 and Section 80 committees.

Administrative Governance

The administrative functions of the city are also under the purview of the mayor and the mayoral committee. However, a city manager role and a chief operations officer (COO) role were also created to manage

Table 11.1   Comparison of Section 79 and Section 80 committees

	Section 79 committee	Section 80 committee
Extent of authority	The council determines functions and may delegate powers and duties.	The executive mayor delegates powers and duties.
Appointment of the chairperson	The council appoints chairperson.	The executive mayor appoints chairperson.
Membership	The committee may coopt noncouncilors.	The committee consists only of councilors.
Objective	The committee is established for the effective performance of functions of the council.	The committee is established to assist the executive mayor.

Source: City of Johannesburg 2005.

the central functions, such as health and social development as well as the administrative functions of the 11 regional administrations. These roles were created in 2002–03, when more administrative changes were implemented to manage the need for constant integration and coordination of overlapping functions in the regions and the inner city (City of Johannesburg 2004). The city manager is in charge of the administration stream but also reports to the executive mayor and the council. The city manager oversees the COO and the Finance and Economic Development, Development Planning, and Transportation and Environment Departments. They are also in charge of utilities, corporate entities, and various agencies. Of these, the Johannesburg Development Agency, which is in charge of the regeneration of the inner city, is the most relevant to this case (see figure 11.2).

Institutional Arrangements for the Regeneration of Johannesburg Inner City

To maximize participation from all of the relevant players, various sectors and institutions collaborated within an institutional framework developed in the 2004–07 business plan. The plans lay out a system of arrangements to divide the tasks among various institutions and to encourage interagency cooperation. Generally, these institutions can be divided into five categories:

- *The Metropolitan Council.* The council includes members from various entities, including the city of Johannesburg, the Inner City Task Force, the Economic Development Unit, the City Manager's Office, the Planning Department, the Finance Department, the Johannesburg Metro Police Department, the Housing Department, and the Contract Management Unit.
- *The private sector.* These include property and business owners.
- *Utility companies, agencies, and municipal-owned corporations.* These include City Power, Joburg Water, Pikitup, the Johannesburg

Figure 11.2 Administrative governance of the city of Johannesburg

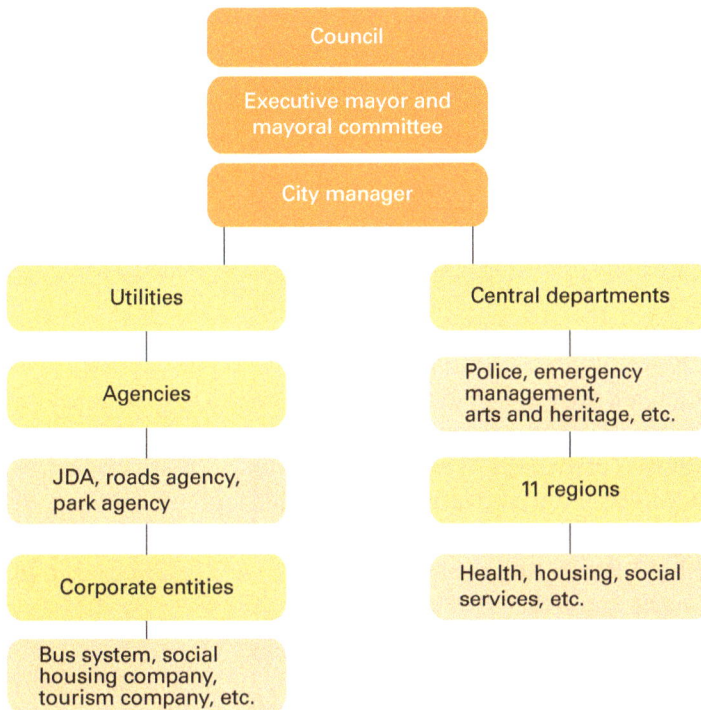

Source: City of Johannesburg 2005.
Note: JDA = Johannesburg Development Agency.

Development Agency, the Johannesburg Property Company, the Johannesburg Roads Agency, and the Metro Trading Company.
- *The provincial government.* Blue IQ (the provincial development plan), an investment agency for strategic economic infrastructure planning, and provincial departments.
- *The community.* The community includes the Johannesburg Inner City Community Forum and the Social Housing Associations (City of Johannesburg 2004).

The 2004 business plan include a framework to maximize the participation from various sectors. These arrangements also strengthened the institutional alignment with regard to delivery responsibilities. In addition, an Inner City Committee was established to monitor the progress. The committee included the inner city member of the mayoral committee, the regional director, the JDA, the Director of Economic Development Unit, a representative from the Planning Department, and the head of the Inner City Task Force (Fraser and Cox 2011). Of these, two are especially significant and are described below.

Inner City Regeneration Office (Region 8 Office)

The inner city used to be called region 8 of the 11 regions constituting Johannesburg. This was changed later in 2006 to cover all of the inner city under one region, namely, region F. At the time of the development of the business plan, the former region 8 office was responsible for various pillars of the Inner City Regeneration Business Plan. The plan assigned the regional office responsibility for community development efforts in the inner city, including housing administration, health, libraries, sports and recreation, and social development. This office consisted of the regional manager and a secretary, supported by staff seconded from time to time on a project-by-project basis.

Johannesburg Development Agency

The JDA was created in April 2001 with the aim of reviving economic activity in the city. The JDA is mandated to work across the Johannesburg metropolitan area, focusing on regenerating the inner city, as well as developing transit areas and working in townships (Clark, Huxley, and Mountford 2010). Its role as an economic development agency is to support the city's growth and development strategy, Joburg 2030 and later Joburg 2040, and to act as a management body to facilitate and initiate development within the CBD.

The JDA has successfully undertaken a range of capital-based projects throughout the city since its inception. During the first stage of operation, from 2001 to 2006, an environment was created to attract new investment and increase occupancy levels in the inner city. It also focused on specific areas of the city to enhance and harness cultural and tourism opportunities. The second stage of operation, from 2006 to 2011, made the logical connection with the 2010 Fédération Internationale de Football Association (FIFA) World Cup. Therefore, the agency concentrated on projects that were vital to the success of this global sporting event. At present, in its third developmental phase, the JDA is working to implement Joburg 2040 and to support the development of the so-called corridors of freedom. These corridors are well-planned transport arteries linked to interchanges where the focus will be on mixed-use development.

JDA's capital budget is supplied by the city of Johannesburg local government, grants from other government departments, the National Treasury, the Department of Public Works, and public and private options defined with regard to specific development initiatives. The JDA draws its operating budget from a 5 percent fee on all projects, including on the capital budget of the city of Johannesburg, and a transfer received from the city to accommodate JDA's nondevelopment based operations (JDA 2011).

To meet its objectives, the JDA has set up four substantive programs to deliver upon and two operational programs to enable cross-cutting functions. These substantive programs include a greenways program, a transit-oriented node development program, priority area planning and implementation, and the inner-city regeneration program (JDA 2012).

The JDA coordinates and manages capital investment and other programs involving both public and private sector stakeholders. Since 2001, for every rand (R) 1 million (about US$63,000) invested by the JDA, private investors have put R 18 million into the inner city of Johannesburg. This enabled the creation of property assets valued at R 600 million and infrastructure assets valued at R 3.1 billion (JDA 2014).

The role of the JDA in the regeneration of Johannesburg has been praised by several sources and is an example of the impact development companies can have in fostering public and private cooperation (Clark, Huxley, and Mountford 2010). However, critics have condemned the JDA for having two major weaknesses: a narrow mandate focused on project implementation and an emphasis on a capital-intensive work load that forces the organization to constantly seek financing (Clark, Huxley, and Mountford 2010). But even with its weaknesses, JDA is viewed as a successful development agency that has implemented many worthwhile development projects within its short 13-year lifespan.

Inner City Summit and Charter

One of the most important planning exercises for the inner city started in 2006, when the executive mayor announced the formation of an Inner City Summit to be held in 2007. The goal of the summit was to bring together various stakeholders to work toward regeneration of the inner city with a recharged energy and to build consensus on which challenges to tackle. The upcoming 2010 FIFA World Cup in South Africa provided additional motivation to achieve some progress in the inner city.

The consultation process took place from November 2006 to June 2007. It involved inner city stakeholders that participated in six working groups on various topics, including (a) urban management, safety, and security, (b) public spaces, arts, culture, and heritage, (c) economic development, (d) social development, (e) transportation, and (f) residential development (Fraser and Cox 2011). Between the third and fourth round of the stakeholder working groups, eight smaller focus groups met to concentrate on issues in greater detail. In addition to these formally organized meetings, further discussions were held directly between stakeholders or groups of stakeholders, as well as various coalitions and interest groups. The summit drew 1,000 participants to observe the culmination of the work.

After months of intense consultation with six stakeholder groups, a charter was published. The charter envisioned the inner city as the vital business core of Johannesburg, which could balance future commercial, retail, and light-manufacturing development with an equally significant residential population. The charter also emphasized creating a desirable urban environment and transportation hub that could serve the whole

Gauteng city region. The charter called for a review of all programs and initiatives to date. The goal was to evaluate and identify the lessons learned, the successes, and failures. The charter also developed a new plan for the regeneration of Johannesburg for the upcoming years using the findings of the six working groups. Finally and most important, it recommended a process to design a spatial development plan for the inner city and Johannesburg as a whole, which would act as a "new Spatial Design Framework for the Inner City" (City of Johannesburg 2015).

Through the charter process, the private sector requested that the city of Johannesburg develop "Partnership Places," which were laid out as public amenities that could be developed and managed jointly by the city and the private sector. Such places would guarantee public accessibility and would include public spaces, parks, walking corridors and the like. The idea, put forward by the Johannesburg Inner City Business Coalition, was to implement a number of public environmental upgrades by selected private sector partners in key areas of the inner city. This, in turn, would be expected to attract private sector property investment. The private sector property owners would also work with the city to upgrade semipublic spaces, where appropriate to improve the streetscape.

The charter also committed the city of Johannesburg and the JDA to look into the development of a major intermodal transport and activity center. It was to be the largest in the country, accomplished by means of a public-private partnership. With regard to housing, the charter addressed the issue of "bad buildings" in the inner city of Johannesburg, committing the JDA to develop an Inner City Housing Action Plan. Explicitly, the private sector was to play a major role with regard to inclusionary housing (City of Johannesburg 2007).

The governance of the charter included the Inner City Section 79 Committee, the Mayoral Inner City Subcommittee, and the Charter Partnership Forum. The forum was to be established by the city and inner-city stakeholders to monitor and evaluate the progress on action plans. In addition, it was to provide a platform for stakeholders to raise issues and find further common ground. The management structure of the charter included the Department of Development Planning and Urban Management. It had responsibility for the coordination and successful implementation of the program, working with the inner-city program manager, various management teams, and cluster team leaders (located in line departments or municipal entities). The inner-city program manager was in charge of delivering a number of outputs including, but not limited to, the formulation, adoption, and implementation of integrated action plans and the budget, as well as the further development of partnerships. To finance the goals outlined in the charter, the mayor allocated R 2 billion (about US$126 million) over a five-year period, as well as an additional R 100 million (US$6.3 million) operating budget for urban management purposes.

The development of the Inner City Charter has been a very significant milestone in the regeneration of Johannesburg. However, some critics view it as less than successful, especially in establishing a platform for effective proactive planning, which was its initial goal. Others argue that while the charter brought together many stakeholders, it was not so successful in achieving the buy-in from the city of Johannesburg officials, as they were unsure about the capacity to produce all of the deliverables in the charter. Most important, the public sector viewed the charter as a general set of shared responsibilities, which had no binding effect on their work as city officials. Indeed, it was not legally enforceable, nor was it included in the later Integrated Development Plan. However, the private sector viewed the charter as a commitment to which they held the city accountable (Fraser and Cox 2011).

Phase 3: Financing and Implemention

The planning and implementation of various initiatives in Johannesburg overlapped. For instance, while many of the larger-scale planning and visioning activities were in place, local-level projects were being implemented. This is an important lesson learned from this case study: in urban regeneration, planning and implementation can occur simultaneously. It is also notable that numerous activities were implemented to revitalize the inner city. However, this chapter only covers the projects that specifically aimed at boosting private sector investment in the inner city. These included mainly the JDA's area-based initiatives (ABIs), crime prevention measures, public arts and public space upgrades, and urban development zones (UDZs). These programs are summarized below.

Area-Based Initiatives

ABIs were targeted rehabilitation of various neighborhoods that seemed strategic to regeneration of the inner city as a whole. The interventions within the inner city of Johannesburg were done in an ad hoc manner under the umbrella of various visions and strategies. Some of the most important projects in the inner city were started by the JDA and were complemented by private sector investors. The JDA followed a property-led regeneration model, investing significant public funds in particular areas in the inner city.

Effect of ABI Investments on Property Vacancy Rates and Values
One major effect of ABI investments by the JDA was the massive decline in property vacancy rates in five years, from 40 percent in 2003 to 17 percent in 2008 (see figure 11.3). Overall, the evidence indicates that most of the areas with ABIs have followed the overall Johannesburg growth trajectory. However, there are exceptions, such as Braamfontein and the High Court Precinct, which have outperformed the city's growth trend. At the same time, rents have also skyrocketed in these areas (JDA 2009). Figure 11.4 shows the growth in rental income from office buildings. Residential rents have also increased significantly. Rental income

Figure 11.3   Office buildings vacancy rates in the inner city of Johannesburg, 2003–08

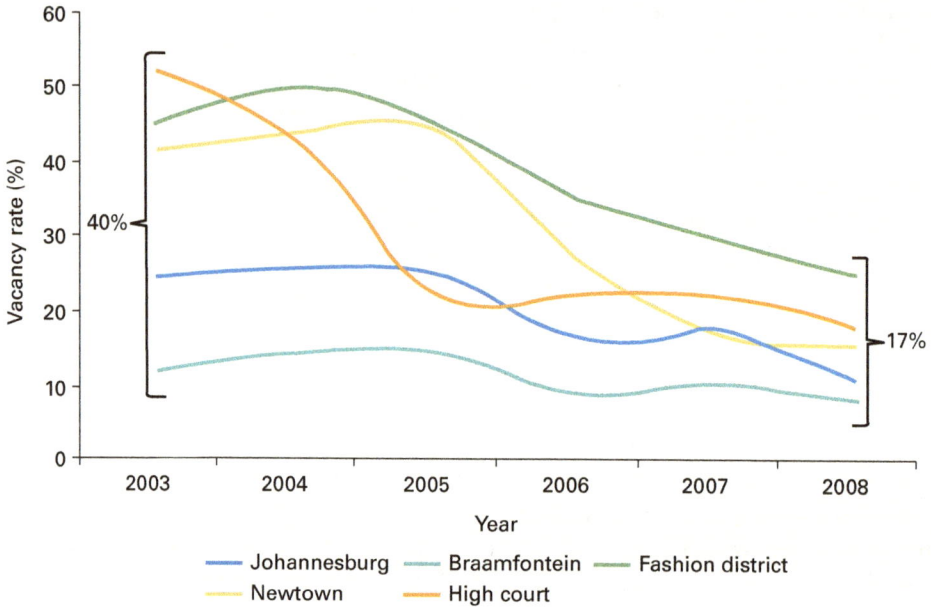

Source: JDA 2009.

Figure 11.4   Growth in rental income from office buildings, 2003–08

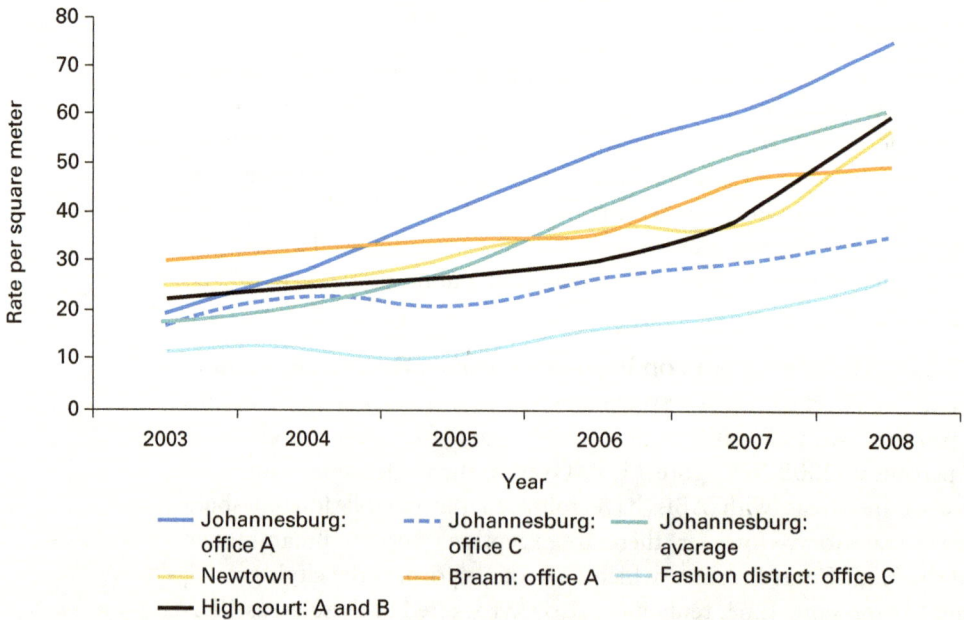

Source: JDA 2009.

prices have increased from R 20 per square meter (sq m) in 2003 to R 50 per sq m in 2008 (Garner 2011).

In addition to vacancy rates, the success of ABIs was also evidenced by the jump in property transaction levels. An evaluation report, which reviewed the deeds registry data since 1997, shows a clear correlation between JDA interventions and increased market activity. This report indicates that from 2001 to 2008, R 7.5 billion (about US$ 473 million) worth of property was purchased. Data also show that much of this transactional activity has been due to residential investment (JDA 2009).

Leverage Ratio of the ABI Investments

Another major indicator of JDA's success in attracting private sector financing to targeted areas is the leverage ratios of public to private investment. Although these ratios differ significantly from one area to another (1:10 for Greater Ellis Park to 1:362 in the High Court Precinct), they show great success even using the most conservative calculations. Table 11.2 summarizes ABI investments and the ratio of public to private investment.

The Role of Improved Public Spaces and the Public Art Program

The JDA partnered with the private sector to upgrade public spaces in Johannesburg using simple interventions, such as improving greenery, lighting, and paving. The Inner City Regeneration Charter set a target for a minimum of 5 percent of the total spaces within the urban development

Table 11.2   Public-to-private investment-leverage ratios, 2001–07

	Total JDA investment (R million)	Total private sector primary investment (R million)	Total private sector investment (R million)	Leverage (primary investment	Leverage (total investment	JDA/ primary private sector investment (%)	JDA/total private investment (%)
Greater Newtown	453	188.7	1,554.2	8.2	14.1	12.1	6.9
Greater Ellis Park	1,635	106.7	689.9	6.5	10.0	15.5	10.0
Braamfontein	622	55.7	2,365.4	42.5	71.2	2.4	1.4
Fashion District	730	33.2	1,267.4	38.2	75.9	2.6	1.3
High Court Precinct	197	8.3	1,617.5	195.7	362.4	0.5	0.3
Total	3,637	393.0	7,495.0	19.1	33.8	5.2	3.0

Source: JDA 2009.
Note: In 2016, 100 South African rands (R) equals US$ 6.30. JDA = Johannesburg Development Agency.

zone of the inner city to be developed as quality public spaces. The need for public spaces became more apparent when various private developers started building and repairing residential property in the inner city, adding to its residential population. The JDA had developed some public spaces; however, many of the quality public spaces have been provided and maintained by the private sector.

The JDA has also been active in public art installations through a program called Precinct for Public Art. This program is financed by a 1 percent contribution of all construction projects within the inner city. The JDA has used this program to include public artwork in all its major area-based initiatives. The goal is not just to provide art but to achieve social cohesion and quality public spaces. Through this program, "the city projects its collective identity and vision, while individuals and community groups in neighborhoods are also empowered to express their unique identities." (City of Johannesburg 2006b).

Urban Development Zone Tax Incentives

To promote private sector participation in urban renewal and accelerate the pace of regeneration, South Africa's Ministry of Finance launched a national tax incentive program in 2003. This national law allowed the municipalities to designate urban development zones around the areas of priority listed in their integrated plans, or areas where "significant fiscal measures have been implemented by that municipality to support the regeneration." (National Treasury 2003). Johannesburg and Cape Town were the first cities in South Africa to start using this program in 2004. The Johannesburg Inner City UDZ included the CBD.

The incentive works in the form of an accelerated depreciation from eligible taxpayers' taxable income—if this income is a result of construction extension, or improvements of, or an addition to an entire building or part of a building within the CBD that is at least 1,000 sq m. The incentive also applies to the purchase of buildings within the CBD (with the same criteria) from a developer, that is, if the developer has not yet claimed any UDZ allowance (National Treasury 2003).

The UDZ incentive distinguishes between construction of a new building and refurbishment of existing ones. In the case of full or partial improvement of an existing building, the UDZ deductibles are equivalent to a five-year, straight-line depreciation or (a) 20 percent of the total cost in the year of assessment during which the building is brought into use by the taxpayer solely for the purposes of trade; and (b) an amount equal to 20 percent of the cost in each of the four succeeding years of assessment, provided that the person engages in continuous use of the building solely for the purposes of trade. In the case of building or extending a building, the deductions conform to the following rules: (a) 20 percent of the total cost in the year of assessment during which the building is brought into use by the taxpayer solely for the purposes of trade, and (b) 5 percent of the cost for the 16 subsequent years of assessment conditional to continuous use for purposes of trade (National Treasury 2003).

The city has praised the UDZ tax incentives as a driving force behind the surge in real estate investments in the inner city in 2005 and 2006. However, it is difficult to analyze the effects of UDZs independent of all other initiatives that were in place at the time. The city claims to have attracted R 2 billion private sector investments to the inner city per year (Garner 2011). Although some smaller scale development companies have complained about the cumbersome bureaucracy of the UDZs, of the 200 UDZs filed, 90 were by smaller development companies. In addition, it is estimated that 65,000 construction-related jobs were created as a result of the UDZ tax incentives (Garner 2011).

The UDZ regulations and conditions have been amended several times since their inception to make them more practical and useful. One important change was the 2005 amendment, which allowed the UDZ benefits to be extended to sectional title ownership. This change resulted in a greater uptake of the incentive by the general public and streamed the benefits from the developers to the buyers of the units. Another amendment allowed for a 25 percent depreciation (over the period of four years) on construction of low-cost, high-density affordable housing. Lastly, the UDZs are now allowed to include developmental leases by the government to the private sector (Garner 2011).

City Improvement Districts

The Central Johannesburg Partnership first introduced the concept of city improvement districts to Johannesburg in 1993. It was a response by local businesses to declining municipal budgets and services. This concept was transferred directly from the North American business improvement districts. The CJP drafted the CID legislation to be revised and approved by the Provincial Government in 1997, which subsequently became effective in 1999.

Generally, a CID is a defined geographic area in which property owners agree to pay for supplementary services and improvements of the urban environment. These services can include security measures, urban area upgrades, litter collection, and design and upkeep of public spaces. In addition, some CIDs also take on additional and complementary services, including web-based communication and information systems connecting all businesses in the area, business attractions; environmental upgrades, business retention, branding and marketing of the CID precinct area, or events management to attract more people to the CID area. It is important to note that these services are supplementary and should represent the needs of the area as identified by the property owners. The local government continues with its standard level of support regardless of the existence of a CID.

In Johannesburg, a CID can be formed when a petition is filed by at least 51 percent of the property owners in the geographic area and is approved by the municipality. Once a CID is legislated, the property owners are required to pay a CID levy for additional services. The CID levy is compulsory and is calculated based on the value of the individual properties and applied on a prorated basis. CID levies may only be spent in the geographic area in which they are gathered. CIDs are established for an initial period of three years but can extend indefinitely unless members file for changes to the original business plan. The CID levy is collected by the municipal council on behalf of CIDs. These are then transferred to the CID without any deduction. In some other cases, the council authorizes the CID to collect the levies on its own.

A board of directors is elected from the member property owners that govern the CIDs. They control the area within the terms of their original business plan. Although nonvoting members of the board may be included, such as a councilor, a tenant, or other stakeholders, property owners must be in the majority. The board usually comprises property owners, business owners, representatives of resident organizations (if relevant), and representatives of the local authority. The board then selects an urban management company to manage the daily functions of the CID, as well as to implement the CID's business plan.

There are three different CID typologies in Johannesburg. They include legislated CIDs, voluntary CIDs, and special projects. The legislated CIDs' responsibilities and functions correspond as noted. Voluntary CIDs and special projects do not fall under the CID legislation. Thus, they are not based on a legally binding agreement between property owners.

The CJP manages four legislated CIDs including the Central Improvement District, the South Western Improvement District, and the Retail Improvement District—all located within the inner city. In addition, the CJP manages Braamfontein and six informal CIDs. A number of other CIDs also exist in Johannesburg. However, these and other voluntary CIDs are not managed by the CJP (see map 11.2).

The CID (inner city) was originally established as a voluntary CID in 1995. Later in 2003, it became a formal CID following approved legislation. The site covers an area of 25 city blocks today, compared with 8 blocks at its inception. The site is mixed use and is located within close proximity to Park Station—the largest multimodal transportation destination in Johannesburg.

CIDs are said to have changed the look and function of a number of areas in the inner city, which required ongoing support by the municipality. But they have also been subject to criticism. Some have argued that the CIDs contribute to the growing spatial inequalities in the inner city and present a risk of political and fiscal fragmentation, which have particular resonance in the postapartheid context (Peyroux 2006). Since lower-income communities cannot afford the additional fees for privatized services, CIDs can be the reason for the widening social and spatial inequalities (Miraftab 2007). Others have expressed concern that CIDs undermine the

Map 11.2   **Johannesburg inner city CIDs**

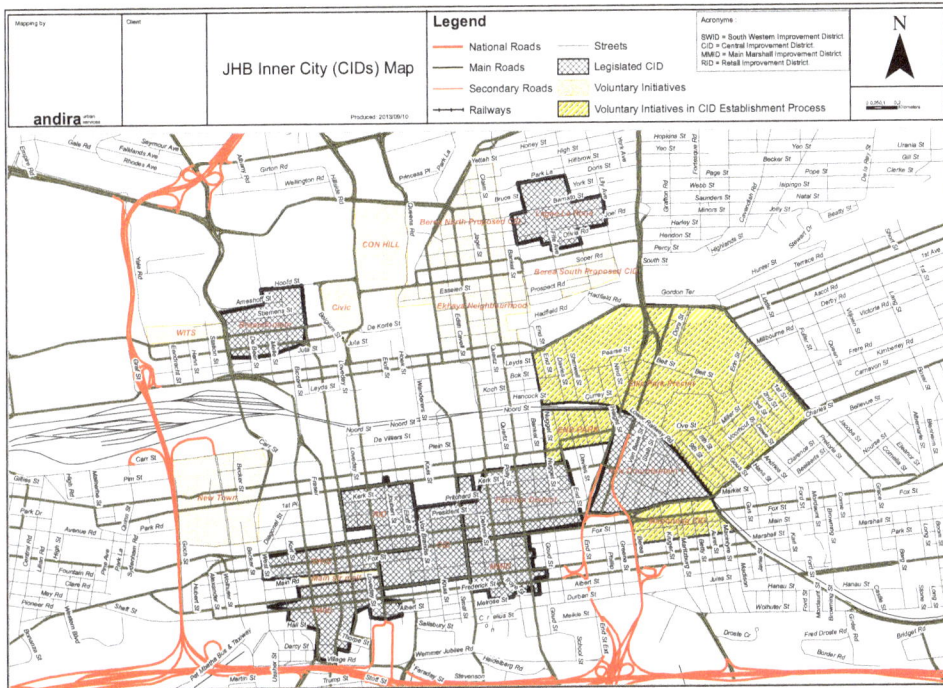

Mapping by	Client		Legend				Acronym:		N
		JHB Inner City (CIDs) Map	— National Roads		⎯ Streets		BWID = South Western Improvement District		
			— Main Roads		▦ Legislated CID		CID = Central Improvement District		
			— Secondary Roads		Voluntary Initiatives		MMID = Main Marshall Improvement District		
andira		Produced: 2013/09/10	⎯ Railways		▨ Voluntary Initiatives in CID Establishment Process		RID = Retail Improvement District		

Source: Johannesburg CID Forum 2015 (resource center), Johannesburg, http://www.cidforum.co.za/content /resources.

efforts of the antiapartheid movement to achieve an integrated city with one tax base (Robinson 1998).

Crime Prevention Measures

Crime and violence are one of the most important barriers to development. In 2002, Johannesburg had the highest crime rate in the country. In order to curb crime, Johannesburg developed a multiagency crime prevention strategy, which involved the Johannesburg Metropolitan Police Department, the South African Police Service, the Gauteng Department of Safety, and the private sector–funded entity, Business against Crime South Africa (BACSA).

BACSA was a wholly private sector–led initiative, established in 1996. It was a nonprofit company with a board of directors comprising local business leaders. The company runs on tax-deductible donations from businesses that benefit from a secure inner city to boost returns on their investments. BACSA complements the criminal justice system by contributing to policy and strategy formulation, implementation support, problem identification and solutions design, and so on.

Funding for BACSA is provided by medium and large businesses, business associations, and some individuals. The top 80 companies usually provide BACSA with R 500,000 to R 1 million (about US$63,000) per year. These funds are then used to fund initiatives approved by the board. One of the most influential works of BACSA was to spearhead the installation of closed-circuit television cameras, which had an enormous impact on the reduction of crime. In a year after installation, the crime rate dropped by 48 percent (City of Johannesburg 2015), and within two years, crime dropped by 80 percent. In addition to BACSA, CIDs, have also had a tremendous impact on reducing crime by designing effective initiatives in their boundaries.

Informal Trade Management

The CJP was established as a partnership between the business community and the local authority. Following its establishment, the CJP founded a joint venture with the Metropolitan Trading Company to manage informal trading in CIDs. It was clear that while CIDs provide services that include partnership development, marketing, landscaping and maintenance, and safety, they could not do so without overlapping with informal trade management in public spaces. This initiative enabled informal surveillance, daily cleaning, and implementation of public safety ambassadors, as well as continual dialogue and communication between all stakeholders. It also ensured better organization of informal trade, which was beneficial to the traders as well as to the community.

In 2014, the city of Johannesburg's Economic Development Department participated in a workshop with CJP. The workshop called for submissions to discuss ideas regarding informal trading within the inner city to improve and implement effective management processes as part of an informal trade management plan. Overall, informal trade initiatives were welcomed as long as they did not prejudice the established commercial sector, and as long as they ensured that stakeholder consultation would be an ongoing part of any process. Discussions were also held around reinstating the joint venture. The main concerns also focused on process, existing rights, and type and quality of facilities. Recommendations included the need to work to enhance and retain the existing economic contribution within the CID and to support pedestrian movement through the CBD as a key driver for informal trade (CID Forum 2014).

Housing Provision

The problem of providing quality housing in Johannesburg dates to the 1980s, when property owners started to rent their (mostly) office buildings to people in need of cheap residential accommodations who were moving to the inner city to find low-paying jobs. The rental income was substantial due to overcrowded units filled with as many as seven to nine individuals. The situation was exacerbated after the fall of apartheid and the emergence of the "sectional title act," which in itself was a positive legislative change.

In the inner city, however, the act resulted in large-scale sectional titling of former office buildings, putting them in the hands of residents who could not possibly pay the city for utilities and taxes. The domino effect of this continued and the banks redlined the inner city properties, refusing to allocate mortgages because of perceived political and financial risks. By the early 2000s, many of the high-rise buildings in the inner city were not eligible for mortgages. This opened up the necessity for rental accommodations as buying became an unviable option (Garner 2011).

In this context, entrepreneurial developers started to move into the inner city with the intention of taking advantage of the new demand for rental accommodations. At the same time, the Trust for the Urban Housing Foundation (TUHF) was established in 2003 to fund the refurbishment of inner city buildings and support residential conversions. The TUHF grants loans to buy or improve residential property in South Africa's inner city areas. It lends money to housing projects in areas of urban decline, with preference given to small and medium-size apartment buildings that are safe and clean—and that have the potential to offer good returns. The TUHF's strategy is to concentrate on small areas and not just individual buildings and use its funds to create residential property markets in the inner cities. Specifically, the TUHF finances projects that will be economically sustainable to generate sufficient income to repay the loans and make a profit. The TUHF also supports projects that will upgrade buildings in the selected inner-city area, giving preference to residential property projects. Finally, it supports projects that will stimulate the economic empowerment of individuals and communities and promote a positive social effect on inner-city communities.[4]

Since its inception, the TUHF has financed over R 4 billion in inner city residential rental property, including 22,000 residential units in South African cities (TUHF 2015). Since commercial banks have been reluctant to invest in the inner city, the TUHF relies on the South African National Housing Finance Corporation for financing. The TUHF has a mandate for residential development, but it also involves itself in mixed-use developments, given its focus on precinct development and regeneration of the inner city.

The TUHF targets mostly freehold buildings. However, to deal with the consequences of the sectional titling act, it also works with investors who can buy at least 50 percent of apartment building complexes. The TUHF has been an outstanding model for refurbishment of housing units in the inner city. Its success lies in its simple corporate structure (Garner 2011) and in the fact that it knows the market well. Indeed, it has been a crucial factor in the expansion of the inner-city housing market.

In addition to the public sector–led efforts, Johannesburg also relies on its entrepreneurial private sector willing to take investment risks to provide housing. These private sector investors used public incentives and saw a market opportunity to develop affordable housing. One example is the Affordable Housing Company (AFHCO), which has taken on housing development in addition to upgrading public spaces and providing educational and recreational facilities (box 11.1). All these efforts helped the city to reach a tipping point in residential development in 2011, when the residential makeover gained significant momentum.

Better Buildings Program

Some argue that the presence of dilapidated and derelict buildings in the inner city of Johannesburg is the single biggest urban management problem contributing to the further obsolescence and blight because of spillover effects on surrounding areas. The Better Buildings Program (BBP) was approved by the mayoral committee and the Economic Development Unit in 2003 to replace the earlier Bad Buildings Program. The former program was developed in 1999 under the management of the ICO. It aimed to develop a mechanism for managing buildings that were classified as "bad"

Box 11.1   The affordable housing company rental model

The Affordable Housing Company (AFHCO) is a successful private sector initiative aimed at providing affordable housing in the inner city of Johannesburg. AFHCO is an exceptional model because it is a for-profit company, taking on the role of a housing agency. It targets younger working-class mixed-race residents of the inner city, with the target earning of R 4,500–12,000 per month. Its portfolio includes 5,500 residential rental units. Its founder saw the opportunity to invest in the inner city and was one of the very first investors to buy cheap, dilapidated properties to rehabilitate them. The AFHCO works with inner city players such as the Johannesburg Inner City Business Coalition, CIDs, JDA, CJP, the city council, and the Property Owners and Managers' Association to redevelop vacant buildings in the inner city. The company expects a rise in its asset prices once the neighborhoods are redeveloped. In order for their financial model to work, AFHCO subsidizes the redevelopments for three to five years until they yield a profit.

To provide affordable accommodations, AFHCO looks for buildings that can be bought for less than R 1,000 per square meter. By using government subsidies for buyers of dilapidated buildings in the inner city, the AFHCO initially set up its financial model on the basis of a deferred ownership. The plan was to buy, refurbish, and sectionalize units for sale. However, like many other residential developers in the inner city, it decided to follow the affordable rental model. Each unit is small and is equipped with high-end finishes and other amenities. In addition, the buildings have full-time staff for cleaning and service. The AFHCO also invests in public spaces, security, and service delivery in partnership with the city council. This is because AFHCO is interested in maintaining the value of their buildings over time. They are active in developing vibrant residential communities by building parks, sports and educational facilities and investing in security.

AFHCO realizes the importance of a high-quality tenant base. It built a school for 350 children (at a cost of R 3 million) and started a community ambassadors program for unemployed young adults. In addition, it also manages a public park located next to one of its developments (Garner 2011). AFHCO has used the UDZ tax incentives, but the company believes that this is not enough subsidy to incentivize private sector participation in residential development in dilapidated areas of the inner city. AFHCO's founder believes that the cost of financing is high and public sector assistance is especially important in the early years of the project, when the project is paying off interest on capital and the tenant base is not yet established.

Sources: Interview with Renney Plitt of AFHCO, February 2013, and Garner 2011.

for a variety of reasons. Bad buildings included abandoned structures and derelict buildings, which were taken over by squatters and in some cases criminal gangs. These properties had accrued various debts to the city. Furthermore, these "bad buildings" were usually overcrowded, illegal, and hubs of criminal activities (Johannesburg Property Company and Economic Development Unit 2005).

The BBP initially identified 122 buildings within the inner city, mainly on the basis of outstanding debts. This program did not result in significant change as only 10 percent of the identified buildings were ultimately transformed through this program. This was mainly because of long processes of litigation, lack of consensus among private and public sector actors with regard to objectives of the program, and the significant focus on debt recovery rather than on broader social and economic development interests (City of Johannesburg 2010). The approach to identifying and evacuating these so-called bad buildings was also criticized for being violent and wild. In several cases the residents pushed back and took the city to the constitution court, and in one case they won. These push backs were the reason for the city to reevaluate its approach.[5]

The new BBP was implemented under the Johannesburg Property Company with assistance from the city of Johannesburg. The main purpose of the new program was to facilitate the expropriation and sale of derelict buildings in the inner city to private sector entities, which had the capacity and capital to rehabilitate and manage them. The difference between the two programs was in their approach to determining "bad" or "problematic" buildings. Whereas the older program focused more on reviving the debt from buildings, the new program methodically identified buildings suffering from physical and social problems throughout the inner city. Such buildings had a negative impact on the urban fabric. In this way, the number of identified buildings grew significantly, representing, at one stage, a value of about R 670 million worth of property, of which about 85 percent owed taxes to the government (Fraser and Cox 2011).

More specifically, the program targeted derelict and overcrowded buildings whose debt owed to the city exceeded its market value. The city also provided the option of writing off the debt or a portion of the debt before transferring the building to a new owner (Fraser and Cox 2011). Parallel to this program, the inner city Housing Upgrading Trust was revived and restructured. Its mission was to provide housing finance to groups of tenants or small private developers who would buy and rehabilitate abandoned buildings.[6] It was also mandated to help tenants apply for national-level subsidies and loans from the National Housing Finance Corporation to add to the additional building stock in the inner city (Beall, Crankshaw, and Parnell 2003).

The BBP achieved moderate success in its goals. The ratio of write-off to refurbishment was 1 to 1.2, meaning for each U.S. dollar of public money in write-offs, 1.2 dollars of private money was invested. Overall, until 2005, the program included 94 structures. At the same time, the private sector took over about 100 bad buildings (without the BBP intervention) to refurbish them. This shows a "ripple-pond effect" of the BBP, with the private sector showing confidence in the inner-city regeneration efforts (Johannesburg Property Company and Economic Development Unit 2005). However, the process of acquiring buildings proved to be lengthy and difficult. After a building was identified and its dues assessed, a legal process would be started to acquire the building. This ranged from outright expropriation to the purchase of the building by the Johannesburg Property Company, which would then identify potential interested investors to repurchase the building (City of Johannesburg 2010). Photograph 11.2 shows examples of refurbished high-rise buildings. While the author cannot confirm that these buildings were financed by BBP, it gives an idea of the progress made in refurbishing dilapidated buildings in the inner city of Johannesburg.

The BBP was an instrument to fight blight in the inner city. However, its limited scope and inflated focus on facilitating market transactions without developing alternative living situations for residents of the bad buildings resulted in displacement of the poor—leaving them without adequate alternative housing options. The importance of providing alternative

Photograph 11.2   **Two examples of refurbished buildings in the inner city**

Source: © Tanya Zack. Used with permission. Further permission required for reuse.

housing was mentioned in the charter in 2007. Nevertheless, it suggested that only 10 of the 250 buildings identified for the BBP be designated as "transitional housing projects in which tenants may reside for a maximum of two years" (Winkler 2006). Given that some of these tenants are among the poorest and most vulnerable groups of inner-city residents, their evictions—without providing suitable alternative accommodations—have been seen as unjust.

In 2008, the city established the Inner City Property Scheme to replace the BBP. Its mandate was to target bad buildings on a case-by-case basis. The innovation in this program was that it established a company in which members would contribute with a minimum equity contribution of R 5 million, in addition to the capital raised by the company. The city would then transfer dilapidated properties to this new company through a lease with an option to buy. Once the property was rehabilitated and converted to a productive economic asset, it would be sold to interested investors. In doing so, a panel of service providers would be established, who could then take on the construction work and related tasks. Through this panel, the city also contributes to job creation and empowerment of the black community. Another advantage of this program is the city's commitment to provide transitional housing for current residents of selected bad buildings through the Transitional Housing Trust. The trust was also tasked with buying the buildings that would later be developed into transitional housing (Garner 2011).

Outcomes and Impacts

In evaluating the regeneration efforts in the inner city of Johannesburg, one should be cognizant of the two parallel streams of interventions: the localized area-based initiatives and the larger visioning process and subsequent strategies. Whereas many of the area-based programs stemmed from the visions and strategies created over the course of two decades, they tended to be linked mostly to the private sector actors that sought to be involved in the implementation of these programs.

This visioning process, which stemmed purely from stakeholders within the inner city, was later broadened and integrated within the metropolitan planning process through instruments such as iGoli 2002, iGoli 2010, and iGoli 2030. Fraser and Cox (2011) argue that these plans did not recognize the critical importance of the inner city to the metropolitan region. They also argue that the weakening of structures, which were developed purely for the regeneration of the inner city (such as the Inner City Committee), denied the very active private sector the ability to comment on various initiatives and plans developed for the inner city.

In terms of planning for inner-city regeneration, the efforts have been ad hoc and largely outside of Johannesburg's Planning Framework. ICO was in charge of coordination of all activities related to the inner city and functioned largely alone. The ICO was never able to lock in the commitment from various city departments around urban regeneration efforts (Fraser and Cox 2011). Further, urban regeneration efforts were never integrated into the planning system of Johannesburg because regeneration initiatives, such as the Integrated Development plan and the charter, did not have the level of granularity needed to become local plans. Rather, the JDA and the ICO developed plans based on projects and priorities identified by the private sector. Indeed, it was the private sector that had already started the development process before the city-wide regeneration initiatives were created. This does not mean that the interventions by the JDA and the ICO were not aligned with the larger regeneration visions; it merely means that there were two parallel processes in place.

Furthermore, numerous urban management and regeneration pilots have been implemented, but the institutional arrangements for coordinating urban management tasks within the inner city have been weak. The communication between various city entities and communications between provincial, national, and local governments could have been more effective. Since the regeneration efforts in Johannesburg have ultimately been very successful, one wonders how much better the impact would have been had there been more coordination among various institutions.

Impacts

Between 2002 and 2007, the inner city has been the largest contributor to the economy of Johannesburg, contributing 20.5 percent of gross geographic product (GGP) growth. Between 2002 and 2007, the average annual economic growth rate of the inner city was just under 6 percent per year, as compared to 6.1 percent for Johannesburg as a whole. The finance and business sectors have been the biggest contributors to inner city's growth, increasing from 25 percent to 35 percent within a decade.

The most obvious fiscal impact of the regeneration efforts in Johannesburg can be observed in the boost in the property market. As a result of JDA's efforts in regenerating the inner city, the private sector has invested an estimated R 4.5 billion in upgrading properties. When combined with new property development, the private sector has invested a total of R 11 billion in inner-city properties since 2000. Nevertheless, in evaluating JDA's interventions in the inner city, it is important to view its massive success in the context of the property boom of 2002–07. More than half of the private sector investors interviewed for an evaluation report of JDA's ABIs said that they did not know about JDA's investments when they decided to invest. They simply perceived the area as a good investment option. Another issue to consider regarding JDA's interventions is that many of them were not allocated a budget for maintenance, and therefore the upkeep and sustainability of these efforts are subject to debate (JDA 2009).

Overall, the establishment of CIDs has been a great success in transforming the inner city. Using private funding, they have contributed to urban management and services. Crime in areas managed by CIDs has decreased by as much as 85 percent. However, some argue that the whole CBD should be covered under one large CID in order to decrease competition among adjoining neighborhoods and aim for a more coordinated effort to revitalize the inner city. Similarly, the UDZs have been very successful in absorbing private sector funds. By 2011, more than 200 UDZ applications had been filed with the city of Johannesburg. Within the 2010–11 financial year alone, UDZs attracted about R 9 billion in private sector investment (Garner 2011).

Involuntary Resettlement

One major criticism of the regeneration process in Johannesburg's inner city has been the lack of provision for displaced residents. In 2003, 39 percent of inner city residents were unemployed and at least 10 percent relied exclusively on the informal sector to survive. The initial efforts in the early 1990s did not include social justice measures to address the extreme poverty in the inner city. At a public meeting in 2003, the executive mayor mentioned that citizens earning less than US$500 per month would not be able to afford to live in the inner city. At the time, this included 62 percent of the residents of the inner city (Winkler 2006). Hence, city officials were aware of the massive displacement that would be involved in vacating the bulk of structures for redevelopment. The city council then committed to providing affordable housing for the poor on the "urban edge," which meant far from economic opportunities and jobs. These displacement and exclusionary acts have been a source of many violent encounters between the City and its residents. A public interest law group took legal actions against Johannesburg's eviction policies and some of these have been escalated to the national level.

The Inner City Regeneration Charter aimed at fixing some of these policies by admitting that earlier initiatives had not taken poorer residents and informal businesses into consideration. The charter made provisions for displaced residents of the BBP. However, only 10 of the 250 buildings identified were planned as transitional housing for two years, and the charter did not specify the plan for such residents after the stipulated two-year period. The residents that are resettled are among the poorest and most vulnerable in the society, usually without knowledge or legal means to defend their rights or demand alternative housing options. Therefore, for an equitable and inclusive inner city regeneration process to succeed, policies to mitigate the impacts of resettlement and exclusion must be included.[7]

Looking Ahead

The Johannesburg inner city must focus on providing more entry-level housing for the poor who choose to live in the inner city to be closer to jobs and economic opportunities. The BBP has been successful in fixing some of the problems of dilapidated buildings in the inner city. However, the scale of such buildings requires a better-coordinated effort among various agencies. It seems that a thorough audit of informal settlements within problematic buildings is needed to get a better sense of scale. Most important, the living conditions and needs of the informal residents of such buildings should be evaluated to avoid further gentrification and displacement. The public transportation network is improving, but there are still many problems with access to the inner city from the townships.

The 2040 plan aims at addressing some of the coordination problems at the city and metropolitan level, but better-coordinated urban management pilots are needed. These should include service-level agreements between the inner city and all of the entities for on-going maintenance and repair of infrastructure. Efforts should be made to translate the visions and subsequent strategies into a more granular systematic urban management program across the entire region. Furthermore, much effort is needed to align inner-city regeneration priorities with those of the metropolitan region to better integrate the inner city into the existing city-region.

Lessons Learned

The most unique characteristic of regeneration of Johannesburg was the multiplicity of actors and stakeholders, such as an active private-sector community, migrant workers, utility companies, and provincial, national, and local governments. Johannesburg inner city regeneration proved that it is possible for such a broad range of stakeholders to collaborate and engage through various loosely connected processes and frameworks. Several lessons emerged from this case study:

- *The process of crafting a vision was used to build consensus in a socially polarized context.* While in many case studies in this volume a mayor or city manager set forth the vision, in Johannesburg the "visioning" process was a collaborative effort. The first comprehensive vision was developed by four different groups of stakeholders through an inclusionary process led by the private sector. A workshop was then conceived to incorporate all four groups of ideas in one vision document. Similarly, the inner-city summit brought together more than 1,000 participants from various sectors. It took months to agree on a shared vision for the inner city. The vision was developed based on discussions in many stakeholder working groups and smaller focus groups. In addition to these formally organized meetings, informal meetings were held between stakeholders or groups of stakeholders, as well as various coalitions and interest groups.
- *Visions should result in solid plans for a set period of time and with assigned financial resources.* Many major plans were developed for the inner city which were later abandoned or revised. This resulted in

missed opportunities and wasted resources and momentum. The Inner City Regeneration Business Plan, developed in 2004, included 63 initiatives and programs, all to be completed by 2007. However, 44 percent of the programs and initiatives did not have an allocated budget and were not implemented properly.

- *The regeneration plan proposed a system to divide various tasks among different institutions and to encourage interagency coopera-tion.* The five entities included in the business plan of Johannesburg were the Metropolitan Council, the private sector, utility companies, the provincial government, and the community through the Johannesburg Inner City Community Forum and the Social Housing Association. The plan aimed at maximizing participation from vari-ous sectors. These arrangements also strengthened the institutional alignment with regard to delivery responsibilities.

- *Establishment of an autonomous agency was instrumental in the regeneration of Johannesburg inner city.* This agency (JDA) was responsible for coordinating all activities and projects related to the inner city. This was especially important as in the beginning, the inner city fell under two jurisdictions, and many other entities from the provincial and national government were also involved in strategizing for regeneration activities. JDA was able to bring all strategies and plans under one umbrella and act as an economic development agency, supporting the city's growth and development strategy. JDA's capital budget was supplied by the city of Johannesburg local govern-ment, grants from other government departments, the National Treasury, the Department of Public Works, and public and private options defined with regard to specific development initiatives. Its operating budget came from a 5 percent fee on all projects, including on the capital budget of the city of Johannesburg, and a transfer received from the city to accommodate JDA's nondevelopment-based operations.

- *In complex political contexts, the process of visioning, planning, and implementing can overlap.* Johannesburg inner city went through many visioning exercises. During this time, the public and private sec-tors continued with planning and implementing smaller-scale neigh-borhood projects.

- *Learning from the international experience matters.* The first CID in South Africa was established following a visit to the United States and Britain by the members of the city council, the community, and pro-vincial government officials. The visit was organized by the International Downtown Association and the British Association of Town Centre Management and included visits to several CIDs to study their effectiveness. South African officials learned from these experiences and copied the concept in South Africa.

- *Ensuring an equitable regeneration process depends on solid solu-tions for gentrification and provisions for displaced residents.*

Regeneration of the inner city of Johannesburg has been criticized for failing to provide sufficient affordable housing for displaced residents of refurbished tenement housing complexes. While the city officials were aware of the potential massive displacement, they failed to provide housing units in the inner city for lower-income residents. Later on, the city council committed to providing affordable housing for the poor on the "urban edge," far from economic opportunities and jobs. The displacements during various redevelopment projects became a source for many violent encounters between the city and its residents, leading to lawsuits and unrest.

Notes

1. Interview with Graeme Gotz, February 2013.
2. To craft a vision, the process followed the guidelines of the International Downtown Association, the consultant to the CJP at the time. These guidelines defined strategic visioning as a "managed collaborative process" with the goal of producing three principal products: a vision for the future, a strategic plan, and a structure for action.
3. These include the 1997 Gauteng Growth and Development Framework, the 1997 Gauteng Trade and Industry Strategy, and the 1996 white paper on urban regeneration by the Gauteng Department of Development Planning and Local Development. This white paper included an integration plan for the city, town, and township centers, and enacted legislation to facilitate the establishment of CIDs and the Blue IQ growth strategy. Most projects initiated under this program were implemented by the Johannesburg Development Agency, when it took over in 2001.
4. See http://www.tuhf.co.za/.
5. Interview with Graeme Gotz, February 2013.
6. This initiative was heavily funded by the United States Agency for International Development.
7. For more information on equitable regeneration and avoiding gentrification, see chapter 3.

References

Beall, Jo, Owen Crankshaw, and Susan Parnell. 2003. "Uniting a Divided City; Governance and Social Exclusion in Johannesburg." *African Political Economy* 30 (95): 171–73.

Bremner, Lindsay. 2000. "Reinventing the Johannesburg Inner City." *Cities* 17 (3): 185–93.

CID Forum. 2014. "Informal Trade Management, City Improvement District Experience."

City of Johannesburg. 1992. *Strategic Initiative for Central Johannesburg*. Johannesburg: city council.

———. 2002. *Annual Report 2001/02*. City of Johannesburg. http://www .joburg-archive.co.za/city_vision/AnnualReport02Ch3.pdf.

———. 2004. "Johannesburg Inner City Regeneration Strategy and Business Plan 2004–2007." City of Johannesburg.

———. 2005. *Integrated Development Plan 2004/05*. City of Johannesburg.

———. 2006a. "Reflecting on a Solid Foundation: Building Developmental Local Government 2000–2005." City of Johannesburg Metropolitan Municipality.

———. 2006b. "Public Art Policy." City of Johannesburg.

———. 2007. "Draft Inner City Regeneration Charter for Discussion." Inner City Summit, May 5, City of Johannesburg.

———. 2010. "Plan for Inner City." City of Johannesburg.

———. 2015. "Reshaping Johannesburg's Inner City." City of Johannesburg.

Clark, G., J. Huxley, and D. Mountford. 2010. *Organising Local Economic Development: The Role of Development Agencies and Companies*. Local Economic and Employment Series. Paris: OECD.

Fraser, Neil. 2007. "Long History Leads to Latest Inner City Summit." City of Johannesburg website.

Fraser, Neil, and Katherine Cox. 2011. "Urban Renewal Models in the Inner Johannesburg City Regeneration Process 1997–2011." Resource Paper, University of the Witwatersrand, Johannesburg.

Garner, G. 2011. *Johannesburg: Ten Ahead: A Decade of Inner-City Regeneration*. Johannesburg: Double G Media.

JDA (Johannesburg Development Agency). 2009. "Analysis of the Impact of the JDA's Area-Baused Regeneration Projects on Private Sector Investments."

———. 2011. "Business Plan 2011/2012." JDA, Johannesburg.

———. 2012. "Business Plan 2013/14." JDA, Johannesburg.

———. 2014. *2013/14 Integrated Annual Report*. Johannesburg: JDA.

Johannesburg Property Company and Economic Development Unit. 2005. "Proposal for Upscaled Better Buildings Programme."

Mabin, Alan. 2007. "Johannesburg: (South) Africa's Aspirant Global City." In *The Making of Global City Regions: Johannesburg, Mumbai/ Bombay, Sao Paulo and Shanghai*, edited by K. Segbers, S. Raiser, and K. Volkmann, 32–63. Baltimore: Johns Hopkins University Press.

Miraftab, Faranak. 2007. "Governing Post Apartheid Spatiality: Implementing City Improvement Districts in Cape Town." *Antipode* 39 (4): 602–26.

National Treasury. 2003. "Revenue Laws Amendment Act (Act no. 45 of 2003).

Peyroux, Elisabeth. 2006. "City Improvement Districts in Johannesburg: Assessing the Political and Socio-spatial Implications of Private-led Urban Regeneration." *Trialog* 2: 9–14.

Robinson, Jennifer. 1998. "Spaces of Democracy: Remapping the Apartheid City." *Environment and Planning D: Society and Space* 16: 533–48.

Segbers, K., S. Raiser, and K. Volkmann. 2007. *The Making of Global City Regions: Johannesburg, Mumbai/Bombay, Sao Paulo and Shanghai*. Baltimore: Johns Hopkins University Press.

Tomlinson, Richard. 2003. *Emerging Johannesburg: Perspectives on the Postapartheid City*. New York: Routledge.

Tomlinson, Richard, Roland Hunter, M. Jonker, Chris Rogerson, and J. Rogerson. 1995. "Johannesburg Inner City Strategic Development Framework." Greater Johannesburg Metropolitan Council. Johannesburg.

Trust for the Urban Housing Foundation (TUHF). 2015. "About us." http://www.tuhf.co.za. Accessed December 2015.

Winkler, Tanja. 2006. "Reimagining Inner-City Regeneration in Hillbrow, Johannesburg: Identifying a Role for Faith-based Community Development." *Planning Theory and Practice* 7 (1): 80–92.

People Interviewed

Sharon Lewis (formerly of JDA)

Graeme Gotz of Gauteng City Region Observatory

Renney Plit of AFHCO

Anne Steffny of Johannesburg CID forum

ECO-AUDIT
Environmental Benefits Statement

The World Bank Group is committed to reducing its environmental footprint. In support of this commitment, the Publishing and Knowledge Division leverages electronic publishing options and print-on-demand technology, which is located in regional hubs worldwide. Together, these initiatives enable print runs to be lowered and shipping distances decreased, resulting in reduced paper consumption, chemical use, greenhouse gas emissions, and waste.

The Publishing and Knowledge Division follows the recommended standards for paper use set by the Green Press Initiative. The majority of our books are printed on Forest Stewardship Council (FSC)–certified paper, with nearly all containing 50–100 percent recycled content. The recycled fiber in our book paper is either unbleached or bleached using totally chlorine-free (TCF), processed chlorine-free (PCF), or enhanced elemental chlorine-free (EECF) processes.

More information about the Bank's environmental philosophy can be found at http://www.worldbank.org/corporateresponsibility.

green
press
INITIATIVE

www.ingramcontent.com/pod-product-compliance
Lightning Source LLC
Chambersburg PA
CBHW080409270326
41929CB00018B/2956

* 9 7 8 1 4 6 4 8 0 4 7 3 1 *